The Authentic Death and
Contentious Afterlife of
Pat Garrett and Billy the Kid

AUTHENTIC DEATH
& CONTENTIOUS
AFTERLIFE OF
PAT GARRETT and
BILLY THE KID

The Untold Story of Peckinpah's Last Western Film

PAUL SEYDOR

NORTHWESTERN UNIVERSITY PRESS
EVANSTON, ILLINOIS

Northwestern University Press
www.nupress.northwestern.edu

Printed in the United States of America

10   9   8   7   6   5   4   3   2

Library of Congress Cataloging-in-Publication Data

Seydor, Paul, 1947– author.
The authentic death and contentious afterlife of Pat Garrett and Billy the Kid :
the untold story of Peckinpah's last Western / Paul Seydor.
    pages cm
Includes bibliographical references and index.
ISBN 978-0-8101-3056-2 (pbk. : alk. paper) — ISBN 978-0-8101-3089-0
(cloth : alk. paper) — ISBN 978-0-8101-6820-6 (ebook)
 . 1. Pat Garrett & Billy the Kid (Motion picture) 2. Peckinpah, Sam,
1925–1984—Criticism and interpretation. I. Title.
PN1997.P366S49 2015
791.43'72—dc23

                                                         2014037057

♾ The paper used in this publication meets the minimum requirements of the
American National Standard for Information Sciences—Permanence of Paper for
Printed Library Materials, ANSI Z39.48-1992.

For Danielle and Samantha:
roses both by other names

I am a child of the Old West. I knew firsthand the life of cowboys. I participated in some of their adventures and I actually witnessed the disintegration of a world.

—Sam Peckinpah

I was obsessed with movement and sound for their own sake, the hero riding on, always riding neither east nor west, south nor north, just riding through space into the unknown Big Empty of the frontier.

—Rudolph Wurlitzer

CONTENTS

Acknowledgments   *xi*

Introduction   *xv*

PART ONE: Authentic Lives, Authentic Deaths   *1*

Chapter One   Brando's Western   *3*

Chapter Two   Garrett's Narrative   *11*

Chapter Three   Neider's Novel   *43*

Chapter Four   Peckinpah's Adaptation   *77*

Chapter Five   Wurlitzer's Screenplay   *113*

Chapter Six   Peckinpah's Changes   *139*

PART TWO: The Versions of *Pat Garrett and Billy the Kid*   *185*

Chapter Seven   The Previews   *187*

Chapter Eight   The Box Set   *227*

Chapter Nine   The 2005 Special Edition   *245*

PART THREE: Ten Ways of Looking at an Unfinished
Masterpiece and Its Director   *271*

Appendix   Credits and Running Times   *317*

Notes   *321*

Bibliography and Filmography   *365*

Index   *375*

ACKNOWLEDGMENTS

Despite what title pages say, few books this side of fiction and poetry are ever the product of a single person. My debts—many and no doubt far from comprehensively recalled—began accruing long ago with Sam Peckinpah himself and his family, friends, and colleagues, who over a thirty-six-year period shared their thoughts and experiences in interviews, correspondence, conversation, and emails: Gordon Carroll, Garth Craven, Gordon Dawson, Gill Dennis, Jerry Fielding, Jesse Graham, Waylon Green, Katy Haber, Jim Hamilton, Monte Hellman, Don Hyde, L. Q. Jones, Walter Kelley, Don Levy, Malcolm McDowell, Daniel Melnick, Kristen Peckinpah, Sharon Peckinpah, Fern Lea Peter, Walter Peter, Marie Selland, Jim Silke, Roger Spottiswoode, Robert L. Wolfe, and Rudolph Wurlitzer. My gratitude for their time and trust is beyond evaluation. Among these for the present book I must single out Katy, Gordy, Rudy, and Roger for special thanks, so graciously and with such patience did they accommodate my innumerable questions—most especially Roger, who remains a close, steadfast, and good-humored friend despite relentless requests to reawaken memories from the better part of a year in his life that I am sure he preferred remain dormant.

Alan Axelrod, Wayne Matelski, Clay Reynolds, Ron Shelton, and David Ward read parts of the manuscript and offered valuable comment and suggestion. Michael Bliss, Robert Merrill, Hershel Parker, Garner Simmons, and David Weddle read it in whole or in part with a care, commitment, and sustained engagement I doubt they could have exceeded with their own work—Bob and Gar especially, with unflagging diligence and dedication. Mark Lee Gardner generously read all the sections that deal with the real Garrett and Billy, directing me to sources I wouldn't have found otherwise, correcting errors of fact, yet also encouraging me to strike out on my own in speculating about all those areas of the history plagued by uncertainty. Of course it goes without saying, though it must be said, that remaining mistakes, misjudgments, and errors of fact or interpretation are solely my responsibility.

This book would not exist but for Nick Redman and Michael Bliss. Nick was brazen enough to pitch a new version of *Pat Garrett and Billy the Kid* before even asking me whether I'd be interested in doing it; and Brian Jamieson, formerly of Warner Home Video, got the ball rolling. A few years later Michael invited me to write an essay for an anthology he was putting together; when I proposed a piece on the preparation of the 2005 Special Edition, invitation became insistence, though at the time I had neither intention nor even a dim intimation it would lead me where it has.

I am indebted once again to Kristen Peckinpah for her generosity in permitting me to quote from and reproduce examples of her father's extensive correspondence and other papers. Don Hyde, Peckinpah's archivist for many years, provided me with a DVD of the second preview of the film. The collector Robert McCubbin graciously opened his home and spectacular library of books, photographs, and other materials about the Old West one afternoon, showing me, among other treasures, an extremely rare first edition of Garrett's book. Bob also generously supplied period photographs from his vast collection. Jeff Slater was unstinting as always in sharing what is unquestionably the world's largest collection of photographs, posters, one sheets, and other memorabilia about Peckinpah and his films. Mike Pitel, a retired Heritage Tourism Development Program Officer in the New Mexico Tourism Department, took me on a morning's tour of Billy the Kid sites in Santa Fe, followed by a lunch and several emails in which he shared his vast knowledge of this history. The Lincoln Historic Site in Lincoln, New Mexico, is without question the best-preserved of all the places associated with the Kid, Garrett, and the Lincoln County War, and it is arguably the best-preserved town of the Old West. Gwendolyn Rogers and the rest of the staff were extraordinarily patient in answering my numerous questions and allowing me to take so many photographs, which are used with the site's permission. Richard Weddle was a source of much information, notably about the ferrotypes of Billy the Kid, and supplied an excellent reproduction of the only surviving one. Scott Arundale, Robert Blenheim, Marcelle Brothers, Steven Gaydos, John Giolas, Karen Mills, Steven Moore, Rich West, and Debbie Zeitman were helpful in their various ways.

I once again happily join the chorus of praise for the Margaret Herrick Library of the Academy of Motion Picture Arts and Sciences: I've never found a more helpful, thorough, and professional staff or a more pleasant and hospitable haven for research. Recognition of five must stand for all: Barbara Hall and Valentin Almendarez, Special Collections Research Archivists; Jenny Romero, Special Collections Department Coordinator; Faye Thompson, Photograph Archive Coordinator; and especially Warren Sherk, Music Specialist, who painstakingly digitized the tape recordings of story conferences, phone calls, and other meetings from the film and the cassette tapes I donated long ago of my interviews with Carroll, Fielding, Spottiswoode, and Wolfe. The reference librarians Graciela Monday of the Alamogordo Public Library and Tomás González of the Roswell Public Library sent me copies of the original news stories of John Meadows's recollections. Susan M. Neider entrusted me with the journals and correspondence of her father, Charles Neider.

Fulsome praise is rarely convincing and never attractive, but I shall risk it for the splendid staff of Northwestern University Press, who embody talent, expertise, enthusiasm, and commitment to excellence in high and equal measure. The following few must stand for the several who go unnamed: Mike Levine, my editor, and Anne Gendler, the managing editor, both of whom in their different and combined endeavors ideally mediate passion, practicality, and wisdom; Marianne Jankowski, for a spectacular cover design that surpassed all expectations; Alma MacDougall, for exacting, meticulous, and sensitive copyediting; Mike Ashby, for eagle-eyed proofreading; and Rudy Faust, for much savvy advice and enthusiasm launching this book into the world.

Last because first in every other way, all my love—thanks is surely too small a word—to my wife Danielle Egerer—the left-brained one in the family and the critic's first, best, most demanding critic, for whose scrupulous reading and unwavering encouragement this book is incalculably better—and our daughter Samantha Rose, who, while we were exploring the New Mexico of Garrett and Billy, asked me, not without some impatience, "Daddy, why is Billy the Kid so important?" At the time I lacked the presence of mind to fashion an answer that seemed likely to make sense to a six-year-old, even a precocious one. But I hope that someday she will find the beginning of one in this book, and even more the answer to another question that has occupied a fair portion of her father's life: why Sam Peckinpah is so important.

INTRODUCTION

Long before Sam Peckinpah finished shooting what would turn out to be his last Western film, *Pat Garrett and Billy the Kid*, there was open warfare between him and Metro-Goldwyn-Mayer. By the time the film was released a few months later, in May 1973, an all-too-frequent pattern in his career was played out yet again: the director accused the executives of recutting the film without his consent or participation and disowned the version released to theaters. A longer preview version was known to exist, with several additional scenes, but fifteen years would pass before it would be shown again publicly; and eventually it was discovered there was a second preview version. As neither had ever been properly dubbed, scored, mixed, or color timed, when Warner Home Video decided to market a DVD package of the Peckinpah Westerns the studio owned, I was asked if it might be possible to add the missing scenes to the theatrical version, which had had the benefit of having been properly finished. Thus began the process that eventually became *Pat Garrett and Billy the Kid: 2005 Special Edition*, which was included, along with the first preview version, in the Warner Bros. DVD box set *Sam Peckinpah's The Legendary Westerns Collection*, and also in a new separate double-DVD set, with the same preview. The story of how I came to do the special edition is the subject of an essay I wrote in 2010 for Michael Bliss's anthology *Peckinpah Today*. It was the third time I had written at considerable length about this film, the others being in the first and second editions of my critical study of Peckinpah's Western films. My intention in the essay was to clear up, once and for all, the controversy, the misunderstanding, and the sheer misinformation that had accumulated about the 2005 Special Edition in particular and this film in general.

That would and should have been the end of it—except the film wasn't finished with me, which meant that, my intentions notwithstanding, I wasn't finished with it. I suppose one is never truly "finished" with anything one really loves. The longer I wrote, the less I seemed to be leading the writing, the more it seemed to be leading me. This is a happy experience for any writer, but it can also be a daunting one if more questions are raised, the answers only ramifying into more questions still, involvement getting deeper and deeper, until it becomes obvious that a single essay, even a long one, will not be sufficient to answer them.

Since the essay in the anthology was already about the versions of *Pat Garrett and Billy the Kid*, the logical place to begin a book about them seemed to lie at the other end of the process: go in search of where it came from. Pauline Kael once called Peckinpah "the youngest legendary American director." It is perhaps fitting, then, that his last Western film is the only one he ever made about actual historical figures of the Old West, men who, like Peckinpah himself, were in the process of becoming legends even while they lived. His films are almost always marked by conflicts between two men or groups of men who represent opposing points of view, philosophies of life, or simply different codes, values, or ways of being in the world. Typically these paired combatants start out as friends and even continue to believe in more or less the same things, but Peckinpah takes them up at junctures in their lives when age or circumstance has forced different, usually opposing choices on them, choices that drive them apart with consequences that are often violent and deadly.

It is perhaps needless to say of so obviously personal and volatile an artist that these conflicts mirrored those in his own massively conflicted life and personality—his inability much of the time to be able, as Emerson said of Thoreau, to feel himself except in opposition. The conflict between Pat Garrett and Billy the Kid in both the screenplay and the history must have cut right straight through to the marrow of Peckinpah's being, because he came to the project at a time when he could see his own internal conflicts and other problems reflected in both men and in the differing ways each defined himself in relationship to the large-scale social, political, and economic changes churning all around them. In retrospect, the irony of the title of Peckinpah's first film, *The Deadly Companions*, would be almost comical were it not so tragic, its implied theme played out on both sides of the camera throughout most of the rest of his career, usually between him and the businessmen, nowhere more rancorously than on *Pat Garrett and Billy the Kid*.

Investigating the writers and historians that Peckinpah and Rudolph Wurlitzer, who wrote the original screenplay, used in making the film would likely provide insights as to what they saw in the materials, why they developed the story as they did, and how the film itself contributes to what one biographer has called "the endless ride" of Billy the Kid and his nemesis Pat Garrett through our history, our culture, and our society. I discovered that despite the distance of ninety-one years, it is possible to draw an almost direct line from the first history of the events—written by one of the two leading protagonists and published only a year after he had shot and killed the other—straight to Peckinpah's last Western film, with only a few degrees of separation between them: a neglected novel that fictionalized the historical events; a screen adaptation of that novel; and a wholly new, original screenplay, developed out of a fresh look at the history, that eventually landed at Peckinpah's feet. Part 1 of this book is taken up with exploring and articulating the line of influence, development, and transformation that led from the historical sources to the several versions of the film.

I also soon discovered that this particular territory in the Old West has a way of becoming a sort of Bermuda Triangle for those who dare to venture in, biographers, historians, and enthusiasts of the Old West getting lost in the maze of its myriad developments, intricacies, byways, ambiguities, uncertainties, mysteries, and the many, many unanswered questions: the early life of William Bonney, his involvement in the intrigue and violence of the Lincoln County War, the nature of his friendship with Pat Garrett (was it a friendship at all?), his legendary jailbreak and Garrett's manhunt to recapture him, his motivation in refusing to leave the territory even as the noose tightened all around him (not to mention the sheriff's motivation in pursuing him), and his death from a single bullet fired near midnight in a dark room, the encounter an accident of circumstance that appears in retrospect to be the very embodiment of the workings of fate and destiny.

This Bermuda Triangle seemed to encompass as well the troubled production of the film and the equally, if not more troubled postproduction, which, though it wrapped over four decades ago, seems to continue on an endless ride of its own in pursuit of some chimerical, mythic "complete" or "final" version that can at last and truly be called Peckinpah's own. Myth is the operative idea here: if the history of the lawman and the outlaw eventually became so enmeshed with its own legend that in places it is all but impossible to separate the one from the other, so too with Peckinpah's last Western, where his own dual legends as undeniable though difficult genius and equally undeniable though brilliant troublemaker collide in such a way that they obscure where the one left off and the other began.

I hope no one will infer from the influences charted and the sources discovered in part 1 any intention to derogate from the originality of the writers and the filmmaker who are my objects of study. Far from it: for me, knowledge of where and how artists learn, by whom they are influenced and what they draw upon, allows the unique contours of their individuality to appear in only sharper profile, their originality to stand out in greater relief, their richness more variegated and abundant. An old saw that never gets dull, variously attributed to Picasso, Stravinsky, T. S. Eliot, and doubtless others, has it that "good artists borrow, great artists steal." Whatever a real artist takes from others is absorbed so thoroughly into the products of his imagination that it is transformed and becomes his own. "The most important form of influence," Charles Rosen once wrote, "is that which provokes the most original and most personal work." Peckinpah was so secure about his own originality that he was forthright to the point of loquacity about what he learned, helped himself to, or brazenly stole from others. (When his close friend Max Evans accused him of stealing the last reel of *The Losers* from Evans's novel *The Hi Lo Country*, Peckinpah replied, "Of course. It just shows you what good taste I have."[1])

To write seriously about Peckinpah and his films is invariably to come face-to-face with issues of authorship: how revision, alternative versions, and outside interference realize or alter intention, impact meaning, and help determine how the work is experienced. In films these considerations are rather more complex and complicated owing to the far greater number of collaborators even directors as personal and singular as Peckinpah must rely upon, to say nothing of the influence of marketing. *Pat Garrett and Billy the Kid* exacerbates these issues because the director not only left the project before it was completed, he refused a later offer by the studio to return and fine-cut the film to his satisfaction. The consequence is that there neither exists nor has ever existed any version of the film which contains everything he wanted in it—even the longest of them is missing important scenes.

This presents a special problem for criticism, because it requires us to write about a film that none of us has ever, strictly speaking, seen. Allow me to provide an example that I will treat at greater length much later. Garrett at home with his wife Ida and later in Roswell with the prostitute Ruthie Lee constitute a pair of scenes obviously intended to resonate off each other. But they were never *both* at once in any version of the film—that is, any version ever shown to the public—until the 2005 Special Edition. The first preview had neither, the second preview had the Ida but not the Ruthie Lee, the theatrical release had the Ruthie Lee but not the Ida, and the short-lived television version (first aired in 1975 on CBS) had the Ida but not the Ruthie Lee. Before I wrote about the film for the first time in the late seventies, I had managed to see the theatrical, the second preview, and the television. Thus I could write about these scenes on the basis of direct experience; but what I could not write about from direct experience is how they played off each other. In order to do that, I had to mix and match versions in my head to come up with a film that had no existence anywhere else.[2] It was not until 2005 and the special edition that I could at last experience both scenes in the continuum of a proper filmic narrative or dramatic structure more or less as Peckinpah and Wurlitzer had intended. Multiply this example several times over and you have some idea of the complications involved in just trying to figure out which *Pat Garrett and Billy the Kid* you're watching. And Peckinpah's thoughts as can be determined or otherwise inferred from his extensive editing notes, reports of what he said, and some of his actions at the time are occasionally ambiguous, indecisive, or contradictory enough that it would be impossible to cull together from the several versions one that could be called definitive.

Problems like these and the issues they raise are taken up in part 2, a greatly expanded version of the original essay, by way of telling the story of the editing of the film, the impossibly rushed postproduction schedule, and how it came to pass that there were five different versions which at one time or another have been shown publicly. In this part I also describe the decision-making behind the 2005 Special Edition, address the aesthetic and ethical issues it raises, answer some of the more uninformed and peremptory criticism it received, and detail the differences between it, the two previews, and the theatrical release.

Because I've written extensive interpretation and criticism, including formal analysis, of *Pat Garrett and Billy the Kid* in my studies of Peckinpah's Western films, I have in part 2 and also in chapters 4, 5, and 6 tried to approach the versions of the screenplays and the film mostly in terms specific to Peckinpah's and Wurlitzer's intentions as dramatists and storytellers, and I've concentrated on their dramatic and narrative strategies and structures. Particularly as regards the scenes, parts of scenes, dialogue, music, and bits of business that are present in some versions and not in others, I've tried to track how these functioned originally and whether they retained, changed, or lost their purpose as the intentions of the writer and director evolved with revisions, deletions, and additions. To a large extent my approach here follows logically from my career as a film editor these last thirty years, where the practicalities of storytelling and the actualities of filmmaking have been my daily professional concern.

But my early years as an academic continue to exert their influence. It is a particular pleasure to acknowledge a groundbreaking work of textual criticism and masterly close reading, one that explores the issues and problems of interpreting an unfinished work, even a masterpiece: Hershel Parker's *Reading "Billy Budd."* "We cannot and should not stop reading *Billy Budd, Sailor* as a classic work of American literature," Parker concludes, "but we should acknowledge that we do not help our reputation as readers and do not help the reputation of the work when we act as if we can offer a complete, coherent interpretation of it." Substitute a few terms and titles and these words could have been written about *Pat Garrett and Billy the Kid.* The reality is that when more than one version of a work of art exists or especially when artists leave their work unfinished, we do not always have the luxury of treating existing versions as sacrosanct, and must as responsible critics and readers or viewers grapple with thorny issues of intention and try, as much as we are able, to think like the artists themselves.

Ever since *The Wild Bunch* established Peckinpah as a filmmaker indisputably of world stature, it hasn't been necessary to justify a study of his work. Still, while book-length studies devoted to single films are by no means rare, they are certainly not usual.[3] Why this one? Three reasons lie readily at hand. The first is that *Pat Garrett and Billy the Kid* affords an opportunity to observe at length and in great detail how a filmmaker navigates his vision through the creative and treacherous waters of collaboration, commerce, and his own self-destructive impulses and behavior. This particular film represents an extreme form of this ongoing struggle, but it is extreme in degree, not in kind. Second, it is practically beyond argument that *Pat Garrett and Billy the Kid* is by far the best and most important of the fifty-plus films about Billy the Kid. That may not say much, since most of them are very bad. But Peckinpah's film also has the higher distinction of being among the very finest of the nearly countless imaginative treatments of this iconic history and legend of the Old West in any medium, possessing a lyricism, a visionary sweep, and a tragic weight that crushes most previous incarnations.

Third, and most important, is the film itself and its place in Peckinpah's work. There are very few films of any kind whose reputation, after almost universally poor reviews upon its initial release, rose so quickly and steeply as this one's did, the ascent beginning almost as soon as the film disappeared from first-run theaters, which happened more or less to coincide with the first reviews in the "little" film magazines and journals in the United States and abroad, whose critics acclaimed it one of Peckinpah's best well before the first preview ever became widely available on VHS and laser disc in the early nineties. Monte Hellman, the director for whom the screenplay was originally written, says the film "brought tears to my eyes because it was so powerful"; Martin Scorsese calls it "a masterpiece, the only other Peckinpah film that came close to *The Wild Bunch*"; David Thomson judges it "one of the great American films"; Richard T. Jameson thinks it "may be the most beautiful and ambitious film that Sam Peckinpah ever made"; and Maximilian Le Cain offers it as one answer to the question, "What was the most important American film of the 1970s?" It often finds a place on most lists of the ten, twelve, or two dozen best Westerns; in 2011 it came in second on *Time Out* magazine's fifty greatest Westerns; in 2008 it placed 126th on *Empire* magazine's 500 best films ever made; and it's in the last few editions of *1001 Movies You Must See Before You Die*. Lists like these are hardly the stuff of high seriousness, but as indices they are not without significance because they cut through a lot of disingenuous respectability to honest passion and enthusiasm, qualities that have always characterized writing about Peckinpah.[4]

Peckinpah's six Western films constitute a body of work that can take its place among the most beautiful and influential ever made. Though their individual achievements vary, as a group they exhibit a thematic, stylistic, and visionary progression that seems almost to have been preordained, so sure is the arc of its trajectory. It would be a mistake to suggest that he intended this from the outset. Very few artists start with a grand plan that extends over several works and years, and almost none who work in mediums as tied to commerce as theatrical films and most forms of theater and music (including classical music), where artistic evolution tends to be rather more fluid, even haphazard, with beginnings recognized as such only in hindsight and destinations often not until quite a while after they've been reached and the artist has moved on to other things. Yet *Pat Garrett and Billy the Kid* unquestionably has a valedictory air about it which, if not quite intentional, nevertheless didn't happen entirely by accident either: Peckinpah became aware, if only after the fact, that he had accomplished something in this film, specifically with respect to the Western as a form, which he'd been working toward for the better part of his career without quite achieving it. The progress of this book has been in some sense about discovering that achievement, articulating it, and seeing how he came to realize it, though I too did not become aware this was where I was headed until very late in the writing.

Peckinpah once said that it was appropriate he should make films about the disintegration of the West as he knew it "through a genre which itself is slowly dying: the Western." No one knew better than he that the Western was losing its popular appeal—indeed, to some, perhaps a large extent because he himself was responsible for all but destroying it. By pushing its dialectics, conflicts, and contradictions, its ambiguities and antitheses, its subversiveness and latent anarchy, its possibilities for exploration of character and psychology, and of course its violence to the farthest possible limits, he forced it to express a ferocious, savage beauty, a depth and range of themes, and an intensity of feeling and emotion which it was scarcely equipped to handle in the first place and which blew it apart in the last. It has sometimes been said there could or should be no more Westerns after Peckinpah's because he both transformed the genre and exhausted its possibilities for meaningful further development. This is an exaggeration, and there have been several very good Westerns since his death. What *is* true, however, is that the Western could never be put back together again quite as it was before, could no longer be made to express its traditional values and certainties as confidently, without appearing naive, silly, perhaps even a little stupid, which is to say that after him the Western could never again be pure, simple, and straightforward—it must embrace irony.

Some good solid reasons, then, these, which will do for the abstracts and summaries, but what they miss is the basis in passion that must inspire all criticism—whatever else that may be, it's another way of saying love. There is at once a special poignancy and a fierce tenacity that attach themselves to the feelings of those of us who love *Pat Garrett and Billy the Kid*, perhaps because it is the only one of Peckinpah's great Westerns that he made a decision to leave before it was finished.[5] Partly for that reason but mostly because of how personally enmeshed was his identification with his protagonists, how deep his emotional investment in their issues, and yet how resistant to resolution these issues were for him, it is arguably the most haunted and haunting of his films: once it gets under your skin or into your head, it neither lets you go nor gives up its secrets easily. In part 3 I explore some different ways of looking at this extraordinary and occasionally problematic and difficult film that nevertheless inspires fresh responses and new insights every time I watch it. Compelling despite (and in part because of) its problems, its vision whole despite its unevenness, *Pat Garrett and Billy the Kid* often puts me in mind of an observation Randall Jarrell made about some lines by Whitman, words that strike me as equally appropriate to this last Western film by Peckinpah: "There are faults in this passage and *they do not matter*."

The Authentic Death and
Contentious Afterlife of
Pat Garrett and Billy the Kid

PART ONE

Authentic Lives,
Authentic Deaths

———◆———

To Hershel Parker,
the better craftsman

Karl Malden, as Dad Longworth, and Marlon Brando, as Rio, in *One-Eyed Jacks*:
"You may be a one-eyed Jack here, but I've seen the other side of your face."

CHAPTER ONE

Brando's Western

Sam Peckinpah's first go-round with the story of Pat Garrett and Billy the Kid came by way of Charles Neider's fictionalized treatment in his 1956 novel *The Authentic Death of Hendry Jones*. After spending some months doing research in New Mexico, Neider set his book in Northern California in and around Monterey and changed the names of the leading protagonists from William Bonney to Hendry Jones and Pat Garrett to Dad Longworth.

Soon after the publication of Neider's book, a producer named Frank Rosenberg optioned it and hired Rod Serling to write an adaptation. Rosenberg didn't like Serling's screenplay and asked Peckinpah, who was a friend of his, to read the novel.[1] Though Peckinpah had at the time no reputation apart from some very good adaptations of *Gunsmoke* radio plays for the then-new television series, Rosenberg was perceptive enough to recognize a promising talent when he saw one, and his gamble paid off. Peckinpah, who appears not to have read Serling's screenplay, loved the novel—"the best Western ever written," he later called it—but said he wanted to research the history himself before sitting down to write. After an intensive six months during the summer and fall of 1957, he turned in a first draft dated November 11, for which he was paid four thousand dollars (far from princely, but very reasonable at the time for an unknown beginner). Rosenberg was impressed and, at Peckinpah's suggestion, sent the script to Marlon Brando, who was likewise impressed, and his company bought it. "Sam was high as a kite," said Marie Selland, his wife at the time. "He really thought Brando could do a fantastic job with the character." Over the next few weeks Brando met with him daily for long script conferences, then nothing much happened for several months until March 1958, when he phoned Peckinpah to tell him an offer to direct was going out to Stanley Kubrick, whom Peckinpah thought a splendid choice. But Kubrick disliked the script and refused to sign on unless another writer was engaged for essentially a page-one rewrite. So Brando fired Peckinpah, which left him, according to Marie, "devastated."

Brando went with Kubrick's suggested replacement, Calder Willingham. But after several starts, not to mention months, it became clear that Willingham wasn't working out to Brando's, Kubrick's, or anyone else's satisfaction. Rosenberg wanted to reenlist Peckinpah, who was by then hard at work on *The Rifleman*, a television series he had helped create, episodes of which he was directing as well. So yet another writer, Guy Trosper, was brought aboard. By this time it was evident that Brando had taken a very personal interest in the project, which in turn led to so many arguments between him and Kubrick about everything from casting to overall development of the characters and the plot that he eventually had Kubrick fired. Brando took over as director and finished the screenplay with Trosper the lone survivor among four (some sources say five) writers who had had a hand in it.

Slightly different versions of these events circulate. Memories are imperfect and, Hollywood being Hollywood, everyone tries or is usually given an opportunity to save face when it comes to the parting of the ways. Willingham, for example, says he resigned, but Brando's partner in his production company recalls that Brando took Willingham out to a dinner and canned him there, at the same time gifting him with a teak-inlaid chessboard. At that point Rosenberg wanted to bring Peckinpah back, but Peckinpah said he was too busy or Brando nixed him (or both). Similarly, when it became obvious that Brando and Kubrick could agree on nothing, Brando asked Rosenberg to have him fired. At the time, however, Kubrick issued a public statement expressing his gratitude to Brando for being so "understanding" of his desire to allow him to resign in order to pursue an adaptation of *Lolita*.

Although several persons associated with the production insist that Brando had for a good while wanted to direct the film, the actor wrote in his autobiography that he tried to hire other directors (among them Elia Kazan and Sidney Lumet); when they turned him down, he had to take over because the start of production had already been delayed a few months, at least one of the stars, Karl Malden, was already on salary and had been paid a substantial amount (in the vicinity of $400,000), and other costs were escalating. By the time the film was completed, an original budget variously reported as $1.8 to $3 million had swollen to $6 million, and the shooting schedule doubled from three to six months. Brando's autobiography provides the reason: "On the first day of shooting," he wrote, "I didn't know what to do," and by "the fifth week, and even the fifth month, I was still trying to learn." He and Trosper

constantly improvised and rewrote between shots and setups, often hour by hour, sometimes minute by minute. Some scenes I shot over and over again from different angles with different dialogue and action because I didn't know what I was doing. I was making things up by the moment, not sure where the story was going. I also did a lot of stalling for time, trying to work the story out in my mind while hoping to make the cast think I knew what I was doing.

In one scene he was supposed to be drunk, but believing he couldn't fake drunkenness, he actually *got* drunk, then too drunk to finish the scene. So he got drunk on another day, but it "still wasn't right, and I had to do it over again on a number of afternoons until it was right." The scene in question never made it into the film. Multiply indulgences like this, add to them Brando's inexperience as first-time director, and it didn't take long before schedules and thus budgets began to soar. After spending several months working with his editor Archie Marshek, Brando gave up, admitting thirty years later in his autobiography, "I was bored with the whole project and walked away from it."

Until Peckinpah's departure, the script retained Neider's title and its story was still recognizably an adaptation of the book. But not long after Peckinpah was let go, the title was changed to *One-Eyed Jacks* and by the time the film was released, in 1961, about the only things it had in common with the novel were some of the characters' names and the Monterey Peninsula setting. So little of Peckinpah's work remained that only Willingham and Trosper received screenwriting credit. Spared all the Sturm und Drang over the screenplay was Charles Neider himself, who seems to have taken it all with great and even amused equanimity, often visiting the set, where he enjoyed his many meetings with Brando, Brando's father, and Karl Malden. One day during dailies Brando's father asked him what he thought of his son's having the six-gun stuck in a wide cummerbund. "First time he'd draw that gun he'd blow his balls off," Neider answered. If the father ever passed this piece of wisdom on to the son, there is no evidence in the completed film to indicate it was heeded.

"The book is spare, sober, tragic," Neider wrote, but "Brando the actor, director, and producer was convinced he had a clear romantic vision, and he clung to it."

> Essentially, the film sentimentalizes the novel. . . . [It] contains wonderful nature scenes, moments of superb acting, a great deal of tension, lots of suspense. It has deservedly become a kind of underground classic, a cult film. It has a romantic, perhaps adolescent, bitter-sweetness that distinguishes it from other Westerns. And it has the sea, the beaches, and Brando's genius.

A far less generous Peckinpah called it "a piece of shit" that ruined "the definitive work on Billy the Kid." He found Brando a study in frustration.

Very strange man, Marlon. Always doing a number about his screen image, about how audiences would not accept him as a thief, would only accept him as a fallen sinner—someone they could love. As it was released, I think I've one scene left in the film—the one where Marlon knocks the shit out of Timothy Carey. The rest is all Marlon's.

Neider's is the more accurate assessment.[2] *One-Eyed Jacks* is one of the strangest Westerns ever made.[3] The film is magnificently photographed, the Monterey setting, with the sand and surf and cypress trees, lending it a look like no other Western's. The entire cast is quite extraordinary, the supporting actors including Ben Johnson, Katy Jurado, and Slim Pickens, all of whom would appear in important roles in Peckinpah's films (the latter two in *Pat Garrett and Billy the Kid*). But it's the power of the central relationship between the one-eyed Jacks of the title that really sets the film apart. Concentrated, brooding, and intense, Brando as Rio gives one of his signature Method performances, while Karl Malden's Dad Longworth is a lying, sadistic opportunist so compleat as to be almost generic. "One-eyed Jacks" refers to the Jacks of hearts and spades, face cards that display only the Jack's profile and are often wild. In the film Rio tells Longworth, "You may be a one-eyed Jack here, but I've seen the other side of your face." The same can of course be said of Rio with respect to Dad. Their story no longer has anything to do with Neider's lean, elegant, focused reimagining of a famous episode in the history of the Old West. In the book Longworth reluctantly and only in the line of duty kills his friend, an unrepentant gunslinger and outlaw who forces the sheriff's hand; in the film, they're outlaw partners, Longworth abandoning Rio in Mexico to the *rurales* and certain imprisonment while he hightails it out and starts a new life as a sheriff in Northern California. Brando and his collaborators turned it into a story of trust and betrayal, vengeance and retribution, their antagonism given a distinctly Freudian slant.

This last is implicit in Neider's novel—he could hardly have been unaware that naming Longworth "Dad" and Hendry "the Kid" slants their relationship in both psychological and mythological directions.[4] Nowhere does he push it, however—they're merely two shadings among several. But Brando and his collaborators added the subplot wherein Rio seduces Longworth's foster daughter, intending to disgrace him by shaming her, which backfires when he falls in love with her. In another scene not in the novel, Longworth lashes Rio to a hitching post, bullwhips him to within an inch of his life while the townspeople look on, then smashes his gun hand with the butt of a shotgun. Against this addition Neider argued that a hard man like Longworth would never put himself in danger like that by potentially angering the Kid's friends, who might ambush the sheriff in revenge. Yet the scene became at once the most notorious and the most powerful in the film. Though by no means graphic, it is a scene of such extreme brutality that even today it is nearly as shocking as it was over fifty years ago, one reason being that its

The Monterey setting gave the picture a look like that of no other Western.

Brando was convinced he had a clear romantic vision and he clung to it.

This scene of such extreme brutality is nearly as
shocking today as half a century ago.

violence does not quite feel fully justified by, thus barely contained in, the immediate dramatic situation or the story at large. (In view of the Freudianism in the material, it was not uncommon for reviewers at the time and since to speculate whether what is being expressed here wasn't a hidden streak of masochism in Brando or some need to punish himself by way of his character for some unconfessed sin or secret transgression.)

Yet it's easy to understand why Peckinpah felt as he did about *One-Eyed Jacks* when you consider his storytelling priorities during these early years of his career. He had already written his first scripts for *Gunsmoke* and he would soon be writing the pilot and other early episodes of *The Rifleman* and developing *The Westerner*. By his own admission he was obsessed with depicting cowboys as truthfully as he could on the basis of what he knew from the hands who worked his grandfather's ranch and from his own considerable research. The title character of *The Westerner*, for example, he intended as "a truly realistic saddle bum of the West. I wanted to make him as honest and real as I could do it." For Peckinpah this didn't necessarily mean a slavish verisimilitude as regards life in the Old West—it's easy to spot all sorts of inaccuracies with respect to details of clothing, props (even firearms), sets, saddles, reins, and so on in his films—so much as a realistic treatment of character, behavior, psychology, attitudes of mind and modes of thought and action, and a clear-eyed, unvarnished look at how cowboys, lawmen, bad men, gamblers, drifters, preachers, farmers, townspeople, frontier wives, schoolmarms, and prostitutes actually lived in their world, what their beliefs and values were. The opening episode of *The Westerner* is about a sadomasochistic relationship between a young whore and her pimp; in another episode a young Easterner's dime-novel illusions of gunplay in the Old West eventually get him killed; an episode of *The Rifleman* is about a marshal who's a drunk, and it does not treat alcoholism humorously. Of course a recurring preoccupation is with serious depictions of violence.

What really seems to have angered Peckinpah most about *One-Eyed Jacks* is that Brando turned Neider's Hendry Jones into a hero "and that's not the point of the story. Billy the Kid was no hero. He was a gunfighter, a real killer." Yet as he must surely have sensed, Neider's attitudes toward Hendry Jones are far from clear-cut, infused with a dark romanticism much akin to his own complex and conflicted feelings about the Old West, Western heroes and outlaws, and the Western itself as they would be given expression in his television and especially his later film work. Neider had taken a slice of Western history and legend and plumbed it for psychological verity and mythic reverberation without allowing it to become in the least self-conscious or pretentious, yet at the same time told a gripping story that could be enjoyed for itself alone. The shocks of recognition the burgeoning filmmaker felt upon first reading it must have been revelatory: here was both a progenitor and a fellow traveler. A closer look at Neider's novel, its primary sources, and Peckinpah's early screenplay will thus help fill a missing chapter in both the director's artistic biography and the story of how his last Western film came to be made. But long before any of these a sheriff wrote a little book about an outlaw he had tracked down and killed in Fort Sumner, New Mexico.

William Bonney, ca. 1879–80, in a portrait cropped and enhanced from the famous tintype. The "missing" left ear is due to a smudge probably caused by someone touching the plate before the emulsion was dry and by degradation over time—evidenced also by scratches on the right side of his face and extensive pitting—which distorts his appearance.

CHAPTER TWO

Garrett's Narrative

I knew both these men intimately, and each made history in his own way. There was good mixed with the bad in Billy the Kid and bad mixed with the good in Pat Garrett. Both were distinctly human, both remarkable personalities. No matter what they did in the world or what the world thought of them, they were my friends. Both were real men. Both were worth knowing.

—Sallie Chisum

Just about everyone who sets out to write something about Billy the Kid and Pat Garrett begins in the same place: a little book, published in 1882, a year after the sheriff shot and killed the young outlaw, that laid the groundwork, established the characters, and set the terms for virtually every history, biography, pulp novel, serious novel, drama, teleplay, screenplay, and movie about them. It carries an almost comically long title:

The Authentic Life of Billy, the Kid,
The Noted Desperado of the Southwest,
Whose Deeds of Daring and Blood
Made His Name a Terror in New Mexico,
Arizona, and Northern Mexico
by Pat F. Garrett
Sheriff of Lincoln Co., N.M.,
by whom he was finally hunted down and
captured by killing him
A Faithful and Interesting Narrative[1]

There is much that is worthy of note here, beginning with the fact that Garrett did not write the book: he had it ghostwritten by a man named Marshall Ashmun Upson, commonly known as "Ash." Born in South Carolina in 1828, Upson lived a peripatetic life that led him to Connecticut, New York, Ohio, Colorado, and Utah, along the way practicing the trades of printer, journalist, newspaperman, and editor (at various times throughout his life he also tried his hand as silver miner, storekeeper, notary, stagecoach agent, and justice of the peace) before settling down as the postmaster in Roswell, New Mexico, where he and Garrett became friends (he eventually lived on Garrett's ranch).[2]

Though it is demonstrably untrue that Garrett was practically illiterate, as rumor had it at the time, the advantages of a professional writer were obvious. In a little over two months after the Kid's death, three pulp "biographies" were rushed into print and five more quickies appeared in the several months that followed. Any new book, even one written by the Man Who Shot Billy the Kid, was facing a lot of competition, even if as biography the competition was all bogus. Garrett had no experience as a writer, Upson a lot. In addition to his newspaper work, he brought—or so he claimed—a small personal connection to the Kid: in 1874 while taking a crack at silver mining in Silver City, New Mexico, Upson boarded for a while at the home of Catherine Antrim and her two teenaged sons, one of whom, fourteen at the time, would be shot dead just seven years later after he had become known as Billy the Kid. If Upson was telling the truth, this made him one of the very few persons living in or around Lincoln, Roswell, and Fort Sumner with any firsthand knowledge of what Billy was like before he fell into a life of crime.

Garrett's stated purpose in writing the book was that he was so disgusted with all the lies and nonsense written about the Kid's life and his own role in bringing it to an end that he wanted to set the record straight. Another was no doubt money. Like most lawmen in the Old West, Garrett was usually in serious need of it—if those who knew nothing about the Kid or Garrett were profiting from the story, why shouldn't he, who had lived it? Unfortunately, the book was to fail on both counts. Upson wanted to shop it back east, but Garrett insisted on a Santa Fe publisher who had no idea how to promote it. Sales were dismal, though the book eventually did gain wide currency, but not for many, many years and much too late to bring either of them any real money.

As for setting the record straight, Upson's elaborate title gives the show away: *The Authentic Life* would fall squarely in line with the dime novels, fanciful popular histories, and other "yellow backs" about the West that proliferated in bookstores and newsstands.[3] Even his assertions of authenticity and promises of fidelity to the truth were such standard practice in the genre that they acquired the status of a convention. But the book was different in one crucial way: Garrett not only played a key role in the history, he was one of the two principal protagonists. And Upson was at the very least an important observer and bystander. According to the historian Robert M. Utley, Upson had

> ample opportunity to know Billy the Kid, who occasionally patronized Roswell's combination store and post office and joshed with other customers. Although not likely intimates, the two were both open and gregarious enough to have been more than casual acquaintances. This intermittent personal connection, together with his own observations from his postmaster's advantage, made him an authority on Billy and his friends and the events in which they figured. (*Violent Life* 198)

The book thus has both a special appeal and a special frustration for historians and history enthusiasts. If a lot of it can be confidently dismissed as pure fabrication, then much of the rest feels tantalizingly close to the real thing, however incomplete, limited in perspective, and melodramatic the presentation. How to separate the one from the other?

The book can be divided into three sections: the first eight chapters take the Kid from birth to the eve of the Lincoln County War; the next seven are preoccupied with the Lincoln County War; the last eight cover Garrett's election as sheriff of Lincoln County to the death of Billy. The first third is almost certainly by Upson alone. As factual history it's worthless, though it's an entertaining ride. It starts with the Kid's birth, in New York City on November 23, 1859, and continues with the death of his natural father, his mother's marriage to a man named William Henry Antrim (portrayed as abusive and neglectful), her early death, leaving Billy an orphan at age fourteen, whereupon he falls in with bad company and eventually becomes a criminal and a killer. The style—florid, inflated, overwrought—is consistent with what was expected of pulp writing: for example, after Billy claims his first life, a man who had insulted his mother, "he went out into the night, an outcast and a wanderer, a murderer, self-baptized in human blood . . . like banished Cain" (11). The text is peppered with verses, poems, lyrics, aphorisms, and the like, as were often found in much fiction, popular and serious, of the nineteenth century. The action is a succession of robberies, jailbreaks, killings, and narrow escapes from the authorities or Indians, perhaps the most outrageous one that has Billy and a pal rescuing a wagon train from an attack by a band of marauding Apaches. At one point, out of bullets, the Kid rushes the attackers using his pistol as a club, then grabs a prairie ax and with "yell on yell . . . fell upon the Reds." Soon the Indians are dispatched and "Billy's face, hands, and clothing, the wagons, the camp furniture, and the grass were bespattered with blood and brains" (29).

It's hard to imagine even Easterners, who constituted a large audience for cheap fiction about the West thinly disguised as fact, being gullible enough to believe any of this. Indeed, it's hard to imagine Upson himself believed it.[4] But perhaps owing to the cachet of Garrett's name, an astonishing number of

Cover of the first edition of Garrett's book as featured
in an early newspaper advertisement

THE

AUTHENTIC LIFE

—OF—

BILLY, THE KID,

THE NOTED DESPERADO OF THE SOUTHWEST, WHOSE DEEDS OF DARING **AND**
BLOOD MADE HIS NAME A TERROR IN NEW MEXICO,
ARIZONA AND NORTHERN MEXICO.

By PAT. F. GARRETT,

SHERIFF OF LINCOLN CO., N. M.,

BY WHOM HE WAS FINALLY HUNTED DOWN AND CAPTURED BY
KILLING HIM.

A FAITHFUL AND INTERESTING NARRATIVE.

SANTA FE, NEW MEXICO:
NEW MEXICAN PRINTING AND PUBLISHING CO.
1882.

Title page of the first edition: note the small discrepancy
between the title here and on the cover (*opposite*).

Upson's fabrications were regarded as fact far into the next century (some of them persist even today). One is Billy's birth city. New York wasn't original even with Garrett-Upson; the first three pulp biographies preceding theirs also located the Kid's birth there. Yet a year before his death Billy told a census taker that he was twenty-five and born in Missouri, only six months later to tell someone else it was in New York City (Gardner, *To Hell* 36), and other accounts place it in Indiana. In fact, no records exist to document when or where he was born or who his father was.[5] His mother was Catherine McCarty, and if, as widely assumed, she was an immigrant from Ireland, New York City was the most likely place of disembarkation and where the boy spent his early years (the city of Five Points and *Gangs of New York* at that). But the name might also have been "McCarthy," and either way no one knows whether it was Catherine's maiden name or a husband's. "Henry" or "William Henry" are the names most historians believe she gave her son at birth; long widowed by the time many years later she met the man who became her second husband, William Henry Harrison Antrim, she took to calling the boy "Henry" in order to avoid confusion.[6] After living in Wichita, Denver, and Santa Fe, where in 1873 the couple were married, the family settled in Silver City in the New Mexico Territory.

There's no evidence to support the stories that Antrim was abusive, but neglectful he surely was, gone long stretches mining for gold. Although he knew his wife's tuberculosis had been steadily worsening, he wasn't even around for the end, leaving Billy and his brother to witness her decline on their own, friends and neighbors attending to the boys' needs as well as their mother's. After four bedridden months of deepening fatigue, increasing difficulty breathing, and coughing spells that probably brought up blood, Catherine died on September 16, 1874, aged forty-five. Once she was gone, Antrim effectively abandoned Billy and his brother to local families (whom Catherine in her last weeks had already asked to take care of her boys after her death) as he pursued his pipedreams of striking it rich. Perhaps resentment at his stepfather's absence during this time was one reason Billy gave up "Antrim" in favor of "Bonney" a couple of years after he cleared out of Silver City. Another, some have suggested, is that "Bonney" might have been the name of his actual father or an ancestor. One of the more plausible explanations came from Sheriff Harvey Whitehill, the first lawman ever to jail Billy (in Silver City, for a minor offense), who said the boy "changed his name in order to keep the stigma of disgrace from his family" (J. Weddle 47). But perhaps out of deference to the memory of his mother, Billy never fully gave up "Henry," always signing his name as "William H. Bonney." Like so much else in his brief life, the complete lack of evidence as regards the reason for the change and the significance of the name serve only to incite rather than restrain speculation.[7] The same for his birth year: it's correct to within a couple of years up or down, but the November 23 day and month are suspiciously identical to Upson's own.[8]

Neither Garrett nor Upson participated in the Lincoln County War. Garrett didn't arrive in the New Mexico Territory until February 1878, when hostilities were just about to flare into the first act of violence that touched off the fighting. But he settled in Fort Sumner, a good four-to-five-days' ride from Lincoln. Upson, however, lived only two days from Lincoln in Roswell, which put him much closer to the action and in frequent contact with the participants. We may safely assume the middle chapters dealing with the war are exclusively his. Though he still can't resist rhetorical asides and flourishes, the style settles down somewhat, becoming less fancy and figurative, while action and incident remain exciting without becoming too outlandish (a notable exception the scene where Billy rescues his friend Charlie Bowdre from a rival gang, the encounter ending in a standoff, the leaders, facing each other like knights of yore across a field of honor, agreeing to withdraw without shedding blood). Maybe one reason was that the events had taken place just four years earlier and were more or less well known, still fresh in memory, and melodramatic enough to require little embellishment or invention: a feud between a pair of rival factions for monopolistic control of government beef contracts, dry goods, and other commerce, not to mention some banking services, such as mortgages. There are chases, shootings, killings, ambushes, and murder for hire, all culminating in the "Big Killing," the five-day battle of the town of Lincoln, at the time the county seat, with the intervention of the U.S. cavalry and the firefight escape of Billy and his allies from a burning house. Here were surely enough action, intrigue, and bloodshed to satisfy the most ravenous fans of Western pulp.

Upson maintained an essentially neutral position with respect to the two warring factions: Lawrence G. Murphy and his partner, James J. Dolan, versus John Tunstall and Alexander McSween. Murphy and Dolan had long held a stranglehold on much of the economic activity in Lincoln County, where they regularly employed a gang of murderous thieves and thugs, called "The Boys" and led by Jesse Evans, for the purposes of rustling cattle and "handling" anyone who got in their way. (Historians disagree whether Billy rode with them for a short time before he threw in with Tunstall.) In Lincoln, Murphy and Dolan built a huge two-story structure, the first floor containing the store, the offices, a saloon, and a gambling hall, the second living quarters. It was alternately called the "Big Store" or "The House," the latter a moniker that was also used to refer to their collective enterprises, legal and criminal. (Three years after the war ended, the store, by then the courthouse, was the jail Billy escaped from.) They had no worries about the law because the sheriff William Brady, heavily indebted to them, was in their pocket, and they had the support of Thomas B. Catron, the U.S. Attorney for the New Mexico Territory and a land speculator who operated out of Santa Fe, had powerful political connections, and was on his way to becoming one of the largest landowners in the United States. Catron and his associates, who included the territorial governor Samuel Axtell as well as Murphy and Dolan, formed the nucleus of the infamous Santa Fe Ring, and they were ruthless in their pursuit of wealth and power. It was Catron who came to the rescue of The House when the ruinous business practices of Murphy, Dolan, and a new partner John H. Riley brought them to the brink of bankruptcy.[9]

Among several questionable schemes and illegal activities, Murphy and Dolan had government contracts to supply beef (and produce) to nearby Fort Stanton and the Mescalero Indian Reservation, most of it with cattle rustled from John Chisum, who for obvious reasons could not compete with pricing based on stolen stock. The Murphy-Dolan herd was often called the "the mystery herd" (Caldwell 78), because no matter how many cattle were sold, the size of the herd remained the same; and they were utterly brazen in their theft of Chisum's cattle, doing so perfunctory a job altering the distinctive Chisum "Jinglebob ear" (the ear cut so that part of it dangled like a flap) and "Long Rail" brand (a straight line from flank to shoulder) as to leave the change insultingly transparent. The rustlers included local thieves (often hired by Murphy and Dolan expressly for that purpose) and even a number of smaller ranchers, cattlemen, and farmers. These "small fellows," as Chisum condescendingly referred to them, struck a kind of common cause with Murphy and Dolan because it was often said (according to Nolan quite truthfully [*West* 71]), that it was impossible to make a living in the Pecos valley without stealing from Chisum, whose herds numbered some eighty thousand cattle and who by 1876 had staked claim to the best available grassland, controlling "nearly 150 miles up and down the Pecos River and fifty miles on either side, extending from the *Eighteen Mile Bend* near Fort Sumner to the mouth of Salt Creek" (Caldwell 63, 75). Although most of it was public land, the size of Chisum's herds and the means at his disposal to enforce his will tended to make it in effect *his* land.

This led to a series of increasingly intense disputes and violent confrontations in 1876–77 that culminated in what is sometimes called the Pecos War or John Chisum's Pecos War in the spring of '77. Upson has been criticized for identifying these as the cause of the Lincoln County War. He was not accurate about this, but he wasn't entirely wrong either. It was partly the combination of the rustling and his inability to compete that led Chisum to partner with Tunstall and McSween, who saw great economic opportunities awaiting them if they entered into competition against The House. Murphy and Dolan did support the smaller ranchers and farmers against Chisum, but it wasn't, contrary to what Upson implied, out of any sense of justice, fair play, or generosity; it was because they wanted the rustling to continue, stolen cattle being the basis of what profits they enjoyed. And if the smaller fellows lent their support to Murphy and Dolan, it wasn't because they particularly liked them, it was because they had to make a living and also because The House owned many of their mortgages and thus could force cooperation through threats of foreclosure, eviction, and violence. Many if not most people in Lincoln County hated Murphy, Dolan, and their associates because the Big Store was said to have engaged in price-gouging for everything it sold, including basic necessities.[10]

John Henry Tunstall was a young Englishman who had come west for the classic reason of seeking his fortune. Not long after settling in the territory, he wrote to his father:

> *Everything* in New Mexico, that *pays at all* (you might say) is worked by a "ring" . . . . My ring is forming itself as fast & faster than I had ever hoped & in such a way that I will get the finest plum of the lot . . . . I proposed to confine my operations to Lincoln County, but I intend to handle it in such a way, as to get half of every dollar that is made in the county *by anyone*. (Nolan, *Tunstall* 213)

He partnered with McSween, a lawyer who was also new to the territory; together they joined with Chisum to start a bank, though Chisum himself was not directly involved in their business activities or the war (his chief concern still putting a stop to the rustling). Tunstall and McSween are generally regarded as having been considerably less ruthless than The House, but they were hardly unmotivated by greed and both had essentially the same goals as their competitors: to acquire power by forming a ring of their own and making pots of money through monopolies.[11] McSween was supposedly against violence as a matter of religious principle, but Tunstall was ready to resort to it, apparently reluctantly, when necessary and surrounded himself with cowhands (including Billy the Kid) who were also proficient gunmen. Tunstall, who had already invested heavily in cattle (on land acquired with the assistance of McSween), soon opened his own store. Now Murphy and Dolan faced direct competition just down the street from the Big Store.

Another thing that helped bring matters to the flashpoint was a dispute involving an insurance policy of a partner of Murphy's named Emil Fritz, who had died a few years earlier. McSween, who, ironically, was through much of this period retained by The House as its legal counsel, was hired to collect the funds. But when he discovered that Murphy and Dolan, desperate for cash, were trying to claim the proceeds of the policy as payment for debts McSween considered highly dubious, he refused to release the funds, nor by then did he trust them to reimburse him for his considerable expenses, including a trip to St. Louis and New York City which he paid for himself. In a further ironic twist, Dolan, alleging that McSween was planning on taking most of the insurance money for his expenses, managed to persuade one of Fritz's heirs to file a suit against the lawyer. There followed a series of complicated legal maneuvers and counter-maneuvers that eventually led to Murphy and Dolan using their political connections to secure a writ of attachment against McSween and, by extension, Tunstall, on the utterly fraudulent pretext that as they were partners, their individual properties were joint, including even Tunstall's personal possessions.

Despite the writ of attachment, Tunstall and McSween were not wholly without support in the legal establishment and might have prevailed had

Tunstall not been murdered and several months later McSween slain in the battle of Lincoln. Tunstall was killed, on February 18, 1878, by a posse deputized to collect the Englishman's cattle per the attachment writ. Billy and several other Tunstall men blamed Brady, but though Brady lent his authority to the posse by deputizing it, he didn't pick most of its members, lead it, or ride with it. Nor has it ever been proved that Tunstall was killed as the result of a specific order; but if one were given, it seems more likely to have come from Dolan, who joined the posse sometime after it had left Lincoln. Once he did, he personally selected and dispatched a group to collect several horses Tunstall and four of his men, including the Kid, were taking to Lincoln. This posse, numbering fourteen (according to most accounts), was led by Buck Morton, a Dolan foreman, and was joined by Jesse Evans and two of The Boys. No one knows for sure if Dolan actually did tell Morton to kill Tunstall, but he certainly knew his foreman's blood was up—"Hurry up, boys, my knife is sharp and I feel like scalping someone!" Morton shouted as he galloped away (Nolan, *West* 104); he knew that Evans, who went along to reclaim a horse he said Billy stole from him, needed no justification whatsoever for killing anyone; and he also knew that passions and conditions were ripe for deadly violence. The killing was surely, as the legal word has it, foreseeable. And violence by proxies like Evans or Morton was standard operating procedure for Murphy and Dolan as long as they had been in business, while The House certainly stood to benefit substantially from Tunstall's death.

Once he was buried, Tunstall's supporters formed a gang of their own—ranchers, farmers, cowhands, rustlers, outlaws—which they called the "Regulators," who even managed, like The Boys, to get themselves deputized for a while. They consisted, among others, of Richard Brewer, Charlie Bowdre, Tom Folliard,[12] Fred Waite, Doc Scurlock, John Middleton, José Chavez y Chavez, Hendry Brown, and the cousins George and Frank Coe. Their most famous member was, of course, William Bonney, which is what he was calling himself by then. In Tunstall's employ for some ten weeks or so, he had developed great respect and affection for his boss (though historians remain divided whether this affection was returned or even particularly noticed, as there is no mention of the Kid in any of Tunstall's extensive correspondence with his family in England). He was also present when Tunstall was killed, though neither he nor the rest of Tunstall's guard actually witnessed the killing and were too far away and too greatly outnumbered to save him. Yet the Kid would neither forget nor forgive. According to George Coe, Billy took the killing "very much to heart," "became discouraged and morose," and told him, "George, I never expect to let up until I kill the last man who helped to kill Tunstall, or die myself in the act" (Otero 103, Coe 63). Each side now had its own motley army of recruits, several of them proficient gunfighters and all with reasons aplenty to start shooting.[13] War was inevitable.

The first acts of vengeance were not long in coming. In early March a posse of Regulators apprehended Buck Morton and Frank Baker, the former a leader

Studio portrait of Pat Garrett, taken in Las Vegas, New
Mexico, 1882, a year after he killed Billy the Kid

of the bunch that murdered Tunstall, and killed them both when they tried
to flee. Less than a month later six Regulators shot down Sheriff Brady and a
deputy in broad daylight in the streets of Lincoln. On both occasions Billy was
an enthusiastic participant. Of the killings of Morton and Baker he confided
to Coe, "Of course, you know, George, I never meant to let them birds reach
Lincoln alive" (132).

The Lincoln County War solidified the Kid's reputation as a brave, daring, and
resourceful gunfighter because he had remained supremely calm and composed
while pinned down by gunfire in the burning McSween house that climaxed
the five-day battle of Lincoln, managing a bold escape for himself and some

others out the back as bullets were flying everywhere (if McSween hadn't panicked, the Kid's plan might have saved him too). But the war wasn't even a
sideshow for Pat Garrett, who doesn't enter the book until it's over. Once he
does and identifies himself, there is an abrupt shift in the point of view and
prose style of *The Authentic Life*, Garrett taking over as narrator in the first
person and Upson ratcheting down the rhetoric considerably. Plain, simple,
and direct, the voice now suggests Upson was almost taking dictation (though
that "almost" is crucial—these last chapters still contain much that suggests
Upson's style, in particular his rhetoric). This is the section on which is based
most of the fiction and films with any pretensions to historical authenticity,
it is also the one to which many historians grant the most credence, and it
contains the two episodes that more than any others are responsible for trans-
forming Henry Antrim–William Bonney into the legendary "Billy the Kid," a
name he did not acquire until a newspaperman conferred it upon him just
seven months before his death.[14] These episodes are his escape from the Lincoln County Courthouse and his death at the hands of Garrett. Although the
day of the escape Garrett was away collecting taxes or acquiring lumber for the
gallows, the account in *The Authentic Life* is generally regarded as in the main
reliable and is consistent with eyewitness accounts and immediate reports in
the newspapers, though there is much variation as regards details and specific
incidents (treated at length in the next chapter). Garrett was, however, a key
participant and one of only three persons in the room when the Kid was shot
two and a half months later on the night of July 14, 1881. The only other participant to have provided a written account is John W. Poe, Garrett's deputy;
but unlike Garrett, Poe was not in the room and he didn't write down his recollections until thirty-seven years later in *The Death of Billy the Kid*.[15]

The night was hot and moonlit. Around midnight, while his two deputies
Poe and Tom "Kip" McKinney waited nearby, Garrett slipped into Pete Maxwell's bedroom through a door that opened into it from the porch, walked
to the head of the bed, and seated himself beside Maxwell, facing the door.
The room was very dark, the only light from the doorway and windows. He
asked Maxwell if the Kid was in town, and Maxwell told him the Kid "was certainly about, but he did not know whether he had left or not." Meanwhile, the
Kid, bootless, carrying a butcher knife and his revolver, was heading toward
Maxwell's house to get some meat from a fresh-killed steer hanging in the
meat room. He noticed a stranger on Maxwell's porch and another squatting
close by. Neither Poe nor McKinney had ever met him before and didn't know
what he looked like. Poe approached him, saying they intended no harm; the
Kid raised his gun and backed into Maxwell's bedroom, asking, "Quien es?"
"Quien es?" then turned toward the bed.

Up until these words Garrett did not know that the backlit figure entering
the room was Billy. "The intruder came close to me," Garrett recalled, "leaned
both hands on the bed, his right hand almost touching my knee, and asked, in
a low tone:—'Who are they Pete?'" Maxwell whispered to Garrett, "That's the

Kid." By then Garrett had already recognized the voice. In the same moment, the Kid realized someone else was in the room and sprung backward, but it was too late. In one swift motion Garrett drew his revolver, cocking it as he did so, fired, then threw himself toward the floor and fired once more. The second shot was wild and in any case unnecessary, as the first had hit the Kid square in the chest just above his heart. Maxwell bolted from the bed and out the door into the barrel of Poe's revolver shoved into his stomach. Garrett pushed the deputy's gun away, saying not to shoot Maxwell, and announced he had shot the Kid. Poe at first didn't believe it, but Garrett assured him that he recognized the voice. Nobody went back in right away. Garrett knew his first bullet struck the Kid and both he and Poe had heard the Kid's body drop to the floor and some sort of sound from him—whether a gasp of breath, a murmur, a soft groan, or a gurgling is not clear. But Garrett could not be sure the wound was fatal or even if it had incapacitated the Kid. Soon enough, however, they ventured back inside and saw a body on the floor with a knife on one side and a revolver on the other: the noted desperado, whose deeds of daring and blood made his name a terror in the Southwest, was dead.

Although there are discrepancies between Garrett and Poe as to how they determined the Kid was in Fort Sumner, their accounts of Billy's approach and the shooting itself differ only in trifling details, such as the order in which Garrett and Maxwell left the room. *The Authentic Life* has Garrett reaching the door first, where he addresses his deputies in the doorway, while Maxwell bolts out past them and Poe draws on him. According to Poe, immediately after Garrett fired the second bullet he was out the door, where he positioned himself close to the wall, followed an instant later by a terrified Maxwell. Poe rings truer here: inasmuch as Garrett exercised caution reentering the room, he surely would not have lingered in the doorway on his way out. (He was no doubt remembering the shooting of Folliard some months earlier. Although Folliard was fatally wounded, Garrett warned his deputies to be careful help-ing him off his horse, as he still might have strength and will enough to try to kill them; as if in confirmation of the warning, they discovered that Fol-liard's revolver was fully cocked.) Another difference is that in *The Authentic Life*, even before he goes back into the room, Garrett is never in any doubt that the man he shot is the Kid, whereas in Poe he has a moment of uncer-tainty, though the deputy is careful to make clear it is a moment only and in response to his telling Garrett he thinks the wrong man was shot. And in Poe both sheriff and deputy linger some moments on the porch before going back in, prevailing upon Maxwell to get a candle, which was placed on the exterior windowsill to throw some light into the dark room.

By far the most contentious aspect of that night concerns whether the Kid was armed with his six-gun (hardly anybody disputes the knife). Though the preponderance of reliable testimony indicates the Kid had his gun with him, there is no available hard evidence to prove the point one way or the other. But this hasn't prevented many writers—and countless Billy the Kid buffs who've bought wholly into the idea of a victimized Billy gunned down in cold blood by a traitorous bought-and-paid-for Garrett—from calling it a "fact" that he was unarmed and labeling both Garrett and Poe liars for reporting otherwise in their books. Their "proof" consists entirely in hearsay from Fort Sumner residents who were absolutely, indeed almost unconditionally sympathetic to the Kid and wholly antipathetic to Garrett. (At least two of those who claimed there was no gun beside the Kid's body were caught in contradictions in later statements.) The most persuasive explanation for why some of the bystanders might not have *seen* the gun is provided by the historian Mark Lee Gardner: "Remember, after he was confident the Kid was dead, Garrett entered the room and at some point examined the Kid's pistol to see if it had been fired. He would not then have placed the pistol back on the floor, which might explain why those who entered the room afterward saw only a butcher knife" (*To Hell* 287). There has also been speculation as to why Billy—uncharacteristically—didn't shoot the moment he became aware of a third person in the room. Garrett himself believed the Kid was "so surprised and startled that for a second he could not collect himself" (Fulton, *History* 401). Another explanation is that Billy couldn't be sure the person wasn't a relative or friend of Pete's or that he wouldn't hit Maxwell himself if he shot quickly. However atypical as regards his behavior, not to mention tragic its consequences for him personally, Billy's hesitation on this occasion actually speaks very well of him.

Discrepancies like those involving the gun in supposedly eyewitness accounts, to say nothing of the lack of solid evidence, or speculations as to why the Kid or Garrett did this instead of that begin to suggest the full extent of the difficulties involved in trying to find out what actually happened that night and why even the most responsible, respected, and conscientious historians and biographers get us only so far. Each one—using the written accounts by Garrett and Poe plus a combination of accounts by other parties (i.e., mostly hearsay, far from disinterested, and recollected many years, typically decades later), deduction, induction, educated guesswork, supposition, speculation, and hunch—pieces together his or her own version of the events, versions often congruent in broad outline yet frustratingly divergent when it comes to details and specifics. Read enough of them and eventually you find yourself right back where you started: Garrett's book, supplemented by Poe's. As Utley has written, "Garrett may have had reasons for tampering with the truth, but until credible evidence can be presented to show that he did, and to show how he did, his testimony may be given more credence than anyone else's" (*Violent Life* 267n).

There are at least three solid reasons for agreeing with this. First, while no one's memory is absolutely reliable, Garrett's is by far the account set down closest in proximity to the events themselves, recalled and written between two years to, in the case of the killing of the Kid, just several months after they took place. Prior to relating his book to Upson, Garrett had in fact given two accounts of the shooting of the Kid: the first a report to the governor the next day, the second an interview with a newspaper three days later. In the former Garrett wrote that the moment the Kid put his hand on the bed, "I felt sure he recognized me." This was because although it

> was my desire to have been able to take him alive, his coming upon me so suddenly and unexpectedly led me to believe that he had seen me enter the room or had been informed by someone of the fact, and that he came there, armed with pistol and knife, expressly to kill me if he could. Under that impression I had no alternative but to kill him or suffer death at his hand. (Fulton, *History* 400–402)

In the newspaper interview he said that the Kid "must have then recognized me, for he went backward with a catlike movement, and I jerked my gun and fired." This is ambiguous. By "he must have recognized me," did Garrett mean that Billy recognized him *as Garrett* or merely that the Kid sensed there was someone else in the room besides Maxwell and himself? Garrett believed he could tell from the Kid's body language that he was aware of another person in the room (perhaps because he heard Maxwell whispering?) and that he could not have mistaken the clicking of the hammer as Garrett cocked it back. But recalling the events again less than a year later, Garrett stated unequivocally that it "will never be known whether the Kid recognized me or not," which is as good an example as any of reason two: Garrett's obvious desire to set down the truth of what happened as best he could know and remember it, including registering doubts and uncertainties when he entertained them.

An even better example may be the nagging matter of the third shot. Garrett and Maxwell, in the room, and Poe and McKinney, just outside, were all absolutely sure they heard three shots. Since Garrett himself fired two, Poe, McKinney, and Maxwell none, the third shot could have come only from Billy's gun. Yet a thorough search of the room turned up no evidence of a third bullet hole, and when Garrett examined the gun, he found "five cartridges and one shell in the chambers, the hammer resting on the shell, but this proves nothing, as many carry their revolvers in this way for safety; besides, this shell looked as if it had been shot some time before." How easy it would have been for him to have declared and published as fact that the third bullet was fired from this shell: no one would have known, likely disputed it, or even examined the gun after Garrett did, and it would have "proved" conclusively that Billy was armed, thus sparing Garrett a lot of criticism (which he had been enduring the several months between that night and the writing of the book). Nevertheless, he told the truth as he found it: all four heard a third shot but the physical evidence that might verify it was not to be found.[16]

The third and perhaps most persuasive reason is that a less honest man or one more concerned with his image would surely have tweaked the facts so as to present himself in a more obviously heroic light. This is just precisely what Garrett did *not* do, yet it hasn't prevented many writers and the same Billy-the-Kid aficionados from vilifying him all the same.[17] Think about it. He didn't depict his final hunting down and killing the Kid as the result of especially dogged tracking or brilliant detective work. Skeptical the Kid was even in Fort Sumner, he went there reluctantly and never pretended the whole encounter that resulted in the Kid's death was anything other than an instance of the most extraordinary luck in which he happened to be dealt the winning hand. He freely admitted that if he had known the Kid was around, he would not have given him even the slim chance that fortune had, the obvious implication being that he would have deliberately, instead of accidentally, ambushed him. That is exactly how he did kill the Kid's two closest partners, Folliard and Bowdre, and he nowhere attempted to varnish over it in his book: he lured Folliard into a trap, warned him to halt, and fatally shot him when he didn't respond to the warning fast enough; and once his posse had sneaked up on and surrounded the gang at Stinking Springs and the hapless Bowdre came out the door to feed the horses, Garrett, thinking Bowdre was the Kid, gave the order to shoot and the outlaw was cut to pieces.[18]

Perhaps even more revealing is the way Garrett relates what happened in Las Vegas, New Mexico, when he, his posse, and their prisoners—the Kid, Dave Rudabaugh, Billy Wilson, and Tom Pickett—were on a train awaiting departure as a large mob, led by the county sheriff, demanded Rudabaugh be handed over because he had killed a jailer there eight months earlier. Garrett had given the prisoners his word they would be escorted safely to Santa Fe for trial. Though the mob, well armed, vocal, and angry, far outnumbered his six-man posse, Garrett remained calm but resolute, threatening to arm the prisoners if it meant saving them from the mob. This did not prove necessary, and after some forty-five tense minutes the train pulled out with posse and all prisoners unharmed and aboard. There was no violence. Gardner, who opens his book with nine gripping pages relating this extraordinary episode, calls it Garrett's "great triumph" as a lawman (3–12). Yet in *The Authentic Life* Garrett himself dispatched it in just two pages, and rather flat, understated pages at that (129–31). The decision to tell it this way must have been his, as one has only to look earlier in the book to see what Upson would have made of it left to his own devices.

If, then, in view of all this, Garrett's intent really had been to make himself the hero, he certainly went about it in an awfully peculiar way; indeed, considering the censure that rained down on him at the time and throughout the decades since, he made a positive botch of it. He has also been called to task for making the Kid the villain of the piece, exaggerating his skills with a six-gun, and inflating his ruthlessness as a killer, assertions that do not survive critical scrutiny of *Garrett's* part of the narrative. To be sure, in the first eight chapters, Upson spins a rousing tale of violence and bloodshed on the part of the Kid, while the section on the Lincoln County War depicts him as a skilled, intrepid gunfighter, with nerves of steel, as well as a vengeful firebrand, albeit one with both explanation and justification for his deeds. But starting with chapter 16 when Garrett takes over, he really doesn't have all that much to say about Billy's personality as such.[19] There are passing mentions of the Kid's "extraordinary forethought and judgment, for one his age," his bravery, his cautiousness when necessary, and his sense of humor and essentially carefree attitude. Garrett also appreciates that the Kid never blamed him for capturing him, rather "evinced respect and confidence in me, acknowledging that I had only done my duty, without malice, by bringing him in" (142). In the appendix he takes aim at those who, after the Kid was dead, called him a coward (itself "a cowardly lie") and is amused "to notice how brave some of the Kid's 'ancient enemies,' and, even, some of his friends, have become since there is no danger of their courage being put to test by an interview with him" (155). At the same time, Garrett refuses to romanticize him or gloss over what he perceives as the Kid's shortcomings and failings. One thing in particular Garrett seems to have disapproved of in Billy's character was the way he tried to make "a plausible excuse for each and every crime charged against him" (133); by contrast, Garrett himself always took his fair share of responsibility for the deaths of his two deputies in the Lincoln jailbreak, writing, "I do not hold myself guiltless" and "now realize how inadequate my precautions were" (139).

Garrett could be accused of exaggeration when it came to Billy's propensity for violence, as when he calls him "daring and unscrupulous," someone who "would sacrifice the lives of a hundred men who stood between him and liberty, when the gallows stared him in the face, with as little compunction as he would kill a coyote" (139). But since the rhetoric here, not to mention the imagery, is almost certainly Upson's, it's impossible to say how close the sentiments are to Garrett's own. More to the point is the context. The specific context is that this comes at the place in the narrative when Garrett has just returned to Lincoln and found his two deputies dead and Billy escaped. The larger context consists in when and why the book was written in the first place: Garrett's intention of correcting what he felt were gross exaggerations, distortions, and falsehoods in the eight books about the Kid that immediately preceded his. Compared to the absurdly wanton, cold-blooded killer the Kid is in them, the portrait that emerges in what are unquestionably Garrett's chapters is convincing precisely because he has toned it down and scaled it back so that Billy seems a recognizable human being, not the bloodthirsty psychopath of the nickel biographies. "Taken as a whole," Maurice Fulton, the first reliable historian of the pair, judged Garrett's "a fair and sympathetic portrayal of the Kid" (*Life* xv). As for Billy's prowess with a six-shooter, several who knew him told of how much he practiced—in the words of one, "continually with pistol or rifle, often riding at a run and dodging behind the side of his mount to fire, as the Apaches did. He was very proud of his ability to pick up a handkerchief or other object from the ground while riding at a run" (Klasner 174). And if Frank Coe is to be believed, the Kid could "ride his horse on a run and kill snow birds, four out of five shots."[20]

Garrett manifestly did not go to Maxwell's to lie in wait for the Kid—if he had, he would've drawn his revolver the moment he began his advance toward the house. Despite vague reports that the Kid was in the area, Garrett still found it hard to believe Billy had not cleared out while he had the chance, perhaps to Mexico. Garrett went to Maxwell's because Maxwell was a friend he felt he could trust. The Kid obviously did not know Garrett was in town because the sheriff, cautious despite his skepticism, had stolen in after dark to avoid encountering anyone who knew him. If the Kid had had any inkling that Garrett and two deputies were around, he would surely have shot Poe and McKinney the moment one of them moved toward him. Lawman and outlaw were thus equally taken by surprise to find themselves brought together in that small room. Though the whole incident was a result of pure blind chance, can it be any wonder that virtually every writer from the crassest pulp hacks to the most serious historians have been unable to resist invoking Fate, complete with a capital F?

According to procedure, the morning after killing the Kid, before leaving Fort Sumner, Garrett convened an inquest that cleared him of any wrongdoing (and also established a solid basis for collecting the reward, the not inconsiderable sum of five hundred dollars). But accusations that the way he killed the Kid was somehow unfair, an ambush, even cowardly, dogged him to the end of his days. It was as if he should have given the Kid a sporting chance to gun him down. In an appendix to *The Authentic Life* Garrett not only answered these accusations forthrightly, without apology or defensiveness; he flung the accusers' words right back at them:

> Suppose a man of the Kid's . . . disposition had warned you that when you two met you had better "come a shooting"; suppose he bounced in on you unexpectedly with a revolver in his hand, whilst yours was still in its scabbard? Scared? Wouldn't you have been scared? I didn't dare to answer his hail:—"*Quien es?*" as the first sound of my voice (which he knew perfectly well), would have been his signal to make a target of my physical personality, with his self cocker, from which he was wont to pump a continuous stream of fire and lead, and in any direction, unerringly, which answered to his will. Scared, Cap? Well I should say so. I started out on that expedition with the expectation of getting scared. I went out counting the probability of being shot at, and the possibility of being hurt, perhaps killed; but not if any precaution on my part would prevent such a catastrophe. The Kid got a very much better show than I had intended to give him. (151–52)

If *The Authentic Life* established Pat Garrett as the sober, serious sheriff, brave but not foolhardy, a responsible professional who pursues his duty without favor, then it also set the terms for a kind of bipolar view of Billy. He was a likable, promising, outgoing, energetic boy who, never having known his natural father and orphaned at fourteen, became an outlaw as a result of defending the weak and helpless against the powerful and corrupt. Alternatively, he was a criminal, pure and simple. Yes, he grew up in a wild, violent, untamed land where the law of the gun ruled, but he had it no worse than many others—indeed, some might argue he had it better. A caring and loving mother raised him through his formative years and saw to it that after her death there were good families who looked after him and tried to keep him on the straight and narrow. If he turned outlaw, it can only have been because he chose to. These two seemingly opposing Billys conjoined in one crucial way: they were both natural-born killers. Neither socio- nor psychopaths, to be sure, but if they thought there was a good reason for killing someone, they did so, evincing absolutely no hesitation before pulling the trigger and no remorse after the bullet left its victim dead on the ground. (Of the Kid's death, George Coe wrote, "For the first and only time in his career [the Kid] spoke first and shot last" [222].) That the killings were reactive to bullying, out of vengeance, in self-defense, for self-protection, or escaping adversaries or the law may be true (often the reasons overlapped), but it doesn't alter the fact that a ready ability to kill seemed to be wired into the genes.

The Authentic Life had it both ways, combining the two Billys into one:

"The Kid's" career of crime was not the outgrowth of an evil disposition, nor was it caused by unchecked youthful indiscretions; it was the result of untoward, unfortunate circumstances acting upon a bold, reckless, ungoverned, and ungovernable spirit, which no physical restraint could check, no danger appall, no power less potent than death could conquer. (5)

These words, obviously Upson's, provide a clue as to why Billy exerts such endless fascination. It's not in spite of but precisely *because of* the contradictions, paradoxes, and antitheses in his character and personality. A killer who is likable is that much more interesting, disturbing, and frightening a killer when he finally kills. A killer who once might not have become a killer, whose descent into a life of crime and violence we are made to sympathize with as we experience step-by-step each wrong decision or stroke of ill fortune, intensifies our emotional involvement and raises the stakes of his killings and his eventual demise in a way not otherwise available. Upson even located the precise episode in the Kid's downward spiral that represents the point of no return: the ambush killing of Sheriff Brady and one of his deputies. Billy was only one of a gang of six who participated in the shooting, but he was the most openly vocal in threatening revenge for Tunstall, which may be one reason only he was ever prosecuted for the crime. Owing to Brady's ties to The House, he was almost certainly less well liked among the populace than Upson claims; the morning of the ambush he had a warrant in his pocket for McSween's arrest, so it's a reasonable guess he was going to take him into custody (or murder him if you buy into Nolan's suspicion that this was tantamount to murdering him: Brady would not do the job himself, but once McSween was in jail, James Dolan would send Jesse Evans to "do his part" [West 121]). Still, it was the sheer cold-blooded, premeditated *way* Brady was gunned down that just plain

Taken in 1879–80, this tintype is the only photograph of William Bonney, the images on this page reproduced actual size. The image on the left, courtesy of Richard Weddle, is of the only remaining plate of the four originals not lost or destroyed. Sold at auction in 2011 for $2.3 million, it is reproduced enlarged on the opposite page. According to Weddle, the irregular shape owes to the haphazard way the photographer cut it, and the two black marks at the lower corners are the photographer's thumbprints left while the emulsion was still wet; for much of its history this tintype was tacked on the wall behind a saloon bar, and for several decades afterward it was kept in a shoebox with other items. The image on the right is a reproduction made by the collector Robert G. McCubbin, on which he superimposed a stiff paper frame of the kind typically sold with tintypes, and is taken from Emerson Hough's 1907 *The Story of the Outlaw*, which marked the first publication of a photograph of an original plate, thus allowing it to be seen without the hundred years of careless handling and neglect that degraded the surviving plate.

This enlargement has been flipped to correct for the
mirror-image reversal of the camera original.

ran against the grain of many people, including quite a number who before then had thought well of Billy. In a detail probably apocryphal, *The Authentic Life* even has the shooters going to the trouble of cutting grooves into the adobe wall they hid behind, the better to steady the barrels of their rifles. "The murder was a most dastardly crime on the part of the Kid," wrote Upson, "and lost him many friends who had theretofore, excused and screened him" (62). From this point on Billy would still have his defenders, especially in the Mexican communities; but his image was irrevocably tarnished, and for many he was both damned and doomed, a killer who must be hunted down and brought to justice, which meant almost certain death by hanging.

If we can see beyond the penny-dreadful goings-on and Upson's over-blown style, it's clear how the dual Billy of *The Authentic Life* influenced just about every subsequent treatment of the Kid in both popular and serious writing. The writers might wholly adopt one Billy or the other or, far more frequently, draw upon both to come up with their own individual composites, but whatever the approach, almost all of them are some variation or other on the pattern set in the Garrett-Upson book. This is as it should be, since there is ample evidence in the Kid's life to support many variations along the spectrum of good to bad, hero to villain, victim of circumstance to preda-tory outlaw. Indeed, it's one of the more amusing ironies that in the name of historical truth, the most revisionist depictions of Billy the Kid in the second half of the last century—*Dirty Little Billy* from 1972 comes immedi-ately to mind, as do *Young Guns* from 1988 and *Young Guns II* from 1990—as an unkempt, unredemptive, literally unwashed punk turn out to be as false as the latter-day Robin Hood celebrated in the first half. The truth is, when he wasn't "working"—that is, rustling cattle or stealing horses—he seems to have been something of a dandy in his dress (favoring a broad-brimmed Mexican sombrero to a Stetson), personally clean and clean-cut, taking much pride in his appearance. (George Coe is reported to have said that if there was a clean shirt in town it was usually on Billy's back.) In fact, he was literate (and a rather avid reader), his penmanship was fine, and everyone, friend and foe alike, remarked upon his intelligence, which was considered to be high.

The famous ferrotype that is the only known photographic likeness of Billy was judged by those who knew him to have done his looks little justice or caught him in a typical outfit; it much displeased Paulita Maxwell, who said, "It makes him look rough and uncouth," adding that "in Fort Sumner he was always careful of his personal appearance and dressed neatly and in good taste" (Burns 195). Because ferrotypes, also called tintypes, were camera originals, they were a mirror image of reality. Throughout their history the tintype of the Kid—there were four plates in all, captured simultaneously from a single exposure—was until recently rarely corrected, that is, flipped, when photo-graphic reproductions were printed in newspapers, magazines, and books, hence the mistaken belief that he was left-handed.[21] (He seems to have been ambidextrous.) Fair-haired and blue-eyed, he was regarded as handsome by most, especially the ladies, despite front teeth that stuck out slightly. At around five feet seven to five feet nine inches in height (reports vary), he wasn't even what most people would probably call short (especially in those days)—I've sometimes wondered if the notion he was short persists because Garrett was so very tall, even by our standards, let alone back then—though he was skinny and apparently rather frail. In any case, neither his skeletal nor his muscular makeup left him well suited to hard labor. He was frequently picked on by bullies, one reason he learned to be so skillful with a gun, he told Frank Coe (Otero 110)—for Billy, "equalizer," the common nickname for guns in the Old West, had a personal significance that was literally physical. The first man he is known for certain to have killed was an actual bully, a blowhard named "Windy" Cahill, a blacksmith who liked to knock him around, throw him to the floor, and humiliate him. Cahill did this once too often. One night in a saloon he called Billy a pimp, threw him down, climbed on top of him, pinning him to the floor, and slapped him about the face. Billy managed to work his gun loose, stuck the barrel into Cahill's stomach, and pulled the trigger. The blacksmith took until the next morning to die. Billy was seventeen, and he hightailed it out of there.

Yet most days he wore a pretty cheerful countenance. Even when he was captured by Garrett and on his way back to eventual trial, he told a reporter who remarked that he seemed to be taking things very easy, "What's the use of looking on the gloomy side of everything? The laugh's on me this time" (Wilcox 303). Will Chisum, John's brother, said of Billy, "Happy go-lucky all the time. Nothing bothered him" (Utley, *Violent Life* 202). He seems to have been especially well liked among Mexicans, who felt he respected them and their culture because he learned to speak Spanish, socialized with them (he was an exceptionally good dancer and a fixture at the weekly *bailes*), and often stayed in their villages. Many of them, it was said, saw his fighting against The House in the Lincoln County War and his subsequent rustling of the big herds as rebellion against their oppressors. This aspect of the Kid's history or legend, as the case may be, was perhaps most succinctly (if condescendingly) expressed by Frazier Hunt in *The Tragic Days of Billy the Kid*, another highly romanticized biography that also has a lot of history in it. "To himself and these gentle, uncomplaining natives he had become a champion, a bright, smiling symbol of revolt lighting up their own dreary and eternal struggles with life," Hunt writes of Billy's return to Fort Sumner after the escape from Lincoln. "And he was touched by their overpowering sense of God's will, their ageless acceptance of destiny. He was their happy warrior, for these were his people and here was his land" (302). How widespread such feelings truly were no one can say for certain, and there is no evidence that Billy and his partners in crime ever thought of themselves as champions of the oppressed, let alone any sort of latter-day Robin Hoods. Still, Yginio Salazar, who, like Billy, only narrowly escaped death when he fled McSween's burning house, said that everyone "who knew him loved him. He was kind and good to poor people, and he was always a gentleman, no matter where he was."[22]

Like many a teenager forced out on his own, Billy was in some ways older than his years. Nearly everyone spoke of his bravery, his sheer cold nerve under pressure, and his ability to shoot fast and accurately. Salazar again: "the bravest man I ever knew"; he "did not know fear"; "in great danger, he was the coolest man I ever knew"; lightning fast, when he drew "his pistol and fired, something dropped; he never missed his mark." Salazar was far from alone in these assessments—Garrett himself echoed them. Though he thought less of the Kid's marksmanship than others did, for Garrett what set the young outlaw apart was that he "shot well under all circumstances, whether in danger or not," and was "as cool under trying circumstances as any man I ever saw" (Fulton, *History* 401–2). Yet many of the same people who liked him were also aware of a disturbingly quick, volatile temper that could erupt into deadly violence. "The Kid was always quick with his gun, but sometimes he was quicker than he ought to have been," said John Meadows, who knew him well enough and always liked him, adding, "He done some things that nobody could endorse, and I certainly do not" (28). A contrary, rebellious, even anarchic streak was used by some to validate their belief that even if he had been led by circumstances into a life of crime, he was so obviously content to remain there that it amounted to a life choice. Not long before her death his mother warned him that if he didn't shape up he would be hanged before his twenty-first birthday; and a sheriff who knew him in Silver City observed, "There was one peculiar facial characteristic that to an experienced manhunter, would have marked him immediately as a bad man and that was his dancing eyes. They were never at rest but continually shifted and roved, much like his own rebellious nature" (J. Weddle 17, 30). As this impression had to have been formed around the time Billy's mother died, a more sympathetic observer might have interpreted the characteristic as a sign of anxiety, trepidation, or heightened awareness in the form of guardedness from a teenager recently orphaned.

Whatever the explanation, once Billy became embroiled in the Lincoln County War, that rebelliousness was in full evidence. Within months to a year of the "Big Killing" in Lincoln, most of the Regulators dispersed, weary of fighting, fearing arrest and jail, or just wanting to get on with their lives. The Coe cousins, Fred Waite, John Middleton, and Hendry Brown all left the state. Doc Scurlock and Charlie Bowdre relocated with their families to Fort Sumner, and soon after that the Scurlocks moved to Texas. Folliard remained at the Kid's side and Bowdre rejoined him in a life of crime. All the others tried to talk Billy into leaving with them or else just clearing out of the territory period. But he "refused to listen to reason," George Coe lamented. Billy's response to Coe was in essence his response to them all:

Well, boys, you may all do exactly as you please. As for me, I propose to stay right here in this country, steal myself a living, and plant every one of the mob who murdered Tunstall if they don't get the drop on me first. I'm off now, with any of my compadres who will follow me, after a bunch

of horses at the Charlie Fritz ranch. He has more horses than he can manage, and I need dinero. I'm broke, fellows, and I've got to make a killing.
(Coe 200)

Although the Coes returned to New Mexico a few years later, they never saw
the Kid again, nor did any of the others once they left the state. As for Billy,
following his escape from the Lincoln County jail, his resolve only hardened.
According to Meadows (front epigraph), in response to increasingly urgent
advice and warnings from several friends, including Meadows himself, to
clear out for a while, the Kid declared, "I am not going to leave the country
and I am not going to reform, neither am I going to be taken alive." And then
there were the killings. It has frequently been reported that he killed as many
men as his twenty-one years; the actual figure was likely not even half that
(and in some of those he was only one shooter among a few to several). But
this still leaves the ones he did kill or was party to, more than enough to
have made a lot of people wary, and some fearful, when Billy the Kid and his
friends were around.

As regards the many assessments of Billy's character and personality, there
is one sphere of influence from the Garrett-Upson book that demands further
study: the ways in which it seems to have insinuated itself into the memories of many of those who knew the Kid, such that when later in their lives
they recall their associations with him, it is in terms that sound suspiciously
reminiscent of Upson's early chapters. Yet neither they nor their interviewers
or ghostwriters, as the case may be, evince any awareness that the memories are laced with incidents, words, phrases, sentences, even whole passages
from *The Authentic Life*. For example, the account in Coe's *Frontier Fighter* of
Billy's early life—including "facts" of his birth, parentage, and the death of his
natural father in Coffeyville, Kansas, after the family moved there from New
York City—are identical to Upson's, including even the assertion that Billy's
stepfather was abusive. In support of this last Coe offers an anecdote: Billy,
in defense of "his mother from Antrim's cruelties," grabs a chair and knocks
the man so thoroughly "out of commission" that he feared he had killed him
(55–56). Even more revealing is Coe's "recollection" of the Kid's daredevil rescue of Bowdre from the Seven Rivers Gang, parts of which are taken almost
verbatim from Upson.[23]

Or notice how in *The Real Billy the Kid* Otero lifts the story of Billy's first
killing, the "idler" who insulted his mother, right out of *The Authentic Life*,
again almost verbatim, and presents it as if he himself had researched and
written it.[24] Then later in the book George Coe "recalls" the incident more or
less in his own words, assuring Otero that he learned of it from Billy himself; after which Frank Coe corroborates it in *his* interview. If the Coe cousins
were telling the truth and they really did hear about this killing directly from
Billy, then it raises some questions. Did Upson invent it, as is often assumed
(though it had some currency before *The Authentic Life*), or did he too get it

from the Kid himself, say, during one of the occasions when, according to Utley, he frequented Upson's store and post office in Roswell? If so, and if the story is still apocryphal, as all serious historians believe, then was Billy often given to such inventions about himself or were some of these old timers "remembering" things they thought they'd heard from Billy though in fact they'd read them in *The Authentic Life* but forgotten they'd read them there?[25]

Consider also how many of the same virtues, personality traits, and descriptions of the Kid's good character recur with remarkable similarity in several recollections about him; these same characteristics—loved by everyone, respectful to ladies, kind to children and old folks alike, adoring of his mother, and so on—are found in *The Authentic Life*, right at the beginning. Upson was also among the first to sound another complex of themes, variations on which turn up in many later histories, biographies, and other accounts: how early in life (aged eight, according to Upson) Billy, energetic and outgoing, "became adept at cards and noted among his comrades as successfully aping the genteel vices of his elders" (8). But soon he has fallen in with harder, rougher elders whose vices are not in the least genteel, whose baleful influences work their ill effects upon the boy, and two pages later he has killed his first man and begun the descent into a life of crime—all because, as Upson put it, "the good influences were withdrawn from his patch" (12).[26] Of course, this could all be coincidental; and if Upson really did know the Kid well, then perhaps he formed the same impressions as several others. Still, so much repetition, including the same or similar words, phrases, and incidents, among several recollections and other accounts, spread out over considerable distances in time, cannot help but invite suspicion.

The one part of the history of Garrett and Billy that is conspicuously absent from the Garrett narrative is their alleged close friendship before fate in the form of the call of duty for the sheriff and the call of the wild for the outlaw puts them on opposite sides of the law. Where did this notion originate? Despite some anecdotal evidence consisting mostly in testimonials and hearsay, the answer in the strictly popular sense is to be found in another book, written forty-three years after *The Authentic Life of Billy, the Kid*: Walter Noble Burns's *The Saga of Billy the Kid*, published in 1925.[27] Burns was a famous reporter (the ruthless editor in the Ben Hecht–Charles MacArthur play *The Front Page* was named after him) who spent a few months in New Mexico interviewing dozens of people who knew Billy or were in Lincoln, Roswell, and Fort Sumner in the old days. Yet despite all this firsthand research, the book he wrote presents essentially the same sorting-out issues as *The Authentic Life*. Like Upson, Burns knew a good story when he found it, and if he had to bend, embellish, or contravene the facts, he had no compunction about doing so if it made for greater excitement, deeper pathos, or richer irony. When you stop to think about it, it was very cagey of him to invoke the archaic by calling it a saga, which implies that if it wasn't quite an actual history, it was at least more (respectable?) than mere fiction. (Pity he wasn't even more inventive—he might have trumped Truman Capote and called it a nonfiction novel.)

The Saga of Billy the Kid in fact reads remarkably like a more thickly textured and expansive, detailed, densely populated, and wide-ranging version of *The Authentic Life*. Most of the characters they share are identical, only more nuanced and fleshed out in Burns without being in any fundamental way transformed or deepened, except when some of the larger-than-life ones are inflated to mythic proportions, hardly surprising from the man who in a later book would call the story of Wyatt Earp in Tombstone *An Iliad of the Southwest*. Like other writers, Burns even helped himself, wholly without attribution, to many of Upson's inventions, including the rescue of the wagon train, and tossed several of his own into the mix. But he must be credited with weaving two new (or at least newly minted) themes into the fabric of the legend, bringing something new to the portrait of Garrett, and trying to account for why against all logic the Kid returned to Fort Sumner after his escape from Lincoln.[28]

Since Billy had "no known tie to bind him," Garrett in *The Authentic Life* claims he could not fathom why the Kid should "linger in the territory"(142). But Garrett had to know of the rumors that Billy was involved with Pete Maxwell's sixteen-year-old sister Paulita. Perhaps Garrett was protecting Paulita's reputation by not mentioning it. Whatever their veracity, the rumors gave Burns exactly what he needed: just as he was unable to keep himself from invoking the gods of antiquity every time history presented him with a coincidence that could be interpreted as momentous, he was unable to resist the opportunity to season his boiling pot with a sentimental love story whereby Billy, despite a girlfriend in every town, village, and settlement in the territory, has but one true love.

> When, later on in his story, Billy the Kid escaped from Lincoln, it is generally conceded he could have got quickly into old Mexico where he would have been safe from pursuit. Life and liberty beckoned him across the Rio Grande. But the love in his boy's heart longed for his sweetheart and he headed straight for Fort Sumner. For the one woman of his dreams he risked his life in his life's most desperate chance. For love of her he died. (180)

By the time Burns interviewed Paulita she was "Mrs. Paulita Jaramillo in her own little cottage in the outskirts" of new Fort Sumner, where stood a railroad, "the iron highway of a modern transportation system" (183). Sitting on her porch crocheting, Mrs. Jaramillo (who seven months after the events of July 14, 1881, married José Jaramillo, a union that did not last) insisted that she and Billy were never sweethearts, only friends, and referred instead to another woman who occupied that place in Billy's heart but who goes unnamed because, Burns coyly remarks, "it is charitable . . . not to rake this ancient bit of gossip out of the ashes" (185).

By indulging Mrs. Jaramillo her little fiction, if fiction it is, Burns was able to be doubly chivalrous while protecting himself by not actually naming the other woman. In fact, self-protection seems to have been his principal motive, as his publishers feared lawsuits if he were to print the truth by naming names. Though Burns claimed he wrote the chapter in such a way that perceptive readers could hardly help but assume Paulita and Billy were lovers, anybody familiar with Fort Sumner gossip in the old days would know, from her description of the other woman as being connected, "not very distantly, by marriage," to Pat Garrett, that she was talking about Celsa Gutiérrez, a married woman herself (to Saval Gutiérrez, probably a cousin) and also the sister of Garrett's second wife Apolinaria, née Gutiérrez. In fact, there were rumors that Billy was carrying on with Celsa (who lived within a stone's throw of the Maxwells)—which of course might further explain why Garrett mentioned neither affair in his book. Mrs. Jaramillo also says that Billy had at least two other girlfriends in Fort Sumner (which if true must have made him a very busy young man indeed).

Were Billy and Paulita lovers? When the posse passed back through Fort Sumner after capturing the Kid and his gang at Stinking Springs, Billy was allowed to bid Paulita farewell. According to James East, "The lovers embraced, and she gave Billy one of those soul kisses the novelists tell us about, till it being time to hit the trail for Vegas, we had to pull them apart."[29] And Paulita later wrote Billy a letter while he was in jail in Mesilla awaiting trial for the murder of Sheriff Brady.[30] Whether these are enough to draw the inference they were lovers is anybody's guess; but in an earlier draft of the chapter devoted to Paulita ("A Belle of Old Fort Sumner"), Burns adduced a good bit of testimony in the form of recollections he gathered from locals between Santa Fe and Fort Sumner to the effect that the Kid was madly in love with her and that they were so determined to marry they kept a pair of horses saddled in her brother Pete's barn, planning to elope as soon as they got some money the Kid was expecting.[31]

The Paulita-Billy romance has been used so often as the explanation for why the Kid returned to Fort Sumner instead of leaving the territory that it may obscure another possible explanation. What if a different question had all along been asked? What if the question were not, why didn't he leave the territory, but rather, would leaving the territory have even occurred to him as a serious option? Granted, as a fugitive who had just killed two deputies in an escape that was on its way to becoming the stuff of legend by the very next day, he was a hunted man with a price on his head, while a great many who had sympathized with him were now turned against him. But that still left a great many who remained on his side, including and especially practically everybody in Fort Sumner and environs. Not all that long after he came back, Billy was doubtless aware of the grumbling among the many in Lincoln and Roswell who had voted for Garrett or helped him win the election that he seemed to be taking his own sweet time resuming the pursuit. Despite warnings to the

contrary from some of his friends, it's likely that so far as the Kid was concerned Garrett appeared to have given up the chase entirely. Indeed, there is
scant hard evidence to suggest Billy even remotely appreciated the precariousness of his situation or the kind of man Pat Garrett really was. On the contrary,
he had his pals to hang out with, card games for money (not to mention rustling and horse stealing, which still paid), dances to go to, and women aplenty.
Why would he want to leave a life like that? Anyhow—no doubt starting to be
seduced by his own reputation—who could draw faster and shoot straighter;
and if he were captured again, well, what jail could hold him? He'd been bust-
ing out of jails since he was fifteen, when he escaped from one in Silver City by
climbing up the inside of a chimney so narrow nobody thought a child could
squeeze through it. If he had learned anything from the Lincoln County Courthouse escape, it wasn't that the circumstances which helped make it possible
were essentially unduplicatable; rather, it was that Lady Luck was still in his
back pocket. This was, after all, a kid, or, rather, an immature young man, and
like many a young man his age, he seems to have believed he would live forever.
As Utley has written (*Violent Life* 1), "More than any other trait, youth shaped
the personality and directed the life of Billy the Kid."

In addition to being made the main reason Billy returned to Fort Sumner, Paulita is also the principal and practically only source Burns adduces to
support his assertion that Pat and Billy were close friends.[32] According to Paulita, they ate, drank, played cards, went to dances, and womanized together.
They sometimes had shooting contests, and on one occasion Pat emptied his
six-gun trying to hit a fleeing rabbit that Billy then dispatched with a single
bullet. If Pat was broke he borrowed from Billy, and if Billy was broke, he went
to Pat. "Oh, yes," was her summation, "Garrett and the Kid were as thick as
two peas in a pod" (197).

Historians have been unable to find any hard evidence to substantiate
Mrs. Jaramillo's assertions, unless more weight than it can bear is laid upon
Garrett's claim at the beginning of *The Authentic Life* to the effect that he knew
the Kid "personally since and during the continuance of what was known as
'The Lincoln County War,' up to the moment of his death" (3). Since the war
started early in 1878 (at about the same time, as has already been pointed
out, that Garrett first arrived in the territory) and since the Kid was dead by
the middle of the summer of 1881, it means that the *totality* of the time they
knew each other in any capacity cannot have exceeded three years. Although
Billy passed through or otherwise spent time in and around Fort Sumner
beginning in July 1878, no one has been able to establish for certain when
or how he and Pat met, but more than likely it was sometime between late
1878 and early 1879 in a saloon Billy and his pals frequented, a saloon where
Garrett worked. No doubt an acquaintanceship of some sort developed; but
given that Billy and his gang were also active *banditos* and often away on jobs,
it could hardly have been a deep friendship or for obvious reasons an old one.
And by the middle of 1880 Garrett had relocated to Roswell so that he would

be eligible to run for sheriff. His statement at the beginning of his book thus appears to have been made to establish his bona fides for writing it, not to claim an intimacy. Far closer to the reality of what existed between them is indicated by what he told an acquaintance in 1880:

> No, we are not friends, neither are we enemies. He minds his business and I attend to mine. He visits my wife's folks sometimes, but he never comes around me. I just simply don't want anything to do with him, and he knows it, and he knows that he has nothing to fear from me as long as he does not interfere with me and my affairs. (Sligh 170)

There is no question that Garrett and the Kid knew each other when Garrett lived in Fort Sumner or that they were at many of the same weekly dances and were part of some of the same card games in the local saloons. They may even have target-practiced together a few times, and Billy and his outlaw friends Folliard and Bowdre were evidently at the party for Garrett's first wedding. So, however, were half or more of the residents of Fort Sumner, since it wasn't yet even a town, only a small settlement of no more than three hundred residents (including the immediate vicinity) where everybody knew or at least had a passing acquaintance with everybody else. But the Kid and Garrett never *rode* together, even once, either as outlaw partners or any other kind, let alone intimates.[33]

Like his counterpart in *The Authentic Life*, Burns's Garrett is a conscientious public servant, a brave and committed professional determined to fulfill his responsibilities to the people who elected him. But he also emerges as an embryonic form of what would later, in the popular culture and even some of the serious fiction and film in the new century, develop into a prominent new hero: men—and much, much later women too—be they police officer, bounty hunter, private eye, bodyguard, soldier, soldier of fortune, mercenary, even some kinds of criminal—whose identity consists almost entirely in their profession, their justification in honing their skills, performing their appointed tasks, and discharging their obligations and responsibilities as perfectly as they possibly can, while setting their emotions completely aside, which usually means suppressing them. Here is Burns:

> No personal feelings of any kind ever clouded [Garrett's] ideas of the law or his duty under the law. He was in a way a legal machine. He moved along his path of duty as crushingly and inexorably as a steam-roller. If he set out to arrest a man, he arrested him or killed him. When he took a trail, he followed it to the end. (301)

This is a figure of genuine honor (though of a disturbing kind, because so narrowly conceived and isolated from normal moral considerations) and his avatars would appear in countless works of fiction, film, drama, and television from low to high, cutting across genres as varied as the Western, detective, police, crime, caper, gangster, war, even samurai and martial arts films. To the extent that this aspect of Burns's Garrett is perceivable, it is only from the vantage point of what came much later and I make no claim there was influence. Where there may have been influence, however, and palpably, was upon Sam Peckinpah, whose Garrett in the prologue to *Pat Garrett and Billy the Kid* is plainly antici- pated in Burns's characterization of the sheriff at the end of his life: "His old geniality and spirit of comradeship were gone. He had become a somber man, sour of outlook, embittered, irascible, easily stirred to dangerous moods" (316).

That is not the only point of congruence. Long before Peckinpah, Burns too realized that the story of Pat Garrett and Billy the Kid could be made to dramatize the end of an era, the Old West giving way to the forces of civiliza- tion, and it is because he wanted to give this drama a tragic *human* dimension that he insisted upon the friendship of his two protagonists. As is most emphatically not the case with Peckinpah, however, no doubts, no ambiva- lences, no uncertainties, and absolutely no ironies cloud Burns's conviction that it has all been for the best: when Billy is finally laid to rest next to Fol- liard and Bowdre, the graves "marked the end of a long campaign to establish law and order west of the Pecos," and "Garrett was the last great sheriff of the old frontier, constructive through destruction, establishing peace on a foundation of graves, the leaping flame from the muzzle of his six-shooter the beacon of prosperity" (289, 312).

Burns was hardly the first to fold the closing of the West into the story of Billy the Kid or to depict Pat and Billy as friends turned foes, but his book is the one that established these aspects of the legend as "facts."[34] He could not have done it without standing on the shoulders of the Garrett-Upson book, but unlike theirs, his was a spectacular success. An immediate best seller and one of the first Book-of-the-Month Club selections, it earned over twenty-five thousand dollars in royalties and in 1930 was made into the hit movie *Billy the Kid* (at Metro-Goldwyn-Mayer, the studio for which Peckinpah would make *Pat Garrett and Billy the Kid* decades later), with King Vidor directing and star- ring Johnny Mack Brown as Billy. Even more significant, however, is that the success of Burns's book, which, like Garrett's, is still in print today, was almost single-handedly responsible, so Nolan has argued (*West* 295), for bringing Billy the Kid and by extension the whole story of Lincoln County out of the obscurity into which all had fallen shortly after Garrett's death in 1908. It was the beginning of what would become in the decades that followed a flood of books and films on the subject that shows no sign of receding—so many, in fact, that in a 2007 review of the most recent biography up to that time, Larry McMurtry quoted a noted bibliographer who told him that "only Napoleon and Jesus had longer bibliographies than Billy the Kid." Yet it wasn't until 1956, thirty-one years after Burns's potboiler and three-quarters of a century after Pat Garrett killed Billy the Kid, that a work of fiction based on their story would be published which is also a first-rate piece of literature.

Charles Neider, ca. 1955

CHAPTER THREE

Neider's Novel

The West as a great myth is one of the most important
products of the American imagination, and yet it has been
touched upon only superficially. Because the old West was
raw, and an object of satire in the East; because many of
its actors seemed childish to sophisticated easterners; and
because those responsible for using western materials are
too often inadequate for the task: because of such reasons
it is usually believed that western materials are adequate
for gunman paperbacks and cowboy movies only, and that
exceptions merely prove the rule. This is an error which
can be rectified by the production of superior art, and such
art, in turn, can only be created out of a profound knowledge and feeling for western materials and the western
experience.

—Charles Neider

There, in a nutshell, is why Charles Neider believed the typical Western
yielded so little first-rate fiction. He had a point. Generally speaking, when
serious writers turned their attentions to the West, they set their stories in
the earlier period of the first explorers and the mountain men or else much
later, including into the next century, when the West was already settled. But
the time of the cowboy, the sheriff, the bandit, the gunfighter, the gambler,
the dance-hall girl—all the character types and conventions Robert Warshow
described in his famous essay "The Westerner"—this relatively brief era was
left, even as its history was happening, mostly to the yellow backs, dime

novels, and newspaper and magazine serials (and, later, movies and Saturday afternoon serials).[1] Though legitimate exception may be taken to the accuracy of Neider's characterization of the field, it is nevertheless how he perceived the background against which he decided to write the book he eventually called *The Authentic Death of Hendry Jones*, one of the finest Western novels ever written. Yet, ironically, its author had no particular connection to the American West until fairly well into his life.

Born in Odessa, Russia, in 1915, Neider was brought to the United States at the age of six and raised in Richmond, Virginia. He later lived in New York City and made his home in Princeton. Over his long career he distinguished himself as novelist, critic, scholar, essayist, journalist, historian, and editor, in the last capacity publishing many excellent anthologies on a variety of subjects, including literature, history, philosophy, and exploration. Insatiably curious and something of an explorer, he often drew on his own experiences, the most dramatic from 1970 on the second of his three trips to Antarctica: a helicopter crash on the slopes of Mount Erebus, an ordeal he documented in *Edge of the World: Ross Island, Antarctica—A Personal and Historical Narrative of Exploration, Adventure, Tragedy, and Survival*. When, aged seventy-eight, he was diagnosed with prostate cancer, personal experience once more furnished material for a book, his last: *Adam's Burden: An Explorer's Personal Odyssey through Prostate Cancer*. The illness claimed him eight years later in July 2001, a month before the book was published. In all, he wrote, edited, or compiled some fifty books, many still in print, a list that does not include *The Authentic Death of Hendry Jones*, his second novel and arguably his finest contribution to the literature of fiction. (His first, *The White Citadel*, published in 1954, garnered high praise from the likes of Saul Bellow, Mark Schorer, Thomas Mann, and E. M. Forster.)

Neider did not visit the American West until 1952, when, aged thirty-seven, he was awarded a residence scholarship at the prestigious Hartford Artists Colony in Los Angeles. As he drove through Texas, New Mexico, Arizona, and the Southern California desert, the experience of directly encountering the landscape for the first time cleared him of both romantic and revisionist preconceptions about the Old West. "I had been washed clean," he declared, a bit dramatically, "and was ready to have, or rather to accept, the new experience in all its dazzle and size and fertility."[2] Although he believed that his "eastern background," "European orientation," and "sophisticated literary intelligence" freed him "to a great extent from the localism and provincialities one finds in Western writers," he nevertheless did a vast amount of research for the better part of three years before starting the writing. Some of it was firsthand, of places and locales, and included extended stays in Northern California and New Mexico. Most of it, however, consisted in historical, literary, and archival sources, and predated any notion of writing the novel. Availing himself of every opportunity to investigate libraries throughout California during those months at the Artists Colony, he discovered "what a gold mine for scholars and writers the literary history of the West contains."

The mother lode was the history of Billy the Kid and Pat Garrett. Once Neider had read as much as he could about them, he drew upon five primary sources as the basis for characters, incidents, and the broad outline of the action. The most obvious and important is of course Garrett's book, to which Neider paid homage by making his title a play on Garrett's. So far as I am aware, however, he nowhere acknowledged his debt to Walter Burns's *The Saga of Billy the Kid*, which I am convinced furnished him with the inspiration, and even a model, for what became perhaps the novel's single most impressive achievement: telling the title character's jailbreak from three distinct points of view and protracting the deaths of the two deputies. The third source is George Coe's *Frontier Fighter* (1934), which Neider read twice.[3] The fourth is John W. Poe's *The Death of Billy the Kid*, from which Neider used the deputy's version of how Garrett learned the Kid was in Fort Sumner (see chapter 5, note 15) and the rumors that the Kid's trigger finger was cut off for a souvenir and that someone else, not he, was gunned down that night. (Neider named his Poe equivalent Andy Webb, but any resemblance to the real Poe stopped with Webb being made the deputy.) The fifth is John P. Meadows.

In 1880 Meadows was a young cowboy down on his luck when he arrived in Fort Sumner, where the Kid took an immediate liking to him and helped him get a cot, a room, and something to eat. They became fast friends, the Kid soon hiring him to deliver and collect on cattle and horses the Kid and his pals were running (which seems to have been the extent of Meadows's involvement in any sort of criminal activity). Meadows first met Garrett briefly in Texas some three years earlier, then renewed the acquaintance in Fort Sumner in 1881, after which they became and remained good friends for twenty-two years, Meadows for a time serving as Garrett's deputy (though never while the Kid was alive). Late in life Meadows often performed as a raconteur and was interviewed about his days in the Old West by reporters and professional historians, many of which interviews were published as newspaper features. Decades later the historian John P. Wilson collected them (including some unpublished material) in a book, *Pat Garrett and Billy the Kid as I Knew Them: Reminiscences of John P. Meadows*.

Obviously Neider could not have known Wilson's book, which wasn't published until three years after the novelist died. But he was a professional critic and scholar, trained in research. Comparisons of passages in his novel to passages in Meadows suggest he was familiar with at least some of the interviews in their original publications, in particular three in the *Roswell Daily Record* from March 1931, a six-part series in the *Alamogordo News* entitled "My Personal Recollections of 'Billy the Kid'" (starting April 1936), and in the same newspaper's series of thirty-nine "as told by John P. Meadows" pieces that ran from August 1935 through June 1936 (when he died). As with the other sources, Neider took what was useful to him: a passage in which Meadows defends the veracity of what he says about the Kid; a key part of the jailbreak; and an important element of the backstory of the relationship between his two main characters (which also found its way into Peckinpah's *Pat Garrett and Billy the Kid*). I will return to these in further detail as they apply.

Neider modeled Hendry Jones, whose nickname is also "the Kid," on William Bonney and Dad Longworth on Pat Garrett, and he confined himself to the last few months of Billy's life, which means the last eight chapters of the Garrett-Upson book. The main incidents he used are the jailbreak from Lincoln, the killing of Tom Folliard, and the Kid's death. But the entire narrative is now in the first person, told by an old-timer Neider created named Doc Baker, "Doc" taken from Doc Scurlock (a leader of the Regulators), "Baker" from Frank Baker (one of the posse that murdered Tunstall). If they had a nice ring of authenticity to them, Neider appropriated the names of actual figures for almost every one of his characters, though the fictional counterpart was not usually based on the person who supplies the name. "Hendry," for example, was taken from Hendry Brown, a close friend of Billy's and a fellow member of the Regulators, and of course in its normal spelling the name Billy's mother gave him at birth. "Jones" Neider probably chose because it's so ironically common, but it also belonged to a family who knew Billy well and treated him as one of their own (see chapter 6, note 15). Dad Longworth's first name came from Sheriff George W. Peppin, whose nickname was "Dad," his last name from Thomas B. Longworth, a constable from White Oaks, New Mexico, who led the posse that tracked the Kid and his gang to the ranch where a blacksmith named James Carlyle was killed in a crossfire (Neider named one of Longworth's deputies Carlyle). Clearly both the nickname and the surname for the Garrett surrogate have significance, the surname in particular suggesting the novelist's attitude toward the character.

In addition to Scurlock, Neider also based Doc on a mix of John Meadows, George Coe, and Charlie Foor. An actual resident of Fort Sumner, Foor at seventy was interviewed by Burns, who put him into the penultimate chapter of *The Saga*, which has "Old Man Charlie Foor" taking us on a tour of the site of the old fort, showing us where Folliard and Charles Bowdre lived, the peach orchard where Garrett hid on the fateful night, Pete Maxwell's house, the very room where the Kid was killed, the gravesites—all gone, covered over with sagebrush and the windswept "bare desert earth" (300). The way Burns calls attention to the return of the old fort into the dust and dirt from which it was built has the effect of pushing the story much farther back into the past, enshrouding it in the nimbus of legend, and edging its principal players toward the status of mythic figures.[4]

The narrator as participant obviously lends both authority and immediacy to a narrative. But as Doc is an old man, immediacy is tempered by the distance of time, which allows him to correct myths and falsehoods that have barnacled what he perceives as the truth. As the novel begins, one of the thousands of tourists who yearly travel to see Hendry Jones's grave tells Baker he "saw a trigger finger in a bottle of alcohol back in Phoenix and there was a label on it and it said it was the Kid's finger. What do you say to that?" Long since fed up with stupid questions, Doc, testy and ornery, replies, "I say it's a damn fool who'll believe every label he reads" (1). Undeterred, the visitor asks about the story that the Kid never got killed back then on the Punta. "The Kid, my friend, is dead these many years." Though the characters are fictional, the substance of the situation is based in fact: for many years after William Bonney's death his alleged trigger finger kept turning up all over the Southwest, and like many another folk hero, he wasn't dead twenty-four hours before sympathetic residents in Fort Sumner started spreading rumors that someone else was killed, not him; he was down in Old Mexico maybe. (Neider ends the novel on such a scene.) Over the years several candidates stepped forward claiming to be him, all discredited; and recently some dyed-in-the-wool aficionados have been lobbying for DNA testing of the remains in his grave.

"Now if you'll just be patient," Doc says at the outset,

> it's the truth I'm getting at and if you're not interested I suggest you run along to the stores and pick up one of the little books full of lies about the Kid's life, written by some smartaleck easterner that never sat in a western saddle, never smelled good horseflesh or a campfire dying in the hills and yet is ready to tell the country about the Kid. I was there and I know what happened. (4)

The claim may echo Ash Upson's assertions of authenticity, but stripped of Doc's orneriness, the tone and even some of the language suggest John Meadows, who said:

> I am well aware of the fact that my version of some of the Billy the Kid lore is not in accordance with that of the story writers and you can do as you please about accepting any of it. I have what I consider good reasons for any of my statements relative to Billy the Kid—I knew him and since that time I have talked with a hundred or more people who knew him. Of course, as I have stated, a great deal of my information about Billy comes from the mouth of Billy himself. (55)

As Doc continues dismantling the myths, it seems clear that Neider is taking cynical aim at some of the sentimental recollections in Miguel Antonio Otero's *The Real Billy the Kid* (which he had read), not to mention a few of those in Burns's book. At the same time, he reclaims others: the stories, for example, "of how we used to dress in those days looking like pigs are mostly untrue," except "of course, living out, hunting, camping, doing a cowhand's work, it was another matter, for then we were at work, wearing shaps, eating dust and not minding how we looked."[5] But in town "we were always well dressed, taking a kind of pride in it," Hendry most of all, "neat and gentlemanly in his manners," cutting "quite a figure," all in black except for his white shirts and his jacket, "always unbuttoned so that he could get at his fortyfour without trouble if he wanted to." The notches on the Kid's gun are another lie (any "real gunfighter knew that notchkeeper was another word for fourflusher"), so too the claim that he killed a man for every year of his life: "He had killed only sixteen men at the time and even that figure was uncertain, for some of the men he had left for dead might have recovered." And then there's the non-sense about his beautiful singing voice—only thing "left out was the guitar." As for sharing his wealth with the poor, if "he gave a native a cow, did that mean he was sharing his wealth? There was plenty more where that had come from and he hadn't worked very hard to get it."

In none of this does Doc have any intention to run Hendry down, but the "truth is the truth and we might just as well get it fixed in the record" (5). The allusion here is not just to Meadows but once more to Garrett, yet the purpose is contrast. When Ash Upson dropped words like "authentic" and "faithful" into the full title of *The Authentic Life*, he was essentially trying to authenticate the outrageous, particularly in the first third where the tales are stretched so tall he himself surely couldn't have believed them. In Neider, however, Doc's claims to telling the truth are there to expose the legend at its silliest so that what remains is the legend at its most authentic, emerging from a lived experience that would plausibly give rise to it as told by a participant. Thus there's nothing to indicate Doc is conceived as an unreliable narrator; and while there are revelations about himself that he doesn't nec-essarily intend or is even aware of, none of them seems to me meant to call into question his credibility as witness or lead us to suspect ulterior motives. By the end, whatever else, the effect of Neider's narrative method is to make us feel that Doc has for the most part brought us much closer to the reality of Hendry Jones's life beneath the encrustations of hearsay, gossip, and pulp melodrama, at least insofar as Doc is in a position to relate it. Of course, there is an irony in the method that doubles back on itself because what Neider called "the *sense* of the Kid as he emerges through the folk legend" was some-thing he tried to realize in the book precisely by sticking "close to the facts."[6] By "facts" here, Neider wasn't necessarily referring only to historical facts as such, but what in the world of the novel Doc distinguishes as fact from fancy. The implicit theme—surely one that wasn't lost on Peckinpah—is that in the Old West fact itself is often the stuff of legend and needs little embellishment and no enlargement.

At the same time, Neider had no desire to write a mere roman à clef about William Bonney and Pat Garrett. Hoping to "avoid too close an identifica-tion" between his novel and the historical characters and to free himself from "all the burdens of mere fact," he cut short his research in New Mexico and changed the setting.[7] The new one had to be near the sea and have a rich Span-ish heritage, both requirements well satisfied by the Monterey Peninsula. As the following pages will show, the characters he created, however inspired by real people in the New Mexico Territory of 1881, are his own creations and exist fully realized with no need of external validation by history. And Neider often ignored the facts when they didn't suit his purposes.

The novel can be divided into roughly three sections after the introductory scene of Doc as an old man with the tourist. The first, which takes up almost a third of the book, consists mostly of the Kid's incarceration in and escape from Dad Longworth's jail in Monterey; the second, the shortest, his trip to Mexico with his gang and their return; the third his reunion with his inamorata Nika Machado; their disintegrating relationship; the deaths of Harvey French, Nika's brother, and Bob Emory; and Dad's killing of the Kid. The novel is compact, concentrated in style, and restricted in scope, particularly with respect to the number of characters and incidents. Almost everything about the Kid's early life is omitted, while the Lincoln County War or any equivalent is dispensed with entirely apart from a single reference. There is only one main character and that is Hendry himself; Dad Longworth, while important, is relegated to a supporting role. The many outlaws Billy the Kid rode with, the gangs he was part of or led, are here consolidated into one with only three members apart from himself: Doc; Harvey French, based on Folliard, with a bit of Charlie Bowdre rolled in (otherwise Bowdre is given no equivalent); and Bob Emory, entirely fictional. The trip to Mexico is wholly invented, but the incidents on either side of it, notably the jailbreak, Harvey's death, and Hendry's death, including the inquest the morning after, hew broadly and often in detail to the accounts in Garrett's book, including replications of dialogue or close equivalents (occasionally lines of dialogue were fashioned from the prose).

A few examples will suffice to indicate Neider's methods and begin to suggest the themes he extracted from his sources. Like Billy, Hendry is a womanizer, but Neider, like Burns, concentrates on just one woman, though the similarities end there. Burns's romance is clichéd and sentimental; Neider's dark, tough-minded, and tortured. Neider clearly based Nika Machado on Celsa Gutiérrez (Garrett's sister-in-law), right down to her marrying her cousin (named Miguel Gomez in the novel); but she isn't made Longworth's sister-in-law and the emotional character of her relationship with Hendry is wholly imagined. Just three days before the Kid is to be hanged, she marries Miguel because he's been in love with her for so long and, soon to die (from a kick by a horse resulting in internal bleeding that will not stop), he wants to leave everything he has to her. She agrees only because she thinks the Kid will also be dead soon. She is desperate to end her destructive relationship with Hendry, who had betrayed her sometime before he went to Mexico by spending a week with another woman. Nor does she want a life with someone whom so many people are gunning for. As in Burns, where Billy returns for his true love, Nika is one reason Hendry comes back to Monterey, but not the sole reason, Dad Longworth being the other and arguably the more important. While Nika is special among the Kid's women, their relationship is clearly meant to indicate the impossibility of a long-term relationship, be it romantic or matrimonial, between any woman and the kind of man he is; and the way he treats her, as an object for his pleasure alone, is distinctly narcissistic. (That Nika cannot bear children suggests their relationship is barren in other ways as well.)

Neider gives Nika a sixteen-year-old brother named Modesto, who worships Hendry; Doc tells us that if there is anyone the Kid really cared about it is Modesto. Modesto is shot down in cold blood by Cal and Curly Bill Dedrick and a cohort named Shotgun Smith out of revenge for the Kid's killing of the Dedricks' brother Lon. Although Modesto is wholly fictional, Hendry's affection for him recalls Billy's affection for John Tunstall, from whose murder Neider appropriates details, including one of the killers going up to Tunstall's dead body and blasting him in the head, then killing his horse and putting Tunstall's hat under the horse's head as a sign of disrespect (Tunstall was proud of his horses and had several very beautiful ones). Curly Bill does the same with Modesto's beloved mare. When the Kid exacts his revenge, Neider stages one of the killings as an ambush reminiscent of the killing of Sheriff Brady, the Kid and Doc hiding behind an adobe wall on which they rest their rifles to steady their aim. Afterward, the Kid goes up to Curly Bill's body and puts a bullet in his head point-blank and he does the same thing after he kills Smith. In a nice touch, Cal escapes only to be killed in Tombstone a couple of years later, character as destiny playing itself out even among the minor figures.

Like Burns with his Garrett and Billy, Neider makes Dad and Hendry friends, but, unlike Burns, not especially close friends, just former outlaw "pards . . . until Dad got the notion he had to be sheriff, with a wife and kids, and so took off to Monterey County" (12). But it's ambiguous how much stock Neider means for us to put in their friendship inasmuch as he never quite allows us to experience it directly. This is partly because not much of the novel is taken up with it—it's mostly backstory—and partly because Doc himself seems unsure. "I think the Kid liked [Dad] and I understand Dad really liked the Kid," he says, "and the only sorry thing about it was that they were no longer operating on the same side" (47). When he says the Kid went to Monterey to make Dad feel sorry he ever gave up the outlaw life, he prefaces it with, "I'm not sure of it, not having heard the Kid tell of it." These are examples of Doc's essential honesty: when he doesn't know something for sure, he tells us so.

As regards Dad, one thing *is* certain, however, and it is that, in contradistinction to most other treatments that cast sheriff and outlaw as former friends, Neider nowhere ascribes disloyalty or betrayal to Dad for going after Hendry, nor does Doc ever think Dad a coward: "[Dad] was no coward. You don't find many fellows like the Kid, who don't have nerves at all and who like to risk it for the hell of it and to test their luck. Dad knew he stood a good chance of being killed by the Kid but it didn't keep him from going after him after the Kid skedaddled" (42). Though Doc admits to hating Dad for killing the Kid, it wasn't for long: "I was never one to hold that grudge against him, seeing as how I knew it was more the Kid's fault than Dad's and seeing as how Dad had no choice in the matter anyhow" (47). Though there are echoes here from the end of Garrett's book, where he writes about his fears pursuing the Kid, equally strong are those from George Coe in *Frontier Fighter*:

> Some critics have claimed it was cowardly of Garrett to kill the Kid with-out giving him the ghost of a chance. They are dead wrong. Garrett was anything but a coward. It took nerve, in no small package, to face danger as he did. . . . I would have done anything reasonable to save the Kid, at the same time I must give Pat Garrett his due. I knew him well, and now feel no bitterness toward him for killing the Kid. (225)

For Doc, Dad is "a fellow who knew his duty," but, far from being a hard-ass about it, Doc gives Hendry every possible warning and chance to clear out, including meeting him "secretly several times and [asking] him to leave the country" (42, 12–13). When at one of them Hendry replies that it's "a free country," Dad asks him to "think it over." Neider got this from Meadows, who said that Garrett personally urged both the Kid and Bowdre to leave the territory for a while and both ignored the advice.[8] So it is with Hendry, who Doc knows has "no intention of thinking it over, his mind being set on what he wanted to do." After Hendry has extracted his revenge killings on behalf of Modesto, he has Old Man Richardson, the owner of the ranch where he's stay-ing, ride into Monterey to tell Dad, "That I'm back" (175). In this, Hendry's relationship with Dad is suggestive of his relationship with Nika: he abso-lutely will not accept the changes the one has made in his life or the other wants to make in hers. Everything must be on his terms alone.

As already noted, the character of Harvey French is based on Tom Fol-liard, who was killed at the hospital on the outskirts of Fort Sumner in a trap carefully laid by Garrett, who lured Billy and his gang into the settlement by spreading false information that he and his posse had cleared out. It worked and it might almost have ended Billy the Kid's career then and there . . . except that riding in front alongside Folliard and Tom Pickett, as they neared the hospital, Billy—as he later told Garrett (with, so Garrett reported, a mischie-vous twinkle in his eye)—had a gut feeling something wasn't quite right.[9] On the pretext that he wanted a chew from one of the gang bringing up the rear who had the best tobacco, Billy dropped back without saying a word, even to Folliard, one of his closest friends. ("The Kid," Garrett dryly noted, "with all his reckless bravery, had a strong infusion of caution in his composition when not excited.") Folliard and Pickett rode straight into the trap. Though Gar-rett, who recognized Folliard, gave both outlaws a moment to surrender (but only just), Folliard reached for his gun and was immediately shot by Garrett and another deputy, while Billy and the rest, including Pickett, spurred their horses and got away. When Folliard, mortally wounded, was carried inside the hospital and laid on a blanket on the floor, what developed was one of those scenes—there are so many of them in the history of Billy and Garrett—that no storyteller or dramatist would likely have dreamed up: the posse returned to their card game, which had been interrupted by the shooting, while Folliard took an agonizing three-quarters of an hour to die. At some point he begged Garrett to put him out of his misery; Garrett refused, but when one of his deputies offered to do it, Folliard cried, "Don't shoot anymore, for God's sake. I'm already killed."[10]

Neider's changes are revealing. First, he moves the ambush from the settlement to a trail and changes the time from evening to later after night has fully fallen, so that Dad cannot clearly see whom he has shot. When the shooting starts Dad thinks he has hit the Kid, only to discover that his shot hit Harvey while Hendry and Doc escape (the mistaken identity taken from the killing of Bowdre at Stinking Springs). Like Poe, the deputy Andy Webb doubts it's the Kid the sheriff killed. "I was sure it was the Kid, I was sure it was the Kid," a shaken Dad protests. "I could have sworn it was."[11] Then he turns and apologizes to Harvey, who, like Folliard, knows he's dying, pleads to be put out of his misery, then changes his mind when a deputy, Juan Carlyle, offers to oblige. Harvey dies a death as agonized as Folliard's, but Neider plays the scene out differently. Harvey's words "Don't shoot anymore. For God's sake I'm killed already!" are taken directly from Garrett's book, but Neider has Carlyle mock him with "I was only kidding," whereupon a furious Dad shoves the barrel of his revolver right into Carlyle's stomach and cocks the hammer. The deputy turns white. "I'm only kidding," Dad says, witheringly. Then he turns to Harvey: "Harvey, you're dying. The game's over for you. Tell us where the Kid is." "Fuck you," is Harvey's answer. By this time Dad—his nerves already rattled by the mistaken killing and worried because they're outside Monterey in a largely Mexican area where sympathies for the Kid run high—advises they'd all better clear out. When Harvey pleads not to be left to die alone, Dad, still worried about the safety of his men, has him slung "face down over his saddle" and sends the horse off with a slap in the direction Hendry and Doc had fled.

The horse carrying the dying Harvey shows up later at the Kid's adobe out on the Punta del Diablo, "Devil's Point," where Hendry and his gang are sequestered. It is here in Hendry's adobe that Neider places the deathwatch, with Hendry and Doc playing cards. Ruminating that Harvey wasn't bad with a horse, but never good with a gun, Doc says, "A fellow like that is bound to get himself killed before he's twenty-five. He would have made a good foreman though." "He just picked the wrong trade that's all," says the Kid, still studying his cards. Meanwhile, Harvey, taking a good long time to die, is thinking, "Why the hell did I get mixed up in all this? . . . Maybe I can get somebody to figure it out. Harvey your time is short you know that?" The death is vividly described: "Suddenly he screamed and we looked up from our game and watched him. He screamed again and then we heard the rattle in his throat. He jerked twice and was still." "Well that's that," says the Kid. "Let's get him buried. I reckon they'll want to have a wake." Doc's reply, "Good old Harvey," is as close as Harvey gets to a eulogy.

By changing the time to after dark and having Dad intending to kill the Kid but shooting the wrong man, Neider is able to allude to and thus dramatize Garrett's frank admission that he was indeed scared when he decided to hunt Billy down. And by taking the exchange between Garrett and Poe outside Pete Maxwell's bedroom just after Billy was shot and using it here, Neider makes it clear that Dad was jumpy enough to shoot hastily and thus carelessly. This will be the first of two times Dad tries to kill the Kid. Here he got it wrong, the next time he'll get it right, but by his own admission wholly by accident, though maybe the accident was helpful in more ways than one: with no time to anticipate, Dad's nerves don't get in the way of his response. His apology to Harvey may be feeble, but the very gesture makes him more sympathetic and provides a small reminder of the ties he once had to Hendry and his friends. Dad's disgust with Carlyle, the deputy who mocks Harvey, resonates from *The Authentic Life*, where Garrett is undeceived about the character of some of the men he must rely on for posses, aware they are scarcely better than those they're pursuing and often much worse. By dispensing with the rather clear implication that Billy all but sent Folliard and Pickett into a trap while protecting his own hide, Neider reinforces our sense of the gang's internal loyalty, which is further reinforced by having Harvey refuse, even on his deathbed, to give up Hendry's whereabouts. (In actuality all Garrett wanted from Folliard was for him to identify who was riding with the Kid, which Folliard did.)

But it's relocating the card game that is the most significant change, one that reveals Hendry in a very unsettling light. Neither he nor Doc loses so little as a second's worth of concentration on their cards while their friend is dying, his fevered last thoughts barely acknowledged. The Kid's reaction in particular is so detached, so lacking in compassion, regret, or even simple sadness as to seem almost wholly without feeling. His response could be called "realistic," except that to have so apparently unaffected a reaction to the death of a friend is not realistic unless one is narcissistic, sociopathic, or so depressed as to be blocked from the normal responses of sympathy. But there is another explanation: a man so completely at home with death, who lives with it so constantly from day to day—meting it out, defending against it, being on the lookout for it—that it is no longer something remarkable, no longer an occasion for sorrow, grief, anger, rage, fear. It is not quite indifference—rather a kind of comfort with it or detachment from it (or both) that keeps emotions at bay or, worse, deadens feeling entirely.

Here is the first clue to what Neider brought to these materials that is fresh and original. It was Neider's Hendry, not the Billy of history, that Peckinpah,

Charles Neider on Chico. During the year Neider spent in Los Angeles,
1952, he became a proficient horseman and enjoyed acting the cowboy.

who got the point sooner than most, had in mind when he remarked that
Billy the Kid was no hero, he was a real killer. Hendry Jones is one of the most
compellingly realistic, psychologically convincing portraits of a gunfighter in
the fiction of the Old West. How did Neider accomplish this? "I . . . tried to
bring to bear upon the materials all of the sobriety and sharp focus of a highly
developed realism," he wrote, "and to treat scene and character with a respect
and care equal to those I would have employed if I had written a novel set in
New York or Boston" (*Great West* 16). In words that anticipate Peckinpah's
stated intentions behind the creation of David Blassingame, the title character of *The Westerner*, Neider wrote, "From the beginning I had in mind writing
a book as authentic in its details as I was capable of making it" (viii). He commenced with the simplest things, asking some pretty basic questions. What is
it like to be on horseback several hours a day for days on end? What is it like
to wear a gun in a holster tied to your leg most of the time? What is it like to
live with a reputation as a fast gun and a price on your head?

From a certain point of view such questions may seem very literal minded, but Neider put his research to good effect and it unquestionably lends the novel an authenticity missing from much fiction about the Old West. He did enough riding to get an idea of what a hard ride does to the body, let alone days of hard riding. When the Kid and his gang leave Monterey for Mexico and return in a total of thirty-eight days, Doc says "that the inside of my thighs and legs were raw, that walking was painful and that my left shoulder blade sometimes woke me at night with its aching."[12] When Doc pronounces the Kid "the greatest gunman alive at his death and one of the very greatest who ever lived," Neider knew that for this to be experienced as anything more than a mere convention of the genre, it needed to be buttressed by something that lends it a palpable reality, and details matter. He bought an old forty-five revolver and holster, strapped them to his right leg, and wore them almost every day all day (except when sleeping) for a couple of months. He soon discovered that his right leg got stronger by way of compensation for the weight of the gun, "so consequently I had an odd walk for a while" (viii). What he also wanted to know was what it was like to walk *without* one after wearing it almost constantly. When Hendry is incarcerated, he "felt as always that there was something wrong with his right thigh" and when "he moved about his right leg thrust itself forward more than necessary, as if the gun was still there." Neider also practiced drawing and shooting so much that he bloodied his fingers trying to grab the gun correctly. By the same token, Doc tells us that when Hendry gave Modesto "his first gun, a nickel-plated Colt's fortyfive," and taught him how to use it, the boy's hand bled and his shoulder ached so much he could hardly lift it. Hendry's only response is to tell him to develop those arm and shoulder muscles. "They say that the great gunmen are born great," Doc says. "All I know is that I practiced almost every day and that the Kid practiced and that Wyatt Earp and Doc Holliday practiced."

But it's more than practice that makes the Kid the best gunfighter of them all. He was born with everything: muscle, speed, terrific nerve, a surefire finger, and a "wild imagination that Wild Bill had and which made him unpredictable. I don't think any other gunfighter had it outside of those two."[13] He is also constantly vigilant and keenly observant, he never loses his nerve, he's an excellent judge of character, and he possesses a near-infallible sense of when to wait and when to strike, nowhere more so than when his life depends upon it. And he has something else as well: luck, "the kind of luck . . . that comes once in a hundred years and that when it comes nothing can change it."

Luck brings to mind card games, to which there are enough references in this novel—not to mention how often various pursuits are referred to as games, including life itself—to make us wonder if we shouldn't pay some attention to them. Neider, whose style and technique recall Hemingway, probably never considered himself much of a symbolist. Many modern storytellers of that period didn't, indeed often reacted resentfully when their work was read that way, perhaps because they felt it made them sound pretentious or artsy. Hemingway seems to have felt this way, so did Peckinpah if you caught him in the wrong mood. But any reasonably attentive reading of the one or viewing of the other soon gives a partial lie to this. I say "partial" because while symbols and metaphors appear in their work (I might even argue that they proliferate in Peckinpah's Westerns), they are so seamlessly integrated into the naturalistic textures and arise so organically from the situations that they don't *feel* like symbols even as they can be seen to function as them. So it is with Neider, who had a gift for bold, stark images of exceptional vivid-ness, and for camouflaging his metaphors in plain sight—card playing, for example.

Card games are ubiquitous in Western novels and films, though mostly as a convention to define the hero against the villain or the villain against a victim or to set up some confrontation, usually an act of violence. But they also served some important socioeconomic functions in the Old West. For one thing, in the New Mexico Territory of Pat Garrett and Billy the Kid, and doubtless most other places in the Old West, gambling was considered a perfectly legitimate way to make money. For another, they were a means of socializing, where you hung out with friends, met new ones (today this would be called networking), made enemies, or just passed the time. Games like poker, faro, and monte also functioned as a kind of school where you sharpened your memory, your wits, your intuitions, your powers of observation and strategy, perhaps most important of all your ability to read *people*. In Neider's novel, card games are a kind of metaphor for the way the world works and how you get along in it. If you're observant enough, detached enough, keep your cool enough, and think enough, then you could exert a certain control over your destiny, could survive and perhaps even win. But only a certain amount—after that, it's all in the cards. When the cards turn against you, there's nothing to do about it except withdraw, fall back, and bide your time until the luck returns, if it does. Sometimes you get the impression Doc believes that a fixed amount of good luck is doled out to each man at birth, and when it runs out, that's it; he has no more to draw on. As Hendry tells Nika, referring to Harvey's death: "When your luck gives out that's the end of the game" (168). Or as Doc observes of the fated meeting in Hijinio Gonzales's adobe that moonlit night when Dad's luck happened to be very good and Hendry's wasn't: "Once the Kid sensed there was someone else in the room besides Hijinio, Dad was a dead man if he didn't shoot first. That was the way the play went and there's no changing the falling of the cards" (42–43).

It's a short distance from card play to gunplay, and luck figures decisively in both. Neider brings together and focuses these motifs in the escape from the Monterey jail: a tour de force of stream of consciousness, shifts in point of view, and the very best kind of action writing because grounded in and reveal-ing of character. The incidents are familiar to anyone who has read Garrett,

Burns, or any of the more recent biographies and histories. Garrett segregated Billy from the other prisoners by keeping him chained to the floor in a large room on the second floor with a window that faced the plaza (Neider puts the other prisoners on the first floor, though in fact they were all kept on the second). He was guarded by two deputies, who watched him in shifts. One was J. W. Bell, well liked by all and decent to the Kid. The other was Bob Olinger, a big bully with a sadistic streak, who despised the Kid because he held him responsible for the killing of a friend, and Billy despised him right back for the same reason: "There existed a reciprocal hatred between these two," observed Garrett, who never liked or trusted Olinger himself, "and neither attempted to disguise or conceal his antipathy for the other."[14] Olinger constantly taunted the Kid, trying to provoke an attack as an excuse to blast him with the load of thirty-six buckshot in his double-barreled shotgun. On the afternoon of Thursday, April 28, 1881, when Olinger took the prisoners to supper at an eatery across the street, a task he performed like clockwork every day between five and six, Billy told Bell he needed to use the privy, which was several yards behind the courthouse.

Coming back the Kid managed to get far enough ahead of the deputy to reenter the jail alone. Though shackled with wrist- and leg-irons, he quickly hauled himself up the steep flight of stairs and down the hallway to the gun-room—he knew the lock was defective, the door needing only a strong shove to force it open—where he grabbed a six-gun and returned to the stairwell just as Bell appeared around the right-angle bend at the landing some twelve steps below. Bell turned to run, the Kid fired, the deputy's body crumpled down the remaining stairs to the ground floor, where he dragged himself outside, mortally wounded. Olinger heard the report of the gun and ran toward the jail, his pistol drawn. As he entered the yard, a voice he recognized—belonging to Gottfried Gauss, a German fellow who boarded at the courthouse—called out from the rear of the building, "Bob, the Kid has killed Bell." In the same moment another voice, also familiar, caught his attention: "Hello, old boy." Olinger looked up, and there, at the second-story window, stood the Kid, smiling and aiming the deputy's own double-barrel shotgun straight at him. "Yes, and he's killed me, too." Scarcely had the words escaped his lips than he was dead on the ground, his right shoulder, breast, and side shredded with buckshot. The Kid went onto the balcony and broke the shotgun across the railing, cursing its owner. "Take it, damn you, you won't follow me any more with that gun."

The events of that day have been told and retold so many times, and figure so prominently into almost every fictional and dramatic treatment, that a brief summary of some of the more prominent versions may be worth the while. The one just provided comes mostly from Garrett's book (though Upson, impeccably genteel when it came to profanity in a book that is from time to time fairly bloody, rendered "damn" as "d—n").[15] As with almost everything else in Garrett's section of *The Authentic Life*, I find no evidence to suggest he endeavored to tell other than the truth as he knew and could piece it together. However, as was not the case with the Kid's death, he was not on the scene—he didn't get back from White Oaks until two days later—so what he had to say was based, like every other account, on hearsay, evidence from the scene, and (one presumes) informed and plausible guesswork. That is the principal reason for so much speculation: the only eyewitnesses to what happened once Olinger left Bell and the Kid alone until the Kid shot Olinger were the Kid himself and Bell, and the Kid never wrote his version down or had it made a matter of record in any form.

Exactly how Billy managed to get the drop on Bell remains the area of greatest uncertainty. The way Walter Burns tells it in *The Saga* is contradicted by evidence. While playing monte, Billy "accidentally" brushed a card to the floor; when Bell bent down to retrieve it, his six-shooter, carelessly wedged under his belt, "projected within reach of the Kid's hand. Leaning across the table, the Kid snatched the weapon. When Bell raised his head, he was looking into the muzzle of his own gun" (244). Though not unique to Burns (e.g., see Coe 218), this would seem to be his or someone else's pure invention, omitting the trip to the privy in its entirety. For the longest time the most widely accepted version has two of Billy's friends leaving a loaded pistol hidden in the privy; the Kid hides it in his clothes until he draws on Bell when they're alone back inside the courthouse. Peckinpah and Rudolph Wurlitzer use this version. Still another, also widely accepted, has the Kid reaching the top of the stairs, where he slipped his hands out of his manacles—because his hands were apparently smaller than his wrists, he could do this easily and often did, laughing in the guards' faces—and coldcocked Bell. Using the chain to swing the full force of the cuffs, he succeeded in cutting two deep gashes into Bell's skull, then grabbed the deputy's gun and shot him as he tried to flee down the stairs. Though Billy was an excellent shot, the bullet that killed Bell, fired in haste, appears to have ricocheted off the wall before going right to left through Bell's body. Robert Utley favors this version, as does Mark Gardner, who points out that forensic tests in 2004 using luminol "revealed substantial blood residue at the top of the courthouse stairs [from] the severe blow Billy delivered to Bell's head." John Meadows's version, which he claimed he got directly from Billy, is a variation of this: Billy gets inside alone, vaults up the stairs in "two or three quick jumps," slips his hands out of his cuffs, waits until Bell catches up to him, then turns and strikes him with both cuffs. The men struggle over the gun, falling to the floor, the Kid wresting the gun away, Bell turning and running, the Kid, still on the floor, shooting him. Neider basically used Meadows through the vaulting up the stairs, then switched to Garrett, eliminating the scuffle at the stairhead.[16]

There is also disagreement whether Olinger said, "Yes, and he's killed me, too," a dispute that has its origin in two short, anonymous letters, purportedly by eyewitnesses or based on what eyewitnesses said, published in the *Santa Fe New Mexican* newspaper on April 30, 1881, just two days after the escape.[17] The first letter, written the day after the escape, refers to "a voice from above that attracted Olinger's attention" as he reached the courthouse, but directly quotes nothing from either man, not even the Kid's "Hello, old boy" (or "Hello, Bob," in other accounts); the only direct quotation is the Kid's curse after he smashes the shotgun, "You damned son of a bitch, you won't corral me with that again." The second letter, written soon after the first, gives the Kid nothing to say before he shoots Olinger, but does directly quote Olinger saying, "Yes and he has killed me too." (This letter is also more detailed in other ways, reporting, for example, that the Kid "expressed himself as being sorry for killing Bell but said he had to do it to make his point.") Those who doubt Olinger ever spoke the dying words attributed to him argue the Kid would never have given the deputy time to say anything. But surely it would not have been out of character for Billy to relish the lethal comeuppance he was about to deliver to the man who tormented him so relentlessly. And why would it occur to an anonymous witness or a mere letter writer—as opposed to a professional journalist looking for a way to juice up a story—to make up something like this? Regardless, what novelist, dramatist, or filmmaker could resist the double irony of the Kid's soft-voiced greeting to the man he's about to kill being answered by the victim's last words that are a confirmation of his own death? Certainly not Neider and certainly not Peckinpah and Wurlitzer. Perhaps it's another instance of printing the legend because it's been so long accepted as fact.

Uncertainty as to whether the Kid emptied both barrels at once into Olinger or one from the window, another moments later from the balcony, is also traceable to these two letters. In the first, since the voice comes from above and the Kid smashes the shotgun across the windowsill, he was clearly inside the building on the second floor at the window when he killed Olinger. The second letter, however, reports only that "a shot was heard" and that Olinger fell dead as he was speaking his last words; but *where* the Kid was standing when he fired is not specified. It isn't until the end of the letter that the smashing of the shotgun is revealed, along with the information that the Kid "had fired upon [Olinger] from the porch, remarking as he did so, 'there you son of a b—— you will never follow me again.'" Both letters place the Kid's curse immediately after he smashes the shotgun, but the second letter locates this event and the firing of the shotgun on the balcony, as opposed to at the window. But inasmuch as this witness is vague as to whether he actually saw the shot that dropped Olinger or only heard it, is he implying that the shot from the balcony was a second shot or is he merely amplifying his description of the first shot? If the latter, then his letter puts the Kid in a different place from where the first letter reports he fired (and quotes a slightly different version of the curse).

There is no ambiguity, however, from Meadows, who locates the Kid at the window and quotes him directly: "I let him have both barrels right in his face and breast." Frederick Nolan, Utley, and Gardner follow Meadows; Garrett and Burns have separate blasts, as do Neider and Peckinpah and Wurlitzer (though in the film both blasts are from the balcony). There is even disagreement whether Olinger's shotgun was filled with eighteen or thirty-six buckshot—that is, nine or eighteen from each barrel—though in an ingenious twist, Peckinpah has Olinger telling the Kid, "I've got my shotgun full of sixteen thin dimes, enough to spread you out like a crazy woman's quilt."[18]

Finally, there was still a *third* anonymous letter, written the next day but not published until two weeks later in a Silver City newspaper, that contains the most detailed report of all. In it the writer says that it "seems" as if the Kid struck Bell both on his head and in back of his ear with the cuffs, breaking his skull and stunning him, then taking his gun. But when Bell unexpectedly recovers from the blows and flees down the stairs, the Kid shoots him, the bullet passing "under Bell's arms and clear through his body." This writer also has the Kid standing at the upstairs window (though, curiously, he misidentifies it as the southeastern one, rather than the northeastern one) and discharging both barrels into Olinger as soon as the deputy enters the gate to the yard beside the courthouse, killing him instantly. After this, the Kid, armed with "two new revolvers, four belts of cartridges, and a new Winchester," holds the entire town hostage from the balcony, threatening "to shoot the first man who started to give any alarm," warning everyone not to approach him too closely, and ordering an old man named Gauss to get him a horse. This goes on for over an hour, during which the Kid somehow manages to break one of the shackles of his leg-irons. He also tells all who are listening that he didn't want to kill Bell but he had to and declares "that he was 'standing pat' against the world": though he would prefer not to, he threatens to kill anyone who tries to interfere with his escape. Just before he comes down from the balcony he smashes Olinger's shotgun over the railing, throwing the pieces at him and saying, "G—d d—n you! You won't follow me with it any longer," then removes his handcuffs and throws them at Bell's body, saying, "G—d d—n you! Take them! I guess you won't put them on me again!" Of the killing of Olinger he later told John Meadows, "I never felt so good in all my life as I did when I pulled trigger and saw Olinger fall to the ground" (Fulton, *Life* 209).

Either before the Kid leaves or while he is riding away, the writer reports being told—though apparently he himself did not hear—that the Kid "made violent threats against those whom he considers have injured him and that he said he did not consider he had been bad heretofore but would let people know what it is to be a bad man." One noteworthy thing that distinguishes this letter from the other two is that while the writer doesn't identify himself by name, he writes in the first person, freely interprets the events, and is unafraid to express his opinion of the participants and the state of affairs. Thus he tells us the Kid rode off with his horse at a walk, "and every act, from beginning to end, seemed to have been planned and executed with the coolest deliberation." He draws attention to the carelessness of the deputies, in particular Olinger, who just two days earlier had "left his revolver loose on the table in front of Kid": the deputy's "over-confidence in himself has been the means of his own destruction, as well as of robbing the gallows of its victim. It is a great misfortune and one that will tell seriously against us. I have about abandoned hope that Lincoln will ever come out of her condition of lawlessness."[19]

Except perhaps for Custer's Last Stand and the Gunfight at the O.K. Corral, Billy the Kid's escape from the Lincoln County Courthouse is the most famous single incident in the history of the Old West, and it is unquestionably the most famous escape. Neider brought something to it that only a gifted novelist can: an interior view of the action that puts us inside the participants' perceptions, emotions, and feelings. Although the novel begins, ends, and proceeds for long stretches from Doc's point of view, Neider, like Melville with Ishmael in *Moby-Dick*, will just as often abandon Doc's voice entirely and slip into what is in effect the third person when he wants to establish a more intimate connection between the reader and characters other than the narrator. He structures the jailbreak from three different points of view, using third person limited for each one. Burns anticipated this in *The Saga*, but Neider's way with it is far more nuanced, sophisticated, and psychologically penetrating.

From the first moment Hendry is led into the Monterey jail—the description suggesting the Lincoln County Courthouse—and is taken upstairs, he at once begins "making himself familiar with it" (25). Why upstairs? We got a special room for you. How many other prisoners? Three. Where're they held? Downstairs. The stairs are steep and not easily negotiated with hand- and leg-irons, but, already laying the groundwork for a plan not yet formulated, the Kid pretends it's harder than it is. Once upstairs he is escorted down the hallway to the last room on the left, along the way methodically taking in everything—the stairs, Dad's office, the layout of the rooms, the contents of his cell, the view of the plaza it affords, anything that might prove handy in making an escape. In the days to come Hendry will start going to the outhouse even when he doesn't have to—he wants the exercise, wants to see what he can learn, but mostly wants to establish a pattern of having to use it several times a day.

In addition to Dad, there are two deputies who guard him. Pablo Patron, a family man with kids, whose wife, Maria Jesús, will bring Hendry his lunches, genuinely likes Hendry. Unlike Bell, Pablo is Mexican and so protective of the position he's earned as deputy in this mostly gringo town that he is especially concerned the Kid doesn't escape on *his* watch. The other deputy, as sadistic as his counterpart in history, is Lon Dedrick, who walks with a swagger and looks like "a traveling arsenal," a pair of six-shooters plus an extra pistol slung over his pommel, and a Winchester rifle and a shotgun. Doc tells us that "he was just a loudmouthed fourflusher and as dangerous out in the open as a kingsnake," but a fellow like that "operated best when a man's back was turned

Earliest existing photograph of the Lincoln County Courthouse, ca. 1886, five years after Billy's escape. There was no exterior staircase to the balcony in 1881.

Stairwell to the second floor: the foreground (*bottom center*) is where the Kid and J. W. Bell struggled before the deputy fled down the stairs in an attempt to get to the landing and cover.

Billy's point of view from the window toward the stone marking the spot where Bob Olinger was standing when the Kid shot him

Olinger's point of view when he looked up after he heard the Kid say, "Hello, old boy"

or when the man was unarmed or shackled" (47). Lon takes great delight in letting the Kid watch him drop the shells into each barrel of his shotgun while goading him to make his play. One morning, when the Kid won't take the bait, Lon cracks him across the face with a pistol.

As the Kid studies Lon's daily routine of taking the three other prisoners to Charley's across the street for their meals, two details strike him: Lon always disappears with his shotgun into the room adjoining the cell; yet moments later, crossing the plaza with the prisoners, he carries no shotgun. Could the room next to his cell be the gun room? He often hears Lon struggling with the door and one day overhears him muttering, "Why don't we get this damn lock fixed? One good shove and that door'll fly open" (56). That's all he needs to hear. One day smoking a cigarette at the window, looking out over the plaza, thinking about what it might feel like to be hanged, it suddenly

> was as though he were not standing at the window with the people watch-
> ing him, as though he were not in the room at all but out in the back yard,
> coming out of the outhouse and running into the house and up the stairs
> and ramming his shoulder against the gunroom door, and he knew in a
> flash what his chance was and knew exactly what he must do and knew
> he would do it tomorrow around noon while Lon was at Charley's and he
> was glad he could make his play. He began to laugh, his face turning very
> red, and the people on the plaza watched him and glanced at each other,
> wondering if he had gone loco. (64–65)

But coming up with a plan is one thing, the carrying out of it quite another. Obviously Hendry cannot practice or rehearse it. Yet he rehearses it all the same *in his head*, reviewing every possible contingency, going over every detail again and again: the back door swung inward—that was good—but the next door might have a chair in front of it—be sure not to catch the shackles on the knob—be careful of any bulging planks or knots he might trip over—the second door was a problem—go over it many times to prepare for it—do everything slowly, make no mistakes—let Pablo and Lon make the mistakes—fourteen stairs—who'd want to build stairs that steep?—but they had a solid banister—he had tested it several times, pretending he had to support himself—using the banister he could vault up the first four in one motion—another leap gets him to eight and then a pair of threes gets him to the top—grip, vault, pause, grip vault pause.

When he gets to the gun room and the defective lock and the realization that then it will be "up to him to know what to do," he relaxes for a moment of rumination:

> They were damn fools not to have shot him in the back and gotten it
> over with. Lon was right. If you were going to kill a fellow it was no good
> playing with him, because the first you knew he might turn around and

kill you. He had gotten just one glimpse inside that gunroom but it was enough. . . . Lon had seen him and said and done nothing and Pablo had said and done nothing too. It was funny how people, who usually claimed they took good care of their lives and put a pretty high price on them, got careless about the crucial things. (67–68)

And then it's back to practicing—the great ones all practiced—and thinking everything through for yet the umpteenth time: ram your shoulder against the door—if it doesn't give, ram it again—keep ramming it even if you hear Pablo coming, even if he shoves his gun into your back—he'll likely just club you with it, because they all want to see you hang—when the door gives way, leave it open—if you close it he can ambush you or pin you down inside—the idea is surprise him and use him as a shield—remember, take plenty of time because "once you've got that door open you've got the town at your feet and so there's nothing to hurry about after that."

My condensation and paraphrase cannot do justice to either the vigor or the energy of Neider's prose in these passages, the way in the headlong rhythms, the cascading phrases, the repeating "ands," the style so adjusts its language as to become the embodiment of what it indicates: Hendry's sensibility, the way his mind works, the processes of his thinking, how he disciplines himself, concentrating intensely on the task at hand, eliminating all distractions, and visualizing the plan so vividly as to make it seem as if he is virtually willing it into existence, like a reality projected into a future that is merely waiting for time to catch up to it.

Come the next day and the trip to the outhouse, Hendry notices Pablo's eyes and

how he had seen nothing in them, which was unlike Pablo. And then he knew that if he made his play he would not live to reach the corridor. Pablo would not hesitate. He would draw fast, shoot straight and to kill. And the Kid knew this so surely that he walked into the adobe and up the stairs and into his cell.

He would have to make his play tomorrow then or not at all. He must be cold in his mind tomorrow and around his heart he must be dead. Cold the way he was cold when someone had the drop on him. Yet he must not freeze up so that his muscles were slow. He hoped Pablo would be sensible when the time came. (72)

We see here how surely Hendry reads people, and we are also given an early clue that anticipates how matter-of-factly Hendry will take the death of Harvey French and that helps us understand why he is able to concentrate so intensely on his card game while Harvey's life slips away. It's the coldness that we first glimpse here: how many times can a man, any man, harden himself into this kind of coldness before the coldness sets in for good? Then, too, there's the importance the Kid places on luck. Luck is the closest thing Hendry has to a belief system. For those who believe in it, luck is of course another name for fate—it's the flip side of fate. "The Kid always used to say," Doc tells us, "that if a bullet has your number on it there is nothing you can do to dodge it" (186).

In one of the more disturbing subplots, Bob Emory advises, not without reason, against going to Mexico right after the jailbreak because "Dad'll be telegraphing to all that country below."[20] All the Kid can ask is, "You aiming to jinx me, Bob?" This becomes such a fixation of Hendry's all the way down to Mexico, in Mexico, and all the way back that even though Doc doesn't like Emory, he does his best to warn him to clear out if he wants to stay alive. After Harvey is killed and Modesto is killed, Hendry, incapable of recognizing his own implication in their deaths, can only think, "That Bob," and Doc "knew right then that Bob was done for, that the Kid was blaming Bob for jinxing his luck." The Kid tells Bob there are some cattle to rustle—Doc can read the Kid well enough to use shoulder pain as an excuse to stay behind—and sometime later he returns "alone, without any steers, and I knew that he had killed Bob. I made up my mind to say nothing about it." By this time, only days before his own death, the Kid's luck, which has been explicitly associated with his youth, specifically the *vitality* of his youth, had, like his youth, long since begun running down. But the morning of the jailbreak, he still has some of both left.

It begins with card games that are mind games: the Kid and Pablo "played draw poker and the Kid kept steadily but deliberately losing, winning only a hand now and then and with poor pots."[21] He even lets Pablo win his forty-four. "The cards are speaking to me today," says Pablo. "Yesterday too," agrees the Kid. And Pablo, "Today better." And the Kid, "It's not in the cards for me." And so Pablo begins to feel flush with exactly the overconfidence Hendry wants him to feel, knowing that the look he saw in Pablo's eyes yesterday, the killer look of resolve, would not be there today. "I've come a long way," Pablo thinks.

> Me a poor Mexican kid. The cards are speaking to me today. Pablo you got yourself a winning streak. Don't change your luck boy.
> "Hombre it looks as if I'm finished," said the Kid. . . . "I think I'll go to the outhouse."
> "Sure," Pablo said.

On the return, the first thing Pablo notices is that the Kid, several paces ahead of him, trips on a rock and stumbles, falling halfway through the doorway, then going out of sight. (Later, when the point of view shifts back to the Kid, we discover the stumble was deliberate, to fool Pablo and keep him from reacting and chasing after him too quickly, thus buying himself more time to get to the gun room.) The deputy isn't frightened—where could the Kid go?— maybe it was even a little joke. He draws his gun and moves forward, then trips just like the Kid. On his hands and knees Pablo suddenly remembers the broken lock and that's all he needs for his mind to start racing—what if the Kid knew just a good shove would force it open?—the Kid with a gun was a terrible thing—he could shoot your eye out at many paces—Pablo fumbles with the exterior door, hands shaking—then the other door and the sound of the leg-irons clanking up the stairs—what have I got to worry about?—I'll catch him before he gets there—then a body throwing itself against the gun room door and Pablo goes "cold from his groin to his feet, running as he was down the corridor to the stairhead"—get out of here—call Lon (that slob, eating)—burn the jail down—Maria Jesús would say, this is white man's business you're only a greaser get out of this pronto—how did he know about that door?—I told Lon we ought to fix it, I told Dad we ought to fix it—damn them they ought to know it's bad luck not to fix a lock like that—another body slam and the door gives way—if the Kid escapes he was through in this town— what would Maria Jesús say, what would his kids say?—better stop him and keep it a secret that it happened at all.

Once more paraphrase is a poor substitute but is perhaps sufficient to illustrate how Neider again uses style to adjust language so as to embody the way a man thinks, this time a very different man. The Kid is sharp, undistracted, and tunnel visioned. He has gone over everything in the minutest of detail; knowing his ultimate goal frees him to narrow his focus on each step necessary to reach it, one step at a time, the order in which they must be followed scrupulously observed and carried out, no mistakes, let Pablo and Lon make the mistakes. Pablo's mind, by contrast, is such a confused welter of scattered thoughts, conflicting responsibilities, cross-purposes, finger-pointing, recriminations, decisions checked by alternatives, then alternatives to the alternatives, the ego that worries even in a crisis where his life is at stake what others will think, the sheer bowel-loosening terror. He is finished long before he reaches the top of the stairs, where, facing a revolver pointed directly at his stomach and the Kid telling him, "Drop it," he freezes. Though he had drawn his gun before he reentered the jail, Pablo rushed up the stairs without thinking to raise it and now, facing the Kid, he's too paralyzed to move. Then his mind starts to racing again and, seduced by the luck the Kid has tricked him into believing has fallen his way, he thinks how lucky he has been so far that day, and, fatally, turns, descending the fourteen stairs two at time, toward the landing where they veer abruptly around the corner and the wall that will shield him, and then "his face struck the stairs and his legs windmilled in a clatter and he fell into the vestibule and against the jamb of the front door, striking the jamb so hard that the Kid felt the vibration in the stairway."

This is followed by the first of three devastatingly intimate scenes of bloody death from shooting which take us right through the moment of expiration. There is no hoary cliché about Pablo's whole life passing before him. Instead, in marked contrast to the confusion of the previous few minutes, Pablo's mind now exhibits an almost radiant clarity, his thoughts orderly, logical, purposive, and he has a destination: he just wants to get outside into the golden light, crawling toward his house and his family. The light looks as if it's evening but that doesn't make any sense because it's around noon and there ought to be plenty of light on the plaza. Then he notices the stack of lumber for the gallows, and it strikes Pablo it's a good idea they "should use some of the lumber to make my coffin, and it seemed to him important that he tell somebody that" and resumes crawling until he suddenly sees "the mission and the altar and the sun blinded him and, sobbing, 'Dios me perdone!' he died."

The Kid knows his shot killed Pablo, but "Pablo oughtn't have run. He ought to have controlled his legs. That little lack of control could cost a man his life. That was why it was important to be ice-cold in your mind and heart when the bad moments came." But this was no time for regrets, now it was time to think of Lon, whom by now he knew "inside out," knew Lon would figure he would avoid the plaza and escape out the back, and so Lon would come around the side of the building where the gun room was, where the Kid would be waiting with "Lon Dedrick's sweet English shotgun." As the themes of luck and fate are brought back in, a new one is introduced: the Kid is revealed to be something of an artist of killing, with an almost formal aesthetics about how to extract the maximum pleasure from it, the form determined, as with so much else in his life, by fate in the form of the cards. "He could kill Lon with one of the Winchesters or even the fortyfive he killed Pablo with, but that was not in the cards," he thinks, "the cards said he must kill him with his own sweet English shotgun."

> He could kill him with a barrelful so that Lon would never know what hit him but that was not the way it was going to be. It was important to let Lon know who killed him and how. Otherwise the fun was gone out of it. There were many ways to kill a man but this was the sweetest. You had to let him know the truth of what happened. You had to give him that last moment of truth before you killed him.

Which he does, but not before one final taunt, "Hi, Lon," and at last the sweet satisfying drink of the fear he takes from the deputy's eyes. As Lon staggers back, crying, "He's killed me too," the Kid pulls the trigger.

This would be an effective place to end the chapter, but Neider knew that once he committed to the Kid's point of view and to Pablo's point of view, storytelling logic required we experience the events through the eyes of one more participant. Lon is basking in the pleasure of the meal he's just eaten, enjoying his coffee, when he hears the shot from the jail. "Shit! That greaser's killed him!" But rushing across he is stopped by "the peculiar stillness of the plaza," broken by someone yelling, "The Kid's killed Patron." By this time Lon is under the gun room window and he hears the voice he has come to know all too well. "He knew from that moment that he was dead and he wished with all his life that he could do it over again, the coming out of Charley's and the crossing of the plaza, for he knew he had made a mortal mistake."

Some reviewers criticized Neider for being too graphically violent. But death by violence, mostly by shooting, saturates the world of this novel, as it did also the years that Billy rode through the New Mexico Territory, where the homicide rate climbed forty-seven times higher than the national average.[22] "Violence was almost a way of life on the frontier," Neider wrote. But fidelity to history wasn't his only motivation; he was also reacting to the way "violence and death are cheapened in the dime novel accounts of Billy the Kid's life, and of the life of other western badmen. I tried to undercut this tradition by portraying death as hard, wrenching, even terrible."[23] The killing of Lon, the most extended passage of really graphic violence, is for at least two reasons as far from gratuitous as it is possible to get. Lon's is the killing that Hendry savors the most. The passage is not from the Kid's point of view, but because we know he is there, looking directly at Lon, it functions as the resolution of the abrupt unresolved ending of the preceding section: "The Kid pulled the trigger of one barrel." The other reason is that Lon, a cruel, violent man who doesn't think much, lives totally at the level of his lower self (if it's even possible to speak of any higher self in him). He would be the least likely of the three to react thoughtfully or in any way spiritually to death. It makes sense that his first thought upon hearing the Kid's voice and knowing he is already in effect dead is self-recrimination: he's been outwitted, outmaneuvered, out*played*. As he "fell to his knees and pitched face first into a pool of his own blood," he sees himself "out on the sea in a skiff in a high wind under the overhanging rocks," but then the skiff "filled with water and the water got into his lungs" and he gasps for breath. Another flash raises him to a great distance from which he can see himself getting shot in the plaza and "the bitterness of it was that the Kid had outlived him": "I'm killed, the son of a bitch has killed me, they'll all be saying he killed me." He urinates again "and at last, drooling blood and pumping blood from his nostrils, he stopped dreaming and it was over." The Kid walks up to him, aims, and blows part of his head off with the load from the other barrel, then breaks the gun and throws the pieces onto Lon's body, saying, "Here Lon here's your shotgun." But he is no longer smiling: "It's a fact he hated that Lon Dedrick as much as he had hated any man."

Luck, fate, violence, and death are all enmeshed in this novel with the themes of youth, loss of youth, aging, and decline. Hendry's luck is the luck of the young, his skills the skills of the young, his pleasures the pleasures of the young, his follies the follies of the young. Although just twenty-five—four years older than Billy the Kid when he was killed—Hendry is already feeling the ravages of a life of hard riding and hard drinking. Although Neider surely knew that the historical model of his character rarely consumed alcohol of any sort and was not in the least morbid or brooding,[24] the story he wanted to tell was that of a gunfighter just past his prime, at the *beginning* of his decline. Scant pages into the story Doc tells us about a new kid—an up-and-coming gunfighter, just "nineteen, fresh, very fast, with several killings to his credit," who is threatening to finish Hendry off—and in passing mentions that "Hendry was running down hill." The new kid turns out to be "a bum who had a streak of luck and he never got a chance to be killed by the Kid" (11–12). But before Doc has finished relating all this in a passage that occupies only a page, he has made three more references to how Hendry "was feeling old," how it was true he "was now rolling down hill," "how tired and rundown" he was (it's a nice touch that in the space of a paragraph the decline is accelerated as "running" becomes "rolling," with its suggestion of loss of volition).

As these references accumulate, recurring with greater and greater frequency, they begin to take on the character of a low but insistent drone that builds with increasing intensity throughout the entire narrative, while Doc applies the word "tired" to the Kid so often it functions like a fixed epithet. Hendry is drinking so much that, deprived of alcohol in jail, his hands tremble when he lights a cigarette. When he is finally reunited with Nika, who is also prematurely aging, feeling old and tired and exhausted, she notices how raw his face had become, his eyes bloodshot, the brittleness in his gestures, and "the grime" that "had settled into the hairline creases of his neck"—her Hendry who "had always been a clean fellow, he had always bathed whenever he could and had liked to use lots of soap." Nika knows in her bones "he would not live to reach his next birthday" and she does not want to be there at the end.[25] One night, following the afternoon when Bob Emory was killed, Doc awakens to find the Kid pointing a gun at him. Too terrified to move, Doc soon realizes that the Kid's *"not all there,"* that his "attention was somewhere else, somewhere he himself didn't know." Finally, Doc, who's been worried the Kid might find out that once he too had slept with Nika, says, "Go on. Get it over with." This snaps the Kid out of it, and he sits in a chair and offers Doc the gun, "butt first, meaning for me to shoot him. I shook my head to say I wouldn't. He began to sob."

The Kid has endured many losses—his mother, Dad, Nika, Modesto, Bob, most of his old gang, and he's facing many more—paramount among them perhaps the one that looms before him: a price now on his head, he will have to leave Northern California, where he feels so much at home. Some of the losses are his fault, some the fault of others. But I do not believe Neider means for us to think of them as explanations for the Kid's decline. At most, they intensify or hasten it, as when, regarding the Kid from a distance when he is informed of the death of Modesto, Doc notices that

> his face looked tired and I can see it now, the weariness that came into it,
> into the eyes and under the eyes and around the nose, the taut weariness
> of luck going sour, and I reckon from that moment on things were never

the same for him, it was that moment that really began the rolling down-hill which ended as it could only end, in his own untimely and mysterious death. (171–72)

There is very little discernible capacity for regret in Hendry's character and almost none for guilt. If Neider really has succeeded in his aim of making Hendry a tragic figure, then the Kid's tragedy inheres less in his character as such than in his literal flesh and blood: his body simply can no longer take the punishment he continues dishing out to it, especially from the drinking. Doc makes a point of telling us the Kid favors rotgut whiskey flavored with coffee and cut with pepper to give it spice. But drinking isn't the only stress. In a revealing passage late in the book Doc describes what it is like to live on the run under the constant threat of death:

> Whenever we used to sit down to a meal it was never side by side but around the fire facing each other. That was the way we always ate or sat around, so we could see behind each other's backs and guard against being surprised. When we ate, our rifles were always across our laps or lying handy close by. It was always like that. Eating is very dangerous when you are being hunted.
>
> In the old days it had been fun to live like that, but now we were very tired. The Kid looked so tired I was greatly surprised. The life of always being hunted was really changing him. And changing me too, I had no doubt. (179)

In stories about Billy the Kid a common theme seems to be choice: the Kid chooses not to change his ways and this represents his decision to live free rather than give in to the forces of regimentation and conformity that are moving in to make the West safe for churches, schools, and businesses. But Hendry seems no more able to change his ways than he can change the color of his skin, and conscious choice as such has little to do with it. For one thing, he is imprisoned by the rigidity and narrowness of his code, a code built around getting even, shooting first so that you can live and shoot another day, and a belief in luck and fate as final determinants of how and why things happen. It is a code that in a very real sense displaces personal responsibility onto a simplistic notion of fate. Nika cannot understand how Hendry can feel no sorrow for Harvey French and, grief stricken to the point of hysteria, she holds him responsible for Modesto's death, which in a sense he was. The Dedricks are part of the same culture as he: a culture of revenge killing that is just as happy to kill a culprit's friends in revenge as kill the culprit himself. But standing there, tears in his eyes as he looks at Modesto's mutilated body, all the Kid can think to do is stifle his tears and any responsibility that might be welling up by blaming the death of Modesto, and Harvey too, on Bob, who he believes has jinxed everyone's luck.

Just as he is unable to go beyond the limitations of his thinking, Hendry is similarly helpless to resist the pull of inertia in the life he is living. His decision to return to Monterey may look like choice, but it has all the earmarks of a species of denial because what he does not realize is that he has no power to halt the one change that inevitably forces all the other changes: his own receding youth and advancing age. The self-destructive drinking is probably something he does at least in part so that he won't have to face this unalterable, implacable fact. When he is at last killed, he doesn't get the final clarity of Pablo crawling toward the mission and God or even the lesser realization by Lon that he's been outplayed. When Dad's gun flashed, Doc figures the Kid "probably never knew what hit him" (190). As Hendry backed, unknowing, into that dark room where death awaited him, his last thoughts were of how tired he was of everything and about how he will have to leave the Monterey he loves so much with its meadows and sea and sand and fog and go down to Old Mex which he doesn't like at all and "then the red flame sprang at him and the fortyfive ball crashed into his chest," and he "heard the roar of the sea and found himself face down on the dirt floor, wondering how he got there, and he was gasping and gurgling, and he said faintly, 'Mother. Help me. I'm strangling.'"

Some ironies should not escape notice here: the image of strangling reminds us that just a month or so earlier the Kid had escaped a death by hanging only to die strangling all the same, now on his own blood and his inability to take in any air, which we might recall is not dissimilar to the way Lon Dedrick died, one of Lon's last thoughts also to ask his mother for help ("Ma you fix it like you always do" [86]). Of course, the crucial difference is that, unlike Lon and even the rest of the gang, including Doc himself, the Kid never believed he would live forever, so "was never surprised about getting killed, despite the way it happened." Even when he was younger the Kid was possessed of a fatalism that grasped his own destiny: he "knew he was going to get killed and was waiting for it, . . . the day and the hour, and would have been disappointed if it hadn't come" (9). But it cannot be accidental that Neider links the crude, gross, disgusting Lon and the beautiful, elegant, gentlemanly gunfighter as killers who, for all their differences in style, meet more or less the same violent end, both choking in their own blood. A further irony is that the Kid is denied the opportunity to appreciate, as it were, the manner of his own death, which, like Lon's, comes from the gun of a man he too could not stop himself from pushing.

Ironies like this permeate the novel, nowhere more so than in the way Neider uses the land and the sea and the wildlife. The blurb on the dust jacket of the original hardcover publication, "A Novel of Old California," should have been the subtitle.[26] There are numerous lovely, lyrical passages that evoke the beauty of Northern California: the very blue sea, the salt air that you could taste, a "good country in those days, full of eagles and hawks," a line of cormorants on a black rock, the mossy trees, "the long snaking brown lines out near the kelp beds," "the blowing water," "the crazy cypresses that the poet said look like witch's fingers, pale gray, with blue shadows."[27] The place Neider calls "Punta del Diablo," the settlement that is the equivalent to Fort Sumner, is Point Lobos, now a nature preserve, three miles south of Carmel, which the landscape artist Francis McComas once called the greatest meeting of land and water in the world. Yet here it is also an area so remote and "so craggy and windbeaten and fogblown" that only "the very poor would have thought of living there." And because of the fog, which rolls in almost daily, it is made to feel, like so much else in the novel, dark, airless, and claustrophobic.[28] The fog "made me feel fenced in," says Doc, "and after a couple of days I'd get so jumpy I'd want to shoot the first thing that crossed my path." Doc will conjure a particularly beautiful scene only to foul it with an image of ugliness and stench.

> There were some pretty spots around there—meadows full of paintbrush, coves full of shallow canyons and glassy pools, the thunder of the surf, the starfish lying steaming on the rocks, the big anemones and the big purple urchins, locoweed, sagebrush, buckwheat, lavagray beaches, bright black and glassgreen water—and all the time the smell of fish and seawolves and rotting kelp and fog and birddroppings, rolling in on the seawinds under the burning light. (118)

Neider's purpose here, it seems to me, is not to undercut the one with the other but to force us to experience them both equally and at the same time.

This opposition, between beauty suggestive of springlike vitality and rot seen as decay due to aging, is developed throughout the entire novel. There is almost no mention of Hendry's youthful beauty, his physical prowess, in the old days—the old days referring to between, say, three to seven or eight years before the main events of the story—that is not accompanied by Doc noticing how the Kid has declined. This antithesis is mirrored in other antitheses. Here is Doc recalling the years before Hendry was caught and his old gang broken up and scattered:

> We were a good bunch all right. Most of our names you've never heard of. We got killed before we made a name for ourselves or we got tired of being hunted and took off for good. But a lot of us were good boys and you could have fun with us all right.
>
> We'd go to cockfights and to the bearbaiting fights in the hills and we'd drink and gamble and whore around and live on the fat of the land. When things were quiet we could always shoot up a town or pick a fight with someone we wanted to kill or start a stampede or a small war. (9)

The ironies come close to being risible here: "good boys" whose "fun" consists in shooting, fighting, killing, starting a stampede or a small war. Neider has no problem with elements of the Kid that are romantic—he knows they are inextricably woven into the fabric of the Billy the Kid legend and cannot be ironed out. But what he can do is never allow us to forget that the Kid, for all his personal appeal and physical attractiveness, is fundamentally a killer.

There is one especially chilling scene that speaks to this very point. The Kid, Doc, and the others go to a dance where an old forty-niner named Murphy starts goosing the girl Hendry is dancing with. This frightens the girl and Hendry tells him to beat it. But Murphy, almost certainly drunk, comes back, does it again, and is then escorted outside by some of the other men. Presumably it could have ended there, as there is no indication the old coot will return. But there's a look in the Kid's "cold slatecolored eyes" that Doc has seen before, "and I knew he wanted to see the corpse of that old bird. Sure enough, about five minutes later he excused himself and went outside, caught up with Murphy in a potato field, cracked down on him and shot him through the chest without a word."[29] Without a word, maybe, but Doc, who had followed Hendry outside, is sure to let us know that when the dying man looked up as if trying to explain that it had all been a mistake, what he saw was "the Kid smiling at him." The Kid's only response was, "Let's get going. That fellow has spoiled my fun." Of all the killings in the novel, this one is without question the cruelest, the meanest, the most senseless and unnecessary, and it is also the most revealing. Early in the story Doc remarks that Lon Dedrick "killed a couple of men but I think it was always without giving them a fair break," and tells us about the time Lon offered to shake the hand of a friend who had committed some offense, then "caught the fellow's right hand, jerked out his gun and killed him."[30] But if Doc fails to question (he certainly doesn't seem to notice) whether there is any meaningful distinction between that and the way the Kid kills Murphy, who wasn't even armed, this doesn't mean we should. The killing of Murphy is Neider's slap in the face of every romanticized treatment of Billy the Kid and other gunslingers. It's almost as if he were saying, I'll give you your romantic outlaw, but you have to take him all or not at all: the young man who enjoys killing *and* the young man who is depleted, dissipated, and in premature decline. None will be allowed to exist in the absence of the others.

It is not difficult to see the parallels here with Peckinpah's depictions of gunslingers and outlaws in the Old West, notably the combination of romance and irony (a term I prefer, after Northrop Frye, to "realism") and the complexity of response to his outlaw heroes which he has always insisted upon. There are other parallels too.[31] Peckinpah was so widely read during his college days and early career that he developed a pretty sophisticated sense of the importance of point of view, how it could be used to shape a story or drama and condition our responses to it. We know by his own admission that he attended the Hemingway academy, where he must have schooled himself quite a lot in how point of view can be used subjectively and how to highlight detail without disrupting the line or flow of a narrative. So did Neider. In rereading *The Authentic Death of Hendry Jones*, in particular those sequences where the Kid is taking in and weighing every detail that might be used to help him formulate a plan of escape, I found myself thinking of how, in *The Wild Bunch*, after Pike Bishop dismounts across from the railroad office, he surreptitiously surveys the surrounding rooftops before giving his men the order to advance—soon enough it's the inept bounty hunters allowing their rifles to stick up over the rooftops that alerts the Bunch they've walked into an ambush. And when the Bunch first enter Agua Verde, Pike pauses to survey the courtyard, the shots framed strictly from his point of view, so that without recourse to a line of dialogue, Peckinpah makes the very tissue of his narrative embody what it is like to live a life on the run, always having to take notice of avenues of escape or places with no exits. No one is his superior, few his equal, when it comes to making you feel what it must be like to live from one moment to the next in the world of his films. And no filmmaker ever made us experience the exhilaration and the mania of killing as profoundly, passionately, and terrifyingly as this one did at the end of *The Wild Bunch*.

The theme of the aging Westerner living beyond his time—whether cowboy, sheriff, outlaw, gunfighter, or rodeo man—is as old as the West itself (its beginnings can be found in the Leatherstocking novels of James Fenimore Cooper). Four of Peckinpah's best films are magnificent treatments of it: *Ride the High Country, The Wild Bunch, Junior Bonner*, and *Pat Garrett and Billy the Kid*.[32] With his Western background, it's pretty certain he would have found this theme without Neider. But no truly original artists, those who develop a worldview uniquely their own, need other artists to discover their vision. What influences mostly do is help them speed up the process, educate them, and, perhaps most important, *inspire* them. You do not quote, Emerson said, but to recognize your own. There is no doubt *The Authentic Death of Hendry Jones* was an important influence that inspired Peckinpah, helped him crystallize some of his thinking, and pointed him toward a few storytelling methods and techniques that he would eventually develop into a filmmaking style of unparalleled dramatic, lyric, and expressive power. But all that was still a while down the road. In the meantime, he was handed an opportunity he always felt privileged to have received: a job turning Neider's novel into a screenplay.

Sam Peckinpah, ca. 1957, the year he wrote his *Hendry Jones* screenplay

CHAPTER FOUR

Peckinpah's Adaptation

Of all Peckinpah's gifts, perhaps least sufficiently recognized are those for adapting plays and works of literature to film. In college he once prepared a one-hour version of Tennessee Williams's *The Glass Menagerie*, the cutting and condensing of which he said taught him more about writing than almost anything else he ever did. In 1953, for his master's thesis in theater arts at the University of Southern California, he staged a performance of Williams's *Portrait of a Madonna* that he also filmed with the then-new three-camera method, which was gaining wide use in television at the time. His television adaptation of Katherine Anne Porter's short novel *Noon Wine* is masterly, his solution at one point to the perennial problem of how to translate the effect of a literary point of view into a filmic equivalent brilliant. *The Siege of Trencher's Farm*, which became *Straw Dogs*, hardly qualifies as good literature, but the differences between the novel and the film—and the obvious superiority of the latter as regards complexity of theme, depth of character, and sheer sensibility—are highly instructive. His adaptation of *The Authentic Death of Hendry Jones* was only his second feature-length screenplay, yet, as David Weddle has written, it "demonstrates a remarkable leap in craftsmanship" over the screenplay he had completed just six months earlier.[1]

That earlier screenplay was also an adaptation of a novel, Hoffman Birney's *The Dice of God*, based on Custer's Last Stand and years later made as *The Glory Guys* (1965), directed by Arnold Laven, for whom Peckinpah wrote the pilot of *The Rifleman*. Much of the harsh realism of Peckinpah's screenplay was either watered down or eliminated in favor of a lot of clichés of "masculine" drinking and brawling and a rather banal love triangle; in retrospect, from what one can tell of the script *as shot*, it looks like a practice run for the tougher, grittier, more hard-edged *Major Dundee* (e.g., Senta Berger plays a classy widow who is virtually the same character in both films, and both male leads vie for her attentions). Though Peckinpah can hardly be held responsible for the film, once the action leaves the fort for the plains, *The Glory Guys* improves markedly and begins to suggest what he might have done with it, including a downbeat, anticlimactic ending that is the most effective thing about it. What attention the film got from serious critics was because of Peckinpah's screenplay, Kenneth Tynan writing, "Peckinpah's shadow is better than most other Westerns' substance."[2]

To my knowledge Peckinpah wrote only two complete drafts of his screenplay for *The Authentic Death of Hendry Jones*. One is dated October 3, 1957, the other a month later, November 11. The earlier one is thirteen pages longer and is almost certainly the draft Peckinpah first showed the producer Frank Rosenberg to get his notes before a proper first draft was submitted to Marlon Brando. As the November version is the one given to Brando, my references, unless otherwise noted, are to it (when I've cited scene number, I've not also cited page number).[3] The differences between the two are not great: a couple of scenes are eliminated, others tightened, nothing to affect the overall meaning of the story, though in two instances our sense of individual characters is altered.

One striking aspect of the *Hendry Jones* screenplay is the extent to which, even this early in Peckinpah's career, the born director is palpably present. Most screenplays contain some description of setting and occasional instructions as to how a line should be read, where the camera is to be placed, and how it is to move. But very few display anything like the detail, extent, and sheer number of these as this one does (or several of Peckinpah's others, for that matter). His visual style and technique have always been in some important respects suggestive of those of an old-fashioned novelist (Dickens was a particular favorite), delighting in the details, textures, and activities of a world and bringing them to life on screen. Here is the introduction to the first scene in old Monterey, which, in order to give something of the flavor of what it is like to read screenplays, is reproduced in a typewriter font similar to the one Peckinpah's typist used. Film industry professionals have become so accustomed to the look of this font and format that they are still in use today, even though screenplays, generated on computers for well over a quarter of a century now, have long been able to use any other font.

```
31. EXT. MONTEREY - FULL SHOT (DAY)

     Monterey in the 80's still retained enough of its
     shipping to give it the excitement of a port. The
     architecture, like the population, is a polyglot
     combination -- whitewashed adobe haciendas, brown
     adobe huts, frame false fronts, brick walls, board-
     walks, whalebone walks, cobbled streets, dusty
```

```
streets, bouganvilla, ivy, fuchsias, pepper trees
and willows, geraniums -- a friendly and still vital
town.

Hendry rides into the outskirts of the city, CAMERA
MOVING -- through a cluster of unpainted adobe huts,
scattered with hangdog looking dogs, vendors, carts,
pot-bellied, jaybird-naked children, mujeras, sleepy
senores, and now and then a black-eyed senorita. As
he rides past, most turn to smile broadly, a few
calling out soft greetings which Hendry answers with
a grin and a wave of the hand.
```

QUICK DISSOLVE TO:

32. EXT. MONTEREY - FULL SHOT - PLAZA -(DAY)

```
The plaza is filled with playing children, shopkeep-
ers, exOhio valley farmers and their wives, Yankee
businessmen in high collars, teamsters, New England
whaling crews, Chinese abalone driers and fisher-
men visiting the stores and shops that are filled
with Chinese teakwood tables, Japanese tortoise
shell bowls, English iron stone china, shawls, lace,
zapatas, linens, gunpowder -- and the open air mar-
kets, cantinas, restaurants, saloons that surround
the square. A sleepy town, full of slow business,
easy pleasure and occasional quick violence. In this
predominantly Anglo section of town, Hendry elicits
nothing more than casual interest as he crosses the
plaza. Then, spotting the jail, he rides toward it.
```

No production designer, set decorator, costume designer, or property master
would have any doubt what the director wants here. Nor would any camera-
man fail to realize that tracks will have to be built and that he or she will
need to prepare to shoot a moving point of view as if from horseback. Notice
also how carefully Peckinpah establishes the divisions between the Anglo
and Mexican cultures and their differing relationships to Hendry, divisions
important to the background of the story. (Later, when Hendry is captured
and escorted back in wrist- and leg-irons, the screenplay calls for the Anglos
to be screaming for a hanging while the Mexicans are "grim and quiet, staying
in the dark shadows" [50].) Notice further how the setting is revealed through
Hendry as he rides into town, much as Starbuck is revealed through Pike
Bishop in *The Wild Bunch* or Coarsegold through Steve Judd and Gil Westrum

in *Ride the High Country*. Already Peckinpah seemed to have a firm grasp of how point of view could serve multiple purposes simultaneously: reveal character, establish a scene, open up a society and a set of social relationships, and plunge viewers immediately into a more physical experience of the world within the film.

Neider's novel, although beautifully realized, is far from an obvious candidate for a film. Despite its grit, hard grain, and violence, it's an essentially ruminative and reflective piece told in the first person; there's a lot of time shifting, relatively little dialogue, not all that many scenes thusly defined, and only one big action sequence plus a few smaller ones. Once Peckinpah sat down and started working on it, he must have discovered that for all its effectiveness as narrative, it isn't very dramatic, being neither plot nor incident driven as such (the long sequence in the Monterey jail and a few others conspicuous exceptions). He must also have noticed that except for those places where Neider drops Doc's voice entirely to put us inside the mind of another character or the places where he does write out scenes, we always experience the characters at one remove, that is, through Doc, so they don't quite fully exist in their own right. Moreover, they are all constellated around the title character because he is the object of Doc's fixation. These things are not flaws, merely the consequence of how Neider chose to tell the story; to put it another way, that distance from the past, the impression of being brought close to it yet prevented from directly experiencing it, is part of the effect and meaning of the novel. But in a film, even if the first-person narrator were retained, the characters and the settings would still exist to a large extent outside the narrator's frame of reference, the effect of their being distilled through a single consciousness impossible to achieve with anything approaching the restrictiveness and precision of prose.

Peckinpah's solution was simple and expedient: he retained Doc as narrator in voice-over, but only to establish a temporal perspective on the story, to sound the theme of how history is falsified or idealized through lies, half-truths, exaggeration, gossip, and hearsay into folklore and legend, and to get the film started by setting a scene for Hendry's entrance. The screenplay opens with Doc an old man camping alone, presumably on a hunting or fishing trip. Even though this scene contains no dialogue, occupies only a page, and would be over in scarcely a minute's worth of screen time, Peckinpah describes in great detail Doc's campsite, the surrounding California mountains, and the old Doc himself, whose voice-over begins, as he does in the novel, with the tourists who visit Hendry Jones's grave and "debate whether his bones are there or not," about how you can buy a hundred guns claiming to be his (Peckinpah will develop this in a comic scene he added later), and "run into four or five old-timers claiming to be the Kid himself" (1). Then Doc immediately shifts to the subject of how good a gunfighter the Kid was. The words again come from Neider, but are here front-loaded from later in the book: "the men who judged those things knew what they were talking about, and they decided that Hendry was the greatest gunfighter alive at the time of his death—and one of the greatest ever." From there Doc launches into the first time he met the Kid as the image dissolves to another campfire where Hendry and his two partners come across a much younger Doc, then a bandit and gunfighter with a reputation of his own, though nothing comparable to the Kid's, and we're off and running. We will not hear from Doc as narrator again until page 48, where Peckinpah brings his voice-over back briefly (though with no corresponding visual return to the old Doc at his campsite) to provide some exposition and ease the transition from the Kid's capture to his trial and incarceration. And that's the last we hear ever from Doc as narrator. Like Neider, Peckinpah leaves the "frame" open.[4]

Once he addressed the issue of the narrator, Peckinpah turned to the structure and the characters. The novel divides into three parts: (1) the incarceration and the jailbreak; (2) the trip to Mexico and the return; and (3) the reunion with Nika Machado, the resolution of Hendry's relationship with her, and the deaths of Harvey French, Bob Emory, Modesto Machado, the Dedrick brothers and Shotgun Smith, and the Kid. Peckinpah conceived his adaptation in three parts as well or, as they are customarily called in filmmaking, three acts. By this I don't mean that the screenplay is literally divided into acts. Rather, perhaps because of cinema's early relationship to theater, most screenplays that tell stories seem, like "classic" plays, to break so naturally into three distinct groups or segments of overall action that it became common for filmmakers to refer to them as acts, a practice that has never gone entirely away, even after mainstream films became much freer in form beginning in the seventies.

Peckinpah must have discovered pretty fast that the incarceration ending in the jailbreak was practically ready-made for filming—it's the part of the novel that required the least adapting—but he must have also worried whether it would work as an opening to a film. He often began his stories, especially in his later films, in medias res, but he was also drawn to elaborate setups that establish the settings and introduce the characters. He managed these so well that they rarely feel like something that is being set up and they certainly don't play like expositions as such, because so much else is going on at the same time. He obviously felt that for a film the long jail sequence needed far more preparation. In the novel Doc can tell us about Dad's and the Kid's past friendship in a paragraph or two, but Peckinpah believed, as he later did also of the original version of Rudolph Wurlitzer's screenplay for *Pat Garrett and Billy the Kid*, that this friendship needed to be made into something dramatized, something *felt*, before audiences could or would make any real investment in the characters. Effectively discarding Doc as narrator led Peckinpah to the next solution: eliminating Neider's time shifting in favor of letting the story play out in strict chronology.

Peckinpah distributed the events of the novel between the second and third acts. The incarceration became the screenplay's second act, about forty

Charles Neider   24 Southern Way   Princeton, N. J. 08540

December 19, 1972

Dear Sam:

I was delighted to get your letter from Durango. I'll be
watching for PAT GARRETT AND BILLY THE KID. All my best for
this, and I hope it sickens Brando by contrast with ONE-EYED
JACKS. Before I left New Hampshire recently I was asked to
speak at Keene State College on the differences between a novel
and a film based on the novel. Many of the classes were assigned
HENDRY JONES for reading, and so I was forced to reread the book
for the first time in many years. Before the talk there was
a screening of ONE-EYED JACKS, which I hadn't seen since about
'62 or '63. I was disgusted by a number of things, among them
the maudlin side of the film, the lack of authenticity and the
amount of sheer padding. You can bet that I spoke my mind on
the subject. Also, I spoke very favorably about your work.

Warm regards,

Charles

Letter from Charles Neider to Sam Peckinpah

20th Century Fox
Box 900
Beverly Hills
California 90213

June 21st 1974

Mr. Charles Neider
24 Southern Way
Princeton NY 08540

Dear Charles:

The Book is in Mexico, I am not. I am up here in foreverland doing a picture.

It has taken me a year of my life and more money than I could borrow, but sometime in the next month there will be a print of my version of PAT GARRETT AND BILLY THE KID.

Some people take up gold, alot of people play tennis, I try to hang on to what I believe in. When it is ready I would like you to see it, because it is something we started together a long time ago.

Your friend,

SAM PECKINPAH

Letter from Peckinpah to Neider

pages, the escape the second-act climax. For the third act, about thirty-four pages, Peckinpah simply grouped the trip to Old Mexico with the other material from the last part of the novel. As for the first act, which is almost fifty pages long, once past the brief one-page prologue, Peckinpah took the scene where Hendry and Doc first meet, a flashback in the book, and used it for the beginning of the story proper. After that he added over forty pages of wholly new material that climaxes in the Kid's capture. Even this early in his career he knew there is a big difference between being literal to a source and being faithful to it. If a novel or a play is any good, one huge reason is that what we loosely call its content bears an organic relationship to its style and its medium. A successful adaptation requires reconceiving the work in a new style for a different medium. It also means that the work of adaptation involves not just deciding what to keep and what to lose but what to change or invent in order to make it work in a new form.

Peckinpah spent six months doing the adaptation, but he said it took him a while to get started writing because he wanted to research the historical materials himself. Although he actually did acquire a good bit of knowledge about Garrett and Billy, which he would put to use many years later in *Pat Garrett and Billy the Kid*, there is scant evidence of it in the *Hendry Jones* screenplay, where almost nothing new from the history of Billy and Garrett was added to what was already in the book (even most of the details with which old Monterey is evoked come from the novel). I suspect that what really occupied so much time was coming up with the new material for the long first act, plus more elsewhere in the screenplay. Peckinpah's *Hendry Jones* is recognizably an adaptation of *The Authentic Death*, but it is also, inevitably, a new work based on the previous work. The first-act additions are without exception effective, especially how Dad, Dad's family, and the relationship between him and Hendry are all deepened and brought to dramatic life as compared to the novel. Some later changes having to do with the title character are less so and a new third-act climax represents a real letdown after the first two acts and by comparison to the novel.

Neider described his novel as "spare," which it is. But Peckinpah favored complex, colorful characters whose relationships he liked to thicken with conflicts and complications that follow upon their needs, emotions, dreams, desires, and ambitions. He also liked to get a lot of things going at once, especially parallel lines of action ripe for development in elaborate and unpredictable ways. Although his big films are often described as sprawling, he was in fact a very careful plotter; a master of long-range thematic, motivic, and structural development; and proud of the way his screenplays, as he once said of *Major Dundee*, were so intricately constructed that "if you removed part of it, something else would fall out fifteen pages later" (Farber 37–38). In Neider's novel, important secondary characters, such as Nika, Modesto, and even the members of the gang, figure mostly in the third section, with only fleeting references to them earlier, and then less as introductions than as passing adumbrations. Peckinpah obviously felt this wouldn't play so well on film, so he added these characters to new scenes he created for the first act. Here is a brief rundown of the first act:

Prologue—campsite: Doc as old man is heard in voice-over as the scene dissolves to . . .

Doc's camp: . . . far in the past as Hendry, Harvey French, and Bob Emory come upon Doc; after a few tense moments, Hendry, recognizing Doc from his reputation, asks him to join his gang.

Doc's camp, middle of the night: Doc is awakened by the Kid off a way practicing his draw. Harvey tells a puzzled Doc that the Kid "don't sleep so good" (7).

Paso Robles bank: The gang rob the bank, Hendry shooting and seriously wounding Marshal Tomlinson, whose deputy Jim Fawcett swears to track the gang down, all the way into Monterey County if necessary. "You got no jurisdiction there," Tomlinson tells him. "Longworth does," Fawcett replies. Will he use it? "We're sure as hell goin' to find out" (9).

Campsite: The gang get fresh horses; Hendry announces he's going into Monterey and sends the others to the Punta del Diablo, a remote area a few miles south of Monterey where the gang headquarter themselves.

Monterey: Hendry rides in and goes straight to the jail, where he meets Lon Dedrick for the first time—instant hatred between them. Then Dad appears. After a tense exchange, he invites Hendry to supper to meet the wife and kids.

La Perla Hotel saloon: Lon commiserates with his brothers Cal and Curly, loudly complaining that he can't arrest the Kid because he's an old friend of Longworth's. The other patrons start gossiping about this, too. Lon's brothers suggest that what with Dad's temper, maybe he and the Kid will wind up killing each other, leaving the sheriff's badge to Lon. Lon gets an idea.

Longworth home: Dad, his wife May, their two children (a three-year-old boy and a one-year-old girl), and Hendry are at the dinner table. Dad explains why he became sheriff and advises Hendry to give up the life of an outlaw at the earliest opportunity; the Kid says he thinks he'll hang around Monterey, as the scene ends on notes of concern, threat, and worry.

La Perla Hotel saloon, same night: Lon tricks a drunk named Johnson into trying to swindle the Kid, figuring it will probably come to bloodshed. Then Lon tells a bystander to go get Longworth and tell him the Kid's going to kill Johnson. Meanwhile Nika's young brother Modesto enters the saloon. He tells the Kid Nika is outside waiting for him, but the Kid only inquires how Modesto's gun practice is coming along. When Johnson calls Modesto a greaser, telling him his kind doesn't belong there, Hendry throws Johnson out of the saloon. Furious, Johnson comes charging back through the swinging doors, his gun drawn. Hendry shoots him twice and Johnson falls dead, "his gun skidding across the floor." The Kid tells Modesto to let Nika know he'll be along shortly, then sits down for another tequila, awaiting Dad, who arrives angry. He tells the Kid that now he'll have to clear out of Monterey County—*all* the way out. The bartender says Hendry shot Johnson in self-defense, whereupon Lon asks, "Yeah, where's his gun?" (The script doesn't explicitly say so, but the implication is that Lon picked Johnson's gun up when it skidded across the floor and disposed of it to make it look as if Hendry murdered Johnson without provocation.) When the Kid leaves, Dad notices a look of anticipation on Lon's face and tells him not to "throw away your deputy's badge, yet—I might outlast both of you" (28–32).

Monterey, outside the hotel: There is a brief scene between Hendry and Nika in which she urges him to take her away with him to Mexico. He tells her he'll meet her at the Punta.

Plaza of the settlement at the Punta del Diablo: Hendry and Nika walk toward Nika's adobe, but they are interrupted by Francesca Zamora, an old Indian woman who has "adopted" Hendry as a kind of grandson.[5] She loves Hendry almost unconditionally, but she doesn't like Nika at all and tries to interest him in the younger, nubile Juanita. The Kid and Nika retire to Nika's adobe, where she tells him that if he doesn't take her with him, she's leaving him. They begin to make love.

Plaza, nearby: Juanita dances as Francesca looks on, then looks in the direction of Nika's adobe.

Longworth bedroom, same night: A pounding on the door awakens Dad. It's Lon and Jim Fawcett, the deputy from Paso Robles. Fawcett tells him about the robbery and the Kid's shooting of Tomlinson, who remains critically wounded. "What do you plan to do?" Dad asks. "Take him," says Fawcett. There's a long pause, then Dad says, "All right," and reluctantly prepares to leave with them (40).

Plaza at the Punta, later that night: Hendry, finished with Nika, has returned to the plaza and is talking with Francesca, who asks if he will take Nika with him when he and his gang leave. She urges him to because she doesn't want Nika around anyhow. They move on to the—

Cantina: —where Doc, Harvey, and Bob are drunk and Juanita is dancing. Soon she turns her attentions completely to Hendry. Miguel Gomez appears; an older man and a friend of Hendry's, he tells the Kid that he was set to marry Nika before Hendry came back. Hendry tells him she's "still my girl." "Perhaps," says Miguel. "No, hombre—no perhaps—entiende?" answers Hendry. "If she is your woman," asks Miguel, "why don't you take care of her?" Hendry regards Miguel for a long moment, then turns and leaves, Juanita running after him (44).

Beach, a short time later: Clad only in a blanket, Juanita flirts with Hendry, then tosses off the blanket and runs into the surf, beckoning him to follow. He watches her for a moment, smiles, then removes his gun belt and starts to take off his shirt. Suddenly Juanita screams, there is a cut to a close-up of Hendry, and Dad's voice offscreen, "Don't try it, Hendry." The camera booms up to reveal "a line of twenty armed men silhouetted on the bluff top."[6] As Lon shackles Hendry, Juanita wrapped in the blanket next to him, there is a cut to a close-up of Nika, who has observed the entire scene. She turns and leaves, Hendry's eyes on her as he is led away by the posse (44–45).

Almost fifty pages make for a long first act by any standard, yet the speed and sureness with which it moves and the economy with which the characters are introduced and the setup is laid out are equally impressive. Even a cursory summary is sufficient to illustrate how tightly Peckinpah has structured the action, knit together the relationships among the various characters, and stayed alert to nuances of expression and gesture. I'll detail three examples. First, in an ironic touch, the Kid is tried and found guilty for the killing of Johnson, which was in fact self-defense, though witnesses claimed the victim had no gun. This much is right out of the novel. But by inventing the business of Lon deliberately removing the gun from the scene of the crime, Peckinpah lets him have a temporary victory over both the Kid and Dad, which adds a dimension of smugness to the swagger, sarcasm, and viciousness he displays all the while he is guarding the Kid, which in turn lends a grimly comic irony to the deputy's eventual demise: all his machinations have gained him nothing but an untimely death at the hands of the man he hates more than any other, the themes of destiny and fate working themselves out, though, typical of Peckinpah, in unexpected and ironic ways. Also typical of Peckinpah is having Dad figure out what's on Lon's mind from the look on his face at the end of the scene.

Second, the business between Hendry and Juanita is in the novel, but only as backstory: Doc informs us that sometime in the recent past the Kid betrayed Nika by shacking up with Juanita for over a week in the Punta, right there where Nika lives, humiliating her before the whole community. However, by dramatizing the betrayal and showing us the Kid responding to Juanita's flirtations within at most an hour after he has made love to Nika, and having Nika witness to it, Peckinpah allows us to *feel* her shame far more sharply while intensifying our sense of just how cruel Hendry really is to her, how coldhearted and selfish in pursuit of his pleasures. Later, when Nika refuses to visit the Kid in jail and agrees to marry Miguel, it works better because we've experienced with her the feelings that led to these decisions.

Third, by introducing Lon's brothers Cal and Curly Bill early in the story and showing the kind of relationship they have with him, Peckinpah is able to make their eventual killing of Modesto seem like a decision made by a pair of individuals who've been well characterized, as opposed to a plot device to get the Kid back into action. In putting it this way, I by no means wish to suggest that they feel like a plot device in Neider's novel. On the contrary, the issue is the difference between how something functions in a novel versus how it might play in a film. Since this novel is a first-person narrative, Neider can introduce and drop characters virtually at will, a few remarks or a paragraph sufficient to explain who they are, where they came from, and where they go. This is far more difficult to manage in a play or a film where there isn't a narrator, and where even a narrator wouldn't necessarily be of much help because the medium is so insistently a dramatic one. Peckinpah had a rare gift for being able to depict characters of extraordinary presence and vitality in a few swift, deft strokes, and he always believed that even minor characters, however briefly they appear, and villainous characters, however evil they may seem, should be realized in the fullness of their humanity. He tended to favor a three-beat structural unit—it's almost like a micro-version of a three-act structure—that was perhaps best encapsulated in what he used to tell his editors: "Introduce. Develop. Finish."

In the case of the Dedrick brothers, they're introduced in the first act when a frustrated Lon, who has been humiliated by both Dad and Hendry, goes over to complain to his brothers in the saloon, where they also humiliate him—Ma says "you can come over Sunday, if you take a bath"—but not before they hit him up for free drinks (15). Later, after he's dead, the brothers, thirsting for vengeance, join Dad's posse—this a change from the novel, where they are not part of the posse. When, in an even more significant change, it is not Dad but Curly Bill who accidentally kills Harvey, thinking he's shot the Kid, they are humiliated by Dad and later take out their frustrations on Modesto, going out to Old Man Richardson's ranch, where he works, and shooting him down in cold blood, then telling Richardson to let the Kid know they'll be waiting in Monterey. Once more themes of fate and destiny resonate, and again in ironic and unexpected ways, Modesto the hapless victim of a vengeance intended for Hendry while the bloviating Dedricks set themselves up for execution. However, because the two brothers have been so well drawn, these conse-quences happen as a function of character.

Of all the new scenes that Peckinpah wrote, the most important, because the most far-reaching in their implications, are the first scene in the Mon-terey jail and its resolution in the Longworth home. I am going to quote the first at substantial length and the second fully, so as to allow Peckinpah's writ-ing to be experienced directly without summary or paraphrase. On entering the jail, Hendry encounters Lon, leaning back in a chair, his legs sprawled across the desk, reading a Ned Buntline Western (a ritzy touch). When Hen-dry inquires where Longworth is, Lon "spits on the floor and goes back to his book. After a moment Hendry crosses to the desk and, placing his hand under Lon's heel, flips him over backwards," saying, "Answer me, you big tub of guts."[7] As Lon goes for his gun, Dad appears. "I was just going to give this smart kid a lesson," Lon tells him. "Go ahead, Lon," says Dad softly, "give him a lesson." Lon stands there looking stupid as Hendry laughs. "You named him, Lon," Dad continues. "Meet Hendry Jones. Most folks call him the Kid." Lon's eyes widen, shocked and confused.

                         HENDRY
                    (after a moment)
          You surprised to see me?

                         DAD
          No -- I figured you'd be in sooner or later.

                         HENDRY
          I waited for you at the Point -- thought you'd
          be out to pay us a visit.
                    (then, tightly)
          We've been there considerable time, Dad.

                         DAD
          I heard . . .

                         HENDRY
          So . . . ?

                         DAD
          So, things have changed.

                         HENDRY
          You want to explain it to me?

                         DAD
                    (angrily)
          Sure, I'll explain it to you, Hendry. Any way
          you want it -- up one side and down the other
          -- I'm sheriff of this county and since I plan
          to keep on being sheriff, I got no reason to
          pay you a visit.

                         HENDRY
          I can find you a reason, sheriff.

```
                        DAD
                  (quieting down
                  a little)
            You know, Hendry -- everybody and his dog are
            claiming that you're responsible for every-
            thing that's happened in this county since you
            pulled in. Now I know that ain't so, but let
            me tell you something --
                  (almost savagely)
            You step out of line just once and I'll bust
            you like I would anybody else -- and don't
            forget it.


                        HENDRY
                  (a death sentence)
            Do you want to try it now, Dad?


39. NEW ANGLE

      For a second it looks as if there'll be bloodshed,
      then Dad shakes off his anger like a dog coming out
      of water and sticks out his hand.


                        DAD
            No, I want you to come over and have supper
            and meet the wife and kids.
                  (softly)
            It's been a long time, Kid.

      Hendry looks at him, then smiles and shakes hands.
      It is obvious that there is a great bond of affec-
      tion and respect between the two men. They look at
      each other for a moment, then, ignoring Lon, move
      out of the office.
```

Peckinpah obviously wants the audience to feel both the past closeness that existed between these two men and the intensity of feeling that still exists between them, even if the feelings are now charged with some antagonism. As with Neider, so with Peckinpah: there is no question of disloyalty or betrayal on the part of Dad toward Hendry. Dad is prepared to turn as much of a blind eye to the Kid's illegal activities as he possibly can, provided Hendry stays out of his jurisdiction in Monterey County. Though the Punta del Diablo may technically be part of Monterey County, it's remote and insular enough that the sheriff is content for the time being to let that hornet's nest go undisturbed so long as it doesn't make trouble for him. There's a lot of unexpressed feeling here as well, notably in Hendry's resistance to the changes in Dad's life, a motif that will be intensified as the story progresses, and the diametrically opposed pulls within Dad of his affection for Hendry and their shared past versus his duties as sheriff and, it will be revealed soon enough, his responsibilities to his family, which is to say the present and the future. Peckinpah's Dad is a much tougher, angrier, and more formidable presence than Neider's and, as we're given just a hint of here, even more fiercely determined to protect his world than the Kid is to destroy it. Against this are Hendry's barely disguised hostility and threats and perhaps also a not quite conscious jealousy that he cannot share in Dad's new life. Finally, a strong current of dramatic irony runs through the scene because we know something the two men don't: Deputy Fawcett is on his way to enlist the sheriff's help in apprehending the Kid for the bank robbery and the shooting of the marshal. For the time being, however, Dad relents, for reasons that will become clear in the companion scene.

46. INT. MONTEREY - CLOSE SHOT - PLATE - (NIGHT)

     THE CAMERA PULLS BACK as LARRY, Dad Longworth's wild-
     haired, rib-thin three-year-old son, picks up his
     full dinner plate and calmly smashes it on the floor.
     For a moment there is a stunned silence. Seated
     around the table are Dad, Hendry and MAY LONGWORTH,
     Dad's wife. May is a full-bodied woman in her late
     20's, and while not unattractive, she is anything
     but a beauty -- blonde hair severely parted in the
     middle, proper manners, proper walk, proper dress,
     improper full-lipped sensual mouth. Seated beside
     May on a pile of books and large cushion is a fat,
     good-natured year-old baby girl. A dishtowel looped
     around her middle holds her securely against the back
     of the chair. The room, a combination kitchen-dining
     area of the Longworth home, is pin-neat, a model of
     the middle-class 80's -- striped wallpaper, framed
     samplers, hand-patched, fresh painted furniture. The
     best silver and incomplete inherited fine china are
     now out of the cupboard and on the table.

47. DIFFERENT ANGLE

     May jumps to her feet and, grabbing Larry by the ear,
     hustles him out of the room. Hendry tips back his
     head and laughs. Larry howls in outraged anguish.

                              MAY
                         (showing her tension)
                    You're going to bed, Larry, and you're going
                    to stay there and stay hungry until you learn
                    to behave yourself . . .

48. MED. SHOT - FEATURING DAD AND HENDRY

    Dad grins at Hendry, a little embarrassed, and takes
    out a cigar. May shoves Larry through the door into
    the hallway, then turns back for a brief instant.

49. CLOSE SHOT - MAY

    She looks at Hendry, her face tight and suddenly
    afraid, then moves out to her squalling son, shut-
    ting the door behind her.

50. INT. PARLOR - MED. TWO SHOT - MAY AND LARRY
    - (NIGHT)

    May, near tears herself, suddenly kneels down and
    holds her boy tight, soothing his crying.

51. INT. DINING AREA - MED. SHOT - (NIGHT)

    Dad, Hendry and the baby sit at the table. Dad
    lights his cigar and Hendry, his laughter spent,
    slumps in his chair, suddenly weary. The baby pounds
    the table with her spoon and smiles delightedly at
    whoever notices her.

                              DAD
                         (laughing a little)
                    The last time we ate together was on horse-
                    back, comin' off the Mongollon Rim -- with
                    that Flagstaff posse just close enough to add
                    taste to the jerky.

                              HENDRY
                    Food's considerable better this time . . .
                         (then, softly)
                    I waited for you in Prescott after that --
                    almost a month.

52. CLOSER ANGLE - FEATURING DAD

>   DAD
>   (trying to explain)
>   After we split, Hendry, I got to thinkin' --
>   I was thirty-four years old and even the horse
>   I rode was stole. My luck was runnin' out and
>   I knew it . . . The kind of luck we needed
>   then is for kids -- and I sure as hell was
>   no kid . . . I figured I had to change or I
>   wouldn't live to make thirty-five.

>   HENDRY
>   (still a little angry)
>   Some change . . .

>   DAD
>   (softly)
>   You're not a kid any longer either.

Hendry looks at him a moment, then laughs softly.

>   HENDRY
>   Don't you worry about my luck, Dad -- it's
>   better than it ever was.

53. DIFFERENT ANGLE - FEATURING HENDRY

>   DAD
>   (after a moment)
>   Why'd you come to California?

>   HENDRY
>   (shrugging)
>   To see you -- see why -- look it all
>   over . . .

>   DAD
>   And now . . . ?

>   HENDRY
>   Quien sabe?

>   DAD
> You goin' to stick around?

>   HENDRY
> Why? . . . make it tough on you?

>   DAD
> A little . . . General feeling is I should run
> you out of the county or shoot you down -- but
> I can handle it a little longer if you behave
> yourself.

>   HENDRY
> We've behaved ourselves, Dad -- so far.

>   DAD
> Look, Hendry, the business we were in -- you
> only get one chance to step away from it. When
> it comes for you, take it.

Hendry sits silently, fiddling with his empty coffee
cup. The baby cries fretfully, then subsides as Dad
hands her a drumstick.

>   DAD
> How many is it now?

>   HENDRY
> Enough.

>   DAD
> They pushin' you?

>   HENDRY
> Once in a while.

>   DAD
> Walk away from it -- and do it now. Country's
> changin' -- growin' up, settlin' down -- time
> for you to do the same.

>   HENDRY
>   (looking at him)
> Here . . . ?

                         DAD
                    (slowly)
          Not here -- old Mex maybe . . .

                         HENDRY
                    (idly)
          Want to come along . . . ?

                         DAD
                    (after a moment,
                    flatly)
          No . . . you can't go back to the way things
          were.
                    (then)
          I like it here. I plan on staying.

                         HENDRY
          Maybe I plan on stayin' too.

                         DAD
          No.

                         HENDRY
                    (curiously)
          You tellin' me to leave?

                         DAD
          Right now I'm askin' you to.

          Hendry tips his head back and laughs softly, almost
          contemptuously.

                         HENDRY
          Old Dad -- Sheriff Longworth.

                         DAD
                    (a little angry)
          That's right -- Sheriff Longworth -- win, lose
          or draw, and don't you forget it.

          Both men look up as May enters.

54. FULL SHOT

 May crosses toward the men, nervously fixing her
hair. Perhaps she has been crying.

      MAY
     (strained)
 I'm sorry, Mr. Jones -- you know how it is
 -- it takes company to make a child act its
 worst.

      HENDRY
 Sure.

      MAY
 Another cup of coffee?

      HENDRY
 No thanks, ma'am. I'll be movin' along now.

 For a moment there is an awkward silence. May stands
looking at the floor, her hands locked, fingers
twisting against each other. Hendry looks at the
baby girl for a moment, then ruffles her hair gently
and awkwardly.

      HENDRY
 You're a very pretty little girl.
   (then straightening)
 I'll see you around, Dad. 'Night Mrs.
 Longworth.

 He moves toward the back door.

      MAY
   (moving with him)
 Can I show you out?

      DAD
   (stopping her
   with a gesture)
 Good night, Hendry.

Hendry nods and moves out through the kitchen to
the back porch, shutting the door behind him. For a
long moment there is silence, then his footsteps can
be heard going down the back steps and around the
house. May, under obvious strain, turns and begins
to clean up the broken dish.

55. DIFFERENT ANGLE

>   DAD
>   Thank you, May -- you did just fine.

>   MAY
>   You could've told me who he was.

>   DAD
>   (drily)
>   You seemed to know right away.

>   MAY
>   How many men has he killed.

>   DAD
>   Considerable.

>   MAY
>   What's he here for?

>   DAD
>   (shortly)
>   Maybe he came here for the same reason I did.

She stands and crosses to the kitchen with the broken dish.

>   MAY
>   And maybe he didn't!
>   (then quietly)
>   Why do you think so much of him?

```
56. NEW ANGLE - FEATURING DAD
```

He turns and crosses to a sideboard, pours himself a
drink.

DAD
(after a moment,
remembering)

He was seventeen when I first met him -- the
best kid I ever knew. Poor as a blanket Indian
-- and ten times as proud.

He sits as May moves to the table and takes the baby
in her lap.

MAY

What made him turn into an outlaw?

DAD

Hell, we never turned -- those things just
happened. One fellow went one way, the next
one another, and the first thing you knew one
of them was called an outlaw and the other was
sheriff of Monterey County.

DAD
(after a long
moment, awkwardly)

I knew his mother -- I knew her very well.[8]

It seems to me the dramatic function of this scene is clear enough to
require little explication. A few lines here come from Neider, but most of the
dialogue, like the scene itself, is entirely Peckinpah's, although some of what
is said represents an attempt to incorporate themes from the novel that are
expressed there in prose, notably the business about luck running out, the
kind of luck that is associated with kids, and the inevitability of change, if
for no other reason than advancing age. Dad's observations about how easy
it was to become an outlaw or a lawman or to slip from one into the other
derive from Doc's ruminations how "in those times things weren't all figured
out the way they are now": hardly anyone ever decided to become an outlaw,
those "things just happened" (Neider, *Authentic Death* 10).[9] Otherwise, taking
up threads from the scene in Dad's office earlier that day, we have two friends,
separated by time, circumstance, and choice, facing each other across a table
that might as well be an unbridgeable chasm, the tension now greater because

the setting is Dad's home, at the dinner table, surrounded by his family, which seems to me the real reason Peckinpah came up with this scene: to give the wife and children a flesh-and-blood reality the better to focus the issues and raise the stakes. It is here also that Dad is first seen to embody the role suggested by his name, and it finds him looking backward and forward: toward his own children and toward Hendry, whom he tries to tell as honestly as he knows how why things can no longer be the same between them, the presence of May and the children evidence of all he has gained and everything he stands to lose. Although the script describes the family as solidly middle class, this is done with no hint of derision or irony. Indeed, as the scene develops, it begins to suggest that Dad asked Hendry to supper in the first place because he gambled that letting the Kid actually meet his family, and witness firsthand the depth of his feelings and the strength of his commitment, might help make the point more emphatically (yet sympathetically) than any words. It doesn't work. One of the subtlest yet most revealing moments comes when, after Dad advises him to go to Mexico, Hendry can actually ask if Dad would like to come along. When Dad tells him there's no going back to the way things used to be, Hendry, as he did in the office, issues another veiled threat, announcing that maybe he plans on sticking around too.

One of the many reasons I would love to see the film Peckinpah might have made is to discover how he would have directed the actor playing Hendry when he asks Dad if he'd like to come along. This is one of the many problems of reading a screenplay: even when it's complete, it remains in a fairly literal sense unfinished, because it's not a final anything, only a stage (a critically important stage, of course) along the way to becoming a film. With that in mind, let's approach the scene not as something to be read but as something to be *played and filmed*. The first thing we notice is that we come into the scene very late, after dinner is over and Dad has brought out the cigars; Hendry has not yet become sullen, but the toddler is throwing a tantrum, which it falls to May to deal with. It makes perfect sense to begin the scene this late, as the dinner conversation was doubtless small talk and it's unlikely Dad would get down to any serious business with the Kid that might prove upsetting to May and the children during dinner. She takes the child into the adjoining parlor, but she pauses at the door and, in close-up, looks back at Hendry, "her face tight and suddenly afraid." She closes the door, disappearing into the next room, where, close to tears herself, she attends to her bawling son. Then we cut back to the kitchen, except that, because of the way Peckinpah has placed the close-up of May to establish the two men from her point of view, our response to everything they say is now conditioned by our experience of *her* fears about what Hendry's presence signifies for her husband, her family, and their life together. This is vintage Peckinpah, yet at the dawn of his career: rarely content to let us experience anything from just one point of view or perspective, always forcing us to multiple ways of looking at things, boxes outside boxes, contexts enveloping contexts.

Dad lights his cigar as Hendry, "suddenly weary," slumps in his chair while the one-year-old daughter pounds the table (yet another perspective). Dad gets down to business but, as was not the case in the office earlier that day, his manner is now mild and easeful and his approach circular, first recalling the last time he and Hendry were together as partners. It's an indication of his strength that he can lead by displaying a little vulnerability. From what the Kid says in response, we may infer that they were forced to separate by the posse pursuing them and that Dad never kept an agreement to reunite later on in Prescott.[10] Forthrightly and without apology Dad explains why he never showed up; Hendry's first reaction is mild sarcasm ("Some change"). Dad, his composure unruffled, ignores the jibe and carries on calmly, his concern for Hendry's future, that he indeed *have* a future, genuine. But it is all to no avail—the only time Hendry seems to pay attention is just before he's about to make a threat: "We've behaved ourselves—so far." There is no direction here, but the dash surely indicates a beat, and "so far" must be full of irony—there might even be a little smile—yet with only the slightest dynamic inflection, if any. Dad still doesn't rise to the bait, but tries a different tack, as the dynamics subtly shift upward, becoming more direct and personal: "Look, Hendry, the business we were in—you only get one chance to step away from it. When it comes for you, take it." In a really good film, the beats, pauses, and reactions are as important as the lines, sometimes more so. ("Play the reaction, not the line," Peckinpah often told his editors.) Hendry has no answer—did he even hear what Dad said?—sitting quietly, fiddling with his coffee cup, the silence filled by the pointed sound of the baby girl crying until Dad placates her with a drumstick.

Dad tries again, the dynamics shifting upward once more, his tone acquiring greater urgency: "Walk away from it—and do it now." Hendry can't be so obtuse as to think Dad seriously means for him to remain in Monterey, yet that is precisely what he asks, so his purpose must be to continue testing the older man. All Dad can do now is say, "Not here—old Mex maybe." Peckinpah's direction calls for this to be said slowly, whether cautiously, as a subtle warning, or as the first inkling that a boundary is about to be set, would doubtless be determined in rehearsal, but at the very least we may safely infer he wanted his actor to apply more gravitas than he has used so far in the scene. Another beat and another shift in the dynamics, this time downward: Dad tells Hendry—"flatly"—that they can't return to the way things were. Another beat, then more declaratively: "I like it here. I plan on staying." This is the opportunity Hendry has been waiting for: "Maybe I plan on staying too." There is no direction as to how this should be played, but surely no one, including Hendry himself, can possibly believe that at this point in the story he has any real desire to stay in Monterey except to make trouble for Dad, to push the confrontation to the inevitable flash-point. Dad's reply, a laconic "No," without further explanation, also comes with no direction, but surely none is needed: the actor probably shouldn't say it loudly, but he must be absolutely resolute. "You tellin' me to leave?" asks Hendry—again, there might be an ambiguous smile. And once again Dad struggles to balance restraint and resolve: "Right now I'm askin' you." Hendry's reply is derisive laughter, followed by what sounds like a sarcastic toast: "Old Dad—Sheriff Longworth." And now, finally, Dad releases his anger: "That's right—Sheriff Longworth—win, lose or draw, and don't you forget it." The moment she hears these words, May comes back into the room.

Peckinpah cannot possibly have chosen the moment of her reentrance randomly. Wherever May was in the house—we left her in the adjoining room, but it's possible the boy eventually fell asleep and she put him to bed—the clear implication is that she was listening to the two men as they talked and she would certainly have recognized when anger entered her husband's voice: it's what makes her come back into the kitchen. (This is another reason why I know in my bones that Peckinpah would have covered her throughout: he rarely passed up an opportunity for paralleling lines of movement, whether emotional or physical.) There's another awkward silence, then Hendry gets up to leave, ruffling the baby's hair: "You're a very pretty little girl." As he walks toward the door, May moves to show him out, but Dad stops her "with a gesture," bidding Hendry good night but remaining by May's side as Hendry is left to find his own way to the back door, walking down the stairs and going around to the front of the house where his horse is tethered. May turns and begins to clean up the broken dinner plate.

As an example of how Peckinpah makes his symbolism grow naturally and unobtrusively out of a scene, this is as good as any in his work. He never got to shoot it, but he envisioned it so exactly that even a production assistant could stage it without obscuring its meanings. Dad's decision to let Hendry find his own way out—literally sending him out of the house and into the world—symbolizes his commitment to the choices he has made, to his family and their future over Hendry and his past—it's almost as if he has drawn a line back over which Hendry may no longer trespass. All this finds the perfect objective correlative in the way Dad gently holds May back, then stays by her side, the camera remaining on the silent couple as the Kid's footsteps echo from the stairs. The stillness is broken only when May bends to pick up the pieces of the plate, which, if we're reading as attentively as the material deserves, we will recall was thrown to the floor at the beginning of the scene by a three-year-old boy whose impulses to destruction mirror those of the equally anarchic "kid" across the table, this one a man who seems never to have grown up, his very presence a threat to everything the family is about.

Although May is a one-scene character, she is still, like Garrett's wife in *Pat Garrett and Billy the Kid*, indisputably a major character in the story. Peckinpah was ever sensitive to the place of women in Western society, especially the way they are dependent upon or otherwise used and victimized by men.

It's a recurring theme throughout his career and was prominent in all his television work and several of his films. Even in the male-dominated world of *The Wild Bunch* we find him periodically referencing the point of view of women and children. Although many women are understandably resentful when they are portrayed as mere victims, there is nothing "mere" about Peckinpah's portrayals: he really did know—all too personally, I am afraid—how men *do* victimize, abuse, or simply disregard women even as they use them. May is no victim of abuse; and though the principal note Peckinpah has her strike is of worry for her family, she nevertheless emerges as a figure of quiet strength and dignity. And in the postlude following the departure of Hendry, Peckinpah wrote a lovely extended moment of warmth, intimacy, understanding, and honesty between this wife and her husband. As for Hendry, May might as well not even exist, or, perhaps worse, exist only to clean up the damage done by men like himself.

In the earlier draft, Peckinpah ended the postlude with a segue into a new scene, wherein Nika and Modesto come to the Longworth house inquiring as to the Kid's whereabouts. When they leave, there is this exchange:

```
                    MAY
        Is your gunman friend "keeping company" with
        Nika?
                (as Dad nods)
        Then she's ruined!

                    DAD
                (bluntly)
        No, she's not. She's a grown woman who knows
        what she wants.

                    MAY
                (bitterly)
        He'll get killed and then what will she do?

                    DAD
                (dryly, taking the baby)
        Then she'll get married and probably have ten
        kids. Don't worry about Hendry, May.

                    MAY
                (her arms around him)
        I'm not worried -- I'm worried about you.

        After a moment they move inside the house and shut
        the door. (10/57, 29)
```

This scene seems to me to constitute the most significant difference between the 10/57 and 11/57 drafts, and in every way its removal was an improvement. For one thing, as exposition, it's unnecessary. For another, folding the introduction of Nika and Modesto into the scene where Hendry kills Johnson is at once more economical and far more effective as drama. Third, having Nika and Modesto come to the Longworth house at night suggests the two families have some sort of social relationship that in turn seems to indicate further development, which never happens and for which there is no room in the structure anyhow. Finally, and most important, however, is that it detracts from and subtly undermines the lovely moment of intimacy between Dad and May and the portrait of marital and familial commitment it draws, which, to repeat, I believe are among the principal reasons Peckinpah wrote the sequence in the Longworth house to begin with. If the sequence is allowed to end as it does in the earlier draft with May worrying about Dad, then as written the cause of the worry is ambiguous. Is it that he might be killed or that he might return to his outlaw ways with the Kid? If the latter (or both), then it speaks little for May's faith in her husband and perhaps even less for the depth of Dad's commitment to his family. Rich for development as either of these themes may be, I see little evidence that Peckinpah wanted them in this screenplay.[11]

Peckinpah's additions to the first act in every instance strengthen the story, making it thematically more complex, emotionally richer, and dramatically more intense and immediate. In the second act, his only major addition is fleshing out a nameless character from Neider's novel, a merchant who wants to buy Hendry's revolver, the one with the notches in it, to profit from his notoriety. Dad informs the fellow the Kid never notched his gun—only fourflushers did that—and the merchant goes off disappointed. But Peckinpah couldn't resist making, if not a meal, at least a substantial side dish of him, assigning him the rather Dickensian name of "Fedderson" and a manner both odious and unctuous: "How do you do, Mr. Jones? I'm here to give you an opportunity—an opportunity of a lifetime, you might say. My pockets are stuffed with money for anything you wish to sell—your pistol, your rifle, your clothes . . . at a price I'm sure is more than fair" (63). Before he's finished, Hendry, to Dad's great amusement, has fleeced the merchant out of two hundred dollars for a beaten-up old pistol owned by the other deputy, Pablo Patron, into which, at the Kid's suggestion, Pablo carved thirty-nine notches. "Thirty-nine—think of that," muses a very impressed Fedderson. (The Kid tells Dad to give Pablo the money.) Elsewhere Peckinpah included the dialogue in which Dad, Hendry, and Pablo talk about belief. "What do you believe in, Kid?" "Nothing." And when the subject turns to God, "I hear he's fast but I'd like to see for myself." "You will," replies Dad (72–74). All of which would eventually find its way into *Pat Garrett and Billy the Kid*.

The deaths of Lon and Pablo, however, are not subjectively drawn out as they are in Neider, nor are they in the later film, where Peckinpah used slow motion for the killings of both Bell and Olinger, somewhat extending the moments immediately preceding the shootings but with no equivalent to the extraordinary interior monologues that Neider fashioned for their deaths. My guess is that in the *Hendry Jones* screenplay Peckinpah toned down these and other instances of the novel's graphic violence owing to strictures against how violence was depicted in mainstream American films in the mid-1950s. One detail worth noting is that the Kid blasts both barrels at once into Lon from the window, not, as in the novel, one from the window and a second in the street standing next to his body. Again in deference to the times, Peckinpah probably figured he could never get away with the second blast point-blank to Lon's head (or else he decided to combine both into one for dramatic concision and to make it easier and more economical to stage and film).

Now to those problematic changes in the third act. Given how much he complained of the way Marlon Brando softened and romanticized Rio, the Hendry figure in *One-Eyed Jacks*, we must ask why Peckinpah dropped all the scenes and incidents that reveal how really cold-blooded, remorseless, and at times even gratuitous a killer Hendry is while retaining those or inventing new ones in which his killings can be justified according to the so-called code of the West. Thus, he didn't use the scene where, with a murderous smile on his face, the Kid guns down an unarmed drunken old forty-niner in cold blood just because he was annoying the girl the Kid was dancing with. Nor did he include the Kid's equally cold-blooded murder of Bob Emory—which was also a premeditated murder—just because he thinks Emory has jinxed him. Likewise dropped was the ambush of Curly Bill Dedrick. Yet Peckinpah not only kept the killing of Johnson, which, as in the book, is in self-defense, he added a touch of gallantry to it by having Hendry first throw him out of the saloon for calling Modesto a greaser. He also kept the killing of Pablo, who, it can be argued, gave the Kid no choice; and he kept the killing of Lon, who is so hateful that even in the novel it feels like proper comeuppance for his viciousness. Nowhere does Peckinpah ever attempt to dramatize the sheer, indeed, the almost addictive pleasure Hendry takes from time to time in killing. The closest he comes to any of this, perhaps, is retaining the card game, with Hendry's shockingly indifferent reaction when Harvey breathes his last breath: "Well, that's that" (110).

The Kid's revenge upon the Dedricks Peckinpah fashions into a more or less conventional climactic Western shoot-out in which the Kid gives them and Shotgun Smith a fighting chance. When he mounts up and announces he's going after them, spurning Doc's offers to come along, I found myself thinking that at this point Peckinpah's Hendry was fairly indistinguishable from Brando's Rio when Ben Johnson's Bob Emory proposes they just ambush the sheriff and Brando answers, "That's not my style." Yet it most certainly *is* the style of Neider's Hendry and also of the real Billy the Kid, both of whom kill in whatever way does the job most efficiently. If that means ambush, then ambush it is. Nobody fretted about being called a coward and any notion of fair play was laughable—the idea was to get it done and get away before getting shot in the process. ("If they move, kill 'em," orders Pike Bishop in a close-up that desaturates to the title card featuring the director's credit in *The Wild Bunch*.) But Peckinpah's Kid not only goes it alone, he rides proudly, brazenly, straight up the middle of the main road and right into the Monterey plaza. Someone alerts the Dedricks and Smith that he's coming. When the Kid sees them run out of the hotel across the street toward the jail, he spurs his horse to a gallop and draws his revolver. The Dedricks make it into the jail, but the overweight Smith isn't so lucky. Crouching and raising his shotgun as the Kid dispatches him, Smith falls to the ground dead, both barrels discharging ineffectually into the dirt. Once inside the jail the Kid encounters another deputy, this one so terrified he throws his gun to the floor and raises his hands high above his head. The Kid tells him to clear out, then climbs the stairs, where he kills both Dedricks, but not before Cal manages to wound him in the shoulder. By this time, Dad, who's been having supper elsewhere in town, has been alerted and rushes to the jail.

331. INT. FIRST STORY CORRIDOR - FULL SHOT -
     HENDRY'S POV - (DAY)

     Dad takes two quick steps into the office, his
     gun coming up as he moves, then stops for a brief
     instant.

                         DAD
                  (almost pleading)
              Drop it, amigo -- now!

332. MED. SHOT - HENDRY

     He raises his gun instinctively.

333. CLOSE SHOT - DAD

     He fires.

334. CLOSE SHOT - HENDRY

     He takes the bullet high in the chest and falls
     backward, the gun skidding from his hand.

335. MED. SHOT - CORRIDOR - DOWN ANGLE

Dad walks slowly toward him, holstering his gun
as he does. Hendry forces himself to a sitting
position.

                    HENDRY
              (trying to grin)
        Lucky shot . . .

                    DAD
              (softly)
        Lucky for me . . .

                    HENDRY
        I guess this takes care of it.

                    DAD
              (moving with him)
        Looks that way . . .

    Granted it's a nice touch to have Dad pleading with Hendry to stay his
hand mirror Hendry pleading with Pablo not to flee. But is it worth the rest of
the trade-off? Here it's almost as if the Kid is now killed as the result of a kind
of misunderstanding—"He raises his gun instinctively" while Dad doesn't
realize Hendry's wounded—as opposed to the freak stroke of fate that in
both history and Neider's fiction sent him backing into a dark room where
the equally surprised sheriff, who thought he was someplace else, had the
presence of mind, not to mention the damn good luck, to make a split-second
decision that saved his life and ended the Kid's.
    Peckinpah's substitution of a shoot-out for Neider's far more effective his-
torically based climax is disappointing, but at least it is worked out with skill,
restraint, and some real inventiveness, which is a lot more than can be said
for the egregious cliché of sentimental camaraderie that follows next. Knowing he's mortally wounded, Hendry tells Doc he wants to go back, so Doc and
Dad help him onto his horse and escort him out to the Punta, where, high on
the bluff, the day drawing toward evening, he takes a last long look before,
backlit against the sky and the ocean and "the thousand twilight colors that
follow a Monterey Sunset," he slumps off his horse to his death (118–20). I
am utterly at a loss to fathom what Peckinpah was thinking when he came
up with this, though I did find myself recalling a letter he once wrote to me
expressing nothing but contempt for the similarly over-the-top sunset that
closes *The Deadly Companions*, claiming the intent was ironic, "a bit of the
finger to 'The West,'" adding, "few people picked up on it." But that was a film

he virtually disowned owing to fights with a fatuous, meddlesome producer. *The Authentic Death of Hendry Jones* is a book he revered. Surely there can be no ironic intent here—what purpose could it possibly serve?

Peckinpah got the screenplay back on track by writing a final scene (121–24) that is virtually a transposition, dialogue and all, of Neider's fine closing pages. The Mexicans accuse Dad of cutting off the Kid's trigger finger. "What would I want with his trigger finger?" he returns in stunned disbelief. "Don't you know that I liked him—that I was once his pard? The only reason I killed him is that it was a groundhog case of him or me." Doc informs them the trigger finger is still on the Kid's hand, pleading, "Hombres, don't disturb his grave." When one of them picks up a shovel, Dad threatens to "kill the first man that touches his grave with a spade." The man relents, but another says it doesn't matter, it wasn't really the Kid who was killed anyway, the Kid got away to old Mex. Yes, agrees one more, "They couldn't kill the Kid that way." And someone else, "I know it wasn't the Kid. I saw him. I knew the Kid. That's not the Kid in there." Francesca, the old woman for whom the Kid was her *chivato*, settles the matter: "It's not the Kid. The Kid's in old Mex," to which Doc replies, "That's very good Francesca." This is the last line of the novel, but Peckinpah appended one more brief moment to his screenplay. As the mourners begin to disperse, there is a time cut to:

```
356. FULL SHOT - GRAVE

    It is deserted, lonely and small on the rugged tip
    of the cypress point. After a moment Nika MOVES INTO
    SHOT and stands looking down, then turns and walks
    away as we

FADE OUT:


                    THE END
```

As a closing sentimental-romantic image, this is lovely enough in and of itself and would not be sufficient to soften the hard-edged ironies of the bickering around the Kid's grave. The trouble is, it doesn't exist by itself, but appears rather to be part of a larger pattern of changes that are worth a closer look. To start with, Peckinpah purged the Kid of much that might make him appear cruel, merciless, and homicidal; instead, as the screenplay goes along, he comes more and more to resemble a conventional good badman, less vicious, more heroic, less morally equivocal, more honorable. At the same time, he seems far less haunted, driven, depressed, dissipated, and self-destructive than his counterpart in the book, and much less mysterious, ambiguous, and frightening, no longer the doomed young man pretty much at the end of his tether, subconsciously looking for a way to get killed without actually pulling the trigger on himself. Ironically, if Peckinpah had managed to get more of *this* Hendry into his screenplay, his newly fashioned climax might have worked better because it might have played like a convention transformed. No filmmaker I'm aware of has anything approaching Peckinpah's gift for revitalizing clichés, conventions, types, and stereotypes: by using them in fresh and often radically original ways, he reendows them with an expressive force and vigor that often astounds us into an appreciation of how powerful they originally were. If the Hendry of the screenplay had by this point not diverged so much from the Hendry of the novel, then his decision to face the Dedricks, Shotgun Smith, and Dad alone might feel like a psychologically plausible resolution to a death wish he cannot acknowledge or realize in any other way. This would lend a resonance and irony to the shoot-out that might elevate it above the merely conventional.

In place of this Hendry, Peckinpah gives us one who seems something of a rebellious and defiant, albeit deadly teenager. In strictly psychological terms what he says and does could almost be interpreted as motivated by a need to get and keep the attention of the only father figure he's ever known in the only way he knows how: forcing a reaction by being contrary. When Dad's reaction is not the one he's looking for, he feels betrayed and lashes out. ("You won't be happy until you break it" crossed my mind more than once reading the screenplay.) To be sure, in the first act Peckinpah does intensify our sense of Hendry's cruelty by showing how he betrays Nika with Juanita; but in the third he reneges on this somewhat by no longer having Nika become so hysterical with grief after her brother's murder that she blames Hendry. Instead, in just about the only really bad dialogue in the entire screenplay, Peckinpah has her actually *thank* Hendry "for being here—it meant a lot—to all of us" (114). But how could Nika possibly be grateful to Hendry for being there? It's precisely because he *was* there—because he didn't leave when Dad asked him to or when Nika wanted him to take her away to old Mex—that the chain of events resulting in Modesto's death was set into motion. Whatever Peckinpah was thinking here, altering Nika's behavior is manifestly no improvement upon the book for psychological truthfulness or dramatic effect. Otherwise, his treatment of their relationship stays close to the novel: Nika remains hopelessly in love with Hendry, but she wants nothing more than for him to clear out because she realizes, as he is too selfish to, that their relationship is destroying both of them.

Yet even this fails to make as strong an impression as it might because of how gingerly Peckinpah handles the parallel theme of Hendry's out-of-control drinking. This is almost relentlessly present in the novel—there are places where it seems as if Doc can't get through a page without calling attention to the toll it's taking on Hendry's body and spirit. But in the *Hendry Jones* screenplay the drinking is so underplayed it made me wonder why Peckinpah kept the detail from the book of the Kid's hands trembling as he tries to light a cigarette in jail. In the novel we are in no doubt this is because the Kid is deprived of his whiskey. But how can we infer this from the screenplay? And if we don't, then the most logical other explanations—nerves, fear, trepidation—are misleading. Whatever failings the Kid may have, his cold nerve never deserts him: that much is built into Neider's conception of the character.

When most of this is added up, it's hard to escape the conclusion that for all his animus toward Brando for sentimentalizing and romanticizing Neider's novel and for making the Kid into a conventional hero, Peckinpah was to some extent guilty of the same thing, though of course to a vastly lesser degree. The screenplay still "works"; it's still broadly speaking faithful enough to the novel; and it still reads as if it would make a really fine Western, albeit one that in the last act inexplicably veers off in a less interesting, more conventional and seemingly compromised direction from the quite remarkable first two acts. But a question still nags: how to reconcile the relatively weak new material in the third act with the intelligence, purpose, point, and effect of that in the first act? Something isn't quite computing here, especially in view of how inconsistent the later changes are with what we know of Peckinpah's enthusiasm for the novel (notably the specific terms of his enthusiasm) and his priorities this early in his career, which were for realism, naturalism, and authenticity. Nor are the romantic elements consistent with his style of romanticism, which is passionate, volatile, deeply felt, ambiguous, and far more radical, even subversive. To pose such questions, however, is to come right back up against one of the central problems of unproduced screenplays long past: do we know exactly who was responsible for what? Yes of course Peckinpah wrote every word of the *Hendry Jones* screenplay, but can we be confident that the decisions as to what was kept, what was dropped, and what was changed were his alone?

I can adduce virtually no evidence of any kind for arguing that they weren't, but I would very much like to believe some of them were ordered by Rosenberg. This was, after all, the very beginning of Peckinpah's career in the film industry, when he had virtually no reputation and therefore no power. Shortly after he turned in the screenplay, he discovered firsthand how insecure even a big powerful movie star like Marlon Brando could be as regards roles he felt audiences wouldn't accept him in and what he was prepared to do about it. Despite his own admiration for Neider's novel, Brando clearly saw it as the springboard to play a more conventionally romantic-mythic Western hero, not a dark ironic one. Though at this point Brando was not yet involved in the project, if the idea of sending it to him had already occurred to Peckinpah and Rosenberg, perhaps concerns such as these were taken into consideration. Viewed from this perspective, the third act changes and the new conception of the title character make altogether more sense.

There is only one difference between the two drafts of his screenplay that might be called upon to suggest Peckinpah was forced to make a change against his will, and that is the scene between Nika and Billy following the death of her brother. Here is the later draft (114):

                          NIKA
                  (trying to control
                  her tears, slowly)
      I want to thank you, Hendry . . . I want to
      thank you for being here -- it's meant a lot
      -- to all of us.

                        HENDRY
                  (looking away,
                  loudly)
      Don't worry -- I'll get them.

Nika walks slowly toward him, her voice breaking.

                        NIKA
      Sure you will -- every one of them. But then
      what are you going to do, Hendry . . . ?

And here is the earlier one (128):

                        NIKA
                  (trying to control
                  her tears, slowly)
      I want to thank you, Hendry -- I want to thank
      you for giving him a gun . . . I want to thank
      you for being here -- it's meant a lot -- to
      all of us.

                        HENDRY
                  (looking away, loudly)
      Don't worry -- I'll get them.

Nika walks slowly toward him, her voice breaking.

                        NIKA
      Sure, you'll kill them -- every one of them.
      But then what're you goin' to do -- what's the
      "Kid" goin' to do when there's nobody left
      to kill?

Nika's tone in the earlier draft strikes me as plainly ironic, if not downright sarcastic: she clearly blames the Kid for Modesto's death and for making the life of a gunfighter attractive to him, the crucial line being her withering "I want to thank you for giving him a gun." In the later draft, this has been removed, along with the equally sarcastic reference to Hendry as the "Kid," and made merely emotional and sentimental. The difference is sufficiently marked that for me it's hard to believe the change originated in a decision from Peckinpah alone. But as any sort of "evidence," this is slender to the point of threadbare.

The reality is that we will never know, as none of the principals survives, nor do notes of meetings, notes Peckinpah might have made for himself, or early drafts rejected before those he submitted to Rosenberg and Brando. In fact, there is only one thing we do know as a matter of absolute certainty: when he next turned to these materials a decade and a half later, it would be during one of the blackest periods of his life, he would be at the helm, and the film he delivered would express that blackness in the most uncompromising terms.

Rudy Wurlitzer, Cuba, 1987

CHAPTER FIVE

Wurlitzer's Screenplay

Not only did Billy the Kid appeal to the writer as a romantic myth signifying the sacrifice of youth and freedom, but at one time in his youth he had been convinced that he was a direct reincarnation of Billy the Kid. The shadowy figure of Pat Garrett, at first illusive and alien, became more and more luminous and dominating. . . . Garrett is actually more interesting than the Kid. The killer of freedom is often the true subject of freedom. If the writer had been Billy the Kid as a youth, he was Garrett as a man. So the echo of Garrett's shooting of the Kid became the echo of the film, or, to be exact, of the script, the two men becoming entwined like lovers even beyond the last bullet which ended the breath of the younger.

—Rudolph Wurlitzer

Rudolph Wurlitzer wrote these words as the introduction to a version of the screenplay of *Pat Garrett and Billy the Kid*,[1] published in July 1973, by which time the film, released just two months earlier in the last week of May, had proved itself a box-office failure.[2] Meanwhile, Wurlitzer, after dealing with Peckinpah at his best and worst for the better part of a year, was still so angry, frustrated, and disgusted by the changes forced on his work that he used the introduction as an occasion for some—no doubt well earned but perhaps not entirely well advised—venting on the trials and tribulations of writers in the film industry, his own on this project paramountly. In Hollywood he was "faced with the usual compromises of being used and courted like a nineteenth-century woman and then inevitably discarded from the hierarchy of power," and he accused Peckinpah, "suddenly thrilled by his own collaborative gifts," of reducing the script "to its most simplistic components." Wurlitzer's resentment was understandable, but Peckinpah always reworked screenplays, whether originally by him or by others, before and during filming, typically (though not always) for the better, and usually in the direction of greater complexity and difficulty: he never liked to make response easy for his audiences, which was certainly the case by the time he was finished with this film. And if time spent and work done on something are any measure, then in view of his adaptation of *The Authentic Death of Hendry Jones*, his claims to this story and these materials were at least as strong as Wurlitzer's.

Wurlitzer has long since wished he could take back a lot of that introduction. In one of the many communications between us, he wrote, "These days, as I look back over forty years and many scripts later, I regret having complained about Sam's intrusions into the script. I now see him as an extraordinary artist, using his dark side along with his extraordinary charm and passionate commitment, to risk creating a story that was close to the bone, intimate and dangerous." In fact, the collaboration began very amicably, evidence for which exists in a taped preproduction story conference between Peckinpah and Wurlitzer in September 1972.[3] Documenting the occasion when Peckinpah first brought up his *Hendry Jones* adaptation, this recording makes clear that it was in absolutely no spirit of his forcing the screenplay upon the writer and no air of superiority or insistence. On the contrary, Peckinpah told him that "there's a lot of shitty things in it, but there's some fucking good numbers and things that might be applicable, but I'll leave that up to you." Wurlitzer, for his part, was happy to have it as a way of getting to a clearer idea of some of what mattered most to the director about the story.

Back then, however, as things went forward, Wurlitzer eventually did have more than enough cause for complaint: between the Sam Peckinpah Papers and the Turner/MGM Scripts in the Margaret Herrick Library, there are twenty-seven copies of scripts for *Pat Garrett and Billy the Kid*. Several are duplicates, some partial, but the sheer number alone gives an accurate idea of how worked over his original screenplay was by the time principal photography wrapped in February 1973. I will discuss the versions of the screenplay and their variants in the next chapter, for they document the start of the process by which Peckinpah would make *Pat Garrett and Billy the Kid* arguably his most personal film (including even *Bring Me the Head of Alfredo Garcia*). But that start had prior beginnings both distant and proximate. The distant ones we have already examined; the proximate one is Wurlitzer's screenplay, which demands a closer and more sympathetic look than it has so far received.

Allow me to begin with a confession: in the first and second editions of my critical study of Peckinpah's Western films, I came down pretty hard on

Wurlitzer's screenplay as published in 1973 and on the criticisms he made of Peckinpah's changes. As a storyteller Wurlitzer's impulses are fundamentally lyrical as opposed to dramatic—whereas Peckinpah's are both dramatic and lyrical—but to call the screenplay "resolutely, almost defiantly undramatic," as I did, is too strong by double. In fact, as I will show, contrary to its reputation, Wurlitzer's screenplay was remarkably tight and focused and had an exceptionally strong dramatic structure. I also cast aspersions on some of the dialogue, which I called "stilted and inauthentic," words I now wholly retract and regret ever having written (*Reconsideration* 260, 263). One of Wurlitzer's great gifts as a screenwriter is his ear for dialogue, and it is anything but stilted or inauthentic. One small but telling example: when Garrett orders Alias to go read the labels on the canned goods, he calls them "air tights." For the longest time I had no idea whether this expression was truly authentic (turns out it is), but it *sounds* authentic and in a story that is really all that matters. And one large example, equally telling: while Peckinpah made a lot of changes, most of the dialogue in the film is either by Wurlitzer or very close to what he wrote, including Garrett's longest and best speech, when on the ride to Chisum's ranch he puts his presumptuous deputy John W. Poe in his place in no uncertain terms.

I have no excuse, only explanation, for why I advanced some of the criticisms I did. I first read the published screenplay after I had gone back to see the film a few more times and was still chafing over the generally unfavorable initial reviews in much of the popular media. Most of them struck me as glib, superficial, and stupid—in those days, alas, oftener the rule with Peckinpah than the exception—the reviewers responding less to the film in front of them than to his reputation as an ornery, hard-drinking misogynist, a brilliant director but also an unruly and undisciplined one whose films were too violent. I was also angered by an emerging pattern: many of the same reviewers who were using (and would continue to use) *The Wild Bunch* as a club to bash what they judged a decline in his work not only failed to appreciate that film when it first came out but were actively hostile toward it. At the time I felt the need to be protective, even though I already knew a great deal about his behavior on the set and during postproduction, the drinking in particular. It also seemed to me churlish for Wurlitzer to be attacking a director who had been responsible for making it possible for his screenplay not only to get made at all but in several key respects to have improved upon it. As with Walon Green's screenplay for *The Wild Bunch*, Peckinpah did not abandon Wurlitzer's but built upon it, changing only what he felt needed to be changed. Yet to my knowledge he never sought an onscreen writing credit, feeling that he didn't change enough to warrant it.[4] Despite some serious and substantial reservations about the screenplay—which he expressed privately to some close friends and of course in preproduction and production memos circulated among himself, Wurlitzer, and the producer and later in story conferences—Peckinpah in interviews and other public statements always referred to it in the most positive, even glowing terms and never ever represented the film as anything other than a true collaboration. In saying these things, he wasn't just being collegial—he said them because he believed them to be *true*, which as a matter of fact they were.

What I had not read at the time, however, was Wurlitzer's first completed draft, which was written three years before the version he published, over two years before the beginning of principal photography, and titled simply *Billy the Kid*. He called his published version "a compromise between the first versions and the final, shooting script," judged it "a good read," and considered it "authentically" his yet still "close enough to the actual film." Given this last sentiment and what he had said about the director's changes, it simply did not occur to me that the publication could be all that different from the first draft, even though I knew that the published version was very different from the film.

The producer Gordon Carroll initiated the Billy the Kid project for the director Monte Hellman, who recommended Wurlitzer write the screenplay. Wurlitzer had done a page-one rewrite for Hellman on *Two-Lane Blacktop*, a counterculture succès d'estime (much admired by Peckinpah) that fared poorly at the box office (though has since become a genuine cult classic). Hellman remained attached until at least the middle of 1971, and Carroll managed to pique the interest of MGM, where he had a development deal. During this period Hellman reportedly got a commitment from Jon Voight for Billy and was talking to Robert Redford and Marlon Brando for Garrett. Trouble was, James Aubrey, the MGM studio head, considered Hellman a "small pictures" director and insisted upon an A-list director and at least one A-list star. The demand for a different director turned out to be propitious for Carroll, because both he and Wurlitzer had already begun to find themselves at odds with Hellman about how to develop the screenplay further and were facing resistance because the screenplay itself was deemed insufficiently commercial. According to Wurlitzer at the time, "it was too existential," "there wasn't enough conventional action," and "the exposition was too spare, too minimal": "The consensus . . . was that the project, if it was to have any chance at all, needed two, no, three, call it four cash-box scenes. Scenes of high action, clichéd exposition, obvious clarity. The writer sat down to write them, trying to eliminate the clichés and keep to the original line." Since these criticisms were filtered through Carroll, Wurlitzer doesn't know the source or sources of them; but when I queried him about them and other matters in 2013, he gave a more detailed and rather different account of this early stage of the project:

> I had just come off writing *Two-Lane Blacktop* for Monte Hellman, which was my first encounter with L.A. and the film scene. Monte left me completely alone to drift through the car scene inside the evolving non-traditional corridors of my imagination, which I accepted, as if that

was the way it was done, being totally innocent of the hierarchies and sublimations involved in being a screenplay scribbler at the mercy of producers and directors. Monte hired me when he read my first novel, *Nog*, which represented a radical departure from traditional narratives, an intuitive and free exploration into movement for its own sake that I was able to continue with *Two-Lane*. So my first draft of *Billy* was written in that mode. Gordon Carroll was the first hands-on company producer I worked with and he influenced the direction of the script, steering me towards a more acceptable narrative structure, although at first, not really knowing where I came from, he left me alone as Monte was still the choice. When it became clear that the studios were looking for a more bankable director, everything changed with the story.

By the time Sam came on, I wasn't concerned with cash box scenes, being more involved with making the over-all drama more intense and theatrical, but with more integrity to the story line. Sam's presence was inspiring as well as somewhat intimidating and in his way, which was full of sudden surprises, he taught me a lot about action and how it serves a greater intimacy with the characters if it's filmed in the right way: lucid, always moving, usually surprising but inevitable.

The germinal idea behind the project, which was brought to Carroll sometime in late 1969 or early 1970, was to explore some parallels between the lifestyles and careers of rock stars and outlaw heroes of the Old West, specifically what it must be like to live your life to its fullest very early, between the ages of, say, nineteen and twenty-three, climaxing "at one incandescent point, then it's over." Carroll told me he considered several outlaws, but the more research he did the more obvious it became that Billy the Kid was really the only choice, despite the sizable history of Billy the Kid movies, most of them bad. When he was introduced to Wurlitzer and told him what he had in mind, the young writer—he was thirty-three at the time—said he had already been researching a screenplay about the Kid. Wurlitzer, who always loved Westerns and identified with Billy in part because he too was born back east (Upson's strategy in giving the Kid a New York birthplace evidently still effective some eighty years later), focused on Billy's "initial innocence and spontaneity and how he became corrupted inevitably by a narrative that he had no control over. In those days I gave myself permission to explore the dark side by intuitively pulling the rug out from traditional narrative (as in *Two-Lane*) and was drawn to explore the creation of myth for its own sake."

Beginning the writing in March 1970, he worked fast and submitted a complete *Billy the Kid* screenplay by June 21, 1970. It is, to my way of thinking, the purest distillation of what he made of these materials and indicates more clearly than any subsequent versions what he brought that was new and original to the retelling of the story. In this specific sense it is also, I believe, superior overall as a finished screenplay to the one he published because, written as it was in a very concentrated period of time that allowed few opportunities for distraction or influence by others, it is through-conceived and fully realized on its own terms in a way that none of the subsequent versions is, whatever dividends in greater richness of character and complexity of theme and texture they eventually yielded on film. Yet apart from Wurlitzer himself and Carroll, it's doubtful anyone involved in the production, including Peckinpah, ever read it. Nor to my knowledge has anyone who has written substantially about the film read it, except for Robert Merrill and myself. But I discovered it only in 2012 and Merrill learned of it from me, too late for it to inform the chapter on the film in his and John L. Simons's *Peckinpah's Tragic Westerns*, which was published in 2011. No one has been more thorough than Merrill in combing through the several screenplays, but it's easy to understand why both he and I, and maybe others too, never discovered the first version: a copy is not among Peckinpah's files and other papers the family donated to the Herrick Library (though most of the other versions are), so it isn't filed with the Sam Peckinpah Papers. Rather, it's in the *Pat Garrett and Billy the Kid* section of the Herrick's Turner/MGM Scripts archives, where it's grouped with several subsequent versions that duplicate some of those from the Peckinpah Papers. The trouble is that the different collections are not yet cross-listed; and the further trouble is that even if they were, this first draft would be easy to miss because it's catalogued as *Pat Garrett and Billy the Kid*, not as *Billy the Kid* or, as the title page has it, BILLY THE KID, complete with caps and broken underscoring.[5]

Right away the title is revealing of Wurlitzer's—and Carroll's and Hellman's—initial emphasis and focus: *Billy*, not Garrett, just the Kid. Although the page counts for their respective scenes are very close in number—a ratio that remained fairly constant in every draft—the overriding impression is nevertheless that the Kid is the main character, Garrett the most important supporting character in what is fundamentally Billy's story. If this appears to contravene Wurlitzer's own statement that Garrett eventually became so much more interesting that he threatened to take over from the Kid, we must remember that he wrote those words fully three years after this first version and from the perspective of the many subsequent versions and the film itself, by which time both he and Peckinpah had irreversibly brought Garrett to center stage. Nor am I persuaded that Wurlitzer's first screenplay dramatizes what he says it does, in particular Billy's innocence, the conflict between him as symbol of freedom and Garrett as killer of freedom, and the themes of loyalty and friendship versus ambition and expediency. His is a far more original take on these materials than that, as is the completed film.

In researching the screenplay Wurlitzer availed himself of four primary sources: Maurice G. Fulton's *History of the Lincoln County War*, Eve Ball's *Ma'am Jones of the Pecos*, John W. Poe's *The Death of Billy the Kid*, and Garrett's *The Authentic Life of Billy, the Kid*. What he specifically took from each will be noted as called for, but the most important source remains Garrett. Like practically everyone else, Wurlitzer went to the last third of *The Authentic Life*, where the sheriff takes over as narrator, but he begins even deeper, specifically with chapter 22, the day of the jailbreak after Garrett has departed for White Oaks to collect taxes. As this version of the screenplay is available only at the Herrick Library, a summary of the action will be a useful prelude to the discussion that follows.

The screenplay opens in medias res in the jail with Billy and J. W. Bell, one of the deputies, playing cards as Billy tells how he shot Buckshot Roberts in the gut. Bell, who reminds him that Roberts was his (Bell's) friend, tells Billy, "I'll still be able to eat good after you swing" (3). Before long Billy engineers his spectacular escape. His first stop after leaving town is a farm owned by an old couple from whom he helps himself to a fresh horse. Garrett returns from White Oaks to find his deputies dead, deputizes Alamosa Bill, orders the formation of a posse, and pays a visit to his wife Ida. Billy rejoins his gang in Fort Sumner. The next morning they awake to find two strangers in the settlement. One is the character we'll soon know as Alias,[6] the other an old man who draws on Billy and whom Billy kills. Garrett travels to Pecos to see if his old friend Sheriff Cullen Baker has any idea of the Kid's whereabouts. Back in Fort Sumner Billy is target-practicing when he is joined by his girlfriend Maria, who urges him to leave the territory before the authorities capture or kill him. Sometime later he, Alias, and Silva steal cattle from Chisum. Billy and Alias take off after some wild turkeys; while they're gone, Chisum's men descend on Silva and shoot him and his horse dead, Billy and Alias watching from too great a distance to be of any help.

Garrett arrives in Santa Fe, where he goes to a cantina and sends a messenger to request a meeting with Governor Lew Wallace. While waiting Garrett plays some cards; a drunk in the bar hassles the messenger, and Garrett, a few drinks under his belt by then, breaks the drunk's jaw in retaliation, then goes off to see Wallace, who reaffirms to Garrett the urgency of apprehending Bonney to "stop all this anarchy" (41) so that the New Mexico Territory will attract investors. He reminds Garrett that he had offered Bonney amnesty, which the Kid refused. He tells Garrett a man named John W. Poe, hired by some Texas cattlemen, will be his deputy, and Garrett asks Wallace to put up a reward for Bonney. Wallace proposes two hundred dollars, but Garrett says the Kid's easily worth five hundred, and Wallace agrees.

Back in Fort Sumner Billy and some of his boys go to a roof-raising party outside the settlement; when they get there, they discover there is no party because the father earlier shot a man named Jake Hawkins for trying to get too close to his daughter. Billy and his friends talk the family into throwing the party anyway, and soon a table is spread with food and there is much merrymaking, Billy getting very drunk and singing "Silver Threads among the Gold." Later three men on horseback show up to avenge Hawkins,[7] but Billy and his boys take their guns, force them to strip naked, and send them on their way.

Poe eventually catches up with Garrett and they go to John Chisum's ranch to see if Chisum knows anything about the Kid's whereabouts. Back in Fort Sumner Billy and Maria are languishing in a stable when a voice calls out to Billy reminding him of a time they rode together. The voice belongs to Tom Ketchum, an outlaw from Billy's past. Seriously rattled that he could be surprised so easily, Billy decides that maybe a while in Mexico mightn't be such a bad idea after all. In the next scene, he leaves for Mexico and after riding for an indeterminate amount of time he comes upon the camp of his friend Paco, an old sheepherder. They get drunk together and Billy again sings "Silver Threads among the Gold" before passing out. Garrett and Poe arrive at Jones's Trading Post,[8] where Garrett sends Poe on ahead. Soon Holly arrives with Beaver and Alias—all three Billy's friends and fellow gang members— and Holly tells Garrett the Kid is headed on down to Mexico. Back at Paco's camp, Billy awakens alone; hearing a sound, he draws his gun and fires only to discover he's killed a burro that has strayed from its owner.

Poe arrives at Tuckerman's Hotel, where he overhears some information about the Kid's whereabouts from a pair of old miners. Elsewhere Garrett, bathing in the Pecos River, hears shots in the distance, scrambles out of the water, and dresses quickly. Soon a large raft with a family on it comes round the bend; a huge red-bearded man, presumably the father, tosses a bottle into the water and shoots at it. Garrett hails the raft, asking the man where they're headed. "Downriver," he replies, firing at the bottle, missing it. When Garrett then fires at the bottle, missing it also, the red-bearded man fires toward Garrett and Garrett fires back, neither bullet finding a mark. The raft drifts on down the river as the two men continue to regard each other warily. Elsewhere Billy, half asleep in the saddle and drunk, wanders aimlessly through the barren landscape. Poe arrives in Fort Sumner pretending he's a miner, and he questions Luke and Eno (both members of Billy's gang) about the Kid; when they become suspicious, Poe leaves. Billy comes upon what appears to be a deserted cabin, goes inside, and falls asleep at the table. When he awakes he discovers a comatose man in the bed across the room. Sobered by the sight, the Kid leaves.

Garrett arrives in Roswell to enlist his friend Kip McKinney as an additional deputy. An exhausted Billy eventually arrives back in Fort Sumner and proceeds to get drunk with his friends. The next morning Garrett and McKinney, now joined by Poe, arrive in Fort Sumner. Garrett says he'll stay outside the settlement until dark when he'll be less easy to recognize. Billy awakens in the afternoon, hung over. After dark Garrett and his deputies split up and enter the settlement. Billy meanwhile goes to a saloon and starts drinking again. McKinney is looking for the house of a woman Billy is supposed to be involved with, but goes into the wrong house and interrupts Alias and a different woman in bed. Alias resumes his business and McKinney rejoins Garrett, who decides to inquire of Pete Maxwell as to the Kid's whereabouts. Billy leaves the saloon on his way to Maria's but, hearing some hammering, walks into the shop of a local carpenter. Meanwhile Garrett and the others pause behind the saloon where the Kid had a drink. Billy finds Maria and takes her to Pete Maxwell's, where they go to one of the bedrooms. But before making love, Billy goes to the outhouse. Garrett enters Maxwell's bedroom and sits beside the bed. More or less as it is described in Garrett's book, Billy on his return comes across McKinney and Poe, draws his gun on the two strangers, and, asking, "Quien es? Quien es?" backs into Maxwell's bedroom, where Garrett shoots him. Garrett walks out, Poe tells him he killed the wrong man, but Garrett assures him it was the Kid. When a confused, crazed Maxwell comes hobbling toward them, Poe raises his pistol but Garrett holds the deputy's wrist down, saying, "It's Maxwell." A distraught Maria shouts, "Garrett, you're a pig. That bullet you put into his body went into you. That bullet will always be in you" (118). The screenplay ends with Garrett, McKinney, and Poe looking on as the yard fills with the populace of Fort Sumner, the low moan of the women's voices rising to a shriek.

A few things are evident from even so sketchy a summary. There is far less violence here than in any subsequent version of the screenplay or the film, and there are only five killings: Billy shoots Bell, Olinger, and the nameless man in Fort Sumner, Chisum's men shoot Silva, and Garrett shoots Billy. That's it. Apart from the killing of the nameless man, there is no shoot-out in Fort Sumner the morning after Billy's return following his escape, no gunfight at Black Harris's (indeed, no Harris and his bunch at all), no death of Sheriff Baker, no killing of some of Chisum's men following the murder of Silva, no visit to the Horrell family where Billy kills Alamosa Bill in a duel (once he is deputized, Alamosa is never seen again), and no goading and killing of Holly by Garrett. Despite the presence of some scenes later dropped and the absence of those later added, and the wholesale reorientation of the story toward Garrett, the broad outline of the plot and the structure of scenes alternating back and forth between Billy and Garrett originate here, as does Wurlitzer's conception of Garrett and Billy never being seen together until the very end when Garrett kills him.

The totality of their friendship as expressed in any sort of dramatic terms is thus virtually nil, or, to put it another way, it's all backstory, and there isn't much of that. This is indicated early on in the scene between Ida and Garrett (19–20) when she tells him "people are probably repeating all those stories about being friends of his" and Garrett retorts, "I don't give a damn what they're saying." If they are meant to be true, then why have Ida refer to them as stories, as in rumors, as in untrue or at least unfounded? Presumably if anyone would know, she would. Throughout, Garrett hardly mentions Billy at all, and he makes no defense of him against Poe's insults (this scene was not written until sometime after the first draft, but even in its earliest iteration Garrett does not defend Billy). That there is some shared past is indicated by Garrett's response when told of the killing of Silva—"I always liked Silva" (37)—and his answer to Wallace asking if Billy is a friend, "I know Billy" (40). Yet both replies are notably terse and lacking in emotion or other sentiment. About all that can be assumed on the basis of what we're given is that there was *some* kind of relationship between Garrett and Billy and his friends, but that it was considerably less than a real friendship and at best more than mere acquaintance, while motifs such as loyalty, camaraderie, and betrayal are nowhere sounded in the screenplay.[9]

A number of scenes appear to be mere distractions or even diversions because so little happens in them. When Garrett visits Sheriff Baker looking for "sign" on the Kid, Baker has no information for him, so Garrett leaves; when Alias, Half-Breed, and Holly walk in on him at Jones's Saloon, they play a few hands of cards, he asks them about the Kid, Holly says he thinks he's in Mexico, then he and his pals walk out, leaving Garrett sitting alone with his whiskey; when Garrett checks in at Roberta's Hotel in Roswell, there isn't a whore in sight and he does nothing in the room he rents except lie down on the bed and stare at the ceiling; for most of the roof-raising party, Billy and his gang do nothing except get drunk, dance, and pass out; on the trip to Mexico Billy does little more than meander around in a drunken stupor until he winds up in the middle of nowhere at the apparently abandoned cabin. Garrett's meeting with Chisum is more substantial inasmuch as it establishes the loan that enables Garrett to buy some land for a ranch near Roswell, reveals the information that Billy once worked for Chisum and claims five hundred dollars in back wages (which Chisum in so many words denies), implies a personal reason why Chisum wants Billy apprehended, and indicates an acrimonious relationship between Chisum and Garrett.[10] But none of this receives any sort of development, and both Chisum's personal reasons and the suggestion of ill feeling between him and Garrett are left vague and unexplored.

When Garrett arrives in Santa Fe to meet with Governor Wallace (39–42), there are no businessmen or politicians awaiting who represent the forces of big business and government descending upon the territory, only the governor himself, a pompous windbag who seems to enjoy nothing so much as hearing himself orate. As if to make up for all the exposition missing elsewhere, Wurlitzer gives Wallace a long monologue that makes explicit the themes of economic development, the collusion of business and politics, the necessity to eliminate the Kid—who as a symbol of anarchy scares away investors and settlers—and other outlaws if the territory is to grow and prosper, and how the "myth" of the Kid makes him even more anathema to the vested interests, thus underlining the urgency to get rid of him. Putting it this way makes the monologue sound terribly clumsy, which it would be except that Wurlitzer ironizes it with a witty touch: a drunken Garrett nods off while the governor drones on. Wallace's monologue also makes conspicuous how absent these themes are elsewhere in the screenplay. Indeed, outside of this monologue, Wurlitzer does almost nothing to introduce, advance, or even much mention such typical Western antitheses as savagery versus civilization, the past versus the future, nature versus industry, natural man versus societal man, individualism and untrammeled freedom versus conformity and uniformity, a heroic past versus a prosaic present, a pure wilderness versus a corrupt and corrupting society built upon the "values" of commerce, a heroic ethos versus a business ethos, and so on and so forth. There isn't even much talk about the precariousness of law and order in a violent, untamed land.

But if the screenplay isn't about any of these things and if it isn't about the betrayal of the outlaw by the sheriff, what is it about? I personally believe the best clue is afforded by the song Billy twice sings, "Silver Threads among the Gold." Best to approach that, however, by way of comparing and contrasting how Wurlitzer characterizes Billy and Garrett. This Billy might be the most unsentimental and unromanticized portrait of the Kid in serious fiction or film. His predecessor is the title character of *The Authentic Death of Hendry Jones*, where Charles Neider was similarly unflinching in portraying the Kid as an unregenerate alcoholic and a near-pathological killer who takes a positive pleasure in killing. On one level Neider's novel can be read as a kind of Rake's Progress in the Old West, Hendry deteriorating into alcoholism, despair, and an early death that spares him the drawn-out, disgusting one from hard living and drinking that might be in store for him were he to survive into middle or old age. Although Wurlitzer ignored Peckinpah's suggestion to read Neider's novel (even to this day he has never read it), his Billy also follows a rake's progress and his early death likewise spares him a more protracted one in Mexico, should he have reached there and stayed. Neider made his Kid attractive in some fairly conventional ways—very handsome, very clean, very well dressed, even very gallant with the ladies—and although he's cruel to his girlfriend Nika, he befriends her brother, weeps when he is killed, and has a near breakdown after he murders a member of his gang in cold blood. Wurlitzer by contrast never softens or glamorizes his Kid, who is at least as cruel and ruthless as Neider's and undergoes a decline into booze, sloth, and sullen, volatile, antisocial hostility which is at once steeper, deeper, and far more extreme: this Billy the Kid is Hendry Jones carried to the nth degree.

Wurlitzer develops the Kid's decline in three stages. In the first, which goes from the opening through to the death of Silva, Billy commands, dominates, and controls the world around him through charisma, intimidation, his prowess with guns, and his readiness to resort to violence, whether against his enemies or his friends and even his lover. After retrieving the pistol hidden in the outhouse, Billy, knowing a man named Carlyle was a friend of Bell's, asks Bell if he knows how Carlyle died (5–6). When Bell says he heard about it, Billy, in a disturbingly vindictive display of sheer power, declares, "I want you to hear it from me": "I shot him three times in the back of the head. I blew his head off." Then he announces, "I'm going to kill you, Bell." Unable to move, Bell says, "I sure hope you don't, Billy," and Billy shoots him dead. As is not the case in the film, Bell here makes no gesture toward flight, so there is of course no pleading from Billy for him not to run and no hesitation, reluctance, or regret in killing him. The same is true of the killing of Olinger, which is also different from the film. Olinger plainly doesn't like the Kid and obviously relishes the thought of his imminent hanging, reminding him that people are "comin' a long way" and "I aim to please 'em by makin' sure you do a proper cakewalk and piss backwards before you swing up stiff" (2). But in marked contrast to Neider and to what was eventually filmed, Wurlitzer doesn't make any sort of big dramatic meal of the deputy's nastiness and he is never shown actually mistreating Billy. This has the effect of throwing our attention toward how much the Kid enjoys having the drop on Olinger: "They say shotguns make a nice pattern. I guess some of us are goin' to find out, Bob." After he breaks the shotgun over the railing, his "face, his eyes in particular, seem extraordinarily alive" (7).

Next Billy orders an old man—not Mexican, as in the film, but German, as he was in actuality—to bring him an ax (to break the leg-irons) and then get him a horse from the livery: "Saddle him and bring him around. You ain't back soon I'll come after you" (9). Later at the old couple's ranch, as Billy helps himself to one of their horses, the husband turns his rifle on him only to be warned, "You can't see well enough, Caleb. And if you miss I'll burn your house down and kill the rest of your hosses and most likely git you to pushin' grass from the underside" (13). The night Billy gets back to Fort Sumner, there's a nice subtle moment that reinforces his absolute dominion over his men and suggests the extent to which it is their fear of him that keeps them in line. Most of the gang are asleep in one of the barracks. Billy sits down on a bunk where Luke and some woman—she will later be identified as Maria—are having sex. Billy starts taking his boots off and without his having to say a word, Luke leaves the bed and Billy takes his place. (The scene ends with an amusing twist: moments after Billy enters her the woman exclaims, "You been inside that jail *casa* too long. . . . Oh, *madre*, you finish already" [23].) The next morning Billy's power is demonstrated in the way he dispatches the nameless man who's come looking for him. Offering him breakfast, Billy tells the story of how John Jones killed U. S. Christmas—though the version here differs from the one in the film and resembles instead the Alamosa Bill duel in the Horrell scene from later scripts—distracting the man enough so that as Billy lowers his plate, he simultaneously draws his gun and shoots the man dead, remarking, "Guess he figured we had to stand up. Times has probably changed" (26).

A different kind of ruthlessness and power is shown when Maria finds him practicing his shooting in a field (30–32). She begs him to leave the territory before he is captured again or killed. Although her entreaties echo sentiments already voiced by others, including Caleb and Luke, Billy will have nothing of it; when she presses the point, he "slaps her cheek, very hard," his expression cold and detached, and says, "Don't ever bother me when I'm standin' in the middle of a goddamn field." Then he draws her close to him and caresses her hair; she resists, he pulls her tighter; when she finally stops resisting, he "walks away, leaving her standing in the field." His short temper and violent response here are the first indications that he may be in considerably less control of his life than he seems and they also suggest there's a lot of denial going on, while feigning tenderness, getting a response, and then deserting her demonstrates his cruelty in a different way.

Although during this stage of the structure there are a few passing references to his getting older and the missed targets are intended to imply he may be losing some of his skills with a gun, what is mostly on display is his control of any situation he finds himself in. All this abruptly changes when he, Alias, and Silva steal some of Chisum's cattle (32–35). Billy and Alias spot some wild turkeys and take off after them, whooping it up, waving their hats, and shooting off their guns, leaving Silva alone with the cattle. The pair disappear over a rise after the turkeys, but soon tire, dismount, and lie on their backs, "winded and exhilarated," looking "at a cloudless sky." Their reverie is disrupted by the distant sound of hoofbeats in the valley below. They see a bunch of Chisum's hands surround Silva and shoot both him and his horse. Too far away to save him and anyhow outnumbered, Billy and Alias can do nothing but watch as the men "arrange Silva's body so that his arms are around the horse's neck and his legs around its belly," in an "obscene necrophilic posture." Once Chisum's men have ridden off after the stolen cattle, Billy and Alias ride up to Silva's body, where Alias (whom Wurlitzer made a stutterer) remarks, "It d-d-don't matter n-n-none once you—you—you're dead."

There are two significant developments here and one setup. In contrast to what has come before, this is the first scene in which the Kid has not been able to control a situation or to exert any power, being forced instead to watch helplessly while a friend is killed. Second, which follows from the first, his inability to control the situation is directly related to how irresponsibly he has acted, for it's difficult to escape the conclusion that both he and Alias are at least in part responsible for Silva's death: it was surely thoughtless, not to say stupid, to leave Silva and go off chasing turkeys, compounding the offense by yelling and shooting. Yet Billy (like Neider's Hendry) is unable to own it, very much as he cannot bring himself to admit that he's in any danger from Garrett. Billy doesn't reply to Alias's remark, but the cold-blooded way Chisum's men murder Silva and disgrace his dead body sets us up to expect reprisals from Billy and his gang against Chisum and the other big landowners, very much as the real Billy did against the Regulators after the murder of Tunstall. But Wurlitzer thwarts this expectation and there are no reprisals.

The second stage begins with Billy and his pals departing Fort Sumner for the roof-raising party, to which Wurlitzer added an odd invention by having Billy go dressed as a woman (43–50). No explanation is given except perhaps Alias's remark that no one will recognize him that way,[11] though up to this point in the story Billy's safety in and around Fort Sumner has not been an issue: as Luke had remarked earlier, the law would "have to send a battalion to roost us out" (22). When I first read the published version of the screenplay

I thought this scene was a complete digression and said so (*Peckinpah* 189); over three decades later I discovered a memo by Peckinpah in which he called it "without purpose."[12] I think we were both wrong. It's a digression only if you miss the point, as Peckinpah apparently did and I certainly did, that the scene marks the first clear indication of Billy's decline, his weakening grip on himself and the world around him, both embodied in his drunkenness. Though he and his boys send the dead Hawkins's three friends or family (whichever they are) packing, Wurlitzer ironizes this not just by the dress Billy is wearing and backing him with lots of help from his gang, but also by having him asleep when the men arrive, the bottle still nestled in his lap. He's awake for the confrontation only because Alias rouses him from his drunken nap.

Billy's situation is thrown into greater relief by the scene that follows at Chisum's ranch, where Chisum and Garrett discuss his fate in the most dire terms, the old cattle baron assuring Garrett the Kid will be dead before the summer is over and Garrett swearing he'll get him first. When the story shifts back to Fort Sumner, it finds Billy and Maria naked in a stall in a stable (57–61). Reminding him he's been in Fort Sumner three weeks now (i.e., since the Lincoln jailbreak), she says, "People know you are here. Garrett, he knows you are here." Billy denies it, Maria insists upon it, Billy denies it, saying, "It don't make no difference." Then he says softly, "You're better 'n Celsa, but you ain't no better than that muchacha in El Paso. I forgot her name." Suddenly their argument is interrupted by a deep male voice that calls out Billy's name. Billy freezes, then carefully straps on his holster as the voice continues, "It's been a while, Billy." "I ain't exactly knowin' the voice," the Kid answers, as he steps out of the stall, still naked except for the holster, and into the next one, where a drunk man is asleep. The unseen voice continues:

> On that drive with S Bar S. Camped two days on the Berenda, near Clayton. You and me got liquored. We rode down to that big ole sheep camp some Mexicans had built. There was that old mother dog and four pups that belonged to that sheep outfit. The pups was about a month old. You been drinkin' more 'n I and you took those dogs, one at a time, and cut their throats. But that weren't nothin'. There was the time me and Wolf Stevens kilt us two women and throwed 'em in the Rio Grande. You wanted out. They hanged Wolf, Billy.[13]

"Tom Ketchum," Billy says. The drunk on the floor has come awake and stares wide-eyed at Billy, who ignores him as he continues talking to Ketchum: "Who you ridin' for, Tom?" By now Billy's "hands are shaking. He holds them in front of him and tries to hold them even, but they have a life of their own. He sees the man looking at him and drops his hands to his sides. Billy is pale with fear." Ketchum, still unseen, says he's just come off being a deputy in Amarillo because, wanted for rustling, he figures "the best thing was to be in the law until it blowed over." Maria flees the stable as Ketchum, still unseen, tells Billy, "I'll catch up with you later." Billy, "his voice quavering," says, "All right, Tom," then urinates over the chest of the drunk at his feet.

This scene is so strange—much more so than the roof-raising party—that it's worth appreciating how Wurlitzer has visualized the setting and the action. It is afternoon in a stable large enough to contain sixty stalls; cobwebs and birds' nests "filter the light that streams through a small window above the stall" where the scene opens with Billy leaning against the wall looking at Maria, who "lies on a thin pile of straw, staring at the ceiling." Though the script is ambiguous whether they've had sex or not—either way serves the story—they're completely naked and their physical and emotional attitudes suggest they're postcoital. The touch of romance from the filtered light is soon undercut by their arguing and even more by the sordid detail that, if they have made love, unknown to them a drunk was asleep the whole while in the adjoining stall. Once Ketchum's voice interrupts their argument, Billy straps on his holster without putting on any clothing—the symbolism so obvious no commentary is necessary—and carefully steps into the next stall, where he finds the sleeping drunk as Ketchum's voice keeps talking.

The information that Ketchum was a deputy and has operated on both sides of the law makes him a pretty clear surrogate for Garrett, who has also been on both sides of the law. And the way Wurlitzer allows Ketchum to disappear without anyone, including the prospective audience, actually laying eyes on him lends an ironic accuracy to Maria's warning moments earlier that Garrett's "been seen in many places." If Ketchum's disembodied voice can be construed so as to suggest that no matter where Garrett may actually be, he's relentlessly closing in, the man on the floor can be seen as a warped reflection of Billy, who, like him, had drunk himself to sleep in a preceding scene and will do so again in several to follow. The ease with which he has been snuck up on cuts right straight through all his denial and leaves him face-to-face for perhaps the first time in his life with an apprehension of his own vulnerability, not to say mortality, which so overwhelms him that he literally loses control of his bladder and pisses his pants, or would have except that he isn't wearing any. It would be hard to imagine a more vivid image of stark fear and sheer loss of control than the one with which Wurlitzer ends this scene: Billy, *his hand still on his gun*, cannot keep his bladder from emptying itself over the drunk's chest.

Come the next morning the Kid is saddled up and off to Mexico. As Wurlitzer envisions it, the journey is little more than one long bender. He comes upon Paco's sheepherding camp (62–66), where the two of them spend the better part of a day getting drunk as Paco tells him about the house he plans to build with his own hands, a speech that in the film was spoken while he was dying after being tortured by Chisum's men. But here Paco doesn't die and he doesn't need saving from Chisum's men. After singing "Silver Threads among the Gold" again, Billy falls asleep. The next afternoon as Paco departs with his herd, he leaves Billy a bottle of mescal and says, "Go to Mexico."

Billy very softly replies, "I'll be goin' directly." But later that day, Paco's herd scarcely out of sight, Billy uncorks the bottle and takes a drink. Then he puts the bottle down, measures off fifty paces, and tries to hit it, shooting from the hip. When he misses twice, he walks back, picks up the bottle, and takes another drink, then another and another until he's so drunk all he can do is lie against a wall staring into the distance under an "immense" and "completely quiet" sky, "the sunset brilliant and overwhelming." Soon he falls asleep again but is awakened by a noise and footsteps. Cocking his gun he calls out, "Name yourself," but there is no answer. "Say something or I'm goin' to stop you," he shouts. The footsteps continue and in a panic he fires until he empties his revolver. He hears a groan and once his eyes adjust to the darkness he makes out the dead body of a burro with a pair of metal trunks on its back. One of them has broken open and spilled out "needles and spools of colored thread, hair tonic and medicine bottles and rolls of fabric." It's obviously a drummer's burro, but there is no sign of the owner. The next morning Billy rides off, averting his eyes from the slain animal.

When next the screenplay returns to him, he is riding "slowly across a mesa," "half asleep in the saddle. He apparently has given the horse its own rein" (82). After a time cut to night, he continues riding past a small settlement of adobe buildings, keeping well away from them, as he "stares straight ahead." Though brief, these images suggest a pretty clear metaphor of a man being carried or driven along by forces to which he has abdicated all control, wandering without volition, purpose, or even much awareness of where he is, where he's going, or what he's doing. As this interlude immediately follows the raft scene, another image of humanity being pulled by currents it has no power but to follow, both scenes together, especially coming as they do back-to-back, reinforce the theme of determinism and lead to the last scene in stage two: the deserted cabin, one of the most eerily haunting scenes I've read in any screenplay (88–91).

In contrast to the desert settings of the rest of the trip to Mexico, the cabin is situated in "a small green valley," "intimate and serene," with a narrow stream running through it. The place "is well laid out and the corral and fences seem unusually immaculate." The Kid dismounts, draws his pistol. The door is closed and there is no sound from inside. "He slowly turns the door handle. Then he slams the door back and quickly steps inside, his six-gun ready." The room is sparsely furnished. A rifle hangs above the fireplace and next to it various animal traps and bowie knives. There are also a dozen skulls ranging from foxes to buffalo, their eye sockets "blank and staring." A wooden bunk is covered with a bearskin, hanging on nails over the bunk are four black scalps and dozens of necklaces made from animals' teeth, and next to the bunk is a small side table with a black-bound Bible on it. "Everything about the room is severely ordered and clean," reads the description. "There is nothing to suggest a woman's touch, or indeed, that of more than one other person. *The effect is ferocious and lonely*" (my emphasis). In the middle of the room sits a simple table with a single chair facing the door. By now Billy must have run out of alcohol, so we may assume he's sober. Once inside, he takes the rifle off the wall and puts it on the table, rummages through the cupboards (perhaps in search of a drink), but finds only some bread, which he sits down at the table to eat. He stares out the open door into the valley and soon falls asleep at the table, not to awaken until morning. He is startled to find the rifle returned to the post on the wall, the bread put away, the door closed, and a fully dressed man lying on the bunk "in tanned leggings and moccasins and a torn long-sleeved undershirt. He lies with his eyes open, staring at the ceiling. His eyes are enormous and unblinking. He is very thin, almost emaciated. His mouth is half-open, showing that he has no teeth. Except for his staring eyes, it is not clear whether he is alive or dead."

Billy is unable to take his eyes off this sight for several minutes, long enough for the light to shift from dawn to early morning. We never find out if the man is the owner of the cabin or another vagabond like Billy who has just wandered in or whether he is actually dead or merely comatose. Such questions matter little to Billy because whatever their answers, they would not alter what the man represents: an all-too-present and terrifying omen of the only fate Billy seems to fear more than death, which is becoming a man without identity, whom no one will remember, whose death is completely anonymous and isolated. This is the first, and by far the stronger, of two epiphanies for Billy, and out of it comes the only decision he seems to make as a matter of choice, which is to go back to Fort Sumner. Whether this decision can support a metaphysical interpretation, whether, as Wurlitzer himself once suggested (Aghed 129), that by accepting the mantle of his burgeoning legend, the Kid is making an existential choice to become Billy the Kid—these are matters for debate. What is beyond question, it seems to me, is that the decision to return is the only decision he appears to make after a mental activity that could be characterized as thought and consideration, one that isn't made through a fog of booze, under a cloud of denial, or as an excited reaction to panic or anger. It represents his desire to reclaim the only identity he knows in the only place he feels at home.

Billy's decision is not, however, sufficient to halt his decline—it appears rather to focus and hasten it. The third and final stage begins when, exhausted upon his arrival back in Fort Sumner—Wurlitzer makes a point of noting that his shirt is ripped, as if to recall the torn undershirt of the man in the bunk and thus further cement the association—Billy goes to a cantina where he finds some of his gang. Though they are happy to see him, he's sullen and hostile toward them, including Maria. Soon he fires off his gun to rouse everyone; but as the atmosphere becomes more and more festive, Billy gets quieter and quieter and so tired that Alias and Maria help him to a corner of the room, where Maria puts a blanket over him as he falls asleep. He doesn't come to until the following afternoon, when he awakens on a four-poster bed in a room where Maria and Eno tell him people have been asking about him, they

know he's in Fort Sumner (104–5). "I reckon," Billy replies, then, staring at
the ceiling, starts rambling about buying a ranch that he'll stock with cattle
stolen from Chisum and maybe raise some quarter horses too. Maria loses
patience and walks out, leaving him in the bed staring at the ceiling, a double allusion to the nameless man in the cabin and to Garrett in the room at
Roberta's, where the bed is also described as having four posters. This too is
an image evocative of death, which is now closer than Billy realizes. But in the
context of the story and where it comes in the screenplay, it is also a picture
of a man so depressed he's unable to make his muscles move. As in the stables
scene, it is left ambiguous whether Billy and Maria had sex the night before,
but, in another detail that suggests his waning power, they for sure don't the
night he dies: he goes to the outhouse *before* any lovemaking commences and
he's killed before he can return to their bed.

If Billy's story inscribes a straight line that figuratively descends, then Garrett's is a slowly narrowing gyre. Yet as the screenplay progresses their paths
have in common an overall movement from outdoors and/or daylight to
indoors and/or night. The further Billy declines and the closer Garrett gets
to him, the darker, more confined and claustrophobic the settings become,
reflecting of course the diminishing options of both men. As a character
Wurlitzer's Billy may be narrowly conceived and lacking in complexity as such,
but it is nevertheless a fully rounded, developed, consistent, and compelling
character. Garrett, however, is considerably less well defined, more elusive
and vague. He has gotten a loan from Chisum for a ranch near Roswell, which
appears to be linked to apprehending the Kid; and he also asks Wallace to
put up a reward. If Garrett were able to collect the reward, it would of course
help him pay off the loan sooner, but the one reason he gives for proposing it
is that it might encourage others to help him capture the Kid sooner, which
entails the possibility that Garrett wouldn't necessarily collect it or would
have to share it if he did. And Billy tells Maria that Garrett's "tied into the
highest hand and it's a game he ain't dealin'" (58). Yet these are dropped like
so many tangents, for us to make of them what we will or not. It wasn't until
later versions that Wurlitzer introduced the representatives of the Santa Fe
Ring at Wallace's; but even then the details of any deal to bring in the Kid, or
whether there even was a deal, are never made explicit, let alone clarified (and
in the later screenplays and the film I've always felt this was something of a
red herring beside other deeper, more complex and gnarled reasons [*Reconsideration* 270–98]). In this early draft Garrett's motivations remain murky, his
moods mercurial, his feelings rarely articulated or even indirectly indicated,
the things he says usually tersely stated, practical, inexpressive, and rarely
betraying his thoughts or emotions.

This is one reason among several why the screenplay feels so much more
like the Kid's story than Garrett's. Another is that it's not only front-loaded

with Billy's scenes, but with Billy at his most powerful and dominating. Later, when his decline starts, his is still the only character *development* that's driving the story. Garrett doesn't develop at all. For much of the script he does little of consequence, seems oddly ineffectual, and at times rather passive. Arriving on the scene after Billy has managed a sensational jailbreak, he is given a distinctly undramatic introduction: he enlists a deputy in Alamosa Bill, who's never heard from again; forms a posse; visits his wife, who complains that he fails to say he's happy to see her while he sighs, "It's going to be a long night," then leaves the house and we never see her again; the posse he had earlier called for turns out to be a motley lot that "thunders by him" and are also never heard from again. This essential pattern is replicated in most of Garrett's scenes: people and places are visited, some questions are asked, they are answered or not, the scenes end, most of the characters never heard from or even mentioned again, and the sheriff drifts on to the next encounter with someone else.

Not that the scenes are of no meaning or significance. They establish that Garrett has ties in the territory and relationships with several people. When he returns from tax collecting and calls for a posse, it's clear that many of the townspeople are against the Kid. One of them says he's glad to help, adding, "Some of us were wonderin' when you'd make your move," to which Garrett replies, "I'm makin' it now" (18). In Pecos, however, Sheriff Baker openly ridicules Garrett for working for the town of Lincoln, tells Garrett he doesn't even like him, and when Garrett leaves turns back to the boat he's building and says maybe he'll just get in and float on down to the Gulf of Mexico. The saloon scene before Garrett meets with Wallace shows that Garrett is well known throughout the territory, can pick up a card game wherever he goes, is tough and not to be messed with, and will avail himself of the services of a prostitute when the urge is upon him. When Holly and the others turn up at Jones's Saloon, there is a distinct tension between them and Garrett, but the card game seems to dissipate it. Other scenes show that he is ill at ease with the people he's working with, including Poe, whom he seems to dislike (but not nearly so much as in later drafts, especially once Peckinpah took charge), and he practically has to coerce McKinney into coming to Fort Sumner as backup. In the aggregate these moments suggest that Garrett seems to have few friends and virtually no intimates (including his wife), but at no point is it ever implied or otherwise suggested that he has any misgivings about the task he is performing ("I don't give a damn what people think"). But this still leaves us with a series of low-key scenes and mostly one-scene characters in which almost nothing happens that advances plot or deepens our sense of him.

By any rules of storytelling or dramatic logic, this shouldn't work. Yet in some difficult-to-define way, it does, at least in the reading. Why? In his introduction Wurlitzer refers to the "shadowy figure of Pat Garrett, at first illusive and alien." For me, it's this very shadowy and alien quality that paradoxically makes the Garrett figure so compelling and effective here. From a certain point of view he's not even a character as such: as befits his status as nemesis, the agent of fate, if not the embodiment of fatality, his function is akin to what in the trade is sometimes called "a ticking clock," that is, some threat, conditioned by time, that lends urgency to the plight of the main character or characters, while as a device he confers a quasi-dramatic irony upon the proceedings (I say "quasi" because, like the audience, Billy too knows Garrett is after him, but, unlike the audience, he is not aware of how tightly the noose is closing around him). A more individuated Garrett wouldn't necessarily weaken any of this—the film demonstrates that readily enough—but in the specific terms of the purity of this early conception, it might blur the focus and it would unquestionably dilute his power as a nemesis. Absent any dramatized or expressed feelings between Garrett and Billy, and without the killings of Black Harris and Holly, there is never any sense that Garrett is taking his own sweet time so that Billy will have a chance to clear out of the territory. Rather the opposite: both the unhurried, methodical, almost plodding manner of his pursuit and the scarcity of information he actually acquires as to the Kid's whereabouts if anything only reinforce the fatalism that informs this story and the idea that he is an agent in a course of action the outcome of which he is powerless to hasten, retard, or alter: hurrying won't bring it about any faster, slowing down won't delay it.

It's a pity that Peckinpah couldn't find a place in the completed film for Billy to sing "Silver Threads among the Gold," not least because it is believed to have been one of William Bonney's two favorite songs (the other "Turkey in the Straw"). More important, however, is that the twin themes of fatalism and determinism are obliquely woven together in the first verse, the only one Wurlitzer has Billy sing:

> Darling, I am growing old,
> Silver threads among the gold;
> Shine upon my brow today,
> Life is fading fast away;
> But, my darling, you will be, will be,
> Always young and fair to me;
> Yes! My darling, you will be,
> Always young and fair to me. (46)

This is a sentimental love song wherein the silver threads obviously refer to gray hairs beginning to appear on a blonde head, and its immediate relevance to Billy the Kid is equally obvious: even at the age of twenty-one he is beginning to feel the first faint pangs of the loss of his youth. (It's a nice touch that the second time he sings the song he falls asleep right *before* the line "Always fair and young to me" [66].) Although Wurlitzer doesn't really develop the motif of the Kid's aging very much (even his diminished target-shooting skills can be read as at least as much a function of his excessive drinking), the theme of life and lives fading fast away does precipitate out such that it eventually soaks through the entire story. (This is not surprising given the origin of the project in the lives of rock stars of the sixties.) It is a cliché of Western fiction and film that the way of life of the Western hero, be he cowhand, sheriff, or outlaw, is being pushed aside by forces of progress that are increasingly fencing in or crowding the vast open spaces. But some of the better Western writers and filmmakers also realize that there is something very sentimental, perhaps even false in the way this theme is typically realized, which often cloaks or obliterates a perhaps even darker theme. This other theme is how the Western way of life itself, transitory by its very nature, contained the seeds of its own destruction, its people, hero and villain, complicit in its (and their own) destruction. I've rarely seen this complex of themes better realized than in Wurlitzer's screenplay and the deeper, richer film Peckinpah eventually made from it.[14]

Once past the opening in Lincoln and apart from the Wallace scene in Santa Fe, the places Wurlitzer sets his screenplay are wholly on the fringes of society, where existence is hardscrabble, mostly hand-to-mouth, dirt-poor, and squalid, the inhabitants barely hanging on by their fingernails. The Kid and his gang are mostly a bunch of feckless layabouts who do little more than drink, screw, and pull occasional jobs like rustling. If they possess virtues like loyalty and any sort of fellow feeling, it's not greatly in evidence. They make no attempt to spring the Kid when he's in jail and it is suggested they never had any intention to. (Neider by contrast was careful to establish, and Peckinpah followed suit in his adaptation, that the three remaining members of Hendry's gang are too much outnumbered by Dad Longworth's posse.) They have no families that we can discern, and their women consist in prostitutes and camp followers who for the most part are passed around as casually as bottles of whiskey. Billy has a "special" girl in Maria, but when we are introduced to her she has taken up with one of his gang while he was in jail awaiting execution. There is no indication she is anything more to Billy than his latest transient attachment; any promise of a relationship that might include marriage and a family he rejects and her along with it. What is most obvious about Fort Sumner and everything associated with it is that there's nothing renewing or renewable about it. It's an abandoned fort and Wurlitzer makes it a point to mention that the buildings are "in disrepair"—as he does also of Caleb's ranch, which "is one of total disintegration," likewise Cullen Baker's house, "as dilapidated as the rest of the Pecos" (12, 21, 28). The unexpressed kicker behind Luke's joke that the law would need a battalion to get them out of there is that nobody seems to care enough to send a battalion, just a single sheriff and a deputy. But give this self-destructive Billy enough time and he and the rest of them may just get around to doing the job on themselves (and there is Chisum's cryptic remark, "Bonney won't live the summer" [54]). By the time Garrett catches up and shoots him, Billy has become almost

The horizontal path through the lower third of the photograph
indicates the location of the Pete Maxwell house in
Old Fort Sumner. None of the original buildings remains.

pathetically ineffectual, a man who starts drinking the moment he gets up in the morning and doesn't let up until he's gone through a few cycles of nodding off, coming to, then drinking some more until he finally drinks himself to sleep for the night.

Besides being harsh, imperiled, and transitory, life in the world of this screenplay is brutally, unyieldingly, punishingly exhausting; it beats you down until there's almost nothing left. When the three strangers show up at the roof-raising party, they are unshaven and bleary eyed; one, whose face is lean and ravaged, is "tired enough to fall out of his saddle" (45). When Billy arrives back in Fort Sumner from Mexico, he's unshaven and "weary to the point of collapse" (99). The motif of exhaustion reaches its most powerful expression in the scene in Tuckerman's Hotel, where Poe learns the Kid is in Fort Sumner from a pair of old miners. Poe doesn't have to beat information out of them, because one of them is such a blabbermouth that it comes out with no coercion at all while Poe just lies there appearing to mind his own business.[15] That's the plot function of the scene. But its meaning lies in the glimpse into the argumentative relationship of the two old men at the end of their partnership, dividing up their meager worldly possessions between them. They can be seen as something of a distorted counterpart to Garrett and Billy and they may also suggest a possible future for Billy and his gang if they should live so long. One is ornery and cantankerous; but the other is just plain bone tired. The scene ends when he rambles through a long, mournful complaint about how used up he and the country are. It so draws together and fuses all the motifs of drifting, aging, exhaustion, and loss that it could almost serve as an epigraph for the whole screenplay:

> I might drift over to Fort Sumner myself now that the army pulled out. Ain't nobody over there but locos ridin' the high line. Hell, I'm tired. Tired of lookin' for yeller rocks. Tired of tryin' not to look at your ugly face. Tired of seein' the land git crowded up. Tired of feelin' my bones stiffen up. Tired of hustlin' a stake. Tired of being snake-bit and sunstruck. Tired of listenin' to myself. Tired of huntin' and fightin' and killin', and waitin' to be killed. (80)

The reference to drifting calls to mind how much movement, images of movement, and references to movement consist in drifting or floating, that is, movement determined not by choice as such and that requires abdication to large, impersonal forces outside the self or equally powerful ones from deep inside. Even Garrett's pursuit of the Kid, though it has the single most important dramatic purpose in the story, has something of the feel of drifting, perhaps because it is so unhurried and because so many of the places he stops at or the people he questions yield such fruitless results. By the time he and Billy are brought together at Pete Maxwell's house, it's almost as if they've drifted into each other's presence—which of course doesn't make the encounter feel any the less fated. Indeed, paradoxically, the more random Garrett's path appears to be along the way the more unalterably fated it looks when viewed from its destination.

Equally telling are the numbingly repetitive "tireds" in the old miner's monologue. Once past the death of Silva, a fatigue sets in that seems to weigh down and burden everyone and everything. The raft floats down the river as if inch by inch. Garrett seems to move slower the closer he gets to the Kid, and the last thing he does before leaving for Fort Sumner is to lie on that bed at Roberta's staring at the ceiling, and he doesn't move or shift his posture from late afternoon to evening on through the night into the middle of the next morning. This sequence follows Billy's in the cabin; placed side by side, they have something of the feel of strange, ironic resurrections or rebirths. When Garrett finally rouses himself, he deputizes McKinney and it's on to Fort Sumner to finish the job he set out to do, though he does not know it will end there. When Billy awakens from his sleep, is transfixed by the horrific sight of the man in the bunk, then shakes himself loose from the spell, it's to return to Fort Sumner and resume his hapless decline, though he does not know it will end so abruptly.

Images of torpor, stasis, death, and life as a living death so proliferate in the screenplay that its action becomes the very embodiment of entropy: all energy, all striving, all force, all will just seem to be drained or draining out of these people. The man Billy kills in Fort Sumner has a "morose, toothless face" (23); the man and wife at the roof-raising party are "dour and expressionless"

(45); the drunk in the stall stares openmouthed and wide-eyed; the wife and boy on the raft "stare with a stern, mournful expression" (81); the skulls on the wall stare sunken eyed; the man on the bed stares with mouth open, toothless, and "enormous and unblinking" eyes; Billy cannot rouse himself out of bed his last day; and Garrett goes into a daze sitting in the dark room before Billy enters. Most everyone is desperate, despairing, and isolated, relationships and other connections always fraught, fragile, threatened by age, violence, and death. One reason why Wurlitzer's concept of Billy and Garrett never meeting until the very end works here is precisely because their friendship is treated as so tenuous from the outset. This may also explain why the several single-scene characters are so effective: people drift into each other's lives for a few minutes or hours, then leave, the spidery strands that connect them dissolving almost before they've turned their backs, closed the doors, or ridden out of sight.

The last of the numerous mirrorings, echoings, and doublings by which Wurlitzer binds together the characters and their destinies comes when Billy leaves the saloon in search of Maria. He hears the sound of hammering, which he follows into a shop where he is surprised to find a carpenter he used to know building a trunk (110–11). The last Billy heard the carpenter was in jail in Amarillo. He was, the carpenter tells him, but he busted out and had to kill some kid whose brother is almost certainly now looking for him. The carpenter relates this in a flat, almost monotone voice while continuing his work on the trunk, which is painted green and gold. The carpenter says he's going to rob the bank at White Oak, stash everything inside the trunk, put a silver lock on it, and "tie her up top of the stage and ride on out the country." Without saying a word Billy elects to stay for a while and watch the carpenter work. It's the Kid's second epiphany: a man who, like himself, has also broken out of jail, killed in the process, and now just waits for fate to catch up to him, the carpenter's talk about leaving the territory with the green and gold trunk no less a pipe dream than Billy's about buying a ranch and raising cattle and quarter horses.

Wurlitzer was told that this script wasn't easy to sell because it didn't have enough action, but I wonder if there wasn't something more basic going on: he took the most enduringly popular legend of the Old West and fashioned it into an uncompromisingly bleak vision of flux, mutability, and impermanence. It is a bleakness which survived all the subsequent changes and which Peckinpah fused with his own and realized in a film of extraordinary power, a film which turned out to be itself also not so easy to sell. It's a vision where everything seems to be separating, unraveling, deteriorating, dissolving, disintegrating, breaking down, breaking apart, blowing away, drifting away, floating away, fading away, dying away. The only tie that cannot be severed and that will survive even the finality of death is the fate that binds together the outlaw and the lawman: if ever two men shared a fixed purpose on a path laid with iron rails on which their souls were grooved to run, they were Pat Garrett and Billy the Kid. Yet in this fine, compressed, almost unendurably dark screenplay, it is a purpose without apparent motive, a path without apparent design, a determinism that serves no higher plan in a world without apparent meaning.

Rudolph Wurlitzer (*left*), in wardrobe as Tom Folliard, and Peckinpah

CHAPTER SIX

Peckinpah's Changes

A lot of the better moments in the script were inspired by Sam's character, his own advancing age and paranoid erosions and confrontations. There were many notches jammed on his fuselage, along with his defiant weariness about his compulsive on-going struggles with the studio, and his addiction to backroom dramas and how he used it to fuel a story about the corruption of innocence and loss of essential identity. So much of the final rewrites were influenced by Sam's instincts and his complex relationships, which is why the film, for the most part, carries such an authentic and personal imprint and almost always carries Sam's signature.

—Rudolph Wurlitzer

Peckinpah has long and rightfully been credited with making *Pat Garrett and Billy the Kid* far more Garrett's story than Billy's. As with so much else on this project, however, the process actually had at least one origin in a seemingly small change by Wurlitzer himself. Less than a month after completing the *Billy the Kid* original, he created a second draft, dated July 10, that was unchanged except for the addition of Garrett's name to the title. Why? To make it easier for Gordon Carroll to attract A-list stars for the part, which would have proved much more difficult with a script named after Billy only. It's surprising the psychological effect alone of the change: "suddenly" Garrett's role looms larger, not least because, despite the Kid's clear dominance, Wurlitzer gave the sheriff first position in the new title. At this period in American filmmaking—the end of the sixties, the beginning of the seventies—somewhat older male stars were bigger draws at the box office. Despite the popularity of *Easy Rider* and some other youth-oriented films, the likes of Dennis Hopper and Peter Fonda could not be counted upon to open a picture, though, according to casting memos, Fonda *was* on the short list for the role of Billy, along with Dustin Hoffman, Al Pacino, Jon Voight, Malcolm McDowell, Paul Le Mat, and Don Johnson. But the list for Garrett, in addition to James Coburn, included Gene Hackman, Marlon Brando, Gregory Peck, Rod Steiger, Paul Newman, George C. Scott, Lee Marvin, Donald Sutherland, William Holden, Robert Ryan, Clint Eastwood, and Jason Robards, not to mention several British actors such as Sean Connery, Michael Caine, Richard Burton, Albert Finney, Richard Harris, Robert Shaw, Alan Bates, and Peter O'Toole.

Several of these could hardly have been serious candidates, but that still left enough who were, and Coburn wasn't a shoo-in. An early preproduction meeting reveals Peckinpah had to work to sell him to Carroll and Wurlitzer, both of whom were worried that after the *Our Man Flint* series and comedies like *Waterhole #3* Coburn's acting had become entirely too broad.[1] (Someone close to the project called him a ham, and his wolfish grin was so famous it's mentioned in the first sentence of his Internet Movie Database entry, where it's described as "amazing.") Though this was neither a fair nor an accurate assessment of Coburn's acting, it was an understandable one at the time: 1972 felt a like a long way from the taciturn knife fighter in 1960's *The Magnificent Seven,* the resourceful "Manufacturer" in 1963's *The Great Escape,* and the detached scout in 1965's *Major Dundee.* Peckinpah stuck by his man, however, advising Wurlitzer to have a look at Sergio Leone's *Duck, You Sucker* (aka *A Fistful of Dynamite*), where, despite Leone's inflated, operatic style, Coburn delivers a sensitive, delicate performance as a haunted Irish Republican explosives expert on the lam in Mexico. (Wurlitzer told me his concerns were actually "minor, mostly because I had only seen Coburn a few times in comedies, and boy, was I wrong, because he was a great Garrett and later on we became close friends.")

Another reason Wurlitzer may have put Garrett ahead of Billy in the title is that even this early in the process he was already beginning to feel his first intimations that maybe the sheriff really *was* the more interesting character. But it would be the better part of two years before he would act on them. In the several months between late June and early November, he did little work on the screenplay. There are five scripts dated November 5, 1970, but most of them are little different from the *Billy the Kid* version apart from the title change. The last in the group, however, has interpolated into it many pages of new scenes or scenes substantially altered, which are dated as late as June 16, 1972: this is the copy that most clearly represents the substantial changes Wurlitzer made on his own before Peckinpah took an active role in the writing and it is also the first copy to have Peckinpah's name as director on the title page. Beyond that it's difficult to date precisely when the new material was written. Once preproduction officially begins on a motion picture, the most recent version of the screenplay is designated the "shooting script," that is, the script that will go into production. Any revisions and additions to it are thereafter referred to as "changes" and are identified with different colored pages, usually dated (e.g., "chngs, 11-16-72"). The shooting script is printed on white pages, the first set of changes on, say, blue, the next on yellow, the next on beige, and so forth, which are distributed to the various department heads, who replace the appropriate pages in their copies of the script. Thus everyone from the actors to the gofers can tell at a glance what the new pages are and how they must be prepared for filming.

Though this particular *Pat Garrett* screenplay was far from a shooting script, the changes are easy to spot because pages from the *Billy the Kid* original are pale green while new pages are off-white. However, the difficulty in trying to establish when the new material was written is that while some of the off-white pages are dated, most of them are not; and one wholly new scene, the Horrell Trading Post, is on pale-green pages and dated November 5, 1970. To the best of his recollection, Wurlitzer believes that all the off-white pages were written more or less in a single concentrated period sometime in the first half of 1972, which is consistent with what Carroll told me when I interviewed him in 1977.

This still leaves the matter of trying to establish exactly what version Peckinpah first read, when he read it, and how he responded to it. Gordon Carroll sent him a script sometime in late 1971 or very early 1972, while he was in preproduction on *The Getaway*. But that particular copy is now missing. It's not among the Sam Peckinpah Papers, where the earliest screenplay is dated July 7, 1972 (with changes as late as July 25). My best guess is that the copy he read was essentially the *Billy the Kid* version only with Garrett's name in the title, some minor changes, and the Horrell Trading Post: in other words, one of the first four November 5 screenplays, but definitely not the fifth (and last) that contains the new material written the following June, well after the December 1971–January 1972 window when from all accounts it was first sent him. What happened to the copy Peckinpah read? As it would have been extremely unusual for Peckinpah (or any director) to have returned it—not if he were really hot on directing it—my guess is that it was lost in the rush to prep *The Getaway*, which included relocating the production offices to Texas (where the film was shot), later on location, or in the return to Los Angeles. As for his response, the story goes that he read the screenplay, loved it, and committed to it immediately; then several months to a year later, once he was finished with *The Getaway*, he read it again and was shocked to discover he no longer liked it.

The first and biggest problem with this scenario is the existence of a two-page memo to Gordon Carroll written while Peckinpah was still filming *The*

Getaway. The first half of the memo covered crew selections, shooting in wide-screen Panavision, and location scouting in Mexico; the second, occupying the better part of three-quarters of a page, was labeled "SCRIPT POINTS," which were highly critical and, though not detailed, very specific in mapping out large areas of concern. This memo is dated April 9, at most four and perhaps only two months after he received the screenplay, not several months to a year. In the Margaret Herrick Library and elsewhere, I've reviewed many drafts of screenplays Peckinpah worked on and have spoken with many people whose work he read and commented upon: to a person they relate what a careful reader he was, how detailed his recall, how specific his notes and precise his suggestions. It's hard for me to believe that, however preoccupied with prepping *The Getaway*, he could have read the *Pat Garrett* screenplay one way and then so completely and so *quickly* reversed himself. The only plausible explanations are that he didn't commit all that enthusiastically or that he withheld his reservations so as not to raise objections that might jeopardize the offer. He was famous (or infamous, as the case may be) for not pulling his punches (in any sense of the word), but he could also be shrewd and cagey when it came to getting what he wanted, and he knew when to play his hand close to the vest.

In the case of *Pat Garrett*, contributing factors intensified Peckinpah's guardedness. Perhaps the most personally important was that he desperately wanted to do this screenplay because it held out the chance to make something like the picture he was not allowed to make fifteen years earlier when he adapted Charles Neider's novel. Another was that, the two years when no one would hire him following the infighting on *Major Dundee* and being fired from *The Cincinnati Kid* (both in 1965) all too fresh in mind, he had entered a phase in his life and career when he seemed to want to be in a constant state of making a film. Between *The Wild Bunch*, which began principal photography in March 1968, and July–August of 1972, as he was completing post on *The Getaway*, he had made five films in four years—*The Ballad of Cable Hogue, Straw Dogs,* and *Junior Bonner* the other three—and here he was prepping the sixth before he had even finished *shooting* the fifth, let alone begun the post. None of these was an easy shoot, involving distant locations, much exterior shooting with all its many exigencies, and considerably complicated and extensive logistics as regards equipment, extras, and many moves. All of which gives the lie to those who accused him of inefficiency and wastefulness: no other major director of the time accomplished anything close to this level of concentrated activity in feature films of comparable scale and quality.

One very real recent setback served only to exacerbate his worries. The previous year Robert Evans at Paramount had given Peckinpah his word the studio would finance *The Emperor of the North Pole*, a screenplay he had been developing for three years, if he would make *The Getaway* first. Peckinpah agreed only to be told that Ken Hyman, the producer who owned *Emperor*, couldn't wait and was paying him off, a betrayal Peckinpah neither forgot nor forgave: "I wanted to direct *Emperor* so badly that I even agreed to do it for an enormous cut in salary." Then Evans reneged on *The Getaway*, which left Peckinpah "out on both pictures" (Simmons 154–55). *The Getaway* was resurrected only because First Artists, a company of which Steve McQueen was one of the owners, stepped into the breach. Knowing how quickly things can change in this business without firm commitments, Peckinpah wanted to get the new picture locked down as soon as possible, preferably with a provision that would cost the studio some serious money if it went into turnaround.

For Gordon Carroll, this was a precarious juncture. James Aubrey, the MGM studio head, had already said he'd green-light it with an A-list director. Peckinpah not only qualified on that count but he had long since established himself as the successor to John Ford as *the* premier director of Westerns. Everyone associated with the project—including, Carroll told me, Aubrey himself—was terrifically excited by Peckinpah's interest: Sam Peckinpah directing a screenplay about Pat Garrett and Billy the Kid seemed almost as fated as the final encounter between the lawman and the outlaw. The last thing Carroll wanted was to let this opportunity slip away, so he did something unusual. Without even asking the director, Carroll went to Aubrey and actually negotiated Peckinpah's deal himself, which included demands for the highest fee the director had ever been paid up to that point in his career, two previews at which his cut would be shown, and his first pay-or-play arrangement (i.e., if the project were canceled he would still receive his full fee). Carroll also told Aubrey he wanted the deal closed in the next twenty-four hours.

Almost miraculously, Aubrey agreed to every one of the terms, including the pay-or-play clause (something he rarely gave any director), and returned with fully executed contracts eighteen hours later—all this before an A-list star had even been signed. That may seem surprising given Aubrey's reputation for destroying directors and his actions once the picture went into production, and even more surprising given that Peckinpah's reputation as a troublemaker, openly hostile toward executives and others on the business end of the industry, was well known and that he was never a "commercial" director in any sense that the businessmen considered reliable (not to mention that he was about to begin production on another picture). But his films were taken seriously, they were talked about, they made their presences known, and in those days unusual films from prestige "personal" directors who were *genuine* auteurs still counted for something at the major studios. If a script were a Western or in any sort of action-oriented genre, someone was usually ready to put up money if Peckinpah were attached. His reputation was also such that few stars who considered themselves serious actors would turn down a chance to work with him.

The deal was signed, sealed, and delivered virtually on the eve of Peckinpah's departure for Texas and *The Getaway*, which left him feeling secure enough to commit his concerns about the screenplay to paper. This he did forthrightly and without euphemism in that April 9 memo:

> Script needs substantial amount of work. As it is at the moment Billy basically does nothing but wait and Garrett less. Suggest you read Charles Nyder's[2] THE AUTHENTIC DEATH OF HENDRY JONES, and concentrate on bringing to some of the dialogue scenes some of the flavour of the period and some purpose.
>
> So many of the scenes are mere set pieces, but maybe that is what the author has in mind, with the look of a man waiting to die. If so I think it should be done much more dramatically and, I hope, in terms of action rather than aimless movement.
>
> e.g. The scene of the [roof-raising] party appears to me to be without purpose, it is almost as if the entire script is a third act.
>
> The importance of correct casting of supporting bits cannot be over-emphasized.
>
> Garrett and Billy briefly talk about their previous relationship, possibly this should be shown.
>
> Because we are dealing with a legend everyone seems to feel that it must be authentic. I am not interested in authenticity I am interested in drama.

Once this memo was dictated, Peckinpah turned back to the picture he was making while Wurlitzer, relieved to be leaving Los Angeles, repaired to the seclusion of Cape Breton, Nova Scotia, a favorite place where he liked to write, happy that he was left alone to do the work essentially on his own. He wrote the next draft "with a few notes from Gordon." Carroll's notes, however, were heavily influenced by what he thought Peckinpah wanted, that is, based on Peckinpah's memo and what Carroll knew about the director's work. As for Peckinpah and Wurlitzer, the memo was the last communication between them until the director read a revised screenplay with the new pages sometime in July or August. Since the memo was quite specific as to *general* points but almost wholly lacking in detail as to how they were to be realized, Wurlitzer was free to invent as he saw fit. Thus, for example, while a larger and more active role for Garrett was plainly implied, the form it would take at this point in the writing would be determined almost exclusively by Wurlitzer. What resulted was the last November 5, 1970, draft with the June 1972 pages, which is also the version closest to the screenplay Wurlitzer published. For book publication he had no compunction about including scenes he wrote at the suggestion of Peckinpah (and others), but none that he didn't feel were pretty much exclusively *his* writing.

Wurlitzer's was the first set of revisions; the second set was done mostly by Peckinpah himself or sometimes by Wurlitzer acting on the director's suggestions or instructions and was spread out from the second half of the summer through the fall to the beginning of production the second week of November, with additional changes continuing during production right through the end of January 1973. "I wrote some scenes in Mexico, mostly about Alias," Wurlitzer told me, "and, of course, the end, and a few other scenes, but by then Sam had taken over and I followed his lead." In the pages that follow I have no intention of detailing every last change from one draft to the next because that will obscure rather than clarify the large-scale changes Peckinpah made from screenplay to film.[3] One reason is that many changes were of little or no long-range importance; a number involved alternatives tried and rejected, including no small number of blind alleys of Peckinpah's making; and others were in scenes discarded altogether at various points along the way, including during editing. Another reason is that many of Peckinpah's most significant contributions came not from modifications or additions to the screenplay as such, but from how he shot, composed, and directed scenes. This last is more important than it may seem. There are some directors who nail down every setup and movement before cameras roll; other directors are more exploratory, improvisational, and spontaneous on the set. Peckinpah unquestionably belongs with the latter, though it would be a great mistake to underestimate how much preparation he did.

The most important reason, however, and the one that looms larger than any other in determining how he would approach the material, is Peckinpah's realization that as a character Garrett was far more compelling and complex than Billy. Wurlitzer agreed, saying Garrett "has much more dimension— he's ambivalent." "Yep," was the director's laconic reply. Peckinpah's thinking can be traced back to his *Hendry Jones* adaptation, where he enlarged Dad Longworth's role to virtually equal footing with the Kid's. I can't state for certain that *Pat Garrett and Billy the Kid* is the first and only fictional treatment to place Garrett center stage and in top position, but I don't know of another.[4] The next logical step was to advance Garrett's age at the time he killed Billy from thirty-one, as he was in history (Wurlitzer's screenplay made him thirty-two), to around the director's own age when he made the film, which was forty-seven. No version of the screenplay I've been able to find explicitly marks this change, but the importance Peckinpah placed on casting in that April memo and the A-list names for the role clearly indicate he conceived Garrett as older virtually from the day he read the screenplay; and it was solidified by Coburn, who was forty-four at the time (but in the film looks an easy fifty or older). This change, of course, mandated an older Billy, who was found in Kris Kristofferson, thirty-six at the time. (The age gap between Kristofferson and Coburn turned out to be almost exactly the same as that between the real Billy and Garrett.) Yet even before Peckinpah began making or dictating changes, Wurlitzer's November 5, 1970, screenplay with the June 1972 changes indicates that he too had begun thinking along the same lines.

Wurlitzer concentrated on four areas: clarifying some exposition; adding some action sequences; fleshing out Garrett; and strengthening what I have identified as the Kid's three-stage decline from control and domination of the world and the people around him at the outset into drink, depression, and dissipation by the end. He also wrote the wholly new scene at the Horrell Trading Post and significantly changed the scene with Paco on the way to Mexico. For purposes of discussion, these additions and changes must be taken up in isolation, but as in all really good storytelling, they achieve multiple objectives simultaneously and are interrelated.[5]

The Opening

Wurlitzer added a long monologue to the very beginning in which Billy describes how Garrett captured him at Stinking Springs. What is most striking about this monologue is how full of himself Billy is. In addition to denigrating Garrett, there's a lot of braggadocio and excuse making:

> Ain't no way Garrett could get the drop on me straight on. . . . I knowed that if'n I could git my hand two inches to my gun butt I got me a chance and I ease my wrist down and this wrist, Bell, and these here fingers attached are oiled and there ain't no blink to them. But I come down an inch and Pat says: "I ain't about to, Billy," and I says, "You're damned right you're not about to, because those good days are over for you, Garrett, when you could go up against a man straight on." He jest pulls the hammer back and I unbuckle. But there was a second there when he wanted to, bad. (3)

It's doubtful Wurlitzer meant for the irony to be lost of the Kid suggesting Garrett's a coward because he won't go up against him straight on when just minutes later Billy will gun down Bell in cold blood without giving him any sort of chance at all. Near the end of the escape, once Billy has Lincoln completely at bay, Wurlitzer added this passage:

> His whole being, if not his consciousness, is deeply aware, as the crowd is deeply aware, that he inhabits a myth, the myth of BILLY THE KID. Billy and the town of Lincoln are suspended for this one moment from mortal time, caught in a ritual that is larger than any one man. They are each dependent on the other to play out their part, to sustain this moment of grace. (10–11)

This marks the first time Wurlitzer made explicit the theme of fatalism, his belief "that once one is trapped inside a myth, the cause and effect becomes fatalistic or pre-ordained." Later he also added several more passing references to the Kid's getting older, slowing down, and being tired. While none of these undermines the stage one concentration on the Kid's control and power, collectively they serve as foreshadowings of the decline that begins in stage two.

Garrett's Wife

In the *Billy the Kid* original this scene was direct, simple, and short. Ida comes right to the point: What are your plans?—The usual. There's talk you used to be his friend—I don't give a damn what people say. You might say you're glad to see me—There's a drunk in town named Alamosa Bill, I've got to take care of him. Will you be blessing this house for dinner?—It feels like it's going to be a long night. This last could possibly be played as humorous, and Ida comes across as a relatively passive woman who accepts her husband's ways. In the new version (20–21A), the exchange comes more or less midway into the scene, is dead serious, and precipitates an argument that almost turns violent. "I'm alone all the time. My people don't talk to me," Ida says. "They say you're getting to be too much of a gringo since you been sheriff. That you make deals with Chisum. You don't touch—" "Not now," Garrett retorts, cutting her off. But she stands her ground: "No, now, or I won't be here when you get back." Garrett, "walking over to the table, picking up a large iron spoon, and slamming it down on the table," turns to her and says softly, "When this is over. Then we'll deal with it." Ida says she hopes the Kid gets away. "He won't," Garrett says, "There's too much play in him"—"And not enough in you," Ida completing the thought. Before he leaves, Garrett walks over and holds "her breast so hard that it hurts," saying, "Wait for me. I need that now," and walks out.

There is a tendency among some critics to give Peckinpah all the credit for this scene, but that is both unfair and manifestly inaccurate. It is true that early on he did tell Wurlitzer that even his lengthened rewrite could be taken further. To that end, Peckinpah added some lines, notably the one of Garrett saying he hopes the Kid has gone to Old Mexico, "where we should be too, if I had any sense"; another in which he says he figures he was elected to bring the Kid in; Ida's "You're dead inside"; and an almost sheepish "I'm sorry" from Garrett.[6] But all of this was at the service of reinforcing or otherwise dramatizing what was already latent in the writing: Garrett's uneasiness about all the changes and new alliances in his life, his reluctance to begin the job he has signed on for (Wurlitzer even added the pressure of obligation with the line, "I'll bring him in. Too much is riding on it fer me not to," though this is susceptible of more than one meaning), the anger, and the barely suppressed threat of violence toward Ida.

In other words, Peckinpah's most substantial contribution was in how he staged, played, and visualized the scene, his customary peerless attention to beats, silences, and dynamic shadings. He added (or allowed) a wonderful ad-lib in the way Ida, instead of saying, "No. Now," reverts to her native tongue when she becomes angry, shouting, "Si, ahora!"; and had Garrett, in his display of temper, pull down a panel of curtains instead of rapping a spoon on the table. He also dropped Wurlitzer's ending so that the scene could go out on the "too much/not enough play" exchange. With his usual masterly sense of structure, Peckinpah no doubt felt that, as Garrett is never shown returning to the house, why anticipate he will, then withhold it? He apparently also wanted to highlight the pun on "play," which reverberates throughout the rest of the story, and contrast Garrett's apparent lack of sexual desire toward Ida to his dallying with the prostitutes later at Roberta's Hotel.[7] It is tempting to lay great emphasis on his lack of affection, his cruelty, and his shrinking from any intimacy with Ida, a temptation I and others have given in to; but in view of Peckinpah's addition of "I'm sorry," Garrett's attitude in the last moment before he walks out is open to several readings, the range of interpretation surely allowing for it to include a component of regret and remorse (perhaps even a suggestion that all his feeling for her has not died).

As to its visualization, Robert Merrill and John L. Simons lay great weight on the way the set is dressed, and they are right to do so, since Peckinpah always paid extremely close attention to that sort of thing. For them, the house represents a respite, a haven of middle-class domesticity—redolent of Peckinpah's description of the Longworth house in his *Hendry Jones* screenplay—that Garrett, instead of appreciating and welcoming, either obtusely or willfully rejects (115–17). This is not only one way of looking at it, but a way it *should* be looked at. As always with Peckinpah, however, more than one angle of vision is possible, indeed is encouraged and typically insisted upon. A different one might find the interior a little cluttered yet fussy, as in too neat and orderly; the pattern of the flowered wallpaper is regimented yet busy; the walls themselves have too much hanging on them; the furniture leaves little space to move around—in a nice subtle touch, when Garrett goes from the dining room to the kitchen he has to move an ironing board out of his path. And in staging the scene, setting up the shots, and composing the images, Peckinpah continually used door frames, walls, tables, and other objects to draw lines, erect barriers, or demarcate spaces that separate the couple or come between them. From this perspective, the house is subtly suffocating and vaguely claustrophobic, and it's not difficult to understand why Garrett can't wait to get back outside. When they face each other with no obstructions between them, the moment turns almost violent as Garrett rips down the curtains to end their argument before he walks out the door. Since Peckinpah always urged his art directors—here one of his regulars, the great Ted Haworth—to overdress the sets so that he could pare them down, the fact that this set was left this full cannot be accidental.

A haven of domesticity or a house too cluttered and claustrophobic?

Note the ironing board (*left of center, bottom*) that Garrett moves aside as he walks into the kitchen.

Compositions emphasizing lines, walls, and objects that separate the husband and wife

Governor Wallace's

Wurlitzer completely rewrote this scene. When Garrett now visits the governor's hacienda in Santa Fe, Wallace is at dinner with a pair of men who represent the collusion of business and political interests that was the Santa Fe Ring. They are putting up the thousand-dollar reward for the capture of the Kid and they make a rather blatant attempt at bribing Garrett by offering him half the reward in advance with, presumably, no obligations. In turning them down he offers a graphic suggestion where they can put their money. As written by Wurlitzer and directed by Peckinpah with very few changes, this scene contains a number of implications that I feel have been overlooked by virtually every critic who has interpreted it. To begin with, if Garrett's refusal of the reward-money advance suggests anything, it's that he's not for sale as such. He has his own reasons for going after the Kid and they are considerably more complex than "selling out" or betrayal. (Here is Wurlitzer: "Garrett was not for sale. Again, he's caught in the envelope of Billy's and, thus, his own myth, which continued to expand. Perhaps the death of Billy would in some way free him from his own dark side.") Holland's remark to the effect that Chisum and the other big cattlemen have been advised to realize that their options are limited indicates, among other things, that Chisum's relationship with the ring is at least quasi-antagonistic and that his interests are by no means at all points congruent with theirs.[8] As I have argued elsewhere (*Reconsideration* 266), for all that Chisum, Garrett, and Billy are at odds with each other, the big thing they have in common is that as larger-than-life individuals, they belong to the Old West that is being pushed aside by the bankers, the politicians, and the large impersonal economic, political, and social forces. The only place in this new West for the likes of the sheriff, the outlaw, and the cattle baron will be in the realm of history, legend, and story.[9]

Shootouts in Fort Sumner, at Black Harris's, and on Chisum's Land

One way in which Wurlitzer and Peckinpah were rather alike is that dollars damned them both. It's difficult to see how the action sequences Wurlitzer and later Peckinpah added made the screenplay fundamentally more commercial, but, with one exception, they did make for better drama, greater thematic density, and a deeper realization of character and character relationships. The morning after the Kid's return to Fort Sumner following his escape, Wurlitzer extended the story of U. S. Christmas and his Wellington boots so that the killing of the stranger who shows up gunning for the Kid could be built up with greater suspense, which Peckinpah relished to its fullest when he filmed it. Giving the man two partners, he fashioned a set piece that dramatized how closely, almost intuitively Billy and his boys work together, each beat in the U. S. Christmas story functioning as a cue for the gang to get themselves ready and set. By the time of filming, with Bob Dylan cast as Alias, Peckinpah devised a kind of three-part introduction for the character: he's unobtrusively spotted in a cutaway as one of the bystanders who react to Billy's escape, then showcased a little later with a perhaps too-clever exchange, answering Garrett's "Who are you?" with "That's a good question," a riposte that even now always gets a laugh. But Peckinpah reserved the big introduction for a Leone-like flourish by which Alias allies himself with Billy's gang. Although Alias arrives with the three strangers, he positions himself in a strategic spot several yards away from them as Billy starts telling the story; once the shooting starts, Alias does his part by dispatching one of the intruders with a knife through the throat, then gives Billy a grinning thumbs-up. One reason Peckinpah gave for ratcheting up this action was that, having seen Billy as a back-shooter, the audience also needed to see him as a deadly gunman face-to-face with other gunmen.[10] Another is doubtless Peckinpah's sense of proportion and contrast: the Fort Sumner shoot-out needed to be bigger the better to balance it against the firefight Wurlitzer added to the Sheriff Baker sequence and also to contrast Billy's group action with the essentially solitary Garrett's.

It could be argued that as originally conceived the Baker scene always seemed to suggest another shoe waiting to be dropped, so Wurlitzer went ahead and dropped it by having Garrett, Baker, and Baker's wife actually go out to Black Harris's hideout to get the "sign" on the Kid that Garrett is seeking—but not before making some important changes in the original scene (30–32). Jettisoned were Baker's lines about how he doesn't like Garrett, though retained was the old man's disapproval for Garrett's "wearing a badge for the town of Lincoln and them what's in it." Yet despite Baker's can-tankerousness, it's clear in the revision that Wurlitzer meant for us to think of them as friends old and true. And he gave Garrett a reply that became one of the most important lines in the film and marks the first explicit reference to the pressures Garrett feels from getting older: "It's a job," he sighs, as he takes a pull from his flask. "A man gits to an age he don't want to spend time figuring what comes next." Peckinpah got the maximum effect out of this moment in the way he had it played, composed, and edited. Filmed in loose medium shots, "It's a job" is played on Garrett's back from Baker's point of view. Then we cut to a new angle, which has Garrett close to and facing the camera, though the framing remains loose, and still turned away from Baker, who is in the background. The sheer tiredness in Coburn's voice and attitude, the really long pause between "There's an age in a man's life when," as he pockets the flask, and "he don't want to spend time figuring what comes next" all express a resignation born less of acceptance than of exhaustion and defeat. But when he asks Baker for help, the old man answers that he doesn't do "nothin' no more lessen there's a piece of gold attached." Garrett tosses him a

"There's an age in a man's life when he don't want
to spend time figuring what comes next."

coin. When they go inside, Mrs. Baker says she has a bad feeling about it: "This
town ain't worth it fer you to go up agin 'em jest fer Garrett." Baker doesn't
like it either, but "Garrett'd git his ass shot off goin' up agin 'em alone." Garrett reaches into his pocket and "hands Baker's wife some more coins," which
she takes and then gathers up two shotguns, another pistol, and a bottle of
kerosene.

Once at Harris's (32–32C), Garrett announces he just wants to know
where the Kid is, but Harris starts shooting, mortally wounding Baker before
being killed by Garrett. Harris's dying words are that the Kid is in "Paris,
France." In addition to punching up the action, the new scene serves some
other functions. Harris's refusal to give up any information reinforces the
tightness of the Kid's network of friends and fellow outlaws and their loyalty to him. Baker's death is without sentiment or even much feeling: he's
shot dead, there's an end to it, and it's difficult not to feel that in some sense
he dies compromised, his death the price he and his wife pay for demanding
and accepting money in the first place. (Garrett's refusal of half the reward in
advance contrasts with the Bakers' demand for money.)

In the film, however, Peckinpah has Baker return the coin before the three
leave for Harris's, and Garrett offers no more money. Wurlitzer's dialogue is
retained except for removing Baker's line about Garrett getting his ass shot
off. All Baker does is echo his wife that he has a bad feeling about it himself.
These changes suggest Peckinpah wanted further to strengthen our sense of
a bond between Garrett and the Bakers, who are allowed to remain people of
some honor and integrity, which justifies the elegiac treatment of Cullen's
death. The old sheriff tries to stem the bleeding by holding his hand against
the wound in his stomach—Slim Pickens plays the role in what is perhaps the
loveliest performance of his career—and shuffles down to the river, where he
sits on the bank and waits to die as his wife, played by Katy Jurado, looks on,
weeping. Beautifully photographed at sunset in melancholy tones of gray and

magenta, streaked by amber rays of crosslight, and edited so that it ends as Garrett's point of view, it inspired the single best piece in Dylan's score, the ballad "Knockin' on Heaven's Door," with the lines: "Mama, take this badge off of me / I can't use it anymore. / Gettin' dark, too dark to see / I feel I'm knockin' on heaven's door."[11]

In the cattle-rustling scene that comes later (33–36), Wurlitzer's major addition is ending with Billy swearing vengeance on Silva's disgraced body: "I ain't forgettin', and I ain't about to be forgot." A setup for reprisals against Chisum that was implicit in the *Billy the Kid* original here becomes explicit, thus making the thwarted expectations when the reprisals fail to happen more pronounced and dramatic and also setting up a pattern that Wurlitzer will exploit later. However, in a curious invention, he decided to have Chisum not only present when his men surround Silva but actually initiate the murder. Peckinpah had Wurlitzer remove Chisum from the scene and eventually added a new ending in which Billy and Alias kill four of Chisum's men before the remaining three disperse.[12] Also cut was Billy's oath of vengeance, a deletion suggested by Wurlitzer, who felt that after all the violence any dialogue would be superfluous and anticlimactic. He got no argument from Peckinpah, who probably felt that since the vengeance is now meted out in situ and the rest of it never carried out, why leave in the oath?

Wurlitzer's last important addition to this section of the story is the exchange between Garrett and Poe en route to Chisum's ranch. "This country's got to make a choice. The time's over for drifters and outlaws and them that's got no backbone," declares Poe with excruciating pomposity. Garrett puts him in his place:

> I'm goin' to tell you this once and don't make me do it again. . . . The country's gettin' old and I aim to git old with it. The Kid don't want that and he might be a better man for it. I ain't judgin' . . . I don't want you explainin' nothin' to me, and I don't want you talkin' about the Kid or nobody else in this goddamn territory. (55)

The issue of Garrett's age is sounded once again, our sense of the depth of his feelings toward Billy is deepened, and his hostility toward Poe is intensified. Peckinpah also made a small but decisive change to the dialogue, instructing Wurlitzer to substitute "*my* goddamn county" for "this goddamn territory."[13] Peckinpah also called for Poe to be "a real shit," an ambitious backstabber and murderer, and he told Wurlitzer that the character "needs to be resolved more," with some sort of confrontation between him and Garrett (the "finish" from his "introduce-develop-finish" formula). The eventual solution—and an instructive example of how Peckinpah built upon and extended Wurlitzer's work—was to take the protectiveness Garrett displays toward Billy when his name is slurred and give it a devastatingly ironic apotheosis: Garrett viciously kicks Poe away as the deputy moves to cut off the Kid's trigger finger.

Jones's Saloon

In the new version (68A–74) the suppressed violence Garrett displays at home is here expressed, though with an iron control that makes it all the more disturbing. Instead of playing just a sociable game of cards with Holly, Alias, and Half-Breed,[14] Garrett forces Holly at gunpoint to get drunk, eventually goading him into going for his knife so that he has an excuse to kill him. But before that Garrett coolly and methodically protects himself by neutralizing everyone else: he orders Alias to take the butt end of Lemuel Jones's shotgun and crack Half-Breed across the back of the head with it; then he orders Lemuel over to the table where he can keep an eye on him and has Alias force the bartender's hat down over his eyes; next he directs Alias "to go over to that shelf of air tights and give us a nice read, loud enough fer me to catch your sound"; and at last he's ready for Holly. As Wurlitzer conceived the scene, we can see that the kind of control and domination the Kid exerts over people and places in stage one of his development in the *Billy the Kid* original has now been transferred to Garrett, who is increasingly the more powerful protagonist and no less ruthless. Though Lemuel tells Garrett he used to be "damn near a daddy to the Kid," Holly seems to contradict this, saying, "Don't take it personal, Pat, but you 'n him been a little short of supplies ever since you been knowin' each other. Ah, hell, I ain't partial to neither one of ya." Just how close Garrett and the Kid once were, the depth and nature of their friendship, is an ambiguity that is sustained throughout the entire screenplay and is never fully resolved, especially from Billy's side, an ambiguity that Peckinpah allowed to survive in the film, albeit in considerably more muted form.

The one addition Peckinpah made to the writing here was quite small but transformative, and it seems to have been one of those inspirations that occurred to him on the set, as it appears in no copy of the screenplay. After shooting Holly dead, Garrett walks to the door, pauses at the threshold, then turns to Alias: "Boy, when you see Billy, tell him we had a little drink together." The line will resonate in a later scene, but it also recalls the drink they shared in the Fort Sumner opening and thereby perhaps helps clarify why Garrett singles out Holly for killing. At Black Harris's, Garrett informs Harris right off he's only looking for information, but Harris starts shooting anyhow, the Bakers immediately returning fire, thus leaving Garrett no play but to back them up. Here at Jones's Saloon Wurlitzer leaves us to figure out Garrett's reasons for ourselves, though one thing is all but explicit: getting information on the Kid's whereabouts isn't among them. Holly brings it up, Lemuel talks about it, but the only actual question Garrett asks is if they're carrying wages to play a few "sociable hands." We can infer many reasons—though playing cards is obviously not among them—including perhaps a latent streak of sadism in Garrett's personality, which will reappear in a new scene Wurlitzer wrote for Roberta's Hotel in Roswell. Garrett's parting salutation to Alias doesn't necessarily negate his other reasons, but it makes abundantly clear the primary reason is to demonstrate his resolve in the deadliest possible terms so that Billy will realize the inevitable and clear out of the territory. But why does he single out Holly, instead of Alias or Half-Breed? There is no clue in Wurlitzer, but there is in the Fort Sumner opening Peckinpah wrote: it's Holly who says to the Kid, "Why don't you kill him?"—only three to four seconds after Garrett has walked out the cantina door and loud enough to suggest the possibility that he just might have heard it.

Horrell's Trading Post

This was the first wholly new scene Wurlitzer added to the *Billy the Kid* screen-play and the one written closest in time to it (64A–64D). Billy's first stop after he departs Fort Sumner for Mexico, the trading post is owned by the Horrell family, friends to whom he wants to pay his respects before leaving the terri-tory. By chance Alamosa Bill happens to have fallen by a short while earlier and is sharing dinner with them. Billy is invited to join. The tension puts everyone on edge. Finally, Alamosa asks if Billy has run across Pat. "Can't say that I did," Billy answers. Mr. Horrell takes advantage of the silence to issue a warning: "He's going to track you till he gits you, Billy. He might not look it, but Pat Garrett has got more sand than most." "I'm outlawed, all right. Alamosa here will see to that," Billy replies. "And it hasn't been long since I was a law ridin' for Chisum and old Pat was an outlaw. Funny thing, the law." This exchange allowed Wurlitzer to make a historical point about the ease with which indi-viduals could find themselves on one side of the law or the other in the New Mexico Territory of the time (in fact, in all of the Old West), a point that was important to Peckinpah as well. Outlawry and law enforcement called for many of the same skills; and since cowboys, lawmen, rustlers, and other criminals hung out in many of the same places, it was not uncommon for those on either side to be acquainted with one another or even to have ridden together. The scene also extends our sense of how well liked Billy is throughout the territory, not just by Mexicans, but also by some gringo families, of whom the Horrells are among the most prominent and the most recognizably ordinary or "normal."

So far, so good, or at least good enough, though one issue is whether Billy as Wurlitzer conceives him is capable of the kind of detachment from his circum-stances which the irony of this remark suggests. I personally am of two minds about it, and I have the additional problem that the remark seems to suggest he now appreciates the reality of his situation with respect to Garrett, an appreciation absent elsewhere in the screenplay. But the biggest problem is the resolution: Billy and Alamosa can't figure out a way to avoid a confrontation, so they agree to a duel at ten paces, which is staged in front of the entire family, including the children. (Would parents, even in the violent world of this story, allow that? When I once queried Peckinpah on this very point, as well as on the uniformity of the children's response, he told me his thinking was that they had already witnessed the shooting death of their brother, which the father refers to, so they know what to expect and are already beginning to be desensitized to violence, a recurring theme in his work.) Alamosa turns and fires after an eight-count but is so nervous he misses; Billy, turning on ten, shoots him dead. Peckinpah filmed this with only one crucial change: Billy turns and draws after the two-count; when Alamosa turns six counts later, Billy shoots him before he has a chance to fire. Either version raises a concern. If it is argued that Billy's failure to realize Alamosa might cheat illustrates diminished power, he remains nevertheless resourceful enough to kill the deputy and survive. If it's argued that his turning after two dramatizes the kind of ruthlessness exhibited in the killings of Bell and Olinger—almost certainly Peckinpah's intention in making the change—this still puts a brief hiatus in Wurlitzer's carefully worked-out progression of the Kid's decline (though by the time Peckinpah made the change, he had already weakened that decline). Structures don't necessarily have to be direct and linear, but as Wurlitzer designed Billy's descent, it is built in and the duel is but one of several changes, most of them initiated by Peckinpah, that disrupt it. That said, I freely grant that the entire scene, including the duel, is so well written and so effectively directed, played, and shot as to render this objection if not irrelevant, then merely formalistic.[15]

Roberta's Hotel

This is another scene that was completely overhauled (92–96). Instead of going to his room and lying on the bed, as in the *Billy the Kid* original, Garrett asks Rupert, the proprietor (and pimp), to send him a young prostitute named Ruthie Lee, Wurlitzer noting that she is at most sixteen. Rupert informs Garrett she's unlikely to want to see him because she's "been with the Kid more'n a few times." When Garrett orders him to send her anyway, Rupert asks, "You want another one? Last time, you had three or four up there." "Shit, man, jest send me something. But make sure Ruthie Lee is in the package." Once she arrives, Garrett asks her where the Kid is and her reply is that he was with her a few weeks ago. When Garrett tells her she's going to have to do better than that, she says, "I figured. But it'll cost you."

He hands her ten gold coins, which she walks over and accepts, putting them in her purse and then stepping warily away.

RUTHIE LEE (*suddenly vicious*): Why don't you pack it in, Pat? You're gettin' too old to follow kids around. But, of course, maybe if you nail him, it might quicken you a bit. God knows you need some . . .

Garrett rises from the bed, steps quickly over to her, and slaps her across the cheek. She reels, but stands up to him.

RUTHIE LEE: Jesus, but it's easy to uncover you. Of course, your old core
    is rotten and soft enough . . .

Garrett slaps her again. She begins to cry.

GARRETT (*thin-lipped*): Tell me.

RUTHIE LEE: You got to do me one more time, Pat. I owe the Kid that.

*Garrett slaps her twice, causing blood to spurt from her lip. As she begins to
fall, he catches her and lays her on the bed.*

RUTHIE LEE: He's been around Fort Sumner. I don't know exactly where.

Garrett rips off her dress and touches her breast.

RUTHIE LEE (*moaning*): I brought a friend. I figured it would take some of
    the harness off me.

GARRETT: It won't.

RUTHIE LEE (*calling out*): Come on in, Sarah. The transaction has been made.

*Sarah comes in. She is equally young, with long dark hair and a red satin dress.
She is half Negro and expert at her trade. She begins to undress.*

SARAH: Is this a party?

GARRETT (*undressing*): It's going to be real quick.

I have quoted this at length as further demonstration of just how much
Wurlitzer added to his conception of Garrett, continuing to play up Garrett's
age, his violence, and his cruelty and also to point up yet again how Peckinpah augmented it without fundamentally altering it, except in a couple of
revealing ways. Wurlitzer clearly intended the detail of Garrett ripping off the
young prostitute's dress and touching her breast to recall the way he had earlier squeezed his wife's fully clothed breast so hard it caused her pain. The hint
of his sadism both there and in Jones's Saloon is here given a more explicit
sexual twist with Ruthie Lee, whom Garrett has apparently treated roughly
in the past. At home sex with his wife is postponed; here, having gotten the
information he wants, he will indulge himself immediately, albeit very fast, as
he's got to get back on the trail now that he knows the Kid's in Fort Sumner.
    Dated January 31, 1973, a week before the end of principal photogra-
phy, Peckinpah's work on this scene marked the last rewriting he did before

production wrapped.[16] Without appreciably toning it down, he condensed and tightened it, eliminating Ruthie Lee's insults about Garrett's age and virility and advancing her age (she is played by Rutanya Alda, thirty-one at the time). When she enters the room, there are no greetings between her and Garrett or even any feigned pleasantries. Already scantily clad, she gets right down to business: "Which way do you want to go?" she asks, unbuttoning her camisole, then sits on the bed and starts loosening Garrett's neckerchief. He tells her he has a few questions, she answers without waiting to be asked. "He was here a few weeks ago. I don't know where he went," whereupon Garrett slaps her face so hard she's knocked to the mattress. The way Peckinpah staged this moment—having Ruthie Lee already on the bed facing Garrett, and the alacrity with which he strikes her (she hardly finishes the reply)—makes the slap even more shockingly vicious than how Wurlitzer visualized it in his screenplay, where it's telegraphed because Garrett has to advance toward her to get close enough to hit her. Peckinpah dropped the business with the gold coins, so that, like the Bakers, Ruthie Lee is no longer tainted by any suggestion she accepts money for the information. Instead, realizing it's inevitable she will be forced to reveal what she knows of the Kid's whereabouts, she in effect asks to be punished in advance of relinquishing it, which Garrett is only too ready to grant: he slaps her twice more, then grabs a handful of her hair and pulls her toward him, saying through his teeth, "Now you tell me." As with the Ida scene, so too here: it seems to me that for all his reputation as a misogynist, there is no question the director's sympathies lie with the women.

This was the extent of Peckinpah's *rewriting*. But on set he went further. Instead of one, four more prostitutes enter the room, making a total of five, and there follows a montage in which they undress and bathe Garrett. It was Wurlitzer who planted the seed for this by way of Rupert's reference to Garrett having had "three or four" prostitutes in the past, but Peckinpah alone must be held responsible for the over-the-top montage it eventually became.

Paco's Death

In Wurlitzer's original, Paco and Billy spend a day and night getting drunk together. In the new version (64–64H–68), when Billy comes upon Paco and his daughter, two of Chisum's men are tying Paco spread-eagled to a wagon wheel while a third is heating a branding iron. When Paco's daughter tries to intervene, one of them drags her behind the wagon and prepares to rape her (as she is described as naked and bleeding, we may assume she's already been raped at least once). Billy dismounts, sneaks up through Paco's herd of sheep, several of which have been shot, and dispatches two of the men in short order. When he asks the third if Chisum knows about what they're doing, the man answers, "He told us to clear the range." After Billy cuts down Paco, he ties the third man to the wagon wheel. Wurlitzer transferred Paco's drunken reverie about his house from the *Billy the Kid* version to his dying monologue here. After the old man is dead and buried, Billy tells the young woman, "You got a horse here. You can ride back to your people. Figure you want to do that alone." She nods. "She'll put my eyes out," pleads the third man as Billy mounts up. "I hope so," he replies, and rides out of the camp.

There is a long-standing debate among textual critics and scholars over which version of a literary text is the most reliable as regards an author's intentions. A widespread though by no means universally held belief is that revisions and other changes made close to the writing of the original text are likely to be more consistent with the overall intention than those made much later, even when the later ones are made by the author. Most of Wurlitzer's new material actually strengthened his original. This is true especially of his more fleshed-out Garrett: if the character no longer functions as a kind of "pure" nemesis, his greater individuality as a human being reinforces the themes of fate and determinism in other ways and makes for a far more layered and rounded character. And most of Wurlitzer's revisions at this point also strengthened Billy because they are consistent with the character as originally conceived. Yet the Horrell scene raised a minor problem and killing Paco off made it much bigger. To start with, inasmuch as Billy now shoots accurately, dispatching two men with ease and assuming command of a horrible situation, there is no evidence of any decline in his power or control. Why did Wurlitzer do this? The most obvious reasons were to answer calls for more action and greater clarification of exposition and motivation. Since we know that at this point in the revision process there was no communication between Wurlitzer and Peckinpah, who was deep into production on *The Getaway*, if these had a source outside the writer himself, they must have come from Carroll, for whom the director's memo loomed large, notably his suggestion that Billy's development "should be done much more dramatically . . . in terms of action rather than aimless movement"—though I believe it's pretty clear from the context that by "action" Peckinpah meant "dramatic action," not "action scenes" as such. This the new Paco scene achieved but with deleterious results.

Although Wurlitzer retained all the remaining scenes of Billy's decline from the original—the roof-raising party, the panicked killing of the burro, the images of him meandering drunk and half-asleep on his horse, the cabin where he sees the comatose man, the drunken ravings once he is back in Fort Sumner—the thematic, structural, and dramatic functions of the last four are compromised because they are no longer set up by the day and night of drinking with Paco, who when he moves on leaves Billy with a bottle of tequila. I suppose it could be argued that in the new version Billy's drinking and meandering might be interpreted as a kind of guilt reaction to his inability to save Paco, who could then be seen as standing in for all the Kid's friends whom he's deserted by going to Mexico. But that's really stretching a point and nowhere is it accounted for or otherwise sounded in the screenplay. And guilt certainly doesn't inform the scene in the cabin, which has lost a good deal of its significance, not to mention its meaning, if Paco's death is now what causes Billy to turn back. The epiphany still has some strength as a revelation of the kind of anonymous end that might be in store for him if he were to reach Mexico and stay there; but its power as the culmination of a development that begins back at the end of the first act is diluted. Paco's death is the only new scene by Wurlitzer that feels like a violation of both the tone and the style of a screenplay that is otherwise lyrical and makes its points indirectly and elliptically. A tight, exceptionally strong structure, with a carefully through-conceived and worked-out character, starts to unravel here, a process that would continue with changes Peckinpah will bring to it, two of which would make a nonsense of it.

Billy's Return to Fort Sumner

When Billy finally returns to Fort Sumner, Wurlitzer greatly expanded the reunion with what remains of his gang (100B–103A). He arrives to find them even more feckless and aimless than they were after his escape from Lincoln. They celebrate at a cantina where he does what he always does—drinks himself to stupefaction. Pretty soon they're all drunk except Maria. Billy has become silent and morose, nodding off and coming to. Nobody notices except Maria, but when she tries to help him leave, he announces—"swaying," as he does—"I'm sayin' a few words." What follows is a rambling, incoherent speech: I been ridin' a long way, I seen a little too much—Well, what I mean is, WE AIN'T RAISED ENOUGH HELL—I ain't finished with Chisum—What I mean is . . . this here's a free country . . . Ain't nobody ridin' us off nowhere—Chisum, the goddamn governor, nor the goddamn President of the United States. By now most of them are cheering him on with a lot of Dutch courage, Luke falling off his chair, calling out, "You say it, Billy. We're with you." But what about Garrett, Eno wants to know. "If Pat ain't shot hisself by now, I'll deal with him," the Kid answers. "Whooeee! You tell 'em, Billy," a nameless drunk shouts. Billy starts a reply but is so wasted he can't think of what to say next, and he allows Maria to drag him out the door. The last line of the scene is from the same nameless drunk shouting, "Old days are comin' back, boys. I said it first." It's not just Billy but most of his friends and hangers-on who are likewise deluded, as Wurlitzer here strengthened the theme of how their way of life and its world are doomed at least as much by forces from within as from without. And the picture of Billy drinking himself to ruin is made much stronger and more vivid.

The next day (105–106A), Billy, a whiskey bottle next to him, awakens to a hangover and finds Maria, Eno, Luke, and an unnamed "stoop-shouldered man" from the night before in the room. Eno tells Billy that Garrett killed Holly at Jones's Saloon, and the stoop-shouldered man tells him that the other day a man with "law written all over him" was asking about him, presumably alluding to Poe. "You boys runnin' scared?" the Kid asks. The stoop-shouldered man answers that "Garrett seems pure loco," so "the best move is fer you boys to clear out for a spell." "Garrett got luck is all," Billy replies. "But if you boys want to git skeered off by a cork-fingered liquored up old man gettin' ready fer an easy chair, I guess that's your business." When Luke protests, Billy tells them they'll make "right good farmers or field niggers," but "I'm goin' after Chisum." Luke reminds him, "We all ready done that." Billy answers, "I'm talkin' ten thousand head, not jest a supper . . . I'm talkin' about goin' up agin' the old man hisself." Eno asks, when "you figure on gettin' to it?" Billy answers, "I jest about got it worked out. Next week, maybe." Then he goes into his fantasy about starting up a ranch with cattle stolen from Chisum and maybe raising quarter horses. Not much later Billy will get drunk and thus repeat the same pattern as when he swore vengeance for Silva: a lot of bold talk followed by drinking and partying and little or no action from a man who increasingly seems reduced to an impotent will, wholly bereft of internal strength, resolve, or energy to implement it.

Wurlitzer ended this scene on a new exchange between Billy and Maria. Having taken about as much as she can of his denial and his self-destructive behavior, she moves toward the door, saying, "I need to be away from you." "We're together," he says, "Isn't that what you want?" "No," she answers. "That isn't what I want." This is one of a few but critical changes whereby Wurlitzer made Maria a stronger, less compliant, more independent, and considerably more tough-minded character from the first draft. She is no longer the woman in bed with Luke when Billy rejoins his gang after his escape. In the previous version of the stable scene she is shocked and reduced to tears when Billy puts her down by referring to other women he's enjoyed; in this version, she slaps him hard and stands her ground: "I am your woman, and I will fight for that. But don't push me, Billy. I will ride away from you and never look back." In their final exchange he tells her she's acting as if she isn't glad to see him. "I am glad to see you," she replies. "And I don't ever want to see you again." He assures her it's going to be different. "No," she answers. "It will never be different." Cumulatively these changes give the character a progression missing from the original. While she never stops loving Billy and never deserts him, she now comes to a realistic, which is to say a tragic, appreciation of the Kid's person and situation: hopeless in his denials of the danger he's in, his needs and wants always before hers or theirs together, he will never change and any future with him is doomed. If she remains with him, it will be only to play out her destined role in a drama that is not hers to write.

Several months after he left *Pat Garrett and Billy the Kid*, Peckinpah told Garner Simmons, "If I'd shot [Rudy's] screenplay, I would have had five hours of screen time. It was an epic confrontation with a great lyric quality to it.

I brought it down some, but I attempted to retain its lyricism, and I was really pleased with it—proud of it. It wasn't all shoot-outs" (171). In the end Peckinpah was true to his word: he did retain much of Wurlitzer's lyricism while adding equal parts and more of his own, though he was a while getting there. But the talk about five hours of screen time and the epic confrontation is simply wrong or the result of faulty or selective memory. The version Peckinpah likely first read—the *Billy the Kid* original with the new title, the Horrells scene, and some very minor other changes—is small-scale, compact, and short enough at 120 pages. The next version he read was either the last November 5, 1970, one or another dated July 7, 1972, with changes as late as July 25, both of which had all of the new material Wurlitzer had written in response to Peckinpah's April 9 memo;[17] but even if shot to the page, neither of these would likely have exceeded two and a half hours in fine cut. After this version, the next few got longer, one numbering 150 pages, many of the new additions by Peckinpah himself. But these were all interim versions, which sometimes have duplicate pages, are incomplete, and contain scenes he had no intention of shooting. It's obvious he was still working through his ideas, trying out alternatives, rejecting some, modifying others—in other words, they constitute work in progress.

In light of the film as shot and edited, it's hard to know what to make of Peckinpah's "I brought it down some" unless he was talking about merely having shortened it. This is because if he did anything, it was actually to have brought it *up*, that is, intensified and made it more dramatic, not throughout, but in several key places, which included adding more violence. The film was never remotely close to all shoot-outs, but he did add the murder of Garrett, the capture at Stinking Springs, the additional killings the morning after Billy's first return to Fort Sumner and during the cattle rustling, and Poe cold-cocking one of the miners at Tuckerman's Hotel. There is nothing epic about the versions Wurlitzer did on his own, as they are too intimate, elliptical, and claustrophobic to qualify—these are indeed among their strengths. As for the film in any version, well, yes, I suppose it could be viewed as an epic, at least along the lines of the looser connotation of the term as any lengthy, sprawling narrative of heroic deeds that have great significance to a society. But if so, it has to be one of the most small-scale and intimate epics ever made, lyrical and muted for long stretches, and also one of the most ironic, bereft as it virtually is of any deeds or action that could be called heroic—and these too are among its strengths.

To judge from dates on the pages of the various screenplays and despite copious notes in one of the July 7, 1972, drafts, Peckinpah did not begin working with Wurlitzer and writing in earnest until sometime after September 9, the day he held a story conference with Wurlitzer, Gordon Carroll, and Gordon Dawson in his offices at MGM. This meeting, which went on for several hours as Peckinpah methodically went through the screenplay scene by scene, was more important than any other in determining the direction the screenplay would take. Matters he covered in great and specific detail included adding scenes; retaining scenes but condensing them, changing their focus or tone, or moving them to different places; rewriting, adding, or dropping lines of dialogue; refining, honing, defining, reducing, or enlarging the characters; describing how scenes might be staged and played and who would be cast; and articulating large-scale concerns such as structure, intention, and the major themes. (Much of this I've already discussed in the previous section.) Peckinpah considered it one of the most productive story conferences he'd ever had and one of the best meetings with a writer. When it was over he told Carroll that he had gone into it with three primary items on his agenda: the new opening, the Maria-Billy relationship, and the cantina scene following Billy's return from the aborted trip to Mexico.

Of more than passing interest here is how Peckinpah approached the opening, which was to apply exactly the same solution he did for his adaptation of Charles Neider's novel: believing that beginning with the jailbreak was beginning far too deep into the action without sufficient setup, he added a pair of new scenes in front of it so that we could observe the two men together. The new opening scene—I make a distinction between the opening *scene* as such and the prologue, which was not yet written—has Garrett arriving in Fort Sumner to ask the Kid and his gang to clear out of the territory. The most immediate effects are two: it dispenses with Wurlitzer's strategy of the title characters never being seen together until the one kills the other at the end and it sets up a pair of opposing arcs of movement that will converge at the climax. Despite the criticisms he voiced in the introduction to his published screenplay, when this new opening was first proposed Wurlitzer was not only not hostile but welcomed it. Conceding it was very different from his approach, he said, "That's what I like about it. The way I see it is that you want to totally know who these two people are in the first five minutes of the film." "That's right," Peckinpah replied. In chapter 4 I draw attention to how the director favored elaborate setups and in *Reconsideration* I several times observe how musical his dramatic and narrative structures are (183–84, 208, 244). This opening is an example of both. He typically liked his characters to be clearly defined or articulated from the outset, much as a melody is in a theme-and-variations piece of music, so that subsequent development, unfolding, transformation, or revelation, as the case may be, will be clearly registered and have something to play against. Years later Wurlitzer came round to embracing the new opening enthusiastically, realizing that it established "their bond of friendship" and "created a more dramatic arc" (Adams).

It was equally important to Peckinpah that their friendship be a *felt* reality in the drama, not an abstract "given" we are asked to accept so that there can be a story at all. "Pat really wants to take enough time to get those guys out, the point is that Pat really doesn't want to see Billy hanged," he told Wurlitzer. "And once [Billy] gets away, it takes a tremendous pressure off him, and he hopes to God the Kid will get out. So we've got to see this warmth and affection in the jail cell and in the shooting match." Yet like all friendships in Peckinpah's films, this one is rent by conflicts that are tragic. Affection in the sheriff collides with obligation corrupted by the necessity to make deals with people he hates; affection in the outlaw collides with freedom corrupted by narcissism and limitations that keep him from imagining a life beyond the meager one he's living that might actually be worth living. Garrett has new responsibilities born at least partially from a desire to escape a life that seems to have lost what meaning it ever had for him, and Billy's response is nihilistic defiance and judgmental scorn: "Sheriff Pat Garrett, sold out to the Santa Fe Ring." For Peckinpah betrayal as such was not at issue here because Garrett's "trying to tell him that he's going to come for him and he's going to kill him— 'It's my job and I'm going to do it.'"

Wurlitzer delivered his first—and apparently only—attempt at writing a new opening two days later. Dated September 11, it consisted of just four pages, with "RW" (his initials) penciled on them.[18] Though it included some exchanges from the *Hendry Jones* screenplay, neither Peckinpah nor anyone else, including Wurlitzer himself, seems to have been very happy with it because it was not expanded upon or incorporated into any full-length copy of the screenplay. Within the next two weeks, however, Peckinpah turned in the first pages that are unequivocally by him alone. Labeled "SP 9/27/72" at the top, the "SP" his initials, they include the Fort Sumner scene, the capture at Stinking Springs, and the jailbreak.[19] In this and succeeding drafts the Fort Sumner scene has lines taken directly or barely altered from his *Hendry Jones* screenplay (e.g., "Win, lose, or draw I'm sheriff of the county"; "You telling me to leave?"; "Right now I'm asking you to. In five days I'm making you, one way or the other") and has Billy's friends, apparently ignorant that Garrett's the newly elected sheriff, welcoming him. In the final version, the pages dated January 10, 1973,[20] the night before it was to be shot, the news that Garrett was elected sheriff has already reached Fort Sumner and most of the old gang are openly contemptuous of him, excepting Billy. This has the effect of placing Garrett in a more sympathetic light, his visit no longer a mere gesture but a farewell and an honest attempt to give the Kid (and the others) an opportunity to leave before matters come to bloodshed. Billy's remark that he didn't think Garrett would bother to make the ride all the way out there is surely one at which Garrett could take legitimate offense, but he doesn't: "Shit, you know me better than that." A vitally significant new line—which appears in no version of the screenplay, thus suggesting Peckinpah added it on the set or Coburn ad-libbed it—is Garrett's question, "Jesus, Bill, don't you get *stale* around here?" (Inasmuch as this is played offscreen, it's possible it was added in postproduction.)

In addition to deepening our sense of the friendship, the new scene also suggests the underlying tensions and pressures caused by changing times and advancing years. The outlaw life no longer has any allure for Garrett, while the rigidity of Billy's response to Garrett's visit hints at cracks and fissures that predate recent developments and anticipate new ones that will soon lead to bloodshed. These are alluded to much later in Holly's "short of supplies" observation at Jones's Saloon, but they are immediately sounded again in the next scene, the capture at Stinking Springs, where Billy tells one of his men, "Ol' Pat's not gonna like this comin' down hard on him the day after he got his new badge."[21] Peckinpah's Billy, like his depiction of Neider's Hendry vis-à-vis Dad Longworth, has every intention of forcing Garrett's hand and pushing the situation to confrontation. The director next wove Garrett into the jail scene, again using some lines from his *Hendry Jones* screenplay (or directly from Neider's novel), and made Olinger a Bible-beater sadistically obsessed with the Kid's salvation. In revising this scene he also wrote new lines as required by Garrett's presence and the new conception of Olinger, but retained as much of Wurlitzer's dialogue as he could, which I believe explains what he meant when he told me he wrote only about half of the new jailhouse scene.

It was sometime in September that Carroll first broached the idea to Peckinpah of opening the film with Garrett's death (though he had talked about it with Wurlitzer long before the director came aboard). Peckinpah leapt at the suggestion; and in the September 9 story conference he quite tellingly and more than once likened it to "the idea of Greek tragedy" and even began to visualize it for his colleagues, describing how the shooting of Garrett would be intercut with the shooting of the chickens as a titles sequence complete with freeze-frames—all this before he had committed a word of it to paper. In the next two weeks or so he had written it down as a prologue that made its first appearance in a draft dated October 4.[22] At this time Peckinpah conceived it as a prologue *only*; he never wrote or filmed a proper epilogue that reprised the prologue and made a framing structure out of it: that was done only much later in postproduction.

One reason Peckinpah was so taken by Carroll's idea is that Garrett's death, still shrouded in mystery and controversy, has long been thought to be the work of a conspiracy. It probably was, although it was at most a strictly bush-league conspiracy of just a very few men whose reasons were mostly, if not entirely, personal and had absolutely nothing to do with the events almost thirty years earlier except for the coincidence of Garrett's involvement. No matter, historical accuracy doesn't necessarily guarantee strong drama, and Peckinpah, all too ready at this time in his life and on this project in particular to believe he was surrounded by plotting against him on all sides, was plainly in the grip of a story in which decisions people make and actions they take have consequences that put them on certain paths which in turn lead to ends that are unforeseen but inevitable and usually fatal. In other words, his story-conference invocation of Greek tragedy was not made lightly.[23] He must have reasoned that since fatalism is by definition built into the story of Pat Garrett and Billy the Kid, why not extend it all the way to the end of Garrett's life by positing a causal relationship between Garrett's death and his pursuit

FADE IN

EXT. FORT SUMNER - DAY

1) SIX CHICKENS ARE BURIED IN THE SAND UP TO THEIR NECKS.

Three shots ring out - heads fly - slow motion -

2) A YOUNG MAN NAMED WILLIAM BONNEY, KNOWN AS BILLY THE
   KID, FIRING twenty five yards away. - Intercut with
   above -

Two chicken heads leave the scene.

3) THREE CHILDREN PULL THEM out of the dirt for plucking
   and cooking. They run to the Festivo Crowd of fifty
   or sixty people - hungry for a good dinner. The
   chickens are plucked into the pot.

4) BILLY TURNS, SMILING - It's obvious he's the best -
   The Crowd whistles, claps, then:

5) A RIFLE FIRES FOUR TIMES - Two hundred yards from
   Billy.

6) FOUR CHICKEN HEADS LEAVE THE SCENE.

The crowd is silent. Billy turns and stares at:

7) PAT GARRETT, who stands by his horse, reloading his
   smoking rifle.

Billy suddenly laughs, shakes his head and opens his arms
wide in greeting and crosses toward Pat.

Garrett, tall and thin, his features lengthened by a long
handlebar mustache, walks slowly forward.

                    BILLY
              (happily embracing Garrett)
         Your luck is running good for an old man.
         Want to try it with a .44?

                    GARRETT
         Hell, no. You'd whip my ass...
         Let's have a drink....I'm buying.

8) THE CROWD SURGES BEHIND Billy and Garrett as they
   walk into the saloon.

                                        CUT TO:

The beginning of Peckinpah's initial draft of a new first scene
in Fort Sumner: identified by his initials (*top right*), it marks
the first revisions he himself wrote for the screenplay.

INT. - SALOON - DAY - GARRETT AND BILLY

The Saloon is a long low-ceilinged room that also doubles
as a kitchen dining room.

Three men play guitars, one a harmonica.

9)   BILLY AND GARRETT ENTER TOGETHER. THE CROWD FOLLOWS

10)   O'FOLLIARD, PACO, DENVER, BEAVER, SILVA and three of
    his closest companions, LUKE, HOLLY and BLACK HARRIS,
    stand next to him. They are rugged, unshaven and
    obviously hard types...Yolanda serves drinks.

11)   J.W. BELL stands on the other side of GARRETT - A
    tough man, with a quiet melancholy air to him.

The crowd noisily greets GARRETT.

                    LUKE
You old son-of-a-bitch, Pat, how are ja?

                    HOLLY
Goddamn, Pat, you ain't never shot
like that in your life.

                    GARRETT
Marriage does strange things to a man -
sharpens the eye.

                    BLACK HARRIS
Yeah, maybe. But the old ying yang,
did it get any longer.

                    GARRETT
                    (laughs)
I only wish it had.

                    PACO
                 ' (to Garrett)
Como te va, Pat?

                    GARRETT
                    (to Paco)
Todo esta bien.

and killing of the Kid at the behest of big investors who want to develop the territory? Following Wurlitzer's example as regards Chisum's loan to Garrett, what the relationship consists in is never made explicit or even very clear, and in the October 4 draft Garrett is surrounded by entirely new associates, who murder him but whom we'll never see again. By the October 18 draft,[24] Peckinpah came up with the idea of making one of these associates John W. Poe, which was further embellished by inventing a partnership whereby he is leasing land from Garrett, thus making him an instrument of Garrett's death, implicating the whole Santa Fe Ring in it, and introducing the theme of betrayal.[25] Leaving the nature of their arrangement vague was probably a wise decision: too much detail might obscure or otherwise detract from the larger themes.

Wurlitzer had already begun to incorporate a strong element of determinism into the story by way of the new Governor Wallace scene. Peckinpah added to it by playing up the role of personal psychology in shaping the characters' destinies. Like the proverbial moth to the flame, regardless of what Billy does, given who and what he is, it is simply not in his nature to be able to leave the territory for good or prevent himself from returning should he try; by the same token, however many delaying or warning stratagems Garrett employs to buy the Kid time or impress upon him the seriousness of the pursuit, Garrett's personality is such that he can never extricate himself from the course to which he is committed, cannot avoid the fated appointment in Fort Sumner. And what sets the whole action into motion are the social, economic, and political forces that want to develop and bring law, order, and business to the territory, upon which Peckinpah plied the added weight of advancing age, not so much by anything he specifically wrote into the screenplay as by the decisive fiat of casting Coburn as Garrett. This was further reinforced with the casting of Billy's gang. Apart from Charlie Martin Smith (nineteen, Bowdre), all the actors were older than what is suggested in the script or their counterparts in reality (if they had them): Donnie Fritts (thirty, Breed/Beaver), Richard Bright (thirty-five, Holly), Rudolph Wurlitzer (thirty-five, Folliard), Luke Askew (forty, Eno), Jorge Russek (forty, Silva), Bob Dylan (thirty-one, Alias), L. Q. Jones (forty-five, Harris), and Harry Dean Stanton (forty-six, Luke). Even Rita Coolidge at twenty-eight was hardly an ingénue, while Peckinpah's first choice for the role was Begonia Palacios, his second wife, then thirty-one, an actress he met on *Major Dundee* (she sexually initiates Trooper Ryan, the youthful bugler), who turned it down (much to his consternation) because she felt she wasn't ready.

Peckinpah must have noticed, or at least intuited, that all the new material Wurlitzer wrote involving Garrett dramatized one theme or complex of themes over and over: the control, power, and domination Garrett exerts over those around him, whether it's bullying his wife into backing down when she wants to talk about their marriage, telling the investors in Santa Fe where they can shove their reward money, killing Black Harris, goading Holly into going for his knife, physically abusing a favorite whore to get information, and guilting a friend into helping him track the Kid. When Peckinpah added new material of his own designed to orient the story even more toward Garrett, he employed essentially the same tactic as Wurlitzer used to make Billy dominant in his original: a strong introduction followed immediately by scenes that depict the character as brave, decisive, and able to work his will upon those around him. These include the reunion in Fort Sumner, where Garrett shows himself to be a better shot than any of the old gang (and easily Billy's equal) and lays down the terms of his new tenure as sheriff directly and without fear or apology; the capture of Billy at Stinking Springs, where two of Billy's friends are dispatched and the Kid is forced to surrender; and the jailhouse, where Garrett threatens to send Olinger back to West Texas if he doesn't lay off badgering the Kid. Throughout the film Peckinpah staged almost every scene with Garrett to show how quickly he sizes up and takes charge of every place, circumstance, and situation in which he finds himself: a nice small example how he uses his horse to herd the petty thief Gates to Cullen Baker's jail, a large one Jones's Saloon, where he controls the room, rendering everyone powerless without getting out of his chair or even raising his voice. But in the large shadow of the prologue, which is to say from the perspective of the long trajectory of history, all Garrett's demonstrations of control, all these impositions of his will, are seen to be illusory. In most retellings of the story Billy is doomed from the outset, so no matter how heroically or otherwise strongly he is depicted, we always know, if only at the backs of our minds, that fate wields the ultimate trump card. With the new prologue Peckinpah drew Garrett's death into the same orbit of this awareness.

At the outset, dramatic irony as it applies to Billy consists in our knowledge that he will die, but it's an event we don't experience until the very end. With Garrett, however, the effect is far more powerful because we are actually shown his death at the outset—more than just shown it, in fact, but made to experience it with him. Peckinpah went even further by intercutting Garrett's murder with the new Fort Sumner scene. The crosscutting between Garrett's body being riddled with his murderers' bullets and the buried chickens getting their heads shot off by Billy and a younger Garrett twenty-seven years earlier makes Garrett himself one of the instruments by which fate will cut him down as surely as it will the Kid, though it will take nearly three decades longer. As realized on film, the crosscutting has the additional effect not just of reorienting the film toward Garrett but also of making it his in an unusually direct and intimate way, such that it conditions our response to everything that follows. In effect, it established the point of view as Garrett's. I do not mean this literally, of course, only that despite the alternating back-and-forth between the two principals once they've gone their separate ways, emotionally and psychologically the film remains Garrett's through and through.[26] But this was implicit even in Wurlitzer's Billy the Kid original, which contains the germ of a mirror-like or symbiotic relationship between the sheriff and the outlaw. By the time Peckinpah was finished, for better or worse—it turned out to be for better *and* worse—Billy was so thoroughly absorbed into Garrett's psyche as a conflicting side of Garrett's personality that the Kid all but ceased to exist as a character in his own right, or at least as a character with any sort of internal consistency.

The only other new material for Garrett that Peckinpah wrote or had Wurlitzer write of any substance was a decidedly bizarre addition to the final confrontation, introduced in the October 4 version. He not only had Billy and Garrett recognize each other in Maxwell's bedroom, but had Garrett force the Kid at gunpoint out into the plaza, where he shoots him dead in cold blood in front of witnesses, including Poe and McKinney. This was preceded by an exchange of dialogue, the last part of which reads:

> BILLY: What you aimin' to do now?

> GARRETT: Git clear out of the law most likely. Got me some bottomland over to Roswell.

> BILLY: They ain't ever goin' to let you forget, Pat. The tell is on you now.

> *They stare at each other. Billy turns to walk ahead.*

> GARRETT: Kid?

> BILLY (*half turning*): Yeah. I know. Jest one thing. Before you start lyin' to 'em, tell 'em about the time I told you I was faster'n God.

> *Billy turns, his arms extended. Garrett takes a step forward and shoots him through the heart.* (128)

As McKinney strides toward him, Garrett says, "Don't say nothin'. Not a word." But McKinney replies, "You poor son-of-a-bitch."[27]

It's hard to know what to make of this scene. Peckinpah often wrote far more about his characters than he ever planned to shoot, including exploring alternative scenarios, because it was one way he had of getting to know them. This could have been an example of that. Or maybe it was a residue from his *Hendry Jones* screenplay, where he felt the need to give Dad and Hendry some moments together before Hendry dies—but to what end here, where Garrett acts so completely out of character? Maybe he wanted to balance a scene Wurlitzer had added in his first rewrite in which McKinney actually identifies himself to Billy when he comes across Billy on his way to Maria's. McKinney reminds the Kid of when they had met before and they talk about Garrett. Eno is suspicious, but the Kid brushes his concerns aside. The encounter, which was written in such a way as to keep us in suspense whether McKinney is going to warn the Kid off or betray Garrett, isn't as strange as the one Peckinpah wrote, but it's strange enough—why would McKinney risk his life by identifying himself to the Kid, especially since he was reluctant, because afraid, to accompany Garrett in the first place?—and serves no purpose that I can see except further to reinforce how much denial the Kid is in, which is hardly necessary by this point in the story. I personally believe the most plausible explanation is that Peckinpah wrote his scene as a decoy to preoccupy the production executives, who were constantly looking for material to cut. This was a favorite ploy of his. In one meeting, talking about another scene he had no intention of shooting and which he knew the studio would want to lose, he said, "Let's leave it in—let them think of it. I'll fight it tooth and nail, and I'll say I need it. With these people, let them be heroes, let them 'save' the script, [otherwise] they're going to save it anyway by taking something out of real value."[28] Cutting this would allow him to drop a day from the schedule and distract the suits from important material he wanted left alone.[29]

Whatever the reasons, both of these unfortunate scenes remained in the shooting script for a surprisingly long time, well into January, when Peckinpah finally went back to his own variant of Wurlitzer's Garrett-based account. At the same time, he turned his attention to the prolixity of the final night, where Wurlitzer had added a lot of extraneous bits of business, such as bickering between Poe and McKinney, Garrett ordering Poe to go find the house of a woman Billy used to know, Pete Maxwell having a fit in his kitchen because he can't get one of his boots off, and Maria going to help him. Wurlitzer also had Garrett not knowing Maxwell all that well, remaining skeptical the Kid is even there (which of course has a historical basis), and at one point talking about going to find some women they can all enjoy once they've talked with Maxwell. None of this represented the best of Wurlitzer's work. By the time Peckinpah was finished, he had condensed, tightened, and focused the final pages to powerful lyric and dramatic effect, though again much of what he did is not evident on the page, only in the film itself, where this became one of the most beautifully extended and sustained lyrical sequences in all his work.

As rewritten, directed, shot, and edited, Billy and Maria now do make love, and when Garrett, who has known since Roswell that the Kid is in Fort Sumner, reaches the porch of Maxwell's house and passes by the window of their room, he is clearly aware of where they are and what they are doing. He halts his progress and sits down on the swing (several moments later he will slump down on another swing after he shoots the Kid). In a final gesture of commingled respect, affection, and resignation, Garrett nevertheless continues trying to dodge his destiny by allowing Billy a final moment of grace and release with his woman. It's only when the Kid finishes and announces he's going to find something to eat that the moment is broken and Garrett resumes his deadly mission, entering the house and stealing down the hallway, past the room where Maria is still in the bed, facing away from the door, and into Maxwell's room, where he seats himself on a chair, draws his revolver, and waits.

If we stop to think about it, it's a curious piece of staging that doesn't make logical sense: why go into Maxwell's bedroom? As was not the case with the real Garrett, Peckinpah's Garrett obviously doesn't need to inquire of Maxwell if the Kid is in town because he already knows. He could have easily—and if it had happened in history anything like this, the real Garrett surely would have—burst in on the Kid and apprehended or killed him without further ado. But Peckinpah is here drawing together and binding the forces of character and of fate, and Garrett is still trying to escape his destiny. Yet he no sooner settles into the chair and draws his revolver than the Kid backs into the room and turns toward him. Peckinpah allows them a moment of recognition. Billy's face, his gun in hand but not raised, breaks into a smile, one of the most enigmatic expressions in all Peckinpah's work—affectionate? sardonic? ironic? assured? pleased? mocking?[30] Garrett, stone-cold sober, betrays no emotion at all, his face expressionless as he hesitates one last time, and to equally ambiguous effect: can he possibly still believe that somehow, miraculously, fate will spare him fulfilling the final terms of the bargain he struck with himself and others months earlier?

However separately they got there, Peckinpah and Wurlitzer eventually wound up on the same page when it came to Garrett: Peckinpah obviously liked what Wurlitzer did because he kept most of it, changed little of it, and reinforced a lot of it with the new material he wrote or suggested, the casting, and the way he directed, filmed, and edited the scenes. What he brought to the character that wasn't in Wurlitzer was a far stronger realization of Garrett's age and the implications it has for the time in his life and the moment in history when we take up his story. He also brought an equivalently stronger and more intimate sense of Garrett's friendship with the Kid and the psychic ties that bind them. The most powerful effect this had was to raise our investment in that friendship, which in turn made its destruction emotionally devastating, and to entwine the friendship with the larger themes of determinism and fatalism, to equally devastating effect.

When it came to Billy, however, Peckinpah was not so much on a different page as on no particular page at all or several at once. In the April 9 memo he complained that Wurlitzer's Billy "basically does nothing but wait." This is obviously untrue. Wurlitzer's Billy "does" a very great deal: he declines and deteriorates, moving inexorably toward his own death, hapless and helpless to stop himself, despite warnings from practically everyone that Garrett is closing in on him. That's a real story and, as Wurlitzer told it, a substantial and compelling one. It's also the story Charles Neider told, albeit quite differently. Peckinpah realized early on that both the novel and the screenplay are about "a man waiting to die," the difference being that for the director the novel was structured "in terms of dramatic action" (the main reason he urged Wurlitzer to read it), while the screenplay had too much "aimless movement." In my opinion that specific judgment was—quite uncharacteristically—obtuse on Peckinpah's part, but it's clear that he was intrigued by a Billy conceived as a kind of passive suicide—he just wanted him to be an *active* passive suicide. Fair enough. Yet the most puzzling aspect of his revisions is that hardly any of them addressed this specific concern. The only wholly new Billy scene of substantial length that Peckinpah contributed and that survives in the film is the capture at Stinking Springs. But this scene is nearly as much Garrett's as Billy's; and coming as it does at the beginning, it's much too early to develop the idea of a Billy waiting to die. On the contrary, as Peckinpah wrote it, Billy doesn't give up until both Bowdre and Folliard have been shot to pieces trying to escape; and he matches Garrett's "I'm alive, though," with a smiling (or smirking, depending on how one reads Kristofferson's performance) "So am I." This is not, or at least not yet, a Billy resigned to his death.

What Peckinpah mostly did was eliminate the scenes that dramatized the Kid's decline, precisely those in which he felt nothing was happening: the old couple from whom Billy steals a horse; all the Maria scenes; and the scenes of his getting drunk, falling asleep, target-practicing and missing, losing control of his bladder, getting drunker and missing more targets, shooting a burro out of panic, wandering aimlessly on his horse, identifying with the comatose stranger in the cabin, and rambling incoherently in the cantina after returning from the aborted trip to Mexico. Most of these were dropped before the summer's end,[31] yet, astonishingly, *Peckinpah wrote hardly anything to replace them.* The most problematic consequence of this is most clearly illustrated by what he did with the cantina scene near the end. He hated practically everything about it and really went after it in the big September story conference, calling for deep cuts in both business and dialogue and for the tone to be "completely changed." After the meeting ended and Wurlitzer had left, Peckinpah told Carroll, "The most important thing, I got that fucking goofy cowboy bullshit out of the picture." By this he meant the drunken partying and Billy's pathetic attempt at a rabble-rousing speech. Carroll agreed, saying he always considered the scene "unplayable." Maybe so, but before they were shot and edited, more than a few scenes and moments in Peckinpah's films could be described that way, yet they play beautifully on screen. The truth is, when Peckinpah really believed in something, he was usually able to make it play.

The issue here, as I see it, is that his conception of the Kid was still evolving. He told his colleagues he wanted Billy to have "some dignity" at the end and for there to be something of the sense of a "last roundup" for him and his gang. He even suggested a new exchange between Billy and Maria: she asks him to come to Mexico with her and he answers, "Not until Chisum's gone, not until Murphy's gone, and not until I settle with Pat." The exchange never made it into the film, though what he says to Eno upon his return is similar, save the governor being substituted for Murphy (who in history was three years dead by then and anyhow is never mentioned elsewhere or in any other version of the screenplay). "You just give us the word, there's enough of us left," Eno says, and the Kid declares, "Nobody's running us off. Not Garrett, not Chisum, or that goddamn governor." Transferring the setting to the fountain in the plaza of Fort Sumner, cutting the scene to the bone by the time it went through revision, shooting, and editing, shearing it of all the irony of the drunkenness of Billy and his gang, Peckinpah played the Kid's return absolutely straight. (He even wanted the "Old days are comin' back" line given to Billy and again played straight, though this was never done.) The effect is to lead us at the very least to expect a series of reprisals against Chisum or Garrett or the governor or the town of Lincoln or—*something*. Instead, Billy not only "basically" does nothing but wait—he does nothing but wait period.

When this very point was raised in the September 9 story conference, Peckinpah's response was that Billy should return, reassert his leadership, have a brief loving reunion with Maria, and take a couple of days' rest after the hard ride back before he and who's left of the gang get down to the business of going after Chisum and dealing with Garrett. He didn't want Billy getting drunk or even taking a drink and he suggested that Billy's delay in going into action right away be covered with a line of dialogue ("I'll be ready to ride in two days"), a delay that would prove ironic inasmuch as fate in the form of Garrett catches up with him in those two days. Yet not only did Peckinpah not write that line into the screenplay, he explicitly told Wurlitzer to weed out anything that suggested Billy was tired or run-down, a motif that is built into both Wurlitzer's and Neider's conceptions of the Kid. And again, months later, when he finally got around to shooting the Fort Sumner scenes that follow Billy's return, he did little or nothing in the playing, staging, and filming that took the story or the character in the new direction, including even the crucial matter of clarifying the timeline—in the completed film, it feels as if far more than a couple of days elapse between Billy's return and Garrett's arrival. What he did instead was add two quite small but significant scenes that hark back toward Billy's return as Wurlitzer had conceived it, only considerably subtler, more low-key, nuanced, and elliptical: Billy target-shooting and the drink he and Alias share.

The first presents us with a suggestion of how pathetic, purposeless, and even marginalized Billy has become by this point, not to mention how narrow his sphere of influence, his following now a nameless pal and some kids registering their pleasure at his "exploits" by banging a stick on a can and applauding when his shots explode some bottles. The other scene is even better and seems to me one of the most thickly allusive in the entire film. It is late in the day, wind sweeping through the plaza blowing up dust, the Kid by himself at a table, Alias joining him to warn that Garrett's "coming in." "Yeah, I reckon," Billy replies, "maybe he wants to have a drink with me." This is an echo of Garrett's line when he left Jones's Saloon after killing Holly and an allusion to the parting drink he had with Billy at the beginning of the film. But a deeper and more important allusion comes by way of the transformation in

"Maybe he wants to have a drink with me."

the plaza itself. At the beginning it is brilliantly sunlit, the air clean and clear, the scene festive, alive with color and vitality. By the end the swirling dust obscures the late afternoon sun and the colors are washed out into dull shades of pink, tan, gray, and brown. The images of Billy sitting alone drinking while his friends watch him in silence from a distance evoke . . . well, it surely cannot be an accident that the word which comes most readily to mind is from Luke's remark when the Kid was about to depart for Mexico: "Hell, in ol' Mex he ain't goin' to be nothin' but another drunken gringo shittin' out chili peppers and waitin' for . . ."—the beat is integral to the meaning—"*nothin'*." How uncannily accurate a description this is of even the deceptively festive life we see in the plaza at the beginning, the life the Kid rode away from when he left for Mexico, and the life he returns to, except that it's not in ol' Mex but right there in Fort Sumner. Staving off boredom by target-practicing on live chickens has given way to doing nothing but waiting for a man who's doing nothing but waiting for another man to come in and finish him off, and the notes sounded of lassitude, entropy, and stasis are the final resolution of the question Garrett asked the last time they had a drink together: "Jesus, don't you get *stale* around here, Bill?" The scene ends as Alias rejoins the others at the fountain, leaving Billy once more alone, brooding, sipping his whiskey, staring off into the distance. In scenes and moments like these it seems to me that Peckinpah had by some circuitous route found his way back to the aimlessness, exhaustion, and fatalism of Wurlitzer's Billy, his gang, and the world they occupy, and it's a pity he didn't realize that he needed more, not fewer, like them.

What remains puzzling in view of Peckinpah's criticisms of *One-Eyed Jacks* is that given two opportunities to tell the so-called real story of Billy the Kid as he saw it, as killer, not as hero, he somewhat romanticized or otherwise softened the character. This is clearer in the *Hendry Jones* screenplay because he didn't do the job consistently in *Pat Garrett and Billy the Kid*. In the killing of Bell, for example, Peckinpah retained Billy bragging about shooting Carlyle three times in the back—"Blew his goddamn head off"—yet he also had him say, "I don't want to kill you, Bell," added a "don't" to the screenplay when Bell starts to turn, and on the set added or allowed Kristofferson to insert a "please" after the "don't." In the Stinking Springs capture Billy gives the order for all three of them to attempt an escape; but once Bowdre and Folliard are shot to pieces in this exercise in futility, he saves his own skin by giving himself up. After Silva's death Billy and Alias kill four Chisum hands from ambush and in the Horrell scene Peckinpah had Billy not just turn on the two-count but draw his gun, raise, and aim it before Alamosa turns, which means that the duel becomes in effect an ambush. The Kid arrives too late to save Paco, but he does save his daughter and coolly dispatches the three Chisum perpetrators; and when he returns to Fort Sumner, he tells everyone that Chisum's killed Paco and that nobody's running them off, then proceeds to do nothing. Who and what is this man: a cold-blooded killer, another bandit just looking out for himself, a romantic outlaw who steals from the rich and powerful and protects the weak and helpless, a nihilistic force of anarchy, an unconscious suicide waiting to be killed? In a sense, he is all that and both more and less.[32]

"I know Billy," Garrett tells the investors in Santa Fe, and "he ain't exactly predictable." Peckinpah liked complex characters or at least characters who are multifaceted with unexpected sides and odd angles to their personalities, and he was clearly drawn to characters divided within and against themselves. Neither Neider's Hendry nor Wurlitzer's Billy is this kind of character, but they are believable in their own terms, they are internally consistent, and they have strongly profiled developments that advance and unify their stories. I am not suggesting Peckinpah should have stuck with Wurlitzer's conception if it didn't speak to him. If he couldn't realize it with full conviction, he was of course right to change it. But the problem is that he didn't change it, really; he merely left it in pieces without putting it back together again. He obviously wanted to take Billy in directions that were more interesting to him, but he never got around to writing any of them down. Instead, he seems to have believed he could make it happen in the shooting. In casting Kris Kristofferson he no doubt hoped that some of the dramatic interest would derive as a matter of course from the singer himself, who is tall, handsome, blue-eyed, charismatic, and radiates an unusual combination of warmth and remoteness.

But Peckinpah also saw, in Coburn's words, a "boyish quality" in Kristofferson, "a brash *naïveté*" that he felt he could use for the Kid (Simmons 182). Drawing upon Kristofferson's celebrity as a singer and a songwriter, particularly of songs like "Sunday Morning Coming Down" and "Help Me Make It through the Night," Peckinpah was able to suggest some of the dissipation of Wurlitzer's Billy by association and perhaps also to embody some sense of Neider's young gunfighter at an early crossroads between a reputation he can no longer sustain and a future he cannot abide or contemplate. At the same time, however, Peckinpah hardly ever has Billy take a drink and never depicts him drunk, which was also what he did with Hendry Jones in the Neider adaptation. Yet while this is historically accurate, it makes the scenes where Billy misses when he is target-shooting rather confusing. In Wurlitzer these were there to show the Kid's waning powers owing to the ravages of drink and hard living. In any version of the film they make even less sense because when Peckinpah got around to staging the killing of the Chisum hands responsible for Paco's death, he had the Kid shooting unerringly, at least once from the hip no less, while on a horse made skittish from the pistol shots. If he's capable of this kind of marksmanship, how can he miss a stationary target while standing still, taking his time, and holding the gun with both hands as he sights along the barrel?

When Peckinpah substituted the "I don't want to kill you, Bell" line, Carroll pointed out this was a big change that they should talk about, because "it certainly makes Billy more sympathetic." "We can use that," Peckinpah shot back, "because I really want him to be colder than shit other places." Evidently his thinking was that an occasional moment of sympathy or softening would have the effect of heightening the Kid's cold-bloodedness, which would appear more shocking for the contrast. In this his model was Neider's Hendry Jones. "Hendry was like Billy," Peckinpah told his colleagues. "He was charming, but he's a killer. I mean, it doesn't bother him at all to kill." When Peckinpah had a characterization this definite in mind, and when he articulated it as clearly as he did here, he usually managed to realize it on film. Why not in this instance?

Any number of answers is possible, but one of the most plausible is that at the time of the September 9 meeting, when Peckinpah said this, Kristofferson was not even a contender for the role. This could be "the definitive" film about Billy the Kid, Peckinpah said, "if we can get the right Billy." The right Billy at this point was Malcolm McDowell, whom the company was trying to attract. Peckinpah thought McDowell "sensational" in *If . . .* , where he played Mick Travis, a teenage freshman in a British private school who stages a rebellion in which he guns down upperclassmen who tormented him, schoolmasters who beat him, and parents and other grown-ups. And in the dystopian *A Clockwork Orange*, released earlier in the year, McDowell played Alex, the leader of a gang of thugs whose amusements consist in "ultra-violence," that is, rape, murder, and destruction to the accompaniment of classical music.[33] It's easy to imagine a dollop of sympathy here, a drop of warmth there making a cold-blooded killer even more cold-blooded when the killer is the McDowell of Mick or Alex. But Kris Kristofferson brought a completely different personality to Billy. Not long after signing he told Peckinpah, "The more I look at the script and that book [i.e., Neider's], the more I identify with that character." This must have been music to Peckinpah's ears, because he immediately told Kristofferson, "Play the book—you play that book!"[34] But whether because of inexperience, insufficient rehearsal, or temperamental disaffinity, Kristofferson was never able wholly to identify with Neider's Kid. One reason might have been that in those days Kristofferson had about him an almost vestigial friendliness—that "boyish quality" Coburn mentioned. Though Peckinpah recognized it, he was unable to integrate it into the darker, harder, colder character he had in mind, nor did he manage to get Kristofferson to shed or sufficiently suppress it.[35]

The evidence of the several drafts of the screenplay once Peckinpah took over indicates that he did much more work on Maria than on Billy. He kept trying out different personas on her. He experimented with softening her, making her essentially worried and compliant. Then he made her defiant and tempestuous, in one scene spurning the Kid's advances until, redolent of Stanley Kowalski, Billy shouts, "Goddamn! I don't need your words . . . I need you as a woman. I need you now," and forces himself upon her, which turns her on so much that, redolent of Stella, she gives herself to him.[36] Next he discarded this only to go back to a Maria who does little more than urge Billy to leave. Yet loath to lose the more volatile previous alternative, he rewrote the first part of what used to be the stable scene, transferred it to a ruined adobe, and created a new (one-scene) character he named "Lupe," a "large buxom woman" who tells Billy that Garrett is on his trail and that if he doesn't clear out he "won't get old here."[37] And one late version, in what was evidently an attempt to introduce Neider's theme of luck (which was important to Peckinpah), has Billy telling Maria that she's such a downer she's bringing him bad luck. The scene ends as Billy manages to lift her out of her funk and they "laugh, rolling over on the bed, they're lost in themselves like kids."[38]

Peckinpah eventually faced the inevitable: the script had become so long that he reduced Maria virtually to a walk-on seen mostly along the periphery of the action. In the film Maria and Billy aren't romantically involved at all at the beginning; later there are some exchanged glances suggesting a flirtation; when or how the pair become lovers is never shown, but by the time he's leaving for Mexico, she's giving him a necklace as a memento;[39] and on his final night he picks her up and takes her to bed. One scene Peckinpah wrote—or had Wurlitzer write—was a "cute" introduction, inserted after the shoot-out with the three men in Fort Sumner, in which the Kid follows her back to her house. Though this was filmed, Peckinpah evidently felt it so expendable he dropped it well before the previews. Indifferently played, shot, and directed, it does little for the Maria character or her relationship with Billy and doesn't add much else to the film, except to show Billy horsing around with some local kids.[40]

Why Peckinpah tried out so many variations on this at best secondary character can only be guessed at. He raised concerns at the September 9 meeting that the relationship wasn't working and Wurlitzer concurred, but neither was specific as to why, except that the director insisted upon expunging anything that suggested Maria is a whore or sexually available to Billy's gang. He clearly wanted her to be "Billy's woman," and advised Wurlitzer to have a look at the scenes between Hendry and Nika in the *Hendry Jones* screenplay for some ideas as to how the relationship might be developed. But as revised by

Wurlitzer earlier that year, the relationship was *already* so similar to the one in the *Hendry Jones* adaptation that it's easy to understand why he must have drawn a blank as to what the director was after. Whatever the answer, as the *Pat Garrett* screenplay evolved in the weeks that followed, perhaps unable to solve the big problem of Billy, Peckinpah allowed himself to become preoccupied with a simpler character. Perhaps with his preference for contrast, once Garrett was given a quarrelsome relationship with his wife, Peckinpah did not want something similar between Billy and Maria. Perhaps he realized that having cut all the scenes of Billy in decline, Maria had lost both her dramatic function and much of her thematic justification. Perhaps once his former wife passed on the offer, he lost interest in the character.

It was eventually cast with Rita Coolidge, which raises another question. Could she act? Or was it an issue of money? In the film Maria has just one line (offscreen and unscripted, thus either ad-libbed or added in post), which means that Coolidge was in effect an extra and probably paid as such. So were the members of Kristofferson's band, most of them likewise cast in nonspeaking parts, with the exception of Donnie Fritts as Breed (since all he does is a few times repeat what other characters say, he too was probably paid as an extra with a "bump" for those lines). Inasmuch as Kristofferson and his band, Kristofferson and Dylan, and Kristofferson and Coolidge all knew each other, Peckinpah more than likely counted on getting enough improvised material among them for editing purposes in postproduction. But as a master of getting spontaneous performances, he knew only too well that improvisation works best from a solid foundation of preparation, when the actors are thoroughly familiar with their characters, and if they're *experienced* actors. Little of this obtained for the Billy half of the story.

With Maria and Billy's relationship effectively out and all the scenes of his decline cut, what was left to carry the brunt of practically the whole development of his character between the jailbreak and the return to Fort Sumner at the end was the Horrell scene and Paco's death, which together constitute the entire aborted trip to Mexico. Having Billy leave the territory was always problematic for a Billy the Kid film intended to be definitive, because he never did. One of the never quite satisfactorily answered questions about his last several months is why he didn't go to Mexico or somewhere else once there was a price on his head. This was less of a problem for Neider because, however historically inspired, his novel is a work of fiction with made-up characters transplanted to a different part of the country. And he accounts for it plausibly in the plot: Hendry has to leave the Monterey Peninsula because he's got lawmen from Monterey and the surrounding counties on his trail and the area is much smaller than the sprawling New Mexico Territory. Neider also has Hendry's whole gang go along with him, and they actually *get* to Mexico. They return only because Hendry can't resist going back to force a confrontation with Longworth and because he feels he's got unfinished business with his girlfriend. In his *Billy the Kid* screenplay, Wurlitzer solved the problem differently, with the Tom Ketchum encounter, the Kid's drunken wanderings, and the scene in the deserted cabin.

Though Peckinpah appears neither to have liked nor gotten the point of Wurlitzer's carefully worked-out decline for Billy, he must have realized that when he cut all the scenes that dramatized it, he was left with a big hole in the development. Billy's return no longer made much sense because there is no follow-through from it. This was a huge issue throughout the entire postproduction, one that was eventually addressed by some desperate measures in postproduction that I will detail in part 2. Yet it wasn't just Billy's return that raised questions; his decision to leave in the first place began to appear rather strange. He says that he figures Garrett's given him about as much time as he can, then he tells his friends that they'd better leave too, as there's "gonna be some hard times comin' down," and rides off, leaving even Maria behind. Does this smack a little of desertion? It's even worse when one of them says they'd be happy to come along, because it invites us to ask why they don't, as there seems to be nothing holding them in Fort Sumner. It's possible to justify the Kid's decision here with reference to the three men who show up looking for him or to the death of Silva by arguing the intent is to see that he's leaving to keep his friends out of danger by way of their association with him. But since they're all outlaws, danger like this is routine for them; and, anyhow, none of the screenplays ever dramatizes or otherwise makes that point.

As Peckinpah continued rewriting Paco's death during production, he came up with the idea of cutting the whole second part, which showed that the Kid has buried the two Chisum men, tied the third up so that Paco's daughter can exact her vengeance, and left her with a horse so she can return to her own people. I don't understand Peckinpah's thinking behind removing all this. Inasmuch as it was done on January 2, the night before the scene was shot, perhaps time and money reared their ugly heads again. The call sheets for that day and the next two were unusually full: finish Stinking Springs; start the exterior sheepherders (i.e., Paco's death); finish the exterior river and raft scene (probably to be handled by the second unit); and complete the sheepherders. But the second part of Paco's death contained only five lines of dialogue among three actors, the set was already dressed and involved no complexities of staging, lighting, props, or extras—why would it have required so much extra time? (All those sheep in the background? But it could have been shot close and in a direction away from the sheep, as Paco's beating and death were.) Whatever the answer, once this was crossed out—a large "X" literally drawn over the scene without even removing the page—the solution Peckinpah devised to keep the rest of the sequence from being utterly ludicrous was to have Alias ride up out of nowhere for a two-line exchange: Billy, "Take care of her"; Alias, "You're going back?" The script reads: "Billy doesn't answer and rides out the same way he came in."[41]

In one October 18 version of the screenplay, the beginning of the scene when Billy arrives back in Fort Sumner after Paco's death carries a note that

BILLY AND RED STARE at each other.   332X18-332X20>
                                                  CONT'D
                        RED   (2)
                  Now listen, Kid...

He stops when he sees the look in Billy's eyes.

EXT. SHEEPHERDERS' CAMP - EVENING   332X21

The sun sets. Three graves have been dug. Red is
still tied to the wagon wheel.

Billy walks two saddled horses over to Yolanda.
She still sits in the same position, staring at the
man on the wagon wheel.

                        BILLY (gently to Yolanda)
                  You got a horse here. You can ride
                  back to your people. Figure you want
                  to do that alone.

                        YOLANDA
                  And you, Billy...Mexico?

                        BILLY
                  Going back.

                        RED
                  Don't leave me, Kid. She'll
                  put out my eyes.

                        BILLY (as he mounts
                        his horse)
                  I hope so.

Billy rides out of camp.
                                        CUT TO:

EXT. - FORT SUMNER - EVENING   333-337

Billy rides slowly through the gates of Fort Sumner.
He is unshaven. His shirt is ripped. He is weary,
to the point of collapse.

A man fixing a wagon wheel looks up and stares as
he rides past.

TWO BUCKBOARDS are filled with belongings, ready to
leave. They are two Indian families'...relatives
watch silently.

BILLY RIDES HIS HORSE to the water trough in the
middle of the Parade Ground. As the horse drinks,
Billy's head drops to his chest. He swings off the

The second half of Paco's death scene literally crossed
out of the screenplay and never filmed

They walk out of the saloon.

CUT TO:

Rewrite. → *Also, when Billy*
returns point
333

EXT. - FORT SUMNER - EVENING

("Samarra"

Billy rides slowly through the gates of Fort Sumner.
He is unshaven. His shirt is ripped. He is weary,
to the point of collapse.

A man fixing a wagon wheel looks up and stares as
he rides past.

BILLY RIDES HIS HORSE to the water trough in the   334
middle of the parade ground. As the horse drinks,
Billy's head drops to his chest. He swings off the
horse and puts his head into the trough. Then he
steps back and shakes his head. He motions to a
young boy (MATTHEW) who has been watching him.

> BILLY (to Matthew)
> Go on in and git me a clean shirt,
> boy.

Matthew runs off. Billy takes off his shirt, wads it
up and throws it on the ground.

ENO WALKS UP and takes Billy's horse by the reins.   335

> ENO
> I was hopin' it was you as soon as
> I seen your dust.

Billy takes a clean shirt from the boy and puts it on.

> BILLY
> I ain't shut of this country.
> I guess I should of known.

Men and women come out of the buildings. They stand
silently, watching. Billy smiles and puts his arm
around Eno's shoulder.

> BILLY
> They been killin' my friends, Eno.
> It don't seem right to let 'em
> git away with it.

Peckinpah's handwritten note, "Samarra," in partial answer
to his own question, "where [is] Billy's return point"

reads: "Rewrite? Also, where is Billy's return point? (Samarra.)"[42] "Rewrite" refers to the whole cantina scene. The most revealing comment, however, is the fleeting, tentative one-word answer Peckinpah appended: "Samarra." This can have only one possible referent: John O'Hara's novel *Appointment in Samarra*, specifically the epigraph about a servant who one day in a Baghdad market encounters a woman whose visage frightens him. Believing the woman is Death, he borrows a horse from his master and flees to nearby Samarra. When the master confronts the woman, asking why she frightened his servant, she replies that she didn't mean to frighten him, her expression merely one of astonishment at seeing him in Baghdad because she has an appointment with him that night in Samarra. There is to me no more poignant an indication of how stressed, strung out, and stretched thin Peckinpah was throughout the project than this note. He kept trying to find a solution to a problem that he had helped create and all the while the answer was right there in front of him. The meaning of O'Hara's epigraph is the impossibility of escaping one's fate regardless of the actions one takes. The connection Peckinpah made here surely suggests a burgeoning awareness that the more Billy is motivated along conventional dramatic lines, the weaker both the character and the theme become. Wurlitzer had it right after all: thoroughly characterize Billy and then send him on an only apparently aimless journey that eventually takes him right back to where fate has determined all along he must wind up, and make it be a function of who and what he is.

Once Peckinpah decided to cut the story of Billy's decline, the next step logically should have been to develop a new characterization of the Kid that would serve the same purpose. Failing that, he might have thought about cutting the entire trip to Mexico, something, as we will see, he actually considered doing during the editing, because it no longer served its original purpose and in fact rather undermined it. Why didn't he? The most obvious answer is that Billy needed to be doing *something* while Garrett is pursuing him, and if Peckinpah wasn't going to write new scenes to replace those he had removed, then all he had left were the two scenes of Billy on his way to the border.

This, then, was the shape of the shooting script in particular and the project in general come the morning of Monday, November 13, 1972, when Peckinpah called "Action" for the first time on his last Western film. One of the two principal characters was a protagonist of extraordinary depth and complexity, one of the strongest in any of Peckinpah's films, and he was cast with a charismatic star who was also a fine actor. The other principal was as yet somewhat amorphous, inconsistent, weak in development and dramatic trajectory, and cast with a charismatic singer who had little acting experience. The contrast on every level could hardly have been more striking. Among the secondary characters, Maria was still being rewritten, while Alias was hardly written in the first place and never completed in the last; both were played by singers with little or no acting experience. The portions of the screenplay that were strong got for the most part much stronger: the whole first act, the great final night in Fort Sumner where the characters seem already to be moving like ghosts, almost all of Garrett's scenes throughout. But the ones that were weak or required more work never got the attention they needed, while the major plot and structural hitch of Billy's return was never fixed.

Even under the best of circumstances this would have been a challengingly difficult shoot. But it wasn't close to the best of circumstances and they would decline vertiginously before production wrapped almost three months later. The film was underscheduled and underbudgeted; equipment failures would necessitate reshoots; a horrible flu would ravage the company; and the studio would prove more meddlesome and hostile than even James Aubrey's terrible reputation promised, an unending stream of micromanagers dispatched to Mexico to watch over the unruly director, which succeeded mostly in just wasting his time and pissing him off even more than he already was, thus exacerbating an increasingly serious drinking problem. It was probably the most difficult shoot so far in his career, more so even than *Major Dundee*, with which it shared at least two identical issues: an unfinished script and a title character not fully worked out. As with the earlier film, the problems were not adequately addressed in the shooting, which meant they would be passed along to postproduction, where the director and his editors would have to grapple with them during the months to follow in the cutting rooms.

PART TWO

The Versions of
Pat Garrett and Billy the Kid

———◆———

To Roger Spottiswoode,
who played his string right out to the end

Peckinpah flanked by Roger Spottiswoode (*left*), his principal
editor, and John Coquillon (*right*), his cinematographer

CHAPTER SEVEN

The Previews

It began inconspicuously over thirty years ago:

> Three cut scenes—Garrett with his wife, Garrett and Chisum, and Billy courting Maria—and several minor excisions were restored to the version on television. . . . Unfortunately, the frame story is still missing, and so much else is either altered or missing . . . that the only way to see an approximation of Peckinpah's original is to try to watch the film on television and at a theater within the same short period of time, then edit the two together in the mind's eye.

Tucked away in a footnote in the first edition of my *Peckinpah: The Western Films* (202n), this seemed the most innocent of observations, hardly practical yet all the times allowed. The first of two preview versions of *Pat Garrett and Billy the Kid* would not become available for another eight years; meanwhile, so much violence and nudity were censored for television that in order to fill two hours of prime time it was necessary to put back some scenes that had been lifted in the preparation of the theatrical release. Counting the theatrical and the two previews, this became the *fourth* version of the film to be shown in public, and it marked the first opportunity afforded anyone outside of preview audiences to see two important scenes that serious filmgoers had only heard about. Of course, this version was otherwise so grotesquely expurgated that my little armchair editing exercise remained the only way to "construct," as it were, a version that brought us closer, if only in the theaters of our imaginations, to the film the director might have had in mind but was never able to persuade the studio to release.[1]

Little did I imagine that a quarter century and a different career later, long after I had left academia and become a film editor, I would be given the opportunity to make something very like that imaginary construction come true. If the germ of what became the special edition of *Pat Garrett* originated in that footnote, the idea of actually doing it came from Nick Redman, the producer of a short documentary I wrote and directed called *The Wild Bunch: An Album in Montage*. In 1996 I reviewed the extant versions of *Pat Garrett* and suggested that none of them can in any sense be considered final or definitive (*Reconsideration* 298–306). There are two preview versions, close but not identical, the first of which was released on laser disc in 1990 by Turner, which then owned the Metro-Goldwyn-Mayer library. Between them and the theatrical release, there is no ideal choice. The previews, too loose and unwieldy to be considered fine cuts or even to play optimally, were conceptually and practically never finished. They contain, however, several significant scenes that make for a richer film. For the theatrical release the studio demanded a shorter film, resulting in the removal of these scenes and overall a more tightly cut narrative that reduced character and stressed action. The theatrical is thus thematically somewhat diminished, eliminates at least two secondary but significant characters (Garrett's wife Ida and the cattle baron Chisum), and reduces the ironies substantially. However, and it is a big "however," as regards all the scenes it shares in common with the previews, which is most of them, it is better edited, shaped, and paced. In a word, it *plays* better. It was also finished in the technical sense of being properly color timed, dubbed, scored, and mixed.

My conclusion was that the previews compromise Peckinpah's artistry and style, the theatrical his vision, yet at the time it never occurred to me that it might be possible to put the missing scenes into the theatrical. But my argument, Nick told me, is what gave him the idea to pitch a special version to Warner Bros. which would do just that. This was in 2002 and the timing couldn't have been better, he said. Having acquired the MGM library from Turner some years earlier, Warner Home Video, thanks to the urging of Brian Jamieson, the division's vice-president in charge of special products worldwide and a great Peckinpah enthusiast, was at last planning a DVD box set of the four Peckinpah Westerns the studio now owned, the two for MGM (*Ride the High Country* and *Pat Garrett*) and the two for Warner (*The Wild Bunch* and *The Ballad of Cable Hogue*). Nick eventually became a de facto producer of the set. Would I agree to be the consulting editor on a new version of *Pat Garrett* that would—here he handed my own words back to me—at last join Peckinpah's vision to his artistry—for as little cash as possible, of course, which was to say none? (Not Nick's condition this last, but Warner's: I had already made the *Wild Bunch* documentary for free—once they know you'll work for love rather than money . . .)

I eagerly accepted, but had three conditions of my own. The first and most important was that whatever form this version eventually took, it would never, ever be used to supplant the Turner preview, only to supplement it. My reservations about the previews are several and substantial; that Peckinpah didn't finish them is a matter of fact beyond denial. Nevertheless, the one Turner released on laser disc remains the only version now in wide circulation which he personally worked on; for this reason alone it must be accorded respect and remain always available. The second condition was that I would not touch this version; it would be left exactly as Peckinpah left it. The third was that I would not in any sense recut or reedit the theatrical in whole or in part, except for the bare minimum necessary to fit the lifted material back into the places where it had been removed. (The one exception to this is the prologue, which I describe fully in chapter 9.)

Warner readily agreed to all three conditions, the job was done, and the set released, with two versions of *Pat Garrett and Billy the Kid*, to which the studio assigned subtitles: *2005 Special Edition* and *1988 Turner Preview Version*. (The year in the latter is somewhat misleading, referring not to that of the actual preview, which was on May 3, 1973, but to the year it was first resurrected for airing on Jerry Harvey's fabled Z Channel.) The reception of the set was gratifyingly enthusiastic from legitimate print and Internet reviewers, an enthusiasm that extended in more temperate but still quite real form to the "new" *Pat Garrett*. Most appeared to grasp the issues involved, including the unique circumstances that render a definitive version impossible; and they accepted it in the terms on which I agreed to do it: not as the version Peckinpah "would" or even "might" have done—something nobody can know—but as a way to take the only version that was ever properly finished and, in a sense, complete it the way his editors who prepared it would have completed it for him had they not been forced to do otherwise.

Far more meaningful to me personally was the response from many who know Peckinpah's work intimately or who had actually worked on the film. Garner Simmons, who first met Peckinpah three months after *Pat Garrett* opened in 1973 and whose early career biography, *Peckinpah: A Portrait in Montage*, will always remain indispensable, considers it the best version likely obtainable from the available materials, and thought it played better than any he had ever seen. Kris Kristofferson and Donnie Fritts told Nick it was the best version they had seen, and it is Kristofferson's preferred version. Owing to the painful memories it stirs up, Roger Spottiswoode, the chief editor, still finds it difficult to watch the film; but he did run my recut of the prologue and thought it an improvement upon its counterpart in the Turner preview. Three film critics I've long known and admired, Michael Sragow, Terrence Rafferty, and Steve Vineberg, all wrote to say how much they appreciated the special edition.

Naturally, there were dissenters: fans mostly, an academic or two, and several Internet commentators, who raised questions that ranged from the specific—why wasn't the wife scene restored to the Turner?—to the general— why wasn't a full-scale restoration done to the Turner, including a new print, correctly timed with a properly mixed soundtrack, instead of yet *another* ver-sion? Fair questions all, which I attempt to answer in the pages that follow.

"I would not say the picture was anything but a battleground from two to three weeks before we started shooting to thirteen weeks after we finished." The observation is the producer Gordon Carroll's and it is how he began the first of the interviews I conducted with him in 1977 for the chapter on *Pat Garrett* in my critical study. I reread that chapter (182–226), the expanded one in my second edition (254–306), and those in Simmons (168–88), David Weddle (445–91), and Marshall Fine (237–63): together these provide a thor-ough and mostly reliable history of the difficulties making the film. I next spoke with Spottiswoode, Garth Craven (the second editor), and Katy Haber (Peckinpah's personal assistant of many years), three persons I've known for years as friends (Roger a very close friend) and colleagues (both Roger and Garth), with whom I've often talked about Peckinpah and his work. I also conversed at length or in emails with Gordon Dawson, the second-unit direc-tor and assistant to the producer, and Don Hyde, for many years the archivist Sam entrusted with prints of his films.[2] I listened again to the interviews I conducted with Roger, Carroll, the editor Robert ("Bob") L. Wolfe, and the composer Jerry Fielding, interviews I hadn't listened to for decades. I reviewed all the *Pat Garrett* editing notes and memos in the Sam Peckinpah Papers at the Margaret Herrick Library. These number roughly two hundred pages, most of them typed by Katy; and from what I can tell, they are complete or nearly so and include those by Sam himself; Roger; Carroll; Dan Melnick, the vice-president in charge of production at MGM; and a few other executives, including James T. Aubrey, the studio head with whom Sam fought from start to finish. These notes constitute an extraordinarily detailed record of the edit-ing process.[3] I examined as well all the drafts of the screenplay in the Herrick. Finally, I ran every available version of the film: the second preview, stolen by Sam from the cutting rooms and donated by his family to the Academy after his death; the first preview (hereafter the 1988 Turner or simply the Turner); and the theatrical release. I did not look again at the television version, as it was created for the initial prime-time airing and thereafter effectively with-drawn (I've never seen it show up again anywhere, even in syndication).

I have long believed the two preview versions do not deserve the so-called definitive status they've been accorded in some circles, mostly by a few aca-demics and many Peckinpah buffs, who typically equate more with better, all the while keeping themselves ignorant of the factual history behind this troubled film. The two previews are works in progress, fairly well advanced, to be sure, but still very much *in progress* when Sam made the decision not to work on them further, even though it was evident to everyone, including Sam himself and his editors, that more work was needed and that both were miss-ing important scenes he wanted in the film. Further, the more the evidence is examined, the more difficult it is to escape the suspicion that Sam *wanted* his version to be left unfinished, at least at the time.

All the while the reputation of the previews was inflated, the theatrical was unfairly maligned. Too many reporters and reviewers, not to mention fans—again ignorant as to how and by whom the theatrical was really prepared—still resort to the knee-jerk "butchered" when referring to it. Not only is this untrue, it is quite opposite the truth. There *was* a severely truncated version: Aubrey had ordered a dupe of the work print and employed a team of studio editors to cut it down to a ninety-six-minute shoot-'em-up that he threatened to release unless Sam cooperated. Sam refused, and Garth sided with him. Meanwhile, Roger and Bob Wolfe realized they'd been handed a Hobson's choice—by both Aubrey *and* Sam. It was precisely to keep Aubrey's version from ever seeing the darkness of theaters that they agreed to prepare a theatrical cut that was shorter and tighter yet as faithful to Sam's vision as they could manage under the circumstances. Far from butchery, their work was so thoughtful, sympathetic, and sensitive we do well to remember that on the basis of the theatrical version *alone*—years upon years before Turner ever brought out the first preview on laser disc—*Pat Garrett and Billy the Kid* came to be regarded by many serious critics and filmgoers as one of Peckinpah's masterpieces.

"To achieve great things," Leonard Bernstein once said, "two things are needed: a plan, and not quite enough time." But what happens when not quite enough time becomes not enough time, period? No examination of the versions of *Pat Garrett and Billy the Kid* can begin without the clear understanding that every stage of its making was rushed. The prep was rushed, the rewriting was rushed, the casting was rushed, the shooting was rushed, the editing was rushed, the previews were rushed, and the release was rushed. Virtually from the moment it was green-lit, the project was sitting on a ticking time bomb. It has long been believed that after completion of principal photography, the studio, in the person of James Aubrey, made a decision to advance the release date several weeks to the Memorial Day weekend, thus depriving the director of valuable time he was counting on to edit the film as carefully as he did his previous ones. The truth is that MGM marketing executives had asked for a Memorial Day release quite soon after the film became a go project, several months before the start of production; both Carroll and Sam agreed to it; and the entire schedule was backed into from there.[4] Production was to wrap the end of the second week in January (Friday the twelfth), which would allow for sixteen weeks of editing before the first formal audience preview in the first week of May. In 1973 the long holiday weekend started on Friday, May 25, which meant the film had to be in theaters two days earlier on the Wednesday.

As points of reference, in those days a twenty-week post was considered tight (it still is), thirty doable, and forty comfortable, with many films taking longer. Then as now, the editor was usually given a week or so following completion of shooting to get his or her cut together, then the director and the editor had ten weeks to get the "director's cut" into a playable form fit to show the studio. After that, depending on everything from how well it appeared to be playing to the director's clout and relationship with the producers and the executives, there was a week or so of additional editing, involving tightening and incorporating notes from the producers and the executives prior to audience previews, of which there were usually two. Then more notes, more changes, occasionally a third preview, until a final cut was agreed upon. After that, several weeks were spent finishing the film, which included sound editing, looping, foley,[5] color timing, negative cutting, and release printing. During this process, many directors continue to fine-cut.

Sixteen weeks was thus risky in the extreme, especially with a director who shot as much footage as Peckinpah customarily did and explored the myriad alternatives as exhaustively in the cutting room. Carroll and Sam both knew this, and Sam certainly knew better but consented because he didn't want to jeopardize a "go" project and could always fight the post battle later *after* he had the film in the can. Under the circumstances most directors would do the same. As for Carroll, though in common with most producers he had little experience of cutting rooms, he was nevertheless experienced enough to be aware of how dangerously short the post schedule really was; yet he was willing to take the chance because he believed the release date gave the picture an advantage. (It didn't, but his reasoning was based on industry wisdom common in those days: big-studio action Western with recognizable stars guaranteed solid or better summer box office.) He felt confident because the editors would be Bob Wolfe and Roger Spottiswoode, who had worked so well together on *Straw Dogs* and were currently completing *The Getaway*, itself on a tight schedule.

On October 2 Gordon Dawson dropped a bombshell. He had just gotten off the phone with Bob, who told him that he and Sam had decided they needed to take a break from each other: he would not be cutting *Pat Garrett*. The explanation made little sense to either Gordon, but it alarmed Carroll, who immediately wanted to know who was going to replace him.[6] Sam's answer, delivered through Dawson—for some reason, on that morning Sam and Carroll were communicating via Dawson rather than directly—alarmed him even more: Garth Craven. But Garth, who had worked on *Straw Dogs* and *The Getaway*, was a *sound* editor. He'd been wanting to edit picture for a good while now, and he would soon demonstrate an extraordinary talent for it. But even highly talented people are beginners at some point in their endeavors, and Garth had never edited a film before. Carroll couldn't believe Sam was promoting a tyro on a schedule like this. But Sam remained adamant, refusing even to discuss a more experienced replacement. Dawson explained to Carroll that Sam said he was going to shoot this one differently from his previous films, simpler, with much less coverage, and a lot more "cutting in the camera." But if Carroll had been able to listen in on the call between Sam and Dawson, he might have noticed that Sam never actually *said* that. What

Sam did was listen to Dawson repeat what Dawson reported saying to Carroll about limited coverage and camera cutting and simply allow Dawson to assume by his silence that he was assenting: "I got no worries about making our dates" is where he left it, and suggested Dawson have Carroll phone him directly if he was still worried. (When I related the substance of these calls to Roger, he said, "Sam never cut *anything* in the camera. He believed in the editing room and shot for it.")

Dawson, who is the first to admit he knew fairly little about postproduction, assumed Sam was telling him the truth; and Carroll had no reason to believe otherwise. But Sam had no intention of shooting this or any other film with minimal coverage and camera cutting—not because he couldn't but because that just isn't the way he made films. Editing is often called "the final rewrite" or the "final directing." For most directors this is at least quasi-figurative, but for Sam it was quite literal: "The dailies are just the beginning," he said.[7] The cutting rooms were where he found his films, where he shaped the performances, where he built those complex structures of shots and images. That kind of thing can't be "cut" in the camera or realized with minimal coverage. It's not that his films needed to be "saved" in the editing—far from it—rather that editing was an integral stage of a process of development and exploration that began with the script and ended on the final mixing stage. According to his close friend Jim Silke, Sam likened the process to several cycles of creation and destruction and creation again. Those who thought it would be different on *Pat Garrett and Billy the Kid* had not studied the filmmaker at hand or were simply allowing themselves to be deluded. And, of course, it wasn't different.[8]

Changes in the editing crew weren't Carroll's only headache. Casting was proving more difficult than expected because sometime in the early fall the studio told Carroll to widen the search and go after bigger names, including for supporting roles. For examples, Barry Sullivan wound up playing the one-scene part of Chisum, but not before Sam held out as long as he could for Robert Ryan; David Warner, Charlton Heston, and Sullivan again were considered for Wallace, which eventually went to Jason Robards (who bore a remarkable resemblance to the real Wallace). All this was fine except that bigger names meant the deals became exponentially more complicated, time-consuming, difficult to schedule, and expensive. Despite the apparent wealth of candidates, casting the two leads proved deceptively difficult. Though Sam still stood by Coburn as Garrett, Coburn's commitments to his then-current project, *The Last of Sheila*, made it impossible for him to be in Durango for the original start date of October 23. So that was pushed a week, then a week again, and finally another week to Monday, November 13. As all these delays were piling up, Sam and Carroll, without exactly putting Coburn on a back burner, were forced to consider others, including Rod Steiger, and, of all people, Marlon Brando, who had read a very early version of the script when Monte Hellman was still involved, was not interested, then suddenly reversed himself once Peckinpah was attached.[9] Despite some still-festering rancor over *One-Eyed Jacks*, Sam too was prepared to go with Brando, but he was even more interested in Steiger. It's tempting to think this must have been from desperation, since both actors were physically wrong and Steiger psychologically. But Sam's enthusiasm was genuine, his admiration high, higher for Steiger even than for Brando (he knew "all the stories" of Steiger's alleged difficulties but had gotten drunk with him—always a rite of passage with Sam—and he loved the actor's work). Deals could not be made with either. For a short time Jack Palance was under consideration (as he was also for Poe). All the while this was going on, Herbert Ross, the director of *The Last of Sheila*, was doing his best to adjust his schedule to accommodate a fellow director, but the earliest he could make Coburn available was midweek or later the first week in November.[10] Eventually Sam and Carroll accepted the inevitable, signed Coburn, and pushed the schedule.

Things were scarcely better on the Billy front. Early on Jon Voight was still committed to Billy even though Hellman was no longer involved, and Gene Hackman was eager to play Garrett; but by the time Aubrey, initially ambivalent about both, gave his grudging approval, they had moved on.[11] Though Sam, Wurlitzer, and Carroll still had high hopes for Malcolm McDowell, when it began to look as if he might not happen due to prior commitments,[12] Carroll courted Al Pacino with "a solid offer of $35,000." Though Sam loved him in *The Godfather*, he personally would have preferred Dustin Hoffman. When Pacino proved unavailable and Hoffman too expensive for the studio, someone (perhaps Patricia Mock, the casting director) proposed Kristofferson. Sam screened *Cisco Pike*, released earlier in the year, Kristofferson's first starring role, in which he played a rock musician who is also a drug dealer. In terms of the association Carroll drew between rock stars and outlaws of the Old West, Kristofferson seemed tailor-made for the Kid and Sam was quite taken with his screen presence and later with the man himself. "I think we found our Billy," he told Carroll. The trouble was, like Coburn, Kristofferson was also finishing a film (*Blume in Love*), and this prevented him starting before Thanksgiving, which meant that scenes without him had to be scheduled for the first couple of weeks. This was yet another reason production was delayed to November 13—if Kristofferson were suddenly further delayed, Sam and Carroll did not want to find themselves two or three weeks into production and still without one of the two leads. (As things turned out, according to the call sheets, Kristofferson didn't start until December 5.) Meanwhile, as a result of the search for bigger names, as late as November 6, just seven days before shooting would start, no deals had yet been made for the roles of Poe, Chisum, Wallace, Holly, Sheriff and Mrs. Baker, Mr. and Mrs. Horrell, Lemuel, Folliard, Bowdre, Beaver, Alias, and Maria, and some of these wouldn't be filled until well after production started. Carroll consoled himself that bigger names were worth it, even as he knew that every delay would come out of an already far too short post schedule.

Throughout these several weeks, Sam's mood fluctuated between almost hubristic self-confidence ("I'll start tomorrow. I'm ready. I got this fucking script in my pocket"[13]) and crazy-making anxiety, worrying that he couldn't complete the rewriting until he knew who the actors were: "We're getting heavy names now, really heavy names, the whole conception now has been changed." His worry had cause given how carefully in past films he wove actors' reputations—their personalities, the images they projected of themselves in the media, the kinds of characters they were known for playing—into the conceptions of the characters they played. As someone who started in the-ater, he had a far deeper understanding than most film directors of how to work with actors to get the best out of them. "I don't direct, I indirect," he said. "I like to see an actor ease into a part, pick up what he's got that's good, then kind of lead him, shape him, you know, slide him into something else, rather than give him line readings, so that all of a sudden *he's* doing it. It's from the inside." But this is a process that takes time. "The only way I've found out as a director to keep from losing them," he warned, is "to listen to what they have to say. These are not people I can tell what to do. . . . They'll do it, but then I've lost my rapport, then I lose at least twenty percent of performance level. If we don't get some of these preliminary things done before we start shooting, then, as you know, it happens on the set."[14] He had particular con-cerns about Kristofferson's relative inexperience ("I should be working with him every night"), and he knew that Coburn liked to probe motivation and discuss it at length. Sam also wanted rehearsal time, "at least a day with Jim and Kris to get together and the other members of the cast to get to know each other so that we're not just running blind." He also complained, again legitimately, that as things were shaping up, he would have no time to walk the many locations with John Coquillon, his cinematographer, so they could get the literal lay of the land, how the light fell, where the sun was throughout the day, how scenes might be blocked, lighted, and filmed.

As with their arguments over casting, the studio executives were likewise talking out of both sides of their mouths when it came to the schedule. They demanded more scenes with more action all the while insisting that Peckin-pah and Carroll pull days out of the schedule. Peckinpah wanted sixty-two, the studio fifty-eight with a fallback to fifty-six. But the trouble is, as those who were actually in charge of working out the schedule—Dawson, Frank Beetson (the unit production manager), and Newt Arnold (the first assistant director)—were trying to tell them, dropping, say, three days wouldn't reduce the budget even by sixty thousand, because that's not where the money was going: it was going into the more prestigious cast. In the end, the extra week's delay for Coburn allowed Carroll to find a few days for Sam to walk the sets. But that was just about the last break he or anyone else caught.

In *Peckinpah* (196) I wrote that the film went "only twenty days over sched-ule and $1.5 million over budget." I now know these figures to be misleading. According to the tapes of preproduction phone calls, conferences, and other meetings, depending on who was doing the talking and which week or even day you happen to listen in on, enough numbers were bandied about that it's impossible to determine exactly how long anybody thought the schedule was supposed to be. When I rechecked my interviews with Carroll, I was reminded there was never an agreed-upon schedule, which he told me was not unusual at the time, indeed, was rather the norm. This in turn means there was no finalized budget either. The studio wanted the picture made for three million dollars in fifty-eight days based more or less on the script as it existed *before* Sam began adding to it—in other words, a script that did not include the prologue or the additional action scenes, all of which were requested of him and approved.[15] Sam insisted he needed sixty-two days, off which he could probably shave two. When the studio people heard that, they immediately took two days out of their fifty-eight, still not acknowledging their figure was based on an out-of-date script. He begged for a meeting at which a set schedule would be determined. Finally he got one, late in October, at which he and Carroll from the production and Melnick and Lewis Rachmil (among others) from the studio were present. Sam here capitulated to fifty-eight days with a grumbling nod to make best efforts to lose another two during shooting. "It's a compromise, but it's a decent compromise," Carroll later told Dawson (tape D-1, 11/3/72). "Sam is balking now and wants to go back to fifty-eight, but he's doing it sensibly and practically." It was also at this meeting that Sam and Carroll were informed it was no longer studio policy to build into budgets the standard 5 percent overage for inclement weather, of which there would be much on this shoot.

The weather was far from the worst of it. To begin with, there was the cracked mounting-flange on a Panavision lens, which resulted in well over a week's worth of out-of-focus footage (see Simmons 175, D. Weddle 468–69, and *Reconsideration* 257–58). The story goes that Aubrey forbade reshooting any of it. This is not true, but he was so parsimonious about what he did allow that Sam and his crew reshot the rest of what he felt was needed on the sly. Quite a number of master shots, for example, were not in focus, including some of those in the Wallace, Ruthie Lee, Ida, and raft scenes; Aubrey's answer was to cut around them—by this he did not mean use coverage to bridge one master take to another, but simply not to use masters at all for the scenes in question! (In fact, the shot of Olinger drawing his gun after Bell crashes through the window is obviously out of focus, but it goes by so quickly the softness hardly registers.) Despite Sam's long experience shooting in Mexico, MGM denied his request for a Panavision repairman on location, a decision he said was responsible for about ten to twelve days' unusable footage—probably an exaggeration, but not by all that much. The influenza epidemic that hit Durango that December devastated the crew: almost everyone contracted it, including Sam himself, who was bedridden for three days with a temperature of 104°, forcing production to shut down. Carroll told me that only he and the editors were spared (according to Simmons [174], "Thousands of people would die of the disease that winter in Durango," among them Bud Hulburd, the special-effects coordinator responsible for the bridge explosion in *The Wild Bunch*).

Some have blamed Sam's drinking for his weakened condition, but Carroll denied this, pointing out that the director was troubled by respiratory ailments his whole life, which were exacerbated by the fine silicon dust always blowing through the air in Durango. Be that as it may, one would have to be naive or cynical to believe that some of Sam's ailments weren't due to the excessive drinking. Beginning in early December he was sick on and off throughout the remainder of production. A handwritten note Carroll appended to the end of his daily producer's log for December 5 (day twenty of the shooting schedule) reads: "The director manifested definite symptoms of illness during the day, i.e., vomiting, diarrhea, and general malaise, to which I was witness in part, which caused a slowed tempo of work, costing the company, in my opinion, one-fourth of a day overall" (SPP, 63-f.786). The next two days' entries bring similar notes and report equal or longer delays, and several more would follow. The tape from the three days of the 104° temperature ("Sam in bed sick," 2/1/73) clearly reveals a man so debilitated by congestion and fever he doesn't sound as if he can breathe, let alone speak. Yet as he goes over with Carroll, Dawson, and Arnold what remains to be shot and what he can delegate to Dawson and Arnold, he is sharp and focused, with an attention to detail little short of astonishing under the circumstances. When he refers to specific shots and the number of setups, over thirty, that will be required for the remaining scenes, it sounds as if it's all from his head, not a written-down list (Dawson told me that Sam never, ever made shot lists). Ironically, perhaps one possible reason he functioned so well here despite his feverish condition is that during those three days he was almost certainly too sick to drink—whatever else, he doesn't sound inebriated on the tape.

So let's recompute those overages. Production lasted seventy-two days. Give the studio the benefit of the doubt and assume a fifty-eight-day schedule reasonable, the overage is now fourteen days, not twenty. Taking out three for the shutdown owing to Sam's fever brings us to eleven, subtract eight for making up the soft-focus footage (though keep in mind, Sam said twelve) and we're now at three days—and this without even factoring in those lost due to weather, not to mention the reduced efficiency of a production crew plagued by flu. As for the $1.5 million (actually a little over $1.6), a roughly 20 percent extension of the shooting schedule accounts for a more or less equivalent share of that, and insurance reimbursed much of the portion due to weather, equipment failure, and Sam's illness. In sum, while even without the flu there is no doubt that Sam was not performing consistently to maximum strength or efficiency, the overages in and of themselves were rather routine and even predictable under the circumstances. Moreover, it was precisely because of his ability when necessary to shoot fast, economically, and well that the film didn't go even more over budget and schedule. And as I

ROGER SPOTTISWOODE
DAN MELNICK
March 1st 1973

Post Production Schedule.

Dear Dan:

The following points seem relevant to the post production schedule sent to us by
Jack Dunning.

1. The First Assembly is shown as being complete one week after the completion of
shooting. (13th Feb). The dailies for the final sequence only arrived on that
day. Therefore it was impossible to complete the cut at that point.

2. The Director's Cut. We will be ready to show Sam's first cut on the date
which we agreed upon

3. Completion of looping for the preview. This is scheduled for the 20th March.
At that time we will still be shipping trims, cut and other material from Mexico
to Los Angeles. We assume that you have prepared for all the actors to be
ready for looping if necessary at that time and the week after. There is still,
however, considerable work to be done in preparation for the looping session.
To allow six days from the screening to prepare dupes, mark them up, schedule
actors, record and fit is totally inadequate.

4. We do not know what a temporary dub is. If it existed, we do not know how
it could be made in three days, nor where the music would come from. We repeat
nor where the music would come from. I understand Mr. Peckinpah has been discussing
this problem with you for some two weeks. We still have no firm answer. The
previews must be scheduled at a much later date to accomodate music and dubbing.

5. Your schedule seems to indicate previewing with a work print. This is very
possible given that you are prepared to re-print approximately 1/3rd of the cut film,
which is in the region of 70,000 feet.

6. The Score. One month has been allowed for the score to be written and
recorded. This is of course totally impossible, particularly in the light of the
fact that you expect us to integrate the material that has already been written.

7. The final dubbing period allowed is 7 days. Naturally you must be assuming
that we will dub 24 hours a day, which we will do if need be. However this is
still far too little time to do the film justice.

8. You have allowed three days between the first trial print and release print.
This is so ludicrous it needs no comment.

9. Finally the schedule is totally unrealistic and impossible in all areas.

                    Kindest regards,

                    ROGER SPOTTISWOODE

                              cc. K. Kerkorian
                                  J. Aubrey
                                  D. Netter
                                  S. Peckinpah

Memo from Roger Spottiswoode to Dan Melnick explaining
the impossibility of the postproduction schedule

pointed out in *Reconsideration* (259), if Sam hadn't had the courage to defy orders and reshoot more than the studio was willing to allow but which he absolutely needed to edit the film at all adequately, then it would have to have been picked up in postproduction, when the costs to reconvene the actors and crew and go back to Mexico would have been astronomical.

After all the setbacks owing to inclement weather, faulty equipment, damaged footage, necessary reshoots (approved and stealth), and illness, the production didn't wrap until February 7. And that is how a ludicrous sixteen weeks of post was reduced to an insane thirteen. The schedule in detail was even worse. The full first cut was to be finished by February 13, a week after completion of principal photography, yet the last few days' dailies from Los Angeles did not arrive back in the Durango cutting rooms until the twentieth. "The postproduction schedule was a 'Fuck you' to Sam," Roger told me. "No director in the world could make those dates. They were arrived at from low-budget TV programming, which is what Aubrey knew, to the extent that he knew anything."

On the basis of every available testimony, Aubrey's personality was such that he hardly needed any provocation for screwing artists. But Sam wasn't taking any chances: production had scarcely wrapped when he fired a shot across the bow that set the terms of their relationship for the rest of post-production. Once back in Los Angeles he staged a scene depicting himself on a hospital gurney looking as if he's being administered Johnny Walker intravenously (though he's holding the catheter assembly between his teeth), his middle finger raised to the camera, the gurney surrounded by several members of the cast and crew. This was photographed, printed on MGM memorandum stationery, and signed by Coburn, Kristofferson, Dylan, Harry Dean Stanton, and John Beck. Directed to "the boys at the Thalberg Building," the memo read, "Sirs: With reference to the rumors that seem to be spreading around Hollywood, that on numerous occasions Sam Peckinpah has been carried off the set taken with drink, this is to inform you that those rumors are totally unfounded. However, there have been mornings......................" According to Katy Haber, Sam did this as retaliation for a remark about his drinking by Melnick that was quoted in the *Hollywood Reporter* a week or so earlier. But instead of keeping the mock memo at the level of a prank for the amusement of a few knowing insiders, Sam ran it as a full page in the *Reporter*, where it was seen by all who opened their issues on the morning of Tuesday, February 13 (as it happened, the date the first cut was supposed to be delivered).

Legitimately angry and disgusted as Sam had every right to be by the way the studio treated him during production, it's still hard to imagine he could have been so tone-deaf as to pull a stunt like this, let alone think that anyone outside his inner circle would find it amusing. Though it had the immediate, predictable effect of infuriating Aubrey, Rachmil, and the other executives (except perhaps Melnick, who probably just rolled his eyes), there was more pernicious long-term fallout, namely, to give pause to a great many industry people who were or would like to have been supportive of the director. As hated as Aubrey was, what Sam did here left many wondering if the studio head didn't have some justification, not least because the director's drinking wasn't exactly a secret around town. Yet no matter how irascible, ornery, and impossible he sometimes acted, Sam was still greatly admired and even loved, because in the Hollywood of those days—the glory years of the seventies— people were ready to get behind a true maverick artist fighting for his vision. They would tolerate a certain amount of self-destructive behavior and even substance abuse when the result was achievements like *The Wild Bunch*, *Straw Dogs*, and *The Getaway* (which right at the moment was making a lot of money). But they tended to draw a line when such behavior was flaunted, when it was *literally* advertised, as Sam did here, then thrown in their faces. That just made things worse for everyone else trying to do good work who had to deal with the moneymen.

There are three separate but related facts that undermine the legitimacy of the two preview versions of *Pat Garrett and Billy the Kid* as wholly adequate representations of his final thoughts. The first is the drastically shortened postproduction schedule. The second is Sam's alcoholism, by an order of magnitude worse on this project than on any previous one (perhaps any in his career). By every available reckoning and source, including his closest friends and longtime colleagues, Sam wasn't just drinking every day but was drunk a portion of many days. This started in preproduction and continued unabated beyond completion of principal photography straight through the second preview on May 10, after which he stopped working on the film. The third is the very real likelihood that he never ever watched the film from start to finish in a single sitting during which he stayed awake and/or sober—not even once. Roger can't remember any. When I asked Garth, reminding him that years ago he had told me he seemed to recall at least one screening where Sam came sober and stayed awake, he replied, "I think you may have misunderstood me. I won't say Sam never arrived at a screening without drink in hand, but I will say he never came to one stone cold sober. But then he never did anything in those days stone cold sober." The implications of this cannot be minimized for the eventual editorial fate of the film. Sam had a respect rare among film directors for audiences; from his roots in live theater, he knew how important watching his films with audiences was for gauging how they were playing. By his own admission, the previews were critical to the final fine-tuning of *The Wild Bunch* (see *Reconsideration* 138–39). Skipping one of the *Pat Garrett* previews and spending the other in his office elsewhere on the studio lot left him in the most compromised position imaginable when it came to defending the length of the cut he wanted released.

This should not be misunderstood: nobody alleges Sam never saw the entire film. Typically directors and editors don't take many notes during screenings because they're *watching* the film, trying to experience it as the audience does and to get a feel for how it's playing. The next day it's run on a flatbed and detailed notes are taken. Like most good directors, Sam let his editors implement the notes and changes without him—he didn't hover, preferring to see what they came up with on their own. So, yes, of course he saw the whole film, but only reel by reel, not necessarily in sequence, in the notes sessions, stopping to discuss this or that, interrupting to accept phone calls, taking breaks for lunch, or stretching his legs. And there are pages after pages of notes to indicate that when he watched he did so very carefully with remarkable attention to detail. But none of this was a substitute for uninterrupted screenings on a big screen with proper reel changes. Moreover, given the schedule, even if Sam had been inclined to hover, it would have been impossible, because Roger, Garth, and Bob and their assistants were working simultaneously.[16] Under the circumstances, he didn't have hours in the day to review all the changes.

Sam's refusal to attend the studio screenings was particularly puzzling because he was more aware than anyone else of the unfinished state of the script once shooting started. As I've shown in the previous two chapters, Wurlitzer's original screenplay, contrary to its reputation, was in fact quite small-scale, focused, logically structured, and far from sprawling. By the time Sam finished with his revisions, he had reconceived the Garrett character and given the overall action a stronger dramatic trajectory; but he had also weakened the Billy character and he never solved the nagging issue of the aborted flight to Mexico. Meanwhile, the screenplay became more episodic with the changes he made or demanded before and during production. In and of themselves, some, perhaps most of these problems were not necessarily insurmountable; many screenplays are episodic, including *Junior Bonner*, one of his most beautiful and beautifully structured films, which he had just finished before he embarked upon *The Getaway*. But what it does mean is that it's going to take more time in the editing room to find the right combination of lyricism and flow, of vertical and horizontal motion, of figuring out how long to let a big scene play and when to move it along. Often a scene will play beautifully at full length by itself only to drag when seen as part of the whole film. Is the problem the scene or its place in the structure; does it need to be tightened, moved, or eliminated? You get only so far with short-range work, that is, trimming the scene and cutting lines and bits, then running it again by itself or in the context of a few scenes, or else moving it and watching it in the context of a few scenes before and after the new location. Eventually, the only way to tell if you're on the right track is to watch the entire film or at least a substantial portion of it, preferably in a theater or screening room with uninterrupted reel changes.

It goes without saying that if you're drunk, your judgment is unlikely to be at its sharpest. Sometimes Sam couldn't remember what he had seen at the editorial screenings.[17] He was usually alert and quite focused at many of the notes sessions, though even at these he sometimes arrived or got drunk. By this point in his life, his alcoholism was so severe that many mornings he needed a drink just to steady himself—quite literally to stop himself from shaking—and it exacted a worrisome toll. Added to this was his sheer physical exhaustion from the arduous shoot and how sick he was toward the end—it would be several more months before he fully regained his strength, long after the post on *Pat Garrett* wrapped.

Then there were the performances. Coburn did some of his finest work in a distinguished career: disciplined, concentrated, inward. But Kristofferson as Billy was just beginning his acting career: hard work, charisma, and sheer conviction, not to mention Sam's direction and, so Garner Simmons informs me, a lot of close work with Coburn, managed a remarkably effective performance; but it still needed a lot of shaping and massaging from the editors. Bob Dylan as Alias proved a surprisingly adept physical performer, but every time he opened his mouth he seemed incapable of uttering a single believable word.[18] And a few other parts had non- or inexperienced actors in them (an old high-school chum of Sam's, Wurlitzer himself as Folliard), not to mention Rita Coolidge and members of Kristofferson's band. But Sam also managed to gather one of the most stellar casts of supporting players in postwar Hollywood cinema, including Jason Robards, Katy Jurado, Slim Pickens, R. G. Armstrong, Chill Wills, Barry Sullivan, Jack Elam, L. Q. Jones, Elisha Cook Jr., Dub Taylor, Richard Jaeckel, Emilio Fernández, Harry Dean Stanton, Richard Bright, Charlie Martin Smith, Gene Evans, John Beck, Matt Clark, Aurora Clavell, and John Davis Chandler. Against these seasoned pros the shortcomings of the inexperienced actors and the amateurs were thrown all the more glaringly into relief.

These varied problems and more came to the fore in the editing of *Pat Garrett*. Not surprisingly, they were concentrated largely in those scenes over which later disputes with the studio arose: the wife scene, the Chisum scene, Paco's death, and Tuckerman's Hotel, as well as the prologue, the opening in Fort Sumner, and the raft scene. But long before the studio got involved, several of these were giving Sam and his editors trouble. The notes indicate they were altered again and again, lines and bits taken out, then put back in, then out once more; or moved here, there, and someplace else. Tuckerman's Hotel—the flophouse where Poe learns the Kid's whereabouts—proved especially intractable.

Another "nightmare"—Garth's word—was Paco's death and the rape/assault upon his daughter Yolanda by three of Chisum's men.[19] Both Sam and his Paco, Emilio Fernández, started the shoot drunk and got drunker as it went along, Sam calling for more and more blood to be smeared on Fernández's lashed body long after it seemed to the crew there was far too much. Sam's instruction upon seeing the edited scene? Print the footage down because the blood looked "bad" (2/19/73, 2). But that was the least of its problems. Once Sam crossed out the second half, which showed that Billy has buried

Paco and the two dead Chisum hands and has seen to Yolanda's welfare, he was left with a scene in which Billy just mounts up and departs, leaving her to deal with a dead husband, a traumatized infant, and three dead cowboys in the middle of nowhere. Sam's hasty patch-job of having Alias appear out of nowhere so Billy can leave the woman with him made so little sense—where did Alias come from, has he been following Billy since Fort Sumner, if so, why in secret at a distance?—that it never survived as far as the first preview, which in turn left what remained as nonsensical as before.[20]

The presence of a fix like this at all is indicative of how chaotic the project sometimes was. As previously noted, it was written in the first place to answer concerns that Billy's decision to return to Fort Sumner wasn't adequately motivated. But this strikes me as a nonexistent issue, and Sam's reference to "Samarra" in the margin of a copy of the screenplay suggests he had a burgeoning sense of the same. In the Arthur Penn version of Gore Vidal's *The Left-Handed Gun* (1958), the Billy character is "motivated" to death with practically every cliché of Freudian psychology popular in the fifties (Vidal called it "a film that only someone French could like"). What Wurlitzer and Peckinpah brought to their retelling of this legend was a sense of implacable doom, an almost Dreiserian determinism that undermines free will and renders motivation as it is commonly understood virtually irrelevant. This Billy needs no "motivation" to return; he comes back because he's already in the process of becoming Billy the Kid, because given who and what he is, he's drawn helplessly to his destiny. Conventional motivation does nothing but weaken this theme. Roger actually came up with the best solution here: in the open desert Billy rides up to the camera as it cranes down to meet him; he pauses, looks ahead, then back, then ahead again. He takes as many beats as the moment seems to need, then turns his horse and rides back in the direction he came from—back into history and eventual legend. This was never shot, but an editorial note by Melnick suggests there was talk of trying to construct it out of unused ride-bys.[21]

These evidently yielded nothing, so, beset by suggestions of some friends who saw early cuts, Sam decided to make it unambiguously clear that Billy is returning out of anger over Paco's death, which he accomplished by cheating in a loop line—in other words, a classic fix-it-in-the-mix solution. When Paco expires, Kristofferson looks down, plunges a knife into the ground, and says, "That ties it . . . I'm going back." The first three words were added while he's looking down and we can't see his mouth, the next three after he rises out of frame, where again we can't see his mouth. But by making Billy so decisive here, the long-range implications obviously made things worse when he returns and basically does nothing. It is little wonder that Sam considered dumping Paco's death entirely (which is what happened in the television version anyhow, owing to Yolanda's nudity).

In addition to problem scenes and performances, there were the usual swings and roundabouts routine in the editing of any long and complex film.

```
                    HORRELLS JONES FORMAT
Billy rides towards Horrells
Pat and Poe ride into Jones
Poe and Pat dismount
Billy dismounts
Walk Billy up to door, Pat and Poe enter.
Billy enters, Pat and Poe walk around bar.
Mrs. Horrell says hello, Chill says hello.
Pat takes glasses and whiskey Billy sits down at table.
Pat and Poe sit down at table.
Billy serves himself Pat and Poe remove hats and drinks.
Alamosa badge dialogue, Pat says he will stay the night.
Norepie dialogue, Poe gets up to leave.

ETC ETC ETC ETC ETC follow through sequence right through cutting
out Hollyw's dialogue "Thought you heard about Alomosa" and having
two deaths at same time
```

Peckinpah's detailed instructions for intercutting
Horrell's Trading Post with Jones's Saloon

One in particular baffled everyone. Two of the strongest scenes played back-to-back: Jones's Saloon, where Garrett kills Holly, and Horrell's Trading Post, where Billy kills Alamosa Bill. From first cut these scenes played so well that, apart from a bit of trimming, all felt they needed no further work for the time being. All except Sam, who got it into his head that they should be intercut, and by intercut he meant line by line and bit by bit, a thankless duty that fell to Garth, for whom it was the most bizarre of the wild geese the editors had to chase.[22] The more obvious it became to him and Roger that this scheme was ruining two splendid scenes without any compensating benefits, the more Sam clung to it. It was jettisoned only after he had managed to sneak a few people, including Pauline Kael, Jay Cocks (film critic for *Time*), and Martin Scorsese, into a screening room on the lot where they were shown a cut of the film—in whatever form the editors had it at the time—and some of them complained that the crosscutting was confusing.

Nor is this the only strange crosscutting Sam experimented with. According to the notes, he also experimented with intercutting Paco's death with the prostitutes' montage, apparently cutting to it right off the bit of Garrett flicking the one girl's nipple, which Melnick thought "cheats Paco's death"; and Sam evidently shot the raft sequence so that it could be edited to look as if Billy is watching the whole thing, which Melnick pronounced "totally illogical."

Roger and Garth managed to have a "very long" director's cut ready to show the MGM executives at the scheduled screening on March 13. The cut was undeniably rough but under the circumstances impressive enough to suggest the measure of the film. Astoundingly, Sam never showed up. Quite apart from being irresponsible, this was an appalling thing to do to his editors, leaving them to deal with an apoplectic Aubrey, who, according to Roger, played to the hilt his reputation as an abusive bully, complaining, criticizing, mouthing obscenities throughout the whole screening. Yet to everyone's astonishment, the notes he handed down a day or two later were reasoned, favorable, and even enthusiastic. "Hell of a first cut," he wrote, "proud and happy . . . what you are reaching for is really unusual and provocative." Others present were if anything even more enthusiastic ("a wonderful film," "this picture is tremendous"). The scenes and areas that gave them trouble were those that had already been giving Sam and his editors trouble, and there was general agreement that the film was too long and unevenly paced.

The most intelligent and penetrating notes came from Melnick, who had in fact seen a similar cut about a week earlier in Mexico City. Now Sam always had his problems with studio executives and producers, and he and Melnick certainly had their disputes on this project, but Melnick was nevertheless one producer whose creative instincts Sam always respected. Like everyone else, Melnick felt the prologue as constructed did not work. He was adamant that crosscutting Jones and Horrell was mutually detrimental to both scenes. He disliked Tuckerman's and suggested it be removed. He felt the same about both the Chisum and wife scenes (though his main problem with the latter seemed to be Aurora Clavell's performance, which he felt needed to be addressed with looping, perhaps because he feared her thick accent made her difficult to understand; Sam appeared to agree). After having fought Aubrey to let Sam shoot the raft sequence, he now felt it didn't quite work but was still prepared to argue for it. Sam by no means agreed with all of Melnick's suggestions, some of his proposed solutions in particular, but he knew that several of them had merit. Sam eventually simplified the Jones/Horrell cutting scheme to its final version, where Horrell's is placed logically in the time cut between the shorter first half and longer second half of the saloon. The intercutting of Paco's death was eliminated. The Chisum and wife scenes would get more attention (including looping Clavell). Sam told Melnick he had some ideas to fix the prologue, and he knew that many other matters had to be addressed as well, notably the trimming of several scenes and still further experimentation with moving scenes around (the raft episode, for one).

And then there was the matter of the obstreperous Tuckerman's Hotel, the only scene in which neither Garrett nor Billy figures. In Wurlitzer's *Billy the Kid* original, this scene worked in a way it doesn't in the film. For one thing, it helped that he wrote *two* scenes of Poe on his own—the other in Fort Sumner, where the deputy questions some of the Kid's gang. In other words, Poe on his own was given a *sequence*, so going to him while losing both Garrett and Billy for a while was less jarring when it occurred twice, as it functioned as pattern rather than as anomaly. The context was also different: Billy has

```
                    EXECUTIVE RUNNING    Tuesday March 13th

Melnick Strucutrally works.

Aubrey  Hell of a first cut. I appreciate seeing all the film.  Some parts are
        slow and some we can do without.  Basically the construction id
        good, with the problem of two people following two stories.  I found
        the opening wonderful but did not understand the freezes.  Everything
        moved alongwell for me until I got bogged down with the intercutting
        óf Horrells and Jones.  Then I felt it deteriorated constructionwise
        around the turkeys, bottle shoot and Paco's leaving.  Something
        should be arranged constructively here.  Up to that point I was
        completely in sync with the picture.
        I found Tuckermans slow.

Melnick We should drop the whole first part.

Aubrey  I don't think the river sequence has any place in the movie.

Melnick  I fought for that seqnence, but now I feel it does not work.

Aubrey   I found Roberta's too sexuqlly explicit.  Instead of the river
         sequence, put a Billy seuqence in between Jones and Robertas to cut
         up Pat's story.  Basicaly it looks great, the characters are excellent
         and it plays. All it needs is compressing and needs to be paced.

Melnick  I think the titles are too long.  People might be confused by Garrett's
         death.

Netter.  Basically a wonderful film and I love the music.  Slows down
         around Jones and Tuckermans and River.  Needs tightening around there.
         Because Billy is off screen too long.

Saul     It's a big picture to look at.  Extremely impressed.  I feel
         wé could  tighten by losing Tuckermans and staying more with Garrett.

J. Dunning Picture is tremendous.

Aubrey    Proud and happy with the amount of film you hdd.  What you are
          reaching for is really unusual and provocative.

Dunning   Not enough history in the beginning to completely understand
          first rell.  Thought Governors was good.

_____

Mike Klein.  Last night we had a meeting and Tony Walner objected to
the use of English editiors when American editors are unable to work in
England.

Jack Dunning  I have not heard from them so I am ignoring them.    Matter
              will be sorted out.

_____

Melnick     Re. schedule as long you meet release date the schedule can
            be juggled acorrding to you.
```

Notes by MGM executives following their first screening of an early cut

drunk himself into a stupor, while Garrett is watching the raft drift along. If the story was going to be moved briefly away from both of them, this was a logical place to do it. Also, though Billy was the dominant character in the first version, the story itself was not in any sense *subjectively* his, as the later versions and the film became progressively Garrett's. Indeed, the tone of Wurlitzer's *Billy the Kid* screenplay, at least as a reading experience, is coolly detached: we observe Billy in decline as objectively as we observe Garrett try to pick off the floating bottles. And in the vignette of the two miners dividing up the spoils of their partnership, Wurlitzer wrote the exquisite lament of the one miner that crystallized the themes of loss, exhaustion, and imperma- nence. When Sam set about rewriting the scene, he created another character, a drunk named Sackett, who interrupts the miners' argument, and he ended the scene with Poe coldcocking one of them to get the information he needs, which leads Sackett to observe, "You handled a crude situation with remark- able skill." The scene goes out with Sackett starting to sing "When the Role Is Called Up Yonder," a pointless allusion to the wedding sequence in *Ride the High Country*.

As rewritten, it still might have been possible to retain the essentially lyrical purpose of the scene, especially the lament, in the playing and the directing. Sam cast the reliable veterans Dub Taylor, a regular of his, as one of the miners, and Elisha Cook Jr. as the other, who utters the lament. So far, so good. But he also cast Don Levy, a high-school friend and fellow theater-arts major from Fresno State and the University of Southern California, as Sack- ett, who is so unremittingly terrible that even Aubrey was alarmed enough to fire off a memo to Sam (1/22/73)—the tone was jocular, and Sam replied in kind, though there was no mistaking Aubrey's meaning. Yet perhaps fearing that the lament felt too much like a set piece, Sam reduced it and treated it almost as a throwaway, with cutaways to the other characters and only one medium close-up, and then allowed it to be wholly upstaged by Poe's violence. Trying to get an adequate performance out of Levy and to make the scene otherwise play effectively gave Sam and his editors no end of trouble: along with the opening montage and Paco's death, it was one of the most worked over in the cutting rooms. But even if it had been better played, it might still feel orphaned now that the companion it had in the original version was long gone. And given how thoroughly Sam had made the film Garrett's, with Billy functioning almost as a kind of introject of the sheriff's personality, a single scene without either of them could not help but have the effect of breaking the structural spine of the narrative.

Considering how much trouble the scene was—surely even Peckinpah's most undiscriminating fans cannot regard it as approaching even his mid- dling, let alone great work—and how much Aubrey hated it, Roger couldn't understand why Sam was clinging to it. For the longest time he believed it another example of Sam's strategy of creating a distraction over a scene he didn't care about in order to protect those he did. But after a while Roger began to suspect Sam was hanging on to it because of his high-school friend. It turns out he was right, and not just about Levy. Don Hyde, Sam's archivist, told me that he personally heard Sam give as the reason he fought so hard to keep Tuckerman's was because both Levy and Taylor (who had appeared in four of his previous films) were in the scene.[23] I've often wondered too if it weren't also the presence of Cook, whom Sam admired so much in *Shane* but with whom he had never worked before.

But the only reason Sam ever put explicitly on record for keeping the scene was his worry that audiences would be confused if after Garrett tells Poe to strike out on his own, they weren't shown that Poe actually did travel someplace else, where he learned the Kid was in Fort Sumner. That Sam's concern was real I have no trouble believing: this is one of those plot points filmmakers can easily get hung up on, and determining whether they matter is a critical function of screenings and previews. The scene was removed from the theatrical version, which is how the film was seen for a decade and a half, over which period I read almost every review published in English and taught it at least a dozen times, all without encountering anyone to whom that plot point even occurred, let alone bothered (and, as Melnick kept arguing, the point would anyhow be covered by restoring the Ruthie Lee scene).[24] The motor force of this film is not its plot as such; it's the entwined destinies of the title characters. I don't believe anybody wonders a damn about Poe or any other secondary characters when they're not around.

The prologue was proving equally difficult, but unlike Tuckerman's, it was considered essential. Nevertheless, Melnick felt it a needlessly complicated opening, by turns prolix and diffuse, to a film the strength of which lay in its directness and simplicity; his worry, shared by others, was that it only delayed the real start, which was Garrett's arrival in Fort Sumner. From the beginning, as I've pointed out, Sam imagined titles and freeze-frames in the prologue, as he did in *The Wild Bunch* and, differently, in *Junior Bonner* and *The Getaway*. But what in those films was a clean technique that served the stories both thematically and stylistically here felt vaguely derivative and cumbersome. As noted in chapter 6, the prologue didn't make its first appearance in a version of the screenplay until about five weeks before production began. At that time it was a prologue only; there was no scripted epilogue that returned to the assassination of Garrett, no indication that there was to be one, no talk of one in any memos or discussions, and none was ever shot. And so it remained until deep into postproduction. Instead, the script ended with Garrett riding out of Fort Sumner the morning after he kills the Kid and disappearing into a fog. Sam also wrote that the prologue be processed in sepia and intercut with Garrett's arrival in Fort Sumner, called for the sequence to be very short, and, though filmed with dialogue, perhaps edited in such a way as to play without the dialogue sounding.

Once he got into the editing room, however, he plainly started thinking along far more elaborate lines than even the freeze-frames he talked about in

EXT. - VALLEY - GARRETT - DAY

(NOTE: This first scene is to be gradually intercut with the beginning of the following scene.)

PAT GARRETT RIDES A BUCKBOARD ACROSS a high desert   1
valley. Seated next to him, holding the reins, is
SAM PECK - white-haired, grizzled, with a turned-
down bitter expression to his face.

Garrett is grey, his features grim, his brow set in
a perpetual furrow. Although he sits rigid and un-
moving, his shoulders and narrowed eyes suggest an
internal pain, a contraction that has forced-him
relentlessly in on himself.

JOHN POE on horseback rides beside the buckboard.   2

                    GARRETT
          Goddamn sheep....Listen you son-
          of-a-bitch, I told you not to run
          sheep on my land.

                    POE
          It's my land, Garrett, it became
          mine.when I signed the lease.

                    PECK
          He's right, Mr. Garrett.

                    GARRETT (angered)
          How long have I known you, Peck?

                    PECK
          Almost a year.

                    GARRETT
          Well, that's long enough. When
          we get back I'm payin' you off.
                    (then to Poe)
          I'm breakin' the lease.

                    POE
          I don't allow the law will agree
          to that.

                    GARRETT
          What law? You and the rest of that
          goddamned Santa Fe ring. Your kind
          of law is ruining the country.

Peckinpah's handwritten note about playing the prologue silent and shorter

preproduction. We begin, a title card informs us, near Las Cruces in 1909—as it happens, off by a year (Garrett was murdered in 1908) and never corrected—and once the guns are pulled on an unsuspecting Garrett, we cut to old Fort Sumner in 1881, over which another card identifies the place and time. Then the crosscutting begins between the chickens getting shot and Garrett being murdered. All the while images are periodically frozen with titles placed over them, which raised additional problems. The prologue was supposed to be processed in sepia, but when Sam started freezing images on the Fort Sumner side of the sequence, he desaturated them to black-and-white, thus adding yet another motif to a sequence already overladen with motifs. Past and present, sepia, color, and black-and-white, freeze-frames and moving images, narrative titles and credit titles, and crosscutting—it's not that audiences would have trouble sorting all this out, just that as both storytelling and filmmaking it was messy. Sam seemed to agree, because immediately he told Melnick he had some other ideas for handling the titles, including putting more than one on each frozen image.[25] But there was never time to work any of it out: the opening is the only laborious opening to any of his films. (Roger once told me he thought Sam clung to this titles sequence against his better judgment as the surest way to protect the prologue, figuring the studio would never pay for a new titles sequence.)

One day in late March, going through reels attending to change notes, Roger came up with the idea of reprising a short part of the prologue as an epilogue in order to create a frame structure.[26] The idea was in theory a good one, and Roger, an exceptionally resourceful editor even this relatively early in his career, did an ingenious job making footage that was shot for one purpose serve another. Did it work? Well enough to try it at both previews. But repeating shots for referential purposes was something Sam tried hard to avoid, and I've always thought the footage in the epilogue looks like what it is—borrowed. When Sam wanted flashbacks, he shot material specifically for that purpose, as in *The Wild Bunch*; and when during editing he discovered he needed flashbacks he hadn't shot, he would if possible use footage from outtakes (i.e., shots not otherwise used) from earlier scenes, as he did in *The Ballad of Cable Hogue, Straw Dogs,* and *Junior Bonner*. Whatever else can be said for or against it, there is no question that if Sam had thought of it while he was still in production, a proper epilogue would have been shot and it would have come out looking very different from the way it did.[27]

The epilogue is also conceptually problematic. If the conceit is from "An Occurrence at Owl Creek Bridge" and the internal story is Garrett's life flashing before his eyes as he dies, why does the prologue leave him plainly dead and the epilogue pick him up alive again, only to end before he hits the ground? And why that oddly composed tight angle of the buggy seat and wheel frozen just at the point where Garrett's body bounces off the ground out of frame while his hat and fingertips remain sticking up from the bottom? This is a pretty flat shot on which to end a supposed epic or any other kind of film.

Visible squib wires coming out of Garrett's pant
leg (*center, bottom*) in the prologue

Whatever the answer, the only way Sam could have adequately evaluated the epilogue was to watch it as part of the whole film and see if the repeated footage bothered him. Which he never did.

As Sam was among the most attentive and sophisticated of all film directors when it comes to point of view, it has always seemed odd to me that in the prologue, the most subjective sequence in the film, he violates Garrett's point of view by revealing the distant shooter before Garrett sees him. Wouldn't it have been more effective, and also more like vintage Peckinpah, to reveal the first shooter *through* Garrett, either by the shock of our experiencing the first hit with him or at least reacting with him to the sound of the first rifle crack? When I asked Roger if this were ever tried, he just threw his hands up and said, "We all had a go at that scene. Nobody was ever completely happy with it, it was never right." The reality is that there was simply not enough time to experiment with the entire framing device to get it as finely tuned, balanced, and structured as it obviously needed to be.

Another piece of evidence that suggests the prologue was by no means in its final form even by the time of the previews is plainly visible squib wires coming out of one of Coburn's pant legs, which were not removed even for the second preview. As it's impossible to imagine no one on the editorial crew noticed, the only explanation is that since removing things like this was a very expensive proposition in those days, the optical would not have been ordered until the picture was unequivocally locked and it was certain the shot would be used.[28] It's entirely possible this also explains why the year of Garrett's death is wrong on the "Near Las Cruces" title card, even though the date is correct in a historical note Sam appended to the second preview. Since it's again unlikely that no one noticed the error, the logical explanation is that the correction was awaiting a decision as regards the final form of the prologue.

As late as the notes for the first preview, Sam still had doubts about the style of the titles, including the color red, which may explain both why the historical note in the second preview is in yellow and why it is not followed by an end-credits crawl: there was time enough to shoot the note in the new color but not enough time to shoot a whole new crawl in yellow, let alone change the titles from red throughout the prologue. Finally, consider also that as early as a February 25 set of notes, Sam gave this blanket instruction: "CLOSE UP LINES ON ALL LONG SHOTS." What he meant was for the editors to cut out any long, unnecessary pauses between lines, which is easy to do in extreme long shots because it doesn't matter if the dialogue goes out of sync, since you can't see it. This is a common practice in fine-cutting, and editors, including the three principal ones here, usually do it on their own without having to be told. Yet in the very first shot of the prologue, an extreme wide shot, there is a long, pointless pause between Garrett's first line and Poe's reply. Why wasn't it tightened, along with other instances of the same thing? The likeliest explanation—really, the only explanation—is that the editors simply ran out of time and these became just more things that fell through the cracks or, in the specific instance of the prologue, something to be attended to once a final decision was made. (Why didn't I tighten it for the special edition? Because there is music and I didn't have access to the separate tracks so that the music could be edited to conform to the shorter length once the pause was closed up.) No matter how you look at the notes, the evidence, and the versions of the film itself, the conclusion is inescapable: when Sam left the picture he left a prologue that was still in flux, about several aspects of which he had not made his final determinations.

One of the most revealing documents is a four-page memo from Gordon Carroll, dated March 19, 1973, that summarizes a lunch meeting between Sam, Gordon, Roger, and Dan Melnick, held four days earlier. There are twenty-four separate, detailed notes that cover the whole film and include such matters as the titles sequence, in particular the freeze-frames (whether there should be single or multiple credits on each one or some with no titles on them, etc.); the wife scene (Melnick wants it dropped entirely but realizes he is alone in this, all agree Clavell's performance must be looped, "and Sam suggested that further cuts be made within" it); the length of the Stinking Springs scene (Melnick feels it's too long, "Sam disagrees, although there are lifts he wants to make"—but since a lift indicates a substantial cut, not a mere trim, does this mean Sam didn't disagree?); the raft scene ("Dan sees no hope" for it, "Sam and Roger both feel it needs some work," and all "agreed to consider repositioning" it); and Tuckerman's (Melnick wants to eliminate it entirely, but "Sam and I want to pre-dub the first half of the sequence, possibly making some cuts in it"). The very last note reads in part: "We agree to eliminate the second of Garrett's two lines immediately following the shooting of Billy" and "Sam has ideas for the whole scene (including a later entrance for Rita), and we left the discussion there."

```
Memorandum for Files
March 19, 1973
Page 4.

    23.  We briefly talked about the actual shooting of Billy.
We all seem to be in agreement on how this is to be revised.

    24.  We agreed to eliminate the second of Garrett's
two lines immediately following the shooting of Billy.
Also, Dan felt that Poe's off-screen lines ("trigger finger")
do not work.  Sam has ideas for the whole scene (including
a later entrance for Rita), and we left the discussion
there.




GC/k
CC: Dan Melnick, Sam Peckinpah, Roger Spottiswoode,
    Garth Craven
```

The last note of Gordon Carroll's March 19 memo as
regards Garrett's lines about killing the Kid

The reference to the second of Garrett's two lines following the killing of
the Kid is ambiguous. Garrett says, "I shot him . . . I killed the Kid." If this is
considered a single line separated by a long beat, then the second line can
refer only to Garrett's "What you want and what you get are two different
things." If the "I shot him" and "I killed the Kid" are regarded as two separate
lines, then "I killed the Kid" was to be removed. Though the qualifier "immediately" suggests the latter, the screenplay is of no help: none of the dialogue
as spoken in the versions of the film matches exactly what is in the shooting
script, where Garrett says, "It was the Kid. I shot the Kid," but there Garrett is
responding to a direct question from Kip, "Did you get him?" The description
calls for Garrett's reply to be delivered in a "flat" voice, with no suggestion
it's in disbelief or doubt and no ellipsis or anything else to indicate a pause
between the two declarations. Meanwhile, the "what you want" appears in no
copy of any screenplay, which means it was likely an ad-lib.

Who can say for certain what to make of any of this? Coburn's reading
of the first line is as if in disbelief, perhaps a nod to reports that the real
Garrett said this or something like it immediately following the shooting.
But that was because despite the moonlit night, the room was pitch-black,
the Kid was backlit against the doorway, Poe told Garrett he had killed the
wrong man, and Garrett had a moment of doubt before setting his deputy
straight. As Sam conceived the scene, however, the room is lighted, Garrett
plainly sees he's killed the Kid, and no one questions him about it when he

goes outside. For reasons I've stated elsewhere (*Reconsideration* 302), I believe the "what you want" line an egregious mistake—Michael Sragow once told me it struck him as "a forced, pallid re-rendering" of Thornton's "What I want and what I need are two different things" from *The Wild Bunch*—and it diminishes one of the supreme moments of drama in all Peckinpah's work: Garrett's great anguished "Nooooooo!" as Poe draws his knife and moves to cut off the Kid's trigger finger. I would like nothing more than to believe Sam himself wanted the ad-lib cut, but there is no way to determine this from the note. All we know for sure from the previews is that the directive was never implemented and that in the theatrical all the lines except the "No" were removed.

Confusion like this and lack of follow-through were typical of the later stages of postproduction. On a film with a normal schedule, the only thing the editors and the director would be doing for the first ten weeks following the end of production is preparing the director's cut to show the studio, which is plenty work enough. But part of what made the *Pat Garrett* schedule so crazy is that most of the tasks that follow the director's cut—such as previews, fine-cutting, and everything necessary to finish the film, including sound editing, looping, scoring, color timing, pre-dubbing, dubbing, negative cutting, checking the answer prints, and release printing—had to be started well before picture editing was anywhere near completion. Processes that would ordinarily begin only after the picture was close to being locked were here done in parallel as Sam and the editors continued cutting, shaping, and refining it. This means that the work print was constantly being changed in *substantial* ways day in day out, and every change, even the smallest ones, required a new wave of conforming the many reels of sound effects and music (and, later, the negative itself) so that everything would stay in sync. Since the position of postproduction coordinator didn't exist back then, the responsibility for scheduling and overseeing the finishing work fell to the chief editor, with the director reviewing and approving the elements as they were completed. But Roger was also editing the film at the same time as he was coordinating everything else, including sound and music, which put a tremendous drain on his time and exacted an inevitable toll on his concentration. Add to this the fact that once Jerry Fielding walked off the show, the score was left to a *songwriter*, not an experienced film composer. Who can wonder that so many things fell through the cracks?

Several notes never got addressed at all, such as removing the shot of Poe's horse turning in the prologue, putting back Garrett slapping Ruthie Lee,[29] and closing up pointlessly long beats. Sometimes instructions to make the same changes recur in more than one set of notes. It's impossible to know how to interpret this. Perhaps Sam changed his mind after dictating them, then forgot he'd reversed himself; perhaps the editors didn't have time to implement them because they were already driven far past exhaustion, long fatiguing hours in front of noisy Moviolas, seven days a week, and still there wasn't enough time. Something that particularly worried Bob Wolfe throughout the whole process was that—as was not the case on Sam's previous films where he shared editorial duties with other editors—here each editor tended for the most part to work almost exclusively on the scenes assigned him, while no one seemed to be monitoring the progress of the whole film, charting the changes, or to have the whole film in his head. Under ordinary circumstances, that person would be the principal editor and/or the director. But Sam was too often—well, let's say distracted or indisposed—and Roger had so many fires to attend to he simply ran out of hours in the day.

None of this should be surprising considering the sheer haste in which everyone had to work and the multitasking required to get it all done. That plus the absence of the usual checks and balances that result when editors work on each other's reels—"Did you already do the changes on this scene?" "Are you sure about this note?" "Does Sam really want the wife scene taken out?"—and things just fell by the wayside. And by falling asleep during screenings, arriving late or missing them, Sam wouldn't necessarily have known whether all his notes were implemented or if they worked as he had hoped they would. Nor were the notes themselves always clear, especially if he had consumed too much alcohol. Then, too, missing the first preview wasn't only professionally derelict, it was suicidal. The editors had done an extraordinary job improving the film over the version the executives saw: the latest cut now realized the beauty of much of what Sam had shot, scenes and whole sequences were so moving as to catch the breath, something clearly extraordinary was here struggling to find shape and form. But even after making every allowance for what was an essentially lyrical, meditative piece, punctuated by moments of violence, the picture still played in fits and starts, sequences meandered and scenes stopped dead, the audience soon grew restless. The next day when Melnick—*Melnick*, not Aubrey—asked for Sam's notes, Sam insultingly replied that fifteen feet could come out of one shot, to which he added the injury of not replying to Melnick directly but delivering it via his editors (specifically, Roger). Why did Sam continue to leave himself in so vulnerable a position?

I have over the years talked often and at length about *Pat Garrett and Billy the Kid* with several persons who worked on it or were very close to Sam at the time, including family members. Their loyalty and love were and are beyond question, and not one of them wastes any sympathy on Aubrey, who all agree deserved his nickname "the smiling cobra."[30] Yet they all believe Sam gratuitously manufactured a lot of the quarrels and that by the time of the previews was leaving Aubrey no choice but to take the film away from him. Garth lamented on more than one occasion, "If only Sam had spent the time and energy working on the film that he did provoking Aubrey and the others," and Garth was far from alone in this. If it was true that Aubrey later ordered scenes removed for no other reason than he knew Sam wanted them, it was also true that Sam deliberately left in scenes that were easily expendable simply because he knew Aubrey especially hated them. There is of course no way of knowing for certain, but some people believe that if Sam had just given up Tuckerman's at a strategic moment, he might have been able to retain most of the scenes he *really* cared about.

One of the strategies Sam apparently had in mind when it came to the previews was to invite members of the cast and some industry notables— Henry Fonda, for one—in the hopes that they would spread the word and thus through some form of peer pressure force the studio into allowing him to complete the film as he wished to. Sam also wanted to invite members of his family. When he was forbidden on both counts, he alleged conspiracy. It's hard to fathom what he must have been thinking here and equally hard to escape the conclusion that he was being either disingenuous or naive. Studios rarely allow friends, family, crew members, industry insiders, and press into formal audience previews. The whole point of previews is to get the closest equivalent that can be managed to paying moviegoers who have no stake in the movie they're watching; and once you get them, you don't want to take a chance on having friends, family, insiders, and other interested parties lead, condition, or otherwise contribute to the response. Sam knew this. So he must also have known that as a gambit it was a feeble one, and no substitute for his failure to fight for his film effectively, as opposed to self-destructively and in ways that seemed to guarantee his defeat.

Why didn't Sam attend them? According to Katy Haber, at some point around the time principal photography was completed, Sam seems to have adopted as his primary strategy for handling the studio an extreme form of passive-aggressiveness that consisted in wholesale avoidance of any sort of *direct* dealings with Aubrey, including never attending conferences, meetings, or occasions at which he knew Aubrey would be present. This is why, Katy told me, Sam skipped all studio meetings, screenings, and previews. Yet when it came to protecting his film from Aubrey, the only man with the personal authority and any power to back it up was Sam himself. But he chose to do so only through intermediaries whom Aubrey either bullied or ignored. Whatever Melnick's sympathies for Sam, deep and many, he was caught in a bind, inasmuch as he was in the employ of the studio; Carroll simply lacked a fighter's temperament, and anyhow Sam abused him as much as Aubrey no doubt did.

Much has been reported about how bitter the relationship between Carroll and Sam was, but little about its beginnings. In fact, the tapes of meetings clearly reveal that they became fast friends and had a solid and rewarding partnership throughout most of preproduction. Sam liked Carroll immensely, greatly respected his ideas, welcomed more of them, and even presented him with an offer he had never extended to any other producer except Dan Melnick on *Straw Dogs*: he freely invited Carroll from first cut forward to come into the cutting rooms and observe whenever he wanted (the only stipulation that he refrain from comment until asked). By the time production wrapped, Sam could hardly stand to be around him. It was a classic case of blaming the messenger and also of Sam's need for a whipping boy. Carroll was the bearer of most of the bad news from the studio; worse, as producer he was technically the enforcer as well, which did nothing but ignite Sam's considerable issues with authority. Dawson, who sympathized with Carroll, wrote me that the

> studio juggernaut of Aubrey, Melnick, Rachmil, and Parsons rolled over the top of [Gordon] and right up Sam's ass. Without a firewall, the constant edicts, criticisms, and interferences were so intense that I often thought we should shelve the picture and release the camp war. We could call it "Suits On The Ground." 80% of our attention was devoted to dealing with the MGM napalm, and 20% to the picture. I'm not saying Sam was innocent or even right, but the result certainly would have been different had we been blessed with a stronger gatekeeper. Gordon hung in there, squarely and hopelessly in the middle, taking more shit than any man should have to take.

Spottiswoode's viewpoint is a little different: "A thoughtful gentleman, Gordon Carroll preferred persuasion to combat. I doubt it was his fault he couldn't defend Sam. From our cutting-room perspective, Sam was usually his own worst enemy. When an opportunity arose to defuse a crisis and put out a fire, Sam would often reach for a can of gasoline and toss it into the flames." Part of the trouble was that Sam was never privy to Carroll's dealings with the studio and so wouldn't necessarily have known how much the producer had pled his cause, which was most of the time. But nobody I've spoken with who worked on the film from start to finish (including Dawson) feels that once shooting started Sam treated Carroll fairly or decently, let alone with the respect and appreciation he had earned and deserved. Gordy Dawson put it best: "Really too bad how it all turned out—for everybody."[31]

For his part, no doubt Carroll was by turns as frustrated and infuriated by the same behavior as Roger, Garth, Bob, Katy, Melnick, even Dawson himself were: they all believed Sam could have outplayed and outwitted Aubrey and gained most of what he wanted because he was so much smarter. Instead, Sam seemed to be maneuvering Aubrey to do exactly what he soon would do: take the film away. That would be Sam's final out, his safety valve and escape hatch, from a project he had begun to fear before production started and in which by the time of the previews his faith had been shaken to its foundations.[32] At last he would have Aubrey where he wanted him. He knew Aubrey would insist on further changes, knew he would *have to* because the film still wasn't playing well. Sam's fear was that it might never play well—but if it were taken away from him, he would be absolved of blame for whatever version was released. And if either of the previews survived—well, let me tell you what *that* film could have been if only "they" had left me alone to finish it my way.

But Aubrey didn't strike just yet. There was a second preview a week later. And whatever else, he was good, if not to his word, then at least to the letter of the contract: Sam would have his two previews and they would be of Sam's cuts, nobody else's. Aubrey even allowed the film to be negative-cut and roughly scored and dubbed Sam's way. Despite this, it would be a mistake to assume that these previews were held in good faith. Aubrey or his representatives were already pressuring Bob Wolfe, who was under contract to the studio, to implement their changes, that is, pulling the scenes they wanted taken out; but Bob kept resisting, telling them they promised Sam his cut would be shown at two previews and they should keep their word.

There is one moderate and a couple of minor differences between the first and second previews. The moderate one is a deep cut in the Garrett-McKinney scene at Roberta's. Sam evidently came to believe the scene was so long it was beginning to feel like a set piece, so he instructed that all the dialogue following Garrett's "there's a couple of young ones there too" be lifted—which accounted for a little over a third of it. The minor changes accompanying this were the removal of the shot of Garrett, McKinney, and Poe riding out of town and the short scene of Rupert clearing the table. As I show in chapter 9, removing the Rupert business was entirely beneficial, but lifting the last part of the Garrett-McKinney dialogue, which includes the reasons why Garrett thinks McKinney owes him, deprived the film of a smartly written and played scene, left McKinney a considerably less interesting character (indeed, hardly a character at all), and stripped their relationship of any history. (Here was an example of Sam himself diluting a vignette and one of the best at that.) Meanwhile, eliminating the ride out of town arguably made for a rougher, not a smoother transition into the last sequence of the film.

But there were also two major differences. In the first preview the end crawl begins with the end titles. By the time of the second preview, these were preceded by a legend Sam personally wrote: a "historical" note that links the killing of Garrett to the Santa Fe Ring to Albert Fall and the Teapot Dome and eventually, by way of a veiled allusion, to Watergate and his own problems at MGM. It reads in full:

This has been the story of a time . . . a legend . . .
not about two gunfighters.

Pat Garrett was killed by hired assassins
on February 29th, 1908
on the road to Las Cruces.

The assassins were hired by the so-called Santa Fe Ring. The
same people who had hired Garrett to kill William Bonney.

Garrett, carrying his guilt with him, had gone against the Ring
and solved the murder in White Sands, New Mexico of Colonel
Albert Fountain and his 8 year old son Henry.

The head of the Ring was Albert Fall.

Although there seemed to be sufficient evidence to substantiate
the murder, four of the suspects were never charged, and Wayne
Brazel, who was indicted for the murder was acquitted.

Albert Fall was the defending attorney.

He later became Secretary of Interior for the United States of
America, was impeached, dismissed from office
and imprisoned for the Teapot Dome Scandal.

So what else is new?

The graphic is a combination S and P, which was how Sam signed his initials.
He had them placed onscreen to make sure no one at the studio could miss
the fact that he himself wrote the note. The presence of the note in the first
place is evidence of an unfortunate tendency toward didacticism in some of
his later films, a disinclination to trust the strength of the tale he is telling.
No filmgoers of sensibility then or now need to have the contemporary relevance of the story pointed out to them, while as history this is so cockamamie
that even the parts which are true are so distorted as to amount to the same
thing.[33] But at this point in the proceedings, none of that seemed to matter:
Sam couldn't pass up any opportunity to flip Aubrey and the others the finger,
even if it was something that damaged his film and made both it and him look
silly.

The other major difference is that the wife scene was not present in the
first preview but it was in the second. The question for which I cannot find
an answer is why the wife scene was removed in the first place. Although it
was one of several that Sam kept fussing with throughout the editing and
there was much discussion about whether to remove it, I can find no written
instruction that he ever actually *ordered* it lifted. But it couldn't have been
removed on orders from anyone else, because the studio was not directly
involved with the editing at this point. Inasmuch as it was a clean picture-
and-track lift, perhaps he just told one of the editors to take it out to get a
sense of how the film might play without it. Roger and Garth don't remember,
but Katy distinctly recalls it was Sam's idea to take Garrett right up to the
gate, where he pauses before pushing it open, and then start the lift there,
which is exactly how it is in the first preview. In the theatrical, Roger or Bob
started the lift slightly earlier, when Garrett and Alamosa Bill separate outside the barbershop and Alias follows them out. This seems to me a more

elegant place to do it, as having Garrett walk up to the gate but not go in actually *accentuates* the absence of the scene. Of course, it's entirely possible this was Sam's purpose: make the lacuna so glaring there was no choice but to put the lifted scene back. The simplest explanation, probably the likeliest too, is that its removal was a mistake or resulted from a miscommunication, which is reinforced by a letter written to Melnick about a year later in which Sam referred to "the foul up on the Ida's house sequence."[34]

Adding to the confusion here are two undated sets of editing notes, each two pages long. The first set, untitled, contains an instruction that reads, "PUT IDA SCENE BACK." It's impossible to know precisely when these notes were dictated; but inasmuch as some of them call for changes that were already implemented in the first preview, it's obvious that they must predate that preview. For example, one note calls for removing all dialogue from the raft sequence; but since any dialogue in the raft sequence had been removed *before* the first preview, this set of notes cannot have come after it. Evidently at some point not long before the first preview, Sam told his editors to remove the wife scene, then changed his mind, and in this set of notes instructed them to put it back in. This still begs the question of why it wasn't. More than likely, in the rush to prepare for the first preview, it was just one more thing that didn't get done or else Sam made the decision too late for it to be done in time for the preview.

Even more confusing is the second set of notes, titled "NOTES TAKEN AT PREVIEW OF PREVIEW MAY 3rd." Since the title identifies a preview of the preview, it suggests these notes were given at some sort of run-through prior to the actual preview. Not only is there no instruction here about either removing or putting back the wife scene, the sole reference to it reads: "Stop the music in Ida's house just as Garrett turns to leave." What again remains unexplained is why at this run-through, relatively soon before the preview, the scene was still there yet wound up being removed by the time of the preview itself. This document also indicates that as the previews approached, Sam's notes more and more addressed technical matters (sound balances, color timings, loop lines, etc.) and musical issues (placement of cues, levels). Does this suggest that at least in his own mind he was more or less satisfied with the cut as it otherwise stood (with the wife scene)? Well, that's certainly one way of looking at it, except that these notes continue to raise many issues of timing, pacing, and performance, and he certainly knew that unless he agreed to cooperate Aubrey was going to take over once the second preview was out of the way.

In fact, it turns out something else was up. As far back as the fall of the previous year, while deep into preproduction on *Pat Garrett* and still revising the screenplay, Sam was also setting up his next project, *Bring Me the Head of Alfredo Garcia*, a script he'd been developing on and off since 1970. In the first week of March he took advantage of being in Mexico City, where the editors were screening a first cut of *Pat Garrett* for Melnick, to scout locations for

Alfredo Garcia. (The expenses of the trip were evenly split between United Artists, which was bankrolling the new project, and MGM.) On May 25, following negotiations that had been going on since at least February—and more than likely much earlier—Sam signed a fully executed director's contract, which called for principal photography to begin on September 3 (which was eventually delayed a month). Uncertain what he had in *Pat Garrett* and fearful the troubles associated with it might undermine his chances to get another picture, he was locking something down as soon as he could and was eager to get started, since it was a sure thing, with a friendly producer in Martin Baum, an artist-friendly studio in UA, and people who respected and supported him as an artist.

Of course, many directors try to get their next project into motion before they've finished the current one, and Sam engineered this as often as he was able. When two years earlier he returned to the States to start shooting *Junior Bonner*, he retained control of *Straw Dogs*, leaving the editing to Bob and Roger, and kept a perfectly good eye on the process as they implemented his notes. The same was true of his prep work on *Pat Garrett* vis-à-vis the completion of *The Getaway*. But the comparisons end there, because he didn't abandon any of those films. *Pat Garrett*, however, was a battleground, still unfinished, and by leaving he was consigning it to *certain* jeopardy in order to begin a new film. From this perspective, his behavior has the look less of a man satisfied with something he had achieved than of one who wants to have done with it so he can move on.[35] Indeed, Roger told me this was pretty much how everyone felt by then: the combination of the poisoned working atmosphere at the studio, the sheer nastiness of the infighting between Sam and Aubrey, frustration with Sam's drinking and his refusal to be even a little reasonable, and mostly seven-day workweeks months on end left everybody's nerves so frayed, patience so thin, and energies so depleted that all any of them wanted was to get the hell out of there as soon as possible. That this or something like it was the case is further suggested by what Bob Wolfe told me when I asked him if there ever existed a version of the film on which there was agreement from all the principals that it was a "final" version, a cut everyone was, if not satisfied with, then at least willing to consent to, Sam paramountly. "No," was Bob's terse reply, and his laconism included both previews.

It's unlikely any of these speculations can be resolved with absolute certainty, but what emerges with blinding clarity is the degree to which the editing process had by then deteriorated into a chaotic, almost inconceivably high-pressure environment in which decisions were made in great haste without full consideration of their potential consequences, review of their actual consequences, or time left over for reconsideration, modification, correction, or reversal. About this Roger was quite explicit: "We'd make the changes, but none of us had the time, including Sam, to watch them in context to see if they were really any better than what was there before." The

Twentieth Century Fox
Box 900
Beverly Hills, Cal 90213

April 30th 1974

Mr. Dan Melnick
MGM
10202 W. Washington Boulevard
Culver City California

Dear Dan:

The following is a summary of our comments on yesterday's running:

1. We need the foul up on the Ida's House sequence squared away, which entails getting the complete dupe of the second preview, and since this was a direct lift, it should be easy to drop back in, using the second preview negative, but in order to match the rest of the picture it should be one generation removed.

2. I will break down and give you an itemised timetable of dates to be added as per our discussion.

3. A lift in dialogue between Kip and Garrett and the Don Levy trim.

4. Sweeten the music cue when Charles Martin Smith cannot see the cards any more.

5. Complete the Ruthie Lee sequence with particular emphasis upon the slapping.

6. Replace the Chisum sequence including the ride away splashing through water.

7. Re-dub turkey sequence for level, both sound and music very low on this reel.

8. Would like your thoughts on places to sweeten the music as Dylan score is more than a little thin.

9. Re-examine the song with words during the Pickens death walk.

Peckinpah's reply to Melnick's invitation to recut the film

10. Re-work the end of Garrett leaving Ruthie Lee Hotel so it is not a set piece and so we can drop the ride out of town. This means that trims have to be pulled on that sequence and the sequence immediately preceeding.

11. Cut of Alias instead of Poe. At the same time I will re-examine losing the line.

12. Both Garth and I feel that until we make our move for dubbing to Metro, if we could have the material now, we are set up to do preliminary work i.e. moviolas, rooms etc here on the 20th lot. And that with some of the spare time that we have in between the work we are both doing on other pictures, we could have most of it completed by the time we make our move to Metro, so that you can have a look at it. I therefore suggest that Garth get together with Jack Dunning to discuss whatever is needed.

Let me say that both professionally and personally I am delighted with your co-operation, ideas and enthusiasm. And let me state further that, if something equitable cannot be worked out between United Artists and MGM regarding cost on these changes, I will hold myself personally responsible, and even put up a bond to that effect. So for the love of God, tell Jack Dunning to keep the prices down.

Best personal regards,

SAM PECKINPAH

cc. Jack Dunning
    Eric Pleskow
    Mike Medavoy
    Lee Katz
    Garth Craven

May 3rd.

I forgot to mention a lift in the Governor Wallace sequence.

rush to prep the second preview took a particularly terrible toll: a couple of music and sound entrances were grotesquely clipped—to my ears, it doesn't even sound as if there was a patch session to finesse the temp mix—and the Garrett-McKinney/Rupert/ride-out-of-town lift was evidently made right in the preview print itself, as the tape splice is plainly visible. Neither Sam nor his editors would ever have allowed something this crude to be shown if they hadn't been forced to. All of which brings us right back up against the three facts of the previews: the insanely accelerated schedule, Sam's drinking and other self-destructive behavior, and his failure to attend them.[36]

There is a curious footnote to the unhappy story of the editing of this film and Sam's relationship to it. By November 1973, seven months after the film disappeared from theaters, Aubrey was gone from MGM while Melnick remained. A few months later he invited Sam to come back and prepare a final cut of *Pat Garrett and Billy the Kid* exactly as he wished it to be. On April 29, 1974, Sam, Melnick, and Garth Craven screened the film (which version is not absolutely clear, but it was almost certainly the first preview[37]). The next day Sam wrote Melnick a two-page letter enumerating several matters he wanted to address immediately (including putting the Ida, Ruthie Lee, and Chisum scenes back, further work on the Garrett-McKinney scene and their ride out of town, reexamining the issue of Dylan's vocals for "Knockin' on Heaven's Door," and fleshing out the score in places he felt it was too thin). "Let me say that both professionally and personally I am delighted with your coopera-tion," he concluded.

But nothing ever came of it. In 1995, when I asked Melnick what had happened, he told me that Sam just wouldn't make himself available.[38] This seemed inconceivable to me, and I finally asked Garth about it. "I got as far as going to the studio one afternoon and looking through the vaults. I found the wife scene, and a couple of other things." And then what? "Nothing," Garth replied. "It occupied Sam's attention for about fifteen minutes, and then, like so much else in his life in those years, nothing came of it. He lost interest." I was incredulous when I heard this. Sam pissed and moaned his whole career about interferences by the moneymen in his work, complained how none of his films had been released in anything like versions he approved,[39] and here he was offered means, budget, place to work, and the postproduction staff and facilities of one of the best-equipped studios in the world to make the final cut of one of his finest films with the editor of his choice . . . *and he lost interest?*

When Garth told me that, I was silent for a moment, because all I could think of was how Garth himself must have felt back then: *Pat Garrett* was his first film as a picture editor and he had put himself in potential jeopardy with a major studio when he quit in support of Sam. And then I wondered about Melnick: he had hired Sam for *Noon Wine* after *Major Dundee* and *The*

Cincinnati Kid when no one else would, produced one of his best films in *Straw Dogs*, protected *Pat Garrett* probably as much as he was able in the last stages of the editing, and was met with indifference after presenting Sam with an opportunity that any director would kill for.

"That's a shame," I said to Garth.

Yes," he answered softly, "isn't it?"

Peckinpah and his producer, Gordon Carroll

CHAPTER EIGHT

The Box Set

Nick Redman and I were unprepared for the tempest the 2005 Special Edition of *Pat Garrett and Billy the Kid* generated in a relatively small but quite noisy teapot of fans and other enthusiasts on some blogs and other Internet sites (including Amazon). Or rather, I was unprepared for it; Nick, who has supervised many soundtrack restorations and follows these things, was not in the least surprised, finding it business as usual. I naively assumed the studio would promote the new version accurately, yet when the first DVDs arrived, a blurb on the back cover trumpeted the 2005 Special Edition as "based on the director's notes and the insights of his colleagues," claims I would never have made and do not make now because they are not true. Studios don't typically run publicity copy past those of us who contribute ancillary materials to their DVD releases, and Warner certainly didn't in this case. It was common knowledge at the home video division that no one, including myself, was working from any "notes" by Peckinpah. In fact, before I researched the essay that served as the springboard for this book, I didn't even know of the extensive editing notes and memos in the Sam Peckinpah Papers at the Margaret Herrick Library. And though I had the imprimatur of Roger Spottiswoode to go ahead with the special edition, he did not participate in its preparation. This was because there was no need for it: the terms of the project had to be strictly defined and my access to the requisite materials was severely limited.

Warner Home Video was determined to spend as little money as possible on the box set of Peckinpah's Western films. The division agreed to a special edition of *Pat Garrett* only because it would be based on the theatrical release, for which there already existed a fully dubbed, timed, and cut negative, into which putting back a few scenes was fairly easy and relatively inexpensive as these things go. By contrast, a full-scale restoration of the previews raises a whole slew of issues both practical and ethical, or at least philosophical. The practical issues concern both expense and feasibility, of which more anon, but let me address terminology first.

The whole reason this new version is called a "special edition" rather than a "restoration" is precisely because a restoration implies something that at one time existed in a purer or more pristine, perfect, or complete state. *Pat Garrett,* however, never existed in such a state in the first place, so there was nothing in the literal sense of the word *to* restore. Many filmgoers, especially those who love this film as much I do, mistakenly regard the previews as final cuts, more or less equivalent to the original releases of *The Wild Bunch.* But there is a crucial difference: Peckinpah was intimately involved in the editing of *The Wild Bunch* from first cut right straight through to previews, fine cut, looping, scoring, dubbing, mixing, color timing, and release printing. He personally allowed the release of two slightly different versions of that film, one domestic, one European, the latter longer by one scene: they are not only true final cuts, they were *his* final cuts, completed by him, his editors, and the rest of his postproduction crew. When Warner decided to reduce the running time to make for more showings per day in the domestic market, it did so by way of ordering the material removed from as many prints as possible in the field. The final-cut negative masters back in Los Angeles were left untouched. When the studio did the restoration for a theatrical rerelease in 1995 as promotion for a new laser disc, it was a simple matter of returning to the negative of the European version.[1] But with *Pat Garrett,* there is no equivalent to any of this: Peckinpah never completed a true final cut, and the only master negative I'm aware of is that of the original theatrical release, which is much shorter than either preview and was of course finished without him.

As for the two previews, the only extant copy of the second one is the print, long since faded to red, in the Herrick.[2] It's unlikely there is any negative equivalent for this print, because the negative used to generate it would have been further altered for the theatrical release. The first preview, the 1988 Turner, may also exist only in a single print, which appears to be the one that was used to generate the laser disc and much later the DVD for the box set. If this is true—and from the look of what is on the DVD, I believe it is—then it's obvious that that print was generated from a negative or IP—that is, interpositive, a special print generated from the original negative and used to make a duplicate negative, so that prints can be struck from it rather than from the original—that wasn't properly timed. (To my eyes, it doesn't even look like a particularly good answer print, and it was without question made in great haste.[3])

Nick and I were as disappointed as anybody by the look of the 1988 Turner in the set. But do the elements even exist to make a new and better-looking print? I have no idea, because my offers to help identify what was in the vaults and to sit in—again for no money—during the online mastering sessions were politely but firmly refused. Nor do I know what exists in the way of negative backup. I assume that a protection IP was made as soon as negative cutting was complete. But I don't know this to be so, and Roger Spottiswoode and Garth Craven can't remember. This would have been an internal decision at Metro-Goldwyn-Mayer post, anyhow, and industry practice at the time was inconsistent. If IPs were made for each preview version, then picture restorations are possible but would be expensive.[4] If IPs do not exist but only negative lifts and trims of cut scenes and sequences, then it would still be possible, but, I am informed, more expensive. This is because, regardless of which preview is selected for restoration, the theatrical negative would have to be conformed to that version. And because many shots in the negative would have to be extended, a certain amount of digital restoration would be necessary, thus adding to the expense. Then there is the condition of the audio tracks, which almost certainly do not conform to either preview. All this was in any case moot: Warner Home Video didn't, wouldn't, and wasn't prepared to spend the money.

This was still no excuse for the studio not doing the minimal spruce-up work that is routine on almost all rereleases of older films, such as cleaning the picture element or elements used to make the DVD transfers. That this obviously wasn't done is evidenced by plainly visible dirt, dust, and scratches, which are not unduly expensive to remove or repair with digital technology. Warner might also have attended to the sound mix. To this day I have no idea, nor does Nick, where the studio found the tracks used to master the Turner preview. Half a line by Kip McKinney drops out completely, there are several places where the beginnings or ends of lines are clipped, and the last few reels suffer from a distinct wobble (listen to Dylan's ballad under the end titles), none of which defects afflicts the old Turner laser disc of the same version. Moreover, it's obvious that it's a temporary mix—aka in industry parlance, a "temp mix" or "temp dub"—because more than a few loop lines are insufficiently covered by background atmosphere (or none at all) and there are places where joins in crossed takes are audibly obvious.

None of this can be blamed on the film editors (when it came to sound Roger was one of the most fastidious editors I've ever known and he's still that way as a director), the sound editors, or the rerecording mixers, because they managed as best they could under the most grueling of time constraints. And they can hardly be faulted that a temp dub intended for two showings only to preview audiences was put into wide circulation because the studio wouldn't do a proper fix on it. Meanwhile, the 2005 Special Edition contains a clipped sound transition following the Lew Wallace scene that I twice noted in the editing sessions but that was never corrected, not to mention, even worse, the shot of Olinger where the line "crazy woman's quilt" is obviously out of sync. As for the picture quality of the DVDs, it's barely adequate at best. Roger was shocked by how off the color timing and brightness levels seemed to him. With John Coquillon (*Straw Dogs*, *Cross of Iron*) the director of photography, this is one of the most beautifully shot and composed films ever made, notably in the steepness of the lighting contrasts and the extraordinary richness and vibrancy of the color palette and textures—all washed out and dynamically flattened to a drab, deadening tan in the current transfer.[5]

How could such a careless presentation have been allowed? The preparation of the Peckinpah box seems to have been caught in an internecine warfare involving the domestic and worldwide departments within Warner's home video division. The domestic side developed a particular animus toward Brian Jamieson, the worldwide executive who had initiated the Peckinpah set and for whom it was a labor of love and a long-nurtured dream. The result was that what should have been a prestige set was treated indifferently, shabbily, even hostilely. A documentary Nick and Brian had planned on Peckinpah and the Western was evidently scrapped because the domestic side refused to shoulder part of the cost, while the worldwide side couldn't underwrite the whole thing, which was budgeted at about three hundred thousand dollars.[6]

I proposed that the theatrical release be included along with the Turner preview and the 2005 Special Edition, a suggestion scarcely even taken up for discussion. (In fact, what I actually pleaded for was that *both* the first and second previews be included, along with the theatrical and the 2005 Special Edition.) In addition to incorrect color timing and brightness levels, the grain is coarse rather than fine; a booklet of essays, interviews, and other materials compiled and edited by David Weddle was not included (though it was offered to reviewers as a press kit); the packaging suggested nothing of prestige or distinction, looking instead rather cheesy; and—well, hell, even the title of the damn thing is grammatically awkward: *Sam Peckinpah's The Legendary Westerns Collection*. It should be either *Sam Peckinpah's Legendary Westerns* or *Sam Peckinpah: The Legendary Westerns*. (Jamieson's original title was *Pure Peckinpah*, which the studio appropriated for the press kit.[7]) Sony Pictures was preparing its *Major Dundee* restoration at the same time and was eager for it to be included as part of the set, but it seems Warner couldn't be bothered to sort out the financial arrangements (which I'm told were quite generous to Warner).[8]

According to Nick, the Cannes Film Festival wanted to give Peckinpah a posthumous lifetime achievement award and was begging to premiere the 2005 Special Edition in connection with it. Incredibly, the studio refused to pay for a print. The final coup de grâce was that instead of releasing the set in the fall of 2005 so that it would be available in time for the holidays, the studio withheld it until the beginning of the following year, releasing it in what Nick aptly called "the toilet of January," the worst time to bring out any special product. But there was an unexpected development: despite Warner's best efforts to dump it on the market with as little fanfare as possible, a number of newspapers, magazines, and other sources picked it up and wrote about it. And twelve months later, when *Entertainment Weekly*, which the Warner

Home Video executives regard as the Bible of the industry, published its year-end roundup, Ken Tucker named the Peckinpah Westerns set the number one, as in the most important, DVD release of the year (112). The reaction at Warner? "The executives at domestic were apoplectic," Nick told me, "because they had done everything they could to ensure it would sink like a stone."

Since, for reasons already stated, a "restoration" as the term is commonly understood is impossible, can one be attempted? The question immediately begs another: which preview do you choose? An initial response is to say the second one, because it has the scene between Garrett and his wife. But it also contains clumsy, unfinished things, including decisions that have nothing to do with aesthetic considerations as such (e.g., the bogus historical note that initiates the end crawl); and there were several matters about which Peckinpah still had not made up his mind (notably music) and other things he wanted which were still not done (such as putting back the Ruthie Lee introduction). Even his thinking as regards the wife scene was at the time not entirely clear. Its removal from the first preview was almost certainly a mistake; but in the unlikely event that it wasn't, then it suggests he was at least entertaining thoughts of dropping it. If this is true, then his decision to put it back for the second preview is meaningful only inasmuch as one of the functions of multiple previews is to see how different versions play. All we know for certain is that about a year later he emphatically wanted it back in, though evidently not enough to make himself available when Dan Melnick handed him the opportunity.

But even to consider choices like these is to take the first step on the slippery slope of presuming we know what Peckinpah had in mind, are prepared to do his thinking for him, and can make these decisions in his stead. In other words, if the idea is to try to be as faithful as possible to what we know Peckinpah did and since it is further true that he refused to participate in the additional editing the studio demanded, then the only legitimacy the previews have consists precisely in their unfinished state: their status as works in progress left incomplete. They cannot be considered his "final" thoughts, merely his latest thoughts at that point in time. Arrogate to yourself the task of finishing the previews and, however good your intentions, you violate the only integrity they have. And every fact about his behavior during this crucial period suggests this is the way he wanted it. Meanwhile, regardless of the duress under which they edited it, the theatrical was a version that was actually fine-cut and finished by Peckinpah's closest editorial colleagues according to his style and sensibility. Disowned by the director—who more than likely never actually *watched* it—disdained by many, it seemed the perfect and logical vehicle to use as the platform for a special edition.

Since writing the essay for the *Peckinpah Today* anthology, I've revisited Sam's April 30, 1974, letter to Melnick for the purpose of inquiring whether it could serve as a guide for doing a "proper" restoration. My answer is a cautious "Yes, but." The letter calls for putting back the wife and Ruthie Lee scenes and leaving out both the deep lift in the latter part of the Garrett-McKinney scene in Roswell and the lift of the return to Rupert and the ride out of town. This much is clear. But there is much that is unclear. What does Sam mean by "replace the Chisum and water scenes," as they were already in both previews? The reference to a lift in the Wallace scene is also confusing. Does it refer to the "obsolete" line? But that was already long out of the previews. Does it refer to the line I restored to the special edition? Maybe, but a cut that short is typically called a trim or a pull, not a lift, which usually implies a larger or deeper cut. Or did he have in mind much bigger changes for this scene? After "re-examining" the Dylan vocals, would he have restored them under the death of Cullen Baker? What about the music being too thin in places? So far as I am aware, there is no way of "thickening" Dylan's score where it exists, unless there are elements that were not mixed in when it was recorded, which is unlikely. Or did Sam mean simply adding more music throughout the film, which the word "sweeten" suggests? If so, this in turn suggests something fairly elaborate, which I consider quite likely: given the film's unfinished state, once he and Garth really got down to business, I'd wager crisp new bills they would have done far more work than the twelve items in the letter because, refreshed after a year away on *Bring Me the Head of Alfredo Garcia*, a project he was really pleased with, and Aubrey no longer a toxic presence, Sam would not be able stop himself from improving *Pat Garrett* in all the ways it obviously needed improving, could not stop himself from making it the best film possible out of what he had shot.

Absent that, and in other words, if we were to prepare a version of the film using one of the previews and Sam's letter to Melnick, we would still have to rely on hunch, guesswork, and supposition, still have to make decisions on our own, and what we would be left with at the end of the day is yet another version that was completed without the director. All of which brings us right back to reality: the only versions of the film that have any integrity as regards Sam's direct, personal involvement are the two previews, which are unfinished.

The web is a great democratizing force, but one serious liability among many is that it allows anybody with a computer and time on his hands to appoint himself an expert and publish anything he likes. In many instances this is salutary, resulting in the dissemination of research and knowledge that wouldn't have surfaced in any other way and giving forums to points of view that need to be heard but would not likely be without it. In many other instances, however, it spreads misinformation, misrepresentation, half-truths, falsehoods, fantasies, and just plain lies because the contributors do not have to subject their work to peer review, fact-checking, or any of the other routine checks and balances which attempt to hold reporting, research, and scholarship accountable. Consider just one example of the kind of thing that passes for and is accepted as "information" or at least informed opinion on the web:

> Two different scenes in the Workprint [sic] appear to be unfinished because Peckinpah didn't shoot them to play on their own. John Poe's harassment of some old miners should intercut with Garrett's harassment of young prostitutes. Neither scene works well without intercutting the other. Instead, Seydor drops Poe's harassment of the old miners entirely, and then organizes all the footage of Garrett with the prostitutes into chronological order for his new version. Organizing the footage into chronological order is merely the first step toward intercutting the two scenes, and perhaps trimming the edges, but Seydor doesn't seem to realize that Peckinpah shot these sequences as two halves of a whole.[9]

Maybe one reason Seydor doesn't realize it is that Peckinpah himself didn't either. I have read every version of the screenplay in the Herrick and spoken at length with Rudolph Wurlitzer; I have read every page of Peckinpah's, Gordon Carroll's, Dan Melnick's, and the executives' editorial notes and memos in the Herrick and over the years spoken at length with all three editors, the producer, the studio executive in charge of the production, and the director himself; and I have never heard or come across even a hint of a suggestion that Peckinpah or anyone else connected with the film ever thought of intercutting those scenes. Perhaps needless to say, this commentator cites no source in support of his assertions.

Even the relatively few negative responses to the 2005 Special Edition from legitimate sources are based on no or insufficient research and are thus filled with so many errors of fact and assumption as to be worthless as anything except uninformed opinion. I've addressed most of these in this part of the book, particularly in the previous and next chapters. However, there remains a handful of items with respect to the special edition and to the audio commentaries on the DVDs that require clarification and correction. For one thing, in the audio commentaries, which were done in 2005, I asserted that Peckinpah participated in the editing of the theatrical. I was wrong about this, or, to be more precise, mostly wrong, which I explain in the next chapter.

For another, the 2005 Special Edition has been invidiously compared to Walter Murch's restoration of *Touch of Evil* because, it is asserted, Welles left detailed notes, whereas Peckinpah's were random, disorganized, and even chaotic. This is proffered with absolutely no reference to any facts or supporting evidence. The truth—as I've shown at length in the previous chapter and as is also plainly evident from the samples reproduced in this book—is that there is in the Herrick a folder of page after page of 8.5 × 11-inch sheets of Peckinpah's copious editing notes, which are for the most part clear, detailed, specific, and *typewritten*, by Katy Haber, who took them down as dictation, and which cover practically the entire postproduction editing of the film. It

ROGER

OPENING SEQUENCE Start on signle of chickens, go to wide shot of
group then to wide shot of chickens.
Then to Billy then to hit.
Loop "How long have I known you Peck"
Pick up dialogue over single on chicken and then to to two shot of
Peck and Garrett ie lose run by.
Shot of poe against sky out, use one that is already in for "Part of the
law".
From time Peck gets off lose guy aiming.
Lose gun not going off.
Have Garrett already falling.
As Garrett is on the ground have him move.
Intercut Garrett's dying more.

CANTINA C/U on "Brought you something down from Lincolcn".

POKER GAME Go completely back to original.

SECOND POKER SEQUENCE Don't need man mopping brown outside window.
Don't need Billy taking off handcuffs in close up.
Need insert of him unlocking footlocks.

LAVATORY
LAVATORY SEQUENCE Start sequence with shot of horses broncing, use
dialogue over horses and dissolve into them coming out of the door.
Don't let Billy reach for the gun let it be surprise.
As Billy comes out of Lav use previous cut of people watching.*
Don't need cutaways after Olinger's death
Don't let Dylan look away just keep him looking up.
Go back to Old Man after "Bring me an axe" ie. see him do it then
go to reactions.
Let Old Man say SI instead of "I understand".
As Old Man goes out have Billy already in motion.
Take heads off all crowd reactions.
Get Back to Billy much quicker after reactions.
"When I caught her " close up.
Use top shot of Ollinger coming out of saloon, through gallows.
Use more of Billy singing, 50% less of crowd reactions.

Billy's EXIT AND GARRETT'S ARRIVAL
Forget the Old Man leading the horse, start Billy coming out of door.
As he is bucked play Dylan watching.
Cut "Thanks Friend".
Can't use Dylan again he has already passed him.
"Old Bob" insert of Ollinger's body.
Trim head of Billy so he is in movement as he receives blanket.
Use shot him passing fires as he leaves.*
C/U on "Kid's gone Mr. Garrett" without pan.
Just use shot of Garrett starting to move, shot of Ollinger's body on
ground and straight to Mirror shot instead cantina.

INTERIOR CANTINA
Start with Dylan watching and making notes, then go to Garrett, then
to Jim Cannon moving in beside Garrett in wide shot.
Trim head of "Okay John".
After "Have a bath" go straight to two shot.
Use close up lines.
As Garrett stops and looks at hisehouse lose puff just throw away cigar.

As the first note indicates (*very top*), Peckinpah
experimented with establishing the chicken shoot in Fort
Sumner before going to the murder of Garrett.

EDITING NOTES TAKEN APRIL 2nd 3.30-8.00

Reel 1 Freezes should be sepia.
Put superimposed title over opening and start ride up closer.
Superimpose title over master Fort Sumner 1881.

Reel 9
Put in one of Billy's later ride bys.
Drop Poe and Pat ride by and just have a head on their arrival at Jones.
Lose Billy's ride by just see him arriving at Horrells.
Don't Lose "Thin as a snake" as per yesterdays notes.
Use close up on "Don't mind if I do..... never tasted anything so good"
Added line "If you run into Alamosa Bill tell him I'm looking for him"
to Poe.
After cut to Pat On "Laws a funny thing" go back to Alamosa in close up
then to Billy in close up.
LOOP Least I'll be remembered.
Trim XXXXXXX Billy's close ride out before long shot of him leaving Horrells

Reel 10
Lose close up of Dylan before he opens his jacket.
Trim "Do it"
Loop "Patronizing him real well" or check other take.
Trim head of Alias after hitting Beaver.
Loop Chill "Trying to drown you boy, getting his bark back etc...."
Loop chill breathing under hat.
Music cue to Jerry.
Loop Holly's groans.

Reel 11
Get to Bryson a little quicker
Drop "better take both", cut to Dub Taylor, "Sample cases" and go directly to
"I'll have some food, steak and eggs ...."
"Naked lady dialogue at end" keep track underneath throughout.
Lose "Never seen such a bunch of churn headed etc....... and go directly
to Dub.
Put back in "Man woman or beast" without "Furthermore"
Fix so Levy doesn't lie down at all.
Repeat "When the road" over Pat.
Raft sequence. Hold longer on end, by adding too more cuts.
Hello Billy and Hello Paco over Billy and Yolanda's close ups.
After Billy stabs knife, LOOP I'm going back" show him getting on horse
Yolanda looks up at him and he rides through sheep.
Music cue.
 Loop Paco's lines.
Lose second of the ride by's and put in static shot of Billy just sitting.
LOOP line over Billy's back after he returns "Paco's dead.

Reel 12
Trim Pat signing the register.
Lose "Howdie yourself Pat" and "I wasn't going to come up but I figured
you'd find me anyway" and go straight to "which way do you want to go.?
Trim Garrett "You'll have to do better than that"
Wild lines and ad libs needed for orgy sequence " Ah yes, where's the bottle
etc, etc.
Bottle shoot. Don't bring Dylan up onto the wall. Either remove
Maria completely or get some different loop lines.
13. Lose "South Texas shindig" dialogue.
 Put in beat at end of "Spell my name right in the papers.
Hang on "I reckon" then go to guys on the trough and end scene there
Hang on Billy longer in between woods sequences.
Let all three of them walk out of the woods, see Pat get up.

In this set of notes some six weeks later, Peckinpah
called for a loop line from Billy, "I'm going back," spoken
after Paco dies (*midway down, under "Reel 11"*).

is also true that Sam's behavior on this project was hardly consistently reliable or some of the time even responsible, and there are notes in which his meaning is not entirely clear—something true from time to time of notes by every director everywhere—but there is none I've ever seen that is positively incoherent. However chaotic the editorial *process* was on this film, his notes were not: the suggestion that they consisted in rambling dribs and drabs, scribbled in the margins of scripts and on whatever scraps of paper he had at hand—should we also add cocktail napkins, matchbook covers, and credit card receipts?—is so grossly at variance with any known account or available evidence of the way he worked with his editors as to suggest that, like those self-appointed experts on the Internet, even the occasional academic is not above making things up when it suits his or her purposes. Peckinpah's life was extraordinarily disorganized in lots of ways and he often liked to create chaos on the set for creative reasons; but when he commented on screenplays or gave notes to his colleagues, he was articulate, remarkably well organized, and to the point.[10] Even on those occasions when he eschewed detail because he wasn't sure what he was after and/or because he wanted to encourage his colleagues' creativity, he was nevertheless usually specific in articulating general points. And in my own experience, whether in interview or by correspondence, he was always focused and answered questions clearly, thoughtfully, and intelligently. Garner Simmons, who knew Sam far longer than anyone else who's written a book on him (except Max Evans), tells me that this jibes with his experience from the beginning of their friendship, which started in August 1973, just three months after *Pat Garrett* opened.

As regards comparisons to the restorations of *Touch of Evil* and *Vertigo*, here is part of an email the critic Michael Sragow wrote to Michael Bliss, the editor of *Peckinpah Today*, shortly after the anthology was published:

> It so happens I followed each of those reconstructions/restorations closely and enthusiastically, writing 6000-word cover pieces on them for *San Francisco Weekly*. I applauded both those editions. But it must be said: Murch had to be more interventionist than Paul—[have Paul's critics] ever READ that famous 60-page Welles memo?—and Universal went to greater lengths than Warners did with *Pat Garrett* to present Murch's cut as a director-preferred version. (Many critics preferred the theatrical cut.) And Harris and Katz's decision to include new foley on *Vertigo* was widely damned (wrongly, to my mind) by Hitchcock-philes and NEVER INDICATED ANYWHERE ON THE REISSUE'S ADS OR PACKAGING. It's almost like a Nabokovian comedy: Paul does the LEAST amount of editing he could and insists that prior versions be preserved . . . and gets pilloried . . .

There is a widespread assumption that Peckinpah regarded the previews as his "final cut," perhaps because David Weddle uses the term in his biography

(482) and also because in *Reconsideration* (300) I wrote that Peckinpah "often showed, without apology, the preview print." But Weddle's use of the term "final cut"—he also uses "fine cut"—is in specific reference to the March 13, 1973, executives' screening, which was around 2:40 in length. For that reason *alone*, Peckinpah couldn't—and wouldn't—have considered it a final or fine cut; for another, he continued absolutely uncoerced to work on the editing for almost two full months. To take just three of the most obvious examples, this cut contained some version of the line-by-line intercutting of Jones's Saloon and Horrell's Trading Post, which we know he ultimately rejected; it certainly had dialogue in the raft scene, which we also know he later told the editors to remove; and Tuckerman's Hotel was longer and so unwieldy that even he found it impossible to defend. If he ever did actually state this version was his final or fine cut—and there is absolutely no evidence that he did—it would have been only to gall James Aubrey, not because he thought it so.

As for his showing the second preview unapologetically the rest of his life, yes, this is true as far as it goes, but putting it that way is also misleading because predicated upon information I didn't have at the time I wrote *Reconsideration* or did the audio commentaries. One thing I didn't know then is that, according to Don Hyde, after the second preview, the print was never again shown in a theater or screening room publicly or privately in Sam's lifetime. What he did do, beginning in 1980, is give videotape copies, made by Hyde, to friends and colleagues.[11] But Sam was more than likely also being to some extent opportunistic here—it was the only version he had, after all—and possibly self-serving: it was easy for him to stand by this version when there was little chance of anyone seeing it. By the time he started handing out tapes, it was only *after* he had begun to realize that critical opinion on the film was shifting upward as the years went by. And make no mistake, Sam kept up with his critics—he always did. But from preproduction through to the release and for a good long time afterward, there is a great deal of circumstantial and anecdotal evidence to suggest he was considerably less confident about just what he had wrought—some would argue he was not sure at all and was thus glad for the escape hatch that Aubrey provided. Why else would he have spurned Melnick's offer scarcely a year later to finish the film as he wished? If it is thought that all this is mere conjecture, know that it is a conjecture not just shared but openly expressed by many, perhaps most who knew him well at the time.[12]

Does the 2005 Special Edition artificially quicken the pace of a film that isn't quickly paced? Not at all. The whole issue of the pacing of the several versions of this film has been obfuscated by a lot of rewriting of history. For one thing, the early negative reviewers of *Pat Garrett* complained *much* less about any narrative incoherence and gaps in the continuity than about how dull and boring they thought it was—even Roger Ebert and Pauline Kael, two of Peckinpah's longtime champions, shared in this judgment—and this was the *theatrical* version they were referring to.[13] The truth is that nobody can make *Pat Garrett* a fast-paced film, which even Aubrey discovered with his ninety-six-minute attempt (and which is why he sought help from Sam's crew), and nobody else tried, least of all Sam's editors when they fine-cut it or me when I prepared the special edition. There is quite a chasm between a film that is slackly paced with loose, sagging rhythms and the same film when it is measured, lyrical, ruminative, with open, elastic rhythms that are also controlled. Yet there seems to be a certain cast of mind that must reflexively think "quick" every time "slow" is used, "tight" if "loose" is said, and if "pace" or its variants are written, then a modifier like "fast" is automatically supplied—as if there weren't infinitely subtle degrees of variation between the extremes or a mean that would feel "just right," as in, appropriate to the material and the desired effect.

Another argument is that the 2005 Special Edition turns an unconventional film into a conventional one by making it a "commercial mainstream" film. Not only does this seem to me rooted in snobbery and muddled thinking, I can't even follow its logic: adding material to the theatrical, which was all that was done to arrive at the special edition, makes it *more* conventional and commercial? To start with, even in its theatrical version *Pat Garrett and Billy the Kid* is a very unusual film, one that is hardly "conventional" in any pejorative sense. Peckinpah was a fine artist and on occasion a great one, with an unusually personal and individual vision, considerable integrity, and certain traits of personality and temperament that made life very difficult for him in the American film industry. Yet he aspired to that industry and once he gained access, he remained there for the rest of his life.[14] Like most of the great American directors—no need to name them, I mean all the usual suspects—he made films that are mainstream, commercial films in the sense that they were financed and/or released by major studios and were expected to or at least hoped would generate returns that were profitable. As a project *Pat Garrett and Billy the Kid* was no different in this regard—in fact, in both inception and conception, an argument could be made that it was *less* different than several of his others were: despite some concerns about the commercial viability of the screenplay (at least before the revisions and the signing of Peckinpah), the subject was the most famous and favorite outlaw of the Old West used as a veiled symbol for declining rock stars; Peckinpah was hired because he was an A-list director (notably of Westerns), prestigious and bankable, whose participation alone guaranteed it would be treated as an "important" picture and would help attract serious filmgoers; Coburn was counted upon to bring in the mainstream audience; Kristofferson was there, not to mention Dylan, to pull in the youth, rock, and counterculture crowd; and the high-profile supporting cast, headed by Jason Robards, Katy Jurado, Slim Pickens, and so on, made it look "distinguished." Man, from the standpoint of the box office, this picture was *covered*.

That was the thinking from the studio side, while for their parts Peckinpah and Rudolph Wurlitzer were pursuing a personal vision, and probably neither paid much attention one way or another to the box office, being more interested in telling the story they wanted to tell. In other words, what we have here is an almost banally commonplace scenario for artists and serious filmmaking in Hollywood. In the event, Peckinpah brought back a film that turned out to be a difficult sell, but this didn't owe to any *deliberate* attempt to make it so—everybody, including Peckinpah and Wurlitzer, wanted it to be successful both financially and critically and Gordon Carroll thought it was going to be "a fabulous picture," by which he meant not just a really good one but financially successful too, just as Phil Feldman, who called the screenplay of *The Wild Bunch* a "gasser," thought it was going to be another *Dirty Dozen* at the box office. Things turned out differently. Of course, they often turned out differently for Peckinpah because he pursued his vision where it took him. Nor would he bow merely to the box office, though a much more accurate way of putting this would be to observe he wouldn't bow to the *moneymen's notions about the box office.* The truth is, there is no way of knowing how well *Pat Garrett* might have done if the release hadn't been rushed, if the director and his editors had the time to do it right, and if the studio had blessed it with the TLC in distribution and promotion it obviously needed and warranted.[15]

The year *Pat Garrett and Billy the Kid* was released the following dozen films were also released, the titles selected from a comprehensive database of all American films released in 1973 (I could have chosen any several different dozen): *American Graffiti, Badlands, The Friends of Eddie Coyle, The Last American Hero, The Last Detail, The Long Goodbye, Mean Streets, Save the Tiger, Serpico, Sleeper, The Sting,* and *The Way We Were.* Some of these were box-office hits, some failures; some are serious, some frivolous; some are genre films, others not; some are dramas, others comedies; some move fast, some slow; some are "personal" projects, others studio projects. However their ultimate status as works of art in the grand scheme of things is judged, one thing they all have in common is that each and every one of them is a commercial mainstream American film financed and/or distributed by the major studios at the time. It is simplistic and condescending to pretend that good, serious, and great work is not possible in the so-called commercial mainstream when our every experience—from opera, the concert hall, and traditional theater to contemporary films and even television and cable—furnishes evidence to the contrary. (As Northrop Frye observed of Shakespeare [*Natural Perspective* 38], "His chief motive in writing, apparently, was to make money, which is the best motive for writing yet discovered, as it creates exactly the right blend of detachment and concern.")

Finally, it has been suggested that when the brief epilogue is deleted in favor of the theatrical ending, then the circular structure is lost, the story itself is turned into a simple flashback, and the narrative becomes merely conventionally linear. First, the epilogue wasn't "deleted" because it was never in the theatrical to begin with. Second, the theatrical ending was *not* retained; it was instead replaced by an existing *alternative* theatrical ending that didn't use the smiling two-shot of Garrett and Billy, a personal selection by Aubrey that the editors hated. (Consistent with how little informed they are, these commentators seem unaware there were two theatrical endings—one prepared by the editors, based on the screenplay, and actually shot by the director to *be* the closing image; the other insisted upon by Aubrey—even though I described them in *Reconsideration* [302] and on the DVD audio commentaries.) Third, regarding the epilogues, perhaps I should toss this one back to my critics. Which do you want: the one in the first preview, without Sam's petty, historically inaccurate note, or the one in the second, with the note?

As for the matters of structure, flashback, and linear narrative, maybe we need to get the picture in focus. If the body of the film—that is, the opening reunion in Fort Sumner through to the ending death in the same place—as enclosed in the previews by the moment of Garrett's death, is not a simple flashback, then what is it? It's certainly not complex, complicated, or multifaceted, like, say, the series of flashbacks and other time-shifting devices in *Citizen Kane* or *8½*. If the *Pat Garrett* flashback has any distinction vis-à-vis conventional flashbacks, it can only consist in how much time is allowed to pass—in effect, the whole film—between the dissolve into it and the dissolve back out, though even a delay that long has plenty of antecedents (*Sunset Boulevard* or *Battle of Algiers* anyone?). The same is true when the epilogue is not there, as in the 2005 Special Edition: the body of the film is *still* a simple, albeit very long flashback, though—it almost pains me to have to point this out—not dissolving back out of it actually makes it *less* conventional than bracketing it with an epilogue (let alone one this transparently makeshift). Regarding the linearity of the narrative that makes up the body of the film, whether there's a closed frame, an open frame, or no frame, it's *still a linear narrative* because one thing happens after another in chronological order with no time shifting. There does happen to be a circular structure built into this narrative, which I will show in the next chapter, but some critics appear to be so fixated upon the frame they're blind to the picture inside in it.

Far too many academic critics seem able to think about films only spatially, that is, as constructions to behold and analyze after the experience of watching them has passed, indeed, in which the motor experience, as it were, of the watching is quite forgotten. But the temporal experience profoundly impacts meaning because, like music, dance, opera, and theater, films are an art conditioned by time and one that we experience fully only in a predetermined block of time the duration of which we have little or no control over. For this reason and others, concerns such as tempo, pace, rhythm, and overall length are of the essence. In much academic and also fan-based commentary I am often struck by the fact that relatively little is written about how scenes or films as a whole *play*, even though directors and film editors typically work harder on that and shaping performances than on almost anything else. Peckinpah was not only very demanding in this regard, he was even more fanatical about it than most.

This deficiency—if I am right in calling it a deficiency—in such criticism and commentary is related to a much larger subject that can only be touched upon here: the radical shift during the last quarter century in how movies have gone from being communal experiences in theaters to private experiences in homes. How a film plays, the way it is experienced, and what it means cannot be fully discussed without also taking into consideration the conditions under which it is viewed. This is especially relevant to any discussion of *Pat Garrett and Billy the Kid*. As scholars, critics, and movie lovers we are all properly outraged when films are taken away from directors and reedited without their consent. But another way in which films are distorted all the time is rarely remarked upon. For the last twenty years, as revival houses close and prints become scarcer (the studios no longer finding it profitable to generate new ones when there is so little demand for them), we are more and more forced to watch films of the past at home. This is an experience that is quite at variance with what Peckinpah and other directors of his generation and previous ones had in mind or likely even imagined as a possibility when they made their films. We must all of course be grateful for advances in technology which now make it possible to watch films at home on larger screens or at least screens with the correct aspect-ratio and with a degree of resolution unprecedented in consumer equipment, and we must be more grateful for the sheer number and variety of films that are now available quickly, easily, and inexpensively. But even home theaters with very large screens and front projection still cannot replicate the experience of seeing a movie in a public theater.

The loss of the theatergoing experience was of great concern to Peckinpah, who despaired of cable television and the rise of videocassettes (he never lived to see laser discs and DVDs, let alone streaming, electronic tablets, smart phones, and other portable devices that make it possible to reduce the grandest of cinematic epics to Lilliputian dimensions). As a man of the theater he believed passionately in the value to society of the communal experience of films and plays. "One of the great things about going to a movie or the theater is the act itself," he once said, "the getting out, the buying of the tickets, the sharing of the experience with a lot of other people. Eighty percent of the people who watch television watch it in groups of three or less, and one of those three is half stoned" (Murray 119).[16] It was not just the loss of the social aspect of moviegoing that worried him, because the social experience has aesthetic implications. I'll wager that few of the younger critics, scholars, and fans who've written about *Pat Garrett and Billy the Kid* have ever seen it on a big screen, so they've never experienced the full effect of Coquillon's magnificently atmospheric cinematography, so compromised in the current DVD transfers and on small screens. This is one reason I always try to see *Pat Garrett* when it's shown in revival houses, even though it's "only" the theatrical version, because that is the only version for which correctly timed film prints were struck. Yes, crucial scenes are missing, so the fullness of Peckinpah's vision is betrayed; but if the print is decent or better, the purely cinematic aspect of the experience is overwhelming, and this honors his vision in a different way.

If many who've written about the film haven't seen it on the big screen, then it's also likely they've never seen it with an audience. If I am correct, then they have at best only an imperfect basis for evaluating how well or poorly it plays. The main reason for this is of course that home viewing rarely allows for a film to be watched all the way through without interruption. Marshall McLuhan was doubtless right when he suggested that a television is another guest in the house or member of the family, to be accorded no more or less respect or privilege than anyone else. When enthusiasts gather to watch a film—significantly, they often refer to it as a "video" rather than a film, a movie, or even a flick—it's almost certain to be disrupted by comments in passing, paused for conversation or refreshments, or in effect altered by playing favorite scenes over again or skipping several scenes to advance to other favorites. Indeed, from one point of view, the entire technology of DVDs, with their chapter divisions and remote handsets that provide instant access to any chapter, has been designed to encourage us *not* to watch the film as a whole but to treat it as if it's a collection of its own greatest hits. (One reason so many movies are now released on DVD with additional scenes is not that directors necessarily want those scenes in their films, rather that fans want it all—the more there is to talk about, the longer the party. Of course, the studios usually withhold extended editions until after the theatrical versions have been released, thus forcing consumers to buy the movie again, only for more money, if they want the extras.)

There is one particular long-range effect of the pacing of *Pat Garrett and Billy the Kid* that cannot be fully experienced in any other way than by watching it all the way through without interruption, or at least long segments of it. I have elsewhere commented upon the tremendous leverage Peckinpah gets from time (*Reconsideration* 201–2, 244–45, 301). No filmmaker is his peer when it comes to manipulating it: real time, theatrical time, cinematic time, compressed time, elongated time. There is a subtle but very powerful tension that is built up between the slow basic pulse of the drama and our foreknowledge of how it must end. Gordon Carroll once described the film to me as "a man who doesn't want to run being chased by a man who doesn't want to catch him." To this end, the entire structure is predicated upon a series of delays, drawings out, and procrastinations, on circlings, detours, doublings back, and long roundabouts, all of which are of no avail in preventing the catastrophe that concludes the tragic action. The only way this can be felt fully is by watching the whole film uninterrupted. If this is not done, then it is not felt; and if it is not felt, then the disparity between the characters' illusions of control over their destinies and their actual lack of it is something we merely "understand" as a thematic or intellectual concept—it's not something we've felt emotionally as the function of a dramatic experience. And as Peckinpah himself liked to say, for him, "feeling it" is what his films are all about.

I by no means wish to suggest that a lot of the writing on *Pat Garrett* is compromised because the writers have based their work insufficiently on the theatrical experience or have not had that experience at all. On the contrary, much of this writing has greatly increased our understanding and appreciation of Peckinpah's work. Nor would I like my remarks to be construed as some sort of jeremiad against television, which I watch quite a lot, and, as with most filmmakers and people seriously involved in film and film studies, it is where I watch most films more than a few years old and with great pleasure. I am merely suggesting that most cinema remains stubbornly a performance-based art form, that it derives much of its beauty and its power to move, enthrall, and overwhelm us from this, and that we do well to remember that it finds its fullest expression when its integrity as a theatrical experience is honored. Films are, of course, no more exempt than the other performing arts from having to adapt to changing conditions of financing, marketing, the market itself, audiences, and new technology, including new means of reproduction and presentation, and society itself. But to recognize these changes, accept them, and make the most of them does not require us to deny the reality of our experiences from watching films the traditional way.

People are often surprised when I tell them that I have never, ever, even once, watched *The Wild Bunch* from start to finish at home. This is because *The Wild Bunch* is shown frequently enough at revival houses where I can see it the way I want to see it (in Los Angeles typically once a year or more often). At home, even with the finest equipment on the largest domestic screens, *The Wild Bunch* is not *The Wild Bunch*—it is only a simulacrum of *The Wild Bunch*. To be sure, it'll do, but why should I have to settle for that when I can still see it like it used to be, on a big screen in a theater with an audience, which is how Peckinpah meant for it to be seen? He would have wanted no less for *Pat Garrett and Billy the Kid* and all the rest of his films.

Peckinpah with his Garrett, James Coburn, and his Billy, Kris Kristofferson

CHAPTER NINE

The 2005 Special Edition

Some of the very same people who've complained about the 2005 Special Edition have also paid me the somewhat contradictory compliment of suggesting I do a full-scale restoration of the 1988 Turner Preview Version. I fully concur that the Turner preview should have been—and now should be—accorded the respect of a proper finish in the strictly *technical* sense of correctly timing the picture, mixing the sound, and fixing the egregious carelessness of the transfer for the box set. But for reasons already stated in the previous chapter, I would draw the line at making any substantive changes in scenes or sequences. The only exceptions I would make are two. The first is the wife scene, which I twice tried to persuade Warners to restore to the Turner preview, but the home video division wanted the special edition to have that as an exclusive cachet. My reason for granting this exception is because its removal at the time almost certainly owed to miscommunication (i.e., Sam's reference to the "foul up" in his letter to Dan Melnick[1]). I would also restore the Ruthie Lee scene for the same reason. But otherwise, any further editing, trimming, or rearranging of scenes and sequences would be presumptuous.

Why? Because once Sam left the picture, who better than his editors and Melnick to carry out the trimming, tightening, and remaining fine-cutting the previews needed? Bob Wolfe was the second editor on *The Wild Bunch* (and edited almost all of the final battle), a principal editor on *Straw Dogs* and *The Getaway*, and the coeditor on *Junior Bonner*. Roger Spottiswoode was the third editor hired on *Straw Dogs*, but he was the one Sam brought back with Bob from England to help with the fine cut, and he was Bob's coeditor on *The Getaway*.[2] Dan Melnick produced *Noon Wine* and *Straw Dogs*. When they brought *Straw Dogs* back to America, Sam went almost immediately to Arizona to start filming *Junior Bonner* and left Bob and Roger to finish the editing under Melnick's supervision with Sam's blessing. I am not suggesting they edited the film without Sam. On several weekends they flew to Arizona to run cut sequences for him and get his notes, and once principal photography was completed he returned to Los Angeles where they could work again in proximity. But with respect to *Pat Garrett*, this is precisely the point: he had already been working with them since editing began back in November, and this was in any case standard operating procedure for him, as it is for most directors: watch, give notes, let the editors make the changes, then approve, disapprove, or modify, and go forward.

The notion that many people, including a shocking number of academics and worshipful fans, have of directors looking over their editors' shoulders, meticulously selecting takes, dictating cut points, choosing reaction shots, deciding when to play lines offscreen, timing how long pauses will be played, and so on, almost never happens—it's certainly never happened to me or other editors I know—even with so-called auteur directors.[3] One reason for this is practical: editing begins as soon as the first full set of dailies comes in (typically one or two days after the footage is shot, though on distant locations like Mexico, where customs are involved, it can take as long as a week, and most of the time did on *Pat Garrett*). Within a week or so of the completion of principal photography, the editor is expected to have a first cut—usually called the "editor's cut"—with temporary music and sound effects, ready to show the director. This is the cut in which most editors, myself included, make a diligent attempt to include and make play everything that is in the script. Then directors start giving notes on these and many other matters in varying degrees of detail, depending on everything from the needs of the scene to the temperament, style, and available time of the directors themselves. But often they will give only general notes about trimming and tightening: "This needs to move along," "Can we tighten this?" "Let's lose this," "Is there a better place for this scene?" "Is this working as well as it can?" and so on. All films run long in first cuts because all the scenes and dialogue from the script are generally in them (assuming they were filmed). Only on the rarest of occasions have I ever had directors want to review a series of takes to decide upon a line reading or a reaction (which isn't to suggest that they haven't watched the dailies on their own). This is because they value the distance and objectivity on the material that is afforded by their *not* being involved in the meticulous details of cutting or the minutiae of editing, which is part of the editor's job. It is also because directors soon learn that if they want the best, most creative work from their collaborators, acting like a helicopter is just about the most counterproductive way of getting it.

In my own work (which includes over twenty-four films, most of them features), once the first cut has been screened, my directors and I usually know without having to do a whole lot of talking about it when this or that scene needs to be shortened, and far oftener than not I will do it on my own or be asked to do it on my own and then run it for them. Much of the time in the second and subsequent cuts they're not even aware of what I've removed, which is of course always both instructive and flattering. But since even in postproduction directors have a lot to attend to beyond the editing—and it's easy to forget what was in a scene if it happens to be playing well, especially if they watch several scenes or a whole reel at once—it is my practice always to remind them of what I've taken out just in case I've removed a line here or a moment there that they might especially value but didn't notice had been removed.

This is the way Sam worked with his editors, especially while they were preparing their first cuts, and it is the way I learned to work when I began editing for Roger Spottiswoode once he became a director.[4] It's not an exaggeration to say that Sam trusted Bob, Roger, and Dan Melnick with his films more than anybody else in the world up to that point in his career, and he soon came to feel the same about Garth.[5] In 1977 Bob Wolfe told me that in the relatively short span of time between *The Wild Bunch* and *Pat Garrett* he noticed Sam was spending less and less time in the cutting rooms. This is true of many directors as they get older or become more experienced, and it doesn't mean they don't care about the editing of their films—far from it. It means rather that when they find colleagues they feel they can trust, they have more confidence in delegation. Not for nothing are director-editor relationships often likened to marriages. Directing feature films is an unbelievably high-pressure job. When directors find colleagues they really like, admire, and trust in principal positions—cinematographer, production designer, production sound-mixer, costume designer, first assistant director, editor, sound designer, rerecording mixers, and so forth—many sources of worry and anxiety are lightened or banished entirely. If a theatrical release of *Pat Garrett* had to be prepared without Sam, the job could not have fallen to better hands.

The reality, however, is that the theatrical version was prepared without Sam mostly because he refused to give an inch for so long that he wound up boxing himself into a corner. Late the night of the second preview, after the audience had dispersed and the personnel handing out the questionnaires and monitoring the focus group were gone, Sam invited some colleagues, close friends, and family to gather in his office at the studio. "Everyone was very quiet," his nephew David Peckinpah told David Weddle. "Sam said, 'They've taken it away from me. They're recutting it right now.' Everyone was crowding around him; it had a very wakelike atmosphere, it was strange. I could see it in his face, he was broken" (484). I've been told about that evening many times by several persons who were there, and their recollections are in remarkable agreement: scarcely any of them could remember when they had ever seen a man who looked so completely as if he had lost everything as Sam looked to them that night. It was as moving a scene as they had ever witnessed. How could it not have been? It was staged by a master director. In putting it this way, I intend no mockery, sarcasm, or suggestion of disingenuousness on

Sam's part: it was surely as black a night as he had ever experienced, he was devastated, and it is impossible not to be heartbroken by his situation. But for those familiar with the whole story, and this included some family members, the source of their heartbreak was less the fate of the film than Sam's own share in having brought himself to this terrible place. "I knew his pain was real," one of his colleagues said, "but a lot of it was self-inflicted."

There are several myths about *Pat Garrett and Billy the Kid* that are still widely held to be true. Two of the most persistent are that Sam was fired and in some accounts even barred from the lot and that the studio took the film away from him and began recutting it. The first is untrue: Sam was never fired and he was never barred from the lot or locked out of the editing rooms; he continued to have an office there and he came to it most days, maybe even every day. The second is true only in a very qualified sense: Aubrey's studio editors had not up to this point yet touched the *work print*, which in those days was the master working-copy for any film still in the process of being edited, only black-and-white dupes made from it. Could Sam have reinvolved himself in the editing if he had wanted to, perhaps with Melnick interceding on his behalf with Aubrey, or had he simply burned too many bridges? Was working covertly with the editors a possibility (as it was unlikely Aubrey would ever have come down to the cutting rooms—executives at his level almost never do)? These are unanswerable because by then Sam had so thoroughly antagonized Aubrey, often gratuitously, that Weddle's portrait (485–88) of a vengeful Aubrey who smelled blood, Sam's blood, and wasn't about to relent is all too easy to believe.[6] Yet according to Roger, the editors believed that Aubrey, though fit to be tied by Sam's refusal to show up for his own two previews, would still have preferred a face-saving agreement for both sides, which just might still have been possible if only Sam had made a few concessions.

This makes sense in view of how the scenario for the remaining editing eventually played itself out. To start with, though Aubrey was often called a sonovabitch, few ever called him stupid. He knew he needed Peckinpah's name at the box office: *The Getaway* had just done spectacular business; *The Wild Bunch* was a tremendously prestigious film and along with *Straw Dogs* one of the most talked about of the period. However much Aubrey may have hated Sam, he knew he could never get away with releasing a version that was not at least recognizably A Sam Peckinpah Film. Did he ever have any real intention of releasing the ninety-six-minute cut he had the studio editors prepare or was this just a threat to demonstrate the kind of power he had if he cared to use it? He was no doubt tempted: the day after the second preview was May 11, a mere twelve days before the picture had to be in theaters, and his studio was still without a releasable movie for the important late spring/ early summer slot. One reason for his almost panicked urgency is that the only other picture in the pipeline that might have been substituted had run into so many problems of its own that it couldn't be ready until midsummer.[7] Worse, Aubrey had to show some cash, any cash, on the books owing to debts being run up building the MGM Grand Hotel in Las Vegas, and his sole source for that was the box office. Call it luck of the draw, the wrong place at the wrong time, or Sam's karma, but *Pat Garrett and Billy the Kid* became the center of this perfect storm of cross-purposes, conflicting necessities, and warring priorities.

Of the three principal editors, only Bob Wolfe was ever approached by the studio to watch the ninety-six-minute cut. As I understand it, since his salary was paid by MGM, not the production company as such, he was not in much of a position to refuse the request; and as a responsible professional he wouldn't have been inclined to anyhow, however personally distasteful it was to him. He was appalled by what he saw and told his colleagues it was a mess—which was at once the expected response and the hoped-for reaction, because Aubrey still wanted the people who really knew what they were doing, preferably Sam, but if not Sam, then Sam's editors, to finish the work. How they did it was their business, just so long as it got done in time. Was his threat to release the ninety-six-minute version a bluff? Impossible to say because nobody called him on it, which is probably what he was gambling on.

I once worked for a producer who said he loved negotiating with artists because the real ones always cared more about the work than about anything else, including and especially the money. This was the kind of man Aubrey was, and the ace he held was his near certainty that he could count on how much Sam's colleagues loved him, were loyal to him (despite his behavior), cared about the film, and were prepared to do to keep it (and him) from being destroyed. They rose admirably, in my view heroically, to the occasion, which only raises the question of where Sam himself was. I do not mean this literally—he was in his office, of course—but psychologically or spiritually. In all the behind-the-scenes stories I've heard and read about *Pat Garrett and Billy the Kid* in postproduction, there is one figure who seems to be conspicuously absent: the Peckinpah of the impassioned anger, the infamous temper, the fearsome rages. When Sam let that Peckinpah loose, studio people usually quaked in their boots. Aubrey was a bully and like many bullies he understood and responded to force. I've often wondered how he might have behaved in those meetings or at those screenings where he was so obnoxious, loud-mouthed, and abusive if Sam himself had been in attendance—a celebrity director with serious access to the media and real personal authority, plus a ferocity that almost certainly exceeded Aubrey's own. Where was that Peckinpah? To pose such a question is only to ask again why Sam behaved the way he did on this project, though one answer was certainly sheer exhaustion owing to overwork, fatigue, illness, and of course alcohol.

When I first met Roger in 1977, he painted a fairly intense picture of bargaining sessions in which Aubrey was so obnoxious that all anybody wanted was to get the work finished as fast as possible consistent with doing a good job so they could leave and get on with their lives. But in the years since, with the advantage of distance from the intensity of the circumstances, Roger has elaborated upon his recollections with a more detailed and nuanced account of the whole experience. Bob returned from the screening of the studio editors' cut with a promise from Aubrey that it would never be released, shown, or used if Sam's editing crew would make some changes, which the editors themselves could select from the studio's list of suggestions. This list contained some scenes that Aubrey apparently wanted out because he knew Sam especially wanted them in, but nothing was absolutely insisted upon. The highest priorities for Aubrey were two: overall length, which was to be around a hundred minutes, and a coherent film. From the evidence of the theatrical and my interviews both early and recent with the editors, Aubrey appears to have kept his word: nothing of the ninety-six-minute cut was used in any way to shape, guide, or form the theatrical (in fact, Roger never saw that cut, Bob never watched it again, I don't know if Melnick ever watched it, and for all anyone knows it was thrown away almost immediately).

This is yet further evidence for why it is not only factually mistaken but insulting to Spottiswoode, Wolfe, and Melnick to refer to the theatrical, as some critics continue to do, as the "Aubrey" version, let alone a "mutilated" or "butchered" one. Once Roger and Bob started in on their work, they had almost no direct dealings with Aubrey because Melnick ran interference. It's not even known for certain if Aubrey ever screened the changes. Roger certainly can't remember that the studio head ever came down to the cutting rooms to watch them, which means that the only place he could have seen them was in one of the screening rooms, which again Roger can't remember setting up (as the chief editor he would have been responsible for seeing to it that such screenings were scheduled), Bob and Melnick are no longer around to ask, and Garth doesn't know because he had left by then. There were rumors that Aubrey ordered additional changes after Roger and Bob turned over their cut; but so far as I have been able to determine, again from numerous conversations with Roger over many years, there is only one thing Aubrey later ordered changed. Once the prologue was removed, the epilogue had to go as well, so Roger used the image Sam originally shot for the end: Garrett riding off into the desert. In what was probably a desperate attempt to give summer audiences a "feel good" ending, Aubrey personally demanded the addition of the freeze-frame of a smiling Garrett and Billy from the first Fort Sumner scene. The editors, Roger in particular, hated it, and I cannot imagine that Sam would have approved, if he ever saw it. (The substitution involved a dissolve transition and the overlay of the end crawl, but ordering up an optical like that was the sort of task an assistant editor routinely handled and probably did.) Also, when would Aubrey have found the *time* to order additional changes? Between updating the sound and music units, patching the dub, timing the film, and generating and delivering release prints, everybody was already up against the wall by the time of the previews.

Roger and Bob finished their work in an unbelievably short period of time, fewer than twelve days, and I suspect fewer even than that. In the end, no doubt aided and abetted by Melnick's negotiating, they gained more than they yielded: Aubrey originally wanted thirty minutes removed and settled for twenty, for a final theatrical length of 1:46, down from 2:06.[8] If ten minutes doesn't seem like much, remember that it's enough to include the Ida, Ruthie Lee, and Chisum scenes and also the raft episode (further evidence that Aubrey, who hated this scene, was not insistent as to the specifics of what came out or was left in).[9] When I told Roger these numbers, he was surprised, thinking they had removed rather more. Much of the theatrical version appears to have been guided by Melnick's earlier notes, this not because he was taking advantage of Sam's absence to get his own way but because his notes made sense given the task at hand: the prologue, epilogue, and scenes involving Ida, Chisum, the prostitutes' montage, and Tuckerman's were obvious candidates *because they could be easily lifted with little or no disruption to the continuity.*

The raft scene was another possible lift for the same reason, but Roger and Melnick couldn't bring themselves to remove it, even though they believed it still wasn't working as placed in the previews. It's perfectly clear why: it comes too late, and is further crippled because it's flanked by the two weakest scenes (Tuckerman's Hotel and Paco's death). *Pat Garrett* is not plot driven in the normal sense of the word, and its pacing will never—can never and shouldn't—be fast. But the interlocked scenes of Garrett killing Holly and Billy killing Alamosa are point-of-no-return moments for each man and the action at large; as such, dramatic logic requires that the tempo, if not quicken, at least intensify to reflect the increased urgency. The last thing there is any time to play is a leisurely scene that doesn't advance us toward the final confrontation. The solution lay in the strategy they had already tried but without going far enough: move it earlier, only now *way* earlier, between Billy's escape from Lincoln and before Poe links up with Garrett. Once this was done, the scene was able to fulfill its function as the lyrical interlude always intended because it now comes at the point in the story when Garrett is still trying to give the Kid as much time as he can to clear out of the territory.

Removing scenes still did not get the film down to the demanded length, so the editors started trimming moments and cutting lines. Again, it's impossible to determine how much of this was on the studio list and how much the editors did on their own. Roger recalls that the studio was responsible for next to nothing of the specifics, that is, the actual selection of lines to be cut or bits and other material to be trimmed. This makes sense. For one thing, some of this involved moments of violence or lifts in action scenes (e.g., the hand of cards in the Stinking Springs scene), which certainly doesn't jibe with Aubrey's alleged edict for action above all else. For another, there is no indication Aubrey possessed anything like the talent, patience, and sensitivity that fine-cutting requires. Lines and bits of business can't just be chopped out and what's left slapped back together: this requires finessing, sometimes going to a reaction shot or a different size or angle, maybe retiming the moment. Whatever else can be said about these changes, they are absolutely superior examples of the film editor's art and craft, implemented by men who were *artists*, not a crude, vulgar executive bully.

Roger and Bob did the remaining trimming and tightening with all the considerable attentiveness to detail for which Sam chose them in the first place and hired them again and again. They knew they had to address his performance as the coffin maker and Walter Kelley's as Rupert, since Aubrey never liked Kelley and of course hated Sam. In the case of Kelley's Rupert, this included several lines when Garrett arrives at Roberta's. Are many of them important? If the film were playing optimally, maybe an argument could be made for keeping them. I confess to being personally very fond of two moments: the cryptic exchange wherein Rupert says he hasn't been to another part of town in a month, Garrett asks, "It's that bad, huh?" and Rupert answers, "Worse than that"; and when, replying to a question about the ladies working for him now, Rupert waxes lyrical about "Mrs. Susan Barnes, who I've been partial to myself." This latter probably could have been accommodated, but the trouble with the former is that it brings Rupert calling Garrett a "shiftless jackass" along with it, which makes no sense in reference to the sheriff we've been observing for the past hour and a half. Nor does the talk about Garrett's rowdy behavior in the past, while Rupert's reference to the number of whores Garrett needed the last time—"four to get it up, five to get it down"—is frankly sophomoric.

Another lift is of Rupert clearing the table after Garrett, McKinney, and Poe have left: in a fit, he sets aright an upended chair and is heard complaining about Garrett "breaking up the goddamn furniture, fucked up all my whores." Yet we've seen no brawl and nothing else to indicate Garrett was in any way even a little rowdy, let alone destructive. As for Rupert's complaint about his ladies, except for Ruthie Lee being slapped, from what we've been shown, they've done or been forced to do nothing outside what must be business as usual. Why was this little tag even filmed? The answer is that in an earlier version of the screenplay there was a brief mention of some commotion behind the closed doors of Garrett's room, which was removed before production began. There then being no indication or suggestion that Garrett leaves Ruthie Lee's room once he arrives, if he caused a disturbance, how could it have happened in the barroom, which is where Rupert turns the chair upright? I sometimes wonder if those who go on about the missing or reduced "character vignettes" notice that a vignette like this, absent the bit in the script to which it originally referred, is left literally bereft of meaning (let alone that it's another violation of the point of view). Sam evidently felt the same way because it didn't survive after the first preview, which means that when he had the editors remove the last half of McKinney's introductory scene for the second preview, he also told them to take out the return to Rupert as well. But the fact that it survived as long as it did is prima facie evidence of just precisely the sort of thing Bob Wolfe worried would happen with each editor attending mostly to his own set of scenes while none had the whole film in his head.

Sam's appearance as the coffin maker was reduced to a brief exchange, eliminating among other dialogue the question hurled at Garrett as he walks away, "When are you going to figure out that you can't trust anybody, Garrett, not even yourself?" In the audio commentaries on one of the DVDs I remarked that I found it hard to believe this would have been removed without Sam's approval. That turned out to be wishful thinking (though I still believe that if the postproduction schedule had not been so truncated, Sam would have come to this as well as several other decisions), and there seems to be no question the scene was one for which Aubrey had a particular animus. But this just begs the same question as the raft episode: if he hated it so much, why wasn't it cut out entirely, which would have been a snap to do? One answer is a combination of persuasive bargaining by Melnick and the adroit solution the editors came up with. But a more plausible one is that as the picture was at or nearing the length he wanted, Aubrey didn't care or even know Sam was still in it. I acknowledge the complaint by Robert Merrill and John L. Simons that the encounter is now so short that Will's lines about burying everything he owns in the child's coffin might profitably have been restored.[10] But after running both versions back-to-back a couple of times, what I continue to see in the Turner is a drawn-out moment of directorial self-indulgence and rather blatant point-making, Sam scarcely articulating his words, and what I see in the theatrical is an effective moment of disorientation and sly self-reference, elegant in its pith and brevity. As with his historical note, Sam's writing here seems to me to suggest a failing faith that the tale has already told the meaning far better than any authorial intrusiveness ever could. Allow me to state my bias forthrightly, unpleasant and no doubt ironic as it is to find myself in this instance coming dangerously close to siding with a smiling cobra: nothing and nobody will ever convince me that the disciplined story-teller of even a year earlier on *The Getaway* and two on *Junior Bonner* would have allowed a performance as flaccid as his own here or done other than send up in flames anyone who came up to him and said, "You know, Sam, what you oughtta have is a scene where somebody—maybe you can play it yourself—announces the subtext of the main character and sends it up in neon lights."

Black Harris's dying words, "Paris, France," were removed. Why I don't know, but I remain of two minds about them. I realize their function was to indicate the full extent of Harris's loyalty to the Kid, not to mention the contempt in which he holds Garrett, but when Wurlitzer originally wrote them they *ended* the scene. But after Sam staged the magnificent improvised coda of Cullen Baker stumbling down to the riverbank and death, they wound up sounding a bit like a "button" to end a scene that isn't over yet.

The first part of Billy's escape from the Lincoln jail—meaning the card game with Bell, the outburst from Olinger, and the killing of Bell—is pretty much the same from preview to theatrical except for a few lines and one bit. The preview has Billy's line, "Yeah, now I'd like you to hear it from me," as he's climbing the stairs before he turns and kills Bell. This is one of the few lines I regret not putting back, and I wish I could remember why I didn't: time maybe, the pressures to get the job done, perhaps something so simple as I had forgotten about it. But this regret does not extend to the Olinger lines that were removed, except for R. G. Armstrong's extemporized "walk across hell on a spider web," which effectively stretches out the moment when he has the Kid on his knees, the barrels of the shotgun at his throat, thus better helping to motivate Bell drawing a gun on a fellow deputy. But happily gone is Olinger's "Why, good people are coming just to see your poor sinning spirit meet the devil, and I'm aiming to please them by making sure you say the Lord's prayer before you do a proper cakewalk and soil your drawers." There is so much sheer verbiage crammed into this that poor R. G. couldn't even get his mouth around all the words to deliver a reading with any sort of rhythm or cadence that sounds in the least natural. Of course it didn't help that as heard in the Turner preview's temp mix it was pieced together from two different takes with the join left nakedly exposed. The difference in microphones or in microphone placement, not to mention the shift in background ambience, is glaringly obvious between the onscreen "Why, good people are coming" and the offscreen "just to see your poor sinning spirit meet the devil."

Later in the scene Billy blasts Olinger with the load of dimes intended for himself and says, "Keep the change, Bob," then blasts him again, with another cut to the spasming body. But does the second blast truly punctuate the wise-crack or merely vitiate it? Cutting to the spasming body again hardly seems necessary (not to mention calling attention to the rather obvious fact that when the shot is used later it hasn't been framed to function as Billy's point of view). In effect, the one cancels the other out—it's the equivalent to what in comedy the director Ron Shelton calls "a joke on a joke." It's true that the script has Billy shooting Olinger a second time; but, as Sam himself often observed, films change considerably from screenplay to fine cut: what matters is what ultimately works or can be made to work. The editors wisely removed the second blast and the additional cuts to Olinger's body.

I think they were also wise to lift the short interlude of the hand of cards the dying Bowdre initiates in the Stinking Springs scene. Bowdre has already said, "They've killed me," several more shots are exchanged, and in the next lull there are some lovely silent cuts between Billy and his suffering friend before Billy says, "Maybe it's time you took a walk." I've never been able to put my finger on quite why the business with the cards has never worked for me until I listened to the "Story Conference" tapes and discovered how it came to be written. Sam greatly admired the passage in Neider's novel where Hendry and Doc play cards while Harvey French dies, and he was very pleased with how he adapted it in the *Hendry Jones* screenplay, which he asked Wurlitzer to have a look at to see if he could figure out a way of getting some part of it into their revisions. A good spot, Sam thought, might be the Stinking Springs scene. But the power of Neider's original and Sam's adaptation lies in the contrast between how long the talkative Harvey suffers and the game of cards Hendry and Doc strike up just to fill in the time while they wait, rather impatiently, for him to die. In other words, they're ignoring him, so that when he finally does die, any pathos is rudely undercut by the shocking coldness of Hendry's response ("Well, that's that").

But by the time this was shoehorned into the screenplay, shot, and edited in the previews, Billy's suggestion that they all take a walk was postponed by playing the hand of cards, and the effect arguably was to weaken both the moment of Bowdre's assent and the character himself. In the theatrical, without the card business and its associated dialogue, Bowdre's reply sounds as if he grasps immediately the implications of the Kid's suggestion: Bowdre knows he's going to die and is ready to step up while he still can, which gives this minor but vividly realized character some real stature (in view of how the scene plays out, rather more than the Kid at this point in the story). It also makes the whole moment a good deal less sentimental, not least because the less time Billy wastes before he capitalizes on Bowdre's misfortune, the more pragmatic, even colder he comes off—and coldness is certainly what Sam by his own admission wanted the character to be. (If I had taken a more interventionist approach or been allowed more time with the material, I might have added the pair of silent cuts between him and Folliard before Billy's "time you took a walk" line when they realize how close Bowdre is to death. That might have afforded the best compromise here between practicality and sentiment on Billy's part.)

The most bloated sequence in the previews is the whole meeting between Garrett and Billy in Fort Sumner at the beginning. Consider the moment when Garrett, trying to ingratiate himself with the old gang, lamely remarks, "Say, I understand those señoritas down here are pretty as ever." "Yeah?" asks Holly. "Yeah," Garrett replies. "Yeah," Holly says again, smiling now (surely the wrong beat), then two of the others also chime in with yeahs of their own. Five yeahs in all. If Sam's idea here was to parody his own peerless way of extending a moment, then he couldn't have done a better job—it beats the notorious Monty Python skit six ways from Sunday. The editors also trimmed the anecdote Billy relates a bit later about the time he and Garrett shared a pair of sisters who were prostitutes. The one Garrett "enjoyed" told him to pay her whatever he felt it was worth; when he tosses a dime on the pillow, she says, "If that's all it's worth, I might as well sew it up." In the previews Billy reminds Garrett that he also told her, "You could use a few stitches." But this doesn't build upon the woman's remark toward any new information that illuminates Garrett's character or the past he and the Kid shared, it doesn't enrich texture or contribute to theme—all it does, really, is make a lame joke on an already limping one, the kind of thing Sam was ruthless about eliminating from his films. (The same is true for Lemuel's joke in the previews at the beginning of Jones's Saloon about the whore who wants cowboys with loose boots so she can "strap them with a little tight pussy and give them a warm place to shit for two dollars"—this was tired and tattered long before it ever found its way into the film.)

In the cantina scene that follows, after Garrett leaves, the editors also removed Bell's "You boys are playing a losing game. I figure on staying alive," to entirely salutary effect. The film hardly benefits from a heavy-handed card-playing metaphor this early, and though Bell's remark about staying alive is a nice ironic foreshadowing of his imminent death at Billy's hands, dropping it allows Holly's "Why don't you kill him?" to follow directly upon Garrett's exit, an instance of dramatic concision surely worth the sacrifice, as was also losing Black Harris's "He sure ain't your friend no more," since it allows Billy's answer, "Why? He's my friend," to climax the scene as it should.

These were the means by which the editors distilled the swollen wodge of the opening in the previews into a dramatically charged encounter that truly generates the drama to follow. It would be tedious to go through the entire film detailing each and every instance of fine-cutting. Suffice it to say that this sort of thing is entirely consistent with the way Sam always edited his films. Implementing it was not a matter of rushing the film or trying to make it more commercial or conventional, and it certainly did not involve reducing its poetry. On the contrary, much of the poetry was in fact intensified, because, like good poetry, it was distilled, focused, and in any of several instances allowed points to be registered more subtly, elegantly, indirectly. This was also the kind of thing that most good directors, Sam included, would expect their editors to do as a matter of course, indeed, would regard with concern or suspicion any editor who had to be instructed to do it. Much of this had already been done in most of the scenes; preparing the theatrical simply allowed Roger and Bob to attend to the rest of it.

Michael Bliss once asked me if in doing the special edition I had made "any decisions based on aesthetics alone." In other words, did I do anything simply because I thought it played better or just because I liked it better? It's a fair enough question, but it doesn't allow for an easy answer. All of the examples I've just detailed were *already* in the theatrical version because they were done by the editors, not by me. As I've already suggested, the project was framed in such a way as to free myself from having to make any more decisions than were absolutely necessary and I most emphatically did not want to reedit a film I thought was already superbly edited by editors I held in the highest esteem. It may be necessary to explain a distinction not apparent to people outside the film industry. The reason I get by turns nervous or annoyed when I hear my work on the 2005 Special Edition described as "recutting" or "reediting"—let alone the "Seydor version"—is that what I did is nothing that I or any other self-respecting editor I know would consider recutting or reediting. When we film editors speak of recutting, say, a scene, what we mean is going back to the dailies, selecting new takes, extending moments or reducing pauses, perhaps altering the balance by playing more lines offscreen or more of the scene on one character than another, changing emphases by using more or fewer close-ups, sometimes removing more lines, sometimes adding lines back. In recutting we take the scene apart in whole or by section and reconceive it in a different way. Another kind of recutting is radically altering the structure by shuffling scenes around. I've done several rescue jobs in my career, where I've had to do practically scene-one recuts of the films. My work on the 2005 Special Edition was as far removed from that sort of thing as it's possible to get. Except for the prologue, in which I had to do a certain amount of reediting because title cards, freeze-frames, and desaturated shots had to be removed, recutting is exactly what I was determined to avoid for all the reasons I've stated. The theatrical is not a work in progress but a finished fine cut, which is why it was used as the platform for the special edition.

This is in fact why for the longest time I harbored the mistaken belief that Sam himself must have been involved at least in *discussions* regarding the decision-making of the fine-cutting in the theatrical: it is all so consistent with his work. Plus, I found it almost impossible to believe that the theatrical could have been prepared—and the sound units conformed, the dub patched and fixed, the negative cut and timed, and release prints generated—in the twelve days between the second preview and the release. It was possible, just barely, but only because the editorial crew was so large (perhaps unprecedentedly so in feature filmmaking up to that time). That and something else: much of this had already been discussed with Sam or among the editors themselves. I say that because this is what you talk about in cutting rooms day in, day out. As much of this work was concentrated in scenes or with performances that everyone, including Sam, felt were problematic, the idea that none of this was on the table for discussion prior to the specific time it was implemented would mean that these cutting rooms operated differently from all other cutting rooms, including those on previous Peckinpah films. Not only is evidence for this not very forthcoming, it is contradicted by the editing notes themselves, which constitute a detailed record of how much effort the director and the editors lavished on trying to find workable solutions to the most troublesome scenes, performances, and structural problems.

The truth is that there is an irreducible minimum that you can rush the editing of any film, because you have to live with it for a certain amount of time, thinking and talking and cutting and trying to make it play better, which typically means tightening, trimming, distilling, and watching it in long sections or better still screenings, even if they're not screenings for audiences. If a film is any good, if it has a life of its own, it will soon begin to tell you how it wants to be edited, and it is the job of the editor and the director to listen to

The sequence that takes Garrett to his house (*opposite*) is in most
versions missing the shot of his hesitation at the gate (*A, above*).
Without it, the resonance is lost in a later parallel moment of hesitation
before he goes through the gate of Pete Maxwell's house (*B, above*).

that voice. But it's a process that takes time, and because of the very nature
of what Peckinpah was trying to do here, to say nothing of the problematic
aspects of some of the footage and script issues that were never adequately
addressed, *Pat Garrett and Billy the Kid* needed that time more than most films
and time is what was tragically not available. (Compare the thirteen weeks on
Pat Garrett to *The Wild Bunch*, which was almost *a full year* in postproduction
and shows it.) The editors weren't trying to make it into a fast-paced cowboy
movie for the summer market, they were still trying to make it *play* better.
Under these circumstances, the theatrical version sometimes seems to me an
almost miraculous piece of film editing: apart from the restored material, it
remains unchanged from how Roger and Bob left it, and I wouldn't have had
it any other way.[11]

But to return to Bliss's question about aesthetics alone, allow me to take
two examples, one that is fairly simple and quite large, the other less so and
subtle. The large one is Dylan's vocals under Sheriff Baker's dying moments,
which I've been "accused" of restoring over Sam's expressed wishes to the
contrary. Of course I did no such thing, as the vocals were *already* in the theatrical. But what would my decision have been if I had set different ground

rules? Well, it's common knowledge that Jerry Fielding, Sam's preferred composer, hated the vocals, feeling they were far too on the nose, and soon after
hearing them he left the picture in disgust. At the time of the editing Sam
sided with Fielding and had them removed. But then there's his letter to Melnick about a year later in which he explicitly stated his intention to revisit the
issue of those same vocals: if it's too much to call this a change of mind, it is
certainly a clear expression of serious reconsideration.

The other example involves Garrett's approach to his house after his bath
and shave. The Turner preview has him leaving the barbershop, walking down
the street, and pausing as he looks offscreen; cut to a POV (i.e., a shot intended
to suggest his point of view) of his house farther down the street, where he
knows Ida awaits him; then back to him as he throws his cigar away and continues out of frame into the next shot, the same one that served as his POV,
which picks him up as he walks to the fence, where he hesitates again, this
time for a fairly long beat, then pushes the gate open. Before he goes through
it, we cut to Billy on the trail, the Ida scene having been removed from this
preview. But when Sam ordered the scene restored for the second preview, he
employed a different cutting scheme for the approach to the house. The two
versions are identical up to the cut back to Garrett following the POV; but in
the second preview, once he exits frame, the next cut is to Ida in the kitchen
reacting to his entrance. In other words, the walk up to the gate and the long
hesitation there are gone.

It's impossible to figure out from the available evidence, including editorial
notes, whether Sam wanted this shot in the film or not. To start with, prior to
the 2005 Special Edition, the only version it was ever in was the first preview,
where it lived without the scene in the house that's supposed to follow it. If
Sam himself called for its removal for the second preview, while at the same
time reinstating the scene in the house, I can't discern a rationale for the
decision, which seems to me to diminish the approach to the house, the scene
between Garrett and Ida, and the film at large. Garrett's hesitation—call it
reluctance or procrastination—is a small but significant insight to his character, to what he is thinking and feeling here, and it anticipates and reinforces
all the tension and friction between him and Ida. Then, too, eliminating the
hesitation takes with it the allusion to it at the very end when Garrett repeats
exactly the same action at the white-picketed gate in front of the Maxwell
house before he moves in for the kill. This is another example of how musical
Peckinpah's structures are and how tightly knit internally.

Since the removal of the Ida scene from the first preview was almost certainly a mistake, I think it safe to assume that Sam would have made good and
sure he watched how the reinstatement was implemented in the second preview,
which in turn would suggest that he was satisfied with it. On the other hand,
everything was so rushed by then that maybe he *didn't* have time to check it,
maybe because the task was so straightforward—a simple drop-in, after all—it
was assigned to one of the standby editors or even an assistant, either of whom

could have inadvertently assumed the shot at the gate should be removed in order to get Garrett into the house faster. (Of course, if Sam had attended the preview, he would have seen right away the shot was missing.) Whether eliminating the moment at the gate represents his slightly later thoughts or was a mistake, here is one instance where I could not avoid making a decision of my own. Do you go the route that serves the film better overall or do you accept the second preview just because it is the later one and *may* be a decision made by the director, even though if so, you know it was made in great haste, under the most extraordinary duress, with no time adequately to weigh the alternatives? To a dilemma like this I have no answers that I'd feel comfortable seeing hardened into a general rule meant to be prescriptive (except maybe, whatever is best administered is best?). But I doubt that even my severest critics would argue the film isn't better with the walk up to the gate than without it.

Things like this are only more testimony to the unfinished state of the film when Sam left it and serve further to undermine the legitimacy of the previews as anything other than works in progress left incomplete. Dylan's "Heaven's Door" vocals, Sam's appearance as the coffin maker, moving the raft scene, trimming some of Chill Wills's lines near the beginning of Jones's Saloon, fixing the Fort Sumner opening, restoring the Ruthie Lee scene, judiciously editing Walter Kelley's Rupert, removing Garrett's egregious "What you want" line, eliminating the historical note in the end crawl, and on and on and on through all the rest of fine-cutting—setting aside the wholesale removal of scenes, which was forced upon them, I believe the editors made the right calls in almost every instance and I was happy the decisions had been made by them. They had worked directly with Sam, they knew the material better than anyone else, and they had long familiarity with his style, especially his editing style (which, not to put too fine a point on it, they had as a matter of literal fact helped develop). Even if I had been inclined to do something more interventionist, the conditions under which Warner green-lit the special edition precluded it. I was required to provide in advance an exact list of precisely defined scenes and other material to be reinstated. A house editor retrieved them from the vaults and, working from notes I provided, inserted them into the theatrical version where I indicated. I was never given direct access to the materials and only once and quite briefly was I allowed to do any hands-on work: this was on the prologue because it would have taken far more time trying to explain what needed to be done than just doing it.

The material on my list consisted of: (1) the Chisum scene; (2) one line of dialogue in the Lew Wallace scene; (3) Paco's original dying speech; (4) the wife scene; (5) the prostitutes' montage; (6) the prologue; and (7) the closing shot of Garrett riding out of Fort Sumner into the desert.

The Chisum scene fills in the relationship the cattle baron once had with the Kid and reveals the information about Garrett's loan. While it's right for the faceless politicians and businessmen of the Santa Fe Ring to be shadowy presences we never see (only their lackeys at Wallace's), it's wrong for Chisum, who must be a real and directly experienced presence. Whatever their differences, Chisum belongs with Garrett and the Kid as larger-than-life individuals whose days are numbered, a theme reinforced by the additional line from one of the lackeys ("I can assure you, Mr. Garrett," etc.). As for why I made an exception for this line, it was easy to restore, augments the significance of the Chisum character, and makes an important point about his essentially obedient relationship to the ring. (Decisions like that have led even some of my sympathetic critics to accuse me of inconsistency. Guilty—but in matters like this, an absolute consistency is surely a foolish one.) Though neither of Paco's dying speeches is good, at least the original, which Sam preferred, is not a sententious exposition but is tied to character.

The wife scene is necessary for several reasons, not least because it intensifies our sense of the pressures Garrett is under to apprehend the Kid and provides a glimpse into his difficult marriage and how uneasily he assumes the mantle of the new life he has chosen for himself. It's also a companion to the Ruthie Lee scene, which the editors had to restore for plot reasons once Tuckerman's was gone. But Ruthie Lee is important for other reasons too. She is one of the best character vignettes in the film; cutting out her introduction reduces the story, removes important revelations about Garrett's character, and weakens the structure: why set up a character—which is what Garrett's insistence that she be among the prostitutes sent to his room does—then eliminate the scene in which she is introduced and her significance revealed? I don't have an answer, but since this scene is in neither of the previews, perhaps it was removed because its plot point—how Garrett knows the Kid is in Fort Sumner—is covered in Tuckerman's, where Poe gets the information from the miners. But that's a guess at best, as I can find neither explanation nor instruction in any of the editing notes for its removal. However, in his letter to Melnick a year later, Sam explicitly called for it to be restored, "with particular emphasis upon the slapping," which suggests that its removal was another foul-up that there was never time to correct (though, as with the shot of Garrett at the gate, if Sam had attended either of the previews, he would have noticed it was gone).

The Ida scene also functions as a contrast to the prostitutes' montage: intimacy with a single woman may be difficult for Garrett, intimacy with five at once hardly possible (or necessary). And though this montage still strikes me as both over-the-top and faintly ludicrous, I freely grant it is much less egregious when seen in the dual context of Garrett ill at ease at home with Ida and later cold-bloodedly slapping information out of Ruthie Lee. Inasmuch as the 1988 Turner, alone among the five versions of the film, has the montage without the two prior scenes that give it the only validity it can possibly have, it represents the *worst* possible alternative.[12] This is because the Ida and Ruthie Lee scenes can exist together or one without the other, but the montage cannot exist without at least one of them because its *only* justification consists in how it develops themes they introduce of Garrett's relationship with his

Clearly intended to play off each other, these scenes between
Garrett with his wife and Garrett with the prostitute were never
both in any version of the film at the same time until 2005.

wife, how he expresses his sexuality, and his issues with women, intimacy,
and psychological and physical violence. Lose these and it becomes little more
than some gratuitous sex and nudity, which is precisely how it comes across
in the Turner preview. Moreover, Garrett's demand for Ruthie Lee is made a
nonsense in both previews inasmuch as she ceases to exist as a recognizable
character, there being no way to identify her among the five prostitutes—and
even if there were, what significance could be attached to her on the basis of
the montage alone?

Finally, losing both the Ida and Ruthie Lee scenes also diminishes an
important perspective that Peckinpah built into the film. I have elsewhere
observed how in *The Wild Bunch* he continually references the action to the
point of view of women and children (*Reconsideration* 159–61). While there is
less of this in *Pat Garrett and Billy the Kid*, there is still enough that reducing
it distorts the film. Mrs. Baker, Maria, and here I would add Mrs. Horrell are
minor characters, but they are important minor characters; Ida and Ruthie
Lee are secondary characters, but very important secondary characters. What
the women do in the aggregate is throw into greater relief the limitations, the
ravages, the losses, the grief and grieving—not to mention the victims—that
men like Garrett, Billy, and the way of life they represent leave in their wake.

There is also a sequence of scenes that is now different from the theatrical version. In the theatrical, the scene in which Paco says farewell and Billy leaves for Mexico follows immediately after the turkey shoot, when Silva is killed by Chisum's men, whereas in the 1988 Turner they are separated by several other scenes. Roger can't remember why or how the two scenes came to be played back-to-back, but it seems to me a clear mistake or at least a misjudgment occasioned by the haste with which the theatrical was prepared. For one thing, even by the considerable latitude of elision of time that scene-to-scene cuts by convention allow, Billy and Alias still seem suddenly to turn into a pair of real Speedy Gonzaleses, so fast do they get back to Fort Sumner. For another, and more to the point, Billy's decision to leave is put so close to the killing of Silva as to make it seem like a prime motivation, which doesn't make a lot of sense, as Silva is killed while doing a job, which could happen any time. Finally, played in tandem the two scenes go against the overall scheme of cutting back and forth between the two protagonists. In restoring the Chisum scene, then, I've left in place, albeit modified to account for the new position of the raft scene, the sequence of scenes as they appear in the Turner preview: the death of Silva dissolves to the raft scene, which cuts to Poe's arrival at Garrett's camp beside the river, which cuts to the next day as Garrett and Poe travel to Chisum's, the meeting with Chisum, and then to Paco's farewell and Billy's departure for Old Mexico.

Inasmuch as the theatrical release already has a beautiful titles sequence, the prologue titles and freeze-frames had to be removed and the sequence adjusted accordingly. As I've said, I can think of no equivalent anywhere in Peckinpah's work for a sequence this labored. It's as if he were saying, Now we begin here, you understand where we are, don't you?—No?—Here's a title card just to clarify things—Now we're going over here, you understand we're someplace else, yes, and deep in the past?—You don't?—Another title then. By this time what was obviously originally conceived as a startling series of shocks and dislocations in the mind of Garrett as he is being murdered became instead a ponderous double setup in which the film seems to start, stop, then start again. It has always seemed to me that the crosscutting should begin with no preparation whatsoever and that the twin fulcrums on which it rests should be Garrett and the chickens both getting shot, the cuts so quick they function almost like subliminals. In fact, this is how Coburn once described it to Simmons (183–84) not all that long after the film was released: the chickens exploding in "flash cuts against the slow motion of my—or Garrett's—death until as I topple out of the buggy, we are into the scene where Billy and the rest of them are shooting up the chickens."[13] This in turn would have made it possible to withhold the high, wide establishing shot of Fort Summer, with its identifying title, until well after the crosscutting has begun, which would likely spare the film the impression it's starting up a second time. The sequence also seems to me more effective when it is less drawn out, which is how Sam originally imagined it. This makes perfect sense when we recall that he had already written the first Fort Sumner sequence as a kind of prologue, that is, a scene to establish the terms of the friendship. Little wonder Melnick and the editors felt the newer prologue, intercut with the first scene and freeze-frames and titles laid over both, was protracted and clumsy.

But I remain of more than one mind still about the openings in the Turner preview and the special edition. Except of course for the title cards, most of the shot-to-shot edits and the sequence of action and event are identical to those in the preview—again, I tried to do as little reordering as possible. Shorn of titles, the new montage has the virtues of being clean, swift, and compact, the crosscutting more staccato and the sense of disorientation more dramatic and unsettling, much closer to Coburn's description. But while I don't care for the excessive languor and distention of the Turner's titled montage, what I do miss is the greater expressive and emotional *weight* of the slow-motion shots of Garrett getting hit, which is no doubt due in large part to their terminating as freeze-frames that are held for several beats to accommodate titles. But once the crosscutting between the two time periods comes to an end, with the deaths of Garrett and all the chickens, and the Fort Sumner scene gets under way as a *scene*, it was surely awkward to have the cards, freeze-frames, and desaturations continue deep into the interior of the cantina.

I realize that Peckinpah delayed his card so that the freeze-frame would italicize Garrett's "But in five days, I'm making you," an effect doubtless intended to be more or less equivalent to placing his name immediately after Pike Bishop's "If they move, kill 'em." Sam liked to do this sort of thing with his credit. But does anyone really think it has anything like the same power here as in the earlier film? In *The Wild Bunch* the titles sequence is a measured but relentless crescendo of ever-increasing tension until it crests in Bishop's close-up, where the whites of his eyes, emphasized by the desaturated freeze-frame, leave us, like the innocent people in the railroad office, in no doubt that he means it. But Garrett's line is played on his back, and the image that freezes is not the expression on *his* face but Billy's silent reaction framed as a loose over-the-shoulder. This was surely an odd choice if emphasis was the desired effect. Moreover, Sam delayed his credit so long—almost three minutes have elapsed since the previous one—that we'd be forgiven for thinking the titles have ended. When they resume for the director's name, it feels a bit like an afterthought, and the effect of punctuating Garrett's warning is rather vitiated, despite the ominous sting from Dylan's guitar. I wonder if reconceiving this, so that the titles could end earlier, was behind Sam's thought that more than one credit could occupy some of the desaturated freeze-frames. On balance I marginally prefer the title-less montage in the special edition to the Turner's, but neither is wholly satisfying, and I am reminded of Roger's remark to the effect that no one was really happy with it, it was never right, and it still isn't.

A more promising solution, I now believe, would have been to retain the titles in the montage, but changing the color to the yellow that Sam wanted, and *judiciously* trim, tighten, and distill the crosscutting to give it more concentration and edge, as the editors already did with the Fort Sumner scene for the theatrical. It would also be of tremendous help to see if something could be done about Dylan's score, a rather simple tune strummed on a guitar for almost six minutes, unvaried in tempo and rhythm, with repetitive chords. (I wonder if Sam was reacting to this when in his letter to Melnick he mentioned sweetening the music—almost anything, including no score at all, would likely be an improvement over what is there.) But doing anything along these lines would have occupied the better part of a day for the editing alone, and probably more—definitely more if it involved going into the trims—this before even re-creating new titles, placing and timing them, changing the font color, and experimenting with sepia and desaturation. In other words, I wish Warners had made available the time, resources, and money to address the problem properly. It's very hard to concentrate on something that requires focus and precision in a small room with three or four persons looking over your shoulder and also at the clock. The hour spent on it barely afforded time enough to lose all the title cards and smooth over any shot-to-shot edits that might be jarring.

As for removing the epilogue, this I'll cop to entirely—or almost entirely, because I didn't actually *invent* anything here. When the prologue was dropped, the epilogue obviously had to go as well, which left the ending as scripted: Garrett disappearing into the early morning fog as he rides off. As Sam shot it, there was no fog, but the image he did shoot conveyed the same effect: Garrett's figure recedes into the bleak dawn as he departs Fort Sumner, the image is frozen, and the end-credit crawl begins. This was how the film ended when Roger handed it over to the studio, an answer print already existed in the vaults with that ending on it, and the elements used to generate it remained intact, so I chose it. Speaking personally, I believe it preferable to the makeshift epilogue (and far preferable to Aubrey's stupid, maudlin last-minute substitution), and it has the advantage of not using obviously recycled footage. The way the lawman appears to be gradually swallowed up by the landscape suggests how the judgment of history in the form of legend will weigh against him; and it draws together and focuses the themes of fate and determinism that inform the whole film.

The best reason, however, for removing the epilogue is what it does for the climax. Once Peckinpah added the opening meeting between Garrett and Billy in Fort Sumner, it determined his basic structure, which, in the best description I've read, Simmons likened to "two halves of a great circle" completing itself (171). This circle encloses, defines, and thus becomes the world of the film, so that in the darkened room when Billy turns and sees Garrett and smiles and Garrett rises up and shoots him, it really does feel as if in the exact moment of completion the world also disintegrates. Then Garrett turns and fires at his reflection in the mirror, leaving a disfiguring hole (itself a distorted black circle) where his heart should be: the physical destruction reflects the psychological destruction which reflects the destruction of a way of life, and the point of symbolic suicide is made with a clarity as blinding as the flash from Garrett's revolver. The epilogue can add little, even in the way of irony, to the devastation of this ending, and a case can be made that it even dilutes it. Inasmuch as the epilogue was already in the 1988 Turner, there seemed to me both value and validity in choosing the alternative for the 2005 Special Edition, where the prologue now functions as dramatic irony perfectly well on its own, as it did also in both the screenplay and the early cuts of the film before the idea of framing it occurred to anyone.

In terms strictly of cinematic and dramatic storytelling, this is why the prologue was edited to end with Garrett's death in the first place: if he is not left unambiguously dead at the beginning, we would have no way of knowing for certain that he does in fact die and the effect of dramatic irony would be, if not lost, certainly diminished. This also means that as originally written, and certainly as filmed and edited, the prologue was never intended to establish an open frame that required closure, and it didn't: on the contrary, as implemented, it was a closed narrative-dramatic device, not least because its main action, the murder of Garrett, was brought decisively to full completion, with no reprise set up, implied, promised, or necessary. But when Roger got the idea for the epilogue, he came up with an ingenious way of realizing it, apparently with Sam's blessing, that involved less repeating the action of the prologue than reprising it in a severely condensed form that begins moments after Garrett is first shot, indeed, before he hits the ground, and that allows the film to end very quickly while he is still alive, though obviously dying. In the absence of an appropriately readjusted prologue, however, it could be argued that this has the effect of making the epilogue feel like authorial intrusion, even something arbitrary. If the prologue had been reedited to end with Garrett still alive though mortally wounded, then at the very least the epilogue would have acquired an organic and structural justification because it would function as the necessary completion of an action left incomplete at the opening. I asked Roger if there was ever any discussion of recutting both the prologue and the epilogue so that they would constitute a *chronological* arc that would carry Garrett's assassination across the long span of the 1881 part of the story:

> I can't remember any of the discussions around the epilogue. But it strikes me now that it might have been added for the most obvious reason. What we see at the beginning tells us the factual ending of one of our two characters. It informs us from the start that Garrett came to an abrupt end. It tells us that this is not a story of Garrett's survival by killing Billy, of justice over lawlessness, of the end of the West. It tells us to look for other themes of greater resonance. Playing the scene again at the

end of the film when the story of Billy and Pat is complete, it becomes a very different experience. Now we can savor the ironies and tragedy of Garrett, who loses his life, perhaps as even he imagined, at the hands of those he had served by killing his closest friend. One might argue that without the epilogue one would still be left with the same emotions. But I suspect it is stronger to see it again.

My feelings about the epilogue remain deeply conflicted, but Roger's is the most eloquent case I've heard anyone make for keeping it; ironically, he makes it by openly embracing the reprise as an undisguised piece of authorial intrusion, the filmmakers' desire to force the audience to recall the opening themes of irony, fatalism, betrayal, and death.[14]

Would I have done the special edition any differently had Warner allowed me access to the trims so I could function as a real editor, with my hands on the controls and my instincts plugged into the material? I'd have still felt uncomfortable about recutting Peckinpah and his editors. But I'd be lying if I didn't admit that, as someone who studied this director for a long time before becoming a film editor and whose editing style was profoundly shaped by his work, I would have liked to try some things and run them by Roger. One that comes immediately to mind, following Sam's early instincts, would be to drop the death of Paco entirely, then comb through the ride-bys again to see if anything was missed that could be made to serve Roger's idea of a purely existential moment of decision from Billy for his return. Another would be to see if the prologue could be edited so that we leave Garrett writhing on the ground as he is riddled with bullets that don't finish him off before we settle into 1881. It would also be better, because less destructive to the flow of the cutting scheme, to withhold the Fort Sumner establishing shot—the one that now carries the title identifying place and time—until all the shooting stops and Garrett starts walking toward the fountain. (I would have made this change in the special edition, but without access to the trims I couldn't see if Garrett's move toward the fountain is covered later in the shot. Barring such access, the shot had to remain where it is because on big screens the mismatch in continuity would easily be noticed.) Then I would comb the footage to see if it were possible to construct an epilogue that picks him up at the same point we left him, so it would function as a true frame, concluding with his actual death and ending on a stronger closing image. Then again, for reasons I've just explained, I might not. The assassination *feels* so right as prologue only; the original ending, with Garrett physically alive but psychically scarred for life, even more right. But one thing I wish I had investigated is how long Peckinpah allowed Coburn to keep on riding before saying, "Cut." If it's a good long while, I'd have delayed freezing the image under the crawl for as long as Garrett's figure keeps receding.

After the original essay was published, Michael Bliss asked me to explain how I would stay with Garrett's point of view as he is shot. Offhand, there are two ways it could be played. One would be to withhold the reveal of the distant shooter sneaking into place in the extreme wide shot. If there's a shot of Garrett actually noticing the man as he raises his rifle, then cutting off Garrett to him in the medium shot where he fires might be one way to introduce him, eventually getting to the wide shot at whatever point it feels right to drop back. Another option would be not to reveal the distant shooter until Garrett is actually hit. In either case, the strategy would be to open out from close to distant and back in again, from inside to outside, and to preserve the sequence of perception and reaction as Garrett experiences them, which is very much a Peckinpah procedure and certainly something that would seem to be appropriate in a sequence as obviously subjective as this one. Of course, this is all speculation, as you can never know how something will work until you actually see what's in the footage and begin manipulating it.

So much for fantasy. In reality, the 2005 Special Edition wound up being a mere nine minutes shorter (give or take several seconds) than the 1988 Turner preview if you compensate for the near three minutes of the wife scene. Yet over three minutes of that nine are accounted for by Tuckerman's Hotel, the only full scene not put back. Now that I have established beyond all question or doubt the actual extent of my so-called recutting—that is, hardly any at all—of the special edition, I trust it leaves me free to offer some long overdue praise for the truly magnificent work of Roger and Bob in protecting Sam's vision as much as was humanly possible and of Melnick in providing sufficient cover for them to do it.

I hadn't watched *Pat Garrett and Billy the Kid* since the last run-through at Warner to ensure that the restored lifts were where they were supposed to be. I've watched it three times since, once with my wife; and we watched it as a film *should* be watched: all the way through, no interruptions. We were thrilled how beautifully it plays. To be sure, it is by no means perfect, some performances remain uneven, and a few scenes still struggle to find a workable shape and timing that I believe will always elude them. But the story now moves so surely that until Paco's death we felt as if there was not one weak moment. And after that, it recovers immediately, which has never been the case in the previews. Best of all, perhaps, the drama now seems to find its own natural pace: measured, at times leisurely, yet forward-leaning, narrative and poetry ideally mediated, with an elegiac lyricism made all the more fragile by a fatality inexorably pulling each and all to their doom.

Peckinpah knew better than anybody that when you slow something down too much, you don't necessarily make it more lyrical, and often as not you make it less so. The particular kind of lyric expansiveness of which he was one of the greatest masters depends upon a fairly strict control of tempo in combination with a certain elasticity of line or rhythm, so that when he wanted to linger in a moment or stretch out a scene or stage one of his peerless set pieces, he could do so without worrying that the structure would distend or fall apart. This is why we remember so many moments, fleeting and extended, from his films: at his best he had an almost unerring instinct for just how high and wide he could let that falcon fly before the center ceased to hold. Form and feeling, style and substance, artistry and vision have always been inseparable in his best work, as they are here in his last Western film, where his editors kept and sustained the faith even as his own was faltering.

The miracle is that *Pat Garrett and Billy the Kid* finally does emerge a masterpiece; the sad irony is that the man who made it seemed only belatedly—and maybe never completely—to have realized the full measure of his achievement. When one admires an artist as much as I do this one, it is not easy to recall his behavior during the making of the film, and no satisfaction has been taken in doing so. Perhaps that gives me leave to bracket this part of the book with another quotation, words I wrote eighteen years ago in my *Reconsideration* (306), a tribute as true now as then and felt even more strongly, to a great film and the ravaged man who wrested it from his demons:

> There was something indomitable at the very core of Sam Peckinpah's being. It was this something, or, rather, its extension or equivalent in his imagination that—despite the flaws, mistakes, and weaknesses of *Pat Garrett and Billy the Kid*—managed to survive, intact and unbroken, the whole long, agonized year of fear, anger, booze, infighting, and desperate self-destructiveness. It is the thing that we call—imprecisely but exactly—vision, and it sweeps all before it. This is one of the few films, and perhaps the only Western film apart from *The Wild Bunch*, in which the effect of tragedy is felt and sustained. Yet *The Wild Bunch* is a triumphant tragedy, and it culminates in transfiguration and redemption. No such light illumines the bleak horizons of *Pat Garrett and Billy the Kid*. When the sun goes down on the dusky, godforsaken world of this Western, it seems also to go out, and the sense of finality is shattering.

PART THREE

Ten Ways of Looking at an Unfinished Masterpiece and Its Director

———◆———

To Garner Simmons and David Weddle,
many thanks—many thanks, until you're better paid—
and
Nick Redman and Michael Bliss,
for opportunity and insistence

Peckinpah on set in Durango

1. "I have never made a 'Western.' I have made a lot of films about men on horseback."

This is one of Peckinpah's more widely quoted pronouncements and one that is sometimes misinterpreted as pretentious, even snobbish, when quoted out of its context, which it almost always is. It originated in an interview with Paul Schrader, then a film critic, for an essay he wrote on *The Wild Bunch*. But Schrader was careful to include what Peckinpah said immediately *before* he made that statement, which was that he did not *mind* being labeled a "Western director," an important mitigating qualification if the inference is snobbery. The larger context is the year, which was 1969, the end of the sixties, a decade characterized by a polarized film market, film audience, and film criticism. Granting all exceptions, most serious film critics and serious filmgoers, especially in colleges and universities, were Euro/Asian-centric. If they took American films seriously, it was usually condescendingly, genre the first object of their high-handedness.[1] If a film were in a genre, particularly a popular genre, then by definition it was less worthy than a so-called personal film by a foreign director. Peckinpah himself loved a lot of films from abroad, and in interviews throughout the latter half of the sixties and early seventies he made enthusiastic and very generous reference to favorites of his by Kurosawa (*Rashōmon*), Bergman (*The Magician*), Fellini (*La Strada*), Antonioni (*Red Desert*), and Satyajit Ray (*Pather Panchali*). Beginning in 1961, he shot five of his six Westerns in that decade, a body of work that has been recognized as some of the most personal and deeply felt films ever made. But because they are Westerns, this took a while, which put him in an almost uniquely qualified position to understand what it felt like to have them judged and all too often dismissed on their face (despite worldwide recognition beginning with *Ride the High Country*). From this perspective, Peckinpah's statement strikes me as rather modest in tone and temperate in expression, with a touch of amused irony. All he was saying was, yes, my films are Westerns, but they are also *my* films—please watch them that way. Soon enough, thanks to *The Wild Bunch*, they would be, but at the time he had real reasons for his concern, and snobbery most emphatically did not figure into it.

Peckinpah's statement was used as the epigraph to the section on his work in the expanded edition of Jim Kitses's *Horizons West*, where Kitses declares the director both snobbish and defensive and then broadens the attack to include those who treat Peckinpah as a personal filmmaker of great originality, as opposed to the master only of a genre:

> The quote marks around "Western" in Peckinpah's declaration are suggestive: advocates of the director who repeatedly refer to the Western *films*, rather than simply the Westerns, reinforce the snobbish hair-splitting suggested here. Like the quotation marks in the director's claim, the persistent qualification of "films" is meant to hint at a profound difference, evidence of a polemical and transparent strategy to lift the film-maker clear of any relationship to the common oater, horse opera and shoot-'em-up. Both the director and his advocates are at pains to distance him from the "conventional Western," as if there are other kinds, as if challenging and subverting the conventions is not using them. These films, we are to understand, really do not belong to a genre; they are sui generis—Peckinpah films. (201)

There's a lot going on here, much of it ax-grinding. Let's begin with "Western films," for which literature offers a parallel. For over a century now, literary critics and readers have made a distinction between dime-novel, pulp, or merely generic Western fiction and the "Western novel." Nobody seems to think this snobbish, and most critics and readers accept it for what is: an attempt, somewhat unwieldy no doubt, even clumsy, to recognize a difference that has an observable basis in reality. To group such diverse novels as *The Authentic Death of Hendry Jones*, *Little Big Man*, *Blood Meridian*, *True Grit*, *Death Comes for the Archbishop*, *Lonesome Dove*, and *The Big Sky* under the rubric "Westerns" and leave it at that is not necessarily wrong but it is misleading; to refer to them as Western novels at least identifies them more precisely as works of seriousness of intent, purpose, and expression and helps them escape a categorization that might limit full consideration and appreciation, not to mention a larger or at least more varied readership.[2]

Insisting so stridently upon genre as the primary and virtually the only legitimate determinant and shaper—in other words, the leading formal cause—of Peckinpah's work and dismissing the non-Western films as "modest" in achievement at best[3] or "dead-ends" (240, 243) together beg a legitimate question: would Kitses treat the Melville of *Typee* through *Moby-Dick* the same way, that is, as a writer only of travel literature or seafaring yarns, both well-established, popular literary genres in the America of the mid-nineteenth century (and which is how he was regarded by many reviewers of the time, particularly those who felt he had lost his moorings with *Moby-Dick*)? (Presumably *Pierre*, *Israel Potter*, *The Confidence-Man*, and the short fiction, not to mention the considerable body of poetry, would be modest achievements or dead ends, with the unfinished *Billy Budd* an eleventh-hour recrudescence?) Or how about Beethoven? Is he an original and innovative composer who uses the classical forms and conventions he inherited from Haydn and Mozart in radically new ways? Yes. Is he an original and innovative composer whose style is greatly influenced and shaped by these same forms and conventions? Yes. Insisting upon one to the exclusion of the other is to fail to experience his music fully or to hear it whole. So it is with Peckinpah and the Western. Surely this is an issue on which the only reasonable position is not either/or but both/and.[4]

There happens to be a passage in the 2004 *Horizons West* that aptly illustrates the pitfalls of a strictly generic approach to Peckinpah. Kitses identifies an image from *Pat Garrett and Billy the Kid* which for him "sums up Peckinpah's qualities and achievements" (244): Billy silhouetted against a sunset sky as reflected in the placid surface of a lake. Kitses writes with great eloquence about this image—as he does about Peckinpah in general—and I believe the points he extrapolates from it as a way to elucidate some of the director's attitudes toward Western myth and American society have both great insight and validity. But it also leads him to a decidedly skewed view of Peckinpah's visual style, which Kitses characterizes as "self-consciously painterly" (245). Interestingly, this particular shot, which *is* self-consciously painterly, is quite atypical of Peckinpah's style and rather unrepresentative because it happens in fact to be one that was filmed and composed not by the director and his cinematographer John Coquillon but by the second-unit director Gordon Dawson and the cinematographer Gabriel Torres. (Peckinpah did not dictate the composition to Dawson and Torres, and Dawson regards the shot as one of the proudest achievements of his career.[5]) Imagistically Peckinpah's films are some of the richest, most densely layered, teemingly abundant, and contrapuntally complex ever made. Restless, energetic, volatile, dynamic, colorful, his visual style is among the least painterly of any great filmmaker I have ever seen. To be sure, there are many beautiful "pictures" in his films—the play of dusk and dawn colors and of chiaroscuro lighting in *Pat Garrett* is among the most delicate, nuanced, and atmospherically telling in all his work—but he is very judicious when it comes to suspending the narrative in order to allow us to luxuriate in them. Unlike, for maximum contrast, the rather static painterly compositions of John Ford or David Lean, Peckinpah's are labile, fluid, and fleeting, rarely held for very long, constantly morphing into new perspectives, rather like modulations through keys in a piece of music.

This is why stills from his films reproduce so poorly on the page and why still images, even when taken as "frame captures" directly from the films, are so misleading as ways to understand how style and meaning mediate each other in his work: his images for the most part have to be experienced kinetically, that is, as *moving* images, or, to put it another way, as complex structures of shots in constant motion and collision.[6] Even the actual effect in the film of Billy's silhouette, despite the classical balance, stillness, and near-abstract simplicity of the image, is somewhat undermined when it is isolated and reproduced as a still, because the image is not static and the composition changes as the horseman moves across the frame. Selecting a single frame for reproduction means that a choice must be made between parts of the shot which show different things: the actual figure silhouetted against the sky becomes the reflected figure silhouetted in the lake becomes the figure obscured by the landscape as he rides on (Kitses opts to print the reflection). Any of these when frozen and isolated distorts the *filmic* experience and, I would argue, some of the meaning, the way the fluidly shifting silhouettes and reflections suggest different perspectives on the man and the legend, the individual and the reputation, the figure alternately highlighted and swallowed up (or drowned) by the landscape—all recurring motifs in Peckinpah's Western films. For Kitses, the negation of myth is the only available meaning here ("America in the dark and dead in the water"); but while this is perfectly valid as one meaning among several, with Peckinpah it's always the mixtures that count. The "mixture" in this shot is the rider at the three principal points: moving from the left backlit against the sunset, pausing in the middle and silhouetted in the reflection, then moving on and out of frame right, the figure constantly evolving very much as the legend itself has done and continues to do. The terms of Kitses's generic dialectics are too simplistic for this director's complexity, ambivalences, and conflictedness. To argue that subverting a convention is also using it and to leave it at that when writing about Peckinpah is to do little more than state a truism: because he rarely subverted conventions or ironized myths except to reclaim them all the more tenaciously, which he did by reinventing them with unprecedented intensity, originality, and audacity. He took almost *everything* about the Western, including the most shopworn clichés, the most banal stereotypes, and realized them with such vitality, power, and depth of feeling as to raise the form to transcendence.

Can Kitses, with all his insight into Peckinpah's Western films, seriously expect us to believe he is oblivious to the director's staggering originality, the force of his artistic personality, the struggle and complexity of his moral vision, the weight and density of his themes, the formal power and intricacies of his narratives, the beauty and intensity of his effects, the boldness of his imagination, and how completely he transforms the Western even as he exploits it? Of course not—look at any page in the Peckinpah section of *Horizons West* ("original and groundbreaking work that touched the very pinnacle of cinema," Kitses writes in one summation [244][7]). Snobbism is not at issue here—rather, it's the visceral, bedrock experience of the films themselves. When I first saw *The Wild Bunch* in 1969 I felt what Emily Dickinson said: you know you're in the presence of poetry when you feel the top of your head coming off. I knew then and there that I had to write about this artist. I was an American literature major in college and I had also loved movies and Westerns as long as I could remember. But I had never had an experience like that at a Western—though I did have similar experiences when I read *Absalom, Absalom!*, heard the *Missa Solemnis*, saw *King Lear*, and watched *The Seven Samurai*. I was not alone. At about the same time, in another part of the country, a young film critic named Michael Sragow, at the outset of what would become a very distinguished career, saw the film six times in two weeks, and years later wrote that "Sam Peckinpah was the man who made me want to write about movies . . . I had to write and persuade others that it isn't just an essay in violence or even a magnificent Western. It is a great original work of art."

I cannot count the number of people I've met since then from all walks of life and under countless different circumstances who've had similar experiences of that film and Peckinpah's other work. The terms of the descriptions differ of course with the individual, but not the essence of the experience, which for every one of us was life changing. John Milius said he saw *The Wild Bunch* the second or third day after it opened "because George Lucas saw it and said, 'This is the best movie ever made! It's better than *The Searchers*, it's better than anything! You all have to go see it!'" Phil Kaufman said, "I don't know if such a thing exists as the greatest American movie ever made, but if there were, *The Wild Bunch* would certainly be a candidate."[8] It is impossible to look at the work of that generation of filmmakers, from America and abroad, without seeing the manifest influence of Peckinpah on many of them— Martin Scorsese, Steven Spielberg, Brian De Palma, Walter Hill, Lawrence Kasdan, John Milius, George Lucas, Michael Mann, Phil Kaufman, Oliver Stone, Paul Schrader, Ron Shelton, Mimi Leder, Volker Schlöndorff, Nicolas Roeg, Monte Hellman, Sergio Leone, John Irwin, Alfonso Arrau, Roger Spottiswoode himself, of course, to name only some of the most obvious. Even in his own generation, scenes of violence in Altman's *McCabe and Mrs. Miller* and *The Long Goodbye* and Kubrick's *A Clockwork Orange* would not have been filmed the way they were if not for Peckinpah's example; for that matter, Kurosawa himself, who influenced Peckinpah, used slow motion very differently after *The Wild Bunch*. In the generation following theirs Peckinpah's influence is admitted and celebrated, evidenced in homage, quotation, or allusion too obvious to miss by Quentin Tarantino, the Coen brothers, John Woo, David Fincher, Paul Thomas Anderson, David Ayre, Guillermo del Toro, Gore Verbinski, Benicio del Toro, Robert Rodriguez, Tommy Lee Jones, John McNaughton, and Kim Jee-woon. There was a young art student in graduate school in New York City who saw *The Wild Bunch* one night and decided to become a filmmaker afterward—I am certain that with her, no less than with me, the "decision" was not a decision as the word is ordinarily understood— because more than anything else she had ever seen Peckinpah represented what she called a "paradigm shift" (in this she was casting the net far beyond the world of film). Her name is Kathryn Bigelow and in 2010 she became the first woman to win an Academy Award for directing, her film *The Hurt Locker*.[9]

The impact of *The Wild Bunch* is incalculable, so much so that many young filmmakers aren't even aware of the influence, which is of course the clearest sign that it has become pervasive and lasting. At a film festival in the late nineties, I saw a short film in which the young director had cut in a brief slow-motion shot of a piece of action, slowed down just enough to freeze the image in our minds. He told me afterward that he had never even *heard* of Peckinpah. It hardly mattered: the influence was evident despite its being several degrees removed, because the innovations Peckinpah brought to the language of film had long before been absorbed into its basic vocabulary.

How is all this possible? How can so many different people from such diverse backgrounds and walks of life have so similar an experience? There are countless answers, but one of the most obvious is that *The Wild Bunch*—like *Major Dundee* and *Ride the High Country* before it and *The Ballad of Cable Hogue* and *Pat Garrett and Billy the Kid* after it—is both a Western and so much more than a Western.

2. "The Western is a universal frame within which it is possible to comment on today."

Is *Pat Garrett and Billy the Kid* historically accurate? Peckinpah thought so, but by this he seems mostly to have meant that he felt he had depicted Billy the Kid as a killer rather than as a hero. Wurlitzer thought so too, but he seems to have meant only that by concentrating on the last three months of the Kid's life when, he believed, nobody knew exactly what Billy was up to, he could be freely inventive without being false to history. In fact, Billy was more than just a killer and quite a lot is known about what both he and Garrett were doing those last three months, and little of it is portrayed with anything like strict accuracy in the film. Does this matter? The question of historical accuracy as regards works of the imagination is in many ways a silly one. People who want history should read histories and biographies or watch documentaries. Novels, plays, and films will always invent, distort, or falsify because their priorities consist not in fidelity to facts but in telling good stories. Using facts as a kind of counter by which to club storytellers is a game the historian-critic is always going to win because adapting history to fiction, drama, or film always involves more elimination than inclusion, more reduction than expansion: composite characters have to be created; events discarded, changed, reordered, or invented for the purposes of structure and plot (which life is all too rarely solicitous enough to supply); most problematic, perhaps because most susceptible of distortion, is the need to find a theme in the historical materials. By this I don't necessarily mean a paraphrasable idea, though it could be that too, so much as a perspective or view of the material— that is, some idea, perception, or emotion—that offers an entrée into it and a way of approaching, shaping, and organizing it. In other words, storytellers are always going to try to find their own meaning in the material, which is something that history doesn't necessarily furnish. And when we have a writer with as distinctive a style as Wurlitzer's, to say nothing of Peckinpah's as a filmmaker—well, still less do we have any business expecting, let alone demanding, what is vulgarly called a biopic or a docudrama.

One fairer question might be, does the story illuminate the history in ways that are valid as interpretations or simply as imaginative leaps that are revealing of certain kinds of truth unavailable by any other means? The answer with respect to *Pat Garrett* is a very easy yes. What we might call the film's synoptic view of the events is more than amply corroborated by the most reliable historians, starting with Maurice Fulton, who wrote, "Scratch beneath the surface and you will find one thing as the prime mover in most of the Lincoln County troubles—money" (*History* 95). Wurlitzer, with Peckinpah's blessing, made this explicit in the scene with the men who represent the collusion of investors and land speculators who make up the Santa Fe Ring, while its setting in the governor's hacienda adds politics to the mix; throughout the rest of the film these forces of commerce and big business in collusion with government are periodically referenced, their iron grip strongly implied. The relationship between Lincoln County and the territorial government in Santa Fe allowed the filmmakers to give this theme an unmistakably contemporary slant, indeed a prescient one, because through so much of the conflict Thomas B. Catron and his associates in the Santa Fe Ring remained background figures, aloof and detached even as they controlled the purse strings and gave orders to Murphy, Dolan, and The House.

In most Westerns Catron and figures like him constitute a stock villain whom the hero, sometimes with the help of rallying townspeople, small ranchers, and sodbusters, defeats. As recently as 2003, in *Open Range*, written by Craig Storper (from a novel by Lauran Paine) and directed by Kevin Costner, this figure took the form of an evil land baron (interestingly, played by Michael Gambon, who is Irish, as were many of the participants in the Lincoln County War), who does battle with a pair of cowhands played by Costner and Robert Duvall. *Open Range* is a really good Western and a serious one, yet it is also for the most part fairly conventional. I mean this not critically but descriptively: after a remarkable sustained first hour in which the life of cowboys on a drive is as plausibly and vividly depicted as I've seen in a film, the story narrows to a struggle with the land baron which resolves itself into a once-and-for-all gunfight that dispatches him and his men and restores order to the community, the hero with a dark past redeemed by the promise of an imminent marriage with the sister of the town doctor. And there is no ironic distance upon any of this, which is just as well: that would be condescending and dishonest because what is so pleasurable about *Open Range* is how forthrightly and without apology Costner embraces the classic Western.

In *Pat Garrett and Billy the Kid*, however, figures like the land baron exist but they are never seen; indeed, they're not even *named* or otherwise identified, and when their lackeys refer to them, it is in a passive construction that makes them seem like inhuman, impersonal forces, so our attention is directed instead to the men they control like pawns: "Chisum and the others *have been advised* to recognize their position" (my emphasis). When I say this is prescient, what I mean is that the film has a particular resonance in our own time of multinational conglomerates where nobody seems to know who is in charge or can be held responsible for anything.[10] I can't think of another retelling of the story of Pat Garrett and Billy the Kid that views the history in *quite* this way, but it is just one more example of what can be done with these materials if only you have writers and directors imaginative enough to do it. The Watergate scandal did not break big early enough to have had much influence as such on the development of the screenplay, but by the spring of 1973 Peckinpah alluded to it in the note he appended to the end of the second preview.[11] Even without that, however, there is enough in the Wallace scene and elsewhere to suggest a society infected by corruption and ruled by powerful, insulated conspirators who commit high crimes and misdemeanors with impunity.[12]

3. "And the mere facts tend to obscure the truth, anyway."

Peckinpah was fairly, if patchily, knowledgeable about the history of Pat Garrett, Billy the Kid, and Lincoln County and in ways that indicate he consulted more sources than just Garrett's book. For examples, he knew the Kid learned to use a gun because he was bullied by men bigger and stronger than he; he knew that Chisum, far from being a cardboard villain, was a man of stature and some principle; he knew that Wallace spent a lot of time writing *Ben-Hur* when he should have been tending to the violence in Lincoln County; he knew the specifics as to how Olinger murdered John Jones; and he knew enough about the Kid's escape from the Lincoln County Courthouse to stage it more accurately than any other film account known to me. Yet it is easy to find all sorts of details at variance with the facts as we know them. But in every case there are good dramatic and storytelling reasons for the variances, and also historical ones. We know that Billy shot Olinger from the window on the side of the building, then went out to the balcony, where he may have shot him again or just broken the shotgun if he had emptied both barrels at the window.[13] Peckinpah placed both shootings on the balcony, however, for reasons of economy and greater suspense: he could crosscut between Billy in leg-irons hobbling as fast as he can to retrieve the shotgun, then out to the balcony while Olinger reacts and starts moving toward the courthouse. The balcony also enabled him to give Billy and Olinger a final face-off, the Kid his moment of satisfaction, the deputy his moment of defeat, without the impediment of a sharp raking-angle toward each other through a partially opened window made from period glass that was probably distorted and dirty. If we believe, as some historians suggest, that Billy did take an almost sadistic pleasure in gunning down his tormenter and that Olinger had a moment enough to observe, "Yes, and he's killed me, too," then Peckinpah has dramatized the psychological truth of the encounter in a way that he could not have by being merely faithful to what has been reported. Here the mere facts really would have obscured the truth.

Later in the same scene, citizens crowd into the street around Billy, most of them mute with wonder or awe or respect or fear or just plain anxiety as to what they should do or how they're supposed to react. According to more than one account, nothing like this happened. Instead, for the better part of an hour Billy remained on the balcony and issued warnings for people to stay away from him, which they apparently obeyed, almost none of them leaving their shops or homes, and the streets remained almost empty. Why did Peckinpah ignore this? Well, he may not have known or forgotten he'd read that's how it was. But even if he had remembered, by staging it the way he did he realized the scene as Wurlitzer described it in his second draft: the Kid and the townspeople find themselves in the grip of a kind of mythic trance in which they are helpless to act other than to play the parts assigned by fate. Peckinpah crossed this passage out of the screenplay, but he seems not to have forgotten it. His staging also dramatized the power of the Kid's charisma, which most who knew him said was real and magnetic. Once again, a storyteller has "lied," but hasn't the lie revealed a truth we might not be able to feel in any other way?

Peckinpah and Wurlitzer were careful to show that many people in the Old West were, if not complicit in their own destruction, so heedless of it that they brought much of it on themselves. This too is corroborated by historians. Almost every biography of Billy the Kid paints the same picture of Lincoln County and the New Mexico Territory: random killing, killing for revenge, killing for land, money, profit, or race, roving gangs of thieves, cutthroats, and murderers, and of course a war over mercantilism and government contracts. As in all drama, these conflicts—between high and low, rich and poor, young and old, powerful and weak, law-abiding and lawbreaking—are brought to life and developed through individual characters, some out of history, others made up. Peckinpah's and Wurlitzer's characters are too individuated to be as allegorical as such, nor are they, I think, representative in any simplistic QED way of the larger conflicts. When, for example, Billy and Alamosa Bill engage in their duel, neither Wurlitzer in the writing nor Peckinpah in the realization suggests it has principally to do with obligation or responsibility; the explicit note sounded is that neither of them can think of anything else to do. As these personal conflicts play out they do not express the larger themes so much as reflect and lend them an urgency and pathos that only a tragedy of recognizably human dimensions can embody, as friendships, relationships, and partnerships are destroyed or destroy each other in a world that is breaking apart before our very eyes. When the vehicle is a story of characters drawn with a flesh-and-blood reality that we experience as directly and intimately as Peckinpah typically manages and as he certainly achieved here, then the themes are felt emotionally rather than intellectually, poetically rather than analytically, and we grasp their human import in ways rarely possible even in colorful narrative histories.

This is why storytellers go beyond the facts, ignore them, or change them: one of the purposes, and unquestionably one of the pleasures, of historically based fiction, drama, and film is to imagine the emotional lives and relationships of historical figures. It appears beyond reasonable doubt that Garrett and the Kid were not close friends, but if they were, what kind of friendship might it have been? Wurlitzer has come under criticism for suggesting that Billy was told to leave the territory—who told him, some have demanded to know—and Peckinpah has come under much stronger criticism for suggesting it was Garrett himself. Is there a historical basis for any of this? Depends on whom you believe. The answer to who told Billy to leave appears to be— practically everybody who knew and cared about him, beginning with Ma'am and Heiskell Jones and some of their sons, the Coe cousins, several of the other Regulators before they left the territory, and John Meadows. The idea that it was Garrett himself seems to have originated with Meadows, who said:

> Garrett himself told me time and time again that when he was elected sheriff of Lincoln County, his first object was to put an end to the Kid's continued defiance of the law without any bloodshed. He said, "I had figured out just how to do it. Before I was elected sheriff, I saw the Kid and talked it over with him. We had a game of poker together, and while we were playing, I told him the best thing he could do was to get up and be gone three or four years. Then he could come back and there would be nothing said or done about what had happened in the Lincoln County War. But the Kid could not see the point of my advice, and decided to stay." (43)

I'm unable to find a single historian or biographer apart from Frazier Hunt who lends any credence to this story. Yet denying it raises questions too: Meadows was not known to exaggerate or deliberately falsify his reminiscences, even after he became a minor celebrity as a raconteur. Did Garrett lie to him? Maybe, but why? He had no need to justify himself to Meadows, who was a close friend, never blamed him for killing the Kid, and held him in the highest regard ("I never met in my life a man who was any more truthful, any more honorable, or any better citizen," Meadows said of Garrett [55]). And he certainly couldn't have known that Meadows would ever be in a position publicly to help raise his posthumous reputation. Was Garrett simply misremembering—that is, did he intend to meet with Billy, fail to do so, then years later remember the intention as the deed? Possibly. Another possibility is that Garrett was recalling a similar warning he issued directly to the Kid's close friend Charlie Bowdre: "The best thing all of you can do is leave the country. Why don't you do like Frank and George Coe? Go off to one side and stay awhile; then come back when this thing is over," adding, prophetically, "If you fellows don't go away, I'm going to arrest you or kill you, or you are going to kill me" (the source for this is also Meadows [44]). Still another possibility is that it wasn't something Garrett planned but rather happened into, say, a casual card game with Billy and some of his friends, around the time he was elected sheriff or weeks or months before; and when the talk turned, as it likely would, to the new governor and his pledge to do something to put a stop to all the criminal activity, the amnesty, the general state of affairs in Lincoln County following the war, Garrett merely suggested to everyone present what he later told Bowdre. Any of these scenarios is a plausible variant of what Meadows recalled.

Plausible or not, however, why should Peckinpah's postulating a friendship need any justification outside itself and the perfectly valid dramatic purposes to which he put it? It answered to his long-standing personal, psychological, and thematic preoccupations, and it certainly embodied a historical truth about the Old West: how blurry the lines sometimes were between lawfulness and outlawry, how easy it was for former outlaws to become sheriffs and marshals (and, less commonly, to revert), and how this left friends, partners, comrades-in-arms, even family members estranged from one another owing to chance, choice, temperament, ambition, changing circumstances, good or bad luck, you name it. (We also know that Peckinpah worked very hard to incorporate this theme from Neider's novel into his *Pat Garrett* revisions.) There must be countless such stories from the Old West; if the Peckinpah-Wurlitzer version is more the story of the legend than of the history as such, that hardly invalidates it as drama or for that matter as history, given that legend is an aspect of history.

Another part of the film that is historically inaccurate is the manhunt itself. Garrett conducted no sustained, relentless manhunt for Billy the Kid following the escape, because the trail dried up pretty fast and Garrett soon stopped looking for him, for which he was the subject of gossip and eventually open criticism by many who elected him. But according to *The Authentic Life of Billy, the Kid*, he wasn't slacking, merely, like many others, unable to imagine Billy was still in the territory, let alone so close as Fort Sumner, and he claimed to be continuing his investigation on the sly (142). Does this make the film a lie? The facts of the gossip and the criticism of Garrett indicate how much pressure he was under to apprehend Billy, who rightly or wrongly, fairly or not, came to symbolize the extent to which the territory was still at the mercy of rustlers, horse thieves, robbers, bandits, and killers. Garrett was also the object of derision by Billy's friends and some (though by no means all) of the Mexican populace for allegedly siding with Chisum and the others. He was caught in a terrible bind. By imagining the story as a manhunt that sends Garrett through a cross-section of the social, economic, and ethnic groups and strata that made up the New Mexico Territory, Wurlitzer devised a structure that enabled him to dramatize the conflicting demands and pressures on the sheriff and the hostility he faced in many quarters. For his part, Peckinpah realized this world with a vividness and attention to detail impressive even by the standards he himself set in *The Wild Bunch*, *Major Dundee*, and *Ride the High Country* and he invested the people in it with an affective reality that brings them alive in a way that no other film and few books on this subject ever have.

A big part of what drew both Peckinpah and Wurlitzer to these materials is that, as the writer put it, "everybody knew everybody. That's where a lot of the sadness and tragedy come in."[14] No one has come close to inflecting this with as much pathos as Peckinpah does in *Pat Garrett and Billy the Kid*: scene after scene plays out as farewells, leave-takings, good-byes, some peaceable, most violent, as individuals or groups find themselves in oppositions that didn't exist a few months ago and may not a few months hence, but they do right then, and so by violent attrition a way of life slowly, almost casually disintegrates before our eyes. It is a very special part of Peckinpah's achievement in this film that his depiction of the death of the Old West is at once so tough-minded yet so elegiac, continually forcing us to question its values, its very worth, even as we are moved by its loss.

Because everybody knew everybody else, Peckinpah also believed that the idea of directness—if not honor, then at least forthrightness among thieves—was a practical value these people lived by, not merely a romantic myth. "When Billy switched from Dolan to Tunstall," the director said, "he told his former buddies he was making the switch."[15] Peckinpah was here alluding to chapter 8 from *The Authentic Life*, where Billy rides out to inform Jesse Evans and the Boys that henceforth he was going to be working for Tunstall. Almost nobody believes this incident occurred—if it occurred at all—anything like as melodramatically as Upson imagined it, with dialogue that never came out of an outlaw's mouth or anybody else's ("Boys," intones Evans, the Kid "didn't sneak off like a cur, and leave us to find out, when we heard the crack of his Winchester, that he was fighting against us" [51]). I personally don't think Peckinpah believed it either, but he seems to have believed there was sufficient historical basis behind it for him to want the idea of it sounded in his film. The first scene in Fort Sumner he intended precisely to dramatize the point that Garrett takes the time and expends the effort to make the ride from Lincoln to inform the Kid and his gang directly and in person that he's now sheriff and that his new responsibilities include clearing the territory of outlaws and rustlers.

Although this scene never took place in history and the real Garrett's relationship with his wife was nothing like what is shown in the film, the character as conceived by Peckinpah and Wurlitzer and as played by James Coburn—surely at this point the actor must be counted among the auteurs—is nevertheless a remarkably credible dramatic embodiment of the historical figure, especially the Garrett seen in the prologue: the disillusioned, irascible, hot-tempered ex-lawman, surrounded by people he detests, is easily recognizable from his historical counterpart, who spent his last bitter years in debt pursuing one failing moneymaking scheme after another. But all this may have been less a function of Peckinpah trying to be accurate than of where he felt himself to be while making the film: long about the time the frame story was written, it was beginning to dawn on him just how much that spectacular deal he had received from MGM was going to cost *him*. "In a film," he once told a reporter (Yergin 91), "you lay yourself out, whoever you are." Even a "historical" film.

4. Hendry and Billy

I am certain Peckinpah did not give a hoot in hell that Kris Kristofferson bore no physical resemblance to the real William Bonney. And knowing how sensitive he was to criticism, I am equally certain he knew it would cost him dearly in any of several circles—film reviewers, historians, Billy the Kid buffs, even perhaps many Average Moviegoers with a smattering of knowledge—but he didn't care because what mattered most to him was that he felt Kristofferson was psychologically and temperamentally right for Charles Neider's Hendry Jones. In a kind of reversal of the novelist's process, Peckinpah would turn the Billy of Rudolph Wurlitzer's screenplay back into the Hendry of Neider's novel, and thus get a chance to do it right for a beloved book he felt had been betrayed by Marlon Brando fifteen years earlier. Like Neider's, Peckinpah's Kid is a few years older and already starting to decline, and he is physically and psychically tired. He has drunk too much, whored too much, ridden too much, thieved too much, and killed too much. He has nowhere to go and no real desire to change. The only meaning he can find is with his friends around Fort Sumner, which he must know is threadbare enough, as they didn't even bother to try to spring him from jail. Anyhow, their number is dwindling fast. He is rebellious or at least once was, but inchoately, perhaps even nihilistically so, his refusal to leave or change based on no values that we are able to discern and none that he can articulate—beyond, perhaps, a certain habitual loyalty and a vague notion of freedom that consists in no restraints on his appetites or desires. He simply can't imagine doing anything else and he is incapable of existing in any other way. There is an aspect to his behavior that suggests a passive suicide: if he's stubborn enough, if he sits and waits long enough, he will be killed before he gets old, and if he has any fears at all, the loss of his youth must lie at the heart of them. Yet death cannot be rushed, it must come in its own time, and it can assume only one form: Pat Garrett, a quasi-father figure and close friend who will function as its instrument.

Something like this is what I suspect Peckinpah had in mind when he first read Wurlitzer's screenplay and wrote the memo in which, among other suggestions, he advised Wurlitzer to read Neider's novel. But it didn't quite turn out that way. Somewhere between that first reading and what Peckinpah eventually shot, this conception of Billy got derailed and it was only partially realized in the film as released. How did this happen? I observed in chapter 6 that when Peckinpah himself started adding new scenes of his own to Wurlitzer's screenplay, he basically adopted the same overall strategy he used in his adaptation of *The Authentic Death of Hendry Jones*; that is, he added scenes he felt necessary to set up the story, in this case, the friendship of Garrett and Billy, and then he strengthened the Garrett character. I assume he always meant to do more work on Billy but what he did was just cut out all the scenes from Wurlitzer's screenplay that dramatized the Kid's decline and dissipation and put nothing in their place. Why did Peckinpah remove all this material?

The beginning of an answer is to recall that he did something of the same thing in his adaptation of Neider's novel, making Hendry a less dark, disturbed, and disturbing character and instead a rather more conventional good badman. Speculating on why he did this, I suggested that one possible reason might have been that between them he and the producer feared Marlon Brando would never play that character, which *One-Eyed Jacks* shows to have been true. But from the perspective of *Pat Garrett and Billy the Kid*, I am even less sure of its adequacy as a whole explanation. Most of us who've written about Peckinpah in general and *Pat Garrett* in particular are struck by the bleakness of its vision and have concluded that it seems to have reflected where he was in both his professional and private lives when he made it. Yet to say that is only to beg another question: why should this have been so? On the face of it, Peckinpah's career and even his life seemed to be going very well for him. *The Wild Bunch* and *Straw Dogs*, though highly controversial, established him as a filmmaker of world stature; he was doing what he always wanted to do, which was make films virtually without interruption. To be sure, he was deeply disappointed that *The Wild Bunch* was snubbed at the Academy Awards, he harbored resentment about it the rest of his life, and he was far from pleased by some of the critical reception of his work. But he courted controversy, it was built into his work, and it was one proof of its seriousness, of how edgy, unsettling, provocative, boundary-pushing, even radical and subversive much of it was and always will be. He wouldn't have had it any other way.

He continued to have his problems with the business side of the industry, yet even here the producers on *Straw Dogs*, *Junior Bonner*, and *The Getaway* were essentially supportive and let him make the films he wanted to make. And all of them made money, even *Junior Bonner*, which, though it opened to lukewarm reviews and has often been called a commercial flop, was in fact so economically made that it turned a small profit (see D. Weddle 433). Before he finished shooting *Pat Garrett*, he would see the release of *The Getaway*, which would prove the biggest commercial hit of his career except for *Convoy*. His personal life was a mess—he married his third wife on *The Getaway* and they filed for divorce four months later as he was about to leave for Mexico and *Pat*

Garrett—but his personal life was always a mess. What was different this time was the extent of the drinking.

Even before *Pat Garrett*, his attempts to control it, successful enough to allow him to get by in the past, were getting weaker and less effective. He started *The Getaway* determined not to drink before five in the afternoon; yet he soon began demanding drinks earlier. When Chalo Gonzalez, his assistant, reminded him of his instruction, Peckinpah came back with a version of that hoary joke beloved of California drinkers: "What time is it in New York?"—"Five-thirty"—"Then bring me a goddamn drink" (D. Weddle 437). Despite this, there is no indication he was off his game on that picture, which is superlatively crafted. But that sort of drinking can continue only for so long, and he was at an age—he turned forty-eight on *Pat Garrett*—where his body just couldn't handle the booze the way it used to. Of course, substance abuse in and of itself always presupposes underlying causes, but as anyone who has dealt with alcoholics soon discovers, those problems are eventually shouldered out of the way by the trouble the drinking itself causes, which always demands immediate attention. It was no different with Sam. Back in 1956 when he wrote the *Hendry Jones* adaptation, his drinking was not nearly so debilitating as it would become later. But there was no question he was already an alcoholic, though a much younger one, his body could take it, and he was far better able to control it. For all the bull some of his colleagues who were also drinking buddies liked to sling about his capacity for alcohol and how it didn't affect his work, the truth is that in those days when he knew he had to finish a writing assignment, produce a series episode, or direct one, he typically hunkered down and really did control his intake (often, I've been told, he even abstained). I've heard conflicting accounts about how much he drank while shooting *The Wild Bunch*, but everyone agrees that it was never to the point that it impaired him in any way and that he was never drunk on the set.

There was always a contradiction in Sam's relationship to his own drinking: he would both own it yet deny that it affected him. This dual attitude was reflected in several of his episodes for *The Westerner* and one for *The Rifleman*, where he treated drinking with unblinking candor and seriousness in some yet as a source of comedy in others. By the time he came to *Pat Garrett*, however, nobody was laughing, least of all Sam himself, and for good reason: Wurlitzer's screenplay depicted a young man who was drinking himself to death, and the reflection Sam saw in the character was so accurate it must have knocked him for a loop. Take the scene in the screenplay, where, after trying unsuccessfully to shoot a bottle of mescal at fifty paces, Billy is found sitting in the prairie all by himself, gun empty and bottle nearly so—and compare it to the picture of Sam himself several months later on his days off in Durango in his hacienda, lying in bed with a bottle of vodka between his legs and firing at his reflection in a mirror. The ironies here are quite literally sobering. Did the screenplay anticipate, even influence life or was Sam imitating by way of acting out something he could not face up to? Whatever the answer, what he cut from the Wurlitzer original and what he left out of the Neider adaptation are too consistent with each other to be coincidental.

Hemingway once said that if a writer "knows enough of what he is writing about he may omit things that he knows and the reader, if the writer is writing truly enough, will have a feeling of those things as strongly as though the writer had stated them." Peckinpah certainly knew enough about drinking to be able to make a film about it truly,[16] so we must assume that its reduction in his treatments of Hendry and Billy originate in choice or denial. In his *Hendry Jones* adaptation, he was able to work around what he left out by retaining Hendry's relationship with Nika and inventing a new ending that provided a resolution that was dramatically (and structurally) satisfying. But in Billy, there isn't enough in the character to grasp what isn't there and what's there is contradictory enough to be considered "complex" and "enigmatic" if it works for you or inconsistent and sketchy if it doesn't. In Wurlitzer's screenplay, after a certain point the Kid drinks constantly and is hardly ever sober. In Peckinpah's film, he drinks just twice: once at the beginning with Garrett and again near the end on his last day, first with Alias and later before he makes love to Maria. That's it. Ironically, while this weakened Billy as a character, it wound up strengthening Garrett, much as Dad Longworth was strengthened, because if Peckinpah saw reflected in Billy and Hendry things he didn't want to admit about himself, he found in each of the sheriffs the kind of men he wished he could be.

5. Dad and Garrett

In 1957, when Peckinpah wrote his screen adaptation of *The Authentic Death of Hendry Jones*, he was still married to his first wife, Marie Selland, and they lived in Malibu when it was a small, funky, unpretentious beach community with nice housing that was actually affordable. It was a good life: they at first lived in a Quonset hut in the hills high above the beach and later in a place right on the beach, they had three daughters (their son was not born yet), a menagerie of pets, a wonderful circle of friends and family, parties almost every weekend, and Sam's career was on the rise. It was as close to a life of more or less "normal" domesticity (though with a distinctly bohemian flavor) as he was ever to have as an adult. But there were already fissures in the marriage, while his drinking was getting to be serious enough that the usual changes in personality due to alcohol were beginning to appear. He would get by turns verbally abusive or morose, behavior by no means exhibited every time he drank or even all that often at first. But it happened often enough that both friends and family were worried, and by the time the family moved into the house on the beach he was drinking most nights. Whether he was unfaithful to Marie before he wrote the adaptation, he certainly was once he started in on *The Rifleman* and was spending far more time twenty-some miles down the coast in Los Angeles.[17]

Yet for all Sam's bad behavior, it's difficult to be completely unsympathetic to his obvious conflictedness during these years. On the one hand he seems to have had a genuine desire to be a good father and husband and on the other he was answering the call of his ambitions as both a director and an artist, working furiously hard for long hours days on end churning out scripts for episodic television and soon enough directing and then producing them. Given his temperament, reconciling these conflicts seems never to have been an option in the first place; given the immensity of his talent, sacrificing it wasn't one either. Frustration, rage, lashing out, guilt, apology, aggressiveness, passivity or at least retreat, avoidance, then lashing out again—this was a pattern of behavior that marked his whole life. Little wonder he drank.

When he read Neider's novel, he found in the title character a young man the self-destructive trajectory of whose life was so clearly a possibility for his own that he softened him in the adaptation and removed most of the drinking. But he also found the seeds of another possibility in a different character. In the novel Dad Longworth had been a hell-raiser in his youth but was now a man who accepted responsibility and had already settled down with a family. In the screenplay Peckinpah retained most of this but completely fleshed it out and dramatized it further by inventing new scenes that showed the strength and depth of Dad's commitment to his family. In the novel Dad's wife is Mexican and never identified by name; Peckinpah made her Anglo, named her May, and drew her as a strong, sturdy, sensual woman fiercely protective of her family and concerned about her husband's past association with men like Hendry, who wants Dad to rejoin him in a life of crime. Dad will have none of it and he remains by May's side, sending Hendry away without even showing him to the door. It's not hard to see that Dad here became for Sam a kind of wish fulfillment, a projection of the man he wanted to be and maybe even believed was still a possibility for him. Thirty-two when he wrote the adaptation, Sam must have noticed that he was suspended about midway between Hendry's age, which is twenty-five, and Dad's, which is late thirties. He could see possible futures in both characters and believe the choice was still his to make.

Fifteen years and three wrecked marriages later, it was all different. By then it was clear that despite any wishes to the contrary, as far as drinking and a life of domesticity were concerned, his future had become Hendry's. In the four to five years leading up to *Pat Garrett* he could still see himself as the relatively youthful Hendry, the Hendry of the escalating reputation and the triumphs—the Kid at the top of his game, before the steep decline and sudden death. In Wurlitzer's Billy, however, Sam saw something much closer to the reality of what his behavior had actually brought him to, someone who couldn't stop drinking, couldn't hold it when he did drink, and couldn't control his temper when he was drunk, becoming irresponsible, nasty, cruel, and abusive with increasing frequency and intensity. The prevalent view of Peckinpah's Garrett—I've argued it myself—is that he was depicting in the character much of what he worried about, feared, or hated in himself: his abusiveness, his ambitiousness, his personal corruptibility, his spiritual emptiness, his own capacity for violence (notably toward women), his attraction to the sordid, his fear that he had sold himself out, his increasing isolation from family and old friends, and of course his alcoholism. This is all true and valid so far as it goes. But it doesn't tell the whole story, because Garrett is a figure who is in many ways also admirable and attractive, with qualities that would answer a real and present need in Sam himself if only he could possess or repossess them, as the case may be. In other words, like Dad Longworth, Pat Garrett too was developed into a kind of wish fulfillment.

Think of it. Unlike Billy, who drinks hardly at all, Garrett is shown drinking in almost every scene in the film. It's easy to infer from this that Sam was here trying to show the truth about himself and his own alcoholism. This is true except for one thing: however much Garrett drinks, *he never seems to get drunk*. With few exceptions, throughout the entire film he comports himself with supreme control and dispatch. Although his killing of Holly is disturbing both in how coldly calculated it is and in the sadistic streak it suggests, when it comes to violence Garrett as a rule exercises greater restraint than just about anyone else in the film and does more to avoid it, beginning with asking the Kid to leave the territory, and he kills far fewer men than Billy does. Once we are past the prologue, Garrett sizes up, manages, and generally dominates almost every situation he's in, beginning with his arrival in Fort Sumner, where his marksmanship is superior to everyone else's, including even the Kid's.[18] In the capture at Stinking Springs, he and his posse surround the shack and never for a moment do Billy and his friends have a chance. When he returns to Lincoln after Billy's escape, he takes charge of the town, orders everyone to do his bidding, deputizes a reluctant Alamosa Bill, and then relaxes for a shave as he awaits his bath and meal while his orders are carried out. At Black Harris's, while everyone is running around shooting, Garrett remains cool, calm, and collected, the literal voice of reason ("I'm lookin' for sign, Black") who never misses his mark. In Jones's Saloon, he practically becomes the director himself, blocking the scene before our very eyes even as it's being played, and all without getting up out of his chair until it's over. (In all the many films about filmmaking, this is by far the most accurate depiction I know about one way a great director sets up and stages a scene, save only for not rising from his chair.) And later at Ruthie Lee's, despite how much alcohol he has consumed and the presence of five prostitutes, there is no hint of drink provoking the desire yet taking away the performance. Once back in Fort Sumner, Garrett encircles and ensnares Billy as deliberately as a spider spinning its web, the sheriff's air of seeming invincibility so strong that none of the Kid's friends dares raise a weapon against him. Only in the prologue do we see the limits of Garrett's ability to control the world around him; only with Chisum do we see him defer to authority; and only at home with his wife does he seem ill at ease, trying to sit down and talk with her but soon getting up and pacing around the house until he can think of an excuse to leave.

But Garrett wasn't for Sam just a model of a certain kind of restraint and control he didn't possess but needed to. Garrett also represented something else Sam both wanted and needed at the time but seems not to have had the will to carry out: a desire to change. We have only to look at photographs from around the time of *Pat Garrett* forward to see that Sam was aging prematurely and alarmingly. "How old was he when he died?" "Fifty-nine going on eighty," someone once answered. This is why there is so much talk about getting old in this film and why it has a sense of both urgency and fatigue missing from *The Wild Bunch, Ride the High Country*, and *Junior Bonner*. At the time of *Hendry Jones*, Sam was young enough that he could still imagine a different future for himself. By *Pat Garrett*, he was feeling that time really was running out for him and if he didn't stop hastening it with his behavior, it was soon going to run out for good. According to his friend the actor Robert Culp, a few years later Sam "became acutely aware that he was in mortal danger from his lifetime of abuse" and asked for help from Coburn, whom he knew to be knowledgeable about "several Eastern disciplines." Although Coburn believed the healer he put Sam in touch with gave him "an extra four to seven years of life," the healer himself apparently felt "that a real cure was not possible—it was already too late" (40). The irony of the character who represented a desire for change being played by the actor through whom Sam later sought a means for it is too obvious to require comment.

Garrett was not just a far more interesting character than Billy was, he may also have been the one Sam envied more and he was certainly the more valuable figure to emulate. From this perspective, I am by no means convinced that even Billy's resistance to changing times necessarily represented something positive, admirable, or even particularly desirable for Sam at this point in his life. Rather, I suspect that what the Billy of Wurlitzer's screenplay might really have represented for Sam personally, were it to be articulated in present-day parlance, would go something like, "Been there, done that, still doing it." Garrett's need to change in order to survive reflected Sam's own need and Garrett's actions represented Sam's fears about what change might actually mean and do to him. His fears were real: he was already beginning to lose friends because they just couldn't deal with his drinking and its associated behavior any longer, and he also knew that if he were ever to give up drinking, he might have to give up those friends who were his drinking buddies. Beyond that, who knew how much of it fueled his creativity? To use Billy as an ethical touchstone in the film, which so many critics appear to need to do in their moral revulsion against Garrett, seems to me to miss much of the source of the film's psychological tension, its emotional anguish, most of its thematic and moral complexity, not to mention just about all of its ironies. It is to impose a cut-and-dried dualism upon a dynamic, multifaceted, and ramified one.[19]

Perhaps one can respond only personally: the emotional core of this film has for me always been Garrett, and the power of that core is his desperation: he is trying to get free from a past that will destroy him as surely as it is destroying both itself and those all around him. Yet a person from that past, someone so close to him that he might almost be a part of him, is determined to keep him bound to it, so much so that Garrett is forced into acts of ever greater cruelty to make him understand that he must be let go. Many critics like to make much of Peckinpah's appearance as the coffin maker late in the film, especially of the imprecations he hurls at Garrett in the preview versions. Fair enough, so long as they do not miss the irony that this still makes it Peckinpah himself who directs Garrett to go on in and get it over with, which is to say that he personally gives Garrett the final permission to finish what he set out to do: get Billy the Kid out of his life one way or another.

6. "Things are always mixed."

David Thomson once observed that "it was in looking that Peckinpah seemed most open or uncertain; he looked to see—whereas John Ford looked to discover what he already knew" (672). Precisely. And when Peckinpah looked he looked not in black-and-white but in color, in the full spectrum of complexity, nuance, and ambiguity which that implies. What he mostly saw left him filled with doubt, worry, confusion, frustration, uncertainty, anger, and irony because he was incapable of seeing from one perspective or angle of vision only. By his own admission the very idea of absolutes drove him crazy and he could not prevent himself from dramatizing or otherwise showing multiple points of view that are typically in conflict. He was so restless, inquisitive, honest, and—why use a lesser word?—truthful that he refused to let his films make figuring things out any easier for us than it was for him.

Peckinpah's critics like to harp on the alleged "limitations" of his thinking, but in order to do this they usually make reference to his so-called ideas, that is, the hopped-up things he liked to say in interviews, often as not to needle the reporters so he wouldn't have to talk about his films, which he preferred speak for themselves. As with most artists who are any good, his artistic grasp of his materials, including his ideas, is so much greater than his personal or intellectual grasp of them. He never meant for us to "choose" between the polarities he sets up here or in any of his other films; he meant for us to experience the tensions and difficulties of having to sustain them, to live with and within them the way he himself did, gnawing at him, worrying him, angering him, tearing him apart, perhaps even mocking him.[20] No doubt he would have agreed with Scott Fitzgerald that the "test of a first-rate intelligence is the ability to hold two opposed ideas in the mind at the same time, and still retain the ability to function." It's also one test of a first-rate storyteller, dramatist, and poet, and there are very few filmmakers who possessed this kind of intelligence and even fewer who put it to such volatile emotional, psychological, and dramatic use as effectively as Peckinpah in his best work.

He was especially proud of how he presented his characters without judging them. Much of the time his methods are intended to make judgment as difficult as possible, to erode even the standard bases for judgment, which often makes life very tough for a lot of his critics, who seem to want more clear-cut alternatives or easily digestible choices. Both Peckinpah and Wurlitzer regarded (still regards, in the writer's case) Garrett as a far more layered and tortured character than Billy, and certainly a more conflicted one, with a correspondingly larger grasp of what was going on in the world around him. For one thing, as regards tone, that is, the author's and thus our attitude toward the material, Peckinpah intended for Garrett's asking the Kid to leave and delaying his pursuit to count for a good deal more than some critics seem willing to grant. He told Carroll and Wurlitzer, "Pat really doesn't want to see Billy hanged, and once he gets away it takes tremendous pressure off him and he hopes to God the Kid will get out." For another, Billy and his friends are about as culpable for the loss of their world as the Santa Fe Ring and its putative agent in Garrett are, a theme that is introduced in the prologue, where Garrett is killed not only by Poe and his partners but also symbolically by Billy, his gang, and Garrett himself, and that resounds in almost every violent encounter in the remainder of the film. For a third, I am bewildered by those who argue that Garrett kills the best part of himself when he kills Billy. The best part of Garrett is a man who can't think of better ways to amuse himself than shooting the heads off chickens buried in the sand? The best part of Garrett is a man who drops in on a family at dinner and then engages a duel with another guest, killing him in front of the whole family, including the children? The best part of Garrett is a man who shoots another man in the back? I don't think so, and I seriously doubt Peckinpah thought so.

I remain equally unpersuaded by arguments that Billy is a romantic, idealistic, incorruptible hero, and I have little patience with attempts to view him, his gang, and their Fort Sumner environs as symbolizing some sort of prelapsarian Western Arcadia (despite the presence—patently ironic—of the shepherd Paco and his sheep). I am aware of the fact that the fatal bullet from Garrett's revolver scarcely marking the Kid's body can be construed to suggest that Billy dies "pure," but I don't believe a really attentive viewing of the whole film will support this interpretation. Peckinpah depicted it that way because he wanted an image that would serve as a further contrast to and thus heightening of the disfigured reflection of Garrett in the shattered mirror. He was so identified with Garrett, so implicated in Garrett's issues, that in this scene he kept Billy unblemished by the bullet that pierces his breast as a way of throwing into clearer relief the psychic damage Garrett is doing to himself. By the time of production, Peckinpah's conception of the Kid had become so fluid and changeable that he was made to assume whatever characteristics the

Billy unblemished in death, Garrett alive but psychically scarred for life

director required of him in any given scene, regardless of what he was in his previous scene or would be in his next.

To see Billy, however likable he is, as free or a symbol of freedom seems to me further to strip the character of most of what makes him both interesting and legitimately ambiguous in a valid aesthetic sense. What, exactly, is free about a man whose thinking and modes of action and behavior are as limited as his or as thoroughly determined by the world that shaped him? If Billy represents anything along these lines, it seems to me to lie in something like the abdication of freedom: by the end he just sits and waits. And throughout the film the lives of Billy and his pals which we see on exhibit in Fort Sumner are less suggestive of vitality, energy, or even "youth" than of stagnation: for all of its opening festivities and the vibrancy of its colors and textures, this is a world that is already in the process of dying with or without a Santa Fe Ring to hasten it along. Peckinpah was a complex and tragic romantic, not a cheap and maudlin one, and he was always a hard-edged one, in this film exceptionally so.[21] More than in most of his films, he here created two deeply flawed protagonists, appealing in some ways, very much not so in others, trapped in circumstances far from their own choosing, who make a series of decisions that eventually wind up destroying them both. I can't think of much in the way of lessons for living that can be extrapolated from their story, but it certainly embodies a powerfully tragic vision in which most choices are Hobbesian, the very idea of freedom may be largely illusory, the bedrock reality is impermanence, and the only inevitabilities are changing, aging, and dying.[22]

It's obvious that in killing Billy, Garrett is killing something in himself. But by identifying with both men did Peckinpah also see himself in some sense allegorized in their story? How could he not? When you've relied on something as long as Sam relied on booze, it obviously becomes something you identify with because it's now a part of you—indeed, it's a cliché of addiction that the substance of choice is your best friend.[23] And you don't think about giving it up without getting scared to death at the prospect of being without it. Garrett wants to change, he needs to change, he has to change, yet the price is so high and the world after the change is such an unknown, hence the shattered reflection in the mirror and his ride out into an arid landscape after he performs the final deed that both liberates and entraps him. For Peckinpah himself, those two images were projections of some of his deepest fears as much as they are objective correlatives of themes, emotions, and psychological states in the story.

That the loan from Chisum complicates, compromises, and even corrupts Garrett's motives is beyond question, not least because it adds the pressures of obligation and urgency, which provide the drama with something of a subtly ticking clock: he's expected to do something and do it fast, but his reluctance and procrastination keep pushing back against him (we see yet again what a master of time and long-range structure Peckinpah is). But the

desire to change predates the loan and is located in dissatisfactions and dis-
contents that run very deep, so deep they cannot be salved and may not be
fixable, and this too seems to have reflected something in Peckinpah himself.
The cause may not matter, it may not even be identifiable; these things just
are in some people, and he knew he was one of them. It was around this time
that he started talking in interviews about feeling rootless, homeless, and
lonesome. After he and Marie divorced, he never really had another place he
thought of as home. In the years following *The Wild Bunch* he lived on film
locations; when in Los Angeles, he rented; once his third marriage fell apart,
the only home he had left, and it would be the only one for the rest of his life,
was the rather forlorn mobile home in the trailer park above Paradise Cove in
Malibu. Otherwise, he was a nomad. This provided no doubt one avenue of
sympathy for Billy and perhaps a basis for envy: Fort Sumner was the Kid's
home; when he tried to leave it, he couldn't, so he came back, regardless of
the cost. Wurlitzer's original screenplay actually dramatized this much better
than the character as gutted by Peckinpah did, but more than a suggestion of
it survived in the film all the same. And in Garrett he saw mirrored his own
open road—a road that in Sam's case led to no home—which may be another
reason why the story inside the frame originally ended with Garrett riding
into a barren landscape and left the frame itself unclosed.

Another avenue, if not of sympathy, then at least of identification between
Peckinpah and Billy, consists in Billy's antipathy toward authority. When Garrett tells him, "The electorate wants you gone, out of the country," and Billy
replies, "Well, are they telling me or are they asking me?"—it's easy to imagine
variants and equivalents of this behind the scenes on any of Peckinpah's films,
nowhere more so than on this one. Garrett becomes from this perspective a
kind of surrogate for all the producers and other intermediate functionaries
between the director and the top executives who control the purse strings.
According to Roger, Katy, Dawson, and several others I've spoken with, all
Gordon Carroll would have to say is, "Sam, we're not allowed to do that," and
Sam would come back with, "Oh, yeah, just watch me!" Exchanges like this
happened time and again during the shoot, usually between Sam and Carroll,
occasionally between Sam and Melnick. Billy's antipathy toward authority is
of course a reflection of Garrett's own, but with a crucial difference: Billy's is
essentially adolescent hostility, a function of his youth; Garrett's, like Sam's
own, is deeply rooted, a visceral hatred fueled from the innermost core of
his personality. Garrett is also able better to control it, which is yet another
reason why he is so anguished and psychically tortured, thus as a character so
much richer and more complex.

In charting the relationship between Garrett and Billy, one argument goes
that if Garrett is seen to question the value of the way of life Billy represents,
then the power of the betrayal is weakened and so is Garrett himself as a
tragic figure. But why the theme of a man who comes to regret the way he
has lived his life, including his values and people he's regarded as his friends,

should be any less tragic than a theme of betrayal I don't see. This is, after all, one theme of *The Ambassadors*; it's a theme of *Death of a Salesman* too, though it's doubtful Willy Loman ever fully apprehends the essentially false values by which he's lived his life and which he's tragically passed on to one of his sons; and variants of it can be found in *To Have and Have Not*, "The Snows of Kilimanjaro," and *For Whom the Bell Tolls*, all by Peckinpah's revered Hemingway. As for betrayal and guilt, well, when Peckinpah wanted to tell stories about betrayal or when he wanted his characters to feel guilt, which he did in films as diverse as *The Deadly Companions, Ride the High Country, Major Dundee, Noon Wine, The Wild Bunch, The Ballad of Cable Hogue, Bring Me the Head of Alfredo Garcia*, and *The Killer Elite*, he had no compunction about showing it and he was certainly the master of whatever techniques he needed to dramatize it, whether in flashbacks, in dialogue, in reaction shots, or in performance.

But what in *Pat Garrett* can we point to that indicates Garrett feels guilty?[24] He himself never articulates or otherwise expresses it. Others try to shame him, notably Lemuel, who reminds him that he "used to be just like a daddy to that boy." But I see little to suggest Peckinpah shared their judgments or expected us to either. (The last question he shouts as the coffin maker—"When are you going to learn you can't trust anybody, not even yourself?"—doesn't lay guilt on Garrett, it exhorts him to self-knowledge.) In none of the principal sources that he drew upon is either guilt or betrayal a motif, including Garrett's book, Neider's novel, the adaptation, and Wurlitzer's screenplay. There is no doubt that Garrett carries out his mission with great reluctance and procrastination, but he does everything he can, including essentially committing murder by killing Holly, to demonstrate his resoluteness to the Kid and to give him time to clear out, and at the outset he all but begs him to do so. When Garrett slumps down on the swing after killing Billy and sits there until morning, I see grief, regret, utter exhaustion, and an almost unfathomable emptiness now that it's finally over and had to end this way. He will doubtless be troubled by it all the rest of his life, and I believe the prologue with its flashback structure is intended to suggest how it haunted him. But one can be haunted by feelings other than guilt, as was true of the real Garrett, who just grew tired of being known as the Man Who Shot Billy the Kid, of seeing the culture of romance that had built up around the outlaw, and of being blamed for not giving the Kid a so-called fair chance in the final encounter. My feeling is that what will trouble the Peckinpah-Wurlitzer Garrett most of all, were he ever to become an introspective man, is less guilt than the extent to which he comes to see both himself and Billy as pawns of fate in a game where the winner takes nothing either.

Some of the same people who view Billy as a tonic to Garrett take a decidedly judgmental view of Garrett in the scene with his wife and suggest that he deliberately rejects the warmth, love, and domesticity of the home Ida has made for them. This might make sense if the marriage were shown to be a mutually loving one, but it appears not to be; and if Peckinpah knew

Ironic closing allusions to a cowboy saying and a classic Western film

anything it was surely that you cannot force a feeling that isn't there. I have the same difficulty with those who argue that the ending isn't as bleak as it plainly is. One of them argues that the presence of the boy who throws stones at Garrett's horse offers "a powerful sense of hope, of the ability for change and growth" (Stevens 274). Really? Even when it's a boy angry, with obviously crushed hopes in a patently ironic allusion to the classic Western *Shane*, where in contrast another boy is pleading for the hero to come back? This is one of the problems with semiotically oriented criticism that relies heavily on signage, stock symbols, and stereotypical significations. Sometimes in Peckinpah's films children indicate possibilities for growth and development, as they do in Angel's village scenes from *The Wild Bunch*, especially when close-ups of a pensive Pike Bishop frame a tracking shot of some of the happiest, most beautiful children you will see in films (though contrast is part of the point here too). But at the end, the boy who hoists a rifle and shoots Pike in the back is also an illustration of the corruptibility of children. Innocence corrupted or, rather, further corrupted is also what we see at Horrell's Trading Post. When Billy cheats first in the duel with Alamosa Bill and Alamosa himself cheats a little later, what does this show us except that the younger generation has learned all too well the lessons of the older one? What can we think will be the lessons learned by the children who witness both cheatings, and who had already seen their brother killed not long before? The adolescent boy throwing stones at Garrett's horse and then turning and walking back dejectedly may be open to more than one interpretation, but it's preposterous to suggest that possibilities for hope and change are among them simply because the boy is *young*.

Yet I share the impulse of these critics to want to protect Peckinpah from the charges of nihilism, cynicism, and misanthropy which even some of his most enthusiastic admirers claim to find in his work. It's not that these things aren't there, rather that the work is by no means *limited* by or to them. The proper way to answer them is with reference to the largeness and generosity of Peckinpah's embrace, to his ability to bring so many characters, including minor and even unsavory ones, to life with such depth and vitality, and to the freedom from judgment in his best work. (It's not for nothing that he's sometimes been likened to Jean Renoir, whose work is also distinguished by a disinclination to judge its characters.) Peckinpah was almost incapable of *not* bringing his characters to life: no one who hates humanity could make films that burst with as much human energy in its myriad forms as *The Wild Bunch, Ride the High Country, Major Dundee, Junior Bonner, The Ballad of Cable Hogue, Pat Garrett and Billy the Kid*, and *Convoy* do. Even those films in which he deliberately limited his range and restricted his palette—*Straw Dogs, The Getaway, Bring Me the Head of Alfredo Garcia, The Killer Elite, Cross of Iron*—are still extraordinary for how most of the characters are brought to dramatic life. (Tom Hedden in *Straw Dogs* may be a hateful man and Cap Collis in *The Killer Elite* a sorry excuse for a human being, but as characters they are realized in something like the fullness of their being.) But like everybody else, Peckinpah would have to have been more or less than human if he did not have his black moods, his long dark nights of despair, his feelings of helplessness and hopelessness. *Pat Garrett and Billy the Kid* was made during one of these periods and it expresses those feelings perhaps more unrelentingly than any of his other films except maybe *Bring Me the Head of Alfredo Garcia*.

In analyzing *Pat Garrett and Billy the Kid* as I have in this part of the book, my intention is certainly not to reduce the film to Peckinpah's life, his drinking, and his other problems. No one has to know anything about either to respond to the film, while the parallels between Peckinpah and the principals in any case go only so far before they break down. I offer this interpretation, rather, as one layer of meaning among many in this richly layered film. But it is also by way of suggesting why I do not believe treating the characters in his Western films as only signs, icons, types, or archetypes can by any means wholly account for their power to affect us as strongly as they do. On this level they are indeed sui generis—*Peckinpah* films: psychologically and emotionally embattled because Peckinpah himself was this way and he wanted his films to embody how it felt to be that torn and conflicted and what it does to a person. "When I work, I become all the characters in the script," he once told his friend John Bryson. "It's very dangerous. I act out for myself in real life for the illusion of what I'm going to shoot" (140). From the mouths of any ninety-nine out of a hundred film directors a remark like that would be pure bull, but not from him, though it might have been more accurate if he had said that he finds in the characters feelings he has felt himself, which the characters then help him articulate or otherwise give artistic form to. Either way, however, he's talking about intense, powerful, disruptive, violent, often scary emotions that came from deep within. His fearlessness in getting them on film is part of what makes his films so powerful and compelling.

Rarely in his work was this process more in evidence than in *Pat Garrett and Billy the Kid*. He identified far more closely with Garrett than with Billy, in whom he nevertheless saw more of himself than he wanted to. But he certainly acted out in real life what he was going to shoot, and it became so dangerous that the closer he came to the core of his protagonists the more he drank and the less, I think, he was able to follow the film through to completion. What I find extraordinary, however, is that no matter how black his depression, how extreme his self-destructiveness, how dissipated his energy, he somehow did manage to marshal his resources, gather the strength he needed, and sustain the wholeness of vision that marks a great film, regardless of its flaws. It will not do to be romantic about this: I am not for a moment suggesting that he consciously did this as a strategy to get inside the film or that in better days he couldn't have done so in other ways. Like Garrett, he would sit for hours on end, just drinking; like Billy, he would "target-practice" at random; like both of them, he seemed to be acting out some dark, tormented ritual of symbolic suicide that almost destroyed him in the process. And yet—the combination of how he acted and the film he pulled from his anguish puts me in mind of Malcolm Lowry when he insisted there was not one moment of his alcoholism that he wasted, not one perception or insight, even when in a stupor, that he did not turn to gold in his work: hyperbole, but like all such hyperbole, it has its parcel of truth.

The emotional truthfulness of *Pat Garrett*, its psychological authenticity, was distilled, through some mysterious, scary alchemy, from Sam's helplessness in stopping himself from going to exactly the darkest places he needed to go to feel what he needed to feel to give the story the reality that validates and justifies it. On this film he was so completely self-destructive that it took the help of all his friends and colleagues to get him through it and bring it to an end. But none of their efforts would have come to anything had he not gone to those terrible places, returned to tell the tale, and told it so beautifully, with such piercing honesty. He may have had, as Coburn once said, only four to six good hours a day, but he mined every last ounce of gold from them, and got it all on the screen.

If Peckinpah had been in better shape, might he have made a better film? It would almost certainly have been a different one—beyond that it's impossible to say. But what I will say is that if I had to sacrifice what I love in this film for that different film, even if it were a better film overall, I wouldn't make the sacrifice. Much of the enduring power of this great work lies in its very instabilities, its irresolutions, its ambivalences, ambiguities, and uncertainties—most of all, perhaps, in how difficult Peckinpah makes it for us to have a simple, fixed, or inflexible attitude toward any of the characters or the antitheses, polarities, and dualities by which he structures the story. In *The Wild Bunch* these are resolved in a magnificent equilibrium of fact distilled into legend and myth. In *Pat Garrett and Billy the Kid*, however, there is no equilibrium, only the bleak early morning emptiness that follows a night in which a friendship and the world that made it possible are destroyed by a single bullet.

7. Roger

Roger Spottiswoode was a young assistant editor in London when he was hired as the third editor on *Straw Dogs*. After that Sam promoted him to coeditor on *The Getaway*. To a person, everyone I've ever spoken with about the postproduction on *Pat Garrett and Billy the Kid* credits Roger as the man who worked harder and cared more deeply about the film than anyone else on it. In saying this, no one wishes to detract from the hard work and dedication of the others, only to emphasize that as the first editor hired and present from the moment there was footage to cut, Roger dedicated himself to the film and the film alone, and what he cared about more than anything else was protecting it from those who were trying to destroy it. Ironically, his efforts wound up ending his relationship with Sam, though more than anything else because of the dressing-down he gave Sam after Sam's despicable treatment of Bob Wolfe for helping prepare the theatrical release (D. Weddle 488). Once the cutting rooms were closed, Roger and Sam never saw or spoke to each other again, even though before the incident, as preproduction memos show, he was Sam's first choice to cut *Bring Me the Head of Alfredo Garcia*.

It's doubtful Roger would have accepted an offer to do another film with Sam, as he was actively pursuing a directing career of his own, though in the short term he edited *Hard Times*, which also starred James Coburn and marked the directorial debut of Walter Hill, who had written the screenplay for *The Getaway*. For the longest time Roger was unable fully to return to the "scene" of *Pat Garrett and Billy the Kid*: the fighting, the trauma, the stress, Aubrey's nastiness, Sam's self-destructiveness, and all the rest reassert themselves too strongly and overwhelm everything else. I am still uncertain whether he appreciates the full measure of the film's achievement and his own vital role in it. His memories of Sam remain conflicted, not least because he is the first to acknowledge how much he learned from him. In the course of many emails and conversations while I was writing this book, he eventually reached back and brought forth some extraordinary impressions and recollections that he has allowed me to share:

> Garrett and Billy are the two sides to Sam and neither particularly exemplifies that part of him with which he could not cope very well, the part we only saw infrequently and his family more often, the side of him that may have been compassionate and generous, kind, and yes even sensitive. He didn't seem able to have this sensitivity fit in with his public persona and was, I think, somewhat conflicted about its very existence . . .
>
> But Sam in all his endless complexities seemed to be on intimate terms only with his demons, and the rest of us were usually at a distance even when we thought we were getting close. He has so much of Pat and Billy inside him and, thanks to Rudy's script, he was able put them on the screen.
>
> I do remember that even back then, towards the end of the sixties, this was a very unusual script. Even now it would be an unusual script, just as *Zebulon* is. There were not so many existential films, let alone existential Westerns, whose main idea seems on the surface, and under the surface as well, to question the meaning and purpose of life. This complexity is compounded by making sure that as the story unfolds nothing of great consequence or that might comfortably be called entertainment value actually occurs. Instead, scene after scene reminds us that most people's lives then (and now?) have little meaning or purpose and may end abruptly for no particular reason. So Rudy's script was far, far out of the mainstream and only because of *The Getaway* and *The Wild Bunch* and Peckinpah's name was it possible to get it made. And of course, only Sam and perhaps Monte Hellman would have wanted to make it. Sam, Gordon,

Rudy were all aware of this. Rudy, more than they, was and is comfortable on this terrain.

But I must say, the more I read your account of the script and particularly towards the end, I felt so strongly that Sam's attraction to the script may have been partly because Sam's own life had become like this story and Billy's character.

In Sam's mind, he was still youthful, inside he was the young gunslinger, the young killer—taking what he wanted, where he wanted—a man who had created a legend in his lifetime through a tough, deeply American brilliance. But his options were playing out. Like Billy, he now spent most of his time drunk, inert or picking fights at random. Jim Aubrey was a perfect example of a Chisum figure, or one of the characters Billy meets along the way. There were all the many members of the crew Sam would fire, arbitrarily. Sam's relationship with the various women who hovered around mirror Billy in the way casual sex and violence were interwoven. So here was a character that had always interested Sam, now realized with a kind of nihilism that had overtaken Sam and with which he was intensely familiar. From then forward, as Sam developed and pushed the script into another direction, adding the kind of character that Sam might have become—James Coburn's Garrett, I mean—rather than Billy, he was giving life to a fantasy of a salvation he was tempted by, but chose not to grasp . . . except by making the film, that is.

Well this 5 cent analysis and $2.45 will get you on a New York bus, but I recall, when I was thinking of quitting the film, going into Sam's Durango bedroom, where he lay naked and drunk with the half empty vodka bottle between his thighs and an oversize six shooter in his right hand, and another month of shooting ahead of him—that morning he was both Billy and Garrett as clear as day. I just didn't see it until I read your chapter this morning. He was a man who couldn't see a future, whose legend was perhaps the only thing he really cared about, and who didn't particularly want to witness his reputation wither into dust for the next thirty years. A decent way to go out the door was always the most attractive option for him. And if he could put his thumb in the eye of some of the villains as he went out the door, so much the better.

And yet that still doesn't do justice to his complexity: it was this very complexity that made him so marvelous and also impossible, beautiful yet endlessly difficult, loving yet cruel—and unforgettable.

8. Rudy

Rudolph Wurlitzer was an avant-garde novelist who had written no screenplays before *Two-Lane Blacktop* and had only heard of Sam Peckinpah by reputation. After the pleasant experience of the previous film, *Pat Garrett and*

Billy the Kid was a trial by fire and it left some wounds that were not healed for a good long while to come. Like Roger, Rudy didn't seem fully to appreciate the beauty of the film and how crucial his own contribution to it was, because at the time all he could see was that Peckinpah had savaged his screenplay. But in the decades since, his feelings have changed. This is less a matter of time healing most wounds—though no doubt it is that too—as the way experience, in the form of growth, makes us see previous experience differently, and since then Rudy has become both a distinguished novelist and screenwriter in his own right. No doubt four decades of pretty dramatic changes in the film industry and society contributed their parts as well. Rudy was exceptionally candid, even frank about both his impressions at the time and how he values the whole experience differently today. It is remarkable to ponder how, knowing as little as he did about Sam when he wrote the original screenplay, he could have written one that so directly, almost intimately tapped into some of Sam's most private and pressing concerns and issues:

> I was unprepared for Sam's war-like, charmingly skillful and dangerous presence, but of course fascinated, thrilled and awed as well as somewhat frightened to be hanging around. As I look back I'm filled with nostalgia and appreciation for what he represented, an outlaw fighting the company, fueling himself with on-going give and take wars, but back then I was still "stuck in my fun" and had my own egoic frontiers to defend, however unconscious and innocent. I wasn't prepared for the necessary sublimations and what seemed like arbitrary dictates of a director or producer. But aside from my being under the thumb of his authority Sam seemed like an outlaw and I was happy to ride in his posse, for he was the real deal.
>
> After Sam came on board I wrote the draft with a few notes from Gordon in Cape Breton, Nova Scotia, a place that I've had for forty years and more, on a large piece of land I bought with Phil Glass, where we still go to in the summers, he and his wife or girl friends in one old farm house and me down the beach in a small house that I built over looking the Gulf of St. Lawrence. It's always been a place where I've been able to be off the grid and allow my imagination to recover from L.A. and New York.
>
> Back in the days with Sam's ongoing wars with authority, his own and as well with the powers that owned the purse and other strings, Sam, Gordon Carroll and MGM introduced me to the dark side of the film world that involved egoic passions and betrayals that served to fuel Sam's creative juices, along with booze, women and anticipations of betrayals. On the other lighter more romantic side stood earned loyalties, rough humors and solidarity, passions that helped the assembled develop the filmed story as it played out, in this case the betrayal of two old friends and always lurking in the background, the powers that sought to control the developing businesses that marked the frontier.

Back in New York several weeks before the first day of filming in Durango Dylan came to see me at my lower east side apartment and said he'd heard I was doing a Billy the Kid film with Peckinpah, and that he always felt that he was somehow connected to Billy and was there any way he could be involved. The next day I called Gordon who said absolutely, don't let him get away, we'll get a great score, write him a part, and soon after I improvised a few scenes, calling the character Alias, which seemed appropriate, and a few days later Bob and I flew down to Durango. When I introduced the two legends, Sam looked at Bob for a long beat and said: "I'm a big fan of Roger Miller." I thought it was a blown deal, but despite Sam's rants and sudden changes throughout the film, Bob appreciated Sam's passions, including his old west outlaw presence and instincts for better or worse that always heightened the narrative drama as well as everyone's participation. It was part of Sam's genius that he could enlist the various elements of rock n roll and old time L.A. and his posse of veteran character actors, and still fight his war with MGM and at the same time saddle up and ride his passions to serve the film, which was a perilous ride but in this case, he crossed the finish line with a wild mix of personal passions, agonies, and triumphs.

Later on I came to regret my youthful and naive complaints about Sam. Now I value his canny instincts along with his almost too human frailties. My complaints had more to do with my own issues with authority and how to protect vulnerable creative instincts when one is sublimated to whoever is driving the ship. *Pat Garrett and Billy the Kid* was Sam's film because of his desperate passions and vulnerabilities. He improved the script and made it into a theatrical narrative enlisting the separate parts of his own complicated damaged but always, in that case, creative psyche.

I miss those days. They'll never come again, which is probably one reason why I haven't been to L.A. in fifteen years. I doubt Sam could survive or would want to in today's corporate grid. And now, well, you know, the corporate boys wouldn't let him in the parking lot much less the room.

I miss him. The good, bad, and ugly. I've never known anyone else like him. He was the last of his kind.

9. "Don't perfect it, finish it."

So Peckinpah was fond of quoting one of his mentors. But *Pat Garrett and Billy the Kid* was neither finished nor perfected. Yet this seems to be the one fact that most of the extensive critical literature on this film seems consistently disinclined to come to terms with. Much of it appears to have been written under the influence, however distant, of the New Criticism, which requires of us that we consider nothing outside the work of art itself and which rests more or less on an assumption of the work's intrinsic unity. New Critics and their progeny have been indoctrinated into that assumption of unity—in our day this often takes the form of detaching the work wholly from any connection or association with its creator—a unity we then proceed to demonstrate using all the formidable equipment of aesthetic analysis that constituted our training as critics. But this kind of analysis breaks down almost completely before a film like *Pat Garrett and Billy the Kid*. Billy, for example, is less a fully realized character than a collection of possibilities and alternatives, some partially realized, some not, a few mutually exclusive. Yet this has not prevented several critics from arguing for a consistency, typically involving a benign view of the character, that requires ignoring or, perhaps worse, trying to justify any attributes that undermine the consistency.[25] Similarly, the flight to Mexico and the return were never adequately thought through and Peckinpah's last-minute attempts to fix it on the set and in the dubbing stage smack of desperation in the first place and were inadequate in the last.

I saw the film several times during its first release in 1973, and my initial reaction was mixed. The whole last sequence in Fort Sumner was more powerful than anything else I'd seen in films at the time. What I loved about the film I continued to love, even more, and some of what I didn't—the Lew Wallace scene, for example—I eventually came round to. But the flaws of execution, performance, and pacing remain, especially in parts of the Billy side of the story. And yet, curiously, as the years pass, the flaws recede, quite overwhelmed by the wholeness of Peckinpah's vision, which survived even his departure. What is even more curious is that the essence of that vision is felt and conveyed regardless of which version is seen. In the theatrical version the irony of how and at whose hands Garrett will die is lost, but the themes of flux, impermanence, and disintegration are felt about as strongly, those of fate and determinism nearly so. Despite our not knowing how Garrett will die, our sense that he has destroyed himself and his world along with Billy also remains strong. It is little wonder that, as I observed in chapter 7, *Pat Garrett* was soon recognized as one of Peckinpah's great films and a masterpiece long before many critics ever saw or were even aware of the missing footage. The principal contributions of the prologue/frame story are a massive irony that hangs over the entire drama to follow and a decisive weighting of the story toward Garrett, which is further reinforced by the scene with Chisum and by the prostitutes' montage. The wife scene would reinforce Garrett's primacy even more, but by the time it was available to be widely seen, the critical reevaluation of the film had already more or less happened.

I share the opinion of John L. Simons and Robert Merrill, who have appreciated this scene more thoroughly than anyone else (they are especially alert to its many and varied nuances and undercurrents), that it is one of Peckinpah's really great scenes—it's surely one of the most emotionally truthful he ever directed—yet its main contribution is to our sense of Garrett's character and the choices and compromises he has made, rather than to the large-scale themes of fate, socio-economic-political determinism, and a way of life that is dying out. In other words, however much the Ida scene richly augments the film, her absence from the theatrical, in terms of overall coherence, was hardly a *crippling* diminishment, particularly since the prostitutes' montage was also removed. And in any case, even in the theatrical, the primacy of Garrett is unmistakable.

In writing this, I do not mean to contradict my own argument in the previous chapter that the five women characters of any prominence—Ida, Ruthie Lee, Maria, Mrs. Baker, and Mrs. Horrell—offer a vitally important social and thematic perspective upon the action. Nor am I suggesting that the unauthorized lifts in the theatrical are salutary or in any sense justified, and I would never want the film to exist without the Ida, Ruthie Lee, and Chisum scenes and the prologue. I am suggesting, rather, that Peckinpah and Wurlitzer, against all odds, came up with a basic structure resilient enough and a story protean enough to preserve their core themes and overall effect in at least four different versions. This would hardly be a first in the director's career. He authorized two different versions of *The Wild Bunch* (one domestic, one European); and while he objected to the post-release cuts the studio made, the film itself remains a great film even without the flashbacks and the scene between Mapache and the boy, simply not as rich a one.[26] By contrast, now that we have an extended version of *Major Dundee*, it's clear that the additional material still doesn't address or fix certain basic structural and conceptual problems of the theatrical release or the script itself, unfinished when production began and never adequately completed by the end of principal photography. Mention of *Dundee* reminds us that it too is a film Peckinpah didn't finish. But, unlike *Pat Garrett*, it *is* incomplete, because its vision is fractured and only partially realized. It wasn't until *The Wild Bunch* that Peckinpah in effect made the film he wanted to make in *Dundee*.

I don't believe Peckinpah really could finish *Pat Garrett* because it was so personal about matters he never did resolve during the remainder of his life (and that in some ways became much worse: on *The Killer Elite* he began doing cocaine). That the unfinished aspect of the Billy character seems to matter less than it once did owes mostly to the effect of the restored scenes, all of which deal with Garrett. Once again, the contrast with *Major Dundee* is instructive. Like *Pat Garrett*, the earlier film pits two former friends against each other who in their case are pledged to a duel in which one of them will die. But Dundee's redemption in the last act was hardly developed at all in the release version and the restored scenes don't make it any more convincing. This means that as strong as the Tyreen character is, he's not strong enough to carry the film because the story remains stubbornly anchored to the title character. In *Pat Garrett*, Peckinpah and Wurlitzer between them made the film principally Garrett's, and therein lies the difference. As a "solution," it wasn't ideal, but it was sufficient to carry the film over its trouble spots, not least because Billy came to function at least partially as a conflicting side of Garrett's personality (though the same cannot be said of Garrett vis-à-vis Billy). Still another way in which *Pat Garrett* recalls *Major Dundee* is that it too can be seen to have been, if not finished, then at least continued in the next film.

In the seventies one of the most popular of all film genres, if it can be called such, one that cut across several other genres (Western, crime, police, comedy, adventure, etc.), was the "buddy movie." Peckinpah took the buddy movie, lacerated it, laying bare its obsessions with death, money, and violence and also its (barely) latent misogyny, and pushed it all the way to psychosis. In *Pat Garrett and Billy the Kid*, one friend kills another and the film ends. In *Bring Me the Head of Alfredo Garcia*, one of the buddies—the title character—is dead before the film begins and the other buddy—Bennie, the piano player–manager of a dive bar in Mexico City, whom Alfredo had cuckolded—eventually claims the head and takes it on the road with him, shares tequila with it, talks to it, argues with it, commiserates with it about their mutual lover, ices it to keep it from stinking, all so that he can claim a reward from a big shot named El Jefe, who wants revenge because Alfredo impregnated his daughter. To that revenge motif Peckinpah added one for Bennie: he winds up putting himself and his prostitute girlfriend Elita into a situation that gets her murdered by El Jefe's henchmen. By the end Bennie gets his vengeance, his reward, and still gets to keep his buddy's head, which he plans to return to its grave, where it will rest beside the murdered woman they once shared. But he is gunned down in the process, taking with him several of El Jefe's men in an exciting but hollow climax the very hollowness of which seems part of the point.

This is the only Peckinpah film in which the main titles are placed at the end, which means that the director's name comes up first and the image we see under Peckinpah's is an extreme close-up of a smoking gun barrel pointed straight at us: so much for the lives of men without women.[27] Was Bennie a possible future for the Garrett who rode away at the end of the previous film? Or was Bennie the Billy, only now older, that Peckinpah saw but turned away from in both Neider and Wurlitzer? Or is he a crazy composite of the worst of each? The answers are unknowable. What we do know, from Peckinpah's own admission, is that *Bring Me the Head of Alfredo Garcia* was the only film of his that came out exactly as he wanted it to, that Bennie was a surrogate for himself—"Peckinpah's everyman," he told his friend John Bryson (138)— and that as director Sam was often addressed as "El Jefe." I think we may also safely assume that none of the characters here was a wish fulfillment.

10. "There. That's what I was trying to do with *The Wild Bunch* and didn't succeed."

These were the first words out of Peckinpah's mouth, Don Hyde told me, after they watched a tape of the second preview of *Pat Garrett and Billy the Kid* on a television in 1980. Peckinpah being Sam, he didn't elaborate, but ever since Don told me this I've been wondering what Sam meant. For one thing, the

Death as elegiac

Death as heroic

Death as ignominious

films are so very different in tone, style, mood, and theme. *The Wild Bunch* is epic and epochal—tremendous, passionate, glorious, celebratory and also raucous, disturbing, lyrical, elegiac. It is the richest of all Western films and the densest thematically, it has some of the most fully realized characters, and it is the most complex, probing, and powerful in its treatments of heroism, masculinity, male groupings, societies in violent upheaval, and the ambiguous, twisted, ironic processes by which history becomes legend and myth. *Pat Garrett and Billy the Kid* is slow, low-key, melancholic, and ruminative. No less beautiful than *The Wild Bunch*, its lyricism is born of exhaustion, defeat, and the detritus of a disintegrating world. *The Wild Bunch* ends in a cathartic bloodbath, but out of it emerge new life and purpose. In an extraordinary extended coda of shifting moods and tonalities, in which the ironies double back on themselves, the Bunch, lately bad men, end up looking like heroic liberators who leave behind a legacy of self-sacrifice for the greater good. But whether *Pat Garrett and Billy the Kid* ends with Garrett disappearing into the desert after the disillusioned boy has pelted his horse with pebbles or in a return to his own assassination as his bullet-riddled body is frozen just out of frame after it hits the ground, the effect is pretty much the same: desolation, despair, and a darkening, all-consuming bleakness. The climactic final battle in *The Wild Bunch* is Homeric, almost hallucinatory in its cumulative force and ferocity, as countless bullets fly, grenades explode, and bodies fall to the relentless deafening chatter of a machine gun that indiscriminately mows down anyone and anything in the path of its fire. The climax of *Pat Garrett and Billy the Kid* is equally devastating except that only two bullets are fired, killing one man and leaving another psychically destroyed in what is clearly a symbolic suicide. How many other filmmakers have it in their creative powers to realize endings this different yet to equally shattering effect?

So what *did* Peckinpah mean by what he said? Perhaps a clue lies in the Bunch's heroism. His original intention when he started on *The Wild Bunch* was to tell a story about bad men in changing times, and whatever else, he did not want them to be taken as heroes: "I tried to make a film about heavies—to break up the myth of the Western gunfighter" (Yergin 87). But as he got deeper into the screenplay and the film, he realized that heroism through violence, with all its complexities and ambiguities, was his subject after all, as well as his own ambivalent attitudes toward it and the men whose story he chose to tell. By the time he got to his incendiary climax, he knew there was no way these bad men would not in some sense emerge as heroes owing to the sheer audacity of the way they go to their deaths and the principle of honor for which they wind up sacrificing themselves, however adventitiously. Whatever terrible things they might have done, nothing became their lives so much as the leaving of them, and for this Angel's countrymen grant them an afterlife in tales that will be told around their campfires for a thousand years.

"But the Bunch do not enter 'Valhalla,'" writes Gabrielle Murray, "they die—and those images that we see reincarnated at this film's conclusion are retrospective highlights of moments of joy and laughter in their lives" (61). True enough, perhaps. But these images are first and foremost the memories of Old Sykes as he and Thornton ride off with their band of peasant rebels, after which the images modulate into the Bunch's exit from Angel's village as the villagers serenade them with "*La Golondrina*." The translation is "The Swallow," and the lyrics tell of a bird tossed about by the winds, condemned to wander because it cannot find its way home. The Bunch die far from home too, but what does home mean for these restless outlaw vagabonds except their own company and wherever they find themselves in their next adventure? So let us make no mistake: the realm we find them in at the end, the realm of folklore and myth, is *their* Valhalla. And when in the last few moments of the film Peckinpah has the frozen image recede before it disappears, so that it is plainly identified as a *filmic* image, we realize that Valhalla is not a "place" in the world of the story but the myth in which the poet-singer-storyteller's warriors are apotheosized as heroes.

But this is not what happens in *Pat Garrett and Billy the Kid*, and if Murray were to say the same thing about it that she does of *The Wild Bunch*, I would concur with her absolutely. Never one to make things easy on himself, Peckinpah took a dark, claustrophobic screenplay about the most famous outlaw and lawman pair in the Old West and did everything he possibly could to render it in just about the most quotidian and ironic ways. It's impossible to think of a single action in the film that could by any definition be called heroic, though there's certainly audacity, bravado, and derring-do to the Kid's escape from Garrett's jail. But in the rest of the story Peckinpah pulls away from these qualities or otherwise undercuts them until in the last act Billy is almost immobile and it is left ambiguous how much real choice on his part figures into his stasis. Northrop Frye wrote that if irony begins in realism, it gravitates toward myth as "the dim outlines of sacrificial rituals and dying gods begin to reappear in it." This is certainly true in *The Wild Bunch*, and it appears to be true in *Pat Garrett*, where images of Billy with his arms outstretched like Christ's on the cross or in silhouette on horseback can certainly be interpreted as evoking dying gods, while his death is nothing if not a sacrifice to all the forces that are taking over the New Mexico Territory and changing it, not to mention a sacrifice also to Garrett's own desperate need to get free from his past.

Yet it seems to me that Peckinpah for the most part keeps these outlines dim to the point of vague and shadowy, which may be one reason among several why *Pat Garrett and Billy the Kid* has the effect of something muted, damped down, and becalmed. The closest we come to a heroic demise is that of Cullen Baker, yet even here Peckinpah will not allow the old sheriff's stature to be magnified or in any way enlarged or mythicized. There are no low-angle setups that force us to look up at him, and as he stumbles gut-shot toward the river, he is filmed from angles that have us looking down on him and once he is framed so loose that it takes a moment to find his figure in the wide-screen image. When he reaches the river and Peckinpah moves in for a more intimate setup, it is not even a medium close-up, but a much looser medium shot that brings us just close enough to see the incomprehension, sadness, and fear in the old man's eyes (the setup is the point of view of his wife, who sits nearby but does not approach beyond a certain distance), yet that still takes in the parched brown landscape around him with its scattering of trees, the river receding into the distance, and the gray overcast late afternoon sky, with one small patch of clearing through the clouds. The effect is objective and unsentimental, though full of sentiment and very moving because it's so elegiac. Yet in the final cadence, Peckinpah cuts away from the dying man and his grieving wife to an extreme wide-shot that reveals them as insignificant specks in the pitiless desert, and then ends on Garrett, who watches silent, almost impassive, having just been an unintentional instrument in the death of an old friend.

It's impossible not to recall here the death of the old marshal in *Ride the High Country*, but the contrast is telling: a low-angle camera forces us to look up at Steve Judd, his figure looming gigantic in the foreground, at once obscuring and dwarfing the high mountains on the horizon. Mortally wounded in an honorable gunfight, Judd dies with grace and dignity, taking a last yearning look at the distant peaks before turning away and, with his own strength, lowering himself to the ground and death, the mountain revealed in its full majesty, as if in mute tribute to his passing, the whole moment bathed in soft tones of gold and green. This scene is alluded to even more ironically in the prologue, where the camera is placed at a still lower angle (practically ground level) for Garrett's death. But here the effect is not to enlarge his stature, but rather to strip him of his dignity: after falling from the buggy, he writhes in agony in the dirt, the assassins' bullets piercing his body as he tries hopelessly to lift himself off his back. When he finally expires, the length of his body is oriented not across the bottom of the frame but perpendicular to it and extending back along the ground, the setup so low the sole of one boot, his legs, knees, and trunk blocking any view of his head. In the background there is no distant mountain, instead a mere hill, a small craggy rise that in its barren puniness seems to mock the slain lawman, while the sepia tinting reduces the color palette to a drab, deadening reddish gray, making it appear as if he is being absorbed into the desert, foreshadowing a similar effect when his figure becomes smaller and smaller as he recedes into the distance riding away from Fort Sumner at the end. The contrast to the death of Steve Judd could not be more stark.

The same is true of the contrast between the deaths of Pat Garrett and Billy the Kid and those of Pike, Dutch, and the Gorch brothers in *The Wild Bunch*. We may know that after Garrett and the Kid died, they lived on in a legend that exceeded every other of the Old West in popularity and staying power. But despite the references Billy's victims or potential victims make to being remembered and hoping the newspapers spell their names right—death from the barrel of his gun their only chance at immortality—and despite the presence of Bob Dylan as Alias and chronicler and his "Billy the Kid" ballad playing over the end titles, Peckinpah does not allow us to take any refuge in a legendary afterlife and he never leaves us there or brings his film to rest in it, as he plainly does in *The Wild Bunch* with the closing image of the outlaws serenaded by a peasant village that believes they've liberated it from its oppressors. When death comes in *Pat Garrett and Billy the Kid*, it is unadorned and disinterested, and nothing survives it. Pike, Dutch, and the Gorch brothers get to choose the time and manner of their death, meet it head-on, walking to it with a deliberation and sense of purpose that seem to enlarge their stature with each advancing step, and die gloriously in a battle that is at once exalted and horrifying. But Garrett and Billy both die as victims of ambush, and when they are dead, they are just dead: nothing is affirmed, redeemed, or transfigured. The last image Peckinpah gives us of Billy is his bare feet sticking out from under a blanket that is too short to cover his body: like his counterpart in history, he too doesn't get to die with his boots on. And if that boy who throws stones at Garrett's horse suggests anything, it's that those Garrett leaves behind in Fort Sumner want nothing more than for him to go as far away from them as possible. His figure disappears into the unknown Big Empty of the Southwestern desert.

So ends Peckinpah's last Western film, with no heroes, no heroics, and no heroic afterlife.

There. He succeeded.

Appendix: Credits and Running Times

Production (above the line): Metro-Goldwyn-Mayer presents. A Gordon Carroll–Sam Peckinpah Production. Music by Bob Dylan. Written by Rudolph Wurlitzer. Produced by Gordon Carroll. Directed by Sam Peckinpah.

The full cast is included here, though not every cast member appeared in all versions of the film. Character names appear as they do in the credits.

Cast: James Coburn (*Pat Garrett*). Kris Kristofferson (*Billy the Kid*). Bob Dylan (*Alias*). Richard Jaeckel (*Sheriff Kip McKinney*). Katy Jurado (*Mrs. Baker*). Chill Wills (*Lemuel*). Barry Sullivan (*Chisum*). Jason Robards (*Governor Wallace*). R. G. Armstrong (*Olinger*). Luke Askew (*Eno*). John Peck (*Poe*). Richard Bright (*Holly*). Matt Clark (*J. W. Bell*). Rita Coolidge (*Maria*). Jack Dodson (*Howland*). Jack Elam (*Alamosa Bill*). Emilio Fernández (*Paco*). Paul Fix (*Maxwell*). L. Q. Jones (*Black Harris*). Slim Pickens (*Sheriff Baker*). Jorge Russek (*Silva*). Charlie Martin Smith (*Bowdre*). Harry Dean Stanton (*Luke*). Claudia Bryar (*Mrs. Horrell*). John Chandler (*Norris*). Mike Mikler (*Denver*). Rutanya Alda (*Ruthie Lee*). Walter Kelley (*Rupert*). Aurora Clavell (*Ida Garrett*). Rudy Wurlitzer (*O'Folliard*). Elisha Cook Jr. (*Cody*). Gene Evans (*Mr. Horrell*). Donnie Fritts (*Beaver*, aka *Breed*). Dub Taylor (*Josh*). Don Levy (*Sackett*).

Crew (below the line): Director of Photography: John Coquillon, B.S.C. Art Director: Ted Haworth. Film Editors: Roger Spottiswoode, Garth Craven, Robert L. Wolfe, A.C.E., Richard Halsey, David Berlatsky, Tony de Zarraga. Unit Production Manager: Jim Henderling. Assistant Director: Newton Arnold. Second Assistant Director: Lawrence J. Powell. Set Direction: Ray Moyer. Property Master: Robert John Visciglia. Special Visual Effects: A. J. Lohman. Music Editor: Dan Carlin. Camera Operator: Herbert Smith. Make-Up by Jack P. Wilson. Wardrobe: Michael Butler. Casting by Patricia Mock. Sound: Charles M. Wilborn, Harry W. Tetrick, C.A.S. Second Unit Director: Gordon Dawson. Second Unit Director of Photography: Gabriel Torres G. Mexican Production

Manager: Alfonso Sanchez Tello. Mexican Assistant Director: Jesus Marin Bello. METROCOLOR Filmed in PANAVISION.

Running times: theatrical version, 1:46; 2005 Special Edition, 1:55:10; 1988 Turner Preview Version, 2:01:42; second preview, 2:01:07 (the timing of the Don Hyde DVD transfer). Because Peckinpah left the film effectively straddled between two previews of different lengths and with different scenes and shots in them, it's impossible to determine what the length of his hypothetical version would have been. If the wife and Ruthie Lee scenes are added to the Turner preview, the length comes to seconds under 2:07; if you add them to the second preview, it times out to around 2:06:22. But the second preview contains a severely shortened version of the first Garrett/McKinney scene, lacks Rupert clearing the table, removes at least one shot, and has the end note but no end-credit crawl.

Notes

The 2005 Special Edition and 1988 Turner Preview Version are currently available on DVD from Warner Home Video, and the special edition has begun to show on Turner Classic Movies (TCM). The original theatrical version plays from time to time on cable channels; though long unavailable on the home-video market, used VHS copies are easily found on eBay. The only print of the second preview, stored in MHL's Pickford Center for Motion Picture Study in Hollywood, is now too fragile for projection, but the Pickford does have available for viewing two DVDs of this print, transferred from a videotape made in the early eighties. When the tape was made the print was not in great condition either and had a lot of dirt on it, and the 1:85 aspect ratio is incorrect; but at least the reddening had not begun. Don Hyde made the videotape copies when he was Peckinpah's archivist and later he also supplied the DVD transfers.

The main-title card on the film reads *Pat Garrett & Billy the Kid*; but everywhere else, including Wurlitzer's published version, the publicity, and all studio and production documents, it reads *Pat Garrett and Billy the Kid*. The Internet Movie Database (IMDb) website opts for the ampersand, but MGM (which financed the picture), Turner Broadcasting (which owns it), and Warner Home Video (which licenses it) all use "and." To the best of Roger Spottiswoode's recollection, at the time everyone agreed the ampersand made for a much better graphic *in the titles sequence*, but no one, including Peckinpah and Wurlitzer, ever intended for it to supplant "and" anywhere else.

Peckinpah took no onscreen credit for playing Will, the coffin maker.

Gordon Dawson was the location manager in the early weeks of preproduction and functioned as associate producer throughout, but received no onscreen credit in either capacity.

Katy Haber was Peckinpah's personal assistant from the second week of production through the end of postproduction, but received no onscreen credit.

Frank Beetson, the unit production manager during preproduction, was replaced, due to differences with Peckinpah, and received no credit.

None of the seven stuntmen received onscreen credit, though Gary Combs, Whitey Hughes (the Chisum hand who exclaims, "Jesus Christ!" when he sees the Kid), and Billy Hart were Peckinpah regulars.

Jerry Fielding, Peckinpah's longtime composer, was supposed to write the original score and incorporate Dylan's songs, but he quit after hearing "Knockin' on Heaven's Door" because he felt it was so wrong for the picture.

Bruce Dern is listed on IMDb as "deputy." No one I've queried who worked on the film has any idea where this falsehood originated.

NOTES

Introduction

My essay on the versions of *Pat Garrett and Billy the Kid* is in Bliss, *Peckinpah Today* (101–36); my chapters on the film are 5 in *Peckinpah* (183–226) and 7 in *Reconsideration* (255–306). The Kael quotation is from "Peckinpah's Obsession" (80), Rosen from *Critical Entertainments* (129), Peckinpah's reply to Max Evans from Evans (4), Parker from *Reading "Billy Budd"* (178), Hellman from *Pure Peckinpah Press Kit* (47), Scorsese from D. Weddle (483), Thomson (672), Jameson from his Amazon editorial review of *Sam Peckinpah's The Legendary Westerns Collection*, Le Cain from *Senses of Cinema*, Peckinpah on the Western from Leroux (no pagination), and Jarrell from "Some Lines from Whitman" (106). *The Endless Ride* is the subtitle of Michael Wallis's Billy the Kid biography.

1. According to Evans, Peckinpah, who optioned the book "at a fair price, and from his own pocket," spent "more time, money, and effort on *Hi Lo* than any other property yet he only got about twelve minutes of it on the screen in *The Losers*. I'm glad now he stole it" (131, 136). (SPP contains several versions of Peckinpah's attempts to adapt *The Hi Lo Country*.) Fourteen years after Peckinpah's death the director Stephen Frears brought the novel to the screen in 1998 with a wholly new adaptation by Walon Green, who had written *The Wild Bunch*.

2. Robert Merrill told me that he once compiled a list divided between critics who've written substantially on the film who he believes actually *saw* the Ida scene and those who relied on the description in my books. This makes sense if you consider that the only two versions to contain the scene before 2006 had extremely limited or zero distribution: the one broadcast on network television in the mid-seventies disappeared fairly quickly (though not quite before the first consumer videocassette recorders hit the market); and the second preview existed as a single print that was only ever shown in public twice (both in Los Angeles), had no circulation apart from a few tape copies that Peckinpah had made for himself and friends in 1980, and thereafter could be seen only by special arrangement with the Margaret Herrick Library of the Academy of Motion Picture Arts and Sciences beginning in the late nineties. Even the screenplay was and remains hard to find. Those who know the film only from VHS tapes or laser discs of the Turner preview have never seen either the Ida or Ruthie Lee scenes, and those familiar only with the theatrical haven't seen the Ida.

3. There are in fact already two book-length studies of individual Peckinpah films: Ian Cooper's very good *Bring Me the Head of Alfredo Garcia* (2011), part of Wallflower Press's Cultographies series; and Stevie Simkin's *Straw Dogs* (2011), an outstanding

contribution to Peckinpah criticism and scholarship. Despite its title, Max Evans's *Sam Peckinpah: Master of Violence* (1972, Dakota Press) is actually a memoir—very colorful and amusing—of his experiences on *The Ballad of Cable Hogue*, in which he played one of the stagecoach drivers; as its subtitle, *Being the Account of the Making of a Movie and Other Sundry Things*, suggests—accurately—it's not a critical study.

4. The amount of writing about an artist may be an imperfect way of establishing his importance, but it is surely a significant indication of interest. I've tallied some thirty-seven books on Peckinpah and his work. Most of them are critical studies of one sort or another; two are full biographies, one a film-by-film career biography; four are anthologies (three with newly commissioned essays); and a book of poetry. At least twelve originate in other countries and/or languages (Great Britain, France, Germany, Italy, Spain, Japan, and Mexico), and quite a number are from reputable presses (often university presses), with only a handful vanity publications. The quality varies wildly, as would be expected, something true of all critical writing. But the mere statistics hide an important fact: Peckinpah's features number just fourteen, which means that a relatively small body of work—smaller still considering that attention is by no means distributed equally among all fourteen—supports an unusually large and intense critical scrutiny and appreciation. Very few filmmakers of so limited an output can claim this distinction—Chaplin and Welles come most immediately to mind, not many others. But no student of classic American literature would find this surprising, the greatness of several of our most important writers predicated on fairly few individual works. This is only one way that Peckinpah's relationship to this tradition is confirmed.

5. I put it this way in order to distinguish a decision by Peckinpah to leave from what happened on his first three films, where he was fired, barred from the studio lot, or had the films recut by the producers (*Reconsideration* 36, 63–64, 82, 88–89).

Chapter One. Brando's Western

1. If copies of Serling's screenplay exist, they are not in the archives that hold virtually all his writings at the Wisconsin Center for Film and Theater Research in Madison or the University of California at Los Angeles, which leads me to wonder if there was ever an actual script, as opposed to only an outline or a long treatment. My main sources for Peckinpah's and Kubrick's involvements with Brando and *One-Eyed Jacks* are Baxter (108–22), LoBrutto (59–65), "Privilege" (1–3), Simmons (28), and D. Weddle (143–46). Brando spends fewer than four disappointing, uninformative pages on the film in his autobiography (256–60). Peckinpah's "best Western ever written" is from the "Story Conference" tape, 9/9/72 (SPP); Marie Selland's remarks are from D. Weddle (145); Neider on *The Authentic Death of Hendry Jones* and *One-Eyed Jacks* is from his preface to the University of Nevada reprint of his novel (vi–xiii). Peckinpah's comments on the novel and Brando are from Medjuck (21), Cutts (59), and W. Murray (112). Peckinpah on *The Westerner* is from Cecil Smith.

2. When Neider was in California during the filming of *One-Eyed Jacks*, he and Peckinpah met and even socialized some, and much later they carried on a lively, though sporadic correspondence while Peckinpah was doing *Pat Garrett and Billy the Kid* and *Bring Me the Head of Alfredo Garcia*. Neider's published comments on *One-Eyed Jacks* are at considerable variance to those he expressed in letters to the director. In 1972,

after screening the film to a seminar on screen adaptations, Neider wrote, "I was disgusted by a number of things, among them the maudlin side of the film, the lack of authenticity and the amount of sheer padding. You can bet that I spoke my mind on that subject. Also, I spoke very favorably about your work" (12/19). After seeing the theatrical *Pat Garrett and Billy the Kid* Neider wrote, "There were fine moments . . . but I guess you got screwed in the final editing. I really regretted this" (9/20/73). Though Peckinpah wanted him to see the longer version "because it is something we started together a long time ago" (6/21/74), if the novelist ever did, he left no written record of it. (These letters are in SPP 147-f.2066.)

3. Because Paramount failed to renew the copyright and the rights have slipped into the public domain, as of this writing all home video releases, regardless of date or format, including DVD and Blu-ray, are from bootleg sources of bad transfers of equally bad prints (especially ironic since the cinematography received the picture's only Oscar nomination). Yet a first-class print exists because I watched what was obviously a high-resolution transfer of it sometime between 2008 and 2010 on one of the HD-movie channels. It should be given a proper, responsible restoration and release, preferably on Blu-ray.

4. Or so I would have thought, but Neider claimed he "first became aware of the meaning of the moniker Dad in HJ in an introduction to an edition of the novel [Harrow's mass-market paperback, 1972] by the teacher and critic Wirt Williams" ("HJ and Violence," unpublished lecture notes, November 13, 1997, 1).

Chapter Two. Garrett's Narrative

The Sally Chisum epigraph is from Burns (18–19). The account of the Lincoln County War in this chapter is based on several of the standard sources: Nolan's *The Lincoln County War* and *The West of Billy the Kid*, Utley's *High Noon in Lincoln*, Fulton's *History of the Lincoln County War*, Keleher's *Violence in Lincoln County, 1869–1881*, and Wilson's *Merchants, Guns, and Money*.

1. Unless otherwise noted, all references to *The Authentic Life* are to the original text as reprinted by the University of Oklahoma Press (1954).

2. The jobs list and other information about Upson are in many sources; mostly I've used Metz (129–31) and Nolan (*West* 92–93).

3. Cheap covers printed on yellow paper were used for the first dime novels published by Beadle and Adams in 1860 and later copied by others. Even though many that followed used other colors, "yellow backs" caught on for them all. According to the collector Robert McCubbin, who has at least three first editions of *The Authentic Life*, the color of the original jackets varied with printing and available paper. The one he showed me is blue. The cover illustration—a woodcut showing three dead Indians in the foreground and what appear to be two gringos on burros—refers to nothing in the book.

4. Considering Upson wrote the entire book in a breathtaking two months, it's reasonable to wonder if before publication Garrett himself actually read it or had any idea what was really in the parts that didn't directly involve him. Over twenty years later he judged it riddled with errors and collaborated with a writer named Emerson Hough to correct them in what became part of a book called *The Story of the Outlaw*. Although Hough perpetuated some of Upson's inventions, for the portions about Garrett he

relied mostly on the last eight chapters of *The Authentic Life*, on his own research, and on conversations with Garrett, including a visit to old Fort Sumner, by then "a scene of desolation," "the great parade ground gone back to sand and sage brush" (306). Of particular interest are the subtle ways the accretions of the legend, then still in its infancy, appear to be coloring Garrett's memories (e.g., after he and Hough visited Lincoln together, Garrett, speaking "reminiscently of the bloody scenes," said, "I knew now that I would have to kill the Kid. We both knew that it must be one or the other of us if we ever met" [305]).

5. See Robert N. Mullin's *The Boyhood of Billy the Kid*, a monograph based on pioneering research into Billy's early life. It was Mullin who discovered the first *official* document anywhere that established the existence of Billy the Kid as a matter of public record: the entry, dated March 1, 1873, in the registry of the First Presbyterian Church of Santa Fe, of the marriage between Catherine McCarty and her second husband William Antrim, noting that the bride's sons, Henry (as Billy, then thirteen, was still being called) and Joseph (around ten), were in attendance.

6. This according to Jerry Weddle's *Antrim Is My Stepfather's Name*, another monograph distinguished for thorough, pioneering research, notably its detailed account of the Kid's life and environs during the two-plus years the family lived in Silver City.

7. See Nolan, *West* 3–6; Mullin 7; and Wallis 151–56.

8. In the pages that follow, references to Billy the Kid's age are predicated upon the still widely accepted 1859.

9. In March 1877, diagnosed with cancer of the bowels, Murphy sold the company to Dolan, who formed the J. J. Dolan Company with John H. Riley. Though Murphy continued to use his influence on behalf of The House, his drinking, heavy to begin with, worsened as he increasingly used it as a way to numb the pain from the cancer. Much of the Lincoln County War he spent in Santa Fe getting treatment. He died in October, three months after the "Big Killing."

10. The Murphy-Dolan finances were in a constant state of huge debt owing to careless, greedy, risky, questionable, and incompetent business practices as well as corruption aplenty. Yet according to Wilson's *Merchants*, little of it seems to have resulted in any real profit, rather just a succession of robbings of Peter to pay Paul owing to a persistent shortage of actual money. Contrary to what is widely believed, Wilson finds little hard evidence to indicate Murphy and Dolan coerced voting preferences out of those whose mortgages they held and he doubts their foreclosures netted much else than land, which in and of itself was of little use in generating the cash for which they were always in need. Moreover, in their attempts to retain contracts they often bid so low as to make effectively no money and sometimes even to lose it. Wilson also suggests their margins in what they charged for goods were "reasonable, then as now," and that "allegations that the House charged exorbitant prices would seem to have little basis," though he concedes we don't know their prices to cash customers (31).

11. Wilson decisively dissents from the view, still widely held, that the Tunstall-McSween faction was essentially honest, upstanding, and fair or even much less ruthless than Murphy-Dolan. He marshals persuasive evidence to suggest that as the Englishman's prices on produce offered "no better values" than The House's did, "it's hard to see why farmers would have been better off dealing with one merchant than the other" (71) (though he concedes that no evidence exists to indicate whether Tunstall charged less for goods his store carried). Once Tunstall and McSween "launched their orchestrated campaign to take over the economic reins in Lincoln County from

Murphy and Dolan," Wilson concludes, "their ethics were right at the same level" and "Tunstall's plans were simply the old Murphy formula repackaged and, it was hoped, shorn of economic liabilities" (71–73). But there was nothing to support that hope, Wilson argues, as Tunstall's ideas about how to achieve his ends were remarkably naive, and he was about as oblivious as Murphy and Dolan seemed to have been toward how changing conditions were making it increasingly difficult to control local markets and means of production. (Utley comes to many of the same conclusions in his *High Noon*.)

12. Though Folliard's name is usually given as "O'Folliard," Clifford R. Caldwell has shown that the "O" was in fact a middle initial, the last name simply "Folliard." Garrett's book had this right all along but spelled the surname with only one "l."

13. "Recruits" is used advisedly here. According to Bob Boze Bell (*Illustrated Life* 71), both sides in the Lincoln County War coerced neutral citizens into fighting for them. The Regulators threatened Mexican farmers with "a $50 fine if they didn't help serve warrants on McSween's enemies" and Dolan's people strong-armed men into joining their posses (many of those dispatched to find Tunstall "had no intention of killing him" and were "shocked and appalled when they realized what a 'few renegade' posse members had done").

14. This was in an article about outlaws in the Pecos valley, written by W. S. Koogler and published in the *Las Vegas Gazette*, Las Vegas, New Mexico (December 3, 1880).

15. Garrett's account in *Authentic Life* (142–49); Poe's from his *Death of Billy the Kid* (27–50). Unless otherwise noted, all quotations or references in the next several paragraphs to their accounts are to these sources.

16. As if all this weren't uncertain enough, there may have been no third shot at all. Poe later wrote that what he thought was the report of a third shot was caused by the "rebound of Garrett's second bullet, which had struck the adobe wall and rebounded against the headboard of a wooden bedstead" (36–37). But this leads only to another mystery: where did Garrett's second bullet lodge? The headboard is unmarked, but decades later it was discovered that the washstand has a bullet hole with a trajectory consistent with a shot fired from a low angle, as Garrett's was when he dove toward the floor after firing his first shot. This furniture was exhibited in an Albuquerque museum, where it was arranged so as to replicate how it might have been in Maxwell's bedroom. "But the trouble," Mark Gardner, who visited the exhibition, told me, "is that nobody really knows where the pieces were placed in Maxwell's room." All we know with reasonable certainty from Garrett's book is that the bed was situated such that he could face the door when he sat at the head of it and that it was close enough to the wall that he couldn't hide behind it. While it's unlikely there is any other plausible explanation for this bullet hole, it remains, like so much other evidence about that night, frustratingly resistant to being called absolute proof.

Some seven or eight years following the Kid's death, the man who bought the Maxwell house noticed in one of the bedroom window-casings a bullet hole that, he was told, was made by the shot Billy fired at Garrett (see Blythe). But others who claimed to have been there told him the Kid only half drew his gun from his holster and never got off a shot. What is noteworthy here is that whether you believe the person who said Billy got off a shot or those who say his gun never cleared the holster, both parties *place a gun in his hand*.

17. Nor has Garrett's restraint prevented many from indulging in conspiracy theories that range from the barely plausible to the manifestly ludicrous. One of these has

Pete Maxwell colluding with Garrett to lure the Kid into an ambush because Maxwell wanted to put an irrevocable end to the romance between his sister Paulita and the Kid. In order to protect Maxwell from reprisal by the Kid's friends, Garrett lied in his book when he identified his informant as Manuel Brazil, the same rancher whose tip led to the Kid's capture at Stinking Springs. Like many conspiracy theories, this one can be made to have a superficial plausibility until you examine it. There is no evidence, even of a circumstantial nature, to support any aspect of it, while believing it requires us also to believe that Garrett's associates went along with the lie, thus escalating it from a two- to a five-part conspiracy (i.e., Garrett, Maxwell, Brazil, Poe, and McKinney). Yet in his own account of that evening, in response to the persistence of these and similar rumors, Poe flatly denied he and Garrett had *any* advance knowledge from Maxwell or anyone else that the Kid would be at Maxwell's (43). Was he still protecting Maxwell? If so, why? By the time Poe first wrote down his account, in 1919, Garrett had been dead eleven years, Maxwell twenty-one, and the Kid thirty-eight, while most of his friends who might exact revenge were dead, gone, or gone legit. Who needed protecting from whom by then?

Consider also that according to this theory, Poe, universally reputed to be an honest man, not only went along with Garrett, but in doing so published a fifty-seven-page narrative in support of a nearly four-decades-old fabrication that nobody was around to give much of a damn about anyway. If he really wanted to support a lie, wouldn't it have been enough, not to mention less risky as regards exposure, just to pay lip service to Garrett's book and say no more? In a nuttier variation on this scenario, Garrett, with Deputy McKinney's help, ties and gags Paulita, hides behind a sofa, waits until a fully armed Billy comes to see her, then rises up and shoots him dead without warning. The "source" for this is a little-known book by one Frederick W. Grey called *Seeking Fortune in America* (ca. 1912). Though Grey implies he got the story directly from McKinney, he refers to him as "Kipp Kinney," calls him "a genuine gunfighter," doesn't seem to know Paulita's name, is apparently unaware of the existence of Poe, and propagates several of the standard Billy-the-Kid myths while adding some of his own (e.g., the Kid "was a half-breed Indian") (110, 118–19).

However much Pete Maxwell wanted to split up the romance, is it at all probable he would have consented to a scheme in which there was a rather good chance his sister might have been caught in a crossfire between the Kid and the sheriff (not to mention "Kinney," who Grey wrote was posted outside to shoot the Kid in case Garrett didn't get him)? And if he had consented, is it probable that Garrett would have gone along with him? Consider too that in virtually every account of that night—including those from friends of the Kid to whom the conspiracy theorists grant great credence—several persons were on the scene within minutes (some reports say moments) of the shooting. Yet I'm unaware of so much as one who mentioned a sofa or reported the room was other than Maxwell's bedroom, as it would have to have been, unless we're to believe the lovers—assuming they even were lovers—used Pete's for their assignations (hardly likely, since Paulita had one of her own across the hall). I do not know if this particular set of rumors predated Grey's book, but Garrett himself made reference to reports, including illustrations, that portrayed him "shooting the Kid from behind a bed, from under a bed, and from other places of concealment." Correcting this sort of thing was among his stated purposes in writing *The Authentic Life* (151).

Yet this stuff is still resurrected from time to time. In 2000 none other than Frederick Nolan muses in his annotated edition of Garrett's book, "Perhaps, then, [the

McKinney-Grey] account . . . is nearer the truth" (xv). In 2004 it was dramatized in *Billy the Kid Unmasked*, one of those dreary "reenacted" documentaries on the Discovery Channel). And in 2010 Bob Boze Bell dusted it off for a *True West* article investigating alternative possibilities of what might have happened that night. Referencing the original 1863 floor plans for the fort buildings, which indicate only windows, not exterior doors, in the rooms along the porch, Bell writes, "if Pete's room did not have an outside door, then historians will be forced to look at the event with new eyes" (63). Maybe so, but conspiratorial ones? As Bell himself writes, Pete's father Lucien renovated the house, "so he might have created doorways when he and his family moved in." On the strength of most reports, including eyewitness accounts, not to mention photographs (Nolan, *West* 284), there doesn't appear to be any "might have" about it (and, anyhow, plans are only plans—who can say they weren't modified in the execution?). (See also Mark Lee Gardner, http://truewest.ning.com/profiles/blogs/the-other-side-of-the-billy.)

18. According to Metz (77–79), Garrett's mistake was an honest one and he deeply regretted it. Believing the Kid meant to act on his threat that he would never again be taken alive, Garrett decided the only way to avoid a protracted gunfight, which might have left several in his posse dead, was to take the Kid out first with no warning. Though the outlaws remained in their hideout for a long time, they eventually surrendered without violence, suggesting perhaps there was something to Garrett's thinking after all: no one could doubt his seriousness. In a letter written almost forty years later, James East (298), one of the posse, remembered the killing of Bowdre differently: Garrett *did* shout a warning, telling Bowdre to throw up his hands; when Bowdre went for his weapon, Garrett and another posse member fired. Did Garrett not consider his warning worth noting in his book or was East misremembering?

19. Though he did on other occasions, e.g., see Gardner, "Pat Garrett" (37). See also Otero, who quotes several remarks by Garrett to the effect that he really liked the Kid, thought him "one of the nicest little gentlemen I ever knew," etc. (71–73). Like Gardner, I am far from persuaded Garrett said these things, not least because Otero uses them as a setup for his declaration that "Garrett wants one to believe that duty called him. All of which to the author's mind, is unadulterated rot" (73). The last part of Otero's book is mostly oral history based on interviews he conducted, from which he strung together a series of testimonials to Billy's good character. Otero's interviewees were mostly people committed to the McSween-Tunstall side in the Lincoln County War (including former Regulators and Susan McSween, by then Susan Barber); former partners in crime; or friends from Fort Sumner, such as Paulita Maxwell and Deluvina Maxwell (see chapter 4, note 5). Recurring themes are how Billy was a perfect gentleman with the ladies, respectful to old people, generous to the poor, nice to children, loyal to his friends, always of good cheer, and absolutely devoted to his mother (all that's missing is a love for dogs, though there were those who attested to how well he treated horses). When Garrett is mentioned, he is a liar, a sellout, a traitor, a thief, a coward, and a murderer.

Otero even got George Coe to state that Garrett's motivations for hunting the Kid were "money and the office of sheriff of Lincoln County. The Kid was a thousand times better and braver than any man hunting him, including Garrett" (109). This seems to me highly dubious. To start with, it completely contradicts what Coe had to say in his own autobiography, published in 1934, two years before Otero's *The Real Billy the Kid*: "Some critics have claimed it was cowardly of Garrett to kill the Kid without giving him the ghost of a chance. They are dead wrong. Garrett was anything but a coward" (225).

Though Otero was unforthcoming as to exactly when his interviews were conducted, he clearly stated that the interview with George took place not long *before* the interview with George's cousin Frank (110), who died in September 1931. This means that although *The Real Billy the Kid* was published later than *Frontier Fighter*, George's recollections as quoted in Otero's book must predate what he set down as his own by a couple of years, if not more. Did Coe in his autobiography then wholly reverse his opinion of Garrett? There is no way to know, but a good clue is provided in what Coe says immediately following the passage about Garrett just quoted from *Frontier Fighter*: "It was some time before I could be reconciled, as I was misinformed concerning the real facts," and he goes on to relate a chat he had with John W. Poe, "in whom I had absolute confidence, and he gave me all the details just as Garrett had told them, and relieved my mind and changed my attitude toward Pat Garrett." In other words, since Poe died in 1923, it means that George had all the information he needed to form his favorable assessment of Garrett in *Frontier Fighter* well before Otero ever interviewed him. Yet it also means he had plenty of time to reverse himself again in his own book if he had wanted to after the interview, but he didn't. No matter which angle you look at it from, none of this augurs well for the integrity of at least some of Otero's interviews: they can by no means be wholly discounted, but they must be read with caution and skepticism.

20. Coe also said the Kid "could take two six-shooters, loaded and cocked, one in each hand" and twirl them in opposite directions at the same time (Bell, *Illustrated Life* 45).

21. See Richard Weddle's "Shooting Billy the Kid" for a fascinating reconstruction of the conditions and circumstances that produced this image, a detailed description of the ferrotype process, and an investigation of the probable fates of the four original tintypes, only one of which survives.

22. Here and in the next paragraph, Salazar is quoted from Otero (98). Otero spells Salazar's first name "Hijinio," but most sources use "Yginio," which is also the spelling on his gravestone.

23. Upson: "The Evans crowd seemed paralyzed. . . . All gazed wonderingly at the apparition of a gray horse, saddled and bridled, with no semblance of a rider save a leg thrown across the saddle and a head and arm protruding beneath the horse's neck, but, at the end of this arm the barrel of a pistol glistened in the sun-light" (66). Coe: "The posse stood almost paralyzed as they beheld Billy's gray nag flying toward them across the valley with no evidence of a rider save a leg thrown across the saddle, a head protruding beneath the horse's neck, and a hand holding something bright and very dangerous looking" (106). The passages in Coe about the Kid's early life and the fight with Antrim are from 55 to 56.

24. Otero 10. The idler incident is not all that Otero took from *The Authentic Life*: whole pages of the first part of his book are virtually copied from it without acknowledgment.

25. Utley has already raised this question (*Violent Life* 217n) about the Jones family's recollections of how they first met Billy as told in Ball's *Ma'am Jones of the Pecos*.

26. This notion of Upson's—that if Billy had had more positive influences he might have turned out better—was in fact sounded several months earlier by Don Jenardo (a pseudonym for the pulp writer John W. Lewis) in *The True Life of Billy the Kid*, according to Nolan (*Reader* 3) the first complete narrative of the Kid's life, published within six weeks of his death. "With proper culture, Billy the Kid might have made his mark

in the world," the book concludes. "His wonderful energy and remarkable bravery, had they been directed in the right channel, might have placed him high on the pinnacle of fame, instead of giving him an early and ignominious grave" (49). Did this influence Upson? Not necessarily. These ideas were part of the common currency of the times. Darwin's *On the Origin of Species*, published in 1859, gave a new lease on life to the nature/nurture debate, which fast permeated the whole culture from high to low.

27. *The Saga* evidently did not reach the market until early 1926, but 1925 is the copyright year as registered by Doubleday, Page and Co.

28. Burns was certainly among the first to popularize the Tunstall-McSween faction in the Lincoln County War as unequivocally the good guys, Murphy-Dolan the villains. "Viewed impartially," he wrote, "it is now clear that Murphy's cause was basically wrong, McSween's basically right; that Murphy was an unscrupulous dictator, McSween the champion of principle; that Murphy stood for lawlessness, McSween for law" (50). Despite most historians' arguments against this melodramatic reductionism, Burns's characterizations have hung on with surprising tenacity.

29. East 300–301. As published in Siringo (107), East's narrative, which was actually a letter, names the woman "Dulcinea del Toboso." It has long since been established that Paulita's name was changed when the letter was published because she was still denying any romance with Billy and wanted her reputation to remain unsullied. The number of her literary protectors increases apace.

30. Nolan conducts a survey of known or rumored girlfriends of Billy in "The Private Life of Billy the Kid," an article that should really be titled "The Many Loves of William Bonney." He comes down decisively for Paulita as the Kid's one true love at the time of his death, pushes hard for the notion that Garrett and her brother Pete conspired to lure Billy into a trap, and even repeats the gossip she was pregnant with his child. Nolan grants there is no evidence to support the conspiracy, and, unless Paulita had a miscarriage or an abortion, none to prove the pregnancy. According to the 1900 U.S. Census, which Nolan himself cites, her son Telesfor, who was supposed to have resembled Billy, was not born until 1893; he was preceded by two daughters, the earlier born in 1884, when the Kid had been dead four years. Nolan also names some other women rumored to have given birth to children who were Billy's. (See also Utley, *Violent Life* 127 and 248n3.)

Gardner wrote me that when Fort Sumner old-timers talked about an illegitimate child by Billy, they had in mind Abrana Garcia's son Patrocinio: "In a private letter Walter Noble Burns wrote to a William H. Burges on June 3, 1926, he stated that, 'The three Fort Sumner sweethearts of the Kid, aside from Paulita, were Celsa, Abrana Garcia by whom he had a child, and Masaria [*sic*] Yerbe who, I was informed, was still living in Las Vegas.' This letter is in the Robert N. Mullin Collection, and my transcription comes from Bob Utley."

31. In further support of the romance Burns also calls upon James East ("The meeting between the Kid and his sweetheart was affecting. He held her in his arms as she wept on his shoulder"), Frank Coe ("She was the only woman the Kid sincerely loved except his mother"), Martin Chavez (who said the Kid told him, "I am going to Fort Sumner to see the girl who is to be my wife. If I die, all right; then I will die for her"), and Garrett ("I was never surprised at the Kid's devotion to this good, pure girl. She was different from most of the girls he had ever known"). Burns also quotes John W. Poe on Paulita's reaction to Billy's death: "It was generally reported that she and the Kid were to be married and I was rather surprised that she showed little emotion

when she stood beside his dead body." Poe's is the only comment about Paulita's reaction to the Kid's death that I've come across from someone who was an eyewitness. (I am indebted to Gardner for providing a copy of Burns's early draft of his chapter on Paulita [which is part of the Walter Noble Burns papers, University of Arizona Archives]; my references are to pages 217–19.)

32. Though in fact there were others (e.g., several of the reminiscences in Otero). Frazier Hunt takes it practically as gospel that Garrett and Billy were close friends: "The Kid probably had rather mixed feelings when Pat Garrett was married for the second time. It meant a slight rift in the close relationship between the tall, reserved, thirty-year-old man and the slender, gay twenty-year-old boy" (197). Hunt had full access to Fulton's research, so his book, beautifully written and expansive, is far more accurate factually than the first two-thirds of Garrett's and much of Burns's, but his approach to history is equally and unabashedly novelistic. Although reported to have had decidedly mixed feelings about his friend's book (McCubbin iii), Fulton did allow of the "continued association" between Garrett and Billy that "possibly it should be termed a friendship" (Life xv).

33. These were exactly the points Garrett's son Jarvis made in a foreword to an edition of his father's book. He pointed out that the friendship could have been close only "if Garrett had become an outlaw himself by joining the gang," which emphatically "did not occur," adding, "Yes, he knew the Kid," but "everyone had a fairly complete knowledge and good acquaintance with anyone who frequented or lived in small communities. This was a commonplace thing in those days; there weren't many secrets about anyone" (20–21). Was Pat Garrett ever seriously on the wrong side of the law? There were rumors that in Texas, before coming to New Mexico, he killed a man and deserted a wife and family, but no evidence has ever been adduced to substantiate them. In his buffalo-hunting days he killed a partner named Joe Briscoe after an apparently trivial dispute that caused Briscoe to attack him with an ax. Garrett shot him dead point-blank. Distraught and guilt-ridden, he turned himself over to the authorities at Fort Griffin, Texas, but they declined to press charges. Another partner from his buffalo-hunting days once asked Garrett to perjure himself; when Garrett refused, the man thereafter spoke ill of him whenever he could and coaxed some others to do the same. None of their allegations has ever survived scrutiny (Metz 10, 18–38). When Garrett worked as a butcher in Fort Sumner, there were rumors that some of the beef he sold was from rustled cattle (Gardner, To Hell 35), but no evidence has ever been found to corroborate them. Richard Weddle tells me that Maxwell family descendants told him that some of those cattle were rustled from Pete Maxwell, but Weddle has been unable to find corroborating evidence to back this up. And Fort Sumner locals also said Garrett rustled as much cattle as the Kid and his pals did (see Otero 71, 91, 98, and 113); if this is true, most of it was more than likely in the form of rustling that consisted in gathering strays, rather common in those days. As the strays were usually abandoned anyhow, most owners turned a blind eye to the practice. It was only when some enterprising cowboy did all the hard work of gathering enough strays for a herd that the owners became suspicious enough or greedy enough (or both) to go after them.

34. Burns also gave John Chisum his fair share of credit for taming the territory. Striking familiar American chords of rugged individualism and ascension by ambition, intelligence, and hard work, the book opens with an outsized depiction of Chisum as "The King of the Valley," a path-breaking entrepreneur-businessman who became an

"unquestioned monarch holding dominion over vast herds and illimitable ranges" by "the divine right of brains and vision" (1). Fearing the cattle king had become "a dim figure," Burns calls it "an unjust estimate not to rank him as one of the great trailblazers and pioneers of the Southwest," not "an architect of civilization, perhaps, but a labourer laying in the sweat of his brow the foundation stones on which arose civilization and law and order" (19).

Chapter Three. Neider's Novel

The epigraph is from Neider's introduction to his *Great West* (14). Unless otherwise noted, all quotations from Neider are from the University of Nevada reprint of his novel (pagination identical to the first edition by Harper and Brothers [1956]).

1. Neider confined these observations almost exclusively to literature; about Western films (including even Peckinpah's) he had little to say, noting only in passing that he enjoyed them.

2. This and the last quotation in this paragraph from *Great West*, 13, 14; the remaining one is from Neider, "Hendry Jones" (unpublished essay, undated), 2.

3. Unpublished journal (September 22, 1954), 46.

4. It also suggests Burns knew *The Story of the Outlaw* (1907), where Emerson Hough ended his Billy the Kid chapter on a similar note of old times vanished, evoked with similar imagery, only it's Garrett who walks us to the windswept graves (312). Neider himself definitely read *The Story of the Outlaw* and greatly admired Hough's writings.

5. The remaining quotations in this paragraph are from *Authentic Death*, 21–22, 102, and 153–54.

6. Charles Neider letter to Maurice G. Fulton (December 13, 1953), 1.

7. "Hendry Jones" 1. Another reason Neider changed the setting was that he and his wife grew tired of the dust storms that blew through New Mexico during the spring of 1954; they longed to return to California, and they especially loved Monterey and Carmel.

8. Meadows, *Reminiscences* 43. Meadows first told of these meetings at a Pioneer Day celebration in February 1931 in Roswell, New Mexico; his remarks were taken down and printed in three articles in the *Roswell Daily Record*, March 2–4, 1931.

9. The killing of Folliard is from Garrett, *Authentic Life* 118–21.

10. The building was called the hospital only because it housed the infirmary in the days when the fort was a U.S. Army post. But the government had closed the fort thirteen years earlier and two years after that sold it to Lucien Maxwell, whose house would loom so large in the fate of Billy the Kid.

11. The ambush and death of Harvey are from *Authentic Death*, 161–67.

12. Unless otherwise indicated, quotations in this paragraph are from *Authentic Death*, 110, 8, 63, 144–45.

13. The two quotations in this paragraph are from *Authentic Death* (8, 17). Neider seems to have gotten this litany of attributes from Frank J. Dobie's description of Billy the Kid: "He was probably the quickest and surest man on the trigger anywhere south or west of Wild Bill Hickok. His nerve never broke; his alertness never flagged"; he "controlled himself as well as he controlled others; never impetuous, he deliberated every act, every robbery, every murder" (169).

14. Garrett, *Authentic Life* 134; the jailbreak is from chapter 22, 135–41.

15. For the paragraphs that follow, Nolan's account is from *West*, 273; Utley's from *Violent Life*, 180–83; Gardner's from *To Hell*, 144–48, 282n; and Meadows's from 48–49.

16. So far as is known, Billy personally related the events of his escape to only two persons, or, to put it more precisely, only two persons have ever claimed to have been told about it in detail by Billy himself, and neither published his recollections of what the Kid said until several decades later. One is Meadows and the other is Paco Anaya, who as a teenager first met Billy when some of the Regulators spent time hiding out at Anaya's father's sheepherding camp near Fort Sumner after the Lincoln County War. In Anaya's account a lady friend of the Kid's slips him a penknife wrapped in a tortita (in *One-Eyed Jacks* Guy Trosper has Longworth's daughter try to sneak Rio a derringer in a bowl of stew). When Anaya's father asks how he kept it hidden, Billy says, "I put it up 'you know where.'" Over the course of many days' visits to the privy, he periodically extricates the knife, cleans it, and carves a wooden key that allows him to unlock his handcuffs (after each visit he returns the knife to its hiding place). One day he unlocks a cuff and throws it at Bell's head, incapacitating him. (Inasmuch as it seems to have been common knowledge the Kid could slip his hands out of his cuffs, why would he need a key? And would merely *throwing* a single handcuff at Bell be sufficient to incapacitate him?) Anaya set down these recollections in the thirties, when he was seventy, in the form of a sixty-page typewritten document in Spanish, which was not translated and published until 1991 as *I Buried Billy* (the jailbreak on 50–56). As in Otero, there are many long unbroken passages of direct quotation from Billy and others that tax credulity, and it is also marked by numerous lapses of memory, confused chronologies, and mistaken dates, which are understandable given Anaya's age and the time that had elapsed before he started compiling it. Although it has value because he actually did know Billy, its many inaccuracies and outlandish stories, ridiculous on their face, require that, like Otero's, it be read with considerable skepticism.

17. These reports are reprinted in Nolan, *Reader* 311–14.

18. Peckinpah said the idea for this came from "a con at Huntsville," who told him that dimes "make such a whistling sound and they do tear you up something awful" ("Story Conference" tape, 9/9/72). The opening of *The Getaway* was filmed at the prison in Huntsville, Texas.

19. "'The Escape of 'The Kid,'" 1. Gardner, who makes extensive use of this report, told me he concurs with a local New Mexico historian named Drew Gomber that this letter was likely written by Sam Corbet, a former clerk in the Tunstall store. Those who believe the pistol was hidden in the outhouse think Corbet the man who slipped Billy the note informing him where to find it (put there by Jose Aguayo, another friend). But if this letter really was by Corbet, then considering how clearly the closing sentence deplores the violence in Lincoln, it's hard to imagine that whatever his sympathies, he would have been a party to secreting Billy a firearm, as he would have known the likelihood of someone getting killed was high. Corbet, who liked the Kid, here expressed a despair that seems to have been shared by a great many people in Lincoln and the surrounding area, who were weary of the violence, wanted it to stop, and held the Kid as responsible as they did other bad men, even while realizing that many of them were very much worse than he.

20. Quotations in this paragraph are from *Authentic Death*, 90, 172, 176.

21. Ibid., Hendry's escape from 73–86.

22. See Wallis, who points out that the "sparsely populated New Mexico Territory accounted for at least 15 percent of all murders in the nation . . . with gunshot wounds as the leading cause of death" (168).

23. Neider, "HJ," unpublished lecture notes (November 3, 1997), 13, and "Preface" (unpublished early draft, ca. 1984), 11.

24. Although the historical record is far from clear about how much the Kid drank, there is neither evidence nor testimony that he drank regularly and he was certainly no alcoholic.

25. This and remaining quotations in this paragraph are from *Authentic Death*, 136, 177–78.

26. According to Neider, his publishers put this blurb on the cover to distance the novel from the genre of Western fiction as such in order to attract a wider readership ("HJ and Violence," unpublished lecture notes, November 13, 1997, 1).

27. Quotations from the novel in this paragraph are from 131 and 115–19. Doc's description of diving for abalone, prying them off the rocks, pounding them tender, and eating them raw must have struck a very personal note for Peckinpah: his brother-in-law Walter Peter told me how he and Sam used to do exactly that before abalone became so popular as to have been depleted.

28. In this sense the novel at times feels reminiscent of Kafka, a particular favorite of Neider's. An effect of claustrophobia is also characteristic of quite a few notable Westerns from the late forties through the early sixties, particularly those with black-and-white cinematography (which Neider thought more appropriate than color for filming the book—understandably so, stylistically his palette for the most part of blacks, whites, and grays), such as *Yellow Sky, The Treasure of the Sierra Madre, The Gunfighter, Winchester '73, High Noon, 3:10 to Yuma, The Man Who Shot Liberty Valance*, and *Lonely Are the Brave*. Several episodes from *The Westerner* easily join this distinguished group. Often called "revisionist," these films could just as easily, and rather more accurately, be called "noir Westerns," given how much they share with film noir, not just the dark settings, but protagonists who are similarly dark, as in tortured, haunted, driven by demons; endings that are for the most part downbeat; and an overall tone of pessimism and attitudes of cynicism and despair.

29. *Authentic Death* 97–98. Neider took this from *Frontier Fighter*, where it involves a man (unnamed but not William Bonney) and an old forty-niner named King who kids around with people by goosing them. He does this to a girl at a dance, which sends her partner, the young man, into a rage. Restrained from going after King that night, he spied him a few days later in a potato patch and "cracked down and killed the old fellow without further parley" (67).

30. *Authentic Death* 48–49. Neider's description here is exactly the way John Meadows describes Olinger's killing of John Jones—even the language is similar: Bob "caught John's right hand with his left, jerked his six-shooter and shot John in the back of the head" (41–42). For alternative versions of this killing, see Nolan, *West* 215–17, and Ball 178–79.

31. Jan Aghed has speculated that one inspiration for Peckinpah's use of slow motion may lie in the way Neider protracts the deaths of Pablo and Lon. This strikes me as highly unlikely because the *effect* of Peckinpah's slow motion is not at all like that of Neider's protracted individual deaths. It's possible, however, that the way Peckinpah drew out the deaths in real time of Sylvus Hammond and Steve Judd in *Ride the High Country* and Cullen Baker and Garrett in *Pat Garrett* was inspired by

Neider. Of course, the longest death in any of Peckinpah's films is that of Cable Hogue, who gets to hear part of his own eulogy in one of the director's most beautifully sustained pieces of lyricism.

32. *The Ballad of Cable Hogue* is unmentioned here because I don't consider it a story of a man who lives beyond his time.

Chapter Four. Peckinpah's Adaptation

1. Peckinpah's remark about *The Glass Menagerie* is from Murray, "*Playboy* Interview" (111); his *Portrait of a Madonna* and *Noon Wine* adaptations are discussed in *Reconsideration* (130–31 and 91–112), and his *Straw Dogs* adaptation in Sragow's superb "From *The Siege of Trencher's Farm* to *Straw Dogs*" (69–81); Weddle's observation on the *Hendry Jones* screenplay is from 144.

2. Although Weddle reports that *The Dice of God* was Peckinpah's first full-length screenplay, in one interview Peckinpah said it was his second (Medjuck 20). Weddle is correct: the completion date on the cover of *The Dice of God* script is March 20, 1957. Tynan's observation is from a clipping (ca. 1965, SPP).

3. As both screenplays are labeled "First Draft," the only way they can be distinguished is by date, i.e., "*Hendry Jones* screenplay, 10/57" and "*Hendry Jones* screenplay, 11/57." As if this were not confusing enough, there is a copy of the 10/57 screenplay in MHL's Paramount Pictures scripts archives that is identical to the 10/57 screenplay except with a new title, *Guns Up*, evidently the first alternative title that Brando et al. came up with before they settled on *One-Eyed Jacks*. Finally, there is still another screenplay in MHL with the *Hendry Jones* title; however, it is not one of Peckinpah's drafts but a much later version of the *One-Eyed Jacks* screenplay to which someone inexplicably attached Peckinpah's title page.

4. Peckinpah opened the 10/57 draft with the procession of mourners carrying the Kid's coffin to the gravesite; the description suggests a lovely "poetic" opening, the processional, with candles, backlit against the sea or the moonlit night. Though we never see the present-day Doc as an old man, we hear him in voice-over. The whole sequence is three and a half pages longer than the later one, most of it given over to descriptions of who the mourners are. It's easy to understand why Peckinpah streamlined all this, not least because he would have no way of conveying to us on film who these people are or their significance, and no dramatic or narrative purpose is really served by beginning at the gravesite—it would be merely a moody opening.

5. Neider based this character on Deluvina Maxwell, a Navajo Indian born in Canyon de Chelly sometime between 1847 and 1851. At nine or ten she was taken by Apaches, who used her as a slave until they traded her to Lucien Maxwell (the father of Pete Maxwell) for some horses. The Maxwell family took her in, gave her their name, and from all reports treated her extremely well. She became the family servant and acquired a local reputation as a healer. Deluvina adored Billy the Kid uncritically and hated Pat Garrett for killing him. On the scene within minutes of the Kid's death, she burst into tears, pounding Garrett's chest and cursing him, calling him, according to some accounts, a "pisspot" (Nolan, *West* 249, 287).

6. In an earlier scene where Fawcett comes to the Longworth house, the draft ended with an additional line, Dad saying, "I want ten more men here within twenty minutes" (10/57, 47). It's easy to see why Peckinpah took this line out, as it completely

vitiates the surprise reveal of the posse on the bluff. Even this early in his career Peckinpah was well on his way to becoming the consummate *visual* storyteller, dramatist, and *editor*. If he had been allowed to film this screenplay, my guess is that in the editing room he would have gone even further, cutting away from the exchange between Fawcett and Dad *before* Dad makes the decision to help. If a scene is resolved in a subsequent scene, suspense is often better served if the earlier scene is left unresolved.

7. This is one of the few lines from Peckinpah's screenplay that survived the succession of subsequent writers and actually made it to the screen in *One-Eyed Jacks*, and it is one of most widely quoted by fans of the film, though by far the most famous is when Brando calls Bob Emory (Ben Johnson) a "scum-sucking pig," which was not Peckinpah's.

8. This obviously suggests some romantic or sexual relationship between Dad and Hendry's mother, but it can't possibly mean that Hendry is Dad's son because the age differences don't add up. Perhaps Peckinpah included it to add a component of guilt to Dad's protectiveness toward the Kid. Alternatively, since Dad would have known Hendry at the same time as he knew his mother "very well," perhaps this is intended to posit a basis for why the Kid is so hostile to Dad's new life, in which another woman has displaced his mother. Plainly, these are way too many perhapses, and this remains a tangent that is never fully absorbed into the story. In the 10/57 draft, there is an additional line from Dad. Reacting to his wife's "unflinching" stare, Dad says, "She's been dead a very long time, May" (27), which tends to confirm the relationship was at least for a time sexually intimate.

9. Peckinpah tried several times to get the line "One fellow went one way, the next one another, and the first thing you knew one of them was called an outlaw and the other was sheriff" into the *Pat Garrett* screenplay. The randomness of whether a man was one or the other was important to him and in a meeting he told Wurlitzer he was going to show him Dad's "we never turned" speech from the *Hendry Jones* screenplay ("Story Conference" tape, 9/9/72). Although the line appears in some of Peckinpah's tentative revisions, he never did find a place for it in the film or even in any of the screenplay drafts.

10. For *One-Eyed Jacks* Brando and Guy Trosper appear to have gotten the idea of having Dad and Ringo be separated (in their case by *rurales*) from Peckinpah, though of course they developed it very differently.

11. Of course it was another matter when he returned to these materials fifteen years later, but then he was in a very different place in both his life and career. In connection with that, it remains only to ask why, as he carried on a lifelong romance with all things Mexican, he made Mrs. Longworth an Anglo, since in the novel she is Mexican, as were also both of Garrett's wives—Garrett's first wife died shortly after their wedding in the fall of 1879 and within a year he remarried—facts Peckinpah surely knew. This question will be taken up in part 3.

Chapter Five. Wurlitzer's Screenplay

1. *Pat Garrett and Billy the Kid* (New American Library, 1973). The passage in the epigraph is from "Introduction by the Author," v–vi. Long out of print, difficult to find, and expensive, a copy of this book is in MHL.

2. According to *Variety* (weekly edition), by the end of its first week (which included the holiday weekend), *Pat Garrett* grossed $576,000 and placed third among the fifty

top-grossing films for that week, behind *High Plains Drifter* (first) and *Hitler: The Last Ten Days* (5/31/73, 11); by the end of its second week it grossed an additional $351,000 and dropped to fourth place (behind *Drifter, The Day of the Jackal*, and *Deep Thrust: The Hand of Death*) (6/13/73, 9); by the third week it had dropped to forty-sixth place (6/20/73, 13); and by the fourth week it was off the list completely and finished with a year-to-date gross of a mere $1,145,181 (6/27/73, 10). These figures are for domestic returns only, but they were low enough that its run was effectively over, despite the considerable prestige of Peckinpah's name abroad.

3. "Story Conference" tape, 9/9/72 (hereafter "Story" tape).

4. In one of the production meetings Peckinpah referred to himself as "the greatest collaborator with my name not being on the script in the world" ("Sam, Gordon, and I" tape, 9/9/72). This wasn't boastful. No doubt remembering all too well his early days as a writer trying to break into directing, he never tried to take credit for writing he felt he did not do or at least do in sufficient amount to deserve. Garner Simmons, who interviewed most of the writers Peckinpah worked with, told me, "In all the time I spent researching *Portrait in Montage*, I never had anyone accuse Sam of jumping a writing credit. Quite the opposite. For instance, despite substantial rewrites on *Straw Dogs*, which David Zelag Goodman, the original writer, was not even present for, Goodman went out of his way to confirm that Sam never once tried to put his name first on the title pages." Likewise David Weddle: "No writers I interviewed accused Sam of trying to steal their credit. On the contrary, going all the way back to his work on *The Westerner*, he did not claim credit on a number of occasions when he could have." And Wurlitzer: "Unlike many directors, Sam was secure enough about his own identity to be always generous with giving credit to the writer. He was passionately intense in his collaborations with writers and actors and grateful for their loyalties."

5. The script is filed as *Pat Garrett and Billy the Kid* because it is the MHL's policy to file all screenplays under the title of the film *as released*, regardless of any earlier titles. Unless otherwise noted, all script quotations or references in this chapter are to Wurlitzer's *Billy the Kid*, 6/21/70, 119 pp. (T/MGMS, f.256).

6. There is absolutely no independent authentication for the existence of Alias outside *The Authentic Life* (where he is confined to the opening chapters), for which reason historians regard him as an Ash Upson invention (though Walter Burns takes him as real). According to Upson, Billy early on had a partner who changed his name so many times the Kid couldn't keep track of them, so he took to calling him "Alias" (14).

7. Or Higgins—though the script uses the names interchangeably, Wurlitzer informs me Hawkins is the correct intended name.

8. When a few months later the scene at the Horrell Trading Post was added to the screenplay, Jones's Trading Post was called simply the saloon. For clarity, I refer to the saloon as Jones's Saloon, since it's run by Lemuel Jones.

9. In the next complete draft Billy still never refers to Garrett as his friend, and when he speaks of Garrett, it is usually in sarcastic or derogatory terms. Early on Bell reminds Billy, "you 'n' him used to be pretty close." But if this is to be regarded as other than a mere sentimental assumption on Bell's part, Billy's reply—that Garrett, "store-bought now and woman pecked," has "signed hisself over to Chisum and every goddamn landowner that's puttin' muscle on this country"—suggests that what friendship there was or may have been is by now pretty tattered (*PGBK*, 11/5/70 with chngs. through 6/16/72 [T/MGMS, f.262], 3–3A).

10. There is basis in fact for Billy's claim of back wages only in the sense that he got it into his head that Chisum owed him money for fighting in the Lincoln County War and even calculated the amount to be five hundred dollars. According to Fulton (*History* 379–80), when Billy and Chisum happened to run into each other in Fort Sumner, in January 1880, the Kid drew on Chisum and demanded payment. The old man remained calm and asked if he could light up his pipe, "for then I can talk better. Now, Billy, listen. If you talked about that money until your hair was as white as mine, you could not convince me that I owed it to you. Billy, you couldn't shoot an honest man, could you, while he was looking you in the eye? You have killed several men, I know, but they needed killing." Billy backed down but "only for the present. If you won't pay me that $500 in money I'll steal your cattle until I get it." Fulton cites no source for this story, but it exists in more than one version. Utley (*Violent Life* 133) and Nolan (*West* 217) based theirs on the account given by Chisum's son Will, who has the old man saying, "I always pay my honest debts. I don't owe you anything, and you can kill me but you won't knock me out of many years. I'm an old man now," and Billy replies, "Aw, you ain't worth killing." Far more melodramatic is the one in *I Buried Billy* (84), where Paco Anaya raises the debt to five thousand dollars and has the Kid ordering Chisum to "Bite this pistol!" then leading "him around the bar two or three times," demanding a check for the amount, and finally booting him out the saloon door.

As for Garrett's loan, I am unable to find evidence to support the existence of any arrangement between him and Chisum, Joseph C. Lea (see chapter 6, note 8), the Santa Fe Ring, or anyone else that involved money, a loan, property, or other kind of financial quid pro quo in exchange for apprehending the Kid. To be sure, Garrett was elected as a law-and-order man who could tame the territory and make it safe for decent folks, not to mention attract business and investment. But Chisum and the others who supported Garrett also wanted to put a stop to all the theft and violence because they were just sick and tired of it, especially the killing, and in that they had a great deal of ardent support from ordinary citizens, who lived in fear of the outlaw gangs that terrorized New Mexico, Lincoln County in particular. As for Garrett's financial situation, according to Metz (89–91), after bringing the Kid and his gang in, Garrett was seriously strapped for cash, not least because he was still out of pocket for the expenses of the manhunt. When he tried to collect the reward money, Acting Governor W. G. Ritch withheld payment, hiding behind one legal loophole after another. Once the newspapers got hold of this, the populace was so scandalized that several prominent citizens put up the funds themselves (Chisum and Lea *not* among them).

Amazingly, when Garrett tried to collect the same reward (still unpaid) after killing the Kid, it took him six months of personal lobbying in Santa Fe and an act of the territorial legislature to get him the money. In the meantime, once again well-to-do citizens (prominent among them James Dolan) sent him private contributions, which amounted to $1,150 but "did little more than pay Garrett's liquor and gambling bills as he lounged around the territorial capital" (Metz 127). If Governor Wallace, who resigned in March 1881, ever tried to assist or otherwise lend support to Garrett's petitions, there is no record of it. Riding high on the success of his new novel *Ben-Hur*, the former governor washed his hands of the sheriff as thoroughly as he did of Billy the Kid and the rest of the New Mexico Territory. In 1901, however, he did help secure for Garrett the position of collector of customs in El Paso under President Theodore Roosevelt.

11. It turns out that there is some vague basis for this in rumor and gossip. Wurlitzer told me he recalled reading it somewhere or at least hearing it when he

kicked around Lincoln and Fort Sumner in 1969. I heard the same thing myself when I traveled through the area in 2013. Taking advantage of his small, delicate hands and slender physique, the Kid was said to have dressed as a girl in order to escape notice by the authorities. Interviewed in a documentary called *Storytellers of Lincoln County* (1994), Chino Silva (1918–2004), whose grandfather Jesus Silva helped bury the Kid, says that Billy let his hair grow long, wore dresses, and actually worked in Fort Sumner cantinas as a waitress, where he took delight in serving lawmen who hadn't the slightest idea the girl waiting on them was a young man barely out of his teens. Silly as this sounds on its face, it's obvious Wurlitzer didn't just pull it out of thin air. Another rumor, which I first heard from one of the personnel at the Lincoln County Museum, has the Kid trying to grow a beard and moustache while experimenting with dyes to darken his skin. Several months later Mark Gardner alerted me to a news story he had just come across in the *Colorado Springs Weekly Gazette* of July 23, 1881, nine days after the Kid was killed, which reported Billy "had allowed his beard to grow and had attempted to disguise himself as a Mexican by darkening his skin by the use of some sort of root" (2).

12. Memo from Sam Peckinpah to Gordon Carroll, April 9, 1972 (SPP, f.770).

13. Born in Texas in 1863 and hanged in the New Mexico Territory in 1901, Thomas E. ("Black Jack") Ketchum was an actual outlaw. Although the real Ketchum had no connection to Billy the Kid, Wurlitzer helped himself to the name; the killings of the puppies and the women are from Eve Ball (199–200), where it is Ketchum who does the deeds.

14. Some conspicuous exceptions notwithstanding—*The Wild Bunch, The Gunfighter, My Darling Clementine*—filmmakers haven't paid as much serious attention to this darker theme as Western novelists have; and even among them, it tends to be more fully exploited in fiction set in the earlier period of the mountain man. A. B. Guthrie Jr.'s splendid *The Big Sky* is one of the finest examples.

15. The two miners are wholly Wurlitzer's invention, but the basic premise of the scene derives from a passage in Poe's book. One day in White Oaks Poe was approached by an acquaintance who told him that while occupying a room in a livery owned by two men who were friends of the Kid, he had one night "overheard a conversation between the two men, which convinced him the Kid was . . . making his headquarters at Fort Sumner" (12–13; see also Gardner, *To Hell* 162–63). Neider also availed himself of Poe here.

Chapter Six. Peckinpah's Changes

1. "Story Conference" tape, 9/9/72 (hereafter "Story" tape). Throughout this chapter, quite a number of remarks by Peckinpah, Wurlitzer, and Carroll originate in this story conference, so unless otherwise referenced, assume this is the source. The epigraph is from an email Wurlitzer wrote to me.

2. Memo from Sam Peckinpah to Gordon Carroll, April 9, 1972 (SPP, f.770). Peckinpah obviously dictated this memo but didn't read it, since he knew the correct spelling of Neider's name.

3. A fair amount of this has already been done with insight and thoroughness by Robert Merrill in the critical study he and John L. Simons wrote jointly (105–53). Merrill, who wrote most of the *Pat Garrett* chapter, documents the changes so

thoroughly and in such detail as virtually to obviate the need for the job to be done again.

4. Although Eugene Manlove Rhodes's 1927 novel *Pasó por Aquí* features Garrett as a main character, neither it nor *Four Faces West*, the 1948 screen adaptation, is about Garrett *and* Billy. To my knowledge, it wasn't until 2004 and the publication of Wilson's volume of Meadows's reminiscences that Garrett would be given a place beside Billy in the title of a serious book about them. And in 2010 came Gardner's *To Hell on a Fast Horse: Billy the Kid, Pat Garrett, and the Epic Chase to Justice in the Old West*, a dual biography that is by far the most fair-minded, evenhanded, and balanced treatment of both men, with absolutely no axes to grind or agendas to push, and its scrupulous, exhaustive research is the most up-to-date as of this writing.

5. In this section, unless otherwise noted, the only screenplay I am discussing and thus citing is the last of the November 5, 1970, versions, the one that contains all the revisions Wurlitzer did on his own in the first part of 1972: *PGBK*, 11/5/70, chngs. through 6/16/72, approx. 140 pp. (T/MGMS, f.262).

6. There is no way of knowing for certain if unscripted lines were added by Peckinpah or someone else (including Wurlitzer, as he was present during the shoot in Mexico) or were ad-libbed by the actors. Most of them were probably added by Peckinpah; in any case, I attribute them to him because they wouldn't have been printed, let alone used in the film, had he not agreed to them. Peckinpah had no ego when it came to using anything from any quarter if he felt it made for a better film.

7. Though the real Garrett availed himself of prostitutes when he was away from home, which was often and for long periods, he seems to have loved his wife truly. At least there appears to be no evidence he ever had any affairs or romances beyond the physical. His letters, which talk of how much he misses her and their children, are remarkable for their tenderness and expressions of love. Her name was Apolinaria (Ida the name of one of their daughters); she was so dark-skinned she was sometimes called "La Negra" and so short that in a widely printed photograph of her standing beside her *seated* husband, a horizontal line drawn from the top of his head would pass just underneath her nose.

8. Prior to and during the Lincoln County War, Chisum, in partnership with Tunstall and McSween, was actually allied *against* the Santa Fe Ring as represented by Murphy and Dolan. Joseph C. Lea, another big cattleman and sometimes called the "father of Roswell," was at least as instrumental as Chisum, probably more, in persuading Garrett to run for sheriff. Billy was scapegoated here owing to his notoriety, which became infamy after his killings in the Lincoln jailbreak, but it is naive to think he was not also part of the problem. Even his friends, such as Sam Corbet and John Meadows, understood this.

9. Fairly few dramatic or fictional treatments of Billy the Kid include Wallace. (Two others are Gore Vidal's *Billy the Kid* [1989] and *Young Guns II* [1990].) As written by Wurlitzer—Peckinpah contributed almost nothing except the casting of Jason Robards and in his direction suggesting that Garrett and Wallace are friends who share a mutual disgust for Holland and Norris—Wallace is something of a missed opportunity. His governorship of the New Mexico Territory still generates controversy. Some historians say he governed in absentia even when he was present, spending far too little time in Lincoln, where he was needed, and far too much in Santa Fe writing his soon-to-be best seller *Ben-Hur* (Wurlitzer's original screenplay called for a map of the Roman Empire in Wallace's office). Others say he made an earnest attempt to stop the

violence and to arrest, indict, and prosecute the guilty, especially the Dolan crowd, but that he was thwarted by the reach and power of the Santa Fe Ring (unlike the previous governor, Wallace not only was not part of the ring, he was actively hostile toward it). The amnesty Wallace declared for the combatants excluded those with indictments predating the Lincoln County War, the Kid under two for previous killings (one of them Brady). In return for testifying against Dolan and others who fought for The House, Wallace promised Billy, "I will let you go scot free with a pardon in your pocket for your misdeeds" (Fulton, *History* 338). But the governor lacked legal authority to force William A. Rynerson, the district attorney, a close friend of Dolan's, and a solid member of the ring, to honor a pardon *from* prosecution (and he didn't). It was a political-legal mess. In the end, Billy's testimony proved useless: according to Utley, "among fifty or more men indicted for offenses in the Lincoln County War, only Billy the Kid was convicted of any crime" (*High Noon* 156). Nolan (*West* 196) believes Wallace's offer "an empty promise" from the moment he made it. For his part, figuring he'd been used and abandoned, Billy one day just up and walked out of the Lincoln store where he was confined and rode out of town in the direction of Fort Sumner, Tom Folliard at his side. Regardless of where one comes down on the question of his guilt for the murders of Brady and Buckshot Roberts, there can be no doubt that Billy was singled out both by the authorities and by the ring.

10. There is basis in fact for the crack teamwork of Billy and his gang in this scene. According to Henry Hoyt, a doctor who knew Billy, one evening in Tascosa the Kid and four of his pals, including Tom Folliard, were at a *baile* when Billy tripped "and sprawled out on his belly in the middle of the floor. Quicker than scat those four men were back to back around him, with a gun in each hand. . . . Where the guns came from we didn't know, as they had parked their guns, but it was about as remarkable an example of efficiency of its kind as I ever saw" (Bell, *Illustrated Life* 87; see also Hoyt 150–53). Billy and his friends were thereafter barred from *bailes* at that site.

11. Wurlitzer told me that Dylan wrote the song "on a plane from Mexico City to Durango. I remember him saying, 'I have to lay down something good for Slim.'"

12. Peckinpah's objections were two. He didn't think that either Robert Ryan, whom he was counting on to play Chisum, or Joel McCrea, his second choice, "would stand for it," adding, "I don't think history would stand for it either. [Chisum] had tough guys riding for him but he was an extraordinarily moral man." Chisum was famous for never carrying a gun on his person—"a six-shooter will get you into more trouble than it will get you out of," he liked to say—and there is uncertainty as to how much force he used to clear trespassers and settlers off his land. According to Fulton (*History* 33–34), his "policy was to keep intruders out by means other than violence if possible." If Chisum were to remain in the scene, Peckinpah suggested Wurlitzer have him ride up later, presumably after a time cut, and say, "Take him to Lincoln. Charge him with rustling."

13. Because I am writing here about the development of the screenplay, lines of dialogue are quoted from the screenplays, even though they do not always conform exactly to what is in the film itself. This is one such instance. Though the sense of it remains the same, the speech is stronger in the film (and is quoted in full in *Reconsideration* 279). This is typical in filmmaking: directors make alterations, additions, or deletions to fit the way the scene plays out in rehearsals and shooting, and sometimes actors do not find a line as scripted congenial and will change it slightly to make it sound more natural, easier to speak, whatever.

14. The character is called "Breed" in the film and identified as "Beaver" in the cast list.

15. Wurlitzer's source for most of the Horrells scene was Eve Ball's *Ma'am Jones of the Pecos*. In 1877 Barbara Jones—everyone called her "Ma'am"—and her husband Heiskell settled in the Seven Rivers area, where they owned a trading post and ranch. They had ten children, nine of them boys. The Horrells themselves were obviously based on the Jones family, though Wurlitzer's renaming them was curious, as Horrell was the name of a virulently racist gang of brothers from Texas who managed to start their own little war, murdering several Mexican men and raping then murdering the women, before being driven out of the territory. (Wurlitzer cannot remember why he made the name change—perhaps because he had already given "Jones" to Lemuel.) Ma'am Jones and her husband eschewed violence, though their sons did not take after them in this respect. She became a local legend, renowned for her generosity, hospitality, and culinary and nursing skills. The family's close friendship with William Bonney began on a night in October 1877 when he showed up at three in the morning exhausted, emaciated, and hungry, his feet blistered raw from being on foot in undersized boots for three days after escaping an attack by Apaches. (At least that is how it is told in *The Authentic Life*, though few historians give Upson's melodramatized account much credence.) After Ma'am nursed the boy back to health, he stayed on for a while and became close friends with the oldest sons, John and Jim. Although he and John fought on opposite sides during the Lincoln County War—John never liked The House, but he always regarded Chisum and other large cattlemen as the bigger threat—they remained close friends until John was murdered by Bob Olinger, which was the start of Billy's hatred for the deputy. He swore vengeance for John's death, even though Ma'am tried to dissuade him, telling him that killing Olinger wouldn't bring her son back.

Wurlitzer based the duel between Billy and Alamosa Bill on a duel John himself fought with a man named Riley, who had just shared dinner with the family, right down to the dialogue about never tasting anything so good as the fried pie and the exchange in which the duelists ask each other if they can think of any other way out of this. Neither cheats, but they pace off, turn, and fire on a ten-count. Wurlitzer also used some key dialogue from a later scene in Ball's book where Billy tells Heiskell how Olinger shot John in the back. When Heiskell tells Billy that he hasn't got a chance against Garrett, Billy replies, "I'm outlawed. And it hasn't been long since I was a law and Old Pat was an outlaw. Funny thing, the law." Bell's monologue about how to make biscuits (nixed by Peckinpah in the first story conference) is also in Ball. (The passages in Ball pertinent to Wurlitzer's screenplay are from 110, 113–20, 174–75, 204–6. For more on the Horrells, see Nolan, *Bad Blood* 51–54.)

16. *PGBK*, 11/3/72, with chngs. through 1/31/73, 115 pp. (SPP, f.759).

17. *PGBK*, 7/7/72, with chngs. through 7/25/72, 134 pp. (SPP, f.750).

18. For some reason Wurlitzer's 9/11/72 opening pages are filed in T/MGMS, f.264, along with a duplicate of the same *PGBK* 7/7/72 screenplay in SPP, f.750.

19. *PGBK*, 134 pp. (SPP, f.751), undated interim draft based on the 7/7 version.

20. *PGBK*, 11/3/72, with chngs. through 1/18/73, 115 pp. (SPP, f.758).

21. Although the screenplays identify this scene as "Line shack—dawn," I refer to it as Stinking Springs because the action is based on Garrett's capture of Billy and his gang there as related in *The Authentic Life* (122–26). In the earliest version of the scene (SP 9/27/72 [SPP, f.751]) Peckinpah even included the business of Garrett shooting one of the outlaws' horses dead in the doorway to block the only exit. In the book

there is also this exchange: "We have no wood to get breakfast," the Kid tells Pat, who answers, "Come out and get some. Be a little sociable." "Can't do it, Pat. Business is too confining. No time to run around." And Garrett, "Didn't you fellows forget a part of your programme yesterday? You know you were to come in on us at Fort Sumner . . . give us a square fight, set us afoot, and drive us down the Pecos." Peckinpah reduced this to "C'mon in, Pat, I'll warm your breakfast," which is answered with more shooting. Another piece of business he incorporated, though with considerable elaboration, was having Billy help Bowdre up for one final rally, the Kid and Folliard using their dying friend as a decoy, pushing him out the door in a desperate attempt to shoot their way free. Although Garrett reported hearing the Kid say, "They have murdered you, Charlie, but you can get revenge. Kill some of the sons-of —— before you die," his book relates no more shooting after Bowdre was first hit, save killing the horse. As four outlaws (not two) remained alive, Garrett, figuring there might be a long siege, arranged for a nearby rancher to bring food and other provisions. "We built a rousing fire and went to cooking," Garrett wrote. "The odor of roasting meat was too much for famished lads. . . . Craving stomachs overcame brave hearts [a little flourish doubtless added by Upson]," and the outlaws soon surrendered. Historians do not agree whether Billy did send Bowdre out to get some of his own back before he died; Peckinpah named one of the outlaws Folliard in the screenplay, but he is never referred to by his surname in the film (though in the longer version of the scene in the previews he is once called "Tom"); and of course the real Folliard had been killed four days earlier by Garrett in Fort Sumner.

22. *PGBK*, 10/4/72, 130 pp. (SPP, f.752).

23. Peckinpah could claim an impressive grasp of tragedy. He once told me that his original idea for his master's thesis at the University of Southern California had to do with the theory and practice of tragedy from Aristotle to the moderns and that he had even gotten as far as Ibsen in his notes and some writing before abandoning it in favor of filming a play (*Reconsideration* 342–43). His first wife told me he was always quoting Aristotle on tragedy.

24. *PGBK*, 10/18/72, 140 pp. (SPP, f.754).

25. Apart from the dispute involving a lease and the grazing of sheep on Garrett's land—an arrangement that had nothing to do with Chisum, long dead by then—there is no basis in fact for any of this, though it certainly pays rich dividends in irony in the film. But the lessee was not Poe, with whom Garrett got along perfectly well, even supporting the deputy's run for sheriff the next election after Garrett decided he'd had enough. From all reports Poe was a widely admired and well-liked man—Garrett named one of his sons after him. As for the Santa Fe Ring, by the time of Garrett's murder it had long since ceased to exist in anything resembling its constitution at the time of the Lincoln County War and the death of Billy, most of its members dead or moved on or away.

26. I catch hell for this from Jim Kitses in the expanded edition of his *Horizons West*, where he complains that my interpretation of the film as Garrett's tragedy rests on the assumption that the narrative is "subjective, a record of events from Pat's point of view, despite the fact that he is off-stage for half the film's action and the absence of any clues in the text that invite or endorse such an interpretation" (246). Though I am uncertain what Kitses means by the word "text"—the script or the film itself?— Peckinpah's substantial prologue seems to me a pretty large clue, and we have the word of Coburn, who said that as Peckinpah conceived and edited the prologue, "the

entire narrative of the film becomes Garrett's flashback at the moment of his death" (Simmons 184). And when Wurlitzer asked whether to open with Garrett's or Billy's point of view, Peckinpah didn't hesitate: "Garrett," to the writer's enthusiastic consent. But it is the tale that must be trusted: I have written so extensively on this aspect of the tale in *Reconsideration* that I see no need to amplify it here except to suggest that since Kitses is surely too sophisticated a critic to have so simplistic a conception of how point of view functions in filmic and dramatic storytelling, he must be making the obvious reference to the scenes without Garrett in the hope that his readers are not.

27. The expression "son-of-a-bitch" wouldn't be particularly worth remarking upon in Peckinpah except that in two different films he used it in this very distinctive way of prefacing it with the word "poor," the other at the end of *Convoy*, when Dirty Lyle says it as he's about to try to kill Rubber Duck. I have often wondered if this was meant to be an allusion to the terse "eulogy" delivered at Gatsby's funeral by the owl-eyed man, who says, "The poor son of a bitch." If so, I don't get its relevance. "Poor" is a profoundly ironic, spectacularly reverberative word for both Gatsby and *The Great Gatsby*, but I don't see how it applies to anything in *Pat Garrett*, let alone *Convoy*. (Peckinpah definitely knew and loved the novel.)

28. "Sam, Gordon, and I" tape, 9/9/72.

29. Another explanation is that there comes a time in the writing or revising of any screenplay when there are "anything goes" sessions, that is, meetings where the suggestion of all ideas, no matter how outrageous they might seem, is encouraged, because you never really know where some valuable ones might come from. (The same goes during the editing of films.) This scene could have been the result of one such meeting; and though Wurlitzer can't recall with certainty, I am also guessing that it was *not* written by Peckinpah but by Wurlitzer on Peckinpah's instructions. This is because Peckinpah did not typically render the "g" in "ing" endings unpronounced by spelling them without the "g," whereas Wurlitzer did all the time. In fact, Peckinpah eschewed colloquialisms and other sorts of slang, not to mention dialects, in his writing, and throughout the September 9 story conference he repeatedly enjoined Wurlitzer to remove them as well. One reason was historical: "Some of these people were reasonably well educated," the director pointed out. "Cowboys did a lot of reading, they had Shakespeare." Another was characterization: "Garrett should have a little more education. Don't have him say 'fer,' say 'for.'" Third and most important was performance: at one point directing Wurlitzer to change "yeah" to "yes," Peckinpah said, "Let the actor supply this if he wants," otherwise, with all these "gits," "if'n's," "hosses," "gonnas," etc., "I'll get actors who'll do shit[-kicker] numbers on me." Peckinpah was unusually sensitive to any dialogue that sounded too "Western," by which he meant generically clichéd. However, the dropped "g's" in his *Hendry Jones* screenplay indicate that he did not always feel this way. What accounts for the change? That screenplay was written before he became a film director; clearly, a few years directing Westerns for television showed him how over the top actors could go if given the slightest opportunity. Best to nip it in the bud at the writing stage.

30. This moment was of supreme importance to Peckinpah: he instructed the editors to avoid all takes where Kristofferson smiles as he turns—only *after* the turn and the recognition should the Kid's face break into the smile. Peckinpah felt so strongly about this that he had the instruction typed in all capital letters ("Editing Notes Taken Sunday April 7" [SPP, f.770], 2).

31. The roof raising, Ketchum, and cabin scenes didn't survive through July; the burro shooting was transferred to a dilapidated mine shack and hung on through one of the October 18 scripts.

32. It's little wonder that in one of the most discerning appreciations of this film, Tom Block refers to the Kid as a "Rorschach test": "The only value Billy clearly believes in is his own mythic stature, but his trump card—that he hasn't sold out—isn't so impressive once one notices how he spends his freedom: blowing the heads off buried chickens (as homely a metaphor for masturbation as the mind can muster), boozing, whoring and showboating over his victims' bodies."

33. It's hard to imagine Peckinpah watching *A Clockwork Orange* and not smiling—though whether in amusement or derision we will never know—at the irony of the director who had had him fired fifteen years earlier now stealing shamelessly from him.

34. "Schedule Meeting" tape, 10/23/72.

35. Here at the beginning of his acting career Kristofferson possessed a lot of raw talent and he developed remarkably fast into an excellent actor. But it's instructive to compare his Billy the Kid to his Charlie Wade in John Sayles's *Lone Star* (1996), where he completely divests himself of that friendliness and delivers a really disturbing performance as a brutal, corrupt sheriff.

36. *PGBK*, 10/18/72, with chngs. through 11/2/72, 139 pp. (SPP, f.755), 74.

37. Ibid., 54. Lupe is handwritten over Maria's name.

38. *PGBK*, 10/18/72 (SPP, f.754), 112–13.

39. According to the script, it's actually a medallion with a likeness of Saint Christopher, a third-century martyr who refused to sacrifice to pagan gods and is sometimes regarded as the patron saint of travelers. But there is no way an audience could know what is on the medallion from the way Peckinpah shot the scene. If this had been really important to him, he would surely have found a way to make it clear, though as it happened, he did shoot an ironic resolution to the farewell: upon his return from Mexico, the Kid gives the necklace back to Maria, saying, "You take this. My luck's running good." Though Peckinpah pulled this line out long before the two previews, it's still in the theatrical trailer. (Because trailers for coming attractions are prepared well in advance, they occasionally contain material not in the film as released. In *The Wild Bunch*, for example, a scene where Dutch tells Old Sykes that Mapache has taken Angel never made it into either version of the final film, but a piece from it is in the trailer: Sykes: "We gotta get him back!" Dutch: "How?" These trailers are included with the DVDs of the films.)

40. Exhumed to fill out the severely truncated network television version (see chapter 7), this scene, about a minute in length, is viewable on YouTube, where it was posted by Robert Blenheim from a copy he made with his iPhone off a dub of the television version (https://www.youtube.com/watch?v=4hFv-4c12Ig). Curiously, when Billy returns the shirt Maria dropped, he addresses the old woman who answers the door in English, even though he has just spoken Spanish moments earlier and elsewhere in the film. Perhaps this also figured into Peckinpah's reasons for removing the scene.

41. *PGBK*, 11/3/72 (SPP, f.758), 91C–CA.

42. *PGBK*, 10/18/72 (SPP, f.755), 113. I am making an assumption this note is by Peckinpah even though the handwriting is clearly not his, which most of the time was borderline illegible. I believe my assumption valid because other notes throughout

the script in the same hand are notes that only a director would make, having to do with matters such as staging; how scenes are to be played, paced, and visualized; moving scenes around; rewrites; deletions; additions; and so forth. According to Katy Haber, Peckinpah's personal assistant from *Straw Dogs* through *Convoy*, he frequently dictated script notes for her to write directly into his working copies of screenplays (perhaps because he feared he wouldn't be able to read his own scrawl later). Haber didn't join the *Pat Garrett* crew until the second week of production, but in her absence Peckinpah had an interim assistant who, she believes, was responsible for entering these notes for him.

Chapter Seven. The Previews

1. Although sales to television generate a lot of money and thus factor significantly into any given film's projected earnings, the filmmakers themselves rarely have anything to do with editing them to conform to network standards and practices, which was certainly the case with *Pat Garrett and Billy the Kid*. (Nor in those days were alternative takes eliminating nudity or objectionable language the common practice it has since become.) The rationale behind the broadcast additions, including the brief scene with Billy, Maria, and some boys (see chapter 6), was strictly expedience. Apart from the opportunity the television version once presented to see the wife and Chisum scenes, it has absolutely no directorial authority or artistic legitimacy.

2. The only exceptions I make to the use of the filmmakers' first names throughout this part of the book are the two Gordons, Carroll and Dawson: though I knew Carroll as Gordon and Dawson goes by Gordy, for clarity I am using their surnames most of the time. Once production commenced, Dawson assumed the post of second-unit director, but during preproduction he was effectively (and often referred to as) the associate producer, and the tapes make it amply clear that he was simultaneously the right-hand man for both Sam and Carroll.

3. All notes and correspondence related to the editing are contained in one folder in SPP: *PGBK*—editing, 1972–1974, f.770. References here cite date and pagination; the few that are undated I identify by title (if they were titled; some weren't) and probable date. I distinguish memos and letters from editing notes as such. The two hundred pages include many duplicates and some memos that deal strictly with technical matters. As with all films, *Pat Garrett* was edited as it was shot, beginning the moment the first dailies were returned from the lab. When he had time, Sam would watch these early cuts but would give few notes, being concerned mostly that he had all the footage he needed and that the scenes were basically working. This is all standard operating procedure in filmmaking. Unless there is some specific technical or performance issue, some directors don't even watch cut scenes during production because they don't want their attention distracted from shooting.

4. I did not discover this information until 2013 when I listened to the extensive collection of tape recordings of *Pat Garrett* meetings and telephone calls in SPP. It so took me by surprise that I immediately rechecked my notes and interviews from 1977: sure enough, everyone I talked with back then spoke as if the Memorial Day release had been sprung on them unawares, and there is no paper trail to indicate otherwise. Yet the recordings reveal the date was widely known, discussed, and fretted over throughout preproduction. Since Carroll died in 2005 and Dan Melnick

in 2009, I phoned Gordy Dawson, who can be heard on almost every tape because he was doing the recording, and told him I had just found out that the Memorial Day weekend was locked in almost from the outset. "It was?" he asked, genuinely surprised. I next phoned Roger, who had more or less the same reaction. How to explain this? Delays beginning in preproduction and proliferating during production had so eaten into the post schedule that everybody making the film just assumed the original release date no longer obtained and simply put it out of their minds.

But when production wrapped, Aubrey, or more than likely Melnick for him, called Carroll to ask if everything was still on track. The producer had no recourse but to tell the truth—that it wasn't humanly possible to have the film ready by Memorial Day. What would it take to make it ready? Carte blanche to hire as many assistants, sound editors, dubbing stages, processing labs, and technicians as required, including and paramountly another picture editor. Then do it. Immediately the editors, their assistants, and hundreds of boxes of dailies and work print were rushed from Durango to Culver City in Los Angeles, where the augmented crew were already setting up a large suite of cutting rooms on the MGM lot. From then on, once the full enormity of the task they had agreed to settled in, no doubt all felt as if a bomb *had* been dropped, and that is how it got set in their memories. In a March 1 memo to Melnick, Roger outlined in great detail why "the schedule is totally unrealistic and impossible in all areas," but it was essentially ignored except to throw more money and personnel at it. When I asked Carroll in 1977 why he hadn't fought the decision, the two reasons he gave were that he didn't believe an extension would result in a materially better film, especially since Roger and Garth would have another editor and a greatly expanded crew, and that by agreeing to the Memorial Day release he thought he could keep the studio off Sam's back and ensure his version would be released, provided it was delivered on time. He was wrong on both counts, but the decision was honestly made and from the best of intentions.

5. Looping, also called ADR (automatic dialogue replacement), refers to replacing production dialogue in the studio. This is done when the production tracks are unusable owing to extraneous noises that can't be cut and filled, distortion, or the desire (or need) to alter performances. Foley consists in sound effects added in the studio by foley "walkers" as the film is projected in front of them. It is done when production tracks are replaced in looping or by dubbing into other languages for foreign markets (e.g., if dialogue between two characters walking on pavement is replaced, then the sounds of their footsteps have to be replaced as well, since they are married to the original dialogue tracks).

6. In fact, in his call to Dawson, Sam accused Bob of falling "apart on the latter part of [*The Getaway*]" and then launched into a litany of Bob's alleged complaints: "He's got a business, he wants to shoot second unit, he wants steaks imported, he doesn't like his house—fuck him, get rid of him, he's out, and both [Roger and Garth] are better cutters than he is" (tape 14, 10/2/72). As none of this makes any sense in view of everything I had heard and knew about Bob and his work, I asked Dawson if he might know of any other reasons why Sam had turned so abruptly against an editor he used on four of his last five films. "Even if I did, and I don't," Gordy told me, "they wouldn't necessarily tell you anything. Sam was so mercurial. I had to fire so many people for reasons that were just trivial or made no sense at all." With absolutely no hint of false modesty, Roger laughed at the suggestion that at the time he and Garth were better

editors—in the case of Garth, how could Sam even know, Garth not having picture-edited for him yet?

But there *is* one other explanation. Like many directors, Sam often expected his closest colleagues to put their lives and careers on hold while he was setting up or deciding on a project. Bob was offered *Dillinger*, John Milius's first feature, which Sam alluded to in the call with Dawson. From this perspective, Bob's "complaints" sound more like negotiating points in a deal. This, together with the surprise, bordering on shock, of nearly everyone on the project when word got out that Bob wasn't doing *Pat Garrett*, constitutes strong circumstantial evidence to suggest that Sam *had* assumed Bob was doing it. This could easily explain Sam's actions, particularly if he thought Bob would be leaving *The Getaway* early or was using *Dillinger* to get a better deal on *Pat Garrett*. When Bob missed out on *Dillinger*—ironically enough because he was still awaiting word about *Pat Garrett*—he told Carroll that he was available as a standby editor if needed. Carroll was grateful, but Sam wouldn't budge—at least not right then. But when the crunch came early in 1973 and the studio approved a third editor, whom did all turn to, despite the fact that any number of big-name editors was available? Bob Wolfe. Though soft-spoken and a real gentleman, he was nevertheless miffed enough by Sam's shabby treatment the preceding fall that he demanded a very high salary from which he retreated not an inch. Once he was on board, his contribution was above criticism and his loyalty absolute, but neither spared him Sam's wrath. The day he dropped by Sam's office to say good-bye, the director subjected Bob to a verbal tirade so mercilessly cruel (and transparently untrue), calling him a "dummy" and "third-rate," that he left almost in tears (D. Weddle 488). Eight years later, on February 28, 1981, at a vital fifty-two and the peak of his powers as an editor, Bob Wolfe died after a struggle with cancer. Shortly after the funeral, I ran into Sam, who hadn't heard. When I broke the news to him, there was a long pause, then he said, "He was the best—*the best!*"

7. "Sam, Gordon, and I" tape, 9/9/72.

8. On *Pat Garrett and Billy the Kid* Peckinpah exposed 367,440 feet of film with 803 setups, on *The Wild Bunch* 333,070 feet with 1,288 setups. The earlier picture's far more numerous and elaborate action sequences alone account for the greater number of setups. But the higher amount of film for *Pat Garrett* is misleading because fully a third of the figure—123,820 feet—represents footage damaged or wasted owing to defective equipment and inclement weather. (Roger told me that because of the lens problem, they "had to double shoot some days, two cameras side by side, and often-times three.") The production reports for *The Wild Bunch* don't break out the data for unusable or damaged footage, but nothing we know about that production suggests it was remotely comparable to the later film. In any case, 243,620 feet of (usable) footage for *Pat Garrett* is certainly proof enough that Sam wasn't "cutting in the camera." (The *Pat Garrett* figures come from Daily Production Report, February 6, 1973 [SPP, 63-f.787]; those for *The Wild Bunch* from Daily Production and Progress Report, June 30, 1968 [SPP, 82-f.1003].)

9. Hellman told me that Brando considered him "too nice a man" to be a really good director, because "all the best directors he had ever worked with were real sons of bitches."

10. As it happened, Coburn didn't wind up getting there until the weekend immediately prior to his start date, and his first week was to say the least both eventful and demanding: day one, scenes between Garrett and Poe on the trail; day two, Ida's

house; the remaining four days, the scene at the Bakers' and the beginning of Black Harris's. These constitute some of the actor's strongest work in a distinguished career and speak volumes for his talent, commitment, and professionalism that he was ready for them right off the dime. Writing this, I was reminded that the very first time I met Sam and told him how I regretted what had happened with the longer version of *Pat Garrett*, the first words out of his mouth were a nod to his star: "Yes, one of Jimmy Coburn's finest performances."

11. In a long phone call (tape 5, undated, probably late September or early October), Sam shamelessly begged, cajoled, and schmoozed Jon Voight, going so far as to tell him he was prepared to walk himself if the actor did not sign on to do Billy. This obviously wasn't true, but Sam's enthusiasm for Voight (and Gene Hackman) was absolute. Though Voight was still smarting over how he was treated by Aubrey and some of the other executives, Sam reassured him that "Gordon and I did every goddamn thing [we could], and all of a sudden the assholes woke up and said, 'Jesus, you're really right, let's get Jon.'" The actor had by then committed to Charles Eastman and *The All-American Boy* and said he couldn't think of any honorable way to back out of it, much as he wanted to play Billy. "Tell Charles I'll rewrite his script for him," Sam answered, "which will absolutely be needed or I'll do second-unit for him, but you come down here and do the picture." Of all the several fascinating "ifs" about *Pat Garrett and Billy the Kid* I came across while researching this book, unquestionably the two most interesting are the effects on the film if Billy had been played by Voight or Malcolm McDowell.

12. On the "Story Conference" tape, 9/9/72, Carroll can be heard telling Sam that McDowell "wants to do it. He wants to work with you. It's a huge part. It makes him an international star" (the actor evidently asked Carroll to reassure Peckinpah that "he's really good with accents"). When I spoke with McDowell in 2013 he told me that at the time he faced a conflict involving *O Lucky Man!*—an original script he had written to which Lindsay Anderson, his *If . . .* director, was committed, a project that was personally very important to the actor. McDowell's recollection is that his representation at the time might not have let him know soon enough or sufficiently stressed how keen Peckinpah's interest really was, otherwise he would have done everything he could to make himself available. "I would have died to have worked with Peckinpah," McDowell told me. "He was a genius, one of the greatest directors who ever lived. It's a regret I will always have that it didn't happen."

13. In this paragraph, this and the next quotation are from "Schedule Meeting" tape, 10/23/72; the remaining two are from "Story" tape.

14. He was also exceptionally considerate to actors in other ways. At one point he said to Wurlitzer, "Let's give the woman a name. It's only polite to whoever plays any parts no matter how small. To call them 'woman' or the 'second man,' it's a downer, it's an upper if they got a name" ("Story" tape). Sam did this from his earliest screenplays, believing that it made actors feel better if they could say, "I'm playing Joe the deputy or Karen the teacher" and also gets a better performance because they can relate to the role as a character, not a mere part as such.

15. See Carroll memo to Melnick, 10/30/72 (SPP, f.784).

16. Reviewers at the time made much of the fact that six editors are credited in the end titles. But this is misleading: Roger and Garth were not yet members of the Motion Picture Editors Guild, so the union required two additional editors be hired as standbys, and a third was later added just to implement changes. As was not the case with Roger, Garth, and Bob, however, in no sense were these other three functioning

as true editors in the creative sense. They were not additional sensibilities, merely additional hands.

17. As I reported in *Reconsideration* (299n), at the end of one of these he accused the editors of plotting against him by substituting a shot of two riders leaving Fort Sumner together the morning after Billy is killed. He demanded to know where they had found this footage because he had shot only Garrett riding into the distance alone, just as it is in the script—doesn't this prove someone was trying to sabotage the film?—and he insisted they show him the proper ending first thing in the morning. The next day they ran the ending for him absolutely unchanged and he was satisfied. The explanation? He was so drunk by the end of the screening that he was seeing double.

18. To give Dylan the benefit of the doubt, Simmons wrote me that "Sam never had Alias fleshed out in the screenplay, so Dylan never felt he was playing a real character." And because it was Carroll who brought Dylan on, several members of the crew felt Sam treated Dylan accordingly, that is, as "Gordon's singer," thus ignoring him while attending to Kristofferson, "Sam's singer." A sad part of this is that Dylan, like most performers, fell completely under Sam's spell. Carroll told me that when he arranged a screening of *The Wild Bunch* in a New York theater for Dylan alone, Dylan had planned to watch only about twenty minutes of it. Two and a half hours later he emerged—shaken, exhilarated, overwhelmed—and immediately wanted to be part of the new film.

19. In Wurlitzer's screenplay she is explicitly identified as the daughter, but Simmons tells me that Don Emilio with his machismo would have consented to play the scene only on condition the young woman be identified as his character's wife.

20. Rudy Wurlitzer told me that one reason Sam may have put Alias into this scene was to answer concerns of Dylan and perhaps Carroll that there wasn't enough of Dylan in the film.

21. Throughout the next several paragraphs I have condensed and summarized notes by Melnick, Aubrey, and the other executives, which were given over a period of several weeks from early March to after the May previews. The relevant documents (all in SPP, f.770) are "Editing Notes Taken at Melnick Showing Tuesday March 6th," "Executive Running" (3/13/73), "Executive Showing Notes" (undated, but within a day or two of the March 13 screening), memo from Gordon Carroll to Melnick, Peckinpah, and Spottiswoode (3/19/73), "Dan Melnick's Notes after Executive Screening April 6th," "April 6th Executive Screening Notes," and "Dan Melnick's Suggestions" (undated, probably early April 1973).

22. "Horrells Jones Format" (undated, probably late February).

23. That Sam used Levy in three of his films (*Bring Me the Head of Alfredo Garcia* and *Convoy* the other two) was due not just to their long-standing friendship, it was also an example of his generosity. It's difficult to believe, however, that, despite encouraging Levy to leave teaching and come to Hollywood, Sam was in any way deceived as to Levy's actual talent—Levy himself certainly wasn't when I spoke with him long ago. Perhaps it was partly out of regard for his friend's feelings that Sam insisted upon the scene.

24. Letter from Katherine ("Katy") Haber, writing for Peckinpah, to Norma Fink, his attorney, August 11, 1975. This letter, drafted more than two years after the film was released, was in specific reference to the television version of the film, from which the Ruthie Lee scene had already been removed. With Tuckerman's also gone, Sam's worry that viewers wouldn't understand how Garrett learns the Kid is in Fort Sumner is entirely justified in a way it isn't when either the Ruthie Lee or Tuckerman's or both are in the film.

25. Carroll memo to Melnick, Peckinpah, and Spottiswoode, 3/19/73, 1.

26. Sam must have taken to the idea right away, because an April 2 note called for opticals to be made.

27. In the audio commentary to the 2005 Special Edition, Simmons speaks eloquently to this very issue, pointing out that what is missing is "the footage to support a return to that scene, and that would probably mean some sort of close-up of James Coburn as Pat Garrett at the moment of death—that's the shot you don't have."

28. In the DVD transfers Warner removed these from the special edition but not from the Turner preview.

29. This important scene was not restored until Roger put it into the theatrical release; see chapter 9 for more on why it may have been lifted before the previews.

30. Though it is widely reported that John Houseman conferred this sobriquet upon Aubrey and that John Frankenheimer called him a "barbarian," no one has been able to cite a specific occasion or source for either remark.

31. As for Carroll's feelings about Sam, I knew Gordon for several years from 1977, when I first interviewed him, through the mid-eighties, when he produced *The Best of Times*, on which I worked. Outside the studio we shared a passion for music and a keen interest in high-end audio equipment. In that seven-to-eight-year association I never once heard him speak ill of Sam. Though his typically reserved manner belied the depth of his emotions, it was evident there were lingering feelings of disappointment, resentment, hurt, and betrayal.

32. In a meeting on October 23, Sam said, "I'll tell you one thing about Gordon Carroll, he has a little more faith than I do. He seems to think we've got a good picture going here. You want to know something? I think he's right. I don't know what I'm going to goddamn do with it yet." Even allowing for the fact that he'd had a few drinks when he said this, it's difficult to resist reading a lot into his implied reservations and explicit doubts, considering how things turned out in the long run.

33. According to Gardner (*To Hell* 195–244), the murderers of Albert and Henry Fountain were almost certainly ranchers from Dog Canyon (about midway between Las Cruces and Roswell) who were also cattle thieves and had nothing whatsoever to do with the Santa Fe Ring, which was in any case a very different ring from what it was in the days of Billy the Kid. Albert Fall appears never to have been even a member, let alone the leader of the ring; in fact, his adversary, the prosecuting attorney in the trial, was none other than Thomas B. Catron, the actual power behind the ring during the Lincoln County War. Fall was friends with the accused ranchers and did everything he could to keep them from going to jail. Despite Garrett's best efforts—he worked long, hard, and diligently on the investigation—his case was largely circumstantial (though persuasively so). The jury deliberated only seven minutes before returning a not-guilty verdict. Garrett's own murder was wholly unrelated to the Fountain case. He was killed by men who were leasing his ranch, a lease he wanted to break so he could sell the land, as he needed money badly. Born of desperation, Garrett's behavior toward them was often bellicose, and their motive for killing him was more than likely fear that he might be so desperate as to do them harm (a fear shared by their families). Albert Fall did successfully defend the man charged with Garrett's murder, later became secretary of the interior in the Harding administration, and served a year in jail for his part in the Teapot Dome scandal. However, once Sam decided to mention Fall, he missed a big opportunity for irony: some two and a half years after Fall got the alleged Fountain murderers acquitted, Garrett, lobbying for the position of collector

of customs in El Paso, found himself on a train to Washington, D.C., with Fall himself, who had switched from the Democrats to the Republicans. Fall was instrumental in winning support for Garrett's appointment.

34. Letter from Sam Peckinpah to Dan Melnick, April 30, 1974, 1.

35. At the meeting following the screening of an early cut for Jay Cocks, Martin Scorsese, and Pauline Kael, Sam announced he was thinking about accepting an invitation to speak at a college on the East Coast, which would have required him to leave almost immediately. According to Cocks, Kael lit into him, "You dumb bastard, you stay here and fight and get this movie finished." She later elaborated: "I thought it was important for him to stay and finish editing the film. They needed him to tell them what to do. But he was abandoning his movie when it needed him. He had worked like a fiend on that movie. Now he was doing himself in over what others were doing to him. It was a crazy, sadomasochistic thing" (Fine 257). This was also the day she was recalling many years later when in an interview she said, "I was there when Peckinpah told the producer he was walking out on the editing of *Pat Garrett and Billy the Kid*" ("Wild Man" 101). Sam was grandstanding on that occasion, but it was neither the first nor the last time he said things like that to Carroll; and in the end, whether consciously or not, Sam managed to arrange things so that he in effect did precisely what he had been threatening all along.

36. The "numbers," as they're called in the trade, were remarkably consistent between the two previews. On May 3, out of 244 attendees, only 64 percent said they would recommend the film; on May 10, out of 258, only 67 percent (SPP, 62-f.782, 63-f.783). From the point of view of marketing, which likes to see recommended percentages in the eighties, these figures were not encouraging.

37. The first is the only preview the studio would have had, and it's unlikely Sam would have brought with him the preview he had *stolen*. Their friendship notwithstanding, Melnick was still an executive at the studio in a very high position, and Sam, notoriously paranoid throughout his career, was especially so during the making of *Pat Garrett* and remained so afterward. I don't know if Sam actually watched the entire film on this occasion, sober or not—though he obviously watched it long enough to see the Ruthie Lee scene wasn't there—but I've already quoted Garth Craven to the effect that Sam never did anything stone-cold sober in those days.

38. Simmons reminded me that Columbia had made the same offer to Sam sometime after *Major Dundee* was released. Sam declined. Where was the upside? Unless he could produce a masterpiece—despite the high achievement of several sequences and despite his claims on various occasions that it was "possibly" his best film, there was no masterpiece in *Dundee*—he was better off with what-might-have-been.

39. It is hardly nitpicking to point out that this is nowhere near the truth. *Ride the High Country*, *The Wild Bunch*, *The Ballad of Cable Hogue*, *Straw Dogs*, *Junior Bonner*, *The Getaway*, *Bring Me the Head of Alfredo Garcia*, and *Cross of Iron* were all immediately or eventually released in versions he approved or extremely close to what he wanted.

Chapter Eight. The Box Set

1. The studio didn't quite return to the full European version of *The Wild Bunch*, which had an intermission complete with entr'acte music (by Jerry Fielding) and a very slightly simplified montage when the Gorch brothers are killed. The 1995

restoration was made from a domestic negative (or IP, I am not sure which) of the film which contained all the additional scenes of the European, but without the intermission and with the slightly more elaborate montage when the Gorches are killed. As of this writing, Warner Home Video has plans to rerelease *The Wild Bunch* again on Blu-ray to commemorate its forty-fifth anniversary, with a newly commissioned documentary by the filmmaker Gary Leva (which looks to be very promising). Yet when I suggested the studio might consider doing a new transfer of the European version complete with the intermission, which has never before been released on DVD, thus giving consumers something new for their money, I was informed the 2005 transfer with its incorrect exposure levels would be used.

2. MHL now has a viewing DVD of this print (see notes in appendix).

3. I had occasion to watch this print projected theatrically in Los Angeles in November 2013. It is worse looking than I remembered: it was developed far too light such that it lacks the richness of the theatrical, looking often soft, grainy, and crude, with little of the remarkable modulation of light to shadow of the theatrical, while the haste with which the temp dub was prepared is even more obvious over a sound system in a large venue, the many loop lines left nakedly exposed without covering atmosphere even more in evidence. Add to this the fact that the opening is still in black-and-white, not sepia tinted, that both the wife and Ruthie Lee scenes are missing, that the titles are still crude and in one instance inaccurate, and the unfinished nature of this version makes a mockery of any suggestion that it represents Peckinpah's final thoughts.

4. Actually, it makes perfect sense if protection IPs were *not* made of the previews or at least of both previews. Inasmuch as they were one-time-only events, and the first would almost certainly be changed for the second, why incur the expense and the risk? The one for the first preview could be used to generate the second preview. Be that as it may, Sam's letter to Melnick makes specific reference to "the second preview negative" (by this, I am sure he meant the IP), which suggests there are in existence IPs for both previews, and the Turner preview was almost certainly struck from its own IP. But without verification, it's impossible to write with certainty about any of this.

5. There have been many calls for a Blu-ray, but unless Warner does a new corrected transfer, all the higher-resolution format would do is more faithfully reproduce the inadequacies of the current one. Inasmuch as the fortieth anniversary of the premiere came and went a year ago as of this writing, the logical occasion for a Blu-ray has passed, and there is no indication the powers that be at the studio have any continuing interest in the film.

6. The absence of a documentary created expressly for the set was criticized by several commentators. Once the Jamieson documentary became a nonstarter, a deal was made to include a documentary on Peckinpah that had already been made for the Starz Channel, a deal that saved at least a hundred thousand dollars—or so it was thought, except that, according to Redman and Jamieson, by the time all the negotiations for rights and clearances (of music, clips, interviews, and other materials) were concluded, the Starz documentary wound up costing the studio three times the budget of Jamieson's. And that loss is considerably higher when you figure that if the studio had gone with Jamieson's, it would have had a documentary that it *owned* lock, stock, and barrel. "Such is life in the corporate world," sighed Jamieson. It makes me think rather of Sam's karma: thirty years after his death and still so little seems to break his way when Warner or MGM is involved.

7. Titled *Pure Peckinpah Press Kit*, it contains a sixty-eight-page booklet with extensive notes and background on the films by David Weddle (who also edited and compiled the selections); "Moments with Mr. Peckinpah," a reminiscence by Jesse Graham (a longtime friend of the director's); "The Operatic Perversity of Peckinpah's Masterpiece," an appreciation of *The Wild Bunch* by Ron Shelton; an interview with me on the preparation of the special edition (which contains several factual errors and suppositions that I've corrected in this book and elsewhere); a filmography; and a bibliography. There is also a data disc of stills. One wonders what could have been on the minds of those executives to have gone through the expense of all this only to restrict it to reviewers. The value that would have been added to the box set is obvious.

8. When Grover Crisp, the executive at Sony Pictures Entertainment in charge of restoration, made the decision to bring out an extended edition of *Major Dundee* on DVD, he located several minutes of scenes that had been cut without the director's approval, put them back in, lovingly attended to both the picture and sound elements, and even went to the expense of having a new score written because Peckinpah famously despised the original. When Crisp prepared the film for the higher-resolution Blu-ray release, he redid all this work even more exactingly. At the same time he also cleaned up the theatrical version, with the original score, so that filmgoers, film students, and film scholars would have both available. Crisp's work on *Major Dundee* is a standing rebuke to Warner's DVDs of its Peckinpah films.

9. In a subsequent posting the same commentator writes that I made a "mistake" by including the shot of "Garrett hitting the ground dead at the beginning. That shot of Garrett hitting the ground dead belongs at the end." First, there is no shot anywhere in the film—or for that matter in existence—of Garrett hitting the ground dead because Peckinpah didn't stage the action that way. Garrett doesn't die until he's shot several more times *after* he hits the ground. And second, as is plain to anyone who expends the effort to compare the 1988 Turner to the 2005 Special Edition, no new shots were added to or substituted in the prologue when it was dropped into the new version: the one of Garrett hitting the ground is also in the previews' prologue and in exactly the same order and position, just as Peckinpah left it. (Spottiswoode did the first cut of the prologue; once Wolfe joined the crew, most of the considerable recutting fell to him, as he was exceptionally gifted with montages—he had edited the brilliant front-titles sequence of *The Getaway*.) In fact, to be really exact about it, the moment of Garrett actually hitting the ground is elided in the prologue, and in the epilogue it happens after he drops below the frame line. In other words, that specific moment is never shown *on camera*, it is only alluded to. And the literal chronology of Garrett's last seconds of life and the moment of his death were always deliberately violated as a creative decision, that is, Garrett clearly expires in the prologue and the epilogue ends well before he breathes his last (see chapter 9 for more on this). (By the way, the preview is *not* a work print: there are no visible tape splices, which there would be if it were a work print or a dupe from it; it has obviously had at least one color-timing pass beyond the one-light with which the dailies were processed.) Elsewhere in this same forum one of the self-appointed Peckinpah gurus claims the wife scene was shortened in the special edition by some two minutes as compared to the television version. Of course this is nonsense (it wouldn't have been even possible): the scene is identical, including length (about 2:45), in both versions.

10. This organization extended to Sam's files as well. Katy Haber told me that he used to drive them all crazy by insisting that his several "large, heavy" filing cabinets,

containing all his scripts, papers, and correspondence (personal and professional), and legal, business, and other documents, be delivered to wherever he was head-quartered while making a film. When it came to keeping records, Katy told me, "Sam went beyond meticulous—he was obsessive about it" (not least because of lawsuits, she added).

11. On the night of the second preview, following the showing, Garth Craven, suddenly remembering the "preview print was still up in the projection booth of the screening room," had Smiley Ortega, one of the assistant editors, get a studio bike; together they loaded the film into the basket and "Smiley pedaled it across the stu-dio and threw it in the back" of the car of Sam's assistant, who drove it off the lot (D. Weddle 485; see also *Reconsideration* 300n). Though no one remembers where the print was stored immediately afterward, it eventually wound up in the charge of Sam's oldest daughter Sharon, who kept it in her garage in West Los Angeles (she can't recall when she first received it). To my knowledge it was never watched after it left the MGM lot until Sharon let me borrow it sometime in 1979 so that Roger could run the missing scenes for me at his cutting rooms at Universal. Once this was done, I returned it immediately to Sharon, who kept it in her garage until Don Hyde, on her father's instructions, picked it up in late 1979 or early 1980, at which time he had some three-quarter-inch tape copies made for Sam. Don told me that the only occasion he knows when Sam ever watched this version all the way through without interruption was of one of the tapes on a television with Don himself in Montana in early 1980. I pressed him on this: "I'm absolutely sure, because it was when we were reading the galleys of your book, which Sam didn't have before 1980 and I didn't have the print before then to make tape copies of it. Also, showing it anywhere would have required double-system, since the sound is separate from the print, and not many places were equipped for that even back then." This means that that viewing—seven years after he left the film—is the only absolutely verifiable occasion on which Sam ever watched *Pat Garrett* all the way through in *any* version (though see chapter 7, note 37). One can only imagine what it must have looked and sounded like on the televisions of the time, not to mention the fact that the transfer is in the wrong aspect ratio and that the print was already showing considerable signs of wear (see the first note in the appendix). Don also told me that, except for the preview, this print was shown publicly on only one occasion, the screening he himself supervised in Los Angeles at the Directors Guild of America in 1985, a few months after Sam's death the previous December. Soon afterward Don turned all Sam's holdings in his posses-sion over to the Peckinpah family, who in 1986 gifted them to the Herrick along with Sam's files and other papers.

12. It is revealing that when Sam sued MGM after he left the project, the suit did not ask that the film be restored. That ship had already sailed, and insofar as his behavior at the time was any indication, he was content to let it sail. As Garner Sim-mons wrote me:

> Personally, I do not believe that with production complete Sam was willing to resume the fight over recutting the film since he had to question whether there existed the footage to make the film work on a dramatic or aesthetic level. I cannot believe he was not keenly aware of the weakness presented by the Paco sequence. Clearly there was no interest on MGM's part to reshoot it and there was nothing Sam could have done short of eliminating it. In other

words, he was aware of the problems but lacked realistic solutions. To mount a legal challenge that would allow him to reedit the film would have required him to temporarily shelve *Alfredo Garcia*, something he clearly did not want to do. It was a no-win situation. Instead, Sam essentially did what he had done on *Major Dundee*—allow people to believe he alone could make the film whole rather than risk a failed attempt.

There were several counts in the suit, including breach of contract, unfair competition, invasion of privacy, damaged reputation, and false attribution. In *Reconsideration* (270) I wrote that the suit demanded either his name not be used for promotion or the cuts be restored. The latter was a deduction I made at the time that *seemed* logical, not something I knew was in the suit, which it wasn't (the brief is in SPP, f.777). In other words, for Sam the suit was about getting his name removed from above the title and precluding any sort of featured prominence of it in the advertising—he wanted the satisfaction of knowing he had deprived Aubrey of using his name to promote the film. In the end MGM prevailed: Peckinpah's name was prominently featured in all the prints and ads and the suit went nowhere.

13. Kael is one of the very few outsiders to have seen a longer cut of the film as it existed prior to the previews. Speaking in 1998, she said, "I saw it assembled before Sam left the editing; he may have left it partly because it was too shapeless for him to attempt to pull it together" ("Wild Man" 101). Apparently not even the theatrical version was sufficient to dislodge her conviction that it's "a woozy, druggy piece of work," with "no motor impulse, no drive." I do not believe the film in either of the two previews and certainly not the theatrical supports the totality of these judgments; but she was certainly right that the early version she saw needed a lot of shaping and pulling together, and no one can wholly argue away certain structural issues and a few weak scenes in any version.

14. Although he often groused about it and spoke from time to time of alternative means of financing and distribution, he seems never to have made serious efforts to seek them out—even *Bring Me the Head of Alfredo Garcia* and *Cross of Iron* were the result of studio financing and/or required studio distribution.

15. Comparison to the release of *The Wild Bunch* is here instructive: once again a Peckinpah Western was released in the summer and expected to generate the kind of reliable business, say, a John Wayne Western would do and once again it was the wrong model. Peckinpah films, whether they were Westerns or not, needed to be handled as *Peckinpah* films.

16. We do well to remember that Peckinpah's films often display a vibrant sense of both family and community, replete with all sorts of internal audiences and spectators, to which he constantly references the main action and characters, and also with communal events such as celebrations, festivals, carnivals, rodeos, dances, socials, parades, marches, weddings, church services, funerals, and the like.

Chapter Nine. The 2005 Special Edition

1. Sam Peckinpah letter to Dan Melnick, April 30, 1974 (SPP, f.770), 1.
2. I've been told that an editor *not* brought back to the States had turned in an assembly of the siege that was ninety minutes long. Sam started watching it and gave

up in disgust after several minutes, saying to Bob and Roger, "I don't want to see this again until it's fixed."

3. And since the mid-nineties when films began to be edited digitally on computers, directors and editors almost never even watch dailies together anymore. The lab sends the digitized footage to the cutting rooms (a separate copy, usually on DVD, goes to the set for the director to look at when he or she can find the time) and the editors begin editing it, their only notes whatever the director may have dictated to the script supervisor on the set. (There have been many occasions when I've gotten scenes into first cut before my directors have had time to watch the dailies.) Even in the days when directors and editors did watch dailies together, really savvy directors knew dailies sessions didn't necessarily afford the best occasions for selecting takes. If what was shot yesterday or the day before was a love scene, by the time the dailies come in the director may be in the middle of an action sequence, hardly the best frame of mind for evaluating performances in the former.

4. My first editing credit—as associate editor, the same credit Bob Wolfe received on The Wild Bunch—was on Roger's The Best of Times, which he directed from a screenplay by Ron Shelton (who shot second-unit) and on which I worked with Garth Craven.

5. On one of the preproduction tapes Sam called Melnick "the worst man with story in the world—I told him that to his face and I'll tell it to him now on the phone" ("Sam, Gordon, and I" tape, 9/9/72). What to make of this statement in view of Sam's lavish praise for Melnick on Noon Wine ("I would say that we made the picture, not me" [Reconsideration 96]) and Straw Dogs is anybody's guess, except that it's the kind of thing a director could believe on one project and not the next. Roger himself told me that Sam left Melnick in charge of the editing while he went to Arizona to make Junior Bonner. An explanation for Sam's new attitude? More or less the same as for the deterioration of his relationship with Gordon Carroll: Melnick was now working for the studio, directly under Aubrey, so for Sam, despite their past as close colleagues on two of his finest pieces of work, Melnick was now a company man, so he had to be made an antagonist. Though Melnick may have been more of a company man than the circumstances absolutely required, and he was certainly among the stream of executives who descended on the shoot, at least one of his trips was at the behest of a mutual friend, Jason Robards. While doing his Wallace scenes, Robards, long one of Sam's closest friends, was so disturbed by the director's drinking that once back in Los Angeles he phoned Melnick immediately, saying, "Sam's in real trouble, you've got to go down there" (D. Weddle 475). We also do well to remember that as soon as Aubrey was gone and Melnick had some real power, one of his first calls was to Sam with the offer to finish Pat Garrett to his satisfaction. And long before then, as I've already documented, several of Melnick's editorial suggestions that Sam initially rejected he later implemented before the previews—in other words, entirely on his own, not because he was forced to. So until I'm presented with compelling evidence to the contrary, I will let stand the statement about Sam's trust in Melnick, along with Wolfe and Spottiswoode, at least as regards the period from Straw Dogs to Pat Garrett.

I should point out that in the Peckinpah Today version of this essay I wrote that I was mistaken in stating in Reconsideration (269n) that the Peckinpah-Melnick friendship developed a rift not healed for some years. After reviewing my notes from 1977, I'm not sure of my earlier correction, being reminded that the first time I ever met Sam and we talked about Pat Garrett, he singled out "Danny Melnick"—not Aubrey—as responsible for the fate the film suffered at MGM. Although very few characters in

Peckinpah films can be easily categorized as "good" or "bad" guys, most of them existing as shades of gray, in life Sam often needed someone on whom he could focus
blame for adversity, so his generosity and sense of complexity were the first things
to go when he searched for targets, producers and studio personnel usually first in
his sights. There is another odd pattern at work here. Though it was obvious that
as vice-president in charge of production Melnick was in the thankless position of
being the studio's "hatchet-man" (Bob Wolfe's word), Sam still held him responsible
for what happened to *Pat Garrett*, just as years earlier on *One-Eyed Jacks* he laid all the
blame for being replaced as writer at Brando's feet, even though it was actually Stanley Kubrick who demanded a new writer. Regardless, it was "Marlon," Sam later said,
who "taught me how to hate" (Fine 42).

   6. Aubrey had a reputation for destroying artists and their work that went back to
his years as president of CBS Television. During his reign there (1959–65) his lowest-
common-denominator programming proved extremely popular and hugely profitable.
Using a formula a colleague of his described as "broads, bosoms, and fun," Aubrey was
responsible for acquiring such series as *Gilligan's Island*, *The Beverly Hillbillies*, *Petticoat
Junction*, and *Gomer Pyle*, yet he had nothing but contempt for the American public, which he once described as something he flew over. Often called the most hated
man in television (and later the most hated in movies), he had a personality that was
abrasive, a mouth that was caustic, tactics that were ruthless, and a disrespect for
the creative side of the business—including writers, directors, producers, performers, even stars—that bordered on the pathological. (It was said that Lucille Ball was
incapable of referring to him by name without prefacing it with "that S.O.B.") His
vulgarity was legendary—when someone proposed CBS might do a new version of *The
Glass Menagerie*, he asked, "Who wants to look at that? It's too downbeat. The girl's
got a limp"—and he had zero sense of social responsibility when it came to the media,
once saying of the news, "If I had my way, we'd have some guy come on at eleven pm
and say, 'The following six men made horses' necks of themselves at the Republican
convention today' and he'd give the names and that would be it." An open (and, it was
alleged, sometimes abusive) womanizer, who threw notorious late-night and early-
morning parties, he served as the model for characters in Jacqueline Susann's *The Love
Machine* and Harold Robbins's *The Inheritors*. Despite the (at the time) unprecedented
revenues his lucrative programming generated for CBS, eventually a combination of
ratings that started to fall, allegations of financial malfeasance (e.g., kickbacks from
producers whose shows he programmed), personal scandal (the precipitating incident
a wild party in Miami, the details of which have never been made fully public), and a
manner the top brass found offensive—all that and more led the chairman, William S.
Paley, who hated him and was disgusted by his programming, to have him fired.

   During his 1969–73 tenure as the president of MGM, Aubrey divested the studio of
its archives, its storied holdings of props and costumes, and most of its property. His
abrasive style continued unabated, as did his practice of destroying films. In addition
to Peckinpah, directors and producers such as Blake Edwards, Bruce Geller, Herbert
B. Leonard, Michael Laughlin, and Paul Magwood all protested publicly about how
Aubrey had butchered their work (Magwood and Laughlin literally locked out of their
editing rooms). A few months after *Pat Garrett and Billy the Kid* was released, Aubrey
resigned (though some say he did so to preempt a firing) and became an independent
producer whose best-known product was a 1979 television movie-of-the-week called
Dallas Cowboys Cheerleaders (more broads, bosoms, and fun). Although something of

a health-food and fitness obsessive who ran four to five miles a day, he died from a heart attack in 1993, aged seventy-five.

There is no full-fledged biography of Aubrey. By far the most detailed account of his rise and fall at CBS that I've found is the *Life* magazine profile by Richard Oulahan and William Lambert, "The Tyrant's Fall That Rocked the TV World: Until He Was Suddenly Brought Low, Jim Aubrey Ruled the Air" (September 10, 1965, 90–107). The allegations of physical abuse are reported in Harlan Ellison's *The Other Glass Teat* (Ace, 1983) and William Froug's *How I Escaped from Gilligan's Island and Other Misadventures of a Hollywood Writer-Producer* (Popular Press, 2005). Leslie Caron wrote about Paul Magwood and her experience on *Chandler* in *Thank Heavens: A Memoir* (Plume, 2010, 204). Aubrey's remarks about *The Glass Menagerie* and the news are quoted in Murray Kempton's "The Fall of a Television Czar" (*New Republic*, April 3, 1965, 9). Lucille Ball's epithet has been quoted in many sources; Aubrey denied he ever used the expression "broads, bosoms, and fun." Peter Bart's *Fade Out: The Final Calamitous Days of MGM* (New York: Doubleday, 1990) covers Aubrey's years at the studio (though some of the material on *Pat Garrett and Billy the Kid* is not accurate).

7. As it happened, the other film, *The Man Who Loved Cat Dancing*, was also a Western. The original director had been replaced and production twice temporarily shut down because Burt Reynolds, one of the stars, was injured with an abdominal hernia during a stunt fight; the business manager of Sarah Miles, the other star, committed suicide, and she wanted to attend the funeral; and in postproduction the composer was replaced. Like *Pat Garrett*, this film also had a big-name supporting cast, albeit a much smaller one—perhaps this was an MGM formula at the time.

8. These figures are approximate owing to the impossibility of determining exactly what the length of Sam's version would have been (see appendix).

9. Sam shot the raft scene in flagrant defiance of Aubrey's direct edict to strike it from the screenplay and drop it from the schedule. In fact, it was shot *twice*, because the first footage was a liability of the damaged camera. According to Roger, the scene was "the big test of wills" between Sam and Aubrey and also between Aubrey and the entire crew, who were prepared to walk en masse if it were eliminated. All this only persuades me even more that Aubrey either never tracked the changes made after the second preview or didn't care what was removed or retained so long as the end result was a coherent film at a length that could be scheduled in convenient two-hour intervals. How could he be sure he would get such a film? Once again, because he knew that the loyalty of Spottiswoode and Wolfe to their director and, more important, to his film was absolute and they would edit the best film possible under the circumstances.

10. But I dispute their assertion that the editors "chose not to discriminate the good from the bad in this remarkable [?] scene" (152). As a matter of fact, at the time Roger rather liked this little interlude and was inclined to keep it, or at least some of it; what wound up remaining was a compromise between what he might personally have wanted and what he and Melnick figured would satisfy Aubrey or else it was a lift made simply for reasons of time. Roger doesn't remember.

11. This is easily verifiable by anyone who wants to take the trouble. The theatrical version is frequently televised on HDNet Movies, Turner, and other cable stations, while it took me all of thirty seconds to locate VHS copies on eBay.

12. Yet another reason I continue to be by turns amused and amazed by the combination of ferocity and ignorance in so many fans of the Turner preview: most of them seem blissfully unaware that it doesn't contain the Ruthie Lee scene, which Peckinpah

certainly regarded as more important than, say, Tuckerman's; and unless they've read my previous books or those by some other critics, a fair number of them appear to have had no knowledge whatsoever of the Ida scene before they watched the 2005 Special Edition.

13. Discussions in preproduction meetings and early notes Sam gave the editors (2/16/73, 1) indicate he originally thought to open on the chickens buried in the sand. This would certainly have been arresting, though one wonders how it would have affected the rest of the film: beginning in Fort Sumner would establish 1881 as the present and Garrett's death would then be a glimpse into a future which hasn't yet happened; beginning as the film now does near Las Cruces establishes 1909 as the present and Garrett's death is the foregone conclusion to a past which has already happened and is about to unfold, thus more effectively embodying the idea of fatalism.

14. It would be churlish not to acknowledge the detailed, closely reasoned, and sophisticated case that Robert Merrill and John Simons make for keeping the epilogue (50–51); but though I find their arguments impressive, they move me less than Spottiswoode's does.

Part Three. Ten Ways of Looking at an Unfinished Masterpiece and Its Director

The Peckinpah quotations in the section headings are from: (1) Schrader 19; (2) "Press Violent" 15; (3) Murray, "*Playboy* Interview" 107; and (6) Harmetz, "Man Was a Killer" 173. The quotations by Sragow from "Sam Peckinpah" 180; Hemingway, *Death* 192; Fitzgerald, *The Crack-Up* 69; and Frye, *Anatomy* 42.

1. The initial hostile reviews of *Bonnie and Clyde*, prior to Pauline Kael's enthusiastic essay in *The New Yorker* (October 21, 1967), provide a capsule summary of these attitudes.

2. This sort of categorization is even more rigid and thus debilitating in film studies. How often, for example, is *The Wild Bunch* mentioned or included in studies or courses on the epic film? Yet in a strictly formal and traditional sense alone, it's far more of an epic than most of the films that are included in such studies. Why isn't it? Because it's categorized as a Western. For a similar reason, *Major Dundee* isn't included in courses on war films, but a war film is precisely what it is, in addition of course to being a Western. I would argue that in films distinctions such as Western versus Western films are even more urgent now than in Peckinpah's day because we live in a time when it has become almost impossible for all but a very few American filmmakers to do good, serious, and lasting work in the American film industry. When film reviewers can without crossing their fingers behind their backs compare a costumed-hero trilogy to the epics of antiquity, as one of those for a major news magazine did, then maybe we should not be afraid to stand a little fast, even at the risk of being called snobs, and insist upon distinctions we both know and feel to be real, however difficult to define or demarcate.

3. There are many things one can say with validity for or against *Straw Dogs, Bring Me the Head of Alfred Garcia*, and *Cross of Iron*, but "modest" seems to me hardly one of them; and though *Junior Bonner* is small in scale, intimate, and quite gentle, its immersion in character and milieu penetrates so deep that it takes an easy place among Peckinpah's finest films.

4. In this context it's hardly irrelevant to point out that back in the day Peckinpah's Westerns were unusual in having acquired a substantial following far beyond the fan base for Westerns alone and even established a beachhead in what used to be called the "art-house" audience. (Surely Kitses knows this?) It seems no one needs a headful of oaters, horse operas, and shoot-'em-ups to respond pretty fully to his Western films. For a good antidote to the kind of restrictiveness that Kitses insists upon, Gabrielle Murray's *This Wounded Cinema, This Wounded Life: Violence and Utopia in the Films of Sam Peckinpah* insightfully places several of Peckinpah's films outside the framework of both the Western and American culture. And the John Simons–Robert Merrill *Peckinpah's Tragic Westerns* locates his work in a tradition that goes all the way back to Aristotle's *Poetics*, arguing that his "major Westerns are formal tragedies and that Peckinpah is in fact the only tragedian among the major Western filmmakers" (3).

5. After they scouted the location Dawson and Torres did tell Peckinpah what they had in mind. "But it was harder than it looked," Dawson told me. "We staked out the sunrise with the photo double ready and in place for five dawns until we struck gold." As the transition from darkness to bright daylight happens so fast in the morning that most dawn shots are actually filmed at sunset, when "magic hour" lasts much longer, I asked him why this was done at sunrise. "Because there was no horizon to the west, only the mountain that rises up behind Chupaderos," he replied, adding, "It's a toss up between that shot and the deer shots at the opening of *The Getaway* as to my favorites. Sam always said I was a lucky S.O.B. because I got to 'shoot all his David Lean shots.' That certainly was one of them."

6. Kitses himself is aware of this. In the 1969 *Horizons West*, he presciently observed: "Although imagery is often continuous with its own depth and play of light . . . increasingly Peckinpah's appears a cinema of montage, the flow of cutting both honouring and distending time, bridging all the elements of his action" (170).

7. Indeed, I find it ironic that for long stretches it's possible to forget all about the generic scaffolding of *Horizons West*, especially in the newer edition, and to read it as what for the most part it actually is: quite excellent criticism and analysis of six individual film directors as "authors" of their films.

8. The Milius and Kaufman remarks are from *Pure Peckinpah*, 30–31.

9. Kathryn Bigelow made the "paradigm shift" remark in the Q&A when she was the featured guest at a screening of *The Wild Bunch* as part of "The Movie That Inspired Me" series, Hammer Museum, Los Angeles, January 21, 2010.

10. In *The Wild Bunch* Peckinpah depicted a variation on men like this, the kind who think they can remain aloof from and unsullied by all the violence for which they are partially responsible. After the Bunch shoot Mapache, Pike Bishop takes a long look around and then spies the German military advisor deep in the background behind Mapache and his men, raises his gun, and shoots him next. Pike's moment of decision here has to be one of the most personally felt and revealing in all Peckinpah's work: it's hard not to think of his remark in the *Playboy* interview that there "are people all over the place, dozens of them, that I'd like to kill, quite literally kill. You know, you put in your time and you pay your dues and these cats come in and destroy you. I'm not going to work for people who do that anymore" (Murray, "*Playboy* Interview" 115). Less than a year after he said this he would be working for James Aubrey at MGM.

11. Don Hyde told me that as regards "the note where Sam alluded to the Teapot Dome and the then current Watergate, he wanted to do a pic about Nixon (he hated him) and Lt. Calley and My Lai." Owing to his subject matter and several of his themes

(not to mention his putative treatment of women), Peckinpah's critics often assume he was politically conservative, but in fact he was a registered Democrat and considered himself a liberal Democrat.

12. According to Wilson (*Merchants* 136–68), after the Kid was killed what happened in Lincoln County is that the violence and other criminal activity actually did abate, the size and herds of cattle and ranches increased, and by the mid-eighties Lincoln itself experienced an economic boom. New homes and buildings were constructed, and in the coming years there was a public school and a baseball team, a telephone line connected the town with nearby Fort Stanton, and James Dolan became a civic-minded community leader. Throughout the remainder of the century and the very early years of the next, the county underwent cycles of prosperity and stagnation. The real blow came when nearby Carrizozo became a railroad terminal. In an election held on a petition to relocate the county seat from Lincoln, Carrizozo won; the people of Lincoln filed a protest suit, with none other than Santa Fe Ring leader Tom Catron himself arguing the case all the way to the Supreme Court, where the justices (including Oliver Wendell Holmes) upheld the decision of the electorate. Today Lincoln is the Lincoln State Monument, which preserves several of the buildings from the days of the Lincoln County War, including the Courthouse, the Tunstall Store, and the Dolan house. Once a year a reenactment of the escape of Billy the Kid is staged.

13. We also know that J. W. Bell did not crash dramatically through a glass window out into the main street but stumbled out a side or rear door and collapsed dead behind the courthouse into the arms of Gottfried Gauss, the man who shouted, "The Kid has killed Bell," and whom Billy ordered to get him a horse.

14. "Story Conference" tape, 9/9/72.

15. Ibid.

16. Richard Burton, a notorious alcoholic himself, once told Peckinpah that if he were to make a film from *Under the Volcano*, he, Burton, would play the consul for free (see *Reconsideration* 304n). What a film that might have been! It could also be argued that Peckinpah finally did face the drinking in *Bring Me the Head of Alfredo Garcia*, which is certainly soaked in booze.

17. This whole period is covered with candor, tact, and sensitivity in D. Weddle (110–66).

18. There is a historical basis for this. Some of those who knew them both said that Garrett was the better shot with a rifle, the Kid better with a pistol. Apropos of which, I've read at least two critics who state that Garrett uses a shotgun, when it is of course a rifle. (The spray from a shotgun would have peppered Billy and his pals before it reached the chickens.)

19. The romantic loyalty, including even a fierce defensiveness, that some critics develop toward the film's Billy mirrors to some extent the way several historians treat the real Billy.

20. A fellow director, the late Sydney Pollack, articulated this aspect of Peckinpah's work with great eloquence:

> [Sam] combined a romanticism and an appetite for violence. It was the friction between these two opposing impulses that elevated the violence to the level of art. His conflict between his romantic and nihilistic sides is something I think happens often with great directors. The conflict between his pessimism and his buried optimism gave his films a tension that made them

interesting. I was never bored in a Peckinpah movie. I can't say that for any-body else's movies, including my own. (*Pure Peckinpah* 12)

21. This same naive and sentimental romanticism that some critics want to impose upon Peckinpah's vision seems to me to lie at the bottom of attempts to elevate Maria to the status of a major character, despite the fact that after trying and rejecting numerous alternatives, Peckinpah all but wrote her out of the screenplay, except to place her on the periphery of the action. There is no doubt that during the preproduc-tion script revisions he intended for her to have a large role and he certainly assigned her a significant symbolic function at the very end by juxtaposing the lovemaking and the solitary Garrett sitting on the swing outside the window while he waits for the couple to finish: the moment itself is powerfully resonant, though I would argue that most of the resonance resounds off Garrett because the lovemaking between Billy and Maria, sweet and gentle, its climax almost serene, is there to show what is lack-ing in Garrett's life by establishing the strongest possible contrast to the sex-for-hire between him and the five whores in Roswell. But no version of the film seen whole allows us to indulge the cheap sentimentality of inferring anything like a romance between Billy and Maria, let alone any sort of commitment from him—after all, he not too long before had paid Ruthie Lee for sex and earlier still had helped himself to the woman in Luke's bed—Maria is simply the latest of countless transient attach-ments and but for his death would certainly not be the last. In conversation Bob Merrill argued that the "touching tryst between Billy and Maria seems to me some-thing Garrett would never be able to match. This doesn't make Billy a superior person or Maria a more important character, but it does highlight Garrett's deficiencies." No argument with that, but more significant, I think, is the grief she displays in the shot past Billy's feet, which recalls a tearful Mrs. Baker looking at her dying husband and Mrs. Horrell and her children silently witnessing the killing of Alamosa Bill not long after they had watched the oldest son gunned down in a similar duel.

22. As one of Peckinpah's favorite films was the Olivier *Henry V*, I've often wondered if he was aware how much of what he brought to the Garrett-Billy friendship mirrors the relationship between Prince Hal and Falstaff (though the ages are reversed, so to speak). Young Hal knows life changes whether we like it or not—if nothing else, our very bodies see to that, a theme that looms large in Neider's conception of Hendry Jones. Hal also knows he has to grow up and enter a world of responsibility and obli-gation; Falstaff is incapable of any such knowledge. Indeed, once the prince becomes king, the old knight and his companions expect the new court will turn a blind eye toward their petty criminal activities. As king, Hal may have killed Falstaff's heart, but, like Billy and Hendry vis-à-vis Garrett and Longworth, did he leave him any other viable options? I wonder also if a relationship between Lear's desire to "Unburden'd crawl toward death" and Garrett's "There's an age in a man's life" isn't worth some investigation. (Peckinpah knew his Shakespeare well enough: in his college years—on his own, not as part of an assigned course—he gave a summer over to reading most of the major tragedies and some of the histories.)

23. In a letter to Pauline Kael, dated December 14, 1976, while finishing *Cross of Iron* in London, Sam wrote,

I enjoy living a life of sobriety and do not look forward to the 17th of this month when my liver will give me the okay to begin again my needed ways of self-destruction. But I have found that being sober constantly is somewhat of a let down, as I have been waking up without a hangover (the one I have been nursing so carefully for some 20 odd years). I feel like I have lost an old friend . . . ("Wild Man" 100)

I had a personal experience with Sam that is reminiscent of this. One Easter Sunday between 1980 and 1982, he was at his sister and brother-in-law's in Malibu. Although most of the several guests were drinking, including myself, Sam wasn't, but he told me that tomorrow was "M" day. He had been on the wagon for some three weeks, but the next day he was off to Hawaii, and when he got there the first thing he was going to do was have a Martini (that was the "M"). But he consumed no alcohol that Easter Sunday.

24. I know that in the note Peckinpah wrote for the end of the second preview, he said that Garrett carried "his guilt with him," but my trust on this matter is in the film, not the maker . . .

25. Though my own considerably darker take on the character is antithetical to that of most of these critics, I do not wholly exempt my past writing on the film from the criticism I am making of theirs, except to say that in both *Peckinpah* and *Reconsideration* my interpretation of Billy is mixed, and in the latter (289–90) I readily allow for the possibility that the character is flawed or incomplete as conceived, after which I then argue that if he does function as design it can only be on the basis of his very amorphousness, that is, of the difficulty of defining him with any precision. Do I continue to believe this argument? Yes, but only with the proviso that this still does not make for the unified character so many critics seem to want him to be and that any "design" is at least partly adventitious.

26. In the shorter version we do not know the source of the enormous guilt that Pike carries, but we still feel its *weight*, another instance, perhaps, of Hemingway's idea that something can be felt even if it is unmentioned or left out.

27. This image is widely interpreted as Peckinpah's rebuke to his stupidest critics and the "Bloody Sam" moniker they long ago saddled him with. Neil Fulwood articulated this more forcibly than most: "*All right then*, he seems to be saying, *if this is all you'll give me credit for, then here it is* . . . Freeze-frame, close-up: the barrel of a smoking gun, 'directed by Sam Peckinpah' stamped across it" (104).

BIBLIOGRAPHY AND FILMOGRAPHY

Abbreviations

MHL: Margaret Herrick Library of the Academy of Motion Picture Arts and Sciences (Beverly Hills, California)
PGBK: *Pat Garrett and Billy the Kid* screenplays in MHL
SPP: Sam Peckinpah Papers in MHL
T/MGMS: Turner/MGM Scripts in MHL

Archival Sources

Sam Peckinpah Papers in MHL
PGBK—editing, 1972–74, in SPP, f.770: All extant notes, memos, and correspondence by Peckinpah, Spottiswoode, Carroll, and studio executives related to the editing of the film in postproduction.

Screenplays

The Authentic Death of Hendry Jones: A Screenplay by Sam Peckinpah. Both the October 3 and the November 11, 1957, drafts are in MHL's core scripts collection. The October 3 is also in SPP, 84-f.1037, the November 11 also in the Paramount Pictures scripts collection, "Production file-Produced, Series 1" file, under the title *Guns Up*. This same file also contains versions by Calder Willingham and Guy Trosper.
Pat Garrett and Billy the Kid: A Screenplay by Rudolph Wurlitzer. It is all but impossible to devise an easy shorthand way of referencing the more than twenty-seven copies of the screenplay in MHL. Different drafts sometimes carry identical cover dates, the only way to distinguish them being dates on new pages inside and/or total number of pages. Distributed between SPP and T/MGMS, the ones listed here are those I've cited and regard as the most significant in tracking the many revisions. Order is chronological, scripts referenced to folder number (prefixed by "f") and filed in SPP unless otherwise noted. Those with marginalia and other notes by Peckinpah are indicated. Most drafts have Peckinpah's name as director on the cover, but the sole credited writer is always Wurlitzer.
Billy the Kid, 6/21/70, 119 pp. (T/MGMS, f.256). Wurlitzer's original screenplay.

PGBK, 11/5/70, with chngs. through 6/16/72, 140 pp. (T/MGMS, f.262). Last of the 11/5/70 scripts, "SECOND DRAFT" on cover and containing revisions Wurlitzer did on his own in response to Peckinpah's 4/9/72 memo.

PGBK, 7/7/72, with chngs. through 7/25/72, 134 pp. (f.750). Contains all of Wurlitzer's new material from 11/5/70, plus additional new material. Several notes by Peckinpah.

PGBK, 7/7/72, with chngs. through 7/25/72, 134 pp. (T/MGMS, f.264). Contains loose pages of attempt at new opening, dated 9/11/72, initialed by Wurlitzer.

PGBK, 134 pp. (f.751). Undated draft based on 7/7/72 containing pages labeled "SP 9/27/72," first draft by Peckinpah of new Fort Sumner opening and capture at Stinking Springs.

PGBK, 10/4/72, 130 pp. (f.752). First appearance of prologue and Fort Sumner opening incorporated into a new draft, plus new dialogue, closer to final film, in jailhouse and Stinking Springs. Also has dialogue between Garrett and Billy before Billy is shot. Notes by Peckinpah.

PGBK, 10/18/72, 140 pp. (f.754). Prologue character named "Files" changed to Poe.

PGBK, 10/18/72, with chngs. through 11/2/72, 139 pp. (f.755). Has "Samarra" note by Peckinpah. Poe gets violent at Tuckerman's and new character "Sackett" added; elsewhere new character "Lupe" added.

PGBK, 11/3/72, with chngs. through 1/18/73, 115 pp. (f.758). Contains Peckinpah's final rewrite of Fort Sumner opening; killing of Billy brought back closer to Wurlitzer original and Garrett's book. Also contains cross-out of the second half of Paco's death plus ride-up of Alias.

PGBK, 11/3/72, with chngs. through 1/31/73, 115 pp. (f.759). Last version of shooting script, with Peckinpah's revisions to Ruthie Lee scene.

Tape Recordings

There are some thirty hours of tape recordings of story conferences, meetings, and telephone calls in SPP which have now been digitized. (Though I listened to them all, I did not total the timings on the labels, which are only approximate.) Recorded by Gordon Dawson, they are limited to meetings or calls he initiated and/or participated in and with a few exceptions are confined to preproduction. They cover a broad and varied agenda, including script, casting, deals, budget, schedule, arrangements in Durango, etc. The tapes themselves were often haphazardly labeled, most numbered, dated, and timed, some not. I've listed only those specifically referenced in the text; principal participants are named (excepting Dawson, since as noted, he is present on all).

"Story Conference": 9/9/72. Five tapes. Peckinpah goes through the entire script, starting on page one, with Wurlitzer and Carroll.

"Sam, Gordon, and I": 9/9/72. Three tapes, after "Story Conference" as such ended and Wurlitzer has gone. Peckinpah, Carroll. How pleased Peckinpah is with Wurlitzer, how he plans to work with him, criticisms of Melnick, importance of editing.

Tape 5: Undated, probably late September, early October. Peckinpah, Carroll, Voight. Peckinpah tries to persuade Voight to play Billy.

Tape 14: 10/2/72. Peckinpah, Wolfe, Carroll. Editorial personnel discussed, including Wolfe not doing the picture.

Tape 17: 10/2/72. Carroll. Scheduling issues, more on Wolfe matter.

Tape 19: 10/11/72. Peckinpah, Carroll. Coburn's availability, frustration with Melnick.

Tape 21: 10/12/72. Wurlitzer on casting.

Tape 23: 10/16/72. Peckinpah, Melnick, Lindsley Parsons. Peckinpah's rewrites without pay; casting of Wallace, Maria, and Chisum; arguing with Melnick about crew.

"Schedule Meeting": 10/23/72. Peckinpah, Carroll, Rachmil, Kristofferson. Much by Peckinpah about casting, getting performances from actors, losing Voight and Hackman, need to walk locations.

Tape 27: 10/24/72. Peckinpah, Carroll, Arnold. Scheduling.

Tape 28: 10/25/72: Carroll, Beetson. Scheduling.

Tape D-1: 11/3/72. Carroll tells Dawson about late-October meeting with Peckinpah and studio executives over schedule.

"Rachmil Meeting": 1/24/73. In Durango. Peckinpah, Carroll, Rachmil. Production delays.

"Sam in bed sick": 2/1/73. In Durango. Peckinpah, Carroll, Arnold. Peckinpah, with 104° fever, discusses what can be shot without him.

"Production Meeting": 2/3/73. In Durango. Peckinpah harangues Carroll about reshooting damaged footage.

Private Holdings

Charles Neider: unpublished journal while writing *The Authentic Death of Hendry Jones*; unpublished essays, including longer version of lecture that became preface to University of Nevada edition; notes toward other lectures; copies of correspondence with Maurice G. Fulton and with Peckinpah. Loaned by Susan M. Neider, the novelist's daughter. Specific sources are identified and described when cited. Peckinpah's copies of his correspondence with Neider are in SPP, 84-f.1037.

Author's Sources

Unless otherwise noted, sources for all quotations and other information on *PGBK* production, postproduction, and related matters come from my interviews, correspondence, phone calls, conversations, emails, and other communications spanning 1977 to 2014 with Gordon Carroll, Garth Craven, Gordon Dawson, Jerry Fielding, Katy Haber, Monte Hellman, Don Hyde, Brian Jamieson, L. Q. Jones, Walter Kelley, Don Levy, Malcolm McDowell, Daniel Melnick, Sam Peckinpah, Sharon Peckinpah, Fern Lea and Walter Peter, Nick Redman, Jim Silke, Garner Simmons, Roger Spottiswoode, David Weddle, Robert Wolfe, and Rudolph Wurlitzer. I have not provided a specific reference for each and every quotation from these sources. With those persons who became friends, I by no means remember such specifics as date, time, place, and circumstance of every chat, phone call, conversation, visit, stroll, lunch, drink, dinner, party, gathering, or other occasion when something said struck me as important, even when I thought enough to jot it down later or simply retain it in memory. But I have made every reasonable attempt where possible to verify the accuracy of remarks I've quoted with the persons to whom they're attributed. Most of my formal interviews were conducted without a recording device, though I took copious notes. My taped interviews with Carroll, Fielding, Spottiswoode, and Wolfe have been digitized and are now available at MHL.

Works Cited

This book is a study of one film that was never properly finished and of how and why it came to exist in several versions. It is also a study of four other works, three of which provided source material for it and in significant ways influenced it: one biography, one novel, one screenplay adaptation of that novel, and the original screenplay for the film and its many drafts and revisions. These are my primary sources, plus of course the versions of the film. For this reason, when it comes to the history of Pat Garrett and Billy the Kid, I make no apology for relying for the most part on several well-regarded biographies of them and other figures associated with them, reminiscences and memoirs of those who knew them, and histories of the New Mexico Territory, Lincoln County, and its war. My subject is in any case less the actual figures than how they are portrayed in my principal objects of study. The lives of Garrett and Billy are so mired in uncertainty, controversy, and dispute that one of my main areas of investigation turned out to consist in comparing and contrasting the many fascinatingly—or frustratingly—divergent versions of the truth and how even the most diligent and responsible of historians, biographers, participants, bystanders, witnesses, and other chroniclers sometimes seem unable to agree on some of the most basic facts. This doubtless obtains to an extent in all historical writing, but it is exceptionally so with Garrett and Billy, about whom mere differences of opinion, to say nothing of interpretation, seem to inflame the passions of even the most temperate of scholars and historians.

Adams, Sam. "Interview: Rudy Wurlitzer." *A.V. Club*. Accessed August 26, 2011. http://www.avclub.com/article/rudy-wurlitzer-60974.

Aghed, Jan. "*Pat Garrett and Billy the Kid*." 1973. Reprinted in Hayes, *Sam Peckinpah Interviews*, 121–36.

Anaya, Paco. *I Buried Billy*. College Station, Texas: The Early West, Creative Publishing Co., 1991.

Ball, Eve. *Ma'am Jones of the Pecos*. Tucson: University of Arizona Press, 1973.

Baxter, John. *Stanley Kubrick: A Biography*. New York: Carroll and Graf, 1997.

Bell, Bob Boze. "Classic Gunfights." *True West* (August 2010): 60–63.

_____. *The Illustrated Life and Times of Billy the Kid*. 1992. Revised edition, Phoenix: Tri Star-Boze Publications, 1996.

Bliss, Michael, ed. *Doing It Right: The Best Criticism on Sam Peckinpah's "The Wild Bunch."* Carbondale: Southern Illinois University Press, 1994.

_____. *Justified Lives: Morality and Narrative in the Films of Sam Peckinpah*. Carbondale: Southern Illinois University Press, 1993.

_____, ed. *Peckinpah Today: New Essays on the Films of Sam Peckinpah*. Carbondale: Southern Illinois University Press, 2012.

Block, Tom. "*Pat Garrett and Billy the Kid*." *The High Hat*. Accessed October 15, 2003. http://www.thehighhat.com/Nitrate/002/pat_garrett.html.

Blythe, Dee. "Melrose Pioneer Once Traded Horses with Geronimo." *Evening News-Journal* (Clovis, N.M.), May 31, 1937.

Brando, Marlon, with Robert Lindsey. *Brando: Songs My Mother Taught Me.* New York: Random House, 1994.

Bryson, John. "The Wild Bunch in New York." 1974. Reprinted in Hayes, *Sam Peckinpah Interviews*, 137–44.

Burns, Walter Noble. *The Saga of Billy the Kid.* 1925. Reprint, Albuquerque: University of New Mexico Press, 1999.

Caldwell, Clifford R. *John Simpson Chisum: The Cattle King of the Pecos Revisited.* Santa Fe: Sunstone Press, 2010.

Coe, George. *Frontier Fighter: The Autobiography of George W. Coe, Who Fought and Rode with Billy the Kid.* 1934. Reprint, Chicago: Lakeside Press, R. R. Donnelley and Sons, 1984.

Culp, Robert. "*The Wild Bunch*—An Appreciation Update." *Perfect Vision* (October 1994): 24–42.

Cutts, John. "Sam Peckinpah Talks to John Cutts." 1969. Reprinted in Hayes, *Sam Peckinpah Interviews*, 53–61.

Dobie, Frank J. *A Vaquero of the Brush Country.* 1929. Reprint, Austin: University of Texas Press, 1957.

East, James H. "The Capture of Billy the Kid." 1920. Reprinted in Nolan, *Reader*, 295–301.

"The Escape of 'The Kid.'" Supplement. *The New Southwest and Herald* (Silver City, N.M.), May 14, 1881, 1.

Evans, Max. "Sam Peckinpah: A Very Personal Remembrance." 1985. Reprinted in Evans, *Hi Lo to Hollywood: A Max Evans Reader.* Lubbock: Texas Tech University Press, 1998, 130–43.

Farber, Stephen. "Peckinpah's Return." 1969. Reprinted in Hayes, *Sam Peckinpah Interviews*, 29–45.

Fine, Marshall. *Bloody Sam: The Life and Films of Sam Peckinpah.* New York: Donald I. Fine, 1991.

Fitzgerald, F. Scott. *The Crack-Up.* 1936. Reprint, New York: New Directions, 2009.

Frye, Northrop. *The Anatomy of Criticism.* New York: Atheneum, 1957.

_____. *A Natural Perspective: The Development of Shakespearean Comedy and Romance.* New York: Columbia University Press, 1965.

Fulton, Maurice Garland, ed. *The Authentic Life of Billy, the Kid.* 1927. Reprint, New York: Indian Head Books, 1994.

_____. *History of the Lincoln County War.* Edited by Robert N. Mullin. Tucson: University of Arizona Press, 1968.

Fulwood, Neil. *The Films of Sam Peckinpah.* London: B. T. Batsford, 2002.

Gardner, Mark Lee. "Pat Garrett: The Life and Death of a Great Sheriff." *Wild West* (August 2011): 29–37.

_____. *To Hell on a Fast Horse: Billy the Kid, Pat Garrett, and the Epic Chase to Justice in the Old West.* New York: William Morrow, 2010.

Garrett, Jarvis P. Foreword. *The Authentic Life of Billy, the Kid.* 1882. Reprint, Albuquerque: Horn and Wallace, 1964.

Garrett, Pat F. *The Authentic Life of Billy, the Kid.* 1882. Reprint, Norman: University of Oklahoma Press, 1954.

Grey, Frederick W. *Seeking Fortune in America*. Ca. 1912. Reprint, Kessinger Publishing, 2008.

Harmetz, Aljean. "Man Was a Killer Long Before He Served a God." *New York Times*, 1969. Reprinted in Bliss, *Doing It Right*, 169–74.

_____. "*Pat Garrett and Billy the Kid*: What You See on the Screen . . . and What You Don't See." *New York Times*, June 17, 1973, D3.

Hayes, Kevin J., ed. *Sam Peckinpah Interviews*. Jackson: University Press of Mississippi, 2008.

Hemingway, Ernest. *Death in the Afternoon*. 1932. Reprint, New York: Scribner, 1960.

Hough, Emerson. *The Story of the Outlaw: A Study of the Western Desperado with Historical Narratives of Famous Outlaws; the Stories of Noted Border Wars; Vigilante Movements and Arms Conflicts on the Border*. New York: Outing Publishing Company, 1907.

Hoyt, Henry F. *A Frontier Doctor*. 1929. Reprint, Chicago: Lakeside Press, R. R. Donnelley and Sons, 1979.

Hunt, Frazier. *The Tragic Days of Billy the Kid*. New York: Hastings House, 1956.

Jameson, Richard T. Editorial review of *Pat Garrett and Billy the Kid*. Amazon.com.

Jarrell, Randall. "Some Lines from Whitman." 1953. In *No Other Books: Selected Essays*, edited by Brad Leithauser, 98–111. New York: HarperCollins, 2000.

Jenardo, Don. *The True Life of Billy the Kid*. 1881. Reprinted in Nolan, *Reader*, 3–49.

Kael, Pauline. "Notes on the Nihilistic Poetry of Sam Peckinpah." *New Yorker*, January 12, 1976, 70–75.

_____. "Onward and Upward with the Arts: *Bonnie and Clyde*." *New Yorker*, October 21, 1967, 147–71.

_____. "Peckinpah's Obsession." *New Yorker*, January 29, 1972, 80–85.

_____. "The Wild Man: Remembering Peckinpah." *New Yorker*, November 8, 1999, 98–101.

Keleher, William A. *Violence in Lincoln County, 1869–1881*. 1957. Reprint, Santa Fe: Sunstone Press, 2008.

Kitses, Jim. *Horizons West: Anthony Mann, Budd Boetticher, Sam Peckinpah: Studies of Authorship within the Western*. Bloomington: Indiana University Press, 1970.

_____. *Horizons West: Directing the Western from John Ford to Clint Eastwood*. London: British Film Institute, 2004.

Klasner, Lily. *My Girlhood among the Outlaws*. Edited by Eve Ball. Tucson: University of Arizona Press, 1972.

Le Cain, Maximilian. "Drifting Out of the Territory: Sam Peckinpah's *Pat Garrett and Billy the Kid*." *Senses of Cinema*. Accessed April 2001. http://sensesofcinema.com/2001/13/garrett/.

Leroux, André. "The Cinema of Sam Peckinpah." *Le Devoir*, October 12, 1974.

LoBrutto, Vincent. *Stanley Kubrick: A Biography*. New York: Da Capo Press, 1997.

McCubbin, Robert G. Foreword to Frazier Hunt, *The Tragic Days of Billy the Kid*. 1956. Reprint, Santa Fe: Sunstone Press, 2009.

McMurtry, Larry. "Our Favorite Bandit." *New York Review of Books*, October 25, 2007. http://www.nybooks.com/articles/archives/2007/oct/25/our-favorite-bandit/.

Meadows, John P. *Pat Garrett and Billy the Kid as I Knew Them: Reminiscences of John Meadows*. Edited by John P. Wilson. Albuquerque: University of New Mexico Press, 2004.

Medjuck, Joe. "Sam Peckinpah Lets It All Hang Out." 1969. Reprinted in Hayes, *Sam Peckinpah Interviews*, 19–28.

Metz, Leon C. *Pat Garrett: The Story of a Western Lawman*. Norman: University of Oklahoma Press, 1974.

Mullin, Robert. "The Boyhood of Billy the Kid." 1967. Reprinted in Nolan, *Reader*, 214–24.

Murray, Gabrielle. *This Wounded Cinema, This Wounded Life: Violence and Utopia in the Films of Sam Peckinpah*. Westport, Conn.: Praeger, 2004.

Murray, William. "*Playboy* Interview: Sam Peckinpah." 1972. Reprinted in Hayes, *Sam Peckinpah Interviews*, 96–120.

Neider, Charles. *The Authentic Death of Hendry Jones*. 1956. Reprint, with author's "Preface: The Novel into Film," 1993 (adapted from his lecture delivered March 23, 1984), and "Commentary" by Stephen Tatum. Reno: University of Nevada Press, 1993.

_____, ed. *The Great West: A Treasury of Firsthand Accounts*. 1958. Reprint, New York: Da Capo Press, 1997.

Nolan, Frederick. *Bad Blood: The Life and Times of the Horrell Brothers*. Stillwater, Okla.: Barbed Wire Press, 1994.

_____, ed. *The Billy the Kid Reader*. Norman: University of Oklahoma Press, 2007.

_____. *The Life and Death of John Henry Tunstall*. 1965. Revised edition, Santa Fe: Sunstone Press, 2009.

_____. *The Lincoln County War: A Documentary History*. 1992. Revised edition, Santa Fe: Sunstone Press, 2009.

_____. *Pat F. Garrett's The Authentic Life of Billy, the Kid: An Annotated Edition*. Norman: University of Oklahoma Press, 2000.

_____. "The Private Life of Billy the Kid." *True West* (July 2000): 32–39.

_____. *The West of Billy the Kid*. Norman: University of Oklahoma Press, 1998.

Otero, Miguel Antonio. *The Real Billy the Kid*. 1936. Reprint, Houston: University of Houston Press, 1998.

Parker, Hershel. *Reading "Billy Budd."* Evanston, Ill.: Northwestern University Press, 1990.

Poe, John W. *The Death of Billy the Kid*. 1918, 1933. Reprint, Santa Fe: Sunstone Press, 2007.

"Press Violent about Film's Violence: Prod Sam Peckinpah Following 'Bunch.'" *Variety*, July 2, 1969, 15.

Prince, Stephen. "The Recutting of *Pat Garrett and Billy the Kid*." In Bliss, *Peckinpah Today*, 82–100.

"'A Privilege to Work in Films': Sam Peckinpah among Friends." *Movietone News*, February 5, 1979, 1–12.

Pure Peckinpah Press Kit. Warner Bros. Home Entertainment, 2006.

Rosen, Charles. *Critical Entertainments: Music Old and New*. Cambridge, Mass.: Harvard University Press, 2000.

Schrader, Paul. "Sam Peckinpah Going to Mexico." Reprinted in Bliss, *Doing It Right*, 17–30.

Seydor, Paul. "The Authentic Death and Contentious Afterlife of *Pat Garrett and Billy the Kid*: The Several Versions of Peckinpah's Last Western." In Bliss, *Peckinpah Today*, 101–36.

_____. *Peckinpah: The Western Films*. Urbana: University of Illinois Press, 1980.

_____. *Peckinpah: The Western Films: A Reconsideration*. Urbana: University of Illinois Press, 1997.

Simmons, Garner. *Peckinpah: A Portrait in Montage*. 1982. Revised edition, New York: Limelight Editions, 1998.

Simons, John L., and Robert Merrill. *Peckinpah's Tragic Westerns: A Critical Study*. Jefferson, N.C.: McFarland, 2011.

Siringo, Charles A. *History of "Billy the Kid."* 1920. Reprint, 3rd edition, Albuquerque: University of New Mexico Press, 2000.

Sligh, James E. "The Lincoln County War: A Sequel to the Story of 'Billy the Kid.'" *The Overland Monthly* (August 1908): 168–74.

Smith, Cecil. "The TV Scene." Ca. fall 1960, clipping (SPP, 137.f.1836).

Sragow, Michael. "From *The Siege of Trencher's Farm* to *Straw Dogs*." In Bliss, *Peckinpah Today*, 69–81.

_____. "Sam Peckinpah: 1925–1984." 1984. Reprinted in Bliss, *Doing It Right*, 177–88.

Stevens, Brad. "*Pat Garrett and Billy the Kid*." In *The Book of Westerns*, edited by Ian Cameron and Douglas Pye, 269–76. New York: Continuum, 1996.

Tatum, Stephen. *Inventing Billy the Kid*. 1982. Reprint, Tucson: University of Arizona Press, 1997.

Thomson, David. *The New Biographical Dictionary of Film*. New York: Knopf, 2002.

Tucker, Ken. "DVDs of the Year." *Entertainment Weekly* (December 22, 2006): 112.

Utley, Robert M. *Billy the Kid: A Short and Violent Life*. Lincoln: University of Nebraska Press, 1989.

_____. *High Noon in Lincoln: Violence on the Western Frontier*. Albuquerque: University of New Mexico Press, 1987.

Wallis, Michael. *Billy the Kid: The Endless Ride*. New York: W. W. Norton, 2007.

Warshow, Robert. "The Westerner." 1954. Reprinted in his *The Immediate Experience: Enlarged Edition*, 105–24. Cambridge, Mass.: Harvard University Press, 2002.

Weddle, David. *"If They Move . . . Kill 'Em!" The Life and Times of Sam Peckinpah*. New York: Grove Press, 1994.

Weddle, Jerry (aka Richard). *Antrim Is My Stepfather's Name: The Boyhood of Billy the Kid*. Historical Monograph no. 9. Tucson: Arizona Historical Society, 1993.

Weddle, Richard. "A Carte de Visite of Billy the Kid." *Wild West* (October 2014): 44–45.

_____. "Shooting Billy the Kid." *Wild West* (August 2012): 56–62.

Wilcox, Lucius M. ("Lute"). Interview with Billy the Kid. *Las Vegas* (N.M.) *Gazette* (1880). Reprinted in Nolan, *Reader*, 302–7.

Wilson, John P. *Merchants, Guns, and Money: The Story of Lincoln County and Its Wars*. Santa Fe: Museum of New Mexico Press, 1987.

Wurlitzer, Rudolph. *Pat Garrett and Billy the Kid*. With "Introduction by the Author." Signet Film Series. New York: Signet/New American Library, 1973.

Yergin, Dan. "Peckinpah's Progress: From Blood and Killing in the Old West to Siege and Rape in Rural Cornwall." 1971. Reprinted in Hayes, *Sam Peckinpah Interviews*, 82–91.

Video

Major Dundee: The Extended Version, DVD. Directed by Sam Peckinpah. Columbia, 1965; Sony Home Entertainment, 2005. Blu-ray, Twilight Time, 2013. Also contains original theatrical version. Audio commentaries by Nick Redman, Paul Seydor, Garner Simmons, and David Weddle.

Pat Garrett and Billy the Kid, DVD. Directed by Sam Peckinpah, 1973. Warner Home Video, 2005. Contains *1988 Turner Preview Version* and *2005 Special Edition*. Audio commentaries by Nick Redman, Paul Seydor, Garner Simmons, and David Weddle.

Requiem for Billy the Kid, DVD. Directed by Anne Feinsilber. Kino International, 2006. Contains interviews with Rudolph Wurlitzer and Kris Kristofferson.

Sam Peckinpah's The Legendary Westerns Collection, DVD. Directed by Sam Peckinpah. Warner Home Video, 2005. Contains DVDs of *Ride the High Country* (1962), *The Wild Bunch* (1969), *The Ballad of Cable Hogue* (1970), and *1988 Turner Preview Version* and *2005 Special Edition* of *Pat Garrett and Billy the Kid* (1973). Audio commentaries by Nick Redman, Paul Seydor, Garner Simmons, and David Weddle on all included films.

Storytellers of Lincoln County, DVD. Directed by Delana Michaels. Old Mill Productions, 1994.

The Wild Bunch: An Album in Montage. Directed by Paul Seydor, 1996. In *Sam Peckinpah's The Legendary Westerns Collection*, DVD (2005), and *The Wild Bunch: The Original Director's Cut*, DVD (2006) and Blu-ray (2007). Warner Home Video.

INDEX

*Page numbers in **boldface** refer to illustrations.*

Academy Awards, 286
Aghed, Jan, 333n31
Aguayo, Jose, 332n19
Alamogordo News, 45
Alda, Rutanya, 158, **263**
Alias, 119–20, 336n6. *See also* Dylan, Bob
All-American Boy, The, 348n11
Altman, Robert, 277
American Graffiti, 239
Anaya, Paco, 332n16, 337n10
Anderson, Lindsay, 348n12
Anderson, Paul Thomas, 277
Antonioni, Michelangelo, 273
Antrim, Catherine. *See* McCarty, Catherine
Antrim, Henry. *See* Bonney, William Henry ("Billy the Kid")
Antrim, William Henry Harrison, 13, 16, 35, 324n5
Appointment in Samarra (O'Hara), 183
Aristotle, 342n23, 360n4
Armstrong, R. G., 202, 254
Arnold, Newt, 195, 197
Arrau, Alfonso, 277
Askew, Luke, 168
Aubrey, James T., 116, 143, 184, 190–91, 194, 196, 199–200, 205, 206, 207, 215, 216–18, 221, 224, 232, 237–38, 240, 248–53 passim, 266, 302, 303, 346n4, 348n11, 350n30, 356n5, 357n6, 358n9, 360n10
Axtell, Samuel, 17
Ayre, David, 277

Badlands, 239
Baker, Frank, 20–21, 46
Ball, Eve, 118, 341n15
Ball, Lucille, 357n6

Barber, Susan. *See* McSween, Susan Ellen Hummer
Bates, Alan, 140
Battle of Algiers, 240
Baum, Martin, 221
Beck, John, 199, 202
Beethoven, Ludwig van, 275, 277
Beetson, Frank, 195, 319
Bell, Bob Boze, 325n13, 327n17
Bell, James W., 57–60, 104, 119, 332n16, 361n13
Bellow, Saul, 44
Berger, Senta, 77–78
Berger, Thomas, 274
Bergman, Ingmar, 273
Bernstein, Leonard, 191
Best of Times, The, 350n31, 356n4
Beverly Hillbillies, The, 357n6
Bigelow, Kathryn, 277, 360n9
Big Store. *See* House, The
Billy the Kid. *See* Bonney, William Henry
Billy the Kid (1930 film), 41
Billy the Kid Unmasked, 327n17
Birney, Hoffman, 77
Bliss, Michael, xv, 236, 256, 259, 269
Block, Tom, 344n32
Blume in Love, 194
Bonney, William Henry ("Billy the Kid"): books about, 3, 11, 27, 33, 35, 36, 41, 45, 47, 118–19, 324n5, 328n26, 339n4 (*see also individual authors*); death, xvii, 22–25, 27–28, 46–47, 106, 123, 325–27nn16–17; early life, xvii, 12, 13, 16, 20, 28–29, 32, 35, 36, 324n5; films about, xix–xx, 32, 41, 117, 203 (*see also individual titles*); Lincoln County jailbreak, xvii, 17, 22, 27, 35, 37, 45,

Bonney, William Henry, *continued*
46, 56–61, **62–63**, 280–81, 361nn12–
13; Lincoln County War participation,
xvii, 13, 17, 21–22, 26, 33, 34, 282,
337n10; marksmanship, 27, 28, 33,
34, 39, 328n20, 332n16, 361n18;
nickname origin, 22; Paulita Maxwell
romance, 37–39, 326n17, 329nn29–
31; personality, 11, 27, 28–29, 32–36,
39, 51, 69–70, 105, 281, 333n24; the
Regulators and, 20–21, 29; relationship
with Garrett, xvi, xvii, 27, 36–37,
39–40, 282; tintype, **10**, **30–31**, 32,
328n21
Bonnie and Clyde, 359n1
Bowdre, Charles, 17, 20, 26, 34, 35, 40, 41,
46, 49, 51, 52, 282–83, 327n18
Boys, The, 17, 20
Brady, William, 17, 20–21, 29, 38, 50,
340n9
Brando, Marlon, **2**, 3–6, **7**, 78, 82, 109,
111, 116, 140, 193–94, 285–86,
335n7, 335n10; on directors, 347n9;
Peckinpah on, 6, 8, 104, 109, 357n5
Brazel, Wayne, 219
Brazil, Manuel, 326n17
Brewer, Richard, 20
Bright, Richard, 168, 202
Briscoe, Joe, 330n33
Brown, Hendry, 20, 34, 46
Brown, Johnny Mack, 41
Bryson, John, 300, 308
buddy movies, 308
Burns, Walter Noble, 36–41, 45, 46, 47,
49–50, 57, 58, 60, 61, 329n28, 329n31,
330n34, 336n6
Burton, Richard, 140, 361n16

Cahill, Francis P. ("Windy"), 33
Caine, Michael, 140
Caldwell, Clifford R., 325n12
Cannes Film Festival, 230
Capote, Truman, 37
card games, 56, 66
Carey, Timothy, 6
Carlyle, James, 46
Caron, Leslie, 358n6
Carroll, Gordon, 116–18, 139, 140, 141–
42, 143, 144, 159, 162–63, 165, 173,
177, 190, 191–97 passim, 212, 216–17,
239, 293, 296, 302, 304–5, 345n2,
345n4, 348nn11–12, 349n18, 350n32;

photographs, **213**, **226**; relationship
with Peckinpah, 216–17, 350n31,
356n5
Cather, Willa, 274
Catron, Thomas Benton, 17, 279, 350n33,
361n12
Chandler, 358n6
Chandler, John Davis, 202
Chaplin, Charles Spencer ("Charlie"),
322n4
Chavez, Martin, 329n31
Chavez y Chavez, José, 20
Chisum, John Simpson, 18–19, 119–
20, 122, 280, 283, 330n34, 337n10,
339n8, 340n12
Chisum, Sallie, 11
Chisum, Will, 33
Christopher, 344n39
Cincinnati Kid, The, 142, 225
Cisco Pike, 194
Citizen Kane, 240
Clark, Matt, 202
Clavell, Aurora, **149**, 202, 205, 212, **258**,
263
Clockwork Orange, A, 177, 277, 344n33
Coburn, James, 140, 145, 164, 176, 178,
183, 193–95, 199, 202, 213, 238,
264–65, 284, 291, 302, 303, 342n26,
347n10; photographs, **149**, **152**, **211**,
244, **258–59**, **263**, **294**, **298**, **311**
Cocks, Jay, 204, 351n35
Coe, Benjamin Franklin ("Frank"), 20, 27,
34, 35, 282, 328n19
Coe, George Washington, 20–21, 29, 32,
33, 34–35, 45, 46, 51, 282, 327n19,
333n29
Coen, Ethan and Joel, 277
Combs, Gary, 319
Connery, Sean, 140
Cook, Elisha, Jr., 202, 207–8
Coolidge, Rita, 168, 179, 183–84, 202,
212
Cooper, Ian, 321n3
Cooper, James Fenimore, 75
Coquillon, John, **186**, 195, 229–30, 241,
275
Corbet, Sam, 332n19, 339n8
Costner, Kevin, 279
Craven, Garth, 190–91, 192, 200–201,
202, 204, 215, 223, 224–25, 229, 247,
250, 346n4, 346n6, 348n16, 354n11,
356n4

Crisp, Grover, 353n8
Culp, Robert, 291
Custer's Last Stand, 61, 77

Dallas Cowboys Cheerleaders, 357n6
Darwin, Charles, 329n26
Dawson, Gordon ("Gordy"), 162, 190, 192–
    93, 195, 196–97, 217, 275, 296, 319,
    345n2, 346n6, 360n5
Day of the Jackal, The, 336n2
Deep Thrust: The Hand of Death, 336n2
del Toro, Benecio, 277
del Toro, Guillermo, 277
De Palma, Brian, 277
Dern, Bruce, 319
Dickens, Charles, 78, 103
Dickinson, Emily, 276
Dillinger, 347n6
Director's Guild of America, 354n11
Dirty Dozen, The, 239
Dirty Little Billy, 32
Discovery Channel, 327n17
Dobie, J. Frank, 331n13
Dolan, James J., 17–20, 29, 279, 324nn9–
    11, 337n10, 339n8, 340n9, 361n12
Dreiser, Theodore, 203
Duck, You Sucker (A Fistful of Dynamite),
    140
Dunning, John D. ("Jack"), 198, 206, 223
Duvall, Robert, 279
Dylan, Bob, 199, 349n18; as Alias, 151,
    168, 179, 183–84, 202, 238, 305,
    315, 349n18, 349n20; "Knockin' on
    Heaven's Door," 153, 224, 259–60, 261,
    319, 340n11; score, 153, 214, 222, 224,
    229, 232, 265–66, 315

Earp, Wyatt, 37, 55
East, James, 38, 327n18, 329n29
Eastman, Charles, 348n11
Eastwood, Clint, 140
Easy Rider, 140
Ebert, Roger, 237
editing procedures, 246–47, 257, 356n3
Edwards, Blake, 357n6
8½, 240
Elam, Jack, 202
Eliot, T. S., xvii
Emerson, Ralph Waldo, xvi, 75
Empire, xx
Entertainment Weekly, 230–31
Evans, Gene, 202

Evans, Jesse, 17, 20, 29, 284
Evans, Max, xvii, 236, 321n1, 322n3
Evans, Robert, 142–43

Fall, Albert, 219, 350n33
Faulkner, William, 277
Feldman, Phil, 239
Fellini, Frederico, 273
Fernández, Emilio, 202, 349n19
Fielding, Jerry, 190, 214, 260, 319, 351n1
film noir, 333n28
Fincher, David, 277
Fine, Marshall, 190
Finney, Albert, 140
First Artists, 143
Fistful of Dynamite, A. See Duck, You Sucker
Fitzgerald, F. Scott, 292, 343n27
foley, 192, 346n5
Folliard, Tom, 20, 23, 26, 34, 40, 41,
    46, 49, 51–53, 325n12, 340nn9–10,
    342n21
Fonda, Peter, 140, 216
Foor, Charlie, 46
Ford, John, 143, 275, 277, 292
Forster, E. M., 44
Fountain, Albert and Henry, 218, 350n33
Four Faces West, 339n4
Frankenheimer, John, 350n30
Friends of Eddie Coyle, The, 239
Fritts, Donnie, 168, 179, 189
Fritz, Charles, 35
Fritz, Emil, 19
Frye, Northrop, 74, 239, 313
Fulton, Maurice Garland, 27, 118, 279,
    330n32, 337n10
Fulwood, Neil, 363n27

Gambon, Michael, 279
Gangs of New York, 16
Garcia, Abrana, 329n30
Gardner, Mark Lee, 24, 26, 58, 59, 325n16,
    329nn30–31, 338n11, 339n4
Garrett, Apolinaria (wife), 38, 40, 339n7
Garrett, Ida (daughter), 339n7
Garrett, Jarvis (son), 330n33
Garrett, Patrick Floyd ("Pat"): *The
    Authentic Life of Billy, the Kid*, 11–16
    (**14–15**), 22–29, 32, 35–37, 40, 41, 45,
    46, 48–53, 56–60, 118–19, 121, 283,
    284, 297, 323nn3–4; background, 16–
    17, 330n33; death, 165, 210, 218–19,
    350n33; finances, 337n10, 350n33;

Garrett, Patrick Floyd, *continued*
    killing of Bonney, 22–26, 27–28,
    46, 51, 121, 145, 172, 213, 297,
    325–27nn16–17; later career, 350n33;
    personality, 11, 25–26, 28, 40–41, 282,
    284–85; photograph, **21**; professional
    archetype, 40–41; relationship with
    Bonney, xvi, 26–27, 34, 36–37, 39–40,
    282, 327n19, 330nn32–33; wives, 38,
    40, 335n11, 339n7
Gauss, Gottfried, 57, 60, 124, 361n13
Geller, Bruce, 357n6
Gilligan's Island, 357n6
Glass, Philip, 304
Glory Guys, The, 77–78
Godfather, The, 194
"*Golondrina, La*," 313
Gomber, Drew, 332n19
Gomer Pyle, 357n6
Gonzalez, Chalo, 287
Goodman, David Zelag, 336n4
Gould, Joie, 286
Graham, Jesse, 353n7
Great Escape, The, 140
Green, Walon, 115, 321n1
Grey, Frederick W., 326n17
Gunfight at the O.K. Corral, 61
Gunfighter, The, 333n28, 338n14
Guns Up, 334n3
Guthrie, A. B., Jr., 274, 338n14
Gutiérrez, Apolinaria. *See* Garrett,
    Apolinaria
Gutiérrez, Celsa, 38, 49, 329n30
Gutiérrez, Saval, 38

Haber, Katy, 190, 199, 216, 217, 219, 233,
    296, 319, 345n42, 353n10
Hackman, Gene, 140, 194, 348n11
Hard Times, 302
Harris, Richard, 140
Harris, Robert, 236
Hart, Billy, 319
Hartford Artists Colony, 44
Harvey, Jerry, 189
Haworth, Ted, 148
Haydn, Franz Joseph, 275
Hecht, Ben, and Charles MacArthur, 36
Hellman, Monte, xx, 116–17, 118, 193,
    194, 277, 302, 347n9
Hemingway, Ernest, 55–56, 74, 288, 297,
    363n26
Henry V (Olivier film), 362n22
Heston, Charlton, 193

Hickok, James Butler ("Wild Bill"), 55,
    331n13
High Noon, 333n28
High Plains Drifter, 336n2
Hill, Walter, 277, 302
Hi-Lo Country, The (Frears), 321n1. *See
    also under* Peckinpah, David Samuel
    ("Sam"), Screenplays and Television
Hitler: The Last Ten Days, 336n2
Hoffman, Dustin, 140, 194
Holden, William, 140
Holliday, John Henry ("Doc"), 55
Hollywood Reporter, 199
Hopper, Dennis, 140
Horrell brothers, 341n15
Hough, Emerson, 30, 323n4, 331n4
House, The, 17–20, 29, 33, 279, 324nn9–
    11, 340n9
Houseman, John, 350n30
Hoyt, Henry F., 340n10
Hughes, Whitey, 319
Hulburd, Bud, 197
Hunt, Frazier, 33, 282, 330n32
Hurt Locker, The, 277
Hyde, Don, 190, 208, 237, 308, 318,
    354n11, 360n11
Hyman, Ken, 142

Ibsen, Henrik, 342n23
If . . ., 177, 348n12
Irwin, John, 277

Jaeckel, Richard, 202
James, Henry, 297
Jameson, Richard T., xx
Jamieson, Brian, 188, 230, 352n6
Jaramillo, José, 37
Jaramillo, Paulita. *See* Maxwell, Paulita
Jaramillo, Telesfor, 329n30
Jarrell, Randall, xxi
Jenardo, Don (John W. Lewis), 328n26
Johnson, Ben, 6, 335n7
Johnson, Don, 140
Jones, Barbara ("Ma'am") and family, 46,
    277, 282, 328n25, 341n15
Jones, John, 280, 333n30, 341n15
Jones, L. Q., 168, 202
Jones, Tommy Lee, 277
Jurado, Katy, 6, 202, 238, **309**

Kael, Pauline, xvi, 204, 237, 351n35,
    355n13, 359n1, 362n23
Kafka, Franz, 333n28

Kasdan, Lawrence, 277
Katz, James C., 236
Kaufman, Philip, 277
Kazan, Elia, 4
Kelley, Walter, 252, 261
Ketchum, Thomas E. ("Black Jack"), 126–27, 338n13
Kim Jee-woon, 277
Kitses, Jim, 274–76, 342n26, 360n4, 360nn6–7
Kristofferson, Kris, 145, 173, 176–79, 183, 189, 194–95, 199, 202, 238, 285, 344n35, 349n18; photographs, **175, 244, 294**
Kubrick, Stanley, 3–4, 277, 344n33, 357n5
Kurosawa, Akira, 273, 277

Last American Hero, The, 239
Last Detail, The, 239
Last of Sheila, The, 193–94
Laughlin, Michael, 357n6
Laven, Arnold, 77
Lea, Joseph C., 337n10, 339n8
Lean, David, 275, 360n5
Le Cain, Maximilian, xx
Leder, Mimi, 277
Left-Handed Gun, The, 203
Le Mat, Paul, 140
Leonard, Herbert B., 357n6
Leone, Sergio, 140, 151, 277
Leva, Gary, 352n1
Levy, Don, 202, 207–8, 349n23
Lincoln County War, xvii, 13, 16–17, 18, 21–22, 26, 39, 279, 282–83, 325n13, 329n28, 340n9, 350n33; "Big Killing," 17, 21–22, 34
Lolita, 4
Lonely Are the Brave, 333n28
Lone Star, 344n35
Long Goodbye, The, 239, 277
Longworth, Thomas B., 46
looping, 192, 346n5
Lowry, Malcolm, 300, 361n16
Lucas, George, 277
Lumet, Sidney, 4

Magician, The, 273
Magnificent Seven, The, 140
Magwood, Paul, 357n6
Malden, Karl, **2**, 4–6
Mann, Michael, 277
Mann, Thomas, 44

Man Who Loved Cat Dancing, The, 248–49, 358n7
Man Who Shot Liberty Valance, The, 333n28
Marshek, Archie, 5
Marvin, Lee, 140
Maxwell, Deluvina, 327n19, 334n5
Maxwell, Lucien, 327n17, 331n10, 334n5
Maxwell, Paulita, 32, 37–39, 326n17, 327n19, 329nn29–31
Maxwell, Pete, 22–25, 27–28, 37, 38, 46, 53, 120–21, **134**, 326n17
McCabe and Mrs. Miller, 277
McCarthy, Cormac, 274
McCarty, Catherine, 12, 13, 16, 29, 34, 35, 324n5
McCarty, Henry. *See* Bonney, William Henry ("Billy the Kid")
McComas, Francis, 73
McCrea, Joel, **310**, 340n12
McCubbin, Robert G., 30, 323n3
McDowell, Malcolm, 140, 177, 194, 348nn11–12
McKinney, Thomas Christopher ("Kip"), 22, 25, 28, 120–21, 326n17
McLuhan, Marshall, 242
McMurtry, Larry, 41, 274
McNaughton, John, 277
McQueen, Steve, 143
McSween, Alexander A., 17, 18–22, 29, 324n11, 329n28, 339n8
McSween, Susan Ellen Hummer, 327n19
Meadows, John P., 34, 35, 45, 46, 47, 48, 58, 59, 60, 282–83, 332n16, 333n30, 339n8
Mean Streets, 239
Melnick, Daniel, 190, 196, 198, 203–6, 208, 210, 212, 215–17, 220, 224, 231, 237, 245–48, 250–51, 253, 269, 345n4; relations with Peckinpah, 199, 205, 215, 216, 245, 247, 296, 351n37, 356n5
Melville, Herman, xix, 61, 274–75
Merrill, Robert, 118, 321n2, 338n3, 362n21; and John L. Simons, 118, 148, 253, 306, 359n14, 360n4
Mescalero Indian Reservation, 18
Metro-Goldwyn-Mayer (MGM), xv, 41, 143, 188, 221, 229, 249, 285, 352n6, 357n6. *See also under Pat Garrett and Billy the Kid*; Peckinpah, David Samuel ("Sam")
Metz, Leon C., 327n18, 337n10
Middleton, John, 20, 34
Miles, Sarah, 358n7
Milius, John, 277, 347n6

Miller, Arthur, 297
Miller, Roger, 305
Mock, Patricia, 194
Monty Python's Flying Circus, 255
Morton, Buck, 20–21
Mozart, Wolfgang Amadeus, 275
Mullin, Robert N., 324n5
Murch, Walter, 233, 236
Murphy, Lawrence G., 17–20, 173, 279,
   324nn9–11, 329n28, 339n8
Murray, Gabrielle, 312–13, 360n4
My Darling Clementine, 338n14
My Lai massacre, 360n11

Nabokov, Vladimir, 4, 236
Neider, Charles: *The Authentic Death of
   Hendry Jones*, 3, 5–6, 8–9, 44–56,
   58, 60–61, 64–75, 80–84, 87–88, 98,
   103–5, 107–9, 123–24, 133, 142, 144,
   165, 172, 174, 176–79, 254–55, 274,
   283, 285–86, 289, 297, 308, 323n4,
   333nn28–31, 362n22; background,
   43–45; on *One-Eyed Jacks*, 82, 322n2;
   on *Pat Garrett and Billy the Kid*, 323n2;
   Peckinpah's identification with Neider's
   characters, 289; photographs, **42**, **54**;
   relations with Peckinpah, **82–83**,
   322n2. *See also under* Peckinpah,
   David Samuel ("Sam"), Screenplays
   and Television, *The Authentic Death of
   Hendry Jones*
Newman, Paul, 140
Nixon, Richard M., 360n11
Nolan, Frederick, 18, 29, 41, 59, 326n17,
   329n30

"Occurrence at Owl Creek Bridge, An"
   (Bierce), 210
Old West conceptions, xvi, xvii, xx, 8, 41,
   43, 44, 48, 69, 104, 106, 117, 123, 150,
   153, 283–84
Olinger, Bob, 57–61, 104, 280, 333n30,
   341n15
Olivier, Laurence, 362n22
O Lucky Man!, 348n12
One-Eyed Jacks, **2**, 3–9 (**7**), 82, 104, 175,
   194, 286, 322–23nn2–3, 332n16,
   334n3, 335n7, 335n10, 357n5
Open Range, 279
Ortega, Sergio ("Smiley"), 354n11
Otero, Miguel Antonio, 35, 47, 327n19
O'Toole, Peter, 140
Our Man Flint, 140

Pacino, Al, 140, 194
Paine, Lauran, 279
Palacios, Begonia, 168, 179
Palance, Jack, 194
Paley, William S., 357n6
Paramount Pictures, 142
Parker, Hershel, xix
Parsons, Lindsley, Jr., 217
Pat Garrett and Billy the Kid: Billy's
   characterization, 293, 295, 296, 306,
   307, 344n32, 363n25; box office, 113,
   239, 335n2; budget, 195–96, 197;
   cast, 6, 140, 144, 145, 168, 193–95,
   202, 317; cinematography, 229–30,
   241, 275; contemporary relevance,
   280, 360n11; crew listing, 317–
   18; epic status, 162, 210; fatalism
   (determinism, destiny) in, xvii, 71, 87,
   132, 136, 159, 169, 172, 181, 203, 242,
   266, 268, 306, 359n13; Greek tragedy
   and, 165, 342n23, 360n4; historical
   accuracy, 210, 278–85, 343n29,
   361n13, 361n18; MGM conflicts, xv,
   113–14, 116, 184, 188, 190–91, 195–
   96, 198–99, **206**, 215–18, 296, 305;
   pacing and treatment of time, 237–38,
   242, 251, 259, 295, 306; Peckinpah's
   appearance in, 252, 253, 261, 292, 297,
   318, 358n10; Peckinpah's opinion of,
   83, 237; Peckinpah's recutting letter,
   222–23, 224–25, 231–32, 237; place
   in Peckinpah's work, xx, xxi, 114, 191,
   308–15; postproduction, 180, 187,
   191–93, 198–216, 221, 224, 233–
   36 (**234–35**), 245–57, 301, 346n4,
   351n35, 354n12; preproduction, 140–
   46, 162–63, 193–96, 359n13; previews,
   187–89, 190–91, 200, 204–5, 211–12,
   215–21, 224, 228–29, 231–32, 236–
   37, 247–48, 253–56, 260–61, 292,
   318, 351nn36–37, 352nn3–4, 354n11;
   production problems, xvii, 115, 160,
   184, 190, 191, 194–97, 199, 347n8;
   reception and critical reputation, xx,
   113, 115, 191, 237, 306; release date,
   191, 345n4, 355n15; rock stars parallel,
   117, 133, 194, 238; score, 198, 212,
   214, 220, 259–60; set designs, 148;
   sources, xvii, 3, 41, 46, 75, 84, 280;
   structure, 260, 266–68, 295, 355n13;
   title orthography, 318; unfinished state,
   xviii–xix, xxi, 187, 189, 190, 201, 212,
   221, 228, 232, 261, 305, 307–8

SCENES: Billy's death, 170–72, 212–
13, 260, 293, **294**, 306, 312, 315,
343n30, 362n21; Billy's return to
Fort Sumner, 160–61, 173–76,
179–80, 203; Black Harris shootout,
151–53 **(152)**, 154, 168, 253;
cantina scene, 129, 160, 163, 173,
181; Chisum scene, 153, 177, 202,
205, 261–62, 264, 306, 340n12; end
crawl, 218–19, 231, 250, 261, 266,
268; epilogue, 210–11, 239–40,
250, 266–68, 353n9, 359n14; Fort
Sumner shootout, 150–51; Garrett
and Poe scenes, 115, 153; Garrett at
home with Ida, xviii, 147–48, **149**,
168, 189, 196, 202, 205, 212, 219–
20, 231, 245, **258–59**, 260–63, **263**,
291, 297, 306–7, 321n2, 353n9,
359n12; Governor Wallace scene,
150, 168, 168, 196, 261, 279–80,
306, 356n5; Horrell Trading Post
(and Alamosa Bill duel), 121, 124,
146, 155–56, 159, 168, 204–5, 237,
281, 299, 341n15, 362n21; Jones's
Saloon, 115, 154–55, 157, 169,
204–5, 237, 256, 261, 290; Lincoln
County jailbreak, 58–60, 104, 123–
24, 163–64, 165, 196, 254, 280–81,
313; opening scene, 146–47, 163–
64, **166–67**, 169, 173, 202, 210,
212, 254–56, 261, 264–66, 341n21,
359n13; Paco's death, 146, 158–60,
176, 180, 202–3, 204–5, 207, 251,
262, 268, 269, 354n12; plaza scene,
174–75; prologue (Garrett's death),
163, 165, 168, 169, 189, 196, 202,
205, 207, 208–12 **(209, 211)**, 214,
250, 257, 261, 264–69, 293, 297,
306, 314, 342n26, 353n9, 359n13;
raft scene, 120, 180, 196, 202,
204, 205, 212, 220, 237, 251, 261,
358n9; Ruthie Lee and Roberta's
Hotel, xviii, 148, 154, 156–58, 168,
196, 204, 208, 214, 218, 231, 245,
252, 261–63, **263**, 306–7, 321n2,
349n24, 350n29, 358n12, 362n21;
Sheriff Baker scenes, 119, 121–22,
131, 151–52, 154, 232, 253, 259–
60, **309**, 313–14; titles sequence,
264–66; Tuckerman's Hotel, 202,
205, 207–8, 212, 216, 237, 251,
262, 269, 349n24
See also under Wurlitzer, Rudolph

Pat Garrett and Billy the Kid: 1975
television version, xviii, 187, 190, 203,
321n2, 344n40, 345n1, 349n24
Pat Garrett and Billy the Kid: 1988 Turner
Preview, xv, 187, 189, 190, 228, 229,
245, 253–54, 260, 262–65, 267, 269,
318, 352nn3–4, 353n9
Pat Garrett and Billy the Kid: 1990 laser disc
preview, 188–89, 191, 321n2
Pat Garrett and Billy the Kid: 2005 Special
Edition: editing of, xv, xviii, 188–89,
227–40, 245, 253, 256–57, 261–68,
318, 350n27, 353n7, 353n9, 358n12
Pather Panchali, 273
Peck, Gregory, 140
Peckinpah, David Ernest, 247
Peckinpah, David Samuel ("Sam"): on
actors, 195, 348n14; alcoholism,
115, 184, 194, 197, 199–200, 201–2,
215, 221, 249, 287–90, 295, 349n17,
351n37, 356n5, 361n16, 362n23;
attitude toward Billy the Kid, 8, 53–54,
255, 291, 293, 303; on audiences and
theatergoing, 200, 241, 243, 355n16;
books about, 322nn2–4; didacticism,
219; on directing, 195; early career,
3–4, 8–9, 74, 77, 109, 288–89, 336n4;
on foreign films, 273; identification
with Garrett and Dad Longworth,
289–92, 293, 295–96, 300, 303;
influence on filmmakers, 277–78;
MGM conflicts, xv, xviii, 171, 184,
188, 190–91, 195–96, 198–99, 215–
19, 221, 354n12, 356n5; personality,
xvi, xix, 142, 143, 217, 236, 238, 249,
270, 288–89, 302–5, 346n6, 357n5,
360n11; photographs, ii, **76**, **138**,
186, **226**, **244**, **272**; on reaction shots,
100; record-keeping, 236n10, 353n10;
self-destructiveness, xix, 72, 200, 216,
224, 248, 270, 289, 300–301, 363n23;
themes, vii, xvi, 48, 74, 75, 80, 101–2;
on Westerns, 273–74; writing credits,
115, 336n4
OTHER FILMS: *The Ballad of Cable
Hogue*, 142, 188, 210, 278, 297,
299, 322n3, 334nn31–32, 351n39;
Bring Me the Head of Alfredo Garcia,
114, 220–21, 232, 297, 299–300,
302, 308, 349n23, 351n39, 355n12,
355n14, 359n3, 361n16; *Convoy*,
286, 299, 343n27, 349n23; *Cross of
Iron*, 229, 299, 351n39, 355n14,

Peckinpah, *continued*
  359n3; *The Deadly Companions*, xvi,
  106–7, 297; *The Getaway*, 141–43,
  159, 192, 200, 201, 221, 245, 248,
  253, 286–87, 299, 301–2, 346n6,
  351n39, 353n9, 360n5; *Junior
  Bonner*, 75, 142, 201, 210, 221,
  245, 253, 286, 291, 299, 351n39,
  356n5, 359n3; *The Killer Elite*, 297,
  299, 307; *Major Dundee*, 77, 84,
  140, 142, 168, 184, 224, 230, 278,
  284, 297, 299, 307–8, 351n38,
  353n8, 355n12, 359n2; *Ride the
  High Country*, 75, 79–80, 188, 207,
  273, 278, 284, 290, 297, 299, **310**,
  314, 333n31, 351n39; *Straw Dogs*,
  77, 142, 192, 200, 210, 216, 221,
  225, 229, 245, 248, 286, 299, 301,
  336n4, 351n39, 356n5, 359n3; *The
  Wild Bunch*, xix, xx, 75, 79, 102, 105,
  115, 142, 188, 197, 200, 210, 214,
  228, 239, 243, 245, 247, 248, 259,
  263, 265, 270, 273, 276–78, 284,
  286, 287, 291, 297, 299, 301, 302,
  307, 308, 312–15, 321n1, 338n14,
  344n39, 347n8, 349n18, 351n39,
  351n1, 353n7, 355n15, 359n2,
  360nn9–10
  SCREENPLAYS AND TELEVISION: *The
  Authentic Death of Hendry Jones*,
  3–5, 77–111, 114, 142, 145, 148,
  163, 164, 170, 175, 177, 178–79,
  254–55, 286–89, 297, 334nn3–4,
  334–35nn6–9, 343n29; *The Dice
  of God*, 77, 334n2; *The Emperor of
  the North Pole*, 142–43; *The Glass
  Menagerie*, 77; *Gunsmoke*, 3, 8; *The
  Hi Lo Country*, xvii, 321n1; *The
  Losers*, xvii, 321n1; *Noon Wine*, 77,
  224, 245, 297, 356n5; *Portrait of a
  Madonna*, 77; *The Rifleman*, 4, 77,
  287, 289; *The Westerner*, 8, 54, 287,
  333n28, 336n4
  TECHNIQUES: action sequences, 117;
  art direction, 148; characterization,
  88, 153, 163, 170, 172, 176–77,
  181, 195, 293, 295, 297, 299–300,
  343n29, 357n5; children's roles,
  299; credits, 265; cutting room
  editing, 193, 204, 207, 208, 210,
  247, 257; dialogue, 343n29; editing
  style and supervision, 247, 256,
  261, 345n3; flashbacks, 210, 240,
  297; freeze-frames, 208, 210, 212,
  264–65; irony, 106–7, 188, 267,
  313; pacing and time, 87, 148, 237,
  240–43, 269–70, 360n6; parallel
  action, 84, 101, 108; point of view,
  74–75, 79–80, 99, 169, 211, 292,
  343n26; revitalization of clichés and
  conventions, 108, 276; romanticism,
  109, 175, 361–62nn20–21; slow
  motion, 104, 277, 278, 333n31;
  structure, 88, 148, 163, 260, 270;
  title cards, 105, 208, 210–11,
  218–19, 264–65; violence, xvi, xxi,
  8, 104, 115, 121, 156, 277, 290,
  361n20, 363n27; women's roles,
  101–2, 263, 307, 362n21
Peckinpah, Sharon, 354n11
Pecos War (aka John Chisum's Pecos War),
  18–19
Penn, Arthur, 203
Peppin, George W. ("Dad"), 46
Peter, Walter, 333n27
Petticoat Junction, 357n6
Picasso, Pablo, xvii
Pickens, Slim, 6, 152, 202, 238, **309**,
  340n11
Pickett, Tom, 26, 51–53
Poe, John William, 22–25, 28, 45, 53, 118,
  120–21, 213, 325nn16–17, 328n19,
  329n31, 338n15, 342n25
Pollack, Sidney, 361n20
Porter, Katherine Anne, 77
Portis, Charles, 274
Pure Peckinpah Press Kit, 230, 353n7

Rachmil, Lewis, 196, 199, 217
Rafferty, Terence, 189
Rashōmon, 273
Ray, Satyajit, 273
recutting procedures, 257
Red Desert, 273
Redford, Robert, 116
Redman, Nick, 188, 189, 227, 230–31,
  352n6
Regulators, The, 20–21, 29, 32, 34, 46,
  125, 282, 325n13, 332n16
Renoir, Jean, 299
Reynolds, Burt, 358n7
Rhodes, Eugene Manlove, 339n4
Riley, John H., 18, 324n9
Ritch, W. G., 337n10
Robards, Jason, Jr., 140, 193, 202, 238,
  339n9, 356n5

Robbins, Harold, 357n6
Roberts, Buckshot, 340n9
Rodriguez, Robert, 277
Roeg, Nicolas, 277
Rosen, Charles, xvii
Rosenberg, Frank, 3–4, 78, 109, 111
Ross, Herbert, 194
Roswell Daily Record, 45, 331n8
Rudabaugh, Dave, 26
Russek, Jorge, 168
Ryan, Robert, 140, 193, 340n12
Rynerson, William A., 340n9

Salazar, Yginio, 33–34
*Sam Peckinpah's The Legendary Westerns
    Collection*, xv, 188–89, 227, 230–31,
    352n6
Santa Fe New Mexican, 58–59
Santa Fe Ring, 17, 150, 209, 218–19,
    279, 337n10, 339n8, 340n9, 342n25,
    350n33, 361n12
Save the Tiger, 239
Sayles, John, 344n35
Schlöndorff, Volker, 277
Schorer, Mark, 44
Schrader, Paul, 273, 277
Scorsese, Martin, xx, 204, 277, 351n35
Scott, George C., 140
Scurlock, Doc, 20, 34, 46
Searchers, The, 277
Selland, Marie, 3, 288, 296, 342n23
Serling, Rod, 3, 322n1
Serpico, 239
Seven Rivers Gang, 35
Seven Samurai, The, 277
Shakespeare, William, 239, 277, 343n29,
    362n22
Shane, 208, 299
Shaw, Robert, 140
Shelton, Ron, 254, 277, 353n7, 356n4
shooting scripts, 141
Silke, Jim, 193
Silva, Chico, 338n11
Silva, Jesus, 338n11
"Silver Threads among the Gold," 119–20,
    123, 127, 132
Simkin, Stevie, 321n3
Simmons, Garner, 161, 189, 190, 202, 236,
    264, 266, 336n4, 350n27, 354n12
Simons, John L. *See* Merrill, Robert
Sleeper, 239
Smith, Charlie Martin, 168, 202
Sony Pictures Entertainment, 230, 353n8

Spielberg, Stephen, 277
Spottiswoode, Roger, **186**, 189–92, **198**,
    199, 200–201, 203–5, 207–8, 210–12,
    214–15, 217, 219, 221, 227, 229, 245–
    53 passim, 256, 259, 261, 264, 265–69,
    277, 296, 301–3, 345n4, 346n6,
    348n16, 350n29, 353n9, 354n11,
    356nn4–5, 358nn9–10
Sragow, Michael, 189, 214, 236, 277
Stanton, Harry Dean, 168, 199, 202
Starz Channel, 352n6
Steiger, Rod, 140, 193–94
Sting, The, 239
Stone, Oliver, 277
Storper, Craig, 279
Storytellers of Lincoln County, 338n11
Strada, La, 273
Stravinsky, Igor, xvii
Sullivan, Barry, 193, 202
Sunset Boulevard, 240
Susann, Jacqueline, 357n6
Sutherland, Donald, 140

Tarantino, Quentin, 277
Taylor, Dub, 202, 207–8
Teapot Dome scandal, 350n33, 360n11
Thomson, David, xx, 292
Thoreau, Henry David, xvi
1001 Movies You Must See Before You Die, xx
3:10 to Yuma, 333n28
Time, 204
Time Out, xx
Torres, Gabriel, 275, 360n5
Touch of Evil, 233, 236
trailers, 344n39
Treasure of the Sierra Madre, The, 333n28
Trosper, Guy, 4–5, 335n10
Tucker, Ken, 231
Tunstall, John Henry, 17, 18–21, 29, 34,
    46, 50, 125, 284, 324n11, 325n13,
    339n8
"Turkey in the Straw," 132
Turner Broadcasting Corporation, 318
Tynan, Kenneth, 78

United Artists, 221
Upson, Marshall Ashmun ("Ash"), 12–17,
    18, 22, 24, 26, 27, 29, 32, 35–37, 41,
    47, 48, 57, 137, 284, 323n4, 336n6,
    341n15
Utley, Robert M., 13, 24, 36, 39, 58, 59

Verbinski, Gore, 277

Vertigo, 236
Vidal, Gore, 203, 339n9
Vidor, King, 41
Vineberg, Steve, 189
Voight, Jon, 116, 140, 194, 348n11

Waite, Fred, 20, 34
Wallace, Lew, 119, 193, 280, 337n10,
   339n9
Wallis, Michael, 321n
Warner, David, 193
Warner Home Video, xv, 188, 227, 229–
   31, 236, 245, 261, 352n1, 352n5,
   352nn6–8
Warshow, Robert, 43
Watergate break-in, 280, 360n11
Waterhole #3, 140
Wayne, John, 355n15
Way We Were, The, 239
Weddle, David, 77, 190, 230, 236–37, 247–
   48, 334n2, 336n4, 353n7, 361n17
Weddle, Jerry. *See* Weddle, Richard
Weddle, Richard, 30, 324n6, 330n33
Welles, Orson, 233, 236, 322n4
Western genre, xx–xxi, 5, 8, 43–44, 54–56,
   109, 123, 133, 143, 273–79, 338n14,
   359n2, 360n4; "noir Westerns," 333n28
Whitehill, Harvey, 16
Whitman, Walt, xxi
Wild Bunch: An Album in Montage, The, 188
Williams, Gordon, 77
Williams, Tennessee, 77, 178, 357n6
Williams, Wirt, 323n4
Willingham, Calder, 4, 5

Wills, Chill, 202, 261
Wilson, Billy, 26
Wilson, John P., 45, 324nn10–11
Winchester '73, 333n28
Wolfe, Robert L. ("Bob"), 190–91, 192,
   201, 214–15, 218, 219, 221, 245–47,
   249–53 passim, 256, 259, 261, 269,
   302, 346n6, 348n16, 353n9, 358n9
Woo, John, 277
Wurlitzer, Rudolph ("Rudy"): as Folliard,
   138, 168, 202; *Nog*, 117; photographs,
   112, 138; production participation,
   140, 194, 233, 303–5, 335n9, 339n6,
   343n29; relations with Peckinpah, 114,
   117, 139, 304–5
   SCREENPLAYS: *Billy the Kid*, 116–37,
   139–41, 147, 153–56 passim, 159,
   162, 169, 179, 205, 207, 304–5,
   336n5, 338n15; *Pat Garrett and Billy
   the Kid*, vii, xvi, xviii–xix, 58–60, 81,
   113–16, 144–47, 150–51, 153–65,
   168–76, 178–80, 183, 201, 203,
   205, 207, 238–39, 253, 255, 278–
   79, 281–85, 287–88, 291, 293, 296,
   297, 302–5, 307–8, 337n11, 339n9,
   343n26; *Two-Lane Blacktop*, 116–17,
   303; *Zebulon*, 302

Yellow Sky, 333n28
Yerbe, Masaria, 329n30
Young Guns, 32
Young Guns II, 32, 339n9

Z Channel, 189